WARS AND SOLDIERS IN THE EARLY REIGN OF LOUIS XIV

Volume 3 – The Armies of the Ottoman Empire 1645–1718

Text and Illustrations by Bruno Mugnai

'This is the Century of the Soldier', Fulvio Testi, Poet, 1641

Helion & Company

Helion & Company Limited
Unit 8 Amherst Business Centre
Budbrooke Road
Warwick
CV34 5WE
England
Tel. 01926 499 619
Email: info@helion.co.uk
Website: www.helion.co.uk
Twitter: @helionbooks
Visit our blog http://blog.helion.co.uk/

Published by Helion & Company 2020
Designed and typeset by Serena Jones
Cover designed by Paul Hewitt, Battlefield Design (www.battlefield-design.co.uk)

Text © Bruno Mugnai 2020
Illustrations © as individually credited
Colour artwork by Bruno Mugnai © Helion & Company 2020
Maps drawn by George Anderson © Helion & Company 2020

ISBN 978-1-913118-84-6

British Library Cataloguing-in-Publication Data.
A catalogue record for this book is available from the British Library.

For details of other military history titles published by Helion & Company
Limited, contact the above address, or visit our website: http://www.helion.co.uk

We always welcome receiving book proposals from prospective authors.

Contents

Ottoman Chronology

1645
June 24   Beginning of the Cretan War
June 26   Great fire in Constantinople
August 19   Ottoman conquest of Chaniá

1646
April 7   Venetians occupy Tenedos
October 15   Ottomans conquer Réthimno

1647
March 12   Ottomans conquer Novigrad in Dalmatia
September   Venetians retake Novigrad and seize the fortresses of Sibenik and Klis in Herzegovina

1648
May 24   The Venetian fleet blockades the Dardanelles
May 29   Earthquake in Constantinople
June 12/Oct 23 First siege of Kandije (Candia)
August 8   Destitution of Ibrahim I. The Sultan is sentenced to death 10 days later, his son Mehmed IV appointed as new sultan.
October 28   Suppression of the *sipahis* and beginning of janissary domination

1649
May 12   Venetian fleet defeats the Ottomans at Foça
July 7   Rebellion suppressed in Constantinople
July 8 /Oct 2 Ottomans unsuccessfully besiege Kandije for the second time

1650
May/June   Venetians defeated in their attempts to expel the Ottomans from Ierapetra and Sitia in Crete
Summer   Ottoman raids against Zadar in Dalmatia

1651
July 7–10   Venetians win naval engagement off Paros and Naxos Island in the Cyclades

August 21	Popular revolt in Constantinople due to debasement of coinage
September 3	Execution of *valide* Mahpeyker Kösem, mother of Ibrahim I
October	Negotiations opened between Venice and Constantinople

1652

February 21	Venetians conquer the fortress of Zadvarje in Herzegovina

1653

Spring–summer	**Lootings and reprisals between Ottomans and Venetians in Dalmatia, Bosnia and Herzegovina**
December	Grand Vzier Tahroncu Ahmed imposes severe policies to settle Ottoman finances

1654

May 16	Ottoman fleet under Murad Paşa prevails over Venetian vessels in the First Battle of the Dardanelles
September	Ottomans fail to conquer Tinos in the Aegean Sea

1655

June 21	Ottoman fleet defeated by the Venetians at the Second Battle of the Dardanelles

1656

March 4/9	Popular revolt in Constantinople
June 26	Venetians defeat Ottoman fleet at the third battle of the Dardanelles
September 15	Köprülü Mehmed appointed grand vizier
October	A new rebellion extends in Anatolia (*segmen* rebellion)

1657

19 July	Venetians defeat the Ottoman fleet at the fourth battle of the Dardanelles, but are forced to leave the Straits

1658

June/Sept	Ottoman campaign against Transylvania
November	Military expedition in Anatolia against the rebels
December	Upper Egypt rebellion.

1659

February 17	*Segmen* rebellion crushed in Aleppo
Spring	Rebellion in Upper Egypt crushed by the Porte
November	Local rebellion in Wallachia

1660

May 13	Transylvanian Great Prince Ferenc II Rákóczy defeated at Szaászfenes
July 24:	Major fire in Constantinople
August 27	Conquest of Várad by the Ottoman army in Transylvania

1661

October 29	Death of Köprülü Mehmed. His son Ahmed succeeds him

1662
January 23   Pro-Habsburg candidate in Transylvania defeated at Nagyszöllös

1663
April 12   The Porte declares war on the Habsburg Emperor
August 16   Köprülü Ahmed lays siege to Érsekúivár, the Imperial garrison surrenders on 8 September

1664
August 1   Imperialists and allies under Montecuccoli defeat the Ottomans at Szentgotthárd
August 10   Twenty years' truce of Vasvár

1665
July 24   Fire at the Topkapı Palace

1666
May 15   Köprülü Ahmed moves to Crete to resume the siege of Kandije

1667
May 25   Beginning of the new siege campaign at Kandije

1668
Autumn   Venice renews the offer of peace to the sultan, but the grand vizier opposes the continuation of talks

1669
September 6   Surrender of the Venetians at Kandije

1672
June 4   Expedition against Poland to support the Cossacks
August 27   The Ottomans seize Kamieniec
October 18   Truce of Buczacz, Poland agrees to pay tribute to the Porte

1673
January   The Polish Diet refuses to pay tribute
August 7   New Ottoman campaign in Podolia to enforce Buczacz agreement
November 10   Ottomans defeated at Chocim

1674
August 18   Ottomans seize Ladyzyn

1675
August 24   Ottoman–Tatar offensive halted by the Poles at Lvov

1676
September 27   Indecisive battle at Żurawno; Ottomans and Poles sign a new truce
October 3   Death of Köprülü Ahmed

October 5	Merzifonlu Kara Mustafa appointed as new grand vizier

1677

May 31	The Porte intervenes against Russia after disagreements between the Cossacks and the Tsar
Aug 14/Sept 7	Unsuccessful Ottoman siege of Çigirin

1678

April 30	New Ottoman campaign against Russia
July 19–Aug 21	Ottomans conquer Çigirin

1681

February 11	Ottoman–Russian truce signed at Bakhchisaray

1682

January 9	The Porte recognises Imre Thököly as ruler of Royal Hungary against the Habsburgs
June 9	The Porte rejects the Emperor's offer to extend the Truce of Vasvár for another 20 years
July 15/Sept 12	Siege of Vienna and Battle of Kahlenberg
October 27	Imperialists seize Esztergom
December 25	Execution of Kara Mustafa

1684

June 18	Formation of the Holy League against the Ottoman Empire

1685

August 16	Imperialists seize Érsekúivár

1686

June/August	Venetian offensive in the Peloponnese
September 2	Imperialists and allies seize Buda

1687

August 12	Ottoman disaster at Harsány
September	Mutiny of the Ottoman army in Hungary
September 25	Loss of Athens, Venetians seize the Peloponnese
November 8	Destitution of Sultan Mehmed IV. Süleyman II is the new sultan

1688

September 8	Ottoman garrison of Belgrade surrenders to the Imperial army
October 30	Venetians leave the unsuccessful siege at Negroponte

1689

July 8	The Imperialists seize the river port of Orsova on the Danube
August 30	Imperial army defeats the Otomans at Batocina
Sept/Oct	Ottomans lose Smedarevo, Nissa and Viddin

1690

June 7/8	Fire in Constantinople
Aug/Sept	Ottomans reconquer Nissa, Smederevo and the other Danube ports
October 8	Belgrade surrenders to the Ottomans under Köprülü Mustafa

1691

June 22	Death of Sultan Süleyman II. Ahmed II succeeds him
August 19	Imperialists defeat the Ottomans at Slankamen; grand vizier Köprülü Mustafa killed in battle

1692

June 12	Imperialists seize Várad; the Porte loses the control of Transylvania
July 18	Unsuccessful Venetian siege of Chaniá in Crete
August	Poles besiege Kamieniec

1693

June 7/Sept 5	Major fires in Constantinople

1694

September 12	Ottomans leave the unsuccessful siege at the Imperial encampment of Peterwardein
September 21	Venetians seize the island of Chios

1695

February 6	Death of Ahmed II and ascension of Mustafa II
February 22	Ottomans reconquer Chios
September 18	Ottoman Naval victory at Mytilene
September 22	Imperial defeat at Lugos

1696

August 6	Russians conquer Azov
August 26	Indecisive Imperialist–Ottoman encounter at Ollaschin

1697

September 11	Imperialists under Prince Eugene destroy the Ottomans at Zenta

1699

January 26	Treaty of Carlowitz

1700

July 14	Treaty of Constantinople between Russia and the Porte; the Tsar holds Azov and Taganrog

1702

May	Uprising in Tunis against Ottoman authority

1703

| August 22 | Janissary revolt in Constantinople. Deposition of Mustafa II and ascension of Ahmed III |

1704

| April | Riots in Baghdad; Mamluk clan seizes control of the province |

1706

| June/Sept | Plague epidemic in Constantinople |

1711

April 9	Russian–Ottoman War
June	Uprising and riots in Cairo
July 19–20	Ottomans surround the Russians on the Pruth
Summer	Plague epidemic in Smyrna
September:	Ottoman officials expelled from Algiers

1712

| April 16 | The Tsar and the Porte signs the Truce Treaty of Constantinople Azov returns to the Ottoman Empire |

1713

| June 24 | Russo-Ottoman treaty of Edirne |
| Summer | Plague epidemic in Thessalonica |

1715

April 1	War against Venice
July 2	Surrender of Corinth
August 7	Ottomans seize Nauplia
August 22	Venetians evacuate the Peloponnese
September 24	Venetian outpost in Crete surrenders to the Ottomans

1716

April 24	Habsburg Emperor declares war on the Porte
August 5	Ottoman defeat at Peterwardein
August 20	Ottomans leave the siege of Corfu
October 14	Imperialists seize Temeşvár

1717

| August 16 | Imperialists defeat the Ottoman relief army at Belgrade |
| August 18 | Belgrade surrenders to the Imperial Army |

1718

| July | Fire in Constantinople |
| July 16/17 | Peace of Passarowitz |

Foreword

It is difficult to know where to begin in describing the importance and value of this book. Bruno Mugnai has created what may become the definitive reference work on a remarkable military machine. The legacy of its achievement echoes across the Balkans and central Europe even to this day. The Ottomans engendered terror in Christendom. Absorption into their cultural, economic and religious orbit was the stuff of continued nightmares for king and commoner alike. Fear created an extremely hazy perspective obfuscated by prejudice, lack of knowledge and a desire to minimize the threat through making it appear amorphous, cruel and in a progressive state of decay. No empire of such size and power could survive for almost five hundred years being all these things.

Bruno takes the widest possible sweep through a huge amount of source material. From this he distils a sharp, clear and objective explanation about the world of the Ottoman soldier. Concentrating on the phase after the empire's apogee, he decodes unfamiliar terms and complex social and military hierarchies in a clear and simple way.

The evolution of the military machine is explained from recruitment to battle tactics. The confusing multitude of names used to describe troop types is clarified. Weapons, standards, allies, campaigns and fortifications are explored in a concise and informative way which is easy to read and packed with data essential for historian, wargamer, modeller and casual reader alike.

Those of us passionate about the 17th century owe a growing debt of gratitude to Bruno Mugnai who is rapidly becoming a leading authority on the period.

Enjoy this masterful work. It sets the benchmark for others to follow.

Barry Hilton
March 2020

Preface to the First (Italian) Edition

The wars between the Christian States and the Ottomans show aspects very different compared to any other conflict fought in Europe. The tone adopted by the western European literature to describe the Ottomans was close to the political propaganda, very similar to the one recently used against the Communist Bloc and the Soviet Union. It is probably not by chance that certain prophecies about the Sultan, such as his arrival in Rome to water his horse in the city's fountain, survived until a few years ago, replacing the Sultan with the Red Army Cossacks.[1]

In the minds of European Christians is permanently imprinted the image of the Ottoman soldier as 'violator of territories, cities, wealth and men'.[2] The struggle turned into a tremendous challenge: 'experienced in embarrassment, shame and fear.'[3] Contemporary accounts interpreted this ideological reaction and described with the most contemptuous terms the Sultan and his subjects, become the most absolute negative symbols.

Of the wars against the Ottoman Empire, reports, accounts and memories of the major events illustrating the struggle were printed in every European country. The notable exception to this is the City Archives of Vienna, which contain no testimonial of epic relief of the city in September 1683, arguably the defining event of the wars between the Ottomans and Christian Europe. Consequently, a larger part of sources was produced by Christian enemies such as Poles, Hungarians, Austrians and Italians. The Ottoman sources,[4] few in number, are not easily accessible and written with tones no less propagandistic.

---

1 G. Vercellin, *Un Infedele in Vaticano*; in 'Storia & Dossier' 5/1995 (Florence: Giunti Editore).

2 M. Ciccarini, *Il Richiamo Ambivalente. Immagini del Turco nella memorialistica polacca* (Bergamo, Jus Juvenilia 1991), pp.25–26.

3 *Ibidem*

4 Some major Turkish sources of this period are the *Mehmet Ağa tarihi* (Mehmet Ağa's chronicle), or the *Silihtar tarihi* (Esquire's Chronicles), by Findiklili Mehmed, written after 1690, and the *Vekayi'-i Beç*, This chronicle is supposed to be an official diary written by the anonymous Master of Ceremonies of the Ottoman court during the siege of Vienna. A third no less important Ottoman source is the *Seyâhatnâme*. This work by the Ottoman Turkish traveller Evliya Çelebi (1611–1682) is also one of the major texts of Ottoman literature and forms a 10-volume series. Although many of the descriptions in the *Seyâhatnâme* were written in an exaggerated manner or were plainly inventive fiction or third-source misinterpretation, his notices remain a useful guide to the culture and lifestyles of the seventeenth-century Ottoman Empire. Among the classical studies concerning the Ottoman army, there is the work in 20 volumes entitled *Etat Militaire Ottoman, depuis la fondation de l'Empire Ottoman jusqu'à nos jours*, written by Colonel Kabaağaçlızade Ahmed Cevad and published in

Therefore, both Christian and Ottoman sources are not always reliable due to the strong ideological characterisation and force the historian to use caution with all information, because in war, it is well known, no evidence is ever certain.

At the end of the 1970s, the British historian Geoffrey Parker published his important work about the technical-military evolution between the sixteenth and seventeenth centuries, expanding on the theory formulated by Michael Roberts in 1950 and focusing on the most representative topics and protagonists of the so called 'Military Revolution'.[5] Examining the confront between the Ottomans and their western enemies, Parker highlighted the progressive technological gap in metallurgy, production of weapons and modern combat tactics.[6] The Ottoman commanders failed to keep up with their opponents and continued to propose an obsolescent military model. The Ottoman society required of every Muslim subject the duty to fight in defence of the faith. Therefore, while in the rest of Europe the armies progressed in the development of stable professional contingents, in the second half of the seventeenth century a significant quota of the Ottoman army was composed of irregulars, unable to remain in campaign for a long periods. In other words, while the Western Christian states were able to specialise to the war a quote of their human and technological resources, the Ottomans, notwithstanding their empire had been founded on the territorial conquests, remained – paradoxically – just amateurs.

In the long cycle of ongoing war since 1645 (the beginning of the Cretan war) to 1718 (date of the Truce of Passarowitz) two worlds and two eras were in opposition, but despite their military weakness and the suffering of tremendous defeats, the Ottomans showed a vitality and a spirit of sacrifice which has not been given proper attention. Their lack of ability to react to the changes of history and their attachment to tradition did not always prevent the implementation of operational and tactical developments by some of the more adept Ottoman military commanders. Even though the measures introduced often prove unsuccessful, or frustrated by the disparity of forces in the field, the Ottomans represented for many years the greatest threat for Western Europe. The final defeat was delayed not only by resorting to the human and material resources of the Sultan's huge empire, but also from the moral and physical resilience of its soldiers.

Lastly, we should remember how long the Ottoman military model has influenced other European armies.[7] Russia, Poland, and not less, Venice and the Habsburg Empire adopted and sometimes improved formations and battle tactics developed by their Ottoman opponents many centuries before.

The Author; Florence, 26 September 1996

Constantinople in 1882. The most valuable work written by an enemy of the Ottoman Empire is Luigi Ferdinando Marsigli's *Stato Militare dell'Imperio Ottomanno*, printed in Amsterdam in 1721.

5   G. Parker, 'The Military Revolution, 1560–1660. A Myth', p.2, in *Journal of Modern History*, 48/1976.

6   *Ibidem*, pp.18–221.

7   In 1636, the Iranian *Shah* raised an infantry corps organised and trained like the Ottoman janissaries. In the Russian *Czar*'s army, the *Streltzi* corps resembled the organisation of the Ottoman professional infantry and in Poland, Jan III Sobieski formed after 1670 a household infantry company dressed and equipped like the sultan's janissaries.

Preface to the Present (English) Edition

This book is an expanded and revised version of my first publication in 1997–1998. For this reason, the period under consideration goes beyond the years that canonically have been chosen for this series. Therefore, readers will read of events that occurred after the death of Louis XIV: I hope it will be a welcome license. Whenever you go back to a topic, there is always some fear. Hasty judgements, sentences that are no longer valid and errors of all kinds. Actually, I did not think I would write again on this subject, but it was the Century of the Soldier series editor Charles Singleton who, with benevolent obstinacy, convinced me to reopen my old pending account with the Sublime Porte.

In the past two decades, the writing of Ottoman history has changed considerably, for the better, I believe. The widening access to Ottoman source materials in Constantinople, Ankara, and elsewhere has supplemented and in some cases supplanted the Ottoman chronicles and Western European correspondences and observations that previously had constituted the documentary core of the knowledge on the Ottoman army. Thanks to this, an increasing number of accurate research has been published on this matter by valiant scholars, such as Virginia Aksan, Rhoads Murphey, Gábor Ágoston, Mark Stein and many others.

The growing interest is widely justifiable because the Turkish–Ottoman 'military' constituted the first great permanent army of the modern era. Moreover, this kind of army represented a completely original model in comparison with western armies of the same age.

Finally, we must not forget how the wars between the Ottoman Muslim Empire and the Christian West continue to influence European history still today. Whoever wants to go deeper on this, can just follow the long-existing discussion on whether or not modern Turkey joins the European Union. Whether the choice is right or wrong, the ominous and dark shadow of the Ottoman past still exerts a strong influence.

The Author; Florence, 22 December 2019.

Acknowledgements

As with every such undertaking, this book owes a great deal to many people. Its first draft was sketched after an exciting journey in Turkey. This trip occurred in my youth, in 1988, when I travelled through Greece and Turkey with my 'custom' motorbike named Huszár together with the woman of my life. The hours spent in the Topkapı museum remain one of my most indelible memories. I remember the patience and kindness of the museum's staff, who did not expect to receive so many questions from a tourist-biker coming from Italy. To them, as well as to the personnel of the Askery and Denizli museums in Constantinople, I renew my most sincere thanks. The research and writing of this book relied upon a number of archives, libraries, and endowments, in Turkey as well as in Austria, Germany, Italy, Hungary and Poland. Especially in this latter country, I found an inestimable help, which opened to me new perspectives on the matter. This book is therefore a posthumous thanks to professor Zdzisław Żygulski (1921–2015).

A Note on Ottoman Currency

Until the sixteenth century, Ottoman territories in Anatolia and the Balkans had a unified monetary system based on three coins: the silver akçe, the gold sultani, and the copper mangir or pul. The akçe was considered the basic unit of payment, and was commonly used in local transactions. While the copper value of the coin fluctuated with changes within the Ottoman government, the standards of the sultani and akçe originally remained identical to gold or silver coins of other states around the Mediterranean, such as the Venetian ducato. In terms of silver coinage, used in daily transactions and to some extent in long-distance trade, the central government chose to continue with the existing monetary units in the newly conquered territories with or without modifications. Concerning the economic valour of the akçe, an annual salary of 2,000 akçe was considered as basic income for peasants and minor artisans. A janissary earned yearly 4,745 *akçe* maximum, a senior infantry officer of the janissary corps earned in one year about 8,000 *akçe*.

1

The Sublime Porte

In the mid seventeenth century, the Ottoman Empire had a territorial extent of nearly 7,000,000 square kilometres with a population of approximately 25,000,000 inhabitants. The huge empire built by the descendants of Osman (or Othman) had reached the maximum of power and splendour, but now it was facing an unfavourable conjuncture. Scholars of Ottoman history used to portray this age as a period of both decline and decentralisation, and of the collapse of the state. The causes of the crisis are complex, but principally there was the poor capacity of the state to follow the economic development of the western European trades. While the affirmation of the major powers had been granted by the growth of trade and manufacturing, made possible by the resources coming from the New World, the sultans intensified the tax burden of their subjects to face the challenge of international trade. Compared to the Western powers, the Ottoman Empire was also disadvantaged by low economic growth, worsened by its peripheral position to the route of the Atlantic Ocean. More recent studies focus on this period in which the classical institutions of the Empire, above all the army and the system of ownership and taxation on which the army was based were degenerating and cracks were beginning to appear in Ottoman society; also it was a time of increasing favouritism. Further problems derived from internal disorders and corruption.

During the reign of Süleyman the Magnificent (1496–1566) the Ottoman Empire had reached the apogee of its political and military power, but his successors, reared in the harem's golden cage, did not have the preparation and maturity to conduct state affairs effectively, and soon neglected any duty to devote himself to court pleasures, luxuries and hunting. The government remained under the control of officials not always able to hold their task. Many of them owed their position to favour granted by the members of the court. The acquisition of high-ranking state offices, thanks to the intrigues of the court, was certainly not exclusive to the Ottomans, but this evil was associated with the degradation of authority, the spread of nepotism, corruption and venality, joined by the disastrous experience of the sale of the state offices. The struggle for power involved the professional army in a fierce rivalry that finally exploded in violent riots inside the household troops, primarily the janissaries and *sipahis*.

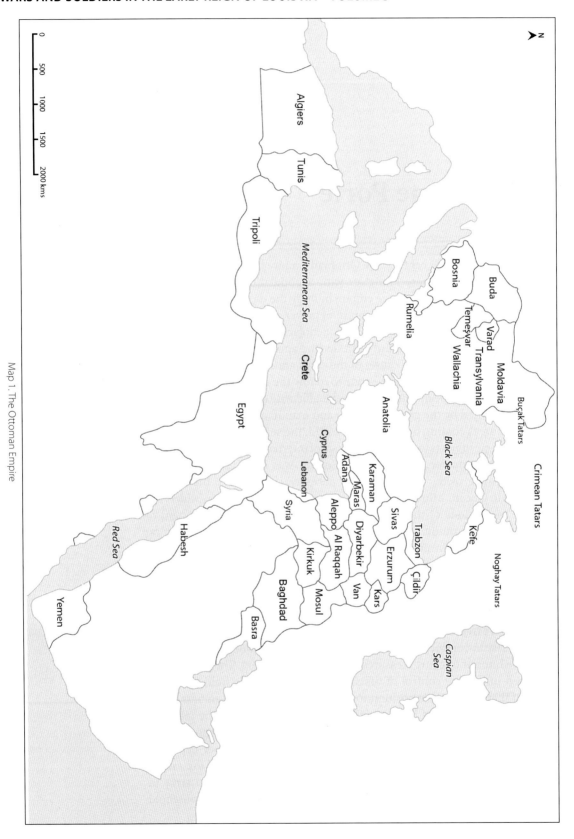

Map 1. The Ottoman Empire

1. Sultan and *silihtar* (esquire), after an eighteenth-century print. In the seventeenth century, Ottomans sultans did not deal with the government, but they embodied the state, which had its centre at the court. Though the period from 1645 to 1718 was one of crisis and change for all elements of the government, the sultan continued to represent the Empire. He had historically been a warrior monarch ruling a state seen as a single household: the sultan was the household head, and under him the dynasty was his family, the territory of the state formed the dynastic patrimony, administered by the ruling class formed by the sultan's slave military retinue. Finally the subject peoples, the *raya*, were the flock whom God had entrusted to the sultan's care.

After the expansive conflict against Venice to conquer Crete, new wars involved the Ottoman Empire against Poland and Russia, until the decisive gamble against the Habsburgs in Hungary. Military defeats suffered at the hands of the troops of the Holy League, and the loss of the Hungarian and Greek provinces at the end of the seventeenth century were seen as direct consequences of the general weakness of the Empire.

Although past historiography has often represented the Ottoman Empire as a highly centralised state, the scenario was very different. As the domain expanded, it became increasingly multinational, both in its subject populations and in its government apparatus. The Ottoman Empire consisted of more than 20 ethnically and religiously different groups. It was a classic example of the plural society, and it is no surprise that today there are more than 30 countries in the former territories of the empire. The fact that the Ottoman government successfully managed to rule many religiously and ethnically different societies for six centuries has attracted many scholars, not only historians, but also social scientists, to investigate the model of administration. Although terms such as 'multiculturalism' and 'pluralism' have recently been explored, their basic characteristics can be seen in the Ottoman policies towards the Muslim and non-Muslim subjects of the empire, especially in the establishment of the *millet* system.[1] Despite their differences in ethnicity and religion the subjects lived together peacefully for centuries under Ottoman

---

1   The word *millet* comes from the Arabic word for nation, 'milla', but in the Ottoman Empire it came to mean a religious community, specifically, non-Muslim religious minorities represented within the empire by an official political leader. The millets were hierarchically organised religious bodies with a decidedly political function, each headed by a cleric, identified as the *millet başi* by the Ottomans, who was appointed by the sultan, usually from a list of candidates provided by the community's leaders. The millet was largely free to order the affairs of his community as long as he remained loyal to the sultan. Non-Muslims were organised into three officially sanctioned *millets*: Greek Orthodox, headed by the ecumenical patriarch of Constantinople, Armenians, headed by the Armenian patriarch, and Jews. Alongside Arabs and Turks, they formed the five fingers of the sultan's hand.

rule. Certainly, coexistence sometimes degenerated into episodes of bitter contrast, but compared to the rest of the world, tolerance and respect between different people and cultures remained at a much better level than elsewhere.[2] From the beginning of their rule, the Ottoman sultans almost never tried to convert the populations of the conquered territories. This decision was due also to the Ottoman fiscal laws, which recognised fewer taxes on the Muslim subjects. Although non-Muslims were excluded from leadership positions, many important activities were entrusted to Greeks, Armenians and Jews, particularly in the supplies for the army and in the merchant navy, such as *sarraf* or bankers and money-changers.

The Ottoman State

The Turkish monarchy is governed by a master; all the subjects are his slaves.

Nicolò Machiavelli, *Il Principe*' chapter III

Several astonished Western commenters noticed that every subject of the sultan, including major dignitaries, accepted without any discomfort the condition of the slaves of their monarch. In the Islamic world, and especially between the Ottomans, the condition of *kul* (slave of the sultan) did not have the same meaning as in Western Europe. All authority derived from the sovereign, who appointed his ministers, the *vezir*, and among them, he designated the first office, the actual director of the state, the *vezir-i âzam* or grand vizier. The government hierarchy had a pyramid shape with the base formed by the common people, the *raya*, subdivided in the rigid craft guilds system. The model of government reflected the Central Asian origins, but soon inherited three major traditions: Turkic, Islamic, and Byzantine. As the Empire expanded, administrative policies became more flexible to accommodate this diversity. There were, therefore, always some local exceptions to the general Ottoman administrative policies.

As successor of the 'Roman' Empire, the sultan considered himself as the only actual emperor. The 'Imperial' sentiment touched a highly sensitive nerve in all external relations, since the Roman–Byzantine Imperial inheritance was constantly claimed and emphasised when the sultan faced

---

However, the debate as to whether the subjects of European states, before the nineteenth century, could be associated with non-Muslim subjects of the Ottoman Empire it is still open.

2   E. Ceylan, 'The 'Millet' System in the Ottoman Empire', in J. Upron-Ward (ed.), *New Millennium Perspectives in the Humanity* (Constantinople-New York NY: Fatih University-Brigham Young University, 2002), p.246: 'As opposed to homogeneity, uniformity and standardization of cultural forms, Ottoman multiculturalism not only ensured the prevalence of different and multiple forms of culture, but it also liberated the non-Muslim groups from the homogenizing logic of majority identity. As a matter of fact, the Ottomans, for many centuries until the nineteenth century, had the ability, authority and power to assimilate social-cultural forms of different ethnic and religious groups, which was the general practice observed in many empires. However, the Ottomans chose heterogeneity and peaceful co-existence.'

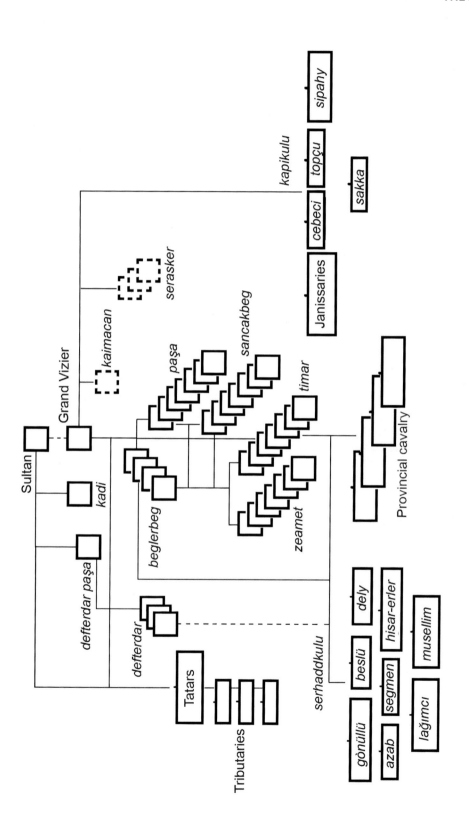

2. The Ottoman Empire's chain of command. (Author's graphic)

Sultan

Grand Vizier

kaimacan

serasker

kapikulu

Janissaries

cebeci

topçu

sipahy

sakka

paşa

sancakbeg

timar

zeamet

beglerbeg

Provincial cavalry

kadi

defterdar paşa

defterdar

Tatars

Tributaries

serhaddkulu

gönüllü

beslü

dely

azab

segmen

hisar-erler

lağımcı

musellim

19

3. Adolescent recruits selected for the court service as an *iç oğlan* (page) completed their training in Constantinople. They were distinguished from the common *acemi oğlani* recruits by the headdress in brocade velvet and their richer clothing, such as the *entari* waistcoat with floral decorations. The Ottoman court had been established in Constantinople after 1453 and was based in the Topkapı Palace. A picturesque crowd of pages, eunuchs, concubines, and employers for the various tasks required by the Imperial protocol resided in the luxurious rooms of the palace. Officials and servants occupied the two branches of the *seray*, the Imperial court: the *enderun* (internal service) and the *birun* (external service). In the first service operated the members of the *has oda* (the Sultan's private secretary), the *hazine-yihassa* (treasurer), *silihtars*, *terçuman* (dragoman or interpreter), the white eunuchs and finally the Sultan's closest attendants, his relatives and the school for the princes. In the *birun* were registered the court Imam, physicians, eye medics, a surgeon and an astrologer. The medical–religious service was followed by the *müteferrika* (the household horsemen), *bostangi* (gardeners), room guardians with their commander, workers and other court personnel. (Ottoman miniature, mid seventeenth century, Bibliothèque Nationale de France, Paris)

the other emperor, the Habsburg one, named simply as 'King of Vienna'.[3] The sultan was also designated with the prestigious title of *padishah*, derived from the Persian language. With equal pride the Ottomans qualified their government with the title 'Sublime Porte',[4] referring to the administration of power that once took place at the entrance of the monarch's tent or palace. The Topkapı palace, the residence of the sultan's court, could be intended as a large pavilion, as the common term referred it as *seray* (the seraglio). Next to the court was located the *divoan*, the state's apparatus of government directed by the grand vizier. In the *divoan* operated the *defterdar paşa* (finance minister) with other ministers, the army and navy senior officers, the religious judges, the caliphs, the provincial governors and the chief of ceremonies. Naturally, in the *divoan* the sultan participated too, secretly observing the government meetings behind a grate. Each political decision would be depend on the sultan's confirmation, who issued a *firman* (Imperial decree).

---

3   Further reading in P. Preto, *Venezia e i Turchi* (Florence: Sansoni, 1975), pp.156–158.
4   The Sublime Porte, also known as the Ottoman Porte or High Porte (Ottoman Turkish: باعلی - ب Bab-ı Ali – from Arabic: ب, báb 'gate' and اع ي ل , alī 'high'), is a metonym identifying the central government of the Ottoman Empire, by reference to the gate giving access to the buildings that housed the government office in Constantinople. The term Sublime Porte as a political centre emerged in the seventeenth century with the increasing ineffectiveness of sultans.

The Ottoman administrative system consisted of two components: the central government and the provincial administrations. In the provincial administration, administrative flexibility was the norm. The provincial government traditionally included two centrally appointed authorities to administer the *sancak* (district): the *beg*, also called *sancakbeg*, who usually came from the military class and represented the executive authority of the sultan, and the *kadi*, who was a member of the *ulema* and represented the legal authority of the sultan. The latter had to be an expert on *sharia* (religious law) as well as the sultan's rules, the *kanun*, laid down in law books, *kanunnames*. These law books legislated taxes, criminal law, tolls, the duties and privileges of officials, and were prepared separately for each *sancak*. In addition to the *beg* and *kadi*, each district had also a *mufti*, who interpreted rather than executed Islamic law. Through his *fetvas*, namely statements regarding legal matters, the *mufti* declared his opinion on legal subjects.

Several *sancaks* formed an *eyalet* or *beglerbegilik*, province, which was administered by the *beglerbeg*, also called *vali*, namely governor. The central government appointed the *beglerbeg*; he was also the *sancakbeg* of the capital district in his *eyalet*.[5] The *paşa* governed and administered major districts, but hierarchically occupied a secondary place. However, the *paşa* could bear title and ensigns like a *beglerbeg*, and outranked all the *paşas* in his province. The *beglerbeglik* numbered four until 1687: Rumelia (Greece), Hungary, Anatolia and Egypt. The *paşalik* formed an overall of 21 in 1683. The *beglerbeg* and *paşa* were also the military commanders of their own provinces, and held authority over the *sancakbegs* for military expeditions, but in civil matters these latter were directly responsible to the sultan. The most important consideration in assigning the provincial posts of governor was their loyalty to the sultan. The specific obligations and responsibilities of *beglerbeg*, *paşa* and *sancakbeg* were not clearly defined and an individual appointed to a provincial or district governor post probably received fairly vague instructions.[6] Equally indefinite was the length of the commission, with some appointments lasting mere days while others extended over a decade. In general, *beglerbegs* and *paşas* were replaced more often than the *sancakbegs*.

The Ottoman lands were divided into three categories: *mülk*, freehold land; *vakif*, land granted for pious or charitable purposes which remained or was revised at the sultan's discretion; and *arazi-i emiriyye* or *miri*, agricultural land that belonged to the state. Revenues for the state were generated exclusively from the latter, which was organised in three types of administrative unit: *timar*, *zeamet*, and *has*. This organisation was called the *dirlik* and usually was known in the West as *timar* system. A *timar* was the smallest unit and produced up to 20,000 *akçe* yearly. *Zeamets* produced from 20,000 to 100,000 *akçe*, and the *has* produced over 100,000 *akçe* as

---

5 The pre-Ottoman legacy is evident in the provincial structure, which had affected elements of the existing system of Byzantine *pronoia* and, more directly, from the *itqà* of the Seljuk. See in A. Bombaci, *Gli Ottomani dalle origini alla conquista di Costantinopoli*, in 'Storia dell'Impero Ottomano' (Turin: UTET, 1981), pp.215–216.

6 G. Ágoston and B. Masters, *Encyclopedia of the Ottoman Empire* (New York: Facts on File, 2009), p.14.

4. The *Beglerbeg* of Rumelia, mid seventeenth century, Ottoman miniature of the Rålamb collection. This collection is one of the most detailed iconographic sources relating to Ottoman dress in the mid seventeenth century. This type of album was popular among collectors, like the Swedish diplomat Claes Rålamb (1622–98), who lived in Constantinople in 1657–58. The book of costumes is a *muraqqa*, a type of picture album usually put together from several different sources. The manuscript contains 121 colourful miniature drawings of Ottoman officials, soldiers, people of various occupations, and different ethnic groups. The drawings are in India ink with gouache and some gilding. Most of the images have notes in Swedish, French, Italian, or Latin describing the character as well as notes made by Claes Rålamb himself. In addition, Rålamb, commissioned a series of 20 wonderful large paintings, illustrating a procession of the *kapikulu* soldiers in full colour. The collection was donated to the Swedish National Library in 1886. This source partially fills the lacking Ottoman iconography during the period of prohibition in depicting human beings, which lasted until the 1720s.

tax revenues. This revenue, which took the name of *mal'i-mukatale*, could undergo variations according to the greater or lesser need of funds for the provincial treasury, or by decision of the government's chief, namely the grand vizier. In any case, the attribution of the posts and related income was entrusted only temporarily: the ownership of the land remained with the sultan, who could replace the curators with approved new officials.[7]

Most *dirlik* holders were military men. The *timar*, village-level revenue, was given to the lowest-level military men for their military service to the sultans. Holders of *zeamet* were generally higher-ranking officers. *Sancakbegs* and *beglerbegs* were granted the *has*, the largest *dirlik*. The peasants were assigned to a *timar*, *zeamet*, or *has*. If a peasant was cultivating the land in a *timar*, he paid his taxes directly to his *timar* holder. If his land was part of a *zeamet* or a *has*, he was responsible to his superiors. Only the *cizye* – the poll tax paid by the non-Muslims – went directly to the central treasury. Every detail concerning the *dirlik* system was specified in the *kanun names*, based on fiscal surveys. In return, *timar* and *zeamet* holders had to maintain a certain number of mounted soldiers, based on their incomes, as specified also in the *kanun name*, and upon request had to come under the *sancakbeg*'s command for military expeditions. This system was applied to the Anatolian and European lands of the Empire.

Egypt represented the major exception. After the occupation of Egypt in 1517, the Ottomans replaced the Mamluk sultan with a *beglerbeg* sent from Constantinople, but the social structure of the province remained unchanged. The Ottomans were pragmatic and realised that the special nature of the Egyptian economy favoured minimal intervention in its administration. Then, Egypt did not become a regular Ottoman province; the *timar* system, which marked the full integration of a province into the Empire, was never applied there, and the province was registered in the *sàlyàne* category alongside Baghdad, Basra, Yemen and Habesh. The governor received an annual salary, the *khazina* (or *khazna*), which he drew from the Egyptian treasury in accordance with the aforementioned *sàlyàne* category. This office was considered one of the most impoertant of the Empire, and often the Egyptian *beglerbeg* was promoted to the grand vizierate after completing his term in the province. Others, less fortunate, were imprisoned or sentenced to death as soon as they reached the sultan's court. Sivar-Oghlu Ghazi Mehmet, governor of Egypt from 1657 to 1659, was a strong governor, who suppressed a rebellion in Upper Egypt. Despite this, he was accused of embezzling a huge sum of money – the equivalent of the annual remittance to Constantinople – for which he was executed in Cairo. The governor's appointment was for one year, but it was usually renewed for another

---

7   In Western sources the Ottoman *timars* were compared to the feudal aristocracy, while in reality the differences were significant. The concept of nobility, in the sense of belonging to a privileged class, did not exist in the Ottoman empire. Usually, the appointments were not transmissible by inheritance and theoretically any Muslim subject could ascend to the rank of grand vizier. The concept of nobility was held only by the sultan's family.

Page 24: 5. Ottoman *çavuş*, 1683. Turban of white silk with dark red *kavuk* cap; yellow silk *kaftan* with silver lace on the lower edge, silver buttons and loops; *kusak* sash of silver brocade silk; carmine red short *hirk*a jacket; *salvar* breeches of white cotton; red leather *mest* shoes; *qilic* sabre scabbard of white metal; natural wood hilt with brass accessories. (Author's illustration. *Kaftan* preserved in the Kremsmünster Museum, Austria, abandoned by an Ottoman officer during the campaign of 1683; late seventeenth century qilij sabre, Heeresgeschichtliches Museum, Vienna)

Page 25: 6. *Yeniceri ağasi*, early eighteenth century. The commander of the janissary corps held a key rank in the Ottoman government and usually the sultan appointed him, choosing from among the candidates submitted by the grand vizier. However, he was not necessarily himself a janissary, but as the janissaries' political role increased in the early seventeenth century, from 1641 the office was held only by former janissaries. The *Yeniceri ağasi* was responsible for checking the newly recruited boys upon their arrival at Constantinople. He had his own residence in the capital, the so-called *ağa kapisi* (Aga's Gate) next to the Suleymaniye Mosque.

Clothing: a *Selimi* turban of white muslin wrapped around a red *kavuk* cap; *divoan-kürkü kaftan* of red velvet with golden and silver brocade embroidery, lined with dark brown sable fur; *entari* waistcoat of yellow silk decorated with green leaves and red corollas, golden buttons; scarlet *salvar* breeches; black leather *kemer* belt with silver accessories and turquoise stones; yellow leather *cizme* slippers; *samsir* sabre scabbard of white velvet with gilded accessories and cattle, ivory hilt with turquoise stones and red corals. (Author's Illustration. Reconstruction after Jean-Baptiste van Moor, *Recueil de cent estampes représentant les diverses nations du Levant*; Iranian *samsir*, about 1640, Topkapı Museum)

two or three.[8] During the seventeenth century the *beglerbeg*, as representative of the sultan's authority, was generally respected and still able to impose his will.

Even the European border provinces did not hold the *timar* system. Between the territories organised as *sancaks* under direct Ottoman rule and the *dar ül harb* (the area open to Holy War), there were frontier regions and vassal states. The *begs* of frontier regions enjoyed greater autonomy than the other *begs* who ruled *sancaks* far from the frontiers. For instance, in Kurdistan, which was a frontier region, the administrative and military systems were very different. As a border province, Ottoman Hungary too held special features. Although the nineteenth-century Hungarian historiography presents a very different scenario, the Ottoman occupation of Hungary was not totally negative, and it allowed the local nobility a certain degree of autonomy. The Ottomans even tolerated the presence of Hungarian soldiers and nobility in their territory. In the sixteenth century the way was opened by the soldiers of the Hungarian fortresses, which collected the taxes in the Ottoman territories, because wide areas across the border were subjected to dual sovereignty. In the following century, by this way, the Hungarian nobility also won back its influence and its right to intervene in the life of the people settled in Ottoman Hungary. The Hungarian officials imposed taxes, gave orders, made arrangements,

---

8   During the 281 years of Ottoman rule in Egypt, 110 *paşas* and *beglerbegs* served as governors of the province, thus making two and a half years the average term. 'In the early eighteenth century, Rami Mehmet won the distinction of being appointed for five years as governor of Egypt. This and other exemplary careers were exceptions, just as it also happened that a governor was sometimes recalled after only a few months in office. Since the *beglerbeg's* terms of office were normally short, they often tried to enrich themselves quickly and were not interested in sponsoring projects whose fruits they would not reap because they required much time, effort and money.' See Michael Winter, *Egyptian Society under Ottoman Rule*, p.32.

regulations and controlled their execution, issued bans, and severely punished the wayward. The people of the occupied regions had to resign themselves to the fact that their returned old masters stayed by the side of the new, and the Ottomans tolerated this actual double domination, a sort of condominium on their territory.[9] However, they could not tolerate limitation concerning the most important question: their military rule over the province. In Hungary, the Porte did not gain a definitive military victory, and could not subjugate the entire kingdom. Throughout the period of their rule, the partial occupation, the half-victory, continued, and this power-sharing became permanent.[10]

A further special category of territory formed the composite Ottoman domains. Alongside the *timar, zeamet* and *has* provinces of Anatolia and Europe, some *beglerbegliks* and *paşaliks* did not included *dirliks* and the tax revenues were paid from the subjects to the governors. These territories were known as *sàlyàne*, and were different in several respects regarding military matters. In these provinces any *timar* and *zeamet* were appointed, and the incomes were collected merely for the treasury, and governors sent from Constantinople were paid in cash from the moneys collected.

The hierarchy established in the civil administration also constituted the military leadership of the Empire. In this regard, the Ottoman Empire resembled a military dictatorship. As discussed before, each governor had command functions over the troops raised in his province. The close relationship between civil society and military organisation was often the cause of changes in territorial divisions. In 1660, for example, was established the *Paşalik* of Várad on the border with Transylvania, in order to better control the turbulent political situation of the tributary princedom. In a similar way, minor land appointments consequent to military conquest may be noted at Crete during the war against Venice, when the island was divided into 17 *zeamets* and 15,130 *timars*.

Major governors' and *sancakbegs'* household heads became 'contractors', taking charge of revenue collection, military recruitment and provisioning for the state. Combining high offices with revenue-farms consolidated this trend. Ottoman dignitaries recognised government finance, particularly tax-farming-*dirlik*, as the best route to wealth; and the posts of their collection agents were held first by household retainers but later often by notables, the *ayan*, of local origin, and became provincial power centres.[11] The reforms influencing military recruitment include the placing of tax collection in the hands of local

---

9   The territories occupied by the Ottomans thus survived until the Holy League War in this ambiguous situation, militarily well subjected and heavily taxed, and for their internal affairs, with ambivalence, in relative freedom but subjected to the service of two lordships. The 'condominium' was not unknown in Eastern Europe and the Balkans. In historiography, this terms designates a relative particularism of certain territories. Scholars consider this phenomenon rather as autonomy. It should be noted that the condominium characterised the Balkan situation before the final Ottoman rule. Further reading: K. Hegyi, *La province hongroise dans l'Empire Ottoman*, in 'Acta Historica Academiae Scientiarum Hungaricae', 33–1987, pp.209–215.

10   *Ibidem.*

11   *Ayan* is the plural of the Arabic word *ayn*, meaning 'something or someone that is selected or special'. The term was used differently by different communities within the Ottoman Empire. The *ayan* included among their ranks wealthy merchants, heads of janissary garrisons, leaders of important craft guilds, and those who had bought the right to collect taxes for the Porte.

men, and the concentration of both mobilisation and supply in many of the same officials, collectively known as *ayans* or 'committees of notables'. In the early eighteenth century came the transformation of the *ayan* into a distinct social class, which differed from both the government-appointed officials such as the *sancakbegs*, governors, and *kadıs*, and the local elites such as wealthy merchants and cultivators. It was a direct result of their growing economic position within the provinces due to the extension of the tax-farming and land tenure systems as well as the social and military responsibilities that came along with it. Regardless of the changes that occurred in the nature of the *ayan*, by the early eighteenth century two very different groups existed within the Ottoman state that both carried the title *ayan*. The first of these and, by far, the most widespread, were small local notables who through their wealth and local influence were able to stand apart from the rest of the local population. The second group, and the one which is of most interest because of its role in the army, is the 'grand *ayan*' (magnate) who exerted influence over entire provinces and received official recognition from the state in terms of titles and honours.[12] Both of these groups could be found throughout the Empire and served an important role in the functioning of Ottoman provincial administration. The prolonged wars in which the Ottomans were involved since the late seventeenth century had a tremendous economic and social impact on the state. No longer was the *sipahi* cavalry which had served as the backbone of the Ottoman military able to compete against Western infantry, which began to dominate the battlefields. The establishment of a well-trained infantry required an increase in tax revenue in order for the central government to equip and train soldiers in this new kind of warfare. The revenues generated by the *timar* system were insufficient to finance the equipment and training of a firearm-equipped infantry, especially with continual currency devaluations.[13]

The wealthiest and most powerful provincial notables were located in the Balkans, which become the Ottoman borderlands in the eighteenth century, alongside the bordering areas located near the Adriatic, Aegean, Black, and Mediterranean seas. The new scenario enabled the local large *ayan* landholders to reap the financial rewards of participating in the trade of soldiers for the Porte. The physical distance of an *ayan*'s landholdings from Constantinople frequently allowed them to disregard the central government, represented often by weak *Paşas* or *beglerbegs*. A quick glance at the peripheral territories of the Ottoman Maghreb, Balkan frontiers along the Adriatic and Danube, eastern Anatolia, and the Arab lands of Baghdad and Egypt, to name but a

---

12 Unlike the lesser *ayan*, those who carried the patronymic titles of –oğlu and –zâde or, even more significantly, had the plural forms of these two endings, could be categorised as being part of the grand *ayan* which were often familial dynasties whose influence over a given region extended for at least a couple generations. See R. Zens, 'Provincial Powers: the Rise of Ottoman Local Notables (Ayan)', in *History Studies – International Journal of History*, vol. 3–3, 2011, pp.433–447.

13 *Ibidem*, p.438: 'In addition, timar revenues were affected in the first half of the seventeenth century by the severe decline in grain prices in the Balkans. The decreasing grain prices encouraged many reaya to shift from land cultivation to livestock herding. This shift towards shepherding was devastating to the *sipahis*, since the sheep tax was reserved for the central treasury and could not be used to fund the needs and activities of the timar holders.'

few, reveal a series of semi-autonomous provincial notables who frequently operated independently of the central government.

Political Crisis and Military Weakness?

In relation to the internal problems of the Ottoman Empire, historians remark that the breakdown of the apparatus of government affected not only the government, but also the whole of the bureaucratic and religious institutions under the Empire. This condition leads to the catastrophic fall-off in efficiency and integrity in methods of training, promotion, and recruitment of the bureaucracy at all levels. This internal chaos would also have affected the army, pushing the Empire into an irreversible decline. However, because the decadence of the Ottoman Empire was not only caused by the weakness of its military power, it is reasonable to say that the decline of Ottoman Empire resulted from complex problems. Some historians also conveyed that the term 'decline' is an inaccurate description of the process where the Ottoman Empire lost its position in the European context. Today, scholars use the terms 'crisis' or 'immobility' instead of decline, emphasising factors such as economic, financial and military changes, as well as the cautious reforms which enabled the Ottoman Empire to endure until 1918 despite the shifts in power. They represent the Ottoman experience from the seventeenth to the eighteenth centuries as a period of transformation in order to adapt the state to the changing international environment. External factors from the penetration of European merchant capital into the Empire, especially French, then Dutch and English, caused huge financial problems for the Ottoman economy. Although this trade system gave many benefit for the merchants, it led to a decline in state revenues and a shortage of raw materials for domestic consumption.[14] And, obviously, without the revenues, the Porte would suffer a serious problem building its armed forces. The conservative governing elite had neither the understanding of economic developments occurring in Western European countries nor was it willing to make drastic changes. The most serious limitation was that the Empire had an outdated agrarian economy, which had limited surplus capacity, was short of ready cash, and was short in the resources required to support the newly evolving gunpowder mass army. The draining of resources became unsustainable. The wars of the seventeenth century were very expensive both in terms of number of soldiers and increasing costs of salary payments: 285.9 million of akçe in 1660, grown to 440.4 million in 1687–88, until the record of 668 million in 1698–99, equal to 55.14 percent of the total state expenditure.[15] The second limitation was directly linked to the first. The government was well known for its dislike of making drastic changes or abolishing any traditional

---

14 See H. Inalcik, 'Military and Fiscal Transformation in the Ottoman Empire', in *Archivum Ottomanicum*, n. 6 (1980), pp.283–337.

15 M. Uyar and E.J. Erickson, *A Military History of the Ottomans* (Santa Barbara, CA; Denver, CO; Oxford: ABC-Clio, 2009), p.87, and G. Ágoston, 'Ottoman Warfare in Europe, 1453–1826', in J. Black (ed.) *European Warfare, 1453–1815* (London: Palgrave Macmillan, 1999), p.137. Further details in the appendix.

military corps or institutions. Understandably, this conservatism resulted from the government's unwillingness to face the socio-political consequences of any radical change.

According to some recent contributions which employ the 'Krause Model' in order to locate capabilities on the scale of international production hierarchy, including arms production, arms transfer and technological diffusion, the Ottoman Empire belonged to an intermediate position between the second and third category or 'Technology II and III'. The four categories are: Technology I: just enough skills to operate and maintain different kinds of weapons; Technology II: sufficient scientific and engineering skills to reproduce or copy basic weapons belonging to the first category; Technology III: appropriate skills through various military and economic organisations to adapt and refine existing weapons for particular battlefield conditions; Technology IV: proper economic, social and political structure to create new weaponry utilising advanced technology. The Ottomans were obviously able to copy and reproduce existing technology, but they had not mastered the underlying process of innovation or adaptation; thus, they were essentially third-tier arms producers.[16] Considering this scenario, Ottoman military thought acted for centuries in an immutable context, where several factors determined choices and mistakes also.[17]

The decrease of resources plus military turmoil was fertile ground for serious political crisis. The attempt to re-establish control of the state had as protagonist the young Sultan Osman II (1603–22), but his courageous attempt to reform the state failed due to the hostility of the increasingly powerful and feared Janissaries, who deposed the Sultan and killed him in May 1622. Since that date every political act had to contend with the prerogative of these turbulent professional soldiers, powerful enough to spread in the rest of Europe the anecdote that now, they constituted more a menace for the sultan than his enemies. The mournful black handkerchief ceremonial, with which were declared forfeited viziers and sultans, following strangulation with a silk rope, served as a deterrent against any unwelcome reform. The major towns and cities of several provinces were surrounded by an unsafe periphery controlled by bandits and rebels. Local authorities were often forced to come to terms with them, or to recognise concessions and paltry compromises. The Empire was transforming in an archipelago, where the main towns remained isolated and without connections with the court and the government. The weakness of central authority and the

16 According to the Krause Model, there was not an actual Ottoman technological decline. Indeed, in its third-tier producer category from the end of the fifteenth century to the early eighteenth century, the Ottoman Empire maintained its original military technological position. In other ways, the general constraints under which the Ottoman army operated are often neglected or underestimated. Five contributory factors influenced in diverse proportions Ottoman military performance in actual deployments: technological constraints; cost constraints; physical barriers and environmental constraints; motivational limits; limits of the state power and coercion. See K. Krause, *Arms and the States. Pattern of Military Production and Trade* (Cambridge: Cambridge University Press, 1992), p.19.
17 See R. Murphey, *Ottoman Warfare, 1500–1700* (London: UCL Press, 1999) p.13, in the chapter 'Material constraints on Ottoman warfare: the immutable context'.

economic crisis affecting many provinces of Anatolia favoured the rebellion of some communities, such as the Druze of Lebanon in 1610, or permitted the neighbouring country to annex a portion of the state, for example as the Zaydi Arabs did of Yemen in 1616, and the Iranians when they conquered Baghdad in 1624. Revolt against the Ottomans had exploded in the Crimea and in the Cossack regions since 1624, while in Anatolia began a new *celali* uprising led by Abaza Mehmed Paşa,[18] who involved the army in hard campaigns undertaken in 1628 after the long siege of Erzurum and the submission of the rebels. Rebellions and unrest occurred also in Syria and Egypt, which involved also the local garrisons. Further problems preoccupied the Sublime Porte in the west. The de facto independence of Montenegro and the persistent Greek guerrillas in Epirus and the Mani peninsula in the Peloponnese, threatened trades and internal security. New disorders happened in Western Anatolia in 1632, while in Constantinople a janissary revolt ended with the murder of the Grand Vizier Hafiz Ahmed. Not only political instability caused concerns: fate also contributed to worsen the scenario when in 1633 a great fire damaged the capital. A period of fragile peace and stability was achieved during the last ruling years of Sultan Murad IV (1612–1640) which, thanks to the work of Grand Vizier Kemankes Mustafa Kara, managed to prevent the collapse of the Empire. In this period were introduced severe restrictions, included the prohibition of tobacco and alcohol to prevent riots. In 1639, the Porte finally signed a treaty of peace with the Safavid Empire. One year previously the Ottomans had achieved the reconquest of Baghdad, but they had lost Erevan in 1636.

The death of Murad IV caused a power vacuum that opened the way to the intrigues of the *valide* Kösem Sultan, who favoured the accession to the throne of his son Ibrahim I. The short reign of this prince (1640–48): 'magnified and exalted so much the ills of the state, which none of the sultans that followed dared to give his name to his children.'[19] The outrageous conduct of '*dely* Ibrahim' (mad Ibrahim) provoked the intervention of the Janissaries, who deposed the Sultan and eliminated him. Ibrahim is also recorded for having ordered the conquest of Crete and for reopening Ottoman expansion to the west after half a century. The long war against Venice (1645–71) reopened also the spiral of inflation and led to the beginning of a frightening economic crisis. The uncontrolled court expenses under Ibrahim I and his unwise measures

---

18 The term *celali* is probably a misnomer. The misunderstanding begins with Ottoman court historians of the seventeenth century who referred to the rebellions as *celali* revolts after a certain Sheikh Celal, who raised a popular rebellion in Eastern Anatolia against the Ottoman authorities in 1519. Historians differ over the reasons for the *celali* rebellions. Some researches cite evidence of severe economic and social pressure in rural Turkey caused by half a century of consistent population growth. Others point to the economic upheaval caused by the influx of cheap silver from the Americas; the drop in the real value of silver destabilised prices and led to rapid inflation. Another factor that contributed to destabilisation in the countryside was the proliferation of muskets among the peasants and the inability of graduates from the state-run religious schools, or madrasas, to find employment. In fact, all these factors probably contributed to the unrest. Further reading: S. White, 'The Climate of Rebellion in Early Modern Ottoman Empire' (Cambridge; Cambridge University Press, 2011).
19 Stanford J. Shaw, 'History of the Ottoman Empire and Modern Turkey' (Cambridge; Cambridge University Press, 1976), part one, p.441.

against Western trade, such as the blockade of foreign ships from the ports of Constantinople and Smyrna, paralysed whole sectors of the Ottoman economy. The currency was devalued repeatedly, and the Treasury resorted to collecting taxes two years in advance.[20] Anatolia was crossed again by the bands of *celali*, to which was added a population exasperated by fiscal measures. Riots and revolts exploded in Constantinople too. The title of sultan went to the teenage son of Ibrahim, Mehmed IV, destined to remain on the throne for 39 years. Between 1645 and 1656, 16 grand viziers were replaced with a bewildering rapidity and the instability of the political situation rushed the Empire into chaos. Since 1646 the Venetian fleet, as reprisal for the attack on Crete, had blocked the entrance to the Dardanelles and the fear of a landing in Constantinople caused the flight of the whole court. The appointment as prime minister of Tarhoncu Ahmed, who previously distinguished himself as governor in Egypt, brought a temporary improvement in internal affairs. The Grand Vizier tried to reform the *timar*, awarding them the collection of taxes to procuring the money desperately need by the Treasury. Tarhoncu Ahmed was the first Ottoman head of government to prepare a budget of estimated expenses; he abolished a large number of costly honorary offices of the court, army and navy, but in 1653, after just a year of reforms, he was eliminated by the intrigues of his opponents. In 1653, the political crisis reached the climax: eight grand viziers alternated in government in just three years, while the struggles of palace and civil unrest continued their usual trend, dominated by the *haseki* (the sultan's concubine) the Janissaries and the major governors. In 1656, a new great revolt began in Anatolia and soon extended into Syria, led by the governor of Aleppo Abaza Hassan Paşa. The scenario appeared desperate and in Western Europe several political observers thought that the Empire was on the verge of collapse. In the fall of 1656, the choice in appointing the new grand vizier fell to the governor of Damascus, the ex-janissary and ultra-septuagenarian Köprülü Mehmed. Thanks to the efforts of the ancient vizier the empire returned to being the menacing power of past centuries. The palace intrigues were opposed with energy, the army's discipline restored, and every dissent cut down with very hard methods. The *celali* revolts resumed their intensity, but soon the disorders ended with the capture and execution of all the rebel leaders. Corruption was equally persecuted with iron hand. In Europe began to circulate the image of Köprülü Mehmed depicted as a ruthless, bloodthirsty despot. He was able to safeguard Constantinople during the most critical events which occurred during the Cretan war against Venice, when in July 1657 the Venetian fleet try to force the Dardanelles channel after its triumph in the fourth battle of the straits. The Grand Vizier personally directed operations from the channel banks and he not hesitate to order the shooting of the routed crews during the most dramatic phase of the naval battle. Despite his bloody methods, Köprülü Mehmed returned to the Sultan a cohesive state and an army capable of resuming expansion against its neighbours. A unique case in Ottoman history, he assured succession in the office of grand vizier to

---

20　*Ibidem*, p.443.

an equally able official like his son Ahmed. Under the Köprülü leadership the Ottoman Empire reached its maximum territorial expansion.

State Government and Army Direction (*a near-perfect military state*)[21]

The hierarchy established across the territorial divisions also constituted the military leadership structure of the empire. Each governor had command over the troops raised in his province. In this regard, the Ottoman Empire resembled a military dictatorship, The Ottoman regime conformed to the pattern of the military patronage state, and the entire governmental machinery, civil administration and military forces, and even religious functionaries were treated as part of the military establishment. The Ottomans defined them as *askeri*, literally meaning 'military' though frequently translated as 'ruling class'.[22] The subject population was the *raya*, the common people. For the Ottomans, the maintenance of the distinction between *askeri* and *raya* was the most fundamental social division within the Empire. Naima Mustafa, a seventeenth-century Turkish chronicler, wrote significantly in this regard, when he describes the Empire as a state governed by a 'circle of justice':

> Because the Ottoman society was separated in classes, the mass of the subjects at base, producer of the state wealth, maintained the military class at the top of power, conforming to an 'equity circle': 1 – State or government cannot exist without the army. 2 – The maintenance of the army requires wealth. 3 – The wealth is produced by the subjects. 4 – The subjects can prosper only in a condition of justice. 5 – Without state or government cannot exist justice.[23]

In war as in peace, the grand vizier held the rank of supreme commander of all the armies. On campaign, he led the main army and appointed his staff of field officers and adjutants without limitation. Like the grand vizier on the field, the offices of *beglerbeg* and *paşa* corresponded usually to the function of *serasker* (senior field commander), whose duties were similar to a Western European general. The commanders of some corps or regional areas were known as *serdar*, comparable to the rank of a modern chief of major staff. The *serdar* and *serasker* were directly responsible of the troops under their command and both had to plan supplies and other logistic needs. Grand viziers, as well as other commanders, were assisted in the task by lieutenants or *kaimakan*.

---

21 Regarding the idea that the Ottoman Empire was 'a near-perfect military state', see P. Sugar, *A Near-Perfect Military Society: The Ottoman Empire*, in L.L. Farrar (ed.), 'War: A Historical, Political, and Social Study', (Santa Barbara, CA: ABC-Clio, 1978), pp.95–104.

22 Subjects of the Ottoman leading class identified them with different terms. In Egypt and Syria, for instance, they were called 'Romai' after the conquest of Constantinople, as the sultans were the successors of the Byzantine–Roman Empire. Curiously, the Ottomans called the Mamluk of Egypt and Syria çerkesy (Circassians) or even *türk* because they came from Turkish-speaking populations of south-western Asia.

23 The 'circle of justice' defined the proper relationship of the *askeri* and the *raya*: the *askeri* received taxation, and the *raya* paid it. Various Authors: *Islamic World Atlas* (Oxford: Equinox, 1982), p.72.

7. Grand Vizier *Fazil* [the wise] Köprülü Ahmed (1635–1676). He was the most successful Ottoman military commander of his age. The portraits of grand viziers and other personalities of the Ottoman Empire are mostly imaginary, however this is considered very faithful, because it was executed after the instructions of the French ambassador to Constantinople, and published by Balthasar Moncornet in the 1660s. (Author's archive)

During a war campaign, the grand vizier assumed the rank of general commander of the army, except when the direction of the army was assumed by the sultan himself. But throughout the period 1645–1718, it happened only once in the two-year period 1695–96, when the army in Hungary was under the command of Mustafa II, the last Ottoman sultan to lead the soldiers in campaign.

Attitudes to command constituted a fundamental requirement to the appointment of grand vizier, however, personalities who distinguished themselves as leaders were few. In this period, there were few grand viziers whose names are associated with victorious episodes. Köprülü Ahmed was certainly the most successful commander of this age. He was born in 1635, at Vezirköprü, in Anatolia, the eldest son of Grand Vizier Köprülü Mehmed. Uniquely in Ottoman history, Mehmed assured the succession of the post of grand vizier to his son Ahmed. The father chose for his son a career in the learned professions, and at 16 Ahmed became a teacher, but entered the Sultan's service when his father became grand vizier. He was made governor of Erzurum (1659) and then Damascus (1660) before he was called up to deputise as grand vizier during an illness of his father. Ahmed became finally grand vizier on 1 November 1661, and proved to be as energetic and skillful as his father in asserting his authority. In 1661, a few weeks after being given the office of grand vizier, he did not hesitate to order the death of a navy captain, who was found publicly celebrating the death of Ahmed's father Köprülü Mehmed.[24] During his first Hungarian campaign in 1663, he learned of a plot against himself, fermented by Şâmî-zâde Mehmed, chief of the secretaries and a member of the faction who brought his father to power. Again, Ahmed did not hesitate to have the man executed. In these decisions, which involved people who belittled him and struggled against him, he always had the support of the Sultan. Contemporary Ottoman sources found in him all the qualities requisite for an Oriental statesman; he was known for his wide knowledge, wisdom, justice, and impartiality. He also distinguished himself in Islamic law and Persian literature. As a military commander, Ahmed showed himself to be skillful and knowledgeable, especially in siege warfare. In open field campaigns, he extensively used the aggressive tactic of raiding, employing Ottoman and Tartar riders. In the war against the Habsburgs of 1663–64, Ahmed strengthened his bonds of alliance with the *han* of the Crimean Tartars, who sent his sons Ahmed Giray and Mohammed Giray, in the summer of 1663 to command a contingent of horsemen estimated to number 30,000.

---

24 J. von Hammer-Purgstall, *Geschichte des Osmanischen Reiches* (Budapest, 1827–1835), vol. XI, p.126.

Ahmed also placed emphasis on the age-old Ottoman policy of protection of the *raya* (non-Muslim taxpayers), which was possible only under a strong central government. He followed his father's reforms, aimed at reducing the power of the janissaries, making them more efficient by restoring discipline into the corps. His measures finally resulted in him attaining the appellation of 'Fazil', the wise. Though his failure at the battle of Szentgotthárd tarnished his earlier success against the Habsburgs – the capture of Érsekúivár and the destruction of Zrínyivár, for example – he was able to make a treaty favourable to the Ottomans at Vasvár, on 10 August 1664. In fact, the Sultan received him with great favour, considering the achievement of Vasvár a great military victory. Fazıl Ahmed won unparalleled prestige when he conquered Kandije in Crete after a siege of 28 months from 1667 to 1669, thus ending a long and expensive war against Venice. During the siege of Kandije, he pursued his objective without worrying about the tremendous losses suffered by his army and the dangerous consequences that could result from his action. In early 1669, one of the most critical moments of the siege coincided with the intense Venetian negotiations to reach an armistice. A rumour began to circulate that the Grand Vizier wanted to continue the siege only to enrich himself further. About 500 menacing Janissaries and *sipahis*, along with many officers, assembled in front of his tent and threatened to stone him. Ahmed was able to restore the dangerous situation only thanks to the intervention of his cousin Kara Mustafa, the *ağa* of the Janissaries and other officers, who dispersed the seditious rebels.[25]

The expedition in Podolia in 1672, in which the Sultan himself took part, was a great achievement for Ahmed. After the Treaty of Buczacz, signed on 18 October 1672, the strategic fortress of Kamieniec was annexed to the Empire, and Polish Ukraine surrendered to the Cossacks under Ottoman protection. Poland was taxed with paying a yearly tribute of 22,000 gold pieces. Nevertheless, the Poles, under John Sobieski, rejected these onerous conditions and took up a counter-offensive, which caused a new war that, continued for four more years until the Treaty of Żórawno, signed on 17 October 1676. Russian intervention in Ukraine forced Ahmed to invade the region in the summer of 1674. Exhausted and ill because of long expeditions and alcohol abuse, he died on 3 October 1676, near Çorlu, in Thrace. He left a fortune of more than 300,000 gold pieces.

His successor and brother, Merzifonlu Kara ('the black') Mustafa, was a man capable of conceiving ambitious expansion plans. Born to Albanian parents in 1634 or 1635, in Merzifon, central Anatolia, Mustafa was educated in the household of Köprülü Mehmed and married into the powerful Köprülü family. In 1659, he became governor of Silistra and subsequently held a number of important offices in the government. Within 10 years, he was acting as deputy for his brother-in-law, Ahmed. Whenever Ahmed was away from the capital, Kara Mustafa was always left as his *kaimakan*.[26] The story reproaches Kara Mustafa for the failure of Vienna, however it is right to outline his quality of a talented organiser. In fact, he was able to gather the largest army of the century and lead it without too much inconvenience to the siege of the Austrian capital, and to supply it conveniently during the 60 days of the siege. He knew war at first hand and he was a bold leader, but his previous experience had been limited to battles against weaker opponents: a minor part in the war for Crete as *kapudan paşa* for two years, later in

---

25 *Ibidem*, p.323.

26 An interesting and lesser-known description of Kara Mustafa and Köprülü Ahmed is that of George Etherege, secretary of the English ambassador to the Porte, and incidentally a notable dramatist, Sir Daniel Harvey, dated 1670: 'The Grand Signor's private council consisted of only five persons, the favourite *kuloglu*, the Caimacam of the Port, the mufti Vani Effendi, a famous Arab preacher, and one of the pashas of the Bench (and counting the grand vizir, there would be five), most of the great men being with the Visier, who is imploy'd in Candia … This kaimakan's name is Mustapha Pasha; hee was formerly captaine pasha or admirall of the galleys, and has married the Visier's sister. Yet this allyance keeps them not from secret emulations and hatreds, and it is thought the kaimakan will dispute the Grand Signor's favour with him at his returne. The Visier, they say, exceeds not the age of two and thirty yeares; hee is of middle stature and has a good mind; hee is prudent and just not to bee corrupted by money, the generall vice of this country, nor inclined to cruelty as his father was. The kaimakan is about the age of forty-five, well spoken, subtill, corrupt, and a great dissembler. Hee flatters the Grand Signor in his inclinations, and ever accompanies him in his hunting, a toyle which nothing but excessive ambition and interest could make him undergoe.' K.M. Setton, *Venice, Austria and the Turks in the seventeenth century* (Philadelphia, The American Philosophical Society, 1991), p.250.

the final phase of the siege, and two campaigns in Moldavia and Ukraine, even if accomplished under the great Köprülü Ahmed. During the campaign of 1674 in Podolia, Kara Mustafa held independent command for the first time. The action presented minor difficulties, but he left a sign of his fierce temperament, at least according to his first biographer:

> The *kaimakan* (Kara Mustafa) marched against the strong city of Human (today Uman in Ukraine) with sixteen *oda* of janissaries, all the feudal troops of Anatolia, Rumelia, Syria and Bosnia, and an artillery train of twenty-six falcons and six culverins. This was the first war expedition of the so far we have him always seen hunting with the sultan, and after his debut in this war at the siege of Kamieniec … The success of the expedition against Human was assured by the superior forces at his disposal. With the help of Doroszenko's Cossacks, Human was stormed and all the inhabitants were massacred, the streets of the city were flooded with blood of the Christians. Prisoners were skinned alive, then stuffed and finally sent to the Sultan. This was the first achievement of Mustafa the Black, whose soul was indeed as black as his name.[27]

On 5 October 1676, Kara Mustafa succeeded to Köprülü Ahmed as grand vizier and was appointed to the command of the army for the new war against Russia. He led the campaign into Ukraine, attempting to shore up the position of the Cossack state of Right-Bank Ukraine, in order to place it under Ottoman vassalage. Eventually, the war against Russia turned into an expensive and difficult series of campaigns, which ended with modest results, except for the conquest of Çigirin.

During the long war against the Holy League, the commanders who took turns after Kara Mustafa collected an impressive series of setbacks, culminating with the loss of the Peloponnese in 1687 and Belgrade in 1688. It fell to another member of the Köprülü family, Mustafa, to assume command of the army on the crucial Balkan front. He was able to arrest the enemy advance and, after 1689, he succeeded in expelling enemies from Bulgaria, Bosnia and Albania. In 1690 his offensive in Serbia closed with the conquest of Belgrade and then his troops penetrated Hungary and Transylvania, but in 1691 Köprülü Mustafa was defeated at Slankamen, where he was killed. After him, pathetic and unprepared commanders took turns, anxious to conclude the campaigns, and hesitant to undertake any offensive action. After the positive experience under Sultan Mustafa II, who achieved success at Lugos in 1695, and arrested the Imperial offensive on Temeşvár in 1696, the war ended with the tremendous disaster of Zenta, in 1697, where ambitions to regain Hungary were finally sunk. A quite miraculous victory arrived in 1711, during the war against Russia, despite the temporising strategy of the Grand Vizier Baltaçi Mehmed. Facilitated by the failure of Moldavian plans to revolt, in July 1711 the Ottoman army surrounded the Russian expeditionary corps near Falltschi on the Pruth River. The Ottomans obtained the Russian surrender and the delivery of all the artillery, and with peace negotiations Azov in Crimea returned to their

---

27 Hammer-Purgstall, *Geschichte des Osmanischen Reiches*, vol. XI, p.401.

possession. The last grand vizier to revitalise for a short time the age of the Ottoman conquests was Damad Ali *kumurçi* (the coalman), who directed the conquest of the Peloponnese in 1715. He led the army in the Balkans when the conflict against Venice involved the Habsburgs. Damad Ali died in 1716 at the battle of Peterwardein, fighting against the most feared adversary, Prince Eugene of Savoy, whose soldiers broke all hope of Ottoman victory in the war of 1716–1718.

Ottoman military history was not without other valuable commanders. In the subordinate ranks is possible to find officers with the traditional Turkish military virtues. Their enterprises are little known and almost never decisive for the development of a campaign, but it is worth mentioning some of these careers, such as the *serasker* Baltaoğlu Hüseyin Paşa (1605?–1659), general commander in Crete for 10 years after 1645. For his eccentric temperament, he gained the nickname *dely* (foul, but in his case bold). His life is seems a literary stereotype of oriental-inspired adventure novels. Known also as *ghazi* (warrior) or *sari* (blonde) Hüseyn, he was born near Bursa in Anatolia and was of Turkish origin. Little is known about his early days in Constantinople. During the reign of Murad IV, he was a member of the palace court's personnel. Hüseyin attracted the attention of his superiors for his skill as an archer. After winning the Sultan's appreciation, he was promoted to various posts: chief stableman and then *sipahi* cavalry officer, participating in the campaigns of Baghdad and Yerevan. Promoted as *paşa* of Silistra, in Bulgaria, he became *beglerbeg* of Egypt in 1635. From the very first day of his arrival in Egypt, when he confiscated the finance minister's and advisors' properties for his own, Hüseyin introduced a series of reforms that made him widely disliked by the local populace. He brought with him to Egypt a large number of Druzes who committed robberies in Cairo, and extorted money from the locals for an upcoming feast celebrating

8. Imaginary portrait of Merzifonlu Kara Mustafa (1634–1683), who succeeded to Köprülü Ahmed as grand vizier in 1677. He served in Crete, Podolia and Ukraine, and in 1682 became the main instigator of the war against the Habsburgs. He undertook the war even though, as the limited achievements of the 1678–81 war had demonstrated, he did not possess the fortune or skill of his predecessors. Encouraged by the successes achieved in the initial phase of the campaigns, Mustafa laid siege to Vienna. Historians condemn his behaviour in 1683 as disastrous, but often they elude the Grand Vizier's talent as an organiser, and able to lead the largest army of the century in besieging the Austrian capital. The defeat of Vienna cost Mustafa his position, and ultimately, his life. On 25 December 1683, the Grand Vizier was executed in Belgrade at the order of Mehmed IV. He suffered death by strangulation with a silk cord, which was the method of capital punishment inflicted on high-ranking persons in the Ottoman Empire. (Author's archive)

the *beglerbeg*'s arrival. Hüseyin also often reportedly rode a horse through crowds of people and animals, swinging a sword, for recreation. Each month, he forced locals to trade in their bullion coin for adulterated metal and sent bureaucrats and officials to remote locations without explanation. During his rule, it was said he had over 1,200 people executed, not including those that he killed by his own hand. Despite his cruelty, Hüseyin was an able leader and skillful commander of the local troops, which was a particularly difficult

9. The gravestone commemorating the valiant *beglerbeg* of Hungary, Arnavut Abdi Abdurrahman, killed in September 1686 during the siege of Buda. Albanian born, he joined the army as a janissary and became commander of the corps in 1667 after a brilliant career. Abdurrahman held this rank during the three fierce campaign in Crete. In 1673, he became *paşa* of Baghdad, and then governor of Egypt in 1676. From 1680 he held the same rank in Bosnia, and in 1684, Abdurrahman finally became *beglerbeg* of Hungary. During the siege of Buda, he skillfully directed the defence for over two months, but the relief forces failed to support him. The city was reduced to ruins, but the *beglerbeg* continued to exhort his men until the bitter end, occurred on 2 September with the surrender of the castle.

A memorial was erected in 1932 in Buda castle, and the inscription, in Hungarian and Turkish, says: 'The last governor of the 145 year long Turkish occupation of Buda, Abdurrahman Abdi Pasha the Albanian fell here on 2 September 1686, when he was 70 years old. He was a brave enemy, may he rest in peace.' (Author's photograph)

task in Egypt. He was attentive to government details and successfully decreased robbery and burglary in Cairo. He was able to maintain the siege around Kandije, despite the precarious situation determined by the Venetian blockade, who left the army without supplies for long periods. And thanks to his efforts failure of the campaign was avoided. But *dely* Hüseyin paid with for his differences with the Grand Vizier with his life, falling victim to the 'normalisation' policy introduced by Köprülü Mehmed. In January 1659, having received the position of *kapudan paşa* (high admiral of the fleet) the year before, Hüseyn was strangled. In his memory arose a multitude of folk songs and poetic composition that kept him alive for centuries in the popular memory.[28]

The echoes of the actions directed by some commanders who arrived in Constantinople were amplified for propaganda reasons, giving birth to legends and nicknames for the protagonists. In the years before the war against the Habsburgs, the enterprises of the *paşa* of Silistra Şyşman Ibrahim, the *saitan* (devil) or 'the fat' had wide echo in the Empire. He gained a remarkable reputation for his unpredictable actions in the war against Poland in 1672–76. His conduct as commander was considerable for the Ottoman standard, but he acted with extreme brutality, exterminating the civilians of the townships which refused to surrender.[29] In the war against Russia, *saitan* Ibrahim did not perform as expected, and lost the command and was then exiled to Anatolia. A characteristic feature of the Ottoman commanding staff was the high turnover, which however did not always end with a death sentence, as happened with Kara Mustafa and *deli* Hüseyin. Usually, the commanders who had failed to carry out satisfactorily a command issued to them, lost their commissions. An Ottoman *askeri* without a position in the army or bureaucracy could not sustain his household, and without the members of his household, he could not hope to perform well enough in the field to receive a new

---

28   E. Eickhoff, *Venedig, Wien und die Osmanen* (Stuttgart, Ernst Klett Verlag, 1988), p.167.

29   O. Bartov, *Anatomy of a Genocide. The Life and Death of a Town called Buczacz* (New York, NY: Simon & Schuster, 2018), p.33.

appointment. This rule did not prevent some commanders from returning in an authoritative post, despite the mediocre service performed until then. Probably the most significant case was that of Genç (young) Hüseyin Paşa, who collected a series of defeats against György II Rákóczy of Transylvania in 1659–60, the Imperialists under Souches in 1664 and, most humiliating, at Chocim, in 1673, against Sobieski. Despite his poor curriculum, Genç Hüseyin distinguished himself for bravery and courage in Ukraine, then, after his appointment as governor of Damascus in 1682, fought valiantly during the siege of Vienna. He died a natural death in Pest, in 1684.[30]

During the War of the Holy League, the enterprises of another Ibrahim Paşa raised Ottoman morale again in the desperate years after 1684. The Bosnian Ibrahim Paşa had become famous after his actions against the Poles and Russians, but his major fame was derived to him with the reckless Hungarian raid of June 1684, when he forced the Imperialists to leave the siege of Buda. Two years later he was appointed to command in Dalmatia, against the Venetians. Set against the same enemies, the *serasker* Halil Paşa gained the name of 'indomitable' by his adversaries. After four years of continued defeats, Halil replaced the brave but untalented Caffer Ismail Paşa, and in 1688 succeeded in arresting the Venetian offensive on the island of Euboea with the bloody siege of Negroponte (today Chalkis). Later, he tried to harass the enemy with a series of well-planned incursions into Attica and the Peloponnese in 1692 and 1694.

However, the singular quality of some officers could not compensate for the almost generally poor military preparation that plagued the Ottoman commanders. In addition, the best Ottoman officers often personally participated in the most dangerous actions and their loss was replaced with difficulty, resorting to replacements who owed their position to the favour of his superiors or to corruption. No military knowledge was learned except experience in campaigns, and this factor aggravated the disparity with their Western counterparts, who in that age were beginning to elaborate modern military theories.[31]

---

30 Hammer-Purgstall, *Geschichte des Osmanischen Reiches*, vol. XII, p.131.

31 The first modern military scholars began to elaborate their thought in the seventeenth century. Montecuccoli, as the most important, is the first author to investigate modern army organisation, tactics and strategies, after studying famous captains such as Nassau, Saxe-Weimar, Wallenstein and Gustavus Adolphus. He wrote important works on the Ottomans, such as *Della Guerra contro il Turco in Ungheria*. As an evident limit of the Ottoman military model, any similar contribution was developed in the Empire and any contemporary Ottoman commander may be compared to the personalities cited above.

2

The 'Ottoman Commonwealth' and the Sultan's Allies

The European political commenters of the seventeenth century noted that in each territorial negotiation the Ottoman delegates tended to leave unresolved some minor disputes.[1] The discussion concerning the borders continued for years before finding an agreement,[2] but this served as a pretext for military interventions, and for maintaining a constant pressure near enemy territories. The instruments of this policy were often the semi-independent States which formed a ring around the western borders of the Empire. In addition to domestic data gathering and home intelligence, taking advantage of their officials in these states, the Ottoman government also collected information about its neighbours. Such intelligence concerned the enemies' military and economic strengths and weaknesses, as well as their policy decisions.[3]

All conflicts that exploded after the Cretan War took place following a single scheme, and were largely fought in the battlefields of Transylvania, Moldavia, Wallachia and Crimea, or at least involved these states in the assaults against Austria, Poland and Russia. Among the tributaries of the sultan there were certain differences related to their conditions of subjection. While the principalities of Wallachia and Moldavia retained in the mid seventeenth century an autonomy little more than nominal, Transylvania benefited a freedom close to complete independence. Although the Hungarian and Serbian political elites had been crushed or driven out, the Catholic and Orthodox Church leaders remained, retaining their authority and autonomy in return for acting as intermediaries for the new government.

---

1   L. Valensi, *Venezia e la Sublime Porta* (Bologna: Il Mulino 1991), p.91.
2   After the Treaty of Carlowitz, in 1699, negotiations with the Habsburg, Russia and Venice concerning the borders in Slavonia, Transylvania, Crimea and Dalmatia continued for a further five years. See Hammer-Purgstall, *Geschichte des Osmanischen Reichs*, vol. XIII, p.95.
3   In the seventeenth century, at least four levels of Ottoman information gathering may be discerned: central intelligence in Constantinople; information gathering by local Ottoman authorities, especially along the Empire's frontiers; intelligence provided by Constantinople's client or vassal states; and espionage and counterespionage carried out by the Sublime Porte's spies and saboteurs in foreign countries. Ágoston-Masters, *Encyclopedia of the Ottoman Empire* (New York NY: Facts on File, 2009), p.277.

In Transylvania, Moldavia and Wallachia, the rulers and local elites were also retained in return for annual tribute to the sultan. The position of these Christian elites remained somewhat equivocal. Though many looked to the Habsburg emperors (and later the Russian tsar) as potential liberators, few were prepared to exchange relatively loose Ottoman control for Austrian absolutism. Transylvania in particular enjoyed special privileges and economic growth, thanks partly to its strategic situation between Poland and the Turkish, and the Habsburg parts of Hungary. Meanwhile, the nobles of Habsburg Royal Hungary tended to look to the Prince of Transylvania or even the Ottoman *beglerbeg* of Hungary as guardians of their traditional constitution, with its elective monarchy and right to resist tyranny. Thus it was much less of a strain for the Porte to maintain its system of fortresses in occupied Hungary than it was for the Habsburgs.

Different appeared the case of the Tatar khanates settled to the north of the Black Sea, who became federated with Constantinople after the treaties concluded by the sultan with the respective sovereigns at the end of the sixteenth century. Differences too may be outlined for the status of the North African regencies of Alger, Tunis and Tripoli, which passed from the condition of vassals to that of allies. The political differences between these states, and their degree of dependence from the Porte, formed a very composite situation, which can be defined as the 'Ottoman Commonwealth'.

Ottoman political influence in the age of Köprülü Mehmed and his son Ahmed involved the neighbouring states and their major enemies. France of Louis XIV was formally allied with the Porte since 1688, but actual military alliances were signed only with the Zaporože Cossack communities from 1668 to 1674, with the Iranian shah from 1696 to 1698 and the King of Sweden from 1709 to 1714. However, every time, the Porte showed some difficulty in managing the alliances and maintaining the stability of the coalition.

The Tatars

The successors of the Golden Horde settled in Crimea formed in the sixteenth century a state that extended to southern Ukraine. Their sovereign yet preserved the title of *khan*, or more exactly *han* of the Great Horde. Their status was considerable in relations with the Porte because, according to the Ottoman court rules, the *han* held the same privilege as the sultan's brothers.

Unfortunately, not many internal Tatar and Turkish sources for the history of the Crimea in the seventeenth and early eighteenth century have survived, because many documents of this period have disappeared in the flames of numerous Russo-Turkish wars, when most Tatar archives were burned. Consequently, data on the internal administrative structure of the Crimea is rather fragmentary and sometimes there is no clear definition of functions fulfilled by some authorities. Moreover, it should also be borne in mind that the administrative division of the Crimea was in general rather vague and inconsistent.

For several years the Crimean Tatars had become sedentary, gradually abandoning the nomadic life of their ancestors. They had founded a city on

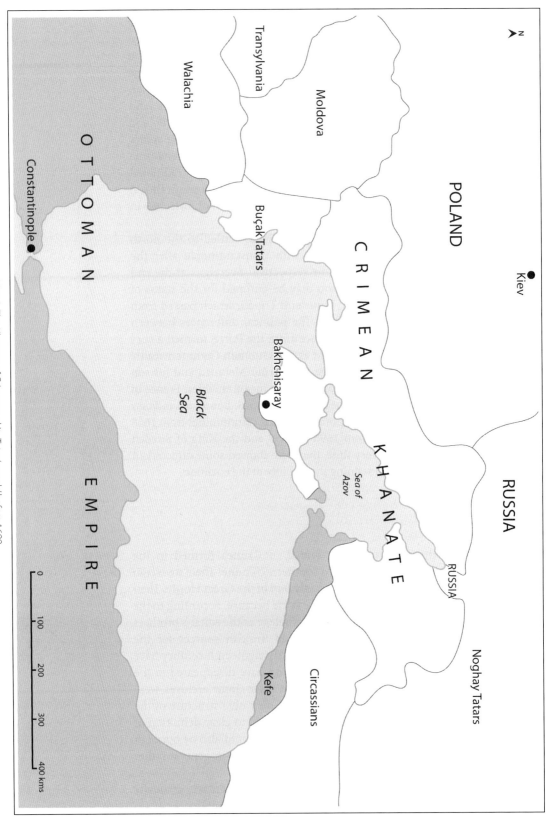

Map 2. The Khanate of Crimea and its Tatar 'vassals' before 1699.

the Black Sea coast, Bakcisaray, famous for trades and treasuries accumulated in the *han*'s palace.[4] The Crimean horde was divided into three large groups: the Sirin, Mansur and Bahrin, each organised in clans with a *mirza* as chief, who usually held the rank of *beg*.[5] This title was in some cases hereditary.

The whole territory of the Crimean Khanate was divided into *qadılık*. Each *qadılık* was under the jurisdiction of a *kadı* (judge); the *kadıs* were appointed by the *qadıasker* or by the *han* himself. The ruler of the Crimean Khanate, a *han* from the Girays' dynasty, who claimed to descend directly from Genghis Khan, was elected on the basis of horizontal lineage. As a rule, the *han* was first succeeded by one of his brothers and then by his sons. It seems that at the end of the seventeenth century, there appeared a position of *qaymaqam* (from Turkish *kaimacan*), who was the *han*'s deputy when the latter was away.[6] Unlike the Ottomans, the Tatars had a kind of aristocracy, which included the leaders of the clans and the relatives of the ruling family. They had an active role in the government, because the most important decisions had been taken not by the *han*, but by the assembly of the *divan*, or council of notables. Sessions of the *divan* were attended by all important officials of the state, representatives of aristocracy and clans. Despite some data about the *han*'s administration, much less is known about the municipal authorities in the Tatar towns of the Crimea. It seems that the Tatar towns were usually ruled directly by representatives of the central power. Most of the Tatar towns were governed by the *emins* appointed by the *han*.

To the north-east of the Crimean Tatars' khanate was the settlement of the horde Noghay, whose borders were not easily defined due to their still strong nomadic culture. The Noghay Tatars had arrived last in the steppes to the north of the Black Sea and their relationship with the Porte was mediated through the Crimean *han*, with whom they did not always maintain good terms. In 1603, a part of the Noghay horde had received from the Ottoman sultan permission to settle in the Moldavian region of Dobrudja, transforming themselves from nomad to semi-sedentary people. The Ottomans welcomed these eastern Tatars to use them against the Polish and to discourage the aspirations for autonomy of the Moldavian princes. The Dobrudjan Noghay established their capitals in Bialogrod and took the name Bucak Tatars.

The Tatars remained allies of the Porte and participated with the Ottoman army in the major wars against Austria, Russia and Poland. The Tatars were masters of long-range military expeditions. And though their forte in mounting long-range raids were those that took them across the Black Sea steppes and into Muscovy or into the Ukrainian lands of Polish-Lithuania, they also carried out operations in less familiar territory not only in the Caucasus but, at the behest of the Ottomans, in central Europe on the Hungarian front, and in Eastern Anatolia on the Iranian front. All such expeditions required skill in organisation, some knowledge of paths and of

---

4   E. Eickhoff, *Venedig, Wien und die Osmanen*, p.281.
5   J. Struys, *Les Voyages de Jean de Struys en Moscovie et Tartarie* (Amsterdam, 1681), p.56.
6   M. Kizilov, *Administrative Structure of the Crimea before and after the Russian Annexation of 1783*, in' Oriens', n. 5, 2016., p.55.

hostile territory, ability to survive in difficult environments, and so forth. On several campaigns alongside the Ottomans, the Tatars performed well-planned and carefully executed military operations. The Porte paid the *han* for military aid, but in addition to this source of income, the biggest gains came from looting.

Spoils of war constituted an important source of income for the Crimean *han* and his subjects. The Tatar horsemen procured plunder and the *han* claimed its percentage. The *han*'s share and the legitimate basis of the collection remain somewhat unclear, but some evidence suggests that the rights of the *han* to a part of the war booty had their roots in both Islamic and Mongol tradition.[7]

The Porte did not interfere in the division of booty, which had already taken by the Tatars. They tried, however, to impose limitations on the countries and people who could be plundered. The Tatars were supposed to respect Ottoman policy towards the neighbouring and tributary states, thus the Porte also limited the possibilities for the Tatars to declare Holy War. For instance, in February 1699 the Grand Vizier Amucazâde Hüseyin reminded the *han* that he was not authorised to launch incursions into Russia and Poland, because of the recently concluded Treaty of Carlowitz.[8]

At the height of the Crimean Tatars' power in the mid sixteenth century, the *han* was able to successfully attack Muscovy and even burn Moscow in 1571 as part of his efforts to extend his domains in the Caspian–Volga region. The following year, however, the Tatars were defeated at Molodi, some 40 miles south of Moscow. This was the last time the Ottomans and the Tatars attempted to invade north of the Black Sea. Ukrainian Cossacks and Russians took advantage of the weakness of the Crimean Tatars in the early seventeenth century and raided at will throughout the peninsula.[9] Therefore, the Tatars assumed the role of the buffer state of the Porte, indispensable to contain the pressure of the Poles and Russians in Moldavia and Ukraine.

In the early seventeenth century, an important change in Tatar–Ottoman relations concerned the sending of the contingents to the sultan's army, recognising the *han* to negotiate a new and higher compensation in proportion to the number of men required for the war. The wars against the Christian European states allowed the Tatars to obtain large gains not only with the rent of the contingents and looting, but also with slavery commerce.[10] Thousands of Austrians, Hungarians, Moravians, Poles, Ukrainians and

---

7   N. Królikowska, *Sovereignty and Subordination in Crimean-Ottoman Relations (16th–18th Centuries)*, in G. Kármán and L. Kunčević (eds), *The European Tributary States of the Ottoman Empire in the 16th and 17th Centuries* (Leiden-Boston: Brill, 2013), p.55. According to Islamic law, one fifth of the booty was delivered to the Muslim sovereign.

8   Hammer-Purgstall, *Geschichte des Osmanischen Reiches*, vol. XII, p.459.

9   The seventeenth century Ottoman travel writer, Evliya Çelebi, refers to the destruction of Crimean cities and the trade routes that had brought the area great prosperity. At the time he thought the only place that was secure was the Ottoman fortress at Arabat. R. Dankoff, *An Ottoman Mentality: The World of Evliya Çelebi* (Leyden: Brill, 2004), p.279.

10   Some researchers estimate that altogether more than three million people were captured and enslaved during the time of the Crimean Khanate and its neighbouring vassals. See A. Fischer, *Muscovy and the Black Sea Slave Trade* (Leiden-Boston: Brill, 1972), p.429.

Russians were chained as prisoners of the brutal *han*'s horsemen, who resold them in Turkey and even in Iran. The Noghays were particularly active in this type of business, becoming principal suppliers of slaves throughout south-central Asia. The ferocity of the Tatar raids was for many years a terrible threat for the civilians living near the frontiers, attracting to the Ottomans the hate of all Christendom.[11]

The Porte tried on several occasions to interfere in the succession of the *han*. In the first half of the seventeenth century, the criteria used to choose the *han* varied significantly. Being the eldest male member of the Giray dynasty did not secure the throne. However, the candidates supported by Constantinople failed to succeeded, and the elected *han* always opposed Ottoman interference. In 1622, Mehmed III Giray took advantage of the recurrent political crisis in Constantinople, and tried to keep away Ottoman interferences from his state. He managed to keep the throne thanks to the domestic support of the Cossacks, and thus the Porte could not remove him for four years. In 1628, autonomy from Constantinople appeared to be complete, forcing the Porte to renew the Tatar alliance with gifts and promises of profitable concessions. However, Mehmed's reign came to an end when he lost the support of the Noghay and the majority of his Crimean subjects. The Ottomans put on the throne a new *han*, Kambay Giray, who confirmed the ancient friendship with the sultan.[12] After these events, the new *han* was more and more frequently appointed by the Porte in the Ottoman capital and sent to Bakcisaray only afterwards to be accepted by the local nobles. In the eighteenth century, the ceremony of election became merely a formality. Nonetheless, the *mirzas*' clans' leaders could still force the sultan to remove an unpopular ruler.

Ottoman military campaigns, considered less useful from a political perspective and which caused them financial loss, constituted another problem in Ottoman–Tatar relations. On such occasions, the *han* had to rise against the Porte, or face a rebellion by his unsatisfied Bucak and Noghay vassals. It is obvious that the Crimean aristocracy preferred to avoid participation in the Ottoman wars, when they felt that these threatened their interests, especially after the negative outcome of the War of the Holy League. Although the Crimean Tatars continued to participate in Ottoman military campaigns, the decline among the Ottomans meant they would return home more often than not without booty to offset their costs. In addition, the financially strapped Ottomans were less and less able to pay for their services.

Relations between Bakcisaray and Constantinople worsened even more at the turn of the eighteenth century, when the Nogay Tatars rebelled in reaction to the provisions of the Treaty of Carlowitz (1699), which stipulated

---

11 Although the practice of slavery was morally condemned in the West (where it nevertheless existed in the equally cruel forms practiced in Africa), some testimonies describe this practice in a much less negative way. In the 1670s, a Russian source reports that Ukrainian slaves freed by the Cossacks following an incursion in Crimea, declared that rather than returning under their former masters, they preferred to remain slaves of the Tatars. See in M. Kizilov, 'Slave Trade in the Early Modern crimea from the Perspective of Christian, Muslim and Jewish Sources', in *Journal of Early Modern History*, vol. II (Leiden: Brill, 2007), pp. 1–31.

12 R. Shaw, 'The Ottoman Empire after 1453', in *Storia dell'Impero Ottomano*, p.439.

their relocation and the ban on raiding neighbouring territories. Gazi Giray, brother of the Crimean *han* Devlet Giray (1699–1702), joined the rebellion. The *han* and Sultan Mustafa II (1695–1703) tried by diplomatic means to put down the rebellion and prevent the Nogays from launching raids that would have endangered the newly established truce between the Ottomans and their Western former enemies. The rebellion interested Russia and Poland, which maintained armed corps on the border, in order to intercept any eventual incursion against them. The *han* called for help from the Porte and the grand vizier authorised the garrisons north of the Black Sea to give support to Devlet Giray against rebels and Noghays. The crisis turned into a civil war, and both factions pillaged each other and destroyed villages who had helped the enemy. Finally, in early 1701, the rebels surrendered. Gazi Giray was arrested and exiled to the isle of Rhodes.[13]

The fortunes of the *han* turned again after the Treaty of Passarowitz (1718). Noghay Tatars gradually turned under the Russian sphere of influence; the Bucak Tatars suffered attacks from the Poles, and reciprocated them with equal ferocity; while the Crimean Tatars remained isolated to face rising Russian power.

The Princedom of Transylvania

In East European history, the first half of the seventeenth century is considered the 'Golden Age of Transylvania'. Thanks to the wise policy of her princes, Transylvania registered an extraordinary development: prosperous trade companies were established; the culture was enriched by influences of the German and Moravian Protestant exiles and the national Hungarian consciousness had the chance to be formed there.[14]

Since the founding of the Princedom in 1548, the *comitates* (counties) became the main units of administration in civil and military affairs, as they were in Hungary. The seven original *comitates* were symbolised in the princedom known in German as *Siebenbürgen* (the 'seven castles'). These were Belső-Szolnok, Dobora, Koloszvár, Torda, Küküllő, Fehér and Hunyad. After the Habsburg recognition of Szápolyai János Zsigmond as Prince of Transylvania, another five counties, the *Partium*, were added in 1570 from East Hungary: Máramaros, Közep-Szolnok, Kraszna, Bihar and Zaránd. Further territories were added in 1606, when some Upper Hungary counties separated from the Habsburg domains after the rebellion of Bocskay István.

The princedom was formed by the 'Three Nations': Hungarian, Saxon and Szekely. The first was the majority and formed the greater part of the aristocracy; the Saxons were the descendants of German immigrants and

---

13   The three contemporary accounts of the 1699–1701 Nogay rebellion, two by Ottoman authors and the extensive description by the Tatar prince Mehmed Giray, provide quite different information about the rebellion. Further reading in D. Klein, 'Tatar and Ottoman History Writing. The Case of the Nogay Rebellion (1699–1701)', in D. Klein (ed.), *The Crimean Khanate between East and West (15th–18th Century)* (Wiesbaden: Harrassowitz Verlag, 2012), pp.125–146.

14   M. Asztalos and S. Pethő, *Storia dell'Ungheria* (Milano: S.A. Editrice Genio, 1930), p.245.

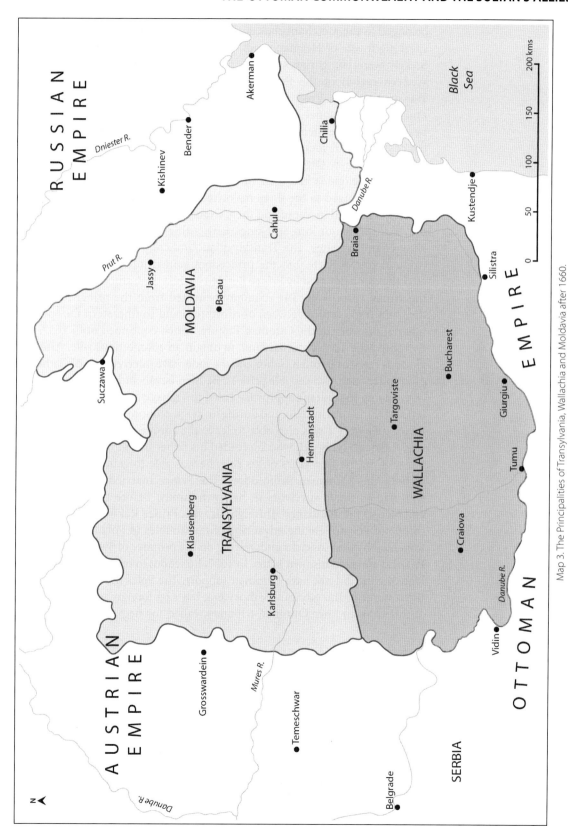

Map 3. The Principalities of Transylvania, Wallachia and Moldavia after 1660.

belonged to the merchant class, and they were concentrated in the German-speaking towns of Hermannstadt, Kronstadt and Clausenburg; finally, the Szekely were Hungarian-speaking people of Turkish origin, settled in the Western region of the Princedom. Alongside these three majorities, in Transylvania also lived Greeks, Armenians, Turks, Jews, Gipsies and a multitude of seasonal workers from Wallachia and Moldavia, principally peasants and shepherds. The Princedom recomposed and miniaturised the cosmopolitan society of the Ottoman Empire. The traditional religious tolerance of their Ottoman neighbours was observed in Transylvania too and all the religions had their ministries and cult places.[15] Political power, however, belonged to the three majority nations, which sent their delegates to the Diet, based in Várad and then, from 1660, in Brassö. The Diet elected the *kiral* (prince or king in Hungarian), a title reserved more often to the Hungarian magnates. The Transylvanian *kiral* continued to pay the *haraci* (tribute) to the Porte, but the princedom gained international reputation after the campaigns led by Prince Bethlen against the Catholic League during the Thirty Years' War. The economy benefited from the princedom being the main trade centre between northwestern and southeastern Europe. The internal disorder in the Ottoman Empire, which continued until 1657, had permitted the Transylvanian *kiral*, to obtain an autonomous rule. After the glorious reign of Bethlen Gábor and the indecisive interregnum of Catherine of Brandenburg, two capable princes, Bethlen István and Rákóczi György I – both having the Sultan's approval – ruled in Transylvania to good effect. The latter became *kiral* in 1630, and during his reign economic growth accelerated. Rákóczi György I was also able to leave the throne of Transylvania to his son, Rákóczi György II, who succeeded his father in 1648. His reign started out well. In the first years of his rule, he was able to gain political control of both the Romanian princedoms. The Prince married Báthory Sophya, who had no male survivors in her own family. Before the wedding, she embraced Protestantism.[16] Through his wife, Prince Rákóczy aspired to the throne of Poland. Taking advantage of the troubles in Poland initiated and fomented by the Cossacks and, relying on the promise of Swedish assistance, Rákóczy pursued his own plans. In 1657, he set out to take the Polish throne. However, he did not have Ottoman support. The Poles did not view him as the restorer of the glorious Báthory era, but as a foreign aggressor. Poland, at this time another Ottoman tributary, called for help from both Vienna

---

15 I. Lázár, *Transylvania, a Short History* (Budapest: Corvina 1997), p.191. Regarding religious tolerance, Transylvania was undoubtedly ahead compared to other European countries. However, we must remember that along with the four recognised religions – Lutheranism, Calvinism, Catholicism, Unitarianism – the Greek-Orthodox religion was not recognised despite the high presence of Romanians, while Judaism was 'tolerated'. There was also rivalry between Catholics and Protestants, which increased with the Thirty Years' War, who in 1619 caused the expulsion of the Jesuits from the country and the subsequent resignation from the office of the Catholic Bishop. Catholicism revived only after 1686, when Transylvania had become a possession of the Habsburg Empire. Concerning religious limitation in Transylvania see also R. Seaton-Watson, *Histoire des Roumains de l'époque romaine à l'achèvement de l'unité* (Brussels, 1941), pp.122–130.

16 Immediately following the death of her husband, she returned to Catholicism and also converted the son and successor Rákóczi Ferenc I, the father of the Hungarian leader in the anti-Austrian rebellion of 1703–11.

and Constantinople against the Swedes and Transylvanians who occupied Cracow in May 1657.

The unscrupulous act of Rákóczy collided with Köprülü policy, which did not permit any aggression against a tributary state, and immediately Köprülü ordered the invasion of Transylvania and the deposition of the Prince. From 1657 to 1660, the Ottoman army and the Tatars overran the Princedom, devastating and firing cities and countryside. Rákóczy fought bravely until the spring of 1660, but he was finally defeated at Szászfenes and died a few days later in Várad, under siege. The pro-Habsburg Transylvanian magnates elected as *kiral* Kemeny János, opposed to Barcsay Akos, supported by the Porte. The war continued, provoking the ruin of the beautiful Princedom and putting an end to any residual hope of independence. Imperialist and Ottoman armies had confronted each other without engagement since 1660; then in 1663, the war extended to Hungary and finally closed in 1664 with the peace of Vasvár, signed after the Imperialist victory in the battle of Szentgotthárd. However, Köprülü Ahmed obtained the election of the pro-Ottoman faction leader

Mihály I Apafy as *kiral*. Transylvania fell under the direct control of the Porte and later the grand viziers used the Princedom to foment the struggle of the Hungarian Calvinist exiles against the Habsburgs. The Hungarian magnate Tököly Imre, leader of the 'malcontents' party', organised his own army in Transylvania, and with French economic help he unleashed a fierce guerrilla war against the Hungarian domains of Emperor Leopold I.[17] Louis XIV's influence in Eastern Europe represented a historic event and a turning point which led to major implications for the following years. Together, the French intervention highlighted the decline of Ottoman foreign policy, no longer able to support alone the fight against Austria. The subsequent victories obtained in Hungary enabled the Habsburgs to become masters of Transylvania in 1686.[18] Two years later France assailed the Emperor in Germany, forcing him to slow

10. Mihály Apafi (1632–1690), Grand Prince of Transylvania from 1661 to his death. As a tributary of the Porte, in 1683 Apafy gathered a force of 6,000 horse and 2,000 foot to join the Ottoman army marching to Vienna. Following the Ottoman defeat at the Kahlenberg, Apafi opened talks with the Austrians and concluded a treaty with Emperor Leopold I on 27 September 1687, obtaining the recognition of his authority in Transylvania, which was finally annexed to Royal Hungary in 1690.

---

17 It is a little strange that a Catholic king and an Islamic vizier helped a Calvinist Hungarian count against a Catholic emperor, but actually, the Ottomans treated the Protestants with particular respect compared to other Christians. Indeed, the common iconoclastic aversion was always mentioned to seal their alliance. See also in F. Cardini, 'Il Turco a Vienna' (Bari: Laterza 2011) pp.220–225.

18 The last Transylvanian *kiral*, Apafy Mihály II, renounced the throne in exchange for the appointment to Count of the Empire and an annuity granted by Emperor Leopold I.

down the offensive in the Balkans, but all Ottoman attempts to regain the control of that region were in vain.

The Princedoms of Wallachia and Moldavia

The history and political structure of both Romanian states in the seventeenth century are very similar. The two principalities were governed by a prince, the *hospodar* in Wallachia and the *voievoda* in Moldavia, elected by the assembly of the nobility – the boyars – with Ottoman confirmation. The population was composed mainly of ethnic Romanians, but in the most important towns lived many Turks, Greeks and Slavs. The internal situation appeared very different compared to Transylvania. In the seventeenth century, the Romanian princedoms did not enjoy autonomy like their neighbour and both the princes ruled two less-advanced countries. The Porte seriously reduced the manoeuvre room available to both Romanian princedoms, and was less and less inclined to allow Wallachia and Moldavia any freedom of initiative in foreign affairs. The local aristocracy, the boyars, were often hostile and unreliable, and ready to replace the *voievoda* or *hospodar*, offering the Sultan increasingly high tributes. After years of intestine struggles and riots, in the mid seventeenth century the huge sums paid by the princes for their enthronement paralysed the economy of both the countries, delaying every social and civil progress. The reigns of Mateu Besarab in Wallachia (1632–54) and Vasili Lupu in Moldavia (1634–53) seem extraordinarily long if compared with those of their successors. In Moldavia 12 princes in just 32 years alternated as rulers; the struggle for power and the boyar conspiracies become so unrestrained as to embarrass even the Ottoman court. While Prince György II Rákóczy was occupied in Poland in his grandiose dream of conquest, the Wallachian *voievoda* Costantin Serban and the Moldavian *hospodar* Georghe Stefanu supported the Transylvanian prince, sending their soldiers to help him against the Ottomans and their Tatar allies. In the summer of 1658 Wallachia and Moldavia were invaded by the Ottoman army, and despite a brief resistance the Princes were replaced with Georghe Ghica in Wallachia and Minhea Radu in Moldavia. But just a few weeks later, Radu sided against the Porte. He ordered the elimination of the boyars who opposed his plans: 'throwing them down from the windows of his palace and covering the screaming with the music of an orchestra';[19] then his soldiers assaulted the Ottoman garrison and finally ordered the massacre of the Turkish residents. In Wallachia, the deposed Prince Costantin Serban joined Rákóczy against the Ottomans and soon returned to the throne, overthrowing Ghica. In 1660, after the final Transylvanian defeat, the Ottoman reaction was ruthless. The Tatars raged into the countrie for three months, devastating town and countryside. In Constantinople, Grand Vizier Köprülü Ahmed examined the possibility of transforming both states into two Ottoman *paşaliks*, but eventually he decided to maintain the integrity of the principalities, entrusting them with rulers chosen exclusively from the Porte. From that date began the

---

19 Seaton-Watson, *Histoire des Roumains*, p.91.

succession to the throne of Albanian, Greek and Hellenised Romanian families from the Greek district of Constantinople, the *Phanar,* for centuries subjected to the sultan, recorded by history as Phanariots.

The last years of seventeenth century are the saddest of Romanian history: conspiracies, betrayals, rebellions and foreign military occupations annihilated every effort towards economic development. The misery of the lower classes reached dramatic levels; in Moldavia – the poorest of the two principalities – according to the writing of an early eighteenth-century French traveller: 'the inhabitants of the countryside feed worse than hunting dogs'.[20]

Although the Porte controlled both principalities through their designated governors, even some Phanariot princes tried to extract their state from the Ottoman orbit. Secret negotiations were conducted from 1686 by the Wallachian *voievoda* Serban Cantacuzenus (ruling from 1678 to 1688), a descendant of the Byzantine Imperial family, with Austrian and Polish emissaries. The Prince contacted also the Greek Patriarch of Athos to obtain the religious imprimatur for the creation of a confessional state in Eastern Europe, but these complex negotiations, often opposed to each other, failed, leaving the Prince alone with his dream of reconstituting the Eastern Roman Empire.[21] His successor, Costantin Brâncoveanu (in charge from 1688 to 1714), managed foreign policy with more balance. He continued to negotiate secretly with the Habsburgs, while simultaneously sending his troops to the Ottoman army to fend off the menace of military occupations. On the contrary, Moldavia was troubled with the passage of foreign armies and in 1686 was occupied by Poles in the north, while Ottoman troops were garrisoned in all the major towns, joined by Tatars with disastrous effects. Here the Porte nominated in 1710 Demeter Cantemir as *hospodar,* to better control Brâncoveanu's aspiration for independence, but the intentions of the new Moldavian prince soon took another course. In April 1711, Cantemir signed a secret treaty with Tsar Peter I Romanov, undertaking to transfer Moldavia to Russian protection and provoke an insurrection against the Ottomans in the north-east. The Tsar had to send his army on the Pruth River to protect the Princedom by an eventual Tatar attack. The plan failed and the *voievoda* fled. Pressed by the enemy he escaped to Russia, avoiding capture by crossing the border wrapped in a carpet inside a wagon.[22] The Ottomans placed on the Moldavian throne Nicolaos Mavrocordatos, son of the famous interpreter of the Porte. Meanwhile in Wallachia, Costantin Brâncoveanu was planning his switch to the Habsburg side, sending an emissary to Vienna and in 1714 transferring his entire treasury to Austrian banks. The desire to seize the throne of Wallachia, more prosperous than Moldavia, induced Mavrocordatos to devise a plan for the deposition of Brâncoveanu. Informed about the secret negotiations of the Wallachian prince by Rákóczy Ferenc's Hungarian refugees, and by the Swedish King's agent Poniatowsky,[23] the new *hospodar* convinced the Phanariot Mihali Racovita to play the role of the traitor and reveal the whole

---

20 A. La Mottraye, *Voyages en Europe, en Asie at en Afrique de A.L.M* (The Hague, 1727), vol. II, p.205.
21 Seaton-Watson, *Histoire des Roumains,* pp.98–99.
22 *Ibidem,* p.108.
23 Ferenc II Rákóczy was the Hungarian prince who led the rebellion against the Habsburgs from 1703 to 1711. The Swedish role in this affair is explained in chapter 2.

matter to Constantinople. Racovita, indeed, had been the candidate proposed by Brâncoveanu to replace Cantemir in Moldavia, but now he could reach the same goal through other means. On 4 April 1714, an Ottoman *ağa* arrived in Bucharest with a small cavalry corps. He entered the *voievoda*'s residence and showed to Brâncoveanu a black handkerchief to reveal his deposition. The Prince tried vainly to exonerate himself: 'He turned to his soldiers and then he called to the population, screaming for help from the windows, but no one raise a finger to save him from the Turks'.[24] Brâncoveanu was transferred in chains to Constantinople and beheaded together his sons and son-in-law: 'then the bodies were thrown into the sea and their heads, exposed outside the door of the Topkapı, remained for three days on top of the lances.'[25]

Brâncoveanu's death closed a disastrous era for Romania. Bitterly, a Romanian historian comments: 'in less than a century, the Romanians had passed from freedom to slavery, from the courage of a lion to the fox's craftiness; from the honourable life to abjection.'[26]

Northern African Regencies

In Eastern Europe Ottoman control on the vassal tributary states became stronger with the progressive weakening of the Porte. In North Africa, instead, from the late seventeenth century began a process of gradual separation from Constantinople, which encountered almost no resistance. The North African Regencies were constituted around the three port-cities of Tunis, Alger and Tripoli. In all these centres, the authority of the Porte was represented by a *paşa*, flanked by officials appointed from Constantinople. The local population were mixed with the descendants of Turkish soldiers, garrisoned in North Africa since 1594, who created the *kul-oglu* social class. They become the most important and organised political group in the countries. The most relevant economic activity of three states was piracy, autonomous as well as corsairs for the Porte. With their actions on the sea, the North Africans caused several incidents with the Christian states in the Mediterranean. At the same time Dalmatian-Albanian, and even Aegean, Ottoman subjects carried out more or less authorised piracy and created squadrons that went plundering together. Events suggest that corsairs taught great piracy (or privateering) to the coast inhabitants; the latter appropriated their flags and started to act along the Adriatic coasts by themselves, blaming their ancient lords for their own massacres and raids.

The Porte's behaviour towards this uncontrolled situation was contradictory: on the one hand, they could not totally disavow the Barbaries' privateering in the name of the sultan; on the other, their unjust attacks risked causing reprisals and clashes in a time that was ill-suited for a declared war. However, the opportunity to obtain large and easy profits with piracy facilitated the arrival of a growing number of adventurers of all nationalities,

---

24 Seaton-Watson, *Histoire des Roumains*, p.110.
25 La Mottraye, *Voyages*, vol. II, p.212.
26 Demeter Xenopol, cited by Seaton-Watson in *Histoire des Roumains*, p.111.

swelling the ranks of the *kul-oglu*. The recognition of their political status was granted by the elective office of *dey*, confirmed to a Creole candidate, and subjected exclusively to the Ottoman *paşa*.[27] In the early seventeenth century the new office of *bey* (after the Turkish *beg*, namely 'sir') was instituted to merge the function of fleet admiral and minister. This office was assigned to a selected corsair captain, the *re'is*, who soon became the most powerful official of the state, and quickly extended his authority on administration and taxation. The function of *paşa* and *dey* was limited and progressively they represented merely the ancient symbol of the Porte granting the *bey* power. In 1640 the *bey* of Tunis, Hamuda ben Murad, obtained the important result of governing the state in complete autonomy. While maintaining in their functions *dey* and *Paşa*, he governed as a monarch extended inheritance of the title to his descendants. The Muradite dynasty conserved Ottoman officials until 1702, when the *bey* was overthrown by a rebellion under a militia officer, the *sipahi* Ibrahim el Serif. In 1705, another *sipahi* named Hussein ben Ali seized power, assuming the title of *paşa* after the sultan's confirmation. The charge of *dey* was suppressed and the power remained with Hussein, whose descendants reigned at Tunis until 1881. The state became completely independent from Constantinople and the unique link with the Porte was secured with the renewal of the *firman* signed in 1705, including military alliance, and the appointment of delegates to embassies.[28]

The evolution of political events followed a similar course in the other states. In Algiers the government affairs passed in 1648 under the direction of a *bey*, following protests against the Ottoman official who tried to impose Sultan Ibrahim's decision to tax the rewards granted to the *re'is*.[29] In 1671 the *kul-oglu* elected a *dey* who limited the prerogative of the Ottoman *paşa*, while continuing to act together him; then, in 1711, the progressive detachment from Constantinople ended with the expulsion of the *paşa* ordered by *dey* Ali Çavuş.

Ottoman authority in Tripolitania had resisted longer, and here the *kul-oglu* remained always loyal to the Porte throughout the seventeenth century. In subsequent years aspirations for autonomy caused recurrent unrest in the country, culminating with the appointment of Karamanli Ahmed as *paşa* in 1711, the office later unified with that of the *dey*.

Georgia

The Kingdom of Georgia collapsed at the end of the fifteenth century and fragmented into three independent kingdoms and five semi-independent principalities. Neighbouring Safavid Iran and the Ottoman Empire subsequently exploited the internal divisions of the weakened country,

---

27   R. Mantran: 'L'evolution des relations entre la Tunisie et l'Empire Ottoman du XVI au XIX siècle', in *L'Empire Ottoman du XVI au XVII siècle* (London: Variourum Reprints, 1984), p.324.

28   *Ibidem*, p.332. In religious matters, the observance of the Ottoman *hanefite* rite, while the rest of the population followed the *malechite* rite.

29   R. Mantran, 'Le statut de l'Algerie, de la Tunisie e de la Tripolitaine dans l'Empire Ottoman', in *L'Empire Ottoman du XVI au XVIII Siècle* (London: Routledge, 1984), p.7.

and at the beginning of the sixteenth century subjugated the eastern and western regions of Georgia respectively. The rulers of regions that remained partly autonomous tried to organise rebellions, but all efforts failed. Furthermore, subsequent Iranian and Ottoman invasions further weakened local kingdoms and principalities. The Porte controlled the southwestern principalities of Mingrelia (Dadian for the Ottomans) and Guria (Guriel), ruled by the Dadiani and Gurieli dynasties, respectively, and the kingdom of Imereti (Açık Baş). However, the strategic relevance of this area was minimal, and compared to Transylvania and the Romanian princedoms, Georgian tributaries represented essentially a buffer zone against the Safavids and the Abkhaz pirates, settled north-west of Mingrelia, who acted against Ottoman trade along the eastern Black Sea coastline. The principalities and the kingdom were regarded as tributary states and allowed internal self-rule. The principal intermediary between the Ottoman court and western Georgian rulers was the Muslim Georgian dynasty of Jaqeli, which was integrated in the Ottoman Empire by having frontier governors in the *Paşalik* of Çıldır, based in Akhaltsikhe. The three states were hereditary monarchies, but their rulers were expected to be confirmed by the Ottoman sultan on their accession, and in return to pay an annual tribute. However, these provisions were not frequently respected and payment of tribute was at times irregular.

By the seventeenth century, both eastern and western Georgia had sunk into poverty as the result of the constant warfare. The economy was so bad that barter replaced the use of money and the populations of the cities declined markedly. The French traveller Jean Chardin, who visited the region of Mingrelia in 1671, noted the wretchedness of the peasants, the arrogance of the nobles and the ignorance of the clergy. The rulers were split between acknowledging Ottoman or Persian overlordship, which occasionally entailed nominal conversion to Islam, or making a bid for independence.[30]

In a series of events, the Imeretian King Simon, favoured by the Porte, was deposed by the powerful Lord Giorgi Abashidze. Simon was then murdered with the help of Mamia III Gurieli, Prince of Guria, in 1701. After Mamia's brief experience as king of Imereti, Abashidze himself usurped the crown in 1702. As his power grew, Abashidze withheld tribute from the Ottomans, as did the princes of Mingrelia and Guria.

In 1703 these events caused immediate Ottoman intervention in western Georgia. While a civil war and break in dynastic succession in Imereti, as well as unilateral acts on the part of the western Georgian rulers, were not uncommon, the massive military response was a change in Ottoman policy in Georgia, further dictated by the necessity of consolidating control over the fluid frontier zone against the background of recent losses in Europe, and the increased activity of the Russians on the Black Sea, especially after the conquest of Azow, which left the eastern coast of the Black Sea under a direct threat of the imaginative Tsar Peter I Romanov.

An unusually large Ottoman expeditionary force was gathered between March and July 1703. All provincial troops of eastern and northeastern

---

30   R.G. Suny, *The Making of the Georgian Nation* (Bloomington: Indiana University Press, 1994), p.52.

Anatolia were required to participate along with contingents of the standing army from Constantinople. The commander-in-chief of this expeditionary force, Köse Halil Paşa, governor of Erzurum, was ordered to conquer Guria, install a new prince in place of Giorgi Abashidze in Imereti, leave Ottoman garrisons in Kutaisi, Imereti's capital, and one in the major provincial town of Baghdati. Another corps under the governor of Çildir was to open the access through the pass of Zekhari to invade Imereti, and a third contingent was ready to land in Mingrelia. These objectives were sized in a short time. Facing the invasion of Imereti, Giorgi Abashidze had secured the loyalty of Gurieli and Dadiani as well as most Imeretian nobles. They blocked roads and evacuated civilians, while the Ottomans took fortress after fortress. After achieving this objective, Halil Pasha conquered Batomi (Batum) on Guria's Black Sea coast and began to erect a new fortress there. Gurieli felt compelled to submit to the Ottoman commander, and the Imeretian Prince Giorgi Mikeladze, Abashidze's foe, defected to the Ottomans and opened the blocked roads. The Abkhaz pirates also intervened, and in their quest for booty sent their ships to join the Ottomans in Guria. A short fight opened the way for the conquest of Baghdati, unable to withstand the Ottoman artillery. The heavily fortified towers of Chalatqe offered stiff resistance, but were eventually blown up by the Ottoman troops. While Guria and Imereti were largely overrun, Mingrelia mostly held out although the Ottomans destroyed the fortress of Rukhi, raided the surrounding countryside, and began fortifying Anaklia as their new outpost on the Black Sea coast.

On 18 July 1703 a second Ottoman expedition was ready at Constantinople, when the janissaries mutinied. On 22 August, Sultan Mustafa was forced to abdicate in a coup. The new sultan, Ahmed III, refused to fund the intervention in Georgia. Thus, the new grand vizier, Kavanoz Ahmed, offered peace, provided Giorgi Abashidze demolished the fortress of Shorapani, gave hostages and tribute, and recognised Giorgi VII as king of Imereti under Ottoman tutelage. Abashidze agreed, but taking advantage of the chaos in the Ottoman command, blocked the road back to Akhaltsikhe. The Georgians ambushed and destroyed the withdrawing Ottoman force. Very few made their way back to Akhlatsikhe.

11. Ottoman foot soldier. The very archaic dress and equipment of this soldier appears in a late nineteenth century photograph depicting some Kevsur highlanders, a population settled on the border with Georgia. This is a very suggestive document, which shows the permanence of an immutable warfare. Very probably, in the late seventeenth century and early eighteenth centuries, Georgian and Mingrelian warriors, as well as the Ottoman bordersmen from the *paşalik* of Çildir wore similar dress and equipment, which comprised musket, dagger, helm and mail coat. (Author's illustration)

12. The kingdoms and princedoms of Georgia in the map of Guillaume De L'Isle (1724).

The Georgian campaign resonated amongst the Empire's eastern European neighbours. In his letter of 3 August 1703, the Ukrainian Cossack hetman Ivan Mazepa informed the Russian government that the Ottomans had suffered a 'considerable defeat in the land of Georgia' and a second army was ready to be deployed against Abashidze.

Western Georgia, albeit not fully conquered, had suffered heavy damage. The costal district around Batumi was irretrievably lost for Guria and the Ottoman garrisons were permanently stationed in the Mingrelian fortresses of Poti, Anaklia, and Rukhi along the coastline and in Baghdati, in Imereti's heartland. Giorgi Abashidze confined Giorgi VII, the Sultan's Imeretian candidate, in the castle of Kutaisi, but his recovery of power was temporary. As Abashidze's power was draining, the unity imposed upon western Georgia crumbled. By 1707, Giorgi VII succeeded in dislodging Abashidze from Kutaisi, but found himself embroiled in fighting with Mamia Gurieli. Giorgi

Dadiani's hold on power also shattered and finally eclipsed under pressure from his own son in 1715.[31]

Cossacks

In 1668, the *hetman* of the *Zaporoszskaja sech* (the river's outer rapids) Cossacks Petro Dorofeyevych Doroszenko, inaugurated a policy of detachment from Poland, signing an alliance treaty with the Sultan. The agreement, the *hetman* hoped, would grant to him full sovereignty of Ukraine at the end of the war against its former Polish masters. In 1667, the pact of Andrusovo had established the division of Ukraine between Russia and Poland, with Russia gaining sovereignty over left-bank Ukraine and Poland acquiring right-bank Ukraine. Once the news reached Doroszenko, he reportedly suffered a seizure upon learning of Ukraine's partitioning. The *hetman* had quickly deserted his pro-Polish position, and after organising a 20,000-man mercenary army to oppose the Andrusovo treaty decided to seek aid from the Ottoman Empire.[32] In 1672 a new war erupted between Poland and the Porte. The *hetman*, with a force of 12,000 cossacks, joined the 100,00-strong Ottoman army in Podolia, and defeated the Polish army in the battle of Chertvenivka. The campaign ended with the capture of the important fortress of Kameniec-Podolski and the signing of the Peace of Buchach. Poland was forced to recognise the *Zaporoszskaja* Cossacks' independence. Bratslav province and the southern portion of Kiev province become, as Cossack territory, administered by Doroszenko under Turkish protection. Meanwhile in the summer of 1672, the left-bank Cossack *hetman*

13. Petro Dorofeyevych Doroshenko (1627–1698) *hetman* of right-bank Ukraine from 1665 to 1672. In January 1668, the Cossack Council supported Doroshenko's intentions to ally with the Ottoman Empire. In 1672, the war against Poland involved the Cossack communities, which suffered the burden of Doroshenko's Tatar allies. The *hetman* soon lost the support of his subjects, who rebelled against the Porte. Despite this failure, the Ottomans supported him in the attempt to re-take power in 1676. Doroshenko abdicated for the first time in 1675, but refused to leave the fortress of Çigirin. In the fall of 1676, 30,000 Russian army crossed Dnieper River and besieged Çigirin. Doroshenko asked his 2,000 *serdiuk* mercenaries to stop resistance and he decided to surrender on 19 September 1676. He never returned to Ukraine.

---

31 D. Rayfield, *Edge of Empires: A History of Georgia* (London: Reaktion Books, 2012), pp. 227–228.

32 In January of 1668 the Council of Officers (Seniors) in Chyhyryn expressed its support for Doroszenko's intentions for the alliance with the Ottoman Empire. In the autumn of 1668 a Cossack delegation was sent to Constantinople with proposal for a military alliance between the Cossack state and the Ottoman Empire. The alliance was once again approved at the 1669 *Korsun* Cossack Council (General Military Council) on March 10–12. The alliance was eventually proclaimed by Sultan Mehmed IV on 1 May, 1669.

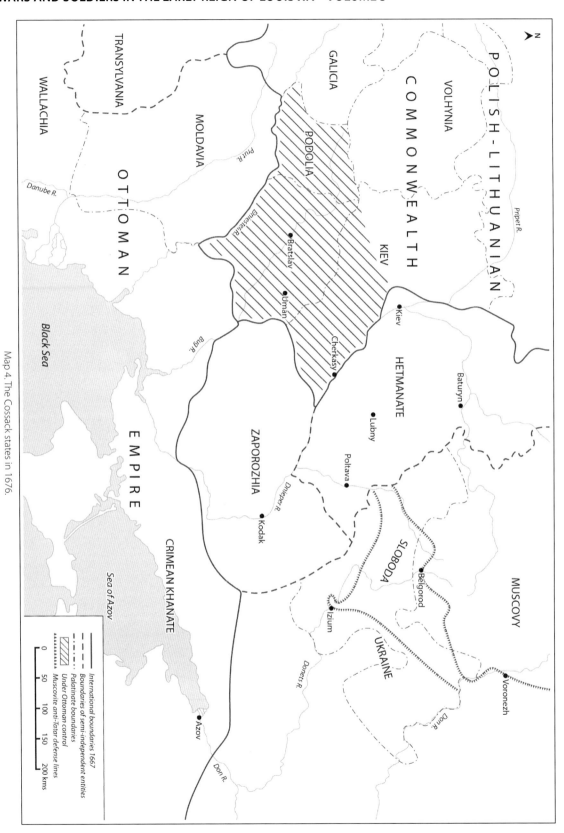

Map 4. The Cossack states in 1676.

POLISH - LITHUANIAN

COMMONWEALTH

TRANSYLVANIA

WALLACHIA

GALICIA

VOLHYNIA

MOLDAVIA

PODOLIA

KIEV

OTTOMAN

Danube R.

Prut R.

Dniester R.

Pripet R.

●Bratslav

●Uman

Cherkasy●

●Kiev

HETMANATE

Baturyn●

Black Sea

Bug R.

ZAPOROZHIA

●Lubny

Poltava●

Dnieper R.

EMPIRE

●Kodak

SLOBODA

●Belgorod

MUSCOVY

CRIMEAN KHANATE

Sea of Azov

Izium●

UKRAINE

Donets R.

●Voronezh

●Azov

Don R.

0   50   100   150   200 kms

International boundaries 1667
Boundaries of semi-independent entities
Palatinate boundaries
Under Ottoman control
Muscovite anti-Tatar defense lines

Demian Mnohohrishny was replaced by Ivan Samoylovych, who was favourable to Moscow. Hostilities resumed in the following year, and Doroszenko joined his troops with the Tatars. Although the alliance did perform an integral part of his successes, the population had suffered greatly in the war. As the right-bank faced devastation, Doroszenko began to lose support from his previously loyal civilians because of his collaboration with the Ottomans and their uncontrollable Crimean Tatar allies. The vast Ukrainian territory was laid waste, cities were burned down, and hundreds of people were taken into captivity by the Tatars. As his forces were weakened by the ongoing war, Doroszenko was forced to rely increasingly on the Ottomans, and this was very unpopular with the majority of deeply Orthodox Christian Cossacks. In March 1674, the Council of Officers in Pereyaslav proclaimed Samoylovych as *hetman* of all Ukraine. However, his title could not be valid until Doroszenko abdicated. In summer 1674, Samoylovych and the Muscovite army under Grigory Romodanovsky launched an expedition against Doroszenko and besieged Chyhyryn, the capital of the *Zaporoszskaja sech*. Grand Vizier Köprülü Ahmed managed to lift the siege in time and drive the Muscovite forces beyond the Dniepr River, but in the autumn of 1675 the Cossack council in Chyhyryn forced Doroszenko to abdicate and pledge his allegiance to Muscovy. However, the Tsar's government demanded guarantees which Doroszenko refused. In the autumn of 1676 Samoylovych with 30,000 men crossed Dniepr and once again besieged Chyhyryn. On September 19, 1676, after several hours of battle, Doroszenko asked his 2,000 garrison to cease its resistance, as he had decided to abdicate. He was arrested and brought to Moscow where he was kept in honorary exile, never to return to Ukraine, and died in 1676. A new war began in 1678 with Muscovy facing the Porte, involving the Cossacks until 1681. Doroszenko's attempt to rescue his country from Polish sovereignty, through a dangerous alliance such as the one with the Porte, had the effect of moving all Ukrainian Cossacks under the protection of Moscow.

Persians

The Safavid dynasty had been for centuries the arch-enemy of the Ottomans in Asia and their temporary alliance, signed in December 1696, represented an episode of great relevance also for the European states. The news of the event aroused the interest in Europe, especially amongst the Holy League members, involved in the war against the Porte of 1683–99. Coeval accounts describe the greeting ceremony of Persian ambassadors in Constantinople: 'who were honoured with gifts and richness by the grand vizier'.[33] The opportunity to conclude this unusual alliance had been further incidents between the Ottoman Empire and Turkmen communities stationed to east of the Caspian Sea. The continuous increase in taxation required of the

---

33 Letter of the English ambassador in Constantinople, Lord Paget, in *K.u.K. Kriegsarchiv, Feldzüge des Prinzen Eugen von Savoyen. Nach den Feldacten und anderen authentischen Quellen hrsg. von der Abtheilung für Kriegsgeschichte des K.K. Kriegs-Archives* (Vienna, 1876–1892), vol. II, p.245.

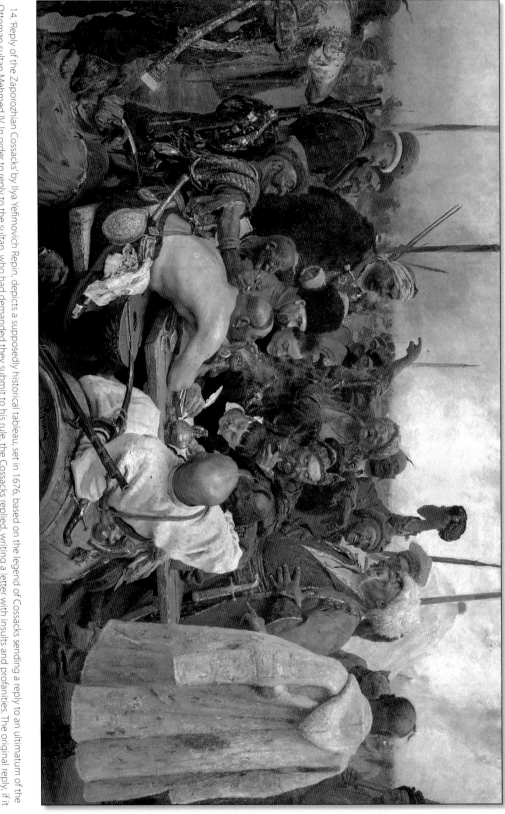

14. 'Reply of the Zaporozhian Cossacks' by Ilya Yefimovich Repin, depicts a supposedly historical tableau, set in 1676, based on the legend of Cossacks sending a reply to an ultimatum of the Ottoman sultan Mehmed IV. In order to reply to the sultan, who had demanded they submit to his rule, the Cossacks replied, writing a letter with insults and profanities. The original reply, if it ever existed, has not survived. Authentic or imaginary, the episode makes explicit the end of the alliance between the Porte and Zaporozhian Cossacks in an anti-Polish key.

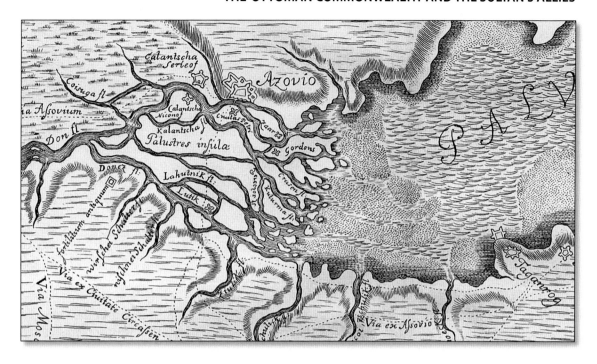

Ottoman merchants who travelled in these regions, had already provoked strong disputes, but in the winter of 1695–96 actual reprisals occurred, culminating with the Turkmen raids in Northern Iraq. Even the Safavids were interested in containing the growing aggressiveness of local Turkmen tribes' leaders, which endangered also Persian trade. The short war took the typical features of the Asian conflicts, culminating in a series of cavalry expeditions against the Turkmen caravan centres, but the forces of the two allies never fought joined.

15. The strategic key fortress of Azov, in the Crimean peninsula, in a 1695 print. The Ottoman strongholds secured the Don River estuary against Muscovite–Russian penetration. Moreover, the Porte ruled a part of the peninsula through the border *paşalik* of Kefe (today Feodosiya in Ukraine).

Swedes

Sweden's King Charles XII was chronologically the last foreigner to join an alliance with the Ottoman Empire. After the disastrous defeat at Poltava in July 1709, during the war against Russia, the Swedish king took refuge in Moldavia with the rest of his army. On the outskirts of Bender, a few miles from Jassi, Charles XII erected a tent city that shortly after took the bizarre name Carlópolis.[34] The King built a 'winter palace' for himself, stables and even a chancellery in his camp and ruled his country from there. His expenses during his long stay in the Ottoman Empire were covered by the Porte as part of the fixed budget negotiated in exchange for Swedish military advice. Sultan Ahmed III, as a gesture of favour to the King, had even ransomed some of the Swedish women and children captured by the Russians at Poltava and turned them to Carlópolis, thus further strengthening the growing community of

---

34 Seaton-Watson, *Histoire des Roumains*, p.106.

the *Karoliner*. From this improvised town he continued his struggle against the Tsar, trying in various ways to involve the Porte. Skilfully, Charles XII used every means, including the resources received from the Ottoman government, to involve the Porte in the war against Russia. In November 1710 the Porte declared war on the Tsar, following the discovery of the secret plans between the Moldavian prince and Peter I Romanov. The Ottomans obtained a surprisingly success on the Pruth River, encircling the Russian army which was forced to drop its arms and surrender. The war closed immediately after the treaty of peace signed in summer 1711, but Charles XII was able to convince the Sultan that the conditions imposed on the Tsar had been too generous. He also caused the dismissal of Grand Vizier Baltaçi Mehmed, who had signed the peace treaty, and with relentless tenacity persuaded Ahmed III to declare war on Russia. The dispute lasted a couple of years, threatened Poland, involved embassies across Europe and menaced the peace with the Habsburg. The Swedish king was even able to gain the support of the Crimean Tatar *han*, Devlet II Giray, in order to move a new war against Russia. Conflict was eventually averted, but the interference of the Swedish king provoked the first signs of discomfort in the Ottoman government. On 1 February 1713, janissaries and townspeople assaulted the Swedish colony. This uprising was called *kalabalık* (Turkish for crowd), and the Janissaries captured Charles XII and put him under house arrest. Defeated and humiliated he was moved to the small city of Demiotica, near Edirne, where he spent six months as a forced resident. In October 1714, he finally left the Ottoman Empire in disguise. His entourage also accumulated huge debts with Bender merchants.[35]

These events allowed the Porte to regain the political consideration which the European courts believed eclipsed after the Peace of Carlowitz, returning to the Sultan confidence in his own offensive means and convincing him to attack the Venetian domains in Greece, regardless of the Habsburg emperor's reaction.

---

35   E. Tengberg, *Från Poltava till Bender* (Lund, 1953), pp.202–210.

3

Ottoman Armies

Show (God) Thy power in our miserable incapacity. Repel today Thy enemies from (their) presumption. Because they rely on huge number, wagoons, horses!

(Vaclav Potocki, 'The War of Chocim' Chodkiewicz's speech to the Polish soldiers, vv. 561–563)

The barbarous nations repose mainly their advantages in the multitude.

(Raimondo Montecuccoli, 'Aforismi applicati alla guerra possibile col Turco in Ungheria' cap. I)

The numerical superiority of Ottoman armies had characterised military confrontation with the West since their arrival in the European scenario, and in the seventeenth century 'huge number' and 'multitude' were still considered the main factors of the Ottoman military power.[1] In fact, the Porte was almost always able to assemble large armies, often greater than those of its opponents. However, it often happened that the actual number of combatants was exaggerated by Ottoman propaganda to enhance the sultan's power, while at other times the overestimation came from their enemies, who incidentally were not always able to know the exact size of Ottoman military strength. In other circumstances, Ottoman commanders too contributed to give uncertain details about their actual force, also of their manpower.

There are primarily two difficulties in obtaining the precise strength of the *Ordû-yi Hümâyûn* (literally, the sacred army of the sultan). Firstly, contemporary chroniclers, Ottoman and Western alike, usually offer obscure and contradicting figures in their narratives, which are deeply affected by the

---

1   In 1662, months before the war against the Ottomans of 1663–64, Montecuccoli presented an analysis of the risks and advantages that a war could entail, and the confrontation between the Turks and the Europeans in a military or, more precisely, tactical key, namely the confrontation between armies that fight with art – evidently the Christian ones – and armies like the Ottomans' which fight with great multitude. From this comparison, Montecuccoli derived the optimistic conviction that 'Christianity had never had such florid weapons, and so refined in military art as it has today.' A. Testa, *Le Opere di Raimondo Montecuccoli* (Rome: USSME, 1988–2000), vol. III, p.133.

inevitable limitations of subjective opinion. For this reason, anyone interested on this matter must be prepared to delve into the complexities of official documents and give meaning to figures randomly appearing in contemporary accounts. This alone, however, does not overcome the complications. The archival sources covering the Ottoman field army are very unwilling to cover all the military corps at a given time, offering instead glimpses of randomly exposed units on different occasions. Taking such hardships into account, a descriptive picture of the Ottoman fighting forces can surface by critically juxtaposing and aligning all relevant and surviving material.

To establish the effective power of the military apparatus of the Porte was obviously the main objective of Venetians, Austrians and Poles, who (especially the first two) created a network of spies and informers worthy of today's best intelligence services.[2] Their activity produced a mass of records, estimates and calculations, sometimes manipulated and circulated by the Ottomans themselves to confuse the work of their enemies. This scenario of uncertainty contributed to strengthen the myth of huge Ottoman armies. Thanks to his unlimited power, the sultan could theoretically allocate large financial resources for the maintenance of his armies. Moreover, the general call to arms of the subjects permitted the Porte to sustain a low average cost for each combatant, calculated as four times lower than in the states of Christian Europe.[3] Obviously, these estimates did not take into account the not negligible amount consumed by the sultan's permanent troops, offering only an average that included all the different forces available. However this figure was regarded with understandable anxiety by the European chancelleries.

In the mid seventeenth century the sultan was believed to have an army of over 300,000 men.[4] In the following century even higher estimates can be found, and even today some works speak with great ease of field armies composed of hundreds of thousands of soldiers.[5] In August 1682, after the Porte declared war on the Habsburg emperor, the Aulic War Council tried to form a picture concerning the actual strength of its powerful enemy. The investigation had been conducted through diplomatic channels, and of course spies sent across borders. The final report included the auxiliary contingents and the troops that governors were mobilising in their provinces. The result was disheartening for the Imperial court: 310,000 soldiers, a number that could increase with the support of the Hungarian rebels, exaggeratedly

---

2   See L. Valensi, *Vienna, Venezia e la Sublime Porta* (Bologna: Il Mulino, 1991), pp.34–35, and K.u.K. Kriegsarchiv, *Feldzüge des Prinzen Eugen von Savoyen. Nach den Feldacten und anderen authentischen Quellen hrsg. von der Abtheilung für Kriegsgeschichte des K.K. Kriegs-Archives* (Vienna, 1876–92), vol. II, p.102, where it is quoted that, briefly, the Aulic War Council appealed against the fact that the information was so scarce, notwithstanding the enormous expenses incurred.

3   This is the reconstruction presented to the Venetian Senate in 1658 by the doge Bertucci Valier, in the opening debate concerning the continuation of the Cretan War. See A. Valiero, *Historia della Guerra di Candia* (Venice, 1679), p.333.

4   K.u.K. Kriegsarchiv, *Feldzüge des Prinzen Eugen*, vol. I, p.530.

5   Among the most exaggerated reconstructions of the strength of the Ottoman Army before Vienna, see D. Frangipane, A. Vigevani and P. Zanetta, *L'Ultimo Crociato* (Udine: Centro Iniziative per l'Arte e la Cultura, 1984), and A. Cremonesi, *La sfida turca a Venezia e agli Asburgo* (Tavagnacco, Arti Grafiche Friulane, 1976).

calculated at about 90,000.[6] It is difficult to establish whether the Ottomans themselves, with clear propaganda intent, spread these figures or if they were the result of calculation errors. Very probably, such high figures often came from the incorrect calculation of personnel who followed the armies on campaign, namely 'the enormous crowd of servants, artisans, slaves and merchants'[7] who contributed to raising every estimate. Even the greatest expert on the Ottoman military of that age, Count Luigi Ferdinando Marsigli (or Marsili), argued this theme in the following way:

> The fame that the Ottoman army's strength under Vienna was three hundred thousand men, could be excused for the large quantity of the Servants, which the Turks have always for their need ... for the great quantity of merchants from all the nations of the Empire, and the people who exercised a job, like happens inside a city.[8]

On the basis of the knowledge acquired during his service in the Venetian embassy in Constantinople, and after examining the state balance, the Count calculated 248,440 as the total fighting force in 1683, namely at the moment of the greatest extent of the Ottoman Empire. This number increased with the Tatar allies alongside Wallachian, Moldavian and Transylvanian contingents, who always (according to Marsigli) fielded another 38,000 men, mostly on horseback. Finally, the Count added 50,572 men of the Ottoman navy, for the remarkable total figure of 337,012 soldiers.[9] Then he enumerated all the specialties of the army and from each subtracted the non-combatants, the unavailable forces and the contingents garrisoned in other provinces, to reconstruct the actual number of soldiers. At the end of these calculations, he established that at the eve of the campaign of 1683 the Ottoman army would be 142,785 men strong, excluding Tatars and auxiliaries. Before Marsigli, another Italian officer and most famous military writer, Raimondo Montecuccoli, had calculated the strength deployed by his adversaries for the Hungarian campaign of 1663. The great Imperial general claimed that the total of standing soldiers in the Hungarian theatre comprised 50,000 men, to which further 40,000 'reservists' were added, and which together

---

6   Österreichisches Kriegsarchiv of Vienna, 'Das Kriegsjahr 1683 nach Akten und andere authentischen Quellen' in *Mitteilungen des K.u.K. Kriegsarchivs* (Vienna, 1883), pp.52–53.

7   K.u.K. Kriegsarchiv, *Feldzüge des Prinzen Eugen*, vol. I, p.531.

8   L.F. Marsigli (henceforth indicated only Marsigli), *Stato Militare dell'Imperio Ottomanno* (The Hague and Amsterdam, 1732), vol. I, p.185. Count Luigi Ferdinando Marsigli (or Marsili) was undoubtedly the greatest writer of Ottoman military history and his work still constitutes the best source of knowledge on the subject. Born in Bologna in 1658, Marsigli entered the service of Venice in his twenties as a diplomat and for 11 months was active in Constantinople as an official of the *Bailo alla Porta* (ambassador) of the Most Serene Republic. In 1682, he volunteered in the Imperial army and the following year was captured by the Tatars in Hungary. Sold as a slave to a *paşa* first, and then to two Bosnian soldiers, Marsigli was able to attend the Vienna siege of 1683 and the subsequent battle of 12 September. Having regained his freedom in 1684, he returned to the Imperial army and participated in all the campaigns in Hungary and the Balkans until the end of the War of the Holy League. In 1699, for his experience in diplomacy and knowledge of the Turkish language, Marsigli was part of the Imperial legation at Carlowitz.

9   *Ibidem*, pp.183–184 and p.191.

with the Tatars and other tributaries increased the Ottoman strength to 120,000 soldiers in all.[10]

Ottoman armies always appeared numerically superior to those of their Christian opponents. On the eve of the war against the Habsburgs the sultan could field a very considerable number of professional soldiers. In 1663, the army mobilised for the campaign in Hungary with 121,600 men,[11] the largest field army in the world. However, it would be wrong to believe the immense figures from contemporary sources, because very often information was deliberately overinflated by the Ottomans to scare the enemy.

Thanks to the research conducted by valiant scholars in the Turkish archives, especially those relating economic matters, military historians have today new light about the actual strength of the Ottoman army. In 1687–88, the permanent army numbered 58,974 soldiers. In 1690–91, there were 69,247.[12] Unfortunately, these figures do not specify if honorary members were included, as usual in the Ottoman army. In 1691–92, the research extends to the provincial force and garrisons. Thus, in this period, the overall force was 134,236 soldiers, increased in 1698–99 to 190,308 in all.[13]

Though the Ottoman army was financed differently depending on the corps that formed it, the aforementioned soldiers of the permanent army, recruited and paid by the royal treasury, represented a significant burden for the state's finances. However, although the maintenance of a permanent military force was expensive, the judgement expressed by Montecuccoli in the 1660s remains significant, because he particularly envied 'the great resources and the always ready troops', namely an actual and large standing army.[14] Furthermore, each *askery* subject of the sultan was obliged to allocate a portion of his wealth for the war, since as a member of the 'rank of believers' he was himself a permanent soldier. However, though in this way it was possible to gather many thousands of men at relatively modest expense, this could only happen for short periods, because most of the warriors of necessity had to return to their own jobs.

When conflicts lasted many years, the fighting strength of the army fluctuated from year to year by tens of thousands of men. The distance of the war theatres and the need to resupply the army on campaign impacted on the formation of contingents. At the end of the nineteenth century, the Austro-Hungarian *Kriegsarchiv* published 20 volumes work on the campaigns of Prince Eugene of Savoy. It quoted the German historian Storck, who calculated as necessary for a field army 100,000 men, 78,000 horses, 5,000 camels, 26,000 tents and 19,000 drivers, without considering the artillery and the huge crowd that always accompanied the armies on campaign.[15] Surely the spectacle offered by an Ottoman army on the march must have

10   R. Luraghi, *Le Opere di Raimondo Montecoli* (Rome: USSME, 1988), vol. I, p.24.

11   Hammer-Purgstall, *Geschichte des Osmanischen Reiches*, vol., XI, p.157.

12   Ágoston, *Ottoman Warfare in Europe*, p.138.

13   *Ibidem*. Further details in the appendix.

14   R. Luraghi, *Opere di Raimondo Montecoli*, vol. II, p.465. Moreover, in this regard Montecuccoli added: 'the permanent army assures experienced, valiant and executive leaders and soldiers'.

15   K.u.K. Kriegsarchiv, *Feldzüge des Prinzen Eugen*, vol. I, p.531.

been grandiose and this may have contributed to its immense fame, but it is difficult to believe that, however clever, the Ottoman commanders were able to manage contingents formed by hundreds of thousands of soldiers in an age in which even the greatest European generals confessed their difficulty leading armies greater than 40–50,000 men.

The crowd following the Ottoman armies also included engineers and other specialists who belonged to the combatant specialties. According to the reports sent to Venice at the beginning of the Cretan War, over one third of the manpower employed in the sieges of Chaniá, Rethymno and Kandije were composed by diggers, pioneers and miners.[16] A similar proportion was evident during the sieges of Kamieniec in 1672, Belgrade in 1690, and Corfu in 1716.[17]

Usually very accurate, Marsigli provides a description of the campaigns in Hungary from 1684 to 1697, and up to 1687 he records the number of soldiers available for the field army. According to his personal calculations, he proposes 70,785 men in 1684, no more than 62,000 in 1685 and 1686 and between 45,000 and 50,000 in 1687.[18] Marsigli referred also to the troops available against the Poles and Venetians in 1684: 25,000 Ottomans with 12,000 Tatars in Moldavia and Ukraine until 1687, and about 35,000 Ottoman troops in Greece and southern Bosnia.[19]

The last two decades of the seventeenth century were marked by the serious defeats in Hungary and Greece; the Empire, attacked simultaneously on four fronts by the armies of the Holy League, had to sustain an effort greater than its possibilities. The economic and political crisis aggravated the dramatic scenario, making it even more difficult to provide the army on campaigns, and even the survival of the state seemed about to be overwhelmed by events. The formation of an army capable of entering the campaign was hampered by the need to defend the extended perimeter of the borders threatened by the enemies. In those terrible years, marked by an uninterrupted series of defeats and territorial losses, the Porte succeeded in deploying a true field army only in the Hungarian war theatre. After the disaster of Kahlenberg and until 1687, the Ottomans faced the Imperialists in open field encounters at Párkány, Vác, Ercsi, Esztergom, Bia and finally at Harsány, where they suffered an even more serious defeat than that at occurred at Vienna four years before. In the following campaigns, the Imperialists faced only modest corps of 25–30,000 men, unable to stop the enemy advance, which reached Bulgaria and northern Albania.[20]

---

16   P. Morachiello, 'Candia, i baluardi del Regno', in *Venezia e la Difesa del Levante* (Venice: L'arsenale, 1986), p.120; the Venetian sources speak of at least 30,000 miners and other auxiliaries out of a total of 80,000 men.

17   Archivio di Stato di Venezia, *Senato Mar*, Dispacci Provveditori da Terra e da Mar, f.808.

18   Marsigli, vol. II, pp.186–187. According to the author, before the campaign of 1686 Grand Vizier Süleyman would spread the tale that he was gathering the largest army ever seen in the Empire after the one that besieged Vienna, but all the efforts made would have resulted in a rather modest number of combatants. This is one of the most significant examples of the Ottoman tendency to magnify the strength of their armies.

19   *Ibidem.*

20   The summer and autumn of 1687 also brought severe shocks to the Ottoman Empire: mutinies and bloody rebellions in Constantinople cost the throne of Sultan Mehmed IV and the grand vizier. The failures and losses since 1683 bore fruit in this way. Passages are also interspersed in

On the other threatened fronts, small contingents of cavalry were able to perform only modest raids, or, as in Moldavia and Ukraine, the Ottoman commanders resorted to the scorched-earth tactic of destroying resources, and reserving the few forces available for the defence of the major fortresses, such as Kamieniec and Azov. Resistance in the Peloponnese was equally unfortunate. Here, except for the fortress of Monemvasia, which held out until 1690, the Venetians succeeded in conquering the whole province in just three campaigns. Dalmatia remained a secondary front, but also here the losses were strategically significant. After two inconclusive and costly assaults against the Venetian forts of Zadvarie in June 1685, and Dolac and Srijane in July 1686, in September the Venetians conquered the strongly fortified Sinj, followed by taking the surrender of Herceg-Novi in September 1687. In 1688, the Venetians succeeded in seizing the strategic fortress of Knin and other minor places in the Lika.[21]

Only after 1688, when the German princes withdrew their troops to face the French on the Rhine, did the emergency diminish and the difference of strength became less unbalanced. However, the decrease of enemy pressure in Hungary, Greece and other fronts did not solve the main problem, namely the setting up of an army capable of carrying out the traditional Ottoman strategy. In 1688, the retreat of the German princes' force from the Balkans and the arrest of the Venetian offensive at Negroponte (today Chalkis in Euboea, Greece) reopened the challenge, but until 1690 the Porte was unable to match the enemy in the open field. After the reconquest of Belgrade in 1690, the Ottomans could retake the initiative, but encountered a new major defeat at Slankamen in 1691. For this campaign the Ottoman treasury resorted to all available resources and the army, under the command of Grand Vizier Köprülü Mustafa, numbered again a significant figure, being estimated around 134,000 men,[22] but evidently including the non-combatants. The presence of large armies returned to being a rare event in the following years, and in fact in the summer of 1694, for the assault on Peterwardein, Grand Vizier Sürmeli Ali was able to gather just 26,000 soldiers.[23] For readers not familiar with the particularity of the Ottoman military, this modest number might seem disappointingly low for an allegedly huge army. Like any other European state of this age, the Porte also had to deal with budgetary problems in order to maintain a standing force that required increasing resources to faceg such a large enemy coalition. However, it should be noted that despite the serious setbacks suffered, the Porte made an exceptional

the reports of the *Theatrum Europaeum*, which testify to a gradual rethinking of the strength of the Ottoman Empire.

21 The capture of Knin marked the end of the successful Venetian campaign to expand its territory in inland Dalmatia, and it also determined much of the final border between Dalmatia and Bosnia and Herzegovina that stands today. The Ottomans besieged Sinj in the Second Morean War, but were repelled. See also A. Nazor, *Inhabitants of Poljica in the War of Morea (1684–1699)* (Zagreb: Croatian Institute of History, 2002).

22 G. Ágoston, 'Ottoman Warfare in Europe, 1453–1826', in J. Black (ed.) *European Warfare 1453–1815* (London: Red Globe, 1999), p.138.

23 G. Payer, *Armati Hungarorum* (Munich: Körösi Csoma Sándor, 1985), p. 115.

effort to maintain, year after year, a force capable of continuing the war on five different fronts.

As occurred in every seventeenth-century army, the actual strength of the field army, even when described in detail, is often uncertain and remains subject to different interpretations. It is often not even clear if figures refer only to the Ottoman troops or include Tatars and auxiliary forces, or whether all these forces rather than those in a specific theatre of war are included in the total. Irregular units, border garrisons, as well as artillery and other specialists were usually included in the documents relating the overall strength, especially in Christian sources. Until the end of the seventeenth century, data continues to be incomplete and unreliable, and only from the first decades of the new century does information show a little better detail. However, even when the details are accurate, often the figures make no distinction between cavalry and infantry, relating only the overall force in the field.

A very accurate report on the Ottoman combatant forces, encamped at Belgrade on July 1697, was sent by the 'secret agent' Kaszpar Sándor to the Imperial headquarters of Peterwardein:

> Sarcan Pasha of Nikopol has under him 400 horsemen; the Pasha of Silistra is here with 800 foot; the janissaries of Adrianopole with 800 men; further 3,000 Bosnian infantrymen are in the encampment, and Kaplan Pasha is here with 1,500 Horse and 8,000 Albanian infantry; there are also 2,500 janissaries with the Sargagi Basci (çarkacybasi); and Sahil Pasha has under him 150 horsemen; further 3,000 janissaries have landed from the ships of the Danube's fleet. The troops under Mizir Ali, governor of Anatolia, alongside the ones under Jarsum Mohammed, beg of Bihac, and Osman Pasha of Damascus, are 4,000 horsemen, while another cavalry corps numbers 5,000 Horse, mainly from the Asian provinces. A further 2,000 Egyptian janissaries and 8,000 *azabs* from Belgrade are camped with 20,000 Horse and Foot arrived days before with the sultan.[24]

The Hungarian spy registered an overall 58,950 combatants, to which were added a further 15,000 men already deployed in the war theatre, and the Tatar horsemen sent by the Crimean *han*. According to the Austro-Hungarian *Kriegsarchiv*, in the campaign of 1697 the overall Ottoman force deployed in Hungary numbered about 135,000 men.[25] Other sources bring to 86,884 men the fighting force gathered for the oncoming campaign.[26] These figures would be very distant from each other, and it could be partially explained only when considering all the auxiliary personnel. The campaign of 1697 ended with the disaster of Zenta, followed by the armistice of Carlowitz in January 1699, which inaugurated a period of peace and of strong reduction of the military forces. However, in 1710 the policy of rearmament returned as the principal matter of the Porte, in sight of the oncoming war against Russia. The mobilisation involved 118,400 men,[27] and a further 30,000 belonged to the

---

24 K.u.K. Kriegsarchiv, *Feldzüge des Prinzen Eugen*, vol. II, p.349.
25 *Ibidem*, vol. I, p.531.
26 Ágoston, *Military Transformation in the Ottoman Empire and Russia, 1500–1800*, p.308.
27 D. Chandler, *The Art of Warfare in thè Age of Marlborough* (London: Batsford, 1976), p.74.

services as drivers, diggers, miners, artisans and other personnel. In this figure were not included the Tatar horsemen usually provided by the Crimean *han*.

Another accurate record concerning the Ottoman troops gathered in prevision of a war campaign is known thanks to the attaché of the French ambassador in Constantinople, the *dragoman* Benjamin Brue, eyewitness in the summer of 1715 of the assembling of the forces in Thebes for the campaign against the Venetians in the Peloponnese. Despite some inaccuracies due to the difficult identification of the specialties, especially in the infantry, Brue estimated at 23,000 horse and 71,000 foot the total strength of the field army.[28] In the monumental work on the campaign of Prince Eugene of Savoy, two volumes deal with the conflict against the Porte of 1716–18. The *Kriegsarchiv* relates several examples that show how it was still very complicated to establish the actual strength of any Ottoman field army. In the spring of 1716, during the frantic preparations for the upcoming campaign on the Danube, information collected in Vienna reported the Ottoman army strength at 200,000 men. Prince Eugene himself declared that, '[There would be] nothing safe to say about the strength and composition of the enemy army. It is certain that this is very great and the enemy say it as well supplied with everything needed for a large-scale campaign.'[29]

The calculation elaborated by the Viennese Aulic War Council in the summer of 1716 reported the total figure of 180,000 combatants, 40,000 of whom were garrisoned on the Hungarian and Dalmatian borders, another 60,000 between Peloponnesus and the siege of Corfu, and finally at least 80,000 gathered for the field army that was preparing to cross the Danube to assault Peterwardein.[30] In contrast to these estimates, the report sent the previous year by the Imperial resident in Constantinople, Count Fleishmann, reported that the sultan could deploy as few as 70,000 men, and that the whole army was in such a deplorable state that an attack by the Emperor would be resolved in an easy success.[31]

Usually, the best way to know actual enemy strength was the interrogation of prisoners and deserters. However, even in these events the information could be discordant. Days before the siege of Corfu, in 1716, the Venetians learned news about the besieging corps from two Ottoman captive soldiers. The first, 'Cussein Giannizero', was captured on 19 August and 'after recovering from his injuries', stated that the field army amounted to about 20–22,000 men, 'composed by various corps of standing troops and militia, alongside 4,000 janissaries from Constantinople, under the command of 20

---

28 B. Brue, *Journal de la Campagne que le Gran Visir Ali Pascha a faite en 1715 pour la conquête de la Morèe* (Paris, 1879), pp.65–68.

29 K.u.K. Kriegsarchiv, *Feldzüge des Prinzen Eugen*, vol. XVI, p.126.

30 *Ibidem*. According to the Kriegsarchiv, in 1716 the Ottoman army would have amounted to a total of 420,000 men.

31 *Ibidem*, p.124: '59,200 Foot and 14,794 Horse, who seem more like marauders than soldiers'. Letter of the Imperial resident Count Fleischmann, dated 28 April 1715. Possibly the Austrian diplomat referred only to the strength of the permanent troops and did not account for the irregulars or the frontiersmen. In fact, the figure relating to the cavalry coincides with the strength of the household cavalry.

colonels and one general'. A further 2,000 *Gibizzi* [*cebeci*],[32] directed by four field officers, 2,000 'volunteers', 1,000 artillerymen with two officers and one artillery general, and 1,500 Asian cavalry came from Constantinople to join the general commander. 'This force had been collected with the promise of wages and other prizes, or, especially the troops of Rumelia, under the threat of retaliation.'[33] The second prisoner, Salì, an artilleryman from Constantinople, reported the presence of about 7,000 janissaries, 'under the command of Çelebi Agà, *Caimecan* in Constantinople', with '3,000 *Gibizzi*, 400 artillerymen, 1,500 cavalry, 3,000 Albanians and various other people'.[34] A third source, a letter of an anonymous officer who collected information from spies and other eyewitnesses, reports another evaluation concerning the Ottoman besieger army that landed at Corfu. It was believed that the enemy landed with '6,000 pioneers and 4,000 janissaries' alongside 15–20,000 further troops. Such were the 'reports of many peasants' who entered the city, leading a prisoner, 'who said he had escaped from a galley and therefore volunteered on the Venetian side to have been Christian.' It is calculated, realistically, that the Ottomans landed at Corfu with 30,000 infantrymen and 3,000 horsemen, This contingent probably included no more than 7,000 infantry and artillery as the only professional troops, while most of the infantry consisted of levies from Thrace and Anatolia, auxiliaries for digging the trenches, and miners. The cavalry belonged to the European provinces and a few hundred came from the provinces close to the border. The largest part of the standing army with the best troops was already on the march to Hungary, where it was about to face the Imperial army.[35]

In 1717, despite the defeats suffered at Peterwardein, Temeşvár and Corfu, the strength of the army would have grown because of the general call to arms proclaimed by the new grand vizier. The army deployed against the Imperialists would have reached the remarkable total of 300,000 men, for a total of almost half a million soldiers mobilised for the campaigns on secondary fronts in Dalmatia, Bosnia and Transylvania.[36] Such numbers obviously arouse great astonishment, but, evidently these figures have a clear propaganda purpose. While narrative sources give inflated figures regarding the strength of the Ottoman armed forces, in light of the above data it is clear that the troops mobilised by the sultans from their standing army no longer outmatched that of Habsburg Austria or Russia by the early eighteenth century.[37] After more than half a century of continuous wars against the West, the Ottomans had not

---

32 *Cebeci*, or armourer. For further detail, see the section in this chapter relating to this corps.
33 Archivio di Stato di Venezia, *Senato Mar*, Dispacci Provveditori da Terra e da Mar, f.808.
34 *Ibidem*.
35 A. Prelli and B. Mugnai, *L'Ultima Vittoria della Serenissima. L'assedio di Corfù, 1716* (Bassano del Grappa: Itinera Progetti, 2016), p.131.
36 K.u.K. Kriegsarchiv, *Feldzüge des Prinzen Eugen*, vol. XVII, p.51. Some of these figures came from a classic of the history of the Ottoman Empire, the *Geschichte des Osmanischen Reiches* by Josef von Hammer-Purgstall. Despite the great merits of this work, the evaluation of the Ottoman military strength is often unreliable, as expressed also by the Kriegsarchiv's authors.
37 G. Ágoston, 'Empires and Warfare in East-Central Europe, 1550–1750: the Ottoman-Habsburg rivalry and military transformation', in *European Warfare, 1350–1750* (Cambridge: Cambridge University Press, 2010), p.129.

abandoned one of their most consolidated and effective strategies: propaganda based on the large number and multitude of their armies. On the other hand, and despite the blown weakness of the Porte, at the beginning of the eighteenth century not even the sultan's enemies seemed prepared to decipher the actual strength of the Ottoman forces, and continued to be deceived by the 'concealment ability' of which Montecuccoli had warned his readers.[38]

The *Kapikulu*

Except for minor changes, the sultans maintained the same military structure established in the sixteenth century. The Ottoman army, as a whole, included three different parts and the most important was represented by the permanent troops of the sultan's household, known as *kapikulu*. The name adopted by this corps means 'slave or subject of the Porte'.[39] These terms indicated also the specific meaning of the court's troops in comparison to the *serhaddkulu*, which was essentially a provincial militia. The other component of the Ottoman army was formed by the cavalry gathered in case of war in the provinces of the Empire, and known as *toprakli*.

The creation of a corps of standing troops, formed by slaves indoctrinated in the Islamic religion and trained as soldiers, dates back to the early fourteenth century, introduced by Grand Vizier Orkhan Paşa. In 1330 this first core of permanent troops numbered 1,000 infantrymen,[40] who assumed the title of *yeniceri*, namely 'new soldiers', to distinguish them from the older corps of combatants, represented by the *sipahi* cavalrymen. Both corps became instruments of the court factions and were often in open conflict with each other and more than once even against the government. The *sipahis*, who recruited among ethnic Turks from Anatolia, and the janissaries coming from Europe, remained a long-lived feature of the Ottoman army. Because of their belonging to the sultan's household, these troops acquired great prestige in Ottoman society and *kapikulu* members were always rewarded with a good salary. Over the years, volunteers were rewarded with admission to the *kapikulu*. In other circumstances, assignment to the *kapikulu* cavalry or janissaries might be obtained after attaining military honours by undertaking a dangerous mission, or volunteering for a placement in some remote and unsafe garrison, such as the Yemen or Crete. In this regard, in 1657 and 1658, in order to procure crew for the Ottoman navy that faced the fearsome Venetian fleet in the Dardanelles, the government promised a place

---

38 Montecuccoli, 'Aforismi applicati alla guerra possibile col Turco in Ungheria', in Luraghi, *Opere di Raimondo Montecuccoli*, vol. II, p.464.

39 In this regard, Marsigli pointed out: 'the name capiculi [*sic*] comprised all the people of the sultan's seraglio alongside other people subjected to the grand lord's authority, and when the sultan goes on campaign they also carry the sword.' Marsigli: vol. II, p.66. The same author adds also that the *kapikulu* included many honorary members who performed no military service.

40 Some historians suggest that the creation of the janissaries was inspired at least in part by the Egyptian Mamluks. The latter were in fact Caucasian and Circassian slaves, but also included ethnic Turks, however the Mamluks were soldiers on horseback, while the Ottoman janissaries were essentially infantrymen. See also J.P. Le Roux, *Histoire des Turcs* (Paris: Fayard, 1988), p.188.

Habit of the Tchorbadgi or Captain of the Janesaries, in 1700.

Capitaine des Janesaries.

18.

16. Janissary ***çorbaci*** (senior officer), after Jean-Baptiste van Moor. Note the size of the ***kalafat*** headdress. In the late seventeenth century, the French diplomat De Ferriol ordered the artist to paint 100 portraits representing court personalities, citizens and soldiers of Constantinople, published in 1708 in the ***Recueil de cent estampes représentant les diverses nations du Levant.*** These drawings are very useful for knowing the changes that occurred between the 'Imperial' period of the sixteenth and seventeenth centuries and the beginning of the eighteenth century, when the trend for the eccentricity of clothing and accessories begins, which would become typical in the following century. (Author's archive)

in the *kapikulu* cavalry to anyone who had served as a sailor or as a marine for one year.[41]

Several records show the strength of the *kapikulu* through the years. In 1652–53, the overall number was about 85,000 men, and then in 1660–61 the number diminished to 61,300. In 1669–70 were registered 95,000 'mouths', while in 1690–91 the overall numbered 83,700. Finally, at the beginning of the eighteenth century, about 59,000 men were members of the *kapikulu*.[42] The fluctuation of strength was the result of the reforms that continually involved the corps since 1622, when the young and clever Sultan Osman II unsuccessfully tried to limit the growing power of his professional 'praetorians'. Other significant reforms and reductions were implemented by Köprülü Mehmed starting in 1658, and later by Merzifonlu Kara Mustafa in the early 1680s.[43]

The variation in number was also due to the fact that registration to the *kapikulu* also occurred as an honorary title or for patronage or clientele reasons. Furthermore, many members were periodically introduced into the *kapikulu* as pensioners and did not participate in war campaigns.

The *kapikulu* was organised like an actual army with its logistical apparatus, a bank restricted to members only, a training school and internal rules configuring it like a very exclusive military corps.

The Janissaries

The infantry was the larger component of the *kapikulu*, and on average represented three fifths of the overall number. The janissaries constituted the main and most famous Ottoman infantry *speciality*. A strong tradition links the institution of this corps with the religious order of the Bektási, whose founder, Haci Bektás Veli,[44] suggested the adoption of the characteristic janissary headgear, inspired by the sleeve with the preacher's blessing hand. Sultan Murad I (reigned 1359–89) gave them the first codex of rules,[45] and already during his reign, their number increased considerably. Originally

---

41 Hammer-Purgstall, *Geschichte des Osmanischen Reiches*, vol. XI, p.58.

42 R. Mantran, 'L'Evolution de l'armée ottomane aux XVI et XVIII siecles', in *Venezia e la Difesa del Levante* (Venice: L'Arsenale, 1984), p.228. Ágoston provides slightly different figures, see 'Ottoman military organisation (up to 1800)', p.4. For further details see the appendix.

43 In 1680–81, Kara Mustafa would have reduced the strength of 17,000 janissaries in all, in order to remove the honorary positions within the corps. See A. Cevad Beg, *Etat Militaire Ottoman, depuis la fondation de l'Empire Ottoman jusqu'à nos jours* (Constantinople, 1882), vol. I, p.82.

44 The Bektaşi order was perhaps most famous for being the interpretation of Islam that was embraced by the janissaries. This relationship between members of the order and officers of the janissary corps gave the group a political dimension as well as a spiritual one. 'In the late fourteenth century, members of the order began serving as chaplains and spiritual guides to the janissary corps, and by the sixteenth century it was established practice that all members of those elite military units were inducted into the order as the founder of the order, Hajji Bektaş Veli, was viewed as the guiding spirit of the Janissaries, not unlike a patron saint in Christian belief.' Ágoston-Bruce, *Encyclopedia*, p.88.

45 The 'five rules' were: 'I: the obedience to officers and chiefs must be like that of a slave. II: the janissaries must be housed as a single corps in a single place. III: no superfluous thing is allowed to be possessed, so that the janissary does not feed luxury. IV: the death sentence must be

discipline was very hard: the janissary could not marry or have children, nor could he work privately until he was on active duty, which ordinarily ended after the age of 45 or for health reasons.[46] In the following centuries, many of the rules were not implemented, especially those relating to private activities, and even the salary was subject to numerous reforms, more or less dictated by contingent reasons. Salary was not identical among the common soldiers and varied according to the year of service. Upon his entry into the corps, the janissary received a daily payment of five *akçe*, then, after the first year of service, he obtained a gradual increase up to 13 *akçe*, which was the highest possible salary for the common soldier.[47] Naturally, earnings could increase thanks to the right that reserved a fifth of the spoils of war to the janissaries, without forgetting the gifts and the various prizes that traditionally were granted to them in the case of special events.

17. 'Janissary who is going to war'. It is well known that Ottoman sources have sometimes been misinterpreted in Western Europe, and very often, in some modern illustrations, the janissaries appear with the same dress on parade as well on campaign. Some fanciful Ottoman miniatures also show the janissaries wearing in battle the uncomfortable *ak börk* headdress and the aulic *dolama kaftan*, but several evidences relate the soldier's true dress on campaign.

(Watercolour of Johannes Löwenklau, from the Hieronymus Beck's *Figurae calamo exaratae variorum Turcarum imperatorum*, late sixteenth century, Österreichische Nationalbibliothek Vienna)

---

applied after accurate consideration … V: in his prayers, the janissary must be the loyal executor of all that has been commanded by Haci Bektás.' Marsigli, I, p.67.

46   Very poor comments circulated about the janissaries' reputation in the seventeenth century. Some Egyptian chronicles stated that the Ottoman soldiers generally were drinkers, hashish addicts and pederasts: 'they did not fast during Ramadan, most of them did not even pray, and they desecrated shrines and sanctuaries. The janissaries often stole food from the shopkeepers or did not pay the right price. People were forced to pull heavy cannons and to load huge stone pillars.' Cited in M. Winter, *Egyptian Society under Ottoman Rule, 1517–1798* (London and New York: Routledge, 2005), p.9.

47   Marsigli, vol. II, p.208.

18. Janissaries in parade dress, after a seventeenth-century Polish collection of Ottoman costumes. One of the peculiar characteristic features of the Ottoman Empire was its liveliness, its incessant activity, its self-realisation in ceremonies, parades, and pageantry. Even the war was for the orthodox Ottomans not a cruel necessity, but a joyful ritual whose effect must always be positive, bringing victory and war's booty, or the delight of heaven so expressly promised by their religion. (Icones Habitus Monumenta Turcarum, between 1586 and 1650, Biblioteka Jagiellońska, Krakow)

In the mid seventeenth century the janissaries formed 196 *ortas*,[48] literally 'chambers' or 'rooms', divided into three categories, and basically maintained the structure received by Suleiman the Magnificent in the first half of the sixteenth century. From that period, the statutes developed and the privileges of the corps expanded. The categories were originally established according to

---

48 *Ibidem*, vol. I, p.68.

the importance of the cities in which they had the garrison. The first category included 101 units, known as *yayabegi* or *cemaat*, the latter a term borrowed from the Arabic meaning 'gathering', or 'assembly'. Another 61 *ortas* constituted the category *bölük* and the remaining 34 were the *segmen*. This latter had been established later than the other two categories and was originally considered as a reserve, therefore they had been the only janissaries who exercised a trade or a job. When joined in a group the *ortas* were collectively identified as the *ocak* (corps, or garrison), distributed throughout the empire. The *ocak*'s responsibility was numerous and varied: collecting taxes, keeping law and order, guarding accesses, and protecting the countryside against marauding parties. Janissaries acted also as gendarmes, and could be dispatched for controlling small posts inside the cities.[49]

The organ of direction of the corps, more or less comparable to a modern major staff, took the name of *divoan*. Alongside the specifically military issues, the janissary *divoan* also dealt with internal justice affairs and central administration. The *divoan* was located in Constantinople, in the residence of its highest member, the *yeniceri ağasi*, who acted as a general commander of the corps. This office was one of the most important not only in the army but also in the Ottoman court. Usually the candidate was chosen from a list of candidates formed by people close to the sultan or to his family. As supreme commander, the *yeniceri ağasi* could promote the officers and propose the commanders of the garrisons. He had two lieutenants who were in charge of specific matters. The *segmenbasci* replaced the *yeniceri ağasi* in Constantinople when the senior officer moved from the capital and contemporarily he was the commander of all the *segmen* units. The other lieutenant was the *kethüda beg*, who had the function of general adjutant of the commander. He held the command of one of the largest *ortas* in the *bölük* category. Furthermore, his rank was particularly profitable, because he received the properties and riches of the janissary officers who died without heirs. In the *divoan*, the *yeniceri ağasi* and his lieutenants occupied the first positions. The *divoan* included also the *fodla katibi*, administrative commissar for the honorific members, and the *yeniceri efendi*, who dealt with justice of the corps, alongside the *muhzir ağa*, the chief of the war tribunal. This latter could replace the *yeniceri ağasi* and even the grand vizier during the process. The subordinate ranks in the janissary *divoan* was occupied by the *kethüda yeri*, who held in Constantinople the office of secretary for the senior commander. He was also the commander of one *orta* quartered in the capital. The *divoan* included also three *çavuş*, who acted like commissars and adjutants of the senior commanders. They had to take care of the exact disposition and number of soldiers during the numerous ceremonies and parade in Constantinople and ensure that all orders and resolutions issued

---

49 In the mid seventeenth century, soldiers of the *ocak* in Lebanon conducted several duties as gendarmerie: 'My order has been issued to station fifteen janissaries in each of the citadels of Sidon and Beirut and ten janissaries in the tower of Emir Muhammad (in Beirut).' Order to Muhammad, çorbacy of the infantry in charge of the citadels of Sidon and Beirut. See A.R. Abu-Husayn, *The View from Istanbul: Lebanon and the Druze Emirate in the Ottoman Chancery Documents, 1546–1711* (London, New York: I.B. Tauris, 2004), p.86.

by the *divoan* were transmitted to the units. The first of them was the *basçavuş*, who dealt with the sentences of the war tribunal. He was also the officer in charge of the entrance ceremony for the recruits: 'to whom he had with a slap to impress the character of janissary to the new arrivals.'[50] The janissary *divoan* included among the subordinates also the provosts and the administrative officials, directed by a *meydanbasi* with a variable number of employees, known as *meydan kethüda*.

There is rarely any indication concerning the strength of a single *orta*. Originally the units residing in Constantinople deployed a strength of 100 janissaries, while the others, destined for the peripheral garrisons, numbered from 200 to 300 rank and file.[51] Some enterprising scholars have tried to investigate this matter in detail in the Turkish archives.[52] Thanks to their effort, several interesting information relating the composition of Ottoman garrisons in Europe came to light. Immediately after the 1663 conquest of Érsekúivár, records show a very large number of janissaries assigned to the new garrison. This increase was the logical result of a successful siege. The besieging Ottoman army at Érsekúivár was a large one, and many of its men were moved into the garrison to establish and maintain control of the newly acquired fortress. The earliest record that remains for this garrison, dated late 1663, shows 1,442 janissaries in three *ortas* of *cemaats* and four of *bölüks*. In early 1664, the janissary contingent was slightly reduced to 1,434 soldiers. The following year, 1676–77, saw one of the smallest recorded number of janissaries serving at Érsekúivár: 638 men in all.[53] This suggests that garrisons and consequently the janissaries fluctuated considerably, due to the constant wars of the seventeenth century.

In wartime, each *orta* had to increase its strength to 500 men,[54] however, according to Marsigli, there were several exceptions and in the seventeenth century the units deployed a large variety of strengths, fluctuating between 100 and 500 men or more.[55] Each *orta* was divided into *odas* (tents), which grouped the janissaries as originally established in order of the ovens in the *orta*. Usually the number of men in each *oda* was 10 to 20. The *oda* may suggest some analogy with the 'company' of the western army, as well as the *orta* resembling the 'regiment', but the *oda* was only an administrative unit, while the *orta* had a tactical role and so was closer to the 'battalion'. Each *orta* had its

---

50 Marsigli, vol. I, p.68. This ceremony took the name of *kapi-cirmak*. At the end the recruit was considered by other janissaries to be a *yoldas*, namely a comrade.

51 *Ibidem*, 'carta dell'Impero Ottomano che mostra le frontiere di terra e di mare…'

52 There are hundreds of archival records of the janissaries from the seventeenth century concerning the pay register. These records seem to have been arranged by region, with one record book listing the janissary troops for the garrison in an entire province, or several neighbouring districts. Thus the records for Kanisza and Érsekúivár can often be found in the same *defter* (register) as those for Sarajevo, Belgrade, Temeşvar, Esztergom, and Buda. Some troops temporarily assigned from Constantinople to the frontier may also still be listed in the capital's payroll. The difficulties arise when one tries to reconcile data from the documents that list only the janissaries with those that list all the other garrison troops. See M. Stein, *Guarding the Frontier. Ottoman Borders Forts and Garrisons in Europe* (London: Tauris, 2007), p.65.

53 *Ibidem*, p.68.

54 A.L. Horniker, 'The Corps of the Janizaries' (part I), in *Gorget & Sash*, vol. III, n. 3, p.9.

55 Cevad, *Etat Militaire Ottoman*, vol. I, pp.143–148.

own commander, the çorbaci, literally 'the one who cooks the soup'. Some of the terminology of the corps derived from the terms used in the kitchen and in military food. This originated from the special meaning that in the Ottoman world was connected to the food received by the sovereign. Therefore, the internal hierarchy reflected the prestige position of those who first received the ingredients.[56] Kitchen tools were also used in the symbols of the body, such as the iron cauldron and the spoon kept on the headgear's case. The use of these symbols also had a special meaning on other occasions, and when the janissaries wanted to show their dissent towards the officers, they showed upside-down cauldrons.

After the çorbaci, the hierarchy continued with the *odabasi*, each commanding its own *oda*, and then their number varied according to how many *odas* formed the *orta*. The *odabasi* may be considered as an NCO as well as the *vekilharc*, in charge as fourier but also as commissar for the supplies of each *orta*. The staff was completed by the *bayrakdar*, standard bearer, and the *asci*, the cook, who was the senior NCO of the *orta*. Among the veteran janissaries, each *orta* had one *basesky*, who carried the flag with the symbol of the unit, which was displayed at the entrance of the quarter or on the çorbaci's tent in the encampment. The *basesky* may be considered similar to the western *corporal* of infantry.

Each *orta* had its own symbol and a number, which did not follow the natural series, because in the hierarchical sequence the first *orta* had '19', the second had '1' and the third had '111'.[57] There were also a couple of vacant numbers, 64 and 65. These numbers belonged to the mounted janissary units licensed in 1623 by Sultan Murad IV, because of their involvement in the murder of Sultan Osman II 'the young'. They had been the only janissary units trained as cavalry.

In addition to the differences in rank established by the assignment of the garrisons,

19. Aşçi, cook, of a janissary *orta*, mid seventeenth century. The *aşçi* was a not commissioned officer but his rank had a great importance in the janissary corps. He was indeed the guardian of the *kazan*, the pot, the main symbol of the *orta*. This *aşçi* wears a dark grey-azure *dolama kaftan* with white lining embroiderd with flowers and leaves, over a green *entari* waistcoat, azure breeches, dark red *kusak* sash under a gilded belt, red gaiters, yellow leather sash, and a couple of knives with silver and brass accessories. A large white metal chain and gilded accessories complete the parade dress of the *aşçi*. Note the *tekke* cap worn under the janissary headdress. (Ottoman Miniature, first half of the seventeenth century, private collection)

---

56 The custom of the ancient Turkish nomads to count the number of fires lit, and then of the pots, to esteem the strength of the army, survived in the Ottoman world and within the janissary corps assumed the meaning of brotherhood of arms and common destiny.

57 K.u.K. Kriegsarchiv, *Feldzüge des Prinzen Eugen*, vol. I, p.524.

some *ortas* also distinguished themselves for traditional duties or for special functions performed in court ceremonies. Count Ferdinando Marsigli collected several notices about this topic, providing a lot of very interesting and almost unknown information. Among the first 'special' units, he refers to *ortas* 60, 61, 62 and 63, known as *solaks*. Each was composed of 100 janissaries, who formed the foot escort for the sultan in Constantinople. They joined the field army only when the sultan marched with his troops, and continued to carry bows and arrows as weapons and to wear a particular and colourful dress very different to that of the ordinary janissaries. The officers of the *solaks* kept the road travelled by the sultan free of obstacles and for this reason they anticipated the procession by riding along the chosen route. *Orta* 63 watched cranes, peacocks and ducks in the Topkapı gardens; while *orta* 64, the *zagarci*, maintained the task of watching the sultan's hunting dogs. In parade this *orta* marched with 34 janissaries on horseback dressed as çorbaci with the leashed dogs. Their commander, the *zagarcibasi*, usually held an important task, not only because on parade he occupied a position close to the sultan, but also because his rank was the antechamber for becoming *yeniceri ağasi*. In the mid seventeenth century, the *zagarci* deployed 600 men.[58] *Orta* 71, the *samsoncu*, and 68, the *turnacy*, also had the task of watching the sultan's hunting animals. On parade, the *samsoncu* marched with the mastiffs trained for bear hunting, while the *turnacy* followed with greyhounds and falcons. The commander of the *samsoncu* took the command of the *zagarci* when the place remained vacant. *Orta* 35 was known as the *avcilar* and had the task of escort and of helping the sultan on hunting trips.[59] Before receiving the appointment as commander of this *orta*, the officer must have covered the entire internal hierarchy. A particular exception was applied to the *odabasi* of the *avcilar*, who were originally the only janissaries who could marry before the end of active service. This *orta* was the only particular unit belonging to the *segmen* category. *Ortas* 14, 49, 66 and 67 were the *hasseki* and from among these were chosen the officer destined to the *turnacy*.

Ortas 1 and 5 were the *deveci*, which originally qualified the drivers and the guardians of the army's camels. Their officers occupied a considerable position in the hierarchy of the corps, because the command of the largest garrison was usually entrusted to them. The commander of *orta* 5 was also the *başçavuş* of the janissaries' *divoan*. *Orta* 84 held the title Imam, because its commander was the religious chief of the janissary corps. *Orta* 54, the *talimhanecilar*, originally had the task of training recruits in the use of the bow, while number 102, the *zemberekci*, performed the same with the crossbow. As a record of these ancient tasks, both the units had as distinctive symbols these weapons. On campaign, these *ortas* had permission to place their tents close to that of the Imam. Also *orta* 51, the *cerge*, had special permission for placing its tents, because they could occupy the space in front of the sultan's pavilion.

---

58   Marsigli, vol. I, p.69.
59   *Orta* 35 was that which deposed Sultan Mustafa II in 1703.

Finally, *orta* 99 was formed by the musicians of the corps, and therefore was designated as the Ottoman military band, the *mehter*.

As always happens when the sources deal with the Ottoman army, there are several contradictory figures that contribute to make the matter very complex. As the strength of the janissaries fluctuated considerably over the years, the problem of the actual number ready to march continues to persist. Moreover, the complete contingent was not always mobilised. What must also be considered, is how very often the Western sources qualify as janissaries all the Ottoman infantrymen, even when they were not present, as happens for example in the Venetian sources dating to the War of the Holy League. However, there is always a considerable difference in the calculation of strength and the estimates coming from authoritative sources that keeps the matter uncertain. For the last quarter of the seventeenth century the Austro-Hungarian *Kriegsarchiv* elevates the strength of the janissaries as never being under 50,000 men.[60]

According to accurate research conducted in the Turkish archives, the overall number of janissaries fluctuated between 51,000 and 55,000 in the 1650s, and decreased considerably in the 1660s, only to reach its peak of almost 79,000 in 1694–5 during the war against the Holy League. The overall force remained high, about 67,700 and 69,600 in the rest of the century, only to decrease again after the war. It was about 36,000 to 40,000 in the first decade of the eighteenth century, but rose again in 1714–18.[61]

In detail, according to the budget of 1660–61, there were 54,222 janissaries enlisted in pay registers. This number seems not to have changed greatly for the succeeding three years. In 1664, the Ottoman central administration paid the salaries of 53,371 men in the janissary corps.[62] However, only a part of these soldiers were employed in the field army of 1663–64. Simon Reniger, a Habsburg resident of Constantinople, who accompanied the Ottoman army during the war as Imperial delegate, claimed that in 1663 the number of janissaries marching to Hungary did not exceed an average of 10,000.[63] He also added that in the coming year this humble figure further dropped to 6–7,000.[64] Further estimates confirmed the assertion concerning the

---

60 K.u.K. Kriegsarchiv, *Feldzüge des Prinzen Eugen*, vol. I, p.523.

61 Ágoston, 'Empires and Warfare in east-central Europe, 1550–1750', in *European Warfare, 1350–1750*, p.128.

62 *Eyyubî Efendi Kânûnnâmesi, Survey and Text*, A. Özcan (ed.), Istanbul, n. 33/1994, p.133.

63 According to a recent study, in March 1663, the Ottoman treasury covered the expenses of pack animals purchased for transporting the equipment of 9,521 janissaries. 'According to an inventory of the ordinance shipped from the Imperial arsenal in Constantinople to the western frontier, the Ottoman troops received exactly 10,000 muskets from March 1663 to June 1664. Although there is a difference of 500 men between the two lists, one should keep in mind that the armourers (cebeci in Ottoman terminology).' In Ö. Kolçak, 'The Composition, Tactics and Strategy of the Ottoman Field Army at Zrín-Újvár and St. Gotthard (1663–1664)', in F. Tóth and B. Zágorhidi Czigány (eds), *A szentgotthárdi csata és a vasvári béke: Oszmán Terjeszkedés-Európai Összefogás – La bataille de Saint Gotthard et la paix de Vasvár* (Budapest: MTA Történettudományi Intézet, 2017), pp.73–92.

64 The final relation of Simon Reniger, the Habsburg resident in Constantinople in 1649–1665, has been published by Alois Veltzé in *Die Hauptrelation des kaiserlichen Residenten in Konstantinopel Simon Renigen von Reningen 1649-1666*, Mitteilung des k. u. k. Kriegs-Archivs. N.F., 12. Bd.

employment of only a part of the whole contingent, but elevated the number of janissaries they confronted to between 8,000 and 12,000.[65]

In the volume dealing with the janissaries, Colonel Cevad Ahmed *beg* affirms that the Cretan War favoured the increasing of the infantry force of the *kapikulu*. The need for foot soldiers would have favoured the recruitment of soldiers to support the exhausting siege campaigns at Kandije in 1667–1669.[66] Unfortunately, the colonel can only partially confirm the figures expressed before, because he gives little information for the period 1645–1718, except for 1698, relating an overall 70,000 janissaries.[67] However, Cevad Ahmed was one of the first authors to investigate the Ottoman archives and to provide the first reliable data regarding the numerical consistency based on the registers of *eulufé*, the salary payroll. While declaring the existence of data difficult to reconstruct, he provides a detailed report concerning the total strength of the three categories of janissaries and the actual one in 1623. In the first category, the *bölük*, he registered 61 *ortas*, with 16,176 janissaries in all, comprising 1,504 honorary salaried members, and 2,406 pensioners, decreasing the effective strength to 12,768 janissaries in all. Concerning the *cemaat* janissaries, he gives the figures for the 101 *ortas* belonging to this category, with 19,546 janissaries in overall, of which 1,462 were honorary members and 1,996 pensioners, for 16,088 effective janissaries. Finally, the 34 *ortas* of the *segmen* category numbered 2,338 in all, with 105 honorary and 202 pensionary janissaries, and 1,931 vacancies.[68]

While the janissaries serving in garrisons close to the front were mobilised for campaigns, the majority dealt with the defence of the Empire's frontiers. According to authoritative sources, some 30 to 60 percent of the janissaries were on frontier duty in the 1650s and the 1710s.[69] Even in 1691–1692, during the War of the Holy League, the proportion of janissaries in frontier garrisons was no less than 42 percent.[70] Not all the janissaries quartered in Constantinople were mobilised for campaigns either. In 1660–1661, only 33 percent (18,013 men); about 30 percent in 1697 (21,000 men); 25 percent in 1701–1712 (9,975 men); and 17 percent in 1710 (7,255 men) of the totals participated in military campaigns.[71]

(Vienna, 900), pp.59–169. For the reference see pp.144–145. In his letter of April 17, 1664 from Belgrade, S. Reniger wrote that the Ottomans had 6,000 janissaries in their army.

65 Montecuccoli claimed to have faced not less of 12,000 janissaries in 1663–64. He estimated the number of janissaries who served in the Ottoman army during the siege of Érsekújvár at around 12,000. See Luraghi, *Opere di Raimondo Montecuccoli*, vol. II, pp.205–220.

66 A. Cevad, *Etat Militaire Ottoman*, vol. I, p.78.

67 *Ibidem*, p.90.

68 *Ibidem*, pp.143–148. The total expenditure for the salaries amounted to 21,742,176 *akçe* for the quarter.

69 Ágoston, 'Empires and Warfare', p.128.

70 *Ibidem*.

71 *Ibidem*, p.129: 'The ratios of mobilised to total troops are similar if one looks at the sultans' standing army as a whole. In 1710, during the Russo-Ottoman war of 1710–11 for instance, out of the total number of 52,337 infantry in the standing army (Janissaries, gunners, gun-carriage drivers, armourers, and their pensioners), only 10,378 men – that is, less than 20 percent – took part in the campaign.

Count Marsigli once again registered the strength and location of the janissary garrisons in 1680.[72] In Hungary there were seven *ocak*; in Eger there were two *ortas* with 200 janissaries in all; Kanisza had one *orta* with 200 men; Buda one with 159; Esztergom one with 121; Érsekúivár housed just 48 men, and Gyor 91, while Nitra, by reason of its position on the border, had the largest *ocak*, formed by seven *ortas* for 962 janissaries in overall. Inside Várad (today Oradea in Romania), close to the border with Transylvania, there were four *ortas* with 622 men, while Kanieniec, the fortress protecting the border with Poland, was manned by 14 *ortas* with 3,600 janissaries. Further south, close to the border with Wallachia, the *ocak* of Lugos (today Lugoy in Romania), deployed two *ortas* with 222 soldiers; Bender, before the Moldavian frontier, had a garrison formed by 470 janissaries. In the Balkan area, there was the *ocak* of Mostar, manned by a single *orta* with 119 men, while the garrison of Sarajevo had a strength of 663 men. Finally, inside Novy Pazar, on the border with Montenegro, there were two *ortas* with 272 soldiers in all. In Crete there were just three garrisons: Rethymno with 60 men, Chaniá with eight *ortas* for 710 soldiers, and Kandije (formerly Candia and today Heraklion), housed 14 *ortas* with 3,200 janissaries overall. Marsigli gave also some notices about the far garrison in Asia. Here, the major *ocak* was Baghdad, where were stationed 19 *ortas* with 3,600 janissaries. Close to the border with Iran, the other major *ocak* was Basra, manned by eight *ortas* with 1,200 janissaries. Further Asian garrisons were located at Arbela, where there was a single *orta* with 117 men; Van housed seven *ortas* with 611 men, and Erzurum had four *ortas* with 626. In Crimea, inside Caffa and Azov, there were respectively a single *orta* with 260 janissaries and eight *ortas* with 1,824. The eastern deployement was completed by the *ocak* of Tripoli of Lebanon, one *orta* with 96 men; Damascus, two *ortas* with 227 soldiers, and Al Raqqah, in Syria, with a single *orta* with 125 janissaries. Altogether Marsigli provides the location and strength of 113 *ortas* out of 196, for a total of 20,396 janissaries.[73] Except for the *ortas* permanently quartered at Constantinople, each *ocak* rotated every three years and then went back to the capital.[74]

In addition to this number, the janissaries resident in the three Imperial cities, namely Constantinople, Edirne and Bursa, should be added, and finally are to be considered also the approximately 4,000 janissaries of the standing garrison of Cairo, cited by Marsigli as 'Egyptian janissaries'. The nomenclature and structure of the Egyptian *ocaks* were similar to the garrison throughout the Empire. The central command in Constantinople exercised control over the Egyptian troops down to the smallest details in accordance with the government's orders. Officers from Constantinople were given position of command in Egypt, and alternatively officers stationed in Egypt were transferred to other *ocaks* in Europe or in Asia as well as to Constantinople.

---

72 Marsigli, vol. I, 'carta dell'Impero Ottomano che mostra le frontiere di terra e di mare…'

73 *Ibidem*, vol. II, p.184. According to Chandler, *The Art of Warfare*, p.74, the Egyptian Janissaries mobilised in 1710 for the war against the Russians would have reached 3,000 units.

74 The rule was applied discontinuously. In fact, analysing the available documents, the same units were assigned to the fort year after year, despite the usual three-year rotation of janissary postings. See Stein, *Guarding the Frontier*, p.70.

The 'Egyptian' janissaries deployed seven *ortas* and concerning their strength, Marsigli states that only 2,000 marched on the war campaigns and alternated with the others 2,000 every two years. In this figure were included the 1,000 janissaries forming the *ocak* of Damascus.[75]

In another part of his work, Marsigli writes that the total number of janissaries in 1680 would have been 54,222 soldiers, and this total included about 10,000 non-combatants distributed among the various *ortas*. These latter were classified as *oturak*, namely veterans and invalids, who received the salary as a prize of their service, and included 34 veteran officers. Among the non-combatants, Marsigli registers also 900 *korucu*, who served as palace corps in the sultan's residences, and finally the *fodlahoran*,[76] honorary members and orphans of the deserving janissaries, who in 1680 totalled 30,022 members. The Italian Count adds further information about the janissaries' strength, closing the argument stating that the final fighting force in 1680 amounted to just 13,266 men.[77] Three years later, Marsigli affirms that the force available for the war campaign would be increased to 19,345 men; the *oturak* were now decreased to 7,000, the *fodlahoran* to 3,000 and finally the *korucu* diminished to 430.[78]

An elite *speciality* par excellence, the janissaries represented the main component of Ottoman infantry, taking part in all the major actions of the army. In the spring of 1645, the janissaries were present at the siege of Chaniá in Crete and subsequently at Réthimno in 1646 and Kandije in 1648 and 1649. Montecuccoli mentions the janissaries at Szentgotthárd, when they crossed first the Raba River opening the decisive phase of the battle fought on 1 August 1664. Again in Crete, at least 15,000 janissaries alternated their presence since 1667 until the end of the siege, closed after three years of the hardest fighting.[79] From 1683 until the peace of Carlowitz in 1699, the janissaries formed the core of the infantry who faced the Imperial army in Hungary and in the Balkans. Later data indicates that the Porte substantially reduced the number of its forces in peacetime, and then increased it before and during major campaigns. In this regard, the treasury paid some 40,000 to 53,000 janissaries in the first decade of the eighteenth century, but the number dropped to its lowest point just before the 1711 war against Russia, only to rise substantially again before and during that campaign.[80] The same trend occurred during the war against Venice and the Habsburgs in 1715–1718.

---

75 Winter, *Egypt under Ottoman Rule*, p.32.
76 Literally it means 'bread eater'.
77 Note that the difference between the figures stated by Marsigli is 13,300.
78 Marsigli, vol. II, p.185. These figures partially coincide with Ahmed Cevad's records, as specified in this chapter.
79 Theoretically, all the janissaries's *ortas* could join the field army, but only in a few cases is it possible to know which of them participated on a war campaign, In Hammer-Purgstall's history of the Ottoman Empire, six *ortas* – numbers 14, 16, 19, 38, 51 and 53 – are mentioned in Crete for the 1648 campaign.
80 Ágoston, *The Ottoman Wars and the Changing Balance of Power along the Danube in the Early Eighteenth Century*, in C.W. Ingrao, N. Samardžić, J. Pesalj (eds), *The Peace of Passarowitz, 1718* (West Lafayette, IN: Purdue University Press, 2011), p.98.

At the beginning of 1716, the total strength available for the campaign in Hungary would be about 40,000 janissaries.[81] Once again, the document of the Imperial Aulic War Council add some light on the details. Among the relations sent to Vienna, the one written by the Imperial resident in Constantinople, Count Fleishmann seems to be the more accurate. The Austrian diplomat wrote that on 30 March about 6,000 janissaries had left for Sophia and further 2,000 were already quartered in Bosnia since the summer of 1715, close to the border with Venetian Dalmatia. Another corps with 7,000 janissaries had been quartered before the winter at Edirne.[82] Overall, in 1716, the Imperialists faced about 26,000 janissaries, who included the men that came from the Peloponnese. At the siege of Corfu remained about 6,000 janissaries,[83] while at least 20,000 of them were involved in the battle fought at Peterwardein on 5 August 1716. Further 2,000 janissaries formed the garrison of Temeşvár, where 'eight banners (*ortas*) had been sent to the city in July.'[84] One year after, the precious letters coming from Fleishmann had failed, and therefore the information is incomplete. However, the Imperial command calculated that at least 25,000 janissaries participated in the campaigns,[85] of which at least 4,000 belonged to the defensive garrison of Belgrade. The battle fought on 5 August 1717 was remembered as one of the bloodiest in the history of the janissaries: over 8,000 soldiers lost their lives in front of the white city on the Sava River.

At another time the different sources partially concur in these figures. Uncertainty is increased by the unreliability of the Ottoman sources. According to the contemporary Mehmed Raşid, who held the position of official court chronicler, between 1714 and 1723, the Porte raised the number of janissaries to 100,000 before the war against Venice, which is a dubious overstatement.[86] The Porte was capable of raising the number of the janissaries from 16,609 in 1709–1719 to 43,562 in 1710–1711 during its preparations for the war against Russia. However, it is unlikely that they could triple the number, from 36,562 in 1712 to 100,000 by 1715. This suspicion is corroborated by the fact that the janissary troops that left the capital with Sultan Ahmed III and Grand Vizier Damad Ali Paşa for the campaign numbered only 13,915. These janissaries were then joined by 6,000 armourers (*cebeci*) and 3,100 artillerymen (of which 3,000 were infantry and 100 mounted). Since these numbers were rather modest, orders were sent to the provinces to recruit new janissaries, artillerymen, and other troops. The number of artillerymen, for instance, was thus raised to 5,000, which is understandable, given the fact that the campaign in the Peloponnese was predominantly siege warfare. However, it is impossible to know the effective number of all *kapikulu* salaried troops who participated in the war against

---

81 K.u.K. Kriegsarchiv, *Feldzüge des Prinzen Eugen*, vol. XVI, p.124.

82 *Ibidem*

83 ASVe, *Senato*, Dispacci Provveditori da Terra e da Mar, f. 808, letter dated 30 August 1716.

84 K.u.K. Kriegsarchiv, *Feldzüge des Prinzen Eugen*, vol. XVI, p.123.

85 *Ibidem*, vol. XVII, p.149.

86 M. Yaşar Ertaş, Sultanın Ordusu, Mora Fethi Örneği, *The army of the sultan: The case of the Morea campaign* (Constantinople: Yeditepe, 2007), pp.218–219, which also quotes Mehmed Raşid Efendi *tarih*, 4 vols. (Constantinople, 1282 A.H.), vol. 4, p.127.

Venice. The situation was similar in the Ottoman–Austrian war. Recent studies estimate the effective strength of the janissaries in the Peterwardein campaign in 1716 at 41,000 men, but this number was reduced after the campaign. According to official accounts, the janissary corps was supposed to have 111,654 men between 18 September 1716 and 14 March 1717, namely after the 1716 campaign and before the 1717 operations.[87]

Notwithstanding that the janissaries represented the elite of the Ottoman army, the soldiers who participated in the eighteenth century campaigns performed poorly. The increased demand for troops required widening the pool of recruitment, and also led to a decline in military skills and put an additional burden on the treasury, which faced recurring deficits. By the late seventeenth century, janissary service had been radically transformed and many soldiers had become craftsmen and shop-owners, though still privileged with tax-exempt status as a reward for their supposed military service, for which they continued to draw pay.[88]

Until the early seventeenth century, the janissaries maintained their firing skills by practising regularly, usually twice a week. However, in 1606, the anonymous author of the janissaries' laws was already complaining about the decline of this practice, noting that the members of the corps were no longer given powder for drills and that the soldiers used their allotted wick for their candles and not for their shooting drills.[89]

The *Acemi-oglani*

Recruitment for the janissaries was regulated by the *devşirme* system, and provided the collection of a certain number of adolescents from the Christian population of the European provinces subject to the Ottoman Empire. The boys were scrupulously selected in the village centre. Orphans were not accepted because they were believed to lack a proper upbringing and to be greedy. Then they were examined for bodily and facial perfection. When the desired number of boys had been chosen, they were organised into groups of 100, 150, or 200 for transport to their destinations. They received a specific dress and headgear in order to discourage any escapes or kidnapping during the transfer. These precautions attest to the generally involuntary nature of the procedure as well as the concern on the part of the authorities to prevent any abuse of the boys during the journey.[90] The *acemi-oglani* had their schools in Bursa, Edirne, Galata and Constantinople. Here the recruits were educated in and converted to Islam, and trained as soldiers or artisans after an apprenticeship in the corps of the *acemi-oglani*. Here they learned some jobs, such as copyists, barbers, carpenters, blacksmiths and, if they showed particular aptitude, they could also learn higher

---

87   Ágoston, *The Ottoman Wars and the Changing Balance of Power along the Danube*, p.102.

88   Cevad, *Etat Militaire Ottoman*, vol. I, p.90.

89   Ágoston-Bruce, *Encyclopedia*, p.297.

90   Gülay Yilmaz, *Becoming a Devshirme: The Training of Conscripted Children in the Ottoman Empire*, in G. Campbell, S. Miers, J.C. Miller (eds), *Children in Slavery Through the Ages* (Cincinnati, OH: Ohio University Press, 2009), p.122.

professions. The great architect Sinan Paşa, famous for the stupendous mosques of Constantinople and Edirne, came from a Greek *devşirme*, while other young *acemi-oglanis* became important physicians or scientists. Further selected students were admitted into the *iç-oglan* corps, where the career of magistrate, *silihtar* or even *sipahi* awaited them. Conscripts who did not accede to the highest offices continued their apprenticeship passed through two-stage training. First, they were hired out by the quarters to a Turkish family in Anatolia or Rumelia – in return for payment – for approximately five years. If a boy was conscripted from Rumelia he would be sent to Anatolia, and vice versa. Placing the boys in locations far from their villages helped prevent them from fleeing. The object was to acquaint the boys with the Turkish language and customs and Islamic practices while they worked for their host families. The second stage of training occurred in the barracks. The boys who had been hired out to Anatolian and Rumelian villagers would be recalled to Constantinople when the existing *acemi oglans* were promoted to the *kapikulu* standing units. The new boys were taught literacy, the principles of governance, and the precepts of the Koran. They were assigned general tasks such as sweeping, carrying, or cooking for themselves and for the city, as well as continuing their training as a professional soldier. They were also used on the ships carrying wood and ice to Constantinople.[91] In the quarters, the recruits destined to become professional soldiers were trained with physical exercises and to use weapons. The teaching period lasted until the recruit turned 18, and after that he remained in the corps for another year, and was admitted into the escort for the *yeniceri ağasi* when he performed the traditional patrol in the streets of Constantinople in search of soldiers outside the barracks without permission.

Until the end of the sixteenth century, the recruitment of young Christians continued to be the only system to provide soldiers to the janissaries and other *kapikulu* infantry corps.[92] However, at the beginning of the seventeenth century, the *devşirme* was no longer able to satisfy the continuous demand for recruits, and was reduced to a vestige of the past, maintained as a mere symbol of authority. In this regard, the aforementioned Colonel Cevad Ahmed states that in 1620, the *yeniceri-ağasi* established in the major garrisons the *bèdjaiç* replacement, namely a reserve of recruits formed by relatives or sons of the serving janissaries.[93] Therefore, after 1620, the janissary corps would have admitted also 'foreigners', who altered the original composition. After 1638, the sons of retired janissaries or those of other *kapikulu* soldiers began to be welcomed, and later also volunteers who agreed to serve in war could join the corps. This mostly happened in the 1650s, when the Empire was under Venetian threat in the Dardanelles. Several times the government faced a shortage of troops in the navy and army during the Cretan War, offering special benefits to those who accepted to serve there, or forming galley crews of volunteers attracted by prizes or by employment in the *kapikulu*. Further need of manpower occurred in 1692, and for completing the infantry for the field army, Grand Vizier Merzifonlu Haci Ali was forced to offer prizes and the admission to the *oturak* corps to all the pensioner janissaries

---

91   *Ibidem*, p.124.
92   Horniker, 'The Corps of the Janizaries', in *Gorget & Sash*, vol. III, n. 4, p.26.
93   Cevad,' Etat Militaire Ottoman' vol. I, p.78.

who returned to their *ortas*.[94] The same problem drastically afflicted the *kapikulu* infantry in 1717.

According to some authors, after the mid seventeenth century the greater part of the janissaries came from western and northern Anatolia, especially from Smyrna, Denizli, Aydin, and even from Sinope in Lazistan or from the Archipelago and Albania.[95] However, the terms *devşirme* continued to identify all the young recruits, including ethnic Turks, destined for the *kapikulu*.

The recruitment of Christian adolescents continued, but with less intensity. However, this recruitment was understandably unloved by the subject populations and contributed to spreading throughout the West the image of the brutal and ruthless power of the Porte, which had caused violent protests and urged entire communities to oppose the officers sent from Constantinople. One of the last *devşirme* is recorded in Greece in 1705 and it was not unnoticed in Constantiople, because the janissaries and officers sent to Thessaly for the recruitment of 50 young Greeks, were massacred by the population of the township of Náoussa.[96]

Marsigli registered 4,012 *acemi-oglanis* in 1683, grouped in 430 *odas*.[97] The corps had its own major staff, which included a çorbaci, a *meydanbasi* as lieutenant and chief of the internal police, and a *kapici* as NCO. The novices received an allowance of seven or eight *akçe* per day, whereas those in the higher ranks received 10 to 12.[98]

Since the *acemi-oglani* recruits destined for the *kapikulu* remained insufficient to fill the ranks of the *kapikulu* infantry, in the early eighteenth century the government turned to other corps. Once these recruits were admitted into the *ortas* they received room and food, and before earning daily pay they had to serve one year or participate in a war campaign. The French historian Jean Guer, citing witnesses, described the enterprise of these turbulent recruits in the street of Constantinople:

> The dress (of the janissary) seems to promise every impunity for their crimes. They walk through the streets insulting Muslims and foreigners indifferently, they beat and rob without distinction: their insolence reaches the point of undermining women in the market and, knife in hand, their comrades oppose the fury of the people. They commit such violence and oppression that, as long as they remain in the city, the inhabitants do not dare to take to the streets.[99]

---

94 Marsigli, vol. II, p.6.
95 R. Mantran, *L'Empire Ottoman du XVI au XVIII siècle* (London: Variorum Reprint, 1984), p.326.
96 D. Brewer, *The Hidden Centuries: Turkish Rule from the Fall of Costantinople to the Greek Independance*, (London: I.B. Tauris, 2011), pp.16–18.
97 Marsigli, vol. II, p.6.
98 Yilmaz, *Becoming a Devshirme*, p.123.
99 J.A. Guer, *Mœurs et Usages des Turcs, avec un abrégé de l'Histoire Ottomane*, vol. II (Paris, 1747), p.205.

The *Cebeci*

The discipline imposed within the *kapikulu*'s corps was regulated by laws devised to avert, as far as possible, any acts of violence. For this purpose, it was forbidden for the janissaries to keep firearms in their residences, or to circulate with them in the city. In Constantinople, all the muskets were kept in the city arsenal and the personnel assigned to their custody belonged to the corps of the *cebeci*. The establishment of this specialised infantry dates back to the second half of the sixteenth century, namely when the use of firearms significantly increased. Their strength was established at 700 rank and file.[100] Their commander was called the *cebecibaşı*. They had to not only repair firearms, but also be able to build them and even make gunpowder. As a specialised technician, a *cebeci* perceived a better salary than the one received by a janissary. The *cebecis* joined the janissaries on campaign and in the garrisons, and participated in fighting like the other infantry. Furthermore, they usually employed special firearms and performed also as marksmen. They also maintained and transported the ammunition for all the *kapikulu* infantry. Originally, each janissary was said to have been issued some 300 musket balls, and sufficient gunpowder for their individual firearms before battles. The *cebecis* were considered a part of the *kapikulu* infantry and were based on the *devşirme* system, but in several respects they could be considered similar to the artillerymen, and in some cases they are associated with them.

Marsigli writes that just two thirds went on campaign, while the rest remained in Constantinople, and like the janissaries, were to serve only three years in a fortress garrison before being rotated back to Constantinople. This schedule was probably an ideal that did not always come to pass.[101] The *cebeci* contingents were usually small, compared to the overall size of the garrison. Most often there were one or two *odas* of around 10 men, plus officers.

Once again, the exact strength of this corps is uncertain. Marsigli affirms that in 1683 there were 630 men, including officers, and they formed 60 *odas*, each under an instructor with the rank of *odabasi*. Other sources raise their number in 1716 up to 3–4,000 men and as many for the following year, mobilised and sent to Bosnia and to the Banat against the Imperialists.[102] It is difficult to establish to what extent these latter figures are correct. However, even the data provided by Marsigli seems too modest and hides ambiguity. In fact, he does not specify whether the *cebecis* he considered were only those in Constantinople, and therefore he excluded any others in the garrisons of the Empire. However, when at the end of his work he summarises and argues his

---

100 J. Stanford-Shaw in *History of the Ottoman Empire and Modern Turkey* (Cambridge: Cambridhe University Press, 1976), vol. I, p.132, reports the original number to 630 men in 1574. Other sources establishes the *cebeci* corps' strength in 1598 to 3,000 soldiers.

101 Stein, *Guarding the Frontier*, p.83. At Kanisza, from the 1650s, records show the same *cebeci* commanders and their troops assigned to the garrison for five years.

102 K.u.K. Kriegsarchiv, *Feldzüge des Prinzen Eugen*, vol. XVI, pp.125–126.

deductions about the current strength of army in 1720, the number of soldiers is the same as 37 years before.[103]

The *Topçu*

The *kapikulu* artillery corps was represented by the permanent artillery personnel known as *topçu*, who, alongside the *humbaraci* (bombardiers), and the *mimar* (carpenters and engineers for the artillery), were considered as 'the most precious corps of the Ottoman army.'[104] The government always invested significant resources for training the gunners and paid them with a higher salary compared to those men destined to be janissaries and even *cebecis*. The *topçus* were entrusted not only with the use of cannons, but also with the preparation of gunpowder, maintenance, and the production of guns in the main arsenal of Constantinople. Further arsenals with gun production workshops existed in Belgrade, Temeşvár and Pera, while laboratories for the production of ammunition were active in Banjaluka and Piravist.[105] In 1696 a new foundry was build in the latter city, which began production before the end of the year.[106]

Despite the occasional importance of local foundries, Constantinople was the core centre of Ottoman cannon casting. During the sixteenth to eighteenth centuries, only about 50 to 60 cannon founders worked at the Imperial foundry; however, if day labourers are counted, the total workforce numbered in the hundreds.[107] With the help of these artisans, the Constantinople foundry was capable of casting hundreds of cannons annually, with a total weight of around 100 metric tons; during some extraordinary years, the weight of the newly cast pieces exceeded 200 and even 300 metric tons (220–330 short tons). Historians outline the production of artillery in the Ottoman arsenals and foundries, including accidents. In 1708, at Gelibolu, 600 people perished following the explosion of a powder windmill; a similar accident killed six labourers in Constantinople, while lightning, falling on another powder magazine, destroyed part of Lemnos castle in the Aegean.[108]

The internal structure of the artillery corps was similar to that of the janissaries and the artilleryman were divided into *ortas* formed by one or more *odas*. The internal hierarchy also appeared similar to the other *kapikulu* corps. The senior commander was the *topçubasi*; he directed the corps from his residence in Constantinople and managed the activity of the city's arsenal. As with other types of *kapıkulu* troops, the commander of the *topçu* was often granted *timar* income, as well as the *ağas*, who served as local commanders in the garrisons. As occurred among the janissaries, the *topçubasi* could also

---

103 See Marsigli, vol. I, p.80 and vol. II, p.82.

104 K.u.K. Kriegsarchiv, *Feldzüge des Prinzen Eugen*, vol. I, p.530.

105 *Ibidem*, p.525.

106 *Ibidem*, vol. II, p.98.

107 G. Ágoston, *Guns for the Sultan. Military Power and the Weapons Industry in the Ottoman Empire* (Cambridge: Cambridge University Press, 2005), p.48.

108 Hammer-Purgstall, *Geschichte des Osmanischen Reiches*, vol. XIII, p.195.

inherit properties and riches of his subordinates who died without heirs. His command was directly subordinated to the authority of the grand vizier, to whom he had to notify the days in which the cannons were cast, an operation which took place in the presence of the head of government. In each main arsenal served a *dökükübasi* as technical director and instructors of personnel. The major staff was completed by the *kátib*, who was the adjutant, a first secretary of the *topçubasi*. These officers had their residence in the capital, where an *oda* under an *odabasi* formed the standing unit in the city.

Data is uncertain regarding the strength of the *topçu* in the mid seventeenth century, and even the well-informed Marsigli merely says that they were less numerous.[109] Numbering about 1,110 in 1514, the size of the corps almost doubled in the 1520s and reached 6,500 men by the end of the sixteenth century. Although strength fluctuated in the seventeenth century, available figures suggest that the Ottomans aimed to maintain artillery power superior to their enemies until about the mid eighteenth century. In the early eighteenth century, some sources relate a strength of 6,000 men, but only 2,000 could be considered as actual gunners.

It is reasonable to suppose that every major fortress had an *oda* of artillerymen, while their number in the field army naturally depended on the cannons used for the occasion. However, the question remains open, because until the early years of the eighteenth century, the Ottoman commanders brought on campaign as much artillery as possible, often more than the availability of personnel, using a train of huge dimensions.[110] The Porte had an enormous reserve of artillery far superior to the personnel it could deploy, but it must be considered that the *kapikulu* gunners were only a part of the servants in the batteries. On campaign, the *topçu* provided the personnel for the direction of the batteries, but for the manoeuvre of the guns and other operations they were joined by the artillerymen enlisted by the governors of the provinces close to the theatre of war. Obviously, this feature increases the difficult of knowing the effective number of the *kapikulu* gunners on campaign.

Raimondo Montecuccoli collected various information on the strength of Ottoman artillery. He reports that for the campaign of 1663, Grand Vizier Köprülü Ahmed had 30 large-calibre cannons for siege artillery, and over 300 'including the light pieces' for the field artillery.[111] During the siege of Érsekújvár the Ottoman artillery fired 18,000 projectiles, which required more than 200 tons of gunpowder. In the summer of 1672, for the siege of Kamieniec, Grand Vizier Köprülü Ahmed again placed 10 batteries with 90 guns of large calibre.[112] After the battle of Kahlenberg in 1683, the allies captured 170 artillery pieces of various calibres, alongside an unconfirmed number of mortars;[113] while four

---

109 Guer, *Mœurs et Usages des Turcs*, vol. II, p.215.

110 Marsigli, vol. II, p.181.

111 Montecuccoli, 'Della Guerra col Turco in Ungheria', in Luraghi, *Opere di Raimondo Montecuccoli*, vol. II, p.211.

112 J. Gierowski, 'Da Chocim a Vienna', in *Atti del Convegno Sobieskiano* (Udine: Università degli Studi di Udine, 17–18 September 1983), pp.20–21.

113 F. Tóth, 'Le Journal de Charles V de Lorraine comme source pour l'histoire de la reconquête de la Hongrie sur les Turcs', in *Histoire, Économie et Société*, vol. 34, No. 3 ; A. Colin, 'La Hongrie Ottomane, XVIe-XVIIe siècles' (Septembre 2015), p.94.

years later at Harsány, the looting included 76 field guns and 10 mortars.[114] In 1716, for the siege of Corfu, the Ottomans deployed eight great batteries with 47 heavy guns.[115] During the preparations for the war against the Habsburgs, Count Fleishmann wrote in his report that in the month of March about 2,000 *kapikulu* artillerymen had left Constantinople for the field army, followed by another 3,000 before the end of the month, but without specifying the number of guns, however related that it was very high.[116] The following year, after the defeats suffered at Peterwardein and Temeşvár, the new grand vizier Bostançi Halil called for reinforcements from the Asian provinces, along with 100 large calibre cannons.[117]

Along with the *topçu* and *mimar*, the aforementioned *humbaraci* also operated, serving the mortars during sieges. They constituted an elite *speciality*, and in addition to their salary, they received the income of a *timar* or a *zeamet* depending on their rank. The *humbaraci* were also involved in the direction of large-calibre cannons and for this reason in Western sources they are identified as 'bombardiers'.

The *topçu* also comprised the drivers and the personnel for the artillery train, known as the *voinac*, with the *top arabacis* as conductors under their own officer, the *top arabacibasi*. Since the number of cannons for the field army was decided by the grand vizier, the *voinac* that resulted was often insufficient and therefore the artillery train was also formed by resorting to civilians and their draft animals, with serious prejudice to the efficiency of the service.

Artillery remained the most critical element of the Ottoman army. Montecuccoli stated that, 'the Turk brings artillery on campaign of a much larger number than us, and consequently makes a much greater impression', but regarding the effect, 'it is much more difficult to move and manage it, and slower to withdraw and position itself.'[118]

Sipahi Ulùfely and *Çavuş*

With the word *sipahi* the Ottomans included all the soldiers on horseback, and this has often generated confusion when, in the Western sources, the permanent household cavalry is associated with the one coming from the provinces. In the coeval sources frequently appear the terms 'salaried sipahi' and 'tribute's sipahi'.[119] The first identified the *kapikulu* cavalry who received their salary directly from the government, while the latter were recruited and administered by the provinces and formed the provincial *toprakli* cavalry. As elite cavalry and mounted lifeguard of the sultan, the household *sipahis*

---

114 K.u.K. Kriegsarchiv, *Feldzüge des Prinzen Eugen*, vol. I, p.531.
115 *Ibidem*, vol. XVII, p.224.
116 *Ibidem*, pp.124–125.
117 *Ibidem*, pp.52–53. For the detailed description of the Ottoman artillery captured at Peterwardein see also in the appendix.
118 Montecuccoli, 'Discorso della Guerra contro il Turco in Ungheria', in Luraghi, *Opere di Raimondo Montecuccoli*, vol. II, p.212.
119 See Marsigli, vol. I, pp.87–99, and Montecuccoli, 'Aforismi applicati alla Guerra possibile col Turco in Ungheria', in Luraghi, *Opere di Raimondo Montecuccoli*, vol. II, p.478.

were the best-paid corps of the *kapikulu*. The common horsemen received 12 *akçe* per day and the salary could increase to four *akçe* after every campaign. As the janissaries, the *sipahis* were 'slaves of the sultan' who received training in the schools close to the Imperial palace of Topkapı.

The senior officers of the *ulùfely* often came from the ruling family, or from the circle of people close to the court. As happened in the janissary corps, some members also came from the *acemi oglani* institutes. To be member of the *ulùfely* was considered a great privilege by every subject; in fact, in addition to the advantages granted to all members of the *kapiculu*, a *sipahi* could aspire to the granting of a fiefdom as *timar*, if his status of service or his behaviour in battle had become the object of reward.

The different parts of the sultan's household cavalry carried particular denominations, originating from their rank within the corps or from special assignments. The most numerous units were the *ulùfelys*, divided into two wings: *ulùfely jessar* (soldier of the left wing) and *ulùfely jemin* (soldier of the right wing). This was the oldest unit of the whole army; its creation was in fact attributed to Osman I (1299–1326), the founder of the Ottoman dynasty. The division into two wings served to distinguish the rank of the cavalrymen: the *ulùfely jessar* occupied the position of honour in the Ottoman cavalry, and therefore during ceremonies and in parade they marched in the first position, and eventually on campaign formed the vanguard. The left wing was divided into three categories: the *yedekçi*, who originally dealt with the training of the sultan's horses; the *buçukçu*, charged with distributing alms during the court's parade in Constantinople, and finally the *cebeci*, who had the honour of carrying the horse-tail ensign, the *tugh*.

The right wing of the *ulùfely* was composed of two sections and it was the only part of the *kapikulu* cavalry to include also non-Turkish horsemen. They were known as *gureba* (or *garib*: foreigners), who had been admitted into the sultan's service for valour shown in battle. The *ulùfely jemin* was divided in two parts, each with their *gurebas* and on campaign, they alternated in forming the guard of the tent of the sultan or the grand vizier, together with the other right wing *sipahis*.

The senior officers of the *ulùfely* formed a major state similar to the one of the janissaries. The corps' commander was the *sipahilar ağasi*, which also boasted the title of first *silihtar*, or esquire of the sultan. The *silihtars* (esquires) formed another component of the *kapikulu* cavalry. Any Ottoman soldier who committed a significant deed on the battlefield could be promoted to the *silahtars*. In official ceremonies, their commander took the position of honour to the left of the sovereign and besides the *sipahi* of the *kapikulu*, the *ağasi* had the supreme command of all the cavalry when the army was in campaign. Under his orders, as lieutenant general, there was the *kethüda*, while the *kethüda yeri* held the post of commissar, chief of the administration as well as auditor of the corps. One *bas-çavuş* with a *çavuş* under him completed the major staff, who included also a secretary and a variable number of *halife*, qualified by Marsigli as an adjutant.[120]

---

120 Marsigli, vol. I, p.88.

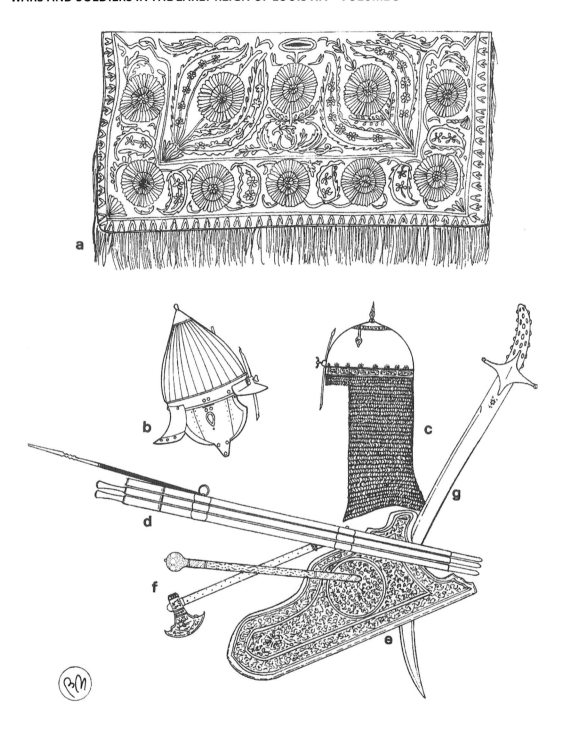

Left: 20. *Kapikulu sipahi* 1650–1700; saddle cover and weapons.

a) At the top is represented a prestigious Anatolian saddle cover, with azure linen weave completely brocaded with silver decorations. The main part is decorated by a sinuous frame with large corollas, with alternating bowed leaves. The same corollas are repeated three times on the field, enclosed between two elongated leaves embellished with minute flowers. A thick silver fringe surrounds the saddle cover around the perimeter, while an oblong hole is set to accommodate the stirrups. (Anatolian manufacture, mid seventeenth century; dimensions 124x131cm. Fine Art Museum, Budapest. A very similar saddle cover is preserved in the Wawel Museum in Krakow, from the Ottoman spoils of 1683)

b) and c) The classical Ottoman helms, the *çiçak* and the *kulah kud*. The first is similar to the Hungarian lobster helm, while the *kulah kud* derives from Iranian models. The metal surface is usually decorated with small flowers and inscriptions with gilded letters. (Seventeenth-century Ottoman *çiçak*, Askeri Museum, Constantinople, and *kulah kud* from the *Türkenbeute* of 1683, Heeresgeschichtliches Museum, Vienna)

d) *Çerid* and case. The *çerid* (javelin), was a typical weapon of the Ottoman cavalry officer. They carried one or two hung on one side of the saddle. Wooden case, covered with black leather with silver accessories; *çerid* with wooden pole, iron hilt and blade. (size 90x14 cm. Ottoman manufacture, 1660, Topkapı Museum, Constantinople)

e) Bow case in leather covered with gilded metal and medallion decorated with floral design; the edge is adorned with a continuous motive of small crossed half palms. Bow cases, quivers, and other small weapons were provided as presents for brave soldiers and diplomatic legations. Bow cases like the one here represented were common in the late seventeenth century, and even the elaborate decoration suggests a high ranking owner. (Size 28.5x67cm. Correr Museum, Venice)

f) The war mace and axe completed the battle equipment of the commander and *kapikulu* cavalry officers. Several examples are embellished with precious stone and corals; other weapons have only the head in silver or gilded metal with wood poles. The Ottoman leading class appreciated the Oriental weapons and imported examples like these from Iran and India. (War mace, 1670–1680, Wawel Museum, Krakow; axe, Moghul India manufacture, early eighteenthh century, Al Sabah collection, Kuwait City)

g) The sabre was the classic oriental weapon and the Ottoman *qiliç* was easily recognisable by the hilt's curvature. Senior officers used sabres manufactured in fine Damascus iron, and the hilt had often ornament with turquoise and corals, as typical of the Ottoman Imperial style. (Ottoman manufacture, late seventeenth century, Topkapı Museum, Constantinople. Author's illustration)

There is some discrepancy among the sources about the size of the corps. According to Marsigli, the *ulùfely sipahis* were tactically divided on the field into five *alays* or 'brigades', composed by a non-established number of *bölükler* (companies), each with a strength of about 20 horsemen under the command of a *bölük basi* with 30 or 40 horseman. Marsigli does not provide information regarding the strength of the left wing and refers only to the number of *yedekçis*, who were constantly maintained at 60 horsemen. The *cebeci* instead depended on how many *tugh* bearers were needed: up to seven if the sultan was present and only five if the grand vizier held the command. Marsigli states that the right wing and the left wing were not necessarily of the same number, however the left wing, as elite cavalry, were as a result less numerous.[121] Other scholars, instead, refer usually six 'divisions', which composed the *kapikulu* cavalry since the age of Süleyman the Magnificent. There were the elite *sipahis*; *silihtars*; right wing *ulùfely*; left wing *ulùfely*, right wing *gurebas* and left wing *gurebas*. The six divisions still existed in the mid seventeenth century, and again in 1661 they are registered in the *kapikulu*. This matter becomes less clear in subsequent years, when the divisions were now five. The French traveller Aubry De La Mottraye, present in Constantinople between 1698 and 1699, left a brief account of the *kapikulu* cavalry, recalling the origins and their most recent history. He confirmed

---

121 *Ibidem*, vol. II, p.181.

21. *Kapikulu sipahi* in campaign dress, early eighteenth century; white turban with red kavuk cap; red coat and azure breeches; red leather footdress (Jean-Baptiste van Moor, *Recueil de cent estampes représentant les diverses nations du Levant*).

the presence of five corps.[122] Very probably, the *kapikulu* reform undertaken by Kara Mustafa in the early 1680s would have affected the *siphais* too, which decreased from six to five divisions.

Strength data does not help to resolve the matter. In 1680, the *sipahis* would have numbered 15,284 men.[123] Twenty years earlier, according to the budget of 1661, the figure was slightly different: 15,248 *sipahis*, who received pay as member of the *kapikulu*.[124]

As for the janissaries, the *sipahis* sent on campaign a part of their force. At the battle of Szentgotthárd, there were about 10–12,000 *kapikulu sipahis*,[125] while in 1674, only 2,000 would have fought at Chocim against the Poles.[126] From as much as can be deduced from this isolated information, in the summer of 1663 the army comprised 352 right and 257 left *gurebas*.[127] When compared to the number of the *kapikulu sipahis* in the 1661 budget, the Porte seems to have mobilised almost 80 percent of the overall *kapikulu* cavalry force. During the spring of 1664, however, the Ottoman army sought relentlessly and with limited success to bring them back on campaign. For this reason, the number of *kapıkulu* cavalry that actually fought at Szentgotthárd can be estimated at fewer than 10,000.

In accordance with the structural characteristics of the Ottoman military, a significant number of these cavalry were scattered across the Empire performing various tasks. However, it seems that the core of the corps resided in the capital. Aubry De La Mottraye states that the overall strength of each 'division' would number 5,000 horsemen, for 25,000 men in all; however he admitted that there were several 'dead wages'.[128]

Since the *kapikulu* participated in the war all together, the household cavalry also followed the main army in all the campaigns. After the siege of Vienna, some 12,000 *sipahi ulùfely* took part in the Hungarian operations in 1684, where they charged with poor results the army of Duke Charles V of Lorraine at Vác and Ercsi.[129] The following year 8,000 *kapikulu* horse

122 A. De La Mottraye, *Voyages en Europe, Asie et* Afrique (The Hague, 1727), vol. I, pp.242–243.

123 Marsigli, vol. I, p.89.

124 Kolçak, *The Composition, Tactics and Strategy of the Ottoman Field Army*, p.83.

125 Luraghi, *Opere di Raimondo Montecuccoli*, vol. I, p.82.

126 Gierowski, *Da Chocim a Viennna*, pp.21–22.

127 Kolçak, *The Composition, Tactics and Strategy of the Ottoman Field Army*, p.85: 'However, according to another account of the campaign, the number of the *gurebas* in the army dropped the following year from a total of 609 to 450.' At this time, there were 503 *ulùfelys* along with their *gureba* colleagues in the army, a number that corresponds only to half of the *ulùfely alay* registered in 1661.

128 Mottraye, *Voyages en Europe, Asie et Afrique*, vol. I, pp.242–243.

129 M. D'Aste (edited by Ernesto Piacentini), *Diario dell'Assedio di Buda del 1686*, in *Diarii degl'Assedii di Vienna del 1683, e di Buda del 1686, distesi e scritti dal Baron Michele D'Aste che vi si trovò presente in tutte le sue Azzioni* (Rome, Budapest: Bulzoni-Corvina, 1991), p.128.

composed the relief corps for the besieged Érsekújvár.[130] In 1686, during the second siege of Buda, 1,000 *ulùfelys* took part in the defence of the city having succeeded in forcing the enemy blockade during a night attack.[131] On this occasion, the cavalry vanguard of the relief army deployed 9,000 *kapikulu sipahis* out of an overall force of 30,000 horsemen.[132]

At the battle of Harsány, in 1687, the *sipahis* fought with the rest of the cavalry in the centre of the Ottoman deployment. This entire sector was overwhelmed by the attack of the Imperialists and the retreat involving the rest of the Grand Vizier Süleyman Paşa's army in a disastrous flight, in which the enemy captured the whole encampment and the artillery. The defeat had such serious repercussions in Constantinople, because almost all the cavalry officers were removed from their rank.[133] Opposed to the Imperial heavy cavalry and the infantry squares, the *ulùfelys* suffered defeat in almost all encounters in the Hungarian war theatre. The many failures provided the pretext for the birth of a proverb, very dear to the janissaries, in which it was said that every foot soldier had to have good eyes and good legs: the first to notice in time the escape of the *sipahis* and the others to save them.[134]

However, during the battle of Zenta, many *ulùfelys* who were already on the other side of the Tisza River, crossed the bridges to resume their position in the defensive deployment. In the battle, almost 20,000 Ottoman soldiers lost their lives, and many were household *sipahis*, fallen in the desperate defence of the bridges: 'and the river was filled with corpses, so as to be possible to cross it even on horseback.'[135]

The rivalry existing between the janissaries and the *kapikulu* knights had always been very heated and more than once had led to serious excesses, such as the

22. Egyptian *çavuş*, mid seventeenth century. (Ottoman miniature, Bibliothèque Nationale de France, Paris)

---

130 *Ibidem*, p.129.

131 *Ibidem*, p.184. The action occurred in the night between 19 and 20 August 1686.

132 *Ibidem*, p.141.

133 Marsigli, vol. II, p.125. The defeat also caused the removal of Sultan Mehmet IV. Marsigli affirmed that after Vienna, the defeat of Harsány had been the major failure suffered by the Ottoman army and 'the most fatal for the dignity of the sultan'.

134 *Ibidem*, vol. II, p.107. Even the Imperial officer Michele D'Aste writes how some prisoners escaped from the Ottomans into the Christian encampment before Buda, and writes about the disagreements between *sipahi ulùfely* and janissaries, and this dispute had been one of the reasons for the failure of the expedition to relieve the besieged city, 'these (the janissaries) are grieving to always remain abandoned by that (the household cavalry), and therefore obstinate in wanting to put themselves in safety.' In Piacentini, *Diario dell'Assedio di Buda*, p.179.

135 K.u.K. Kriegsarchiv, *Feldzüge des Prinzen Eugen*, vol. II, p.140.

23. Sakka, water supplier, early eighteenth century. These personnel were recruited among the poorest people of the Empire, in charge of supplying water for officers and soldiers of the *kapikulu*. According to Luigi Ferdinando Marsigli, the *sakkas* were 'the more rugged people of the army, well recognisable for the deformity of their faces and their poor clothing, usually in dark natural leather.' (Jean-Baptiste van Moor, *Recueil de cent estampes représentant les diverses nations du Levant*)

at-meydan massacre in 1657,[136] which provoked the flight of a large number of *sipahis* to the *celali* rebels.[137] In April 1703, internal struggles once again involved the *kapikulu* horsemen when they again opposed the janissaries, to prevent the deposition of Mustafa II. In the early eighteenth century, the *ulùfelys* had lost much of their influence and were no more able to face the ever more powerful janissaries.

In 1710, the *sipahis* were sent against the Tsar, and their strength still numbered about 20,000 horsemen,[138] and about 15,000 left Constantinople for Moldavia. During the operations in Morea, in the spring of 1715, 1,000 *sipahi ulùfelys* formed the escort of Sultan Ahmed III, who was in Thrace to be promptly informed on the progress of operations,[139] while another 6,000 household's horsemen formed the vanguard of the army camped at Thebes.[140]

In the months preceding the conflict against the Habsburgs, the Imperial resident Count Fleischmann informed Vienna that at the end of March 1716 the cavalry of the sultan had headed to Edirne with 2,000 horsemen.[141] Other dispatches that reached the Imperial command in Hungary stated that the right wing *sipahis* had left Constantinople in mid June with 5,000 men, while the left wing followed with another 1,000.[142]

One year later, in the general climate of emergency, the whole *kapikulu* cavalry was mobilised, also resorting to the recruitment of volunteers by offering fiefs and promotions. No less than 20,000 *ulùfely sipahis* would join the field army for the campaign ended with the defeat of Belgrade on 16 August 1717.[143]

Besides the *ulùfely*, the corps of the *çavuş* were also included in the *kapikulu* cavalry. They were horsemen employed as junior officers or adjutants as well as messengers for the sultan, grand vizier or other commanders. Their rank in the army was particularly elevated, because on the hierarchical scale they immediately followed the *bölükbasis*. When important orders were sent, the *çavuş* formed an escort for the messenger. A *çavuş*basi had the command of the corps. The overall strength of the *çavuş* was unknown to Marsigli and other coeval commenters.

---

136 Bombaci-Shaw, *L'Impero Ottomano*, p.445.
137 J. Matuz, *Das Osmanische Reich* (Darmstadt: Wissenschaftliches Buchgesellschaft, 1985), p.180.
138 Chandler, *The Art of Warfare*, p.74.
139 K.u.K. Kriegsarchiv, *Feldzüge des Prinzen Eugen*, vol. XVI, p.14.
140 Brue, *Journal*, pp.68–69.
141 K.u.K. Kriegsarchiv, *Feldzüge des Prinzen Eugen*, vol. XVI, p.125.
142 *Ibidem*.
143 *Ibidem*, vol. XVII, p.52.

24. *Timar*, provincial cavalryman. White cotton turban with green velvet *kavuk* cap; dark green *kaftan* with wood buttons; white breeches; natural leather boots and belt with brass accessories; wood *kalkan* shield covered with dark red fabric and black polished metal accessories. (Late seventeenth century mail coat, Wawel Museum, Krakow; turban and *kalkan* shield, 1683; Heeresgeschichtliches Museum, Vienna. Author's illustration)

25. Provincial *sipahi*, late seventeenth century. Much of the early history of the Ottoman Turks is still confused in the myth and legendary tales of battles, which included a recurring image of the sultan's cavalry, who suddenly arrived on the battlefield, resulting in immediate victory to its side. The word *sipahi* explicitly referred to the primary role assumed by Turkic horsemen, because its precise translation means 'soldier'. For centuries, the Ottoman *sipahis* were accustomed to launching raids into enemy territory with evasive actions that required particular tactics, with ambushes and sudden assaults. With great skill, the Ottoman cavalry was easily able to perform the tasks of reconnaissance and screening for an army on the march. (Author's illustration)

Among the *sipahis*, the grand vizier chose his personal lifeguard, formed by one squadron of elite horse. Köprülü Ahmed, the commander-in-chief of the Ottoman army and head of the Ottoman financial resources at hand from 1661 to 1676, naturally commissioned the largest life corps. He maintained a permanent force of 400 men whom were recruited among the able-bodied young population of Albanian and Bosnian lands.[144] Coeval commenters were of the opinion that the grand vizier deliberately chose Albanians as his personal guards to whom he had ethnic and regional links, as his father Köprülü Mehmed Paşa had done before him.

The *Sakkas*

The *kapikulu* include also the personnel in charge of the water supply service, which was necessary not only for beverages and cuisine, but also for the ritual ablution required to every Muslim before the pray. The *sakkas* were recruited before the war campaign. This service was a particularly tiring task and undoubtedly the least showy, carried out by men coming from the poorest Muslim population of Constantinople. Their number was established according to the *kapikulu* troops engaged on campaign. There were no differences of rank between the *sakkas* and therefore they depended on the officers of the units to which they were assigned.

Marsigli states that dozens of water carriers were allocated to both the janissaries and the other *kapikulu* units, and that even the senior officers and the grand vizier had many *sakkas* at their service.[145]

Sipahi Toprakli (Provincial Cavalry)

In the mid seventeenth century, the Ottoman cavalry amounted to over 45 percent of the entire armed force, while in the rest of Europe it rarely reached an average of 30 percent.[146] The larger part of this cavalry was gathered from the provinces of the Empire through the calculation of provincial revenues.[147] Marsigli refers to this contingent with the name *toprakli*, while the Ottoman sources usually identified it as *timarli*, *askeri elayet* or simply *sipahi*.

---

144 Paul Rycaut, *The History of the Present State of the Ottoman Empire, Containing the Maxims of the Turkish Polity, the most Material Points of the Mahometan Religion, their Sects and Heresies, their Convents and Religious Votaries* (London, 1686), p.379.

145 Marsigli, vol. I, p.80.

146 Chandler, *The Art of Warfare*, p.30. According to the author, between 1648 and 1715, only Poland could deploy a higher percentage of cavalry; Sweden equalled the Porte, while Prussia and Denmark reached 40 percent.

147 According to Murphey, *Ottoman Warfare* pp.49–63, the typical seventeenth-century Ottoman field army comprised two or sometimes even three mounted soldiers for a single infantry one. This assumption, however, rests upon Ottoman officials' nominal figures which were intended for estimating the size of the provincial troops, commonly believed by many scholars today to have been composed exclusively of mounted soldiers. Some authors, instead, suggest that provincial troops may well have been infantry forces as discussed in this chapter. See also Kolçak, *The Composition, Tactics and Strategy of the Ottoman Field Army*, p.77.

The calculation of the recruit quota was based on the income of each province and district. This system, in which the *sipahis* were allocated *timar* or land estate, continued without significant variations for centuries. In the sixteenth century, the *sipahi* collected and kept the *öşür*, or tithe, and related land taxes, usually half in kind and half in money, as a compensation for the military service the *sipahi* was assigned to render. As representatives of the government, the land holder *sipahis* acted as administrators, policemen, and tax collectors in their own *timar* or *zeamet*. The requirements for military service and supply were determined in proportion to the annual value of the *timar* holdings, which ranged from 5,000 to 20,000 *akçe*. These resources permitted them to recruit fully equipped horsemen from each village and township, known in the Ottoman sources as *cebelü*. The criteria used for the calculation of the soldiers to be mobilised was fixed to one horseman for every 5,000 *akçe* of income. The provincial *sipahi* corps constituted the core of the Ottoman army in the classical period. They supported the permanent *kapikulu* army mounted units, who could also completed their ranks by recruiting the bravest horsemen. This system continued to provide troops until the nineteenth century, despite that they represented just a social group, before disappearing in 1847. However, they fulfilled the request of cavalry for the war and characterised the Ottoman rule in Asia as well as in Europe and Africa.

Only Muslims were admitted into the corps, notwithstanding there were some limitations for Arabs and Bedouins. The most large contingents came from the major governors, namely from the *beglerbegs* and *paşas*, who could gather all the troops of their region. Each governor dealt with the war equipment, the appointment of the *ağas* and other officers, and with the control of the recruits assigned to the governors of the minor divisions, namely the *sancakbeg*, *zeamet* and *timar*. *Sancakbeg* and *zeamet* were both taxed with a contingent of soldiers to be led on campaign, while each *timar* had to present himself to the call of arms along with another equipped and mounted soldier. In alternative, he could pay the *bedel*, a tax for recruiting a substitute, but if a *timar* declined to join any military campaign for seven years, he lost his status. Though the condition of *timar*, as all the offices of the state, was not in principle hereditary, sons of *timars* killed in a war campaign could be commissioned by the government to administer his father's property.

Turks still use five completely different terms to name the horse, outlining the importance of this animal in the history and culture of this people. Traditionally, the Turkish cavalry enjoyed a considerable reputation, both for the boldness of its actions, and for its undeniable resistance to fatigue and privations, acquired in the desolate and inhospitable inner regions of Asia. Many records handed down, halfway between myth and legend, recall the special breed of Turkic riders who were able to survive without food for several days, feeding only off the blood of their horses, sipped through a small cut made at the base of the neck.

All the major eyewitnesses agree in outlining the beauty of the Arabian mounts and the hardiness of the horses selected in Anatolia.[148] The breeds from Hungary and that from northeastern Anatolia were particularly appreciated as warhorses. Marsigli remembered having seen many Ottoman officers choose Turkmen horses, or others bred in Bulgaria, all of them required not only for their strength, but also for their particular beauty and fine proportions.[149] Though the Arabian horses, numerous in the contingents from Syria and Egypt, were admired for their strength and speed, they were not always sufficiently trained. According to Western commentators, Arabian horses were not accustomed to the noise of musketry and cannons. Moreover, they had a tendency to become ill with the grass that grew in Europe and suffered from the climate of Hungary and the Balkans, getting sick and dying in high numbers as soon as the climate became colder.[150] In the mountainous regions of Bosnia, in Serbia and in Albania, small but very resistant horses were bred and, according to Marsigli's opinion: 'they had tolerable features'.[151]

Most of the people who entered the provincial cavalry belonged to the rural classes, especially from those related to horse breeding and trade and to a lesser extent from people living in urban centres. Many recruits were often sons of businessmen or their relatives, friends and clients.[152] For this reason, these tended to be non-professionals, though not necessarily inexperienced in a combat role, who usually preferred long-range combat to fighting in close quarters, which required proper military training. In any case, it was a heterogeneous crowd of semi-professional soldiers, and therefore of unequal skill and valour, and often with inadequate equipment compared to the Western standard. Once the war campaign was over, those who returned hastened to resume their original occupations, and if a campaign ended favourably, just as quickly these troops tended to return to their countries of origin.

Only the major governors, such as the *beglerbegs*, *paşas* and *sancakbegs*, could maintain a standing force, occasionally established in corps known as *alay*. These permanent forces were raised by governors at their own expense, and joined the army on campaign. This system of recruiting seems to have become firmly established in the course of the seventeenth century. In fact, from the 1660s, members of the ruling elite provided the Ottoman army with numerous troops.[153] However, these mercenaries enlisted by governors were by definition out of the Ottoman military network, a fact that makes any attempt to estimate their exact number extremely difficult. According to Hasan *ağa*, the grand vizier's personal seal-bearer, at the time his master

---

148 Montecuccoli, 'Aforismi applicati alla guerra possibile col Turco in Ungheria', in Luraghi, *Opere di Raimondo Montecuccoli*, vol. II, p.42.

149 Marsigli, vol. II, p.42. This particular is confirmed also by Mottraye, *Voyages*, vol. I, p.216–217.

150 *Ibidem*, p.43. At this regard Marsigli adds: 'and I remember how, already in late August during the siege of Vienna, the horses from Asia and Africa was beginning to perish because of the cool nights, and in fact coming back, once concluded the campaigns in Hungary, the cavalry was always all ruined.'

151 *Ibidem*.

152 *Ibidem*, vol. II, p.42.

153 Kolçak, *The Composition, Tactics and Strategy of the Ottoman Field Army*, p.77.

rushed to the aid of the Ottoman garrison of the besieged Kanizsa in the spring of 1664, about 5,000 men of his own accompanied Köprülü Ahmed.[154] This figure is not far from the one included in a list compiled by a German eyewitness who was in Érsekújvár when the Ottoman army camped around the city nearly eight months earlier, which states the grand vizier led a private corps of 4,000 soldiers.[155] Further accounts seem to confirm the formation of private contingents by the senior dignitaries.[156]

In terms of military practice, the nature of these 'private troops' is well established, but concerning the strength of the units there were no rules and for a long time even the establishment of permanent corps was not always accomplished by junior officials such as the *sancakbegs*. These latter represented the key role in the provincial cavalry and their sphere of activity included both military and civil matters. As commander of the cavalry formed by *zeamet* and *timar* holders, the *sancakbeg* had numerous military duties both in war and during times of peace. Usually he called to arms the *sipahis* and their retinues, judged whether those who did not appear had acceptable reasons for their absence, and found an appropriate person to substitute him while he was on campaign. In peace, he signalled for new allotments to valiant soldiers or an increase in revenue for *timar* holders who had excelled in the battlefield or elsewhere. The *sancakbeg*'s civil duties included legal and financial matters with issues of public security.

In every province there was an office directed by a *defter katiby*, with the task of treasurer and administrator of the province, who also supervised the *timars* through a *timar defterdari*. All matters concerning revenues, their variations and the calculation of the contingents to be recruited were recorded and preserved in the archives of the province's capital. In

154 *Ibidem*, p.81.
155 *Diarii Europaei insertis quibusdam, maximè verò Germano-Gallo-Hispano-Anglo Polono Sueco-Dano-Belgo-Turcicis Actis Publici* (Frankfurt am Main, 1664), vol. X, p.680.
156 Kıbleli Mustafa Pasha, the governor-general of Damascus and brother-in-law of Grand Vizier Köprülü Ahmed was among the leading decision-makers in the Ottoman camp. He was a member of the wider network of the Köprülü household and, most probably by exploiting these familial connections, was generously supported by the Ottoman treasury: he received at least 1,320,000 *akçes* in loans at different times – the single largest amount of money allocated to an Ottoman notable during the Ottoman–Habsburg war of 1663–64. Unfortunately, although there are several references in Ottoman chronicles to the military actions of Mustafa *paşa*'s troops, none of these sources contain a specific figure for his soldiers. The list describing the Ottoman siege army in 1663, however, asserts that Kıbleli Mustafa *paşa* commanded a force of 2,500 men at the time of the siege; 500 men of these were taken from the garrison of Damascus and were not a part of his personal household troops. The German eyewitness seems to be the only source promulgating a figure, a fact that casts a shadow of doubt on his account. However, Ottoman narratives and archival sources firmly confirm that Kıbleli Mustafa, as the *paşa* of Damascus, had among his troops 500 cavalrymen from the garrison of Damascus: 'The fact that the anonymous German eyewitness was aware of such minute details of the Ottoman army's composition encourages confidence in his narrative. Moreover, it is certain that although officially holding the title of the governor-general of Damascus, Kıbleli Mustafa was not accompanied by the province's land-holding *sipahis* who had been excused from military service in return for a lump sum of money paid to the Ottoman treasury. In other words, Kıbleli Mustafa's household troops most likely comprised 2,000 men recruited for a limited time period.' Kolçak, *The Composition, Tactics and Strategy of the Ottoman Field Army*, pp.82–83.

Constantinople, there was the general register of the laws, the *kanuname*, which was maintained up to date.[157]

The main division of the contingents was established according to their origin, there was therefore an Asian cavalry, a European one and an African one. When the sultan or his grand vizier joined the army in the east of the Dardanelles, the Asian cavalry occupied the position of honour and in marches they had precedence over the other provincial cavalry. If the horsemen of two or more Asian *sancaks* were present at the same time, the first place belonged to the one coming from the oldest province. The same privileges passed to the European or African cavalry as appropriate.[158] Further divisions existed on the basis of the commander's rank; therefore there was a cavalry of the *beglerbegs*, the one of the *paşas*, *sancakbegs*, *zeamets* and so on. According to Marsigli, the *kanuname* made a further administrative distinction by dividing the district into two categories: the *hass* and *sàlyàne*. The first group comprised the provinces whose manpower quotas for the army were calculated on the basis of the *akçe* revenues, while in the second group there were the provinces that paid an annual tribute to Constantinople, which included the salaries for governors, and the resources for the military expenses managed by the *beglerbeg* or the *paşa* sent from Constantinople. Marsigli states that the Asian provinces of Anatolia, Karaman, Sivas, Maras, Cildir, Diarbakir, Mosul, Aleppo, Damascus, Tripoli of Lebanon, Kars, Erzurum, Van, Al-Raqqah, Kirkuk, and the European ones of Rumelia, Buda, Temeşvár, Bosnia and Crete belonged to the *hass* category. In the second category, Marsigli registered the *beglerbegliks* of Egypt and the *paşaliks* of Baghdad, Yemen and Basra, but he says nothing about the *Paşaliks* of Várad in Europe and Habesh in Africa.

Marsigli affirms to have consulted the *kanun-name* for the year 1670 and he would have transcribed, with the usual care, hundreds of figures referring to the revenues in *akçe* of each province and minor district, with its relative military contingent.[159] On paper, the *toprakli* formed an impressive force. In the 1670s, the provincial cavalry would have been able to field a theoretical force of 126,292 men.[160] The European provinces could provide 28,000 mounted soldiers if the governors proclaimed the general call. To understand the theoretical level of mobilisation required, it is possible to cite the case of the *Paşalik* of Sivas, in Anatolia, which had to provide 8,526 horsemen. The *paşa* himself had to gather one corps of 216 men; alongside the *zeamet* and *timar* living in his province, he could lead a maximum of 3,353 horse

---

157 Marsigli refers to the *kanuname* as a register established exclusively for military purposes. In fact, the *kanuname* dealt with the land survey, which summarised the main regulations regarding taxation and taxes, copies of Imperial decrees, and a host of financial records which provided the Porte with institutional memory. Provincial law codes were attached as prefaces to cadastral surveys or tax registers, and established the taxes and fines that the tax-paying subjects of a given administrative unit (*sancak*, *zeamet* and *timar*) owed to their fiefholder landlords and the sultan. See also Ágoston, *Encyclopedia*, p.277.

158 Marsigli, vol. II, p. 105.

159 *Ibidem*, vol. I, pp.104–134.

160 *Ibidem*, p.134.

on campaign.[161] Strong differences existed between the allocations provided by each province; for instance, in Europe, the *paşa* of Viddin in Bulgaria managed a mounted force of 499 horses, whilst his neighbour, the *paşa* of Silistra, had under his command 8,338 men, on paper.[162]

Sometimes Marsigli's maniacal accounting allows him little licences and superficialities, which can be explained to demonstrate the weakness of the Ottoman Empire. However, he makes a very pertinent observation when he notes that the contingents coming from the most remote provinces encountered considerable difficulties in reaching the Danube, Podolia, Dalmatia or Greece, every year, for a new campaign and in the numbers established by the *kanun-name*.

Marsigli argued that in 1687 the actual number of the provincial cavalry would be reduced to one sixth of the original strength.[163] It is obvious that a full provincial mobilisation could only be maintained with difficulty, even for the apparently inexhaustible Ottoman resources. The more serious problem for Ottoman stability was that *zeamets* and overall *timars* could no longer support the cavalryman's obligations on war campaigns. By the end of the seventeenth century, the revenues of entitlement from the *timars'* revenues were not sufficient, and many *timars* simply could not afford the cost of campaigning. The horsemen who did turn up for a campaign were ill-equipped to face the firepower of the Western armies, and were increasingly reluctant to fight. This scenario was also the result of internal dispute and misrule, favoured by the pretension of the increasingly demanding *kapikulu* permanent troops.[164] This was also the period when local notables known as *ayan* began to extend their power in many parts of the Empire.

Although paper figures for the provincial cavalry rose spectacularly, only a small portion of the *timar*-holders could actually be mobilised at any given time. Therefore, the expected force estimated at more than 100,000 horsemen available on paper, numbered only a few thousand men in reality. Though the whole force was not assembled, the provincial cavalry had suffered a significant lost of relevance in the first half of the seventeenth century.[165] The causes are different and cannot be explained simply as a consequence of the Porte's relaxed authority and the corruption of the local leading classes. The story of the dissolution of the *timar* system starts far earlier than 1700, in fact, as part of the Ottoman realisation of the need for more massed firepower against the Western enemies. The evolution to favour fire armed infantry and

---

161 *Ibidem*, vol. II, pp.201–202.
162 *Ibidem*.
163 *Ibidem*, p.196.
164 Aksan, *Ottoman Wars*, pp.54–55: 'The question of who owned the timar lands became decidedly muddy after the early 1600s, and the right to distribute them more diffuse. The tendency was to convert the fiefs into tax farms, and large numbers fell out of the jurisdiction of the *sipahis*, part of a general trend of the seventeenth century, by which revenue collection devolved to emerging gentry households, consistent with similar trends in other parts of the early modern world. Beneficiaries of the evolving system were the sultan household, administrative officials and janissaries, the latter coincidentally … were sent into the provinces to quell the celali revolts; by the mid seventeenth century, reassigned *timars* regularly went to members of the Janissary corps, sometimes in lieu of pay.'
165 Matuz, *Das Osmanische Reich*, p.177.

massed formal field battles in Podolia or in Moldavia and Crimea was not as evident as in Danubian and Greek warfare. The campaigns in Hungary and Greece in 1684–99 involved the army in a series of sieges, with occasional open field battles. The increasing numbers of infantry with firearms, first as corps of soldiers for a single campaign, and then as provincial militias, complicated the scene.[166]

The Ottoman Empire was essentially an agrarian state, which could extract surplus resources from its subjects with increasing difficulty. This evolved in order to produce regular and predictable cash flows to meet the expenses of modern warfare, introducing several expedients for collecting taxes. However, the only possible lands available were the *timar* and *zeamet* estates of the *sipahis*, but the government was already unhappy with the combat performance of the provincial cavalry, who were militarily useless against the Western European musketeers and artillery. Additionally, they were increasingly unwilling to take part in long campaigns, preferring instead to pay exemption fees. Therefore, the government chose to finance new infantry units at the expense of the provincial *sipahis*. However, it began to reassign the estates slowly because of institutional conservatism, the continuing need for light cavalry against non-European enemies, and potentially disruptive socio-economic problems.

Before 1663, the Porte had no longer collected large cavalry contingents against a Christian enemy. It is interesting to note that Grand Vizier Köprülü Ahmed used the Hungarian campaigns against the Habsburgs to test the actual capacity of mobilisation of the provincial forces for a war in Europe. In the events preceding the conflict of 1663–64, the sources mention the approximately 16,000 European and Asian horsemen,[167] who under Ali Paşa of Temeşvár carried out numerous raids in northern Hungary in the spring of 1661. Two years later, the Ottoman cavalry under the command of Köprülü Ahmed numbered 32,500 men.[168] In 1663, the provincial cavalry came mostly from Rumelia (Greece and Bulgaria), Bosnia, Temeşvár and the Buda provinces, for 12,000 horses in total. Another 4–5,000 provincial *sipahis* arrived from Anatolia, but, with the exception of the *paşa* of Damascus' contingent, the larger part joined the army when the campaign was ending.[169] One year later, according to several sources, the provincial cavalry strength did not exceed 10,000 men. After the battle of Szentgotthárd, 15–17,000 horsemen arrived as reinforce troops from Asia, and they camped

---

166 According to V. Aksan, *Ottoman Wars, 1700–1800* (London-New York: Routledge, 2007) pp.54–55, there is a relationship between displaced *timar* holders, or other demobilised combatants, and the very serious extended rebellions (the *celali* revolts). This topic has long been a source of discussion among Ottoman historians: 'Ottoman fear of an armed countryside is palpable in the documents that survive which were issued in an attempt to control the distribution and use of handguns. Sorting out how these potential soldiers were reabsorbed into the system, or forced into banditry, is one of the tasks of the military historian looking at the evolution of the Ottoman army after 1650. It has proved no less difficult for European military historians in like contexts.'

167 Montecuccoli, 'Della Guerra contro il Turco', in Luraghi, *Opere di Raimondo Montecuccoli*, vol. II, p.396.

168 *Ibidem*, p.410.

169 Hammer-Purgstall, *Geschichte des Osmanischen Reiches*, vol. XI, p.141.

not far from Székesfehérvár.[170] Despite this drawback, in 1667 Köprülü Ahmed mobilised enough forces in Crete from every corner of the Empire to resume the siege of Kandije. In 1672, during the war against the Poles, little more than 6–7,000 horse took part in the campaign in Podolia; mostly of them came from the European provinces. The cavalry was not sufficient for supporting the field army and forced the *serasker* Şyşman Hüseyin to recall the Tatars from their raids in Poland.[171]

However, in the mid seventeenth century the Ottoman commanders continued to ask for well-armed mounted soldiers, probably in the hope of launching cavalry offensives in enemy territory. Financial circumstances seem to have played a part and, although a higher wage was promised to volunteers in possession of a warhorse, there were still few who could meet the recruitment requirements. Furthermore, those who enrolled as mounted soldiers among household troops or in a mercenary band contracted by the Ottoman administration for military service did not favour fighting on foot. However, mounted soldiers in household or provincial troops directly contributed to Ottoman firepower, particularly in siege operations.

If scholars normally find problems in calculating the overall strength of an Ottoman army, the difficulties are even greater to form a reliable picture of the provincial cavalry in the field. The uncertainty about the number of soldiers during a campaign was also due to the inaccurate calculation of these troops and to their arrival in the war theatre, which for obvious reasons could not be simultaneous. Sometimes the calculation becomes even more complicated when the provincial cavalry were included in the garrison of some fortified place along with the infantry. In fact, the Ottomans often used this cavalry like the dragoons of the Western coeval armies.[172] Eyewitnesses relate that the provincial cavalry fought on foot during the siege of Érsekúivár (1663), the siege of Vienna (1683), the defence of Esztergom (1685), the battle of Harsány (1687), the defence of Negroponte (1688) and the sieges of Nauplia (1715) and Corfu (1716), just to mention the major episodes.

To give an idea about the mobilisation of these troops and their heterogeneity, the siege of Vienna in 1683 surely represents the most interesting and crucial event. The campaign was the major organisational effort of Ottoman military history, and several months before the arrival of the army before the Austrian capital, there was already circulating much information about the composition of the contingents. Soon a great number of relations, enriched by particulars not always verifiable, spread in every European capital unto the most remote city. Though these sources are often unreliable, they show interesting details about the provenance of the

---

170 Montecuccoli, 'Della Guerra contro il Turco', in Luraghi, *Opere di Raimondo Montecuccoli*, vol. II, p.450.

171 Gierowski, *Da Chocim a Vienna*', p.18.

172 Kolçak, *The Composition, Tactics and Strategy of the Ottoman Field Army*, pp.77–78. Another interesting detail is provided by the Venetian attaché in Constantinople, Antonio Benetti, who in 1682 refers to a corps of 170 mounted *segmens* equipped with muskets in Grand Vizier Kara Mustafa's household. See A. Benetti, *Osservazioni fatte dal fu A.B. nel viaggio a Costantinopoli dell'Illustrissimo et Eccellentissimo Signor Gio. Battista Donado, spedito Bailo alla Porta Ottomana, dall'anno 1680* (Venice, 1690), pp.21–25.

troops. Several figures appear improbable even considering the origin of the contingents. In 1683, the Habsburg Aulic War Council tried to learn the enemy strength by trusting disparate sources, which evidently exaggerated the actual size of the troops gathered, such as the 24,000 soldiers from Upper Egypt and a further 18,000 from Lower Egypt.[173]

The Italian nobleman Odorico Frangipane, who arrived at Vienna as a volunteer in the fateful summer of 1683, collected in his memoirs much data concerning the strength and provenance of the Ottoman troops.[174] In his report the figures are very approximate and exaggeratedly magnified. However, his detailed description, probably as result of different coeval sources, is particularly interesting, because he lists troops from the most distant provinces:

> Then arrived the Mesopotamians, armed with sabres and bows, numbered thirteen thousand. They were followed the troops of Babylon and Assyria, who for the most part were on horseback, with swords and javelins, they ascended to fourteen thousand men. After them, came twenty-four thousand Syrians, experts in riding, but poor as warriors. Then appeared the troops of Asia Minor, now called Anatolia, good archers and good horsemen, in number of thirty thousand. The peoples of Palestine passed in number of eighteen thousand, who were more able as thieves than as soldiers, followed by the troops of Karaman and Cilicia, armed with bow, sabre and mace: rough and crude people who numbered eight thousand … Troops from Cappadocia and Armenia, armed mostly with spear and sword, and some of them also with musket, in number of twenty-four thousand. … Finally followed the Georgians with other their neighbours, in number of twenty-eight thousand.[175]

The Italian volunteer collected information about the cavalry coming from the Asian provinces, but concerning the European and African troops, such information is curiously absent. Another well-informed eyewitness of the siege, Ferdinando Marsigli, argued that the provincial cavalry had come only from the Asian provinces of Diyarbakir, Aleppo, Damascus, Erzurum and Kars, and from the European ones of Rumelia and Bosnia. According to Marsigli, 64,000 *toprakli* horsemen would be mobilised for the campaign of 1683,[176] of which about 26,000 were from Europe.[177] Marsigli provides little information about the Egyptian cavalry, while the troops from Temeşvár and Buda are only indirectly mentioned. It is known that the troops from the Hungarian *beglerbeglik* secured the bridges on the Raba River and later they joined the besieging army at Vienna. One year later, in early June, in the attempt to relieve Buda during the first Imperial siege, Grand Vizier

---

173 Österreichisches Kriegsarchiv of Vienna, *Das Kriegsjahr 1683*, p.53.
174 Odorico Frangipane, 'Libro Primo di memorie estere, abozate da O.F.', in D. Frangipane, A. Vigevani, P. Zanetta, *L'Ultimo Crociato* (Udine: Centro Iniziative per l'Arte e la Cultura, 1983), pp.79–80.
175 *Ibidem*, pp.79–80.
176 Marsigli, vol. II, p.183. According to the author, the total would be 64,829 horsemen.
177 *Ibidem*. In detail they were 25,890 horsemen from Rumelia and 772 from Bosnia.

Kara Ibrahim sent the troops of the provinces of Adana, Karaman, Srem, Smedarevo, 'together with eight *sancaks* of horse from [the *paşalik* of] Buda' under Cerkes Ahmed and Abdulmumin Paşa to relieve the city.[178]

Contingents from Egypt participated at the battle of 12 September 1683, when they abandoned some of their ensigns, and Marsigli himself remembers how the Egyptian horsemen were easily recognisable for certain peculiarities of the dress.[179] The Egyptian *ocaks* were typical Ottoman garrisons, although a particularly large, strong force of approximately 10,000 men, of which about 8,800 were 'native Egyptians' and formed the permanent 'ready to march' armed force.[180] Some 1,000 troops, a tenth of the army, was stationed in Upper Egypt alone. Notwithstanding the Ottoman presence, the strong ascendancy of the local elites, represented by the Mamluk emirs, continued to be a serious problem in maintaining the Porte's authority in Egypt and Syria.[181]

Egypt's pre-Ottoman military traditions established military classes that continued after 1517, maintaining a strong influence in the country. Unrest and rebellions marked the history of these provinces since 1604, when a major uprising forced the Porte to react with severe punishment.[182] In the early seventeenth century, the local leadership accepted the formal recognition of the sultan's sovereignty represented by the *beglerbeg* and other Ottoman dignitaries and envoys, proclaiming the sultan's name in the Friday sermons in the mosques, and minting coins bearing his name and title. The agreed conditions included the sending of the annual remittance and some points concerning the Ottoman army stationed in Egypt. The most important concerned the demand a contingent of soldiers – usually up to 3,000 men – to fight in the campaigns in Asia, Europe or the Mediterranean.[183] As long as these major objectives were achieved, Constantinople was satisfied, no matter how independent the local emirs in Egypt seemed. However, the repression did not resolve the situation. Rivalry between the military corps, especially

---

178 Hammer-Purgstall, *Geschichte des Osmanischen Reiches*, vol. XII, p.175.

179 Marsigli, vol. I, p.94.

180 Winter, *Egyptian Society under Ottoman Rule*, p.38.

181 Less destructive, but equally persistent, the Ottoman garrisons caused unrest also in Damascus and Aleppo. In the latter city, the janissary were quartered in the north-east side, sparing the rest of Aleppo from disorder and robberies. See H.Z. Watenpaugh, *The Image of an Ottoman City. Imperial Architecture and Urban Experience in Aleppo in the 16th and 17th Centuries* (Leiden-Boston: Brill, 2004), pp.171–172.

182 In 1604, the Porte reacted swiftly by organising a force of loyal troops and Bedouin Arabs, which crushed the revolt. 'Many mutineers were killed; 300 were exiled to Yemen. It is not clear whether the uprising was much more than an attempt by angry soldiers to hold on to their illegal privileges in face of the pasha's determination to restore order and justice. Modern historians try to regard the uprising as a Mamluk secessionist movement to restore the sultanate.' Winter, *Egyptian Society under Ottoman Rule*, p.19.

183 T. Öztürk, 'Egyptian Soldiers in Ottoman Campaigns from the Sixteenth to the Eighteenth Centuries', in *War in History*, 2016, vol. 23, (1) p.10: 'When the Porte decided to enter war, it issued a decree containing the reasons for recruiting soldiers to the Egyptian beys and asked them quickly to make the soldiers get ready for a specific campaign In these decrees, Egyptian *beys*, senior officers, and *ağas* were mentioned. Upon receiving a decree, the *beglerbeg* immediately called the members of his provincial council, the *sancakbeg*, and the seven *ocak ikhtiyars* (senior officers). If a commander had already been appointed, he was also called and presented with the campaign *hil'at* (robes of honour), while local notables were assigned to gather supplies.'

between Ottoman and local troops, favoured the affirmation of the local Mamluk clans, the *qazdughliyya*, which become the best organised 'political' force in the region. The chief exponents of the *qazdughliyya* were Circassian Mamluks and their descendants, although admittedly membership of it was not limited to them: many *beys* were neither Circassians nor Mamluks. In addition, the Ottoman historian and traveller Evliya Çelebi, who visited Egypt during the 1670s, stated that Mamluks came from various regions and ethnic groups. Although the Circassians seem to have been the outstanding element, there were Abazas, Georgians, Russians, Imeretians, Mingrelians and other Caucasians.[184] Gradually, in the seventeenth century, military power shifted to leading emirs, who were soon appointed as effective Ottoman *sancakbegs*.[185] The Mamluks, who until the early eighteenth century continued to fill their ranks by recruiting young people in the Caucasus, increasingly supplied the recruits for the cavalry.[186] Though in Egypt the title *sançakbeg*, or *bey*, never acquired a territorial connotation, local elites controlled territories and the people linked to them like clients and protégées. It was the intention of the government that the number of *beys* in Egypt should not exceed 12, yet it is obvious from numerous decrees that, contrary to the Porte's wish, the number reached at least 40 by the 1650s.

Egypt provided a significant contribution during the long Cretan War. In 1645, Egyptian soldiers are mentioned in the garrison in charge of guarding Suda harbour, while in 1648 an additional 2,000 men disembarked from the ships at Chaniá with ammunition and supplies for a direct participation in the siege of Kandije. In 1667, Evliya Çelebi noted 3,000 Egyptian soldiers who were involved in several assaults against the enemy earthworks.[187] At the end of the siege, in 1669, a further 1,000 Egyptian soldiers landed at Ierapetra harbour with supplies under the command of their *bey*.[188] At the end of the seventeenth century, the Porte's need for soldiers increased and Egyptians were regularly employed in multi-front operations. Egyptian horsemen joined the Ottoman field army at Belgrade in 1690 and Temeşvár in 1697. Furthermore, about 1,300 Egyptian soldiers participated in 1697 at the battle of Zenta.[189]

At the end of the seventeenth century, Egypt still paid the annual tax of 300,000 *serifs* to the Porte,[190] with which the government could pay military expenses and eventually enlist other recruits. However, Egypt's budget had to cover the heavy expenses of the continuous struggle against the rebellious Arab tribes in Yemen, whether the *beglerbegs* and the *beys* approved or not.

---

184 Hathaway, *A Tale of Two Factions*, p.152.

185 The Egyptian *begs* are often called *sançakbegs* in the Ottoman sources, but this rank, which was standard in the Empire, was not used in Egypt. Moreover, while elsewhere in the Ottoman Empire the title was that of a *beg* or *bey*, that is an emir in charge of an administrative and territorial unit. See also A. Hathaway, *The politics of households in Ottoman Egypt. The rise of the Qazdaghs* (Cambridge-New York NY: Cambridge University Press, 1997), pp.27–30.

186 I. Lebedinsky, *Les Armes Orientales* (La Tour du Pin: Editions du Portail, 1993), p.45.

187 Öztürk, *Egyptian Soldiers in Ottoman Campaigns*, in *War in History*, p.12.

188 *Ibidem*.

189 Özcan, *Anonim Osmanlı Tarihi, (1099–1116/1688–1704)* (Ankara: Türk Tarih Kurumu, 2000), pp.120–123 and p.131.

190 Marsigli, vol. I, p.126.

The governor often sent troops into Yemen without sufficient provisions and salaries, passing the responsibility to the Ottoman *paşa* of Yemen, with the result that the Egyptian soldiers did not receive regular salary for months. During the seventeenth century, however, a regional army of Egypt with an esprit du corps and interest of its own began to emerge, opening the way to the transformation that occurred after 1700.[191]

In the early eighteenth century, the French historian Jean Guer reported that the command of the army was entrusted to the 12 Mamluk *beys*, who managed a permanent force of 20,000 horsemen.[192] Among the tasks performed by these troops, there was the obligation to provide for the escort of pilgrims to Mecca, under the command of the *amir al-hajj*.[193] Another 18,000 horsemen could be recruited by the local *beys*, but as Jean Guer pointed out, their military effectiveness was very poor.

Like Egypt, also the *paşaliks* of Habesh, Basra, Baghdad and Yemen belonged to the *sàlyàne* category. These latter provinces did not appear on the *kanun-name* consulted by Marsigli and therefore not even he knew the total number of troops provided by these provinces.

During the seventeenth century, the Porte turn to the *timar* system on several occasions, without completely resolving the matter. Under Köprülü Mustafa the provincial cavalry returned under a more strict control of the government, and the obligations fixed on the *kaduname* were complied with more solicitously. Offices were set up for the recruitment of soldiers, appointing directors chosen among the notables of the province,[194] the *ayans,* but the most significant reform was undertaken only after the peace of Carlowitz, in 1699.

Grand Vizier Köprülü Amcazàde Hüseyn established the obligation for *sançakbegs* to present annual reviews of their contingents and to provide for the regular training of recruits, as well as *zeamets* and *timars* did with their men. A further important novelty was the obligation to establish standing units of provincial cavalry.[195] The discontent of the janissaries and the dramatic economic scenario caused the overthrow of the grand vizier, and the reform of the provincial cavalry remained incomplete. Despite this, a significant innovation regarding the military was the establishment of the *imdad-ı seferiye*, an emergency wartime tax, which became a regular, annual imposition after 1718. However, the revenues were once again assigned to

---

191 The term *Misir kullari*, soldiers (or slaves) of Egypt, appears in some documents dealing with clashes between them and the *kapikulu*, who had been sent to Egypt to support the local *beglerbeg*. See Winter, *Egyptian Society under Ottoman Rule*, p.39.

192 Guer, *Mœurs et Usages des Turcs*, vol. II, p.223.

193 The office of *amir al-hajj* was extremely important, which brought with it great political influence and religious prestige, as well as a considerable economic value. Given the significance of the pilgrimage in Islam, the protection of the caravan and its pilgrims was a priority. The main duties entrusted to an *amir al-hajj* were securing funds and provisions for the caravan, and protecting it along the desert route to the Muslim holy cities of Mecca and Medina in the Hejaz, modern-day Saudi Arabia.

194 E. Werner, 'Das Osmanreich im XVII. Jahrhundert: System verfall und System stabilisierungversuche', in *Die Türken vor Wien*, pp.70–75.

195 Bombaci-Shaw, *Storia dell'Impero Ottomano*, pp.451–452.

local officials and inadvertently contributed to the ongoing empowerment of the provincial magnates.[196]

Many indications suggest, however, that Ottoman commanders relied less and less on provincial cavalry, at least in the campaigns against modern Western armies. For instance, in 1697, provincial *sipahi* forces comprised only 11.62 percent of the 86,884 troops mobilised for the campaign in Hungary.[197]

The majority of the provincial forces were recruited from the *ayan* and the total mobilised strength of these provincial forces could reach 50,000 to 70,000 men in the early eighteenth century. As a result, the ancient *timar* system entered an irreversible crisis, with serious damage to discipline and mobilisation.[198] The increase in the size of the permanent army, especially the janissaries, was also related to the deterioration of the *timar* system and the provincial cavalry. New research dates the beginning of the crisis to the mid seventeenth century. Revenues became administered by a gradually expanding corps of beneficiaries and provincial elites, and most never made their way to the central government treasury. While in the first half of the century, the treasury administered some 58 percent of revenues, this share decreased to 25 percent in the following decades.[199] This in turn led to the financial and military independence of the provincial elites, the *ayan*, whose attempts to appropriate ever larger shares of resources increased the burden on taxpayers, and thus added to the economic and social strains that led to revolts and rebellions amongst the peasant population.[200] According to the British traveller Aaron Hill, in 1709 the provincial cavalry actually available for a war campaign numbered 2,504 *zeamets* and 51,579 *timars*.[201] Another coeval source states that the provincial *sipahis* assembled just one sixth of their force for a campaign.[202] As a result, during the 1711 campaign against the Tsar, Grand Vizier Baltaçi Mehmet could deploy a lower number of provincial horse than the *kapikulu* cavalry.[203] During the war in the Peloponnese against the Venetians, in July 1715, the field army gathered in Thebes 4,394 European and 3,750 Asian and African horsemen; of these troops the majority came from Western Anatolia, while 1,000 were native to the *paşalik* of Sivas, 500 men came from Syria, 300 from Karaman, a further 100 from central Anatolia and just 50 from Karahisar. Altogether, the

---

196 M. Uyar and E. J. Erickson, *A Military History of the Ottomans. From Osman I to Atatürk* (Santa Barbara, CL: ABC Clio, 2009), p.90.

197 Ágoston, *Military Transformation in the Ottoman Empire and Russia, 1500–1800*, p.308.

198 Matuz, *Das Osmanische Reich*, p.71.

199 Ágoston, 'Empires and Warfare in East-Central Europe', p.130.

200 *Ibidem*: 'Since a good proportion of the emerging new elite came from the ranks of the janissaries, their growing control over the local resources once distributed as timar s to the provincial sipahi cavalry led to competition and friction on the local level between janissaries and *sipahis*.'

201 A. Hill, *A Full and Just Account of the Present State of the Ottoman Empire* (London, 1709), p.25. Aaron Hill, dramatist and miscellaneous writer, provides the number of the provincial cavalry in 21 Ottoman provinces. However, he includes also Trabzon and Cyprus, which did not provide *sipahis* but sailors for the Ottoman navy. Further details in the appendix.

202 Guer, *Mœurs et Usages des Turcs*, vol. II, p.200.

203 Chandler, *The Art of Warfare*, p.74.

provincial cavalry did not equal even half of the mounted troops mobilised for the campaign.[204]

In 1716, when the war had already involved the Habsburg emperor, it was necessary to resort to threatening the *timars* at the general call to arms. In the climate of exaltation and frenzy that reigned in those months in Constantinople, calculations and promises were made to set up a huge contingents: the *beglerbeg* of Rumelia estimated he could field nearly 40,000 men; the *paşa* of Anatolia guaranteed more or less the same number.[205] The Asian troops under the *paşa* of Erzurum and the *sancakbeg* of Kaiseri began to be gathered in Nissa, but in the summer of 1716, the news regarding the *sipahis* encamped around Belgrade related that their strength remained low.[206]

The vanguard of 10,000 *sipahi ulùfely* and *toprakli*, under the *carkacibasi* Cürd Pasha, successfully assaulted the Imperial cavalry at Carlowitz, in the first military action of the campaign.[207] The following year, the overall force devised by the government remained high but, due to the serious defeats suffered in Hungary, enthusiasm and morale were very low. In the early spring, the claimed 80,000 horse from the European and Asian provinces, alongside the 40,000 men mobilised in Egypt,[208] were only 20–25,000 mounted troops gathered at Edirne. The Imperial spies reported: 'the Turks are very dismayed … many of them are deserting' and that the Ottomans were seriously late on the gathering programmes.

Before the arrival of the relief army in Belgrade, the *beglerbeg* of Rumelia, with only 6,000 men,[209] received the order to guard the bridges on the Danube to prevent the Imperialists crossing the river. From Egypt no more than 4,000 horsemen mobilised.[210] In June 1717, they arrived at Edirne together with the janissaries of Cairo.[211] The *serasker* Regeb Paşa of Damascus, who held the command for the incursion in Transylvania, had to assemble 30,000 men from Syria, Basra, Baghdad and Palestine,[212] but by mid June he was still on the Lower Danube awaiting the arrival of the Tatars, because without them, he had insufficient troops. In mid June he received the order to be reunited with the main army marching to Belgrade, along with a part of the Ottoman and Tatar cavalry. Until then, the *serasker* had only 20,000 horsemen under his command, of which just a quarter belonged to the Middle Eastern provinces.[213] The command of operations in Transylvania passed to the prince of Moldavia Mihály Rakovita, who, on 19 August 1717, crossed the border. The operation was initially crowned by some success, then it fragmented into looting and hundreds of isolated actions, and finally

---

204 Brue, *Journal*, pp.65–69.
205 K.u.K. Kriegsarchiv, *Feldzüge des Prinzen Eugen*, vol. XVI, p.128.
206 *Ibidem*, p.129.
207 *Ibidem*, p.156.
208 *Ibidem*, vol. XVII, p.52.
209 *Ibidem*, p.53; information reported in June 1717 by a Greek tradesman coming from Edirne.
210 *Ibidem*.
211 *Ibidem*.
212 *Ibidem*, p.54.
213 *Ibidem*, p.184.

the news of the defeat suffered at Belgrade dissolved the corps, which hastily crossed back over the border.

In the battle fought on 5 August, the provincial horsemen formed the second line of cavalry during the counter-assault against the Imperialists. In the morning darkness, shrouded in a deep fog, the *sipahis* clashed against the infantry battalions led by Prince Friedrich Ludwig of Württemberg. The struggle turned into a confused melee in which the Ottoman cavalry had the worst. Some squadrons managed to reach the Danube, beyond the defensive embankment, but they were repulsed and put to flight after a charge of the enemy cuirassiers.

The test of the 1716–17 war proved once more that history's chapter on provincial cavalry, if it was not to be considered concluded, certainly needed a drastic reform. The age of the great masses of mounted soldiers who fought under the flags of the sultan was definitely facing its sunset.

The *Mehter*

The provincial contingents went to the gathering places accompanied by their commanders and military bands, the *mehter*, which joined each major group. These musical formations constituted one of the typical symbols of authority of the Ottoman dignitaries and their origin was lost in the far past. Recently the origin of these bands has been identified in the early Turkish kingdoms in Central Asia.[214] From the literal meaning of the Persian word *mihtar*, namely 'high' or 'elevated', is possible understand how important music was in Ottoman ceremonial. Composers and instrumentalists formed the court of the Sultan's *mehter* in Constantinople, while in the janissary corps *orta* 99 comprised only musicians.

Like all the activities of Ottoman social life, the *mehter* also had its own specific role and such was the reason for its regulations, similar to the military ones. The instruments were the same traditionally used by the Arab, Persian and Mamluk armies, and over time they also moved into Western orchestras, specifically to perform military music.[215] With the exception of the *kos*, the gigantic tambours reserved for the band of Topkapı, each *mehter* consisted of five instruments: *davul*, drum; *nakkàre*, kettledrums; *zuma*, Turkish oboe; *boru*, horn; *zil*, bells. Each group of five instruments formed a *kat* (order); the smallest of the formations usually consisted of three *kat*; the great mehter of Constantinople could deploy up to 40 *kat*.[216]

Starting from the *sancakbeg*, each governor used to maintain his own *mehter*. The grand vizier could deploy a band formed from eight to 12 *kat*;

214 A. Masala, *La Banda Militare Ottomana, il Mehter* (Rome: University of Rome, without date), p.5.
215 The characteristic 'alla turca' music dates to the seventeenth century. Many times this kind of music emphasised more the oriental exotic aspect than the martial one, but in the mid eighteenth century the 'military' character of Ottoman music became particularly explicit in the compositions of European classical composers. See C. Hogwood, Franz Joseph Haydn's 'Military Simphony' n. 100, Decca 311833-1.
216 Masala, *Il Mehter*, p.31.

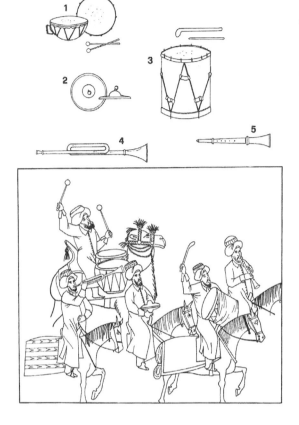

26. The *mehter*, military band, early eighteenth century, and its instruments, after the *Surname-i Vehbi*: 1) *nakkare*; 2) *zil*; 3) *davul*; 4) *boru*; 5) *zurna*.

This illustrated book is preserved in the Topkapı museum, and contains 137 brilliantly-coloured miniatures by Levni, the renowned court painter to the court of Ahmed III. This work interrupted the iconoclast period of Ottoman art during the prohibition of depicting human beings. The miniatures illustrate a fifteen-day festival held on the occasion of the circumcision of four of the sultan's sons in 1720. The miniatures represent parades, musical performances, acrobatics, and fireworks displays, all of which were brilliantly captured and executed by Levni in his miniatures. With one exception, the miniatures occupy double pages. The text for the book was composed by the court poet Vehbi. (Author's illustration)

from six to seven *kat* for a *beglerbeg*, from four to five to a *paşa* and only three to a *sancakbeg*. The spectacle offered by the columns of the provincial cavalry must have been clearly audible in all its noisy solemnity. The *mehter* was led by a *mehterbasi*, assisted by the *aga*, who directed each group of instruments. The band therefore constituted a distinctive rank and also a particularly prestigious honour. When a governor was removed from office, he was also deprived of the right to retain his own *mehter*.

Similarly to Western armies, *mehter* musicians accompanied the troops engaged in combat with music. However, the military music of the Ottomans was not used to communicate commands to troops, but simply supported the morale of soldiers in combat. Testimonies about the alternative use of the *mehter* in battle are reported during the siege of Chaniá in 1645, when the music was used to divert the defenders' fire from the troops hidden with them in a cloud of artificial smoke.[217] During the siege of Vienna, the Ottoman musicians played their instruments to encourage the troops that fought furiously before the ramparts of the Burg and Löbel, while the bands of the Imperial regiments responded from the besieged city. The chroniclers report that the respective music was mocked by both sides.[218]

The *Serhaddkulu*

The corps of the *serhaddkullari* was originally formed in order to dispose the permanent troops on campaign, and to replace them in the garrisons with other soldiers. In particular, the transition from a cavalry-based to a foot-based army composed of musketeer units, favoured the raising of corps recruited only for a campaign or for the duration of a war. The increasing of the *serhaddkulu* strength registered a significant impulse during the long Turkish War against the Habsburgs (1593–1606), when the need for

---

217 G. Brusoni, *Historia dell'Ultima Guerra tra Veneziani e Turchi* (Venice, 1673), *Libro* II, p.46.
218 J. Stoye, *The Siege of Vienna* (Edinburgh: Birlinn, 1964–2006), p.153.

musket-armed units represented the immediate countermeasure against the Imperialists and their Western allies.

Since its presence was originally requested in the border regions, the *serhaddkulu* is often considered to be composed by frontiersmen, but over the years the corps significantly developed and comprised various infantry and cavalry specialties, until it became similar to a modern 'national guard'. Initially the call to arms involved all Muslim subjects living in the border regions, who served for the duration of the campaign; then, at the end of the sixteenth century, some permanent units were created, recruited in every province, to reinforce the garrisons. They received their salary from the *beglerbegs* and *paşas*, who appointed the officer ranks, including an *aga* in charge of the command of the local corps.

Even the *serhaddkulu* was divided into troops on horseback and on foot. The mounted force were represented by three specialties: *beslü*, *gönüllü* and *dely*, and the infantry by a further five: *azab*, *segmen*, *hisar-erler*, *lağımcı* and *musellim*. This pattern had been the result of the evolution of the borderland of the Ottoman Empire.[219]

As for the strength of the *serhaddkulu*, most of the information on these troops concerns the regions involved in the wars against the sultan's enemies. However, reliable estimates with regard both theoretically resourced and actually deployed troops are hard to come by. In the 1660s almost 16,000 *serhaddkulu* soldiers native to the Hungarian territories could join the army, and a further 6–7,000 came from Temeşvár,[220] while up to 30,000 militiamen flocked to the border with Dalmatia under the ensigns of the *paşa* of Bosnia. Finally, the contribution provided by Serbs, Hungarians, Bulgarians, Armenians and Greeks, recruited as drivers for the army train, or enlisted as miners and for all the auxiliary services necessary for the operation of the Ottoman field army, could also be considered.

Towards the end of the seventeenth century, the *serhaddkulu* underwent a significant evolution of its original role. This happened with the growing power of the *ayan* magnates, or notables, who began to exercised a monopoly in recruiting volunteers, especially in Bosnia and Albania, until they became actual warlords. When the balance tipped away from central authority, the government lost its monopoly over the collection of taxes. The privileges conferred upon the highest bidder, who was known as a 'tax farmer', stabilised at the beginning of the 1690s, coincidental to the serious military crisis during the War of the Holy League. In the eighteenth century, these notables gained strength as tax farmers and provincial governors in the peripheral provinces of the Ottoman Empire. Arguably the most important aspect of these borderland locations was that the holders of these territories became indispensable as the front line of defence for the state, namely in the Balkans, northeastern Anatolia and along the border with Persia. To cite just two examples: the

---

219 Today, this world in which Greeks, Slavs, Latins, Turks and Hungarians (Christians, Muslims and Jews) lived together can only be evoked. It is unpleasant to notice that we are talking about it in an epitaph style, but its traces have almost disappeared, and unfortunately in a very tragic way.
220 Montecuccoli, 'Della Guerra contro il Turco', in Luraghi, *Opere di Raimondo Montecuccoli*, vol. II, pp.396–398, and Payer, *Armati Hungarorum*, p.106.

ayans dominated the province of Mosul for about a century starting in early eighteenth century due to their invaluable role as protectors of this key border area with Persia; while from the Mediterranean fortress city of Acre, a series of Ottoman magnates dominated the Palestinian coastal region, frequently ignoring the government's orders.[221]

Azab and *Segmen* – Garrison Infantry and Foot Militia

The *azabs* constituted the semi-regular component of the troops on foot, They were a kind of peasant militia of originally unmarried soldiers (*azab* means also bachelor) serving as foot troops in the garrisons. Usually well equipped and with their own logistical organisation, the *azabs* can be compared to the infantrymen of the Prussian Landwehr of the Napoleonic wars. The *azab* normally served in his own region, but he could also join the field army alongside the janissaries and the other *kapikulu* infantry, especially in sieges or for the defence of strategic points in the war theatre.

Their presence was relevant also in distant theatres of war, such at Crete. According to the Muhurdar's chronicles, the casualties suffered by the *azabs* in the final phase of the war, from 1667 to 1669, suggest that they represented two thirds of the overall infantry force at Crete.[222] In 1659, during the punitive expedition against Transylvania, the corps under the *paşa* of Buda was also composed of local soldiers, and the *serhaddkulu*'s troops represented more than half of the total force, amounting to 17,000 men, of which at least 4,000 were *azab* infantrymen.[223] When they were garrisoned in a city together with an *ocak* of janissaries, the *azabs* carried out all the duties of service, including patrols, especially at night, the *kapikulu* soldiers thus avoiding the most burdensome tasks.[224]

In certain operations, a couple of janissaries supervised the service of the *azabs*, because the members of the *kapikulu* exercised authority over all the *serhaddkulu*'s recruits. Differences of status were reflected in different salaries, thus a common *azab* could earn eight *akçe* maximum at the peak of his career.

Each province organised one or more *azab* corps, usually divided into seven *odas*,[225] each commanded by an *azab-ağasi*, assisted in administrative matters by an *azab-kàtibi*.[226] Often the appointment to the rank of officer was granted after the payment of money, and the same could happen for

---

221 Zens, *Provincial Powers: the Rise of Ottoman Local Notables*, p.440.
222 Figures cited by Rhoads Murphey in 'The Ottoman Resurgence in the Seventeenth-Century Mediterranean: The Gamble and its Results', in *Mediterranean Historical Review*, n. 8 – 1993, p.193, after Mühürdar's history, *Ottoman Casualties at the Siege of Candia, June 1667–9 September 1669*. The same figures are listed in the manuscript copy found in the Topkapı Palace Library: Ms. III Ahmed 3605, f.57a.
223 Payer, *Armati Hungarorum*, p.106.
224 Marsigli, vol. II, p.160.
225 K.u.K. Kriegsarchiv, *Feldzüge des Prinzen Eugen*, vol. I, p.526.
226 Marsigli, vol. I, p.83.

27. Ottoman *azab* soldiers in Pāshānameh.

Azab infantrymen marching in a mid seventeenth century Ottoman miniature. They wear **kaftans** of red, blue, brown and grey cloth. Each **azab** is equipped with a matchlock **tüfek**, but it seems that not all carry the sabre. (Miniature from the *Paşaname*, 1640–45, in Hans Sloan's album, *The Habit of the Grand Signor's Court*; British Museum Library, London).

the lower ranks.[227] The subordinate ranks of an *oda* were completed by 10 *yery* NCOs and one *bayrakdar*, charged with the task of carrying the unit's ensign. When housed in border fortresses they served under the authority of a *dizdar*, responsible for the place.

Regarding the strength of each *oda*, little information is available. According to the Austro-Hungarian *Kriegsarchiv*, each unit took the name of the city or township in which its commander resided, who at the same time held the office of government representative.[228] The commander also exercised control and delivery of the weapons and ammunition, generally entrusted to the *yeris* who kept them in the fortresses' arsenals near the border. To provide for the maintenance of the weapons, a sum was deducted from the soldiers' pay; in some cases the delivery of equipment included the payment of a small sum to be allocated to the cult fund.[229]

The call to arms took place through the gathering of the *sancaks* (banners), which formed a procession led by the *paşas* through the inhabited centres of the province. The formation of the contingents took the name of *cemaat*. This word also means the gathering of the contingents for the war. During these ceremonies, further volunteers could be recruited and welcomed into the corps of the *segmen* infantry. They represented the second infantry *speciality* of

227 In Albania this custom survived until the beginning of the twentieth century. See W. Peinsipp, *Das Volk des Skipetar* (Graz-Vienna; Böhlau Verlag, 1985), p.203.
228 K.u.K. Kriegsarchiv, *Feldzüge des Prinzen Eugen*, vol. I, p.526.
229 Marsigli, vol. II, p.6.

28. *Azab* 1660–90. *Azab* of the Hungarian *beglerbeglik*, 1660–80. The *azab* infantry wore the dress of their country of origin. Montecuccoli and Marsigli relate that the Ottoman *azabs* of Hungary and the Imperial bordersmen *hayduk* wore the same clothing and carried similar weapons. (Author's illustration)

the *serhaddkulu*. The terms *segmen* (also *sekban* or *segban*) identify several types of soldiers and militia. Except for the janissary *segmen* category, in the seventeenth century there were further two types of *segmens*. The first were often hired by provincial *paşas* and *begs*, and were the troops used against the state in what are known as the *celali* rebellions. The second type of seventeenth century *segmen* were irregular auxiliary troops recruited to fill the manpower needs of the Ottoman military. These troops were also referred to as *sarıca*, and are the *segmen* who are found in frontier garrisons. In the Ottoman sources, the *segmen* militia sometimes appear under the name *yaya* or *peyade*, which simply means soldier on foot. These soldiers were initially used in the retinues of local governors, but the need for musket-carrying men in the army led to their use in garrisons and on campaign. *Segmens* performed many of the same roles as *azab* troops and were usually recruited by a janissary officer, usually a *çavuş*, sent out to the province or district. Landless men would be taken into the new units, and would be promised pay from the central treasury. The officer would carry with him an order from the sultan authorising the enlistment of *raya* peasants. The presence of the *segmens* in the army was decided depending on the emergency, and in fact, they were very similar to a levy en masse.[230] It is also notable that the *segmens* were recruited in all parts of the Empire, and that men of varied backgrounds were enlisted, including Christians. Marsigli writes that 'Turks, Greeks (namely Muslims and Orthodox Christians) and Catholics,' all served as *segmen* soldiers.[231] Ottoman sources also refer to large numbers of Christian *segmens* among the siege forces at Vienna in 1683.[232] The sources agree that Muslim *segmens* were more trusted than Christian ones, and there is evidence that some units defected to the enemy.

Each *segmen* unit had a force of 60 men and took the name *bayrak* (ensign): the command was entrusted to a *segmen bolük-basi*, with a *bayrakdar* (ensign bearer) as a lieutenant. The two or more *bayraks* formed corps under the orders of the *serçesme*, a field officer designated by the governors of the province.

---

230 *Ibidem.*
231 *Ibidem*, vol. I, p.85.
232 I. Almond, *Two Faiths, One Banner: When Muslims Marched with Christians across Europe's Battlegrounds* (Cambridg, MS: Harvard University Press, 2011), pp.102–102.

Unfortunately, sources relating the strength of the *serhaddkulu* infantry are very scarce. Scholars who have investigated this matter have produced interesting works relating the number of the *serhaddkulu* troops in all, while the size of single specialities remain uncertain.[233] According to some hypotheses, the strength initially should at least be equal to the janissaries; but later, with the growing demand of infantry armed with firearms, the *azab* presence considerably increased in the field army. Much more difficult are the estimates of the *segmen* corps, which, like all irregular militias, was considered very summarily.

Recent investigation focusing on some fortresses in Hungary, shows several interesting details about these troops. *Azabs* often made up the largest single contingent in a fort. In smaller forts and *palankas* the entire garrison often was formed by *azab* troops. Payroll records show at least 12 and usually 15 *cemaats* of *azabs* assigned to the garrison of Kanisza, between 1621 and 1658, totalling between 660 and 850 men.[234] Close to half the garrison in these years were *azab* soldiers. On the other hand, Érsekúivár housed in the same period a smaller garrison, with fewer *azab* units. Extant records for the period of Ottoman control of the fort list only two *cemaats* totalling between 120 and 200 troops.[235]

However, the presence of both specialties must not have been marginal even in the war theatres where the janissaries operated. In fact, Marsigli defined the *azabs* as 'the nerve of the modern Ottoman infantry'.[236] Unfortunately, not even he was able to provide data on their numbers, since *azabs* and *segmens* did not depend on the central administration, but on the provinces and therefore were not registered on the *kanun-name*. In another part of his work, Marsigli stated that the strength of *segmens* was negligible, both regarding the number of the units and their level of preparation.[237]

Fig: delli archibuſieri pedoni delli Baſſá chiamati Seimeni.

29. *Segmen*, infantry militiaman, recruited in the Empire's provinces, mid seventeenth century. A speciality of the **serhaddkulu**, the **segmen** corps constituted a reserve territorial infantry however, the same terms identified the mercenaries recruited by local notables and even by tributary princes of Moldavia and Wallachia. Note the double powder flask, the ammunition bag carried on the breast, and the gaiter-bends at the legs. (Illustration from Hieronymus Beck's *Figurae calamo exaratae variorum Turcarum imperatorum*, late sixteenth century; Österreichisch Nationalbibliothek, Vienna)

---

233 Further details in the appendix.
234 Stein, *Guarding the Frontier*, p.77.
235 *Ibidem*.
236 Marsigli, vol. I, p.85.
237 *Ibidem*, vol. II, p.138.

According to coeval western sources, in the campaigns fought against the Imperialists in Hungary, until the loss of the *beglerbeglik* of Buda, the *azabs* recruited in the province numbered several times the figure of 9,000 men.[238] During the first siege of Buda, in 1684, almost 10,000 *serhaddkulu* infantrymen participated in the defence of the city; two thirds of whom were *azabs*. One year later, 2,000 men of the Hungarian *beglebeglik* formed the garrison of Érsekújvár.[239]

In 1686, inside the newly besieged Hungarian capital, some 6,000 *azabs* formed the garrison;[240] Buda's commander, Abdi Arnavut Abdurrhaman, also called to arms the civilian population, including non-Muslims.[241] In defending the Ottoman strongholds in Hungary, local *azab* and *segmen* infantrymen resisted until 1690, the year in which even the last major fortress in their possession fell into the hands of the Imperialists. After Érsekúivár, Nitra and Sárospatak in 1685, and Buda in 1686, also Simontomya, Pècs, Siklòs, and Kaposvár surrendered in 1686, then followed Pápa in 1687, Székesfehérvár, Peterwardein and Szeged in 1688, Szigetvár in 1689, Kanisza in 1690, and finally Várad in 1692, which marked the stages of the ill-fated Ottoman resistance in the Hungarian theatre. Isolated and without supplies, the garrisons surrendered one after the other. Marsigli found words of praise to remember the value of this militia, adding that its destruction was actual the cause of the 'collapse of Ottoman arms' in Hungary.[242]

Even in the nearby *paşalik* of Temeşvár, the *serhaddkulu* infantry was mobilised several times against the Imperialists. In the war of 1663–64, under their Pasha Ali, *serdar* of Transylvania, the local *azabs* were engaged in the occupation of the Carpathian principality. In 1696, when Temeşvár was subjected to an attempted siege by the Imperialists, the garrison included about 5,000 *azabs*.[243]

Finally, in 1716, when the city fell into enemy hands, almost half of the 18,000 defenders were represented by local militiamen. Even during the siege of Vienna in 1683, the *serhaddkulu* infantrymen joined the field army, and were thus used very far from their country of origin. Marsigli states the presence of 6,000 *serhaddkulu* infantry from Rumelia and Anatolia and nearly 20,000 Albanians and Bosnians.[244] It was not uncommon for the *azab* infantry, and especially for the *segmens*, to be used in actions destined to failure, as happened to the garrison of Esztergom in the aftermath of the defeat of Vienna, or in the desperate defence opposed in 1689 by the 1,000 *serhaddkulu* inside Viddin;[245] not entirely wrongly, the editors of the Austro-

238 Montecuccoli, 'Della Guerra contro il Turco', in Luraghi, *Opere di Raimondo Montecuccoli*, vol. II, p.396 and p.410.
239 Payer, *Armati Hungarorum*, p.111.
240 D'Aste, 'Diario dell'assedio di Buda', in Piacentini, *Diario dell'assedio e liberazione di Buda*, p.115.
241 *Ibidem*. The Italian officer relates the capture of a Hungarian deserter.
242 Marsigli, vol. II, p.151.
243 K.u.K. Kriegsarchiv, *Feldzüge des Prinzen Eugen*, vol. II, p.161.
244 Marsigli, vol. II, p.129.
245 *Ibidem*.

Hungarian *Kriegsarchiv* considered these troops as 'cannon fodder destined to be sacrificed.'[246]

Despite the poor results performed by this infantry, on the war fronts where the permanent troops were not present, the *serhaddkulu* formed the only infantry of the Ottoman armies. This is the case for *cemaat* raised against the Venetians in the Ionian and Peloponnese starting from 1684. According to the numerous reports compiled by the enemy officers, valuable information may be deduced regarding the composition of the Ottoman garrisons in Greece. The contingents formed by the inhabitants of the besieged fortresses are particularly interesting. After the surrender of Levkas, on 26 July 1684, to the 1,200 soldiers granted of free evacuation, more than 750 were those who left the city with their families;[247] a similar outcome occurred after the surrender of Prevesa, the following month, when 1,000 people followed the garrison after the capitulation. The Greek campaign of the 'Peloponnesian' Francesco Morosini represented for Venice the long-awaited opportunity to avenge the loss of Crete, but the Ottoman troops who opposed the Venetian army were not the veterans of Kandije. The rapid loss of the Peloponnese focused faults and weakness of the defensive system of the Porte. The *azabs* and the *segmens* raised by the local *paşas* to defend the Greek strongholds reached the considerable figure of 25,000 men,[248] but the fortresses fell one after another into the hands of the enemy. In 1687, the situation on this front became unsustainable: Corinth, Athens and other major strongholds were conquered by the Venetians with such ease as to surprise the same allied commanders. Thousands of Muslims fled from the Peloponnese and Attica.

Only in 1688 was it possible to re-establish a defence thanks to the reorganisation of the troops undertaken by the new Ottoman commander and the exhaustion of the Venetian offensive thrust. During the campaign of 1688 in Euboea, the *seraker* Ismail Paşa had formed under his command a *cemaat* of almost 10,000 well equipped and trained *serhaddkulu* infantrymen, who performed successfully in the defence of Negroponte. However, training and equipment of their men certainly constituted a serious problem for the Ottoman commanders, almost never able to obtain a homogeneous standard. The different quality of the troops became evident in field actions. While in Navarino Vecchia (today Pylos in Greece), in 1686, the garrison surrendered almost without a fight; the year before, in Corone, a garrison of 4,000 'well-armed soldiers' rejected the Venetian assaults for 57 days.[249] The definitive conquest of the city required a bitter home fight, which caused 'a great massacre among the defenders.'[250] Even more commendable was the behaviour of the Ottoman garrison of Menekşe (the Venetian Malvasia, today Monemvasia in Greece), who prolonged the defence until 1690, after

---

246 K.u.K. Kriegsarchiv, *Feldzüge des Prinzen Eugen*, vol. I, p.532.

247 C. Ciano, *Santo Stefano per Mare e per Terra* (Pisa: ETS, 1985), p.100: 'Relazione del conte Vandomi, Gran Priore del reggimento Mediceo'. The garrison included 500 Albanians and 400 Greeks.

248 Archivio di Stato di Venezia, Senato, *Mar – Dispacci di Provveditori*, da terra e da mar, f. 1123, n. 42, dated 12 August 1690.

249 Ciano 'Relazione Vandomi', p.106.

250 *Ibidem*.

30. Arnaut, Albanian footman;
early eighteenth century
(Jean-Baptiste van Moor,
*Recueil de cent estampes
représentant les diverses
nations du Levant*).

almost two years of bitter siege. When the fortress surrendered, the Venetian commander Girolamo Corner informed the Senate that the garrison still numbered 1,200 soldiers, but only 300 were capable of bearing arms.[251]

Another siege in which the resilience of the Ottomans stood out was the prolonged defence of Kamieniec, in Podolia, which lasted from November 1674 to September 1676. The 6,000 –strong garrison successfully opposed the long Polish siege, although not always conducted with the same energy.[252] Operations were interrupted in December 1673, to restart the following spring and finally end with the cold season. The truce signed in Żurawno ended the attempts to seize the stronghold. Kamienec represented a goal of conquest even in the successive War of the Holy League, but its mighty walls did not undergo further assaults. Kamieniec returned to the sovereignty of Poland with the treaty of Carlowitz, but it was a victory of diplomacy.

Among the sieges that ended between alternate events and concluded only after several attempts was that of Azov in the Crimea. From 1686, the year in which the Russians joined the Holy League, the fortress represented the main goal of their offensive against the Porte. But the resolving effort came only in 1697, when Tsar Peter I himself directed the assault on the fortress. Although Azov was included within the confines of the Crimean Tatar khanate, the Ottomans possessed the fortress since 1641, after they reconquered it from the Cossacks, and maintained there a strong garrison, which included *kapikulu* infantry as well as *serrhadkulu* troops. After the fall of Azov, another fortress was built to guard the Black Sea. The new fortification was erected at Atsu, at the mouth of the Kuban river, with a garrison under the orders of a *sancakbeg*.[253]

The Ottoman *azabs* clashed once again with the Tsar's soldiers in 1711, during the Russian invasion of Moldavia. In the autumn of 1710, the grand vizier had already mobilised 20,000 *serhaddkulu* infantry soldiers, and another 35,000 irregulars,[254] including engineers, diggers and other auxiliaries; among these troops there were also the bands of rough warriors from the mountains

251 Archivio di Sato di Venezia, *Provveditori da terra e da mar*, f.1123, n. 42, dated 12 August 1690. The Venetians captured 78 cannon, some of bronze, others of iron, as well as two mortars, ship's biscuit enough for some months, gunpowder, and various other pieces of military equipment.

252 Gierowski, *Da Chocim a Vienna*, p.19.

253 K.u.K. Kriegsarchiv, *Feldzüge des Prinzen Eugen*, vol. II, p.76.

254 Chandler, *The Art of Warfare*, p.74.

of Bosnia and Albania. Though they belonged to the *serhaddkulu* infantry, these 'Arnauts' (or Arnavuts) represented a separate category.

They were irregular footmen recruited only for a single campaign, but soon they were highly appreciated for their skill and loyalty. The Albanian presence in the Ottoman army had ancient roots and strengthened during this age. Several Albanians held important positions in the government and in the various places of the Empire. The family Köprülü came from Albania, as well as the *beglerbeg* of Buda, Koca Ibrahim, the unfortunate opponent of Kara Mustafa, and also the brave defender of the Hungarian capital, Abdi Arnavut Abdurrhaman, came from the country of the eagles. Initially, the Albanians who had reached positions of prestige entered the Ottoman service as *devşirme*, but throughout the seventeenth century further Albanians joined the armies attracted by the adventurous life and the possibilities of enrichment offered by the war. Strong links existed with the Albanian clans and the Köprülü, as proved on several occasions. In March 1664, in an attempt to replenish the human resources of the exhausted Ottoman army, Köprülü Ahmed sent a few of his Albanian *aga* officers to Albania to gather a mercenary troop of 1,000 infantrymen. The Albanian *ağas* offered a regular pay to the volunteers who accepted service in the army as long as the Ottoman forces campaigned in Hungary.[255] In the following months this newly-recruited military unit played a significant role in the siege of Zrínyivár and the battle of Szentgotthárd.

Most of the volunteers came from the southern regions of Albania and from Macedonia, where Islam had quickly taken root until it became the main religion of the region in the first half of the sixteenth century. However, Christians were not rare among the Arnauts.[256] The social structure of Albania, where the population was divided into clans similar to Scotland, allowed the expansion of mercenary careers.[257] In addition, the Porte was able to take

---

255 Kolçak, *The Composition, Tactics and Strategy of the Ottoman Field Army*, p.80: 'They were not enlisted in the personal household of Köprülü Ahmed and therefore, as can be deduced from the date of the payment, the Ottoman treasury delivered 500 *akçe* in advance for each mercenary, a sum most likely intended to cover initial expenses.'

256 Albanians also fought for Venice, along with the *schiavoni* units, belonging to the Roman Catholic or Greek Orthodox communities living in the regions between Scutari and Kotor. During the Cretan war, the Venetians tried to enlist the Albanians who served in the Ottoman army. However, also Albanians who were in the Venetian garrisons agreed to enter Ottoman service. Historians rarely compared the experience of these soldiers with those of the Swiss mercenaries, who fought contemporarily for more sides in the conflicts of Western Europe. 'In this ages, an Albanian shepherd or peasant knew no other way to get out of their humble condition and ascend on the social life, just the one offered by the profession of arms. For him, the job of mercenary meant not to serve a cause, but to measure and affirm his courage in battle. The only glory to which an Albanian aspired was the military one, which was the culmination of his virile life.' A. Consiglio, *Storia dell'Albania* (Florence, 1942), p.34.

257 For a discussion of the history of Albanian clans, see R. Elsie, *The Tribes of Albania: History, Society and Culture* (London, New York: I.B. Tauris, 2015). The author prefers to translate the primary Albanian patrilineal kinship-group concept of *fis* as 'tribe', though he acknowledges that the term also generally is, and can be, translated as 'clan'. Elsie distinguishes and describes altogether 74 discrete tribes (rather than '69 different tribes' according to the book cover), including semi-tribes and sub-tribes, in 11 separate chapters covering distinct areas within Northern Albania, and occasionally bordering areas in Southern Albania within the stats of Albania, Montenegro, Kosovo, Macedonia and Greece as well.

advantage of the rivalries among the local leaders by converting them as a recompense to buy their favour. Progressively the Albanian clans turned into *beglik*, in which the chief became a governor trusted by the sultan.

However, the Albanian scenario was not always idyllic for the Porte. Several uprisings occurred at the beginning of the seventeenth century. After the first riots and clashes in the north of the country in 1615, 10 years later the intervention of a Turkish army became necessary.[258] New disorders broke out in 1649 and 1683, led by the Christian clans. However, the larger part of the Albanians remained loyal to Constantinople: the major clans offered to the sultan contingents of thousands of soldies, also employed on fronts very far from their home locations.[259]

Thanks to some maps of Albania and Dalmatia made by the Venetian cartographer Francesco Maria Coronelli, we know the distribution of some garrisons formed by Arnauts and Ottomans around 1683. The information collected by the maps' author came from spies and merchants active in the region, and in view of the imminent war. The fortress with the most numerous garrison was Antivari, manned by 2,000 soldiers; then Ulcinj and the neighbouring villages deployed further 2,000 Arnauts in all; finally Grabalu, a wooden fortress on the mountain, had a garrison of 200 soldiers.[260]

The other region of the Balkans from which the Porte obtained many excellent soldiers was Bosnia, in particular the central northern territory, where adherence to Islam was favoured by the presence of the Bogumil sect.[261] Like the Albanians, numerous Bosnians held high offices in the Ottoman state, including grand viziers. Also the *serdar* Ibrahim, nicknamed *saitan* (the devil) for his elusiveness, was a native of Bosnia. The two soldiers who had bought Count Marsigli were Bosnian, and he followed them to the siege of Vienna as a personal servant. Albanians and Bosnians fought on almost all the fronts in which the Ottoman army operated, both indicated

---

258 In the spring of 1648 Venetian agents, in concert with general provveditor Lunardo Foscolo, contacted the majority of Durrës to plan an insurrection against the Ottoman garrison. The Albanians assured the Venetian emissaries that they could supply 10,000 men in arms, but at the decisive moment, the uprising was discovered, and all the conspirators executed. See Valiero, *Historia*, p.213.

259 According to Jean-Claude Faveyrial, the presence of Albanian soldiers in war theatres far from their settlements dated from the first half of the seventeenth century. The author refers to the arrival of 12,000 'Epirotes' in 1636 who joined the Ottoman army for the campaigns against the Persians in northern Iraq. The Albanians still carried their original Christian ensign with the image of Saint George: 'ayant [the Albanians] arboré le drapeau chrétien au fort d'une bataille contre les Persans, les généraux turcs s'en étaient trouvé offensés et en avaient écrit au sultan.' J.C. Faveyrial, *Histoire de l'Albanie* (Monastir, 1889), p.273.

260 F.M. Coronelli, 'L'Atlante Veneto', in L. Genovié, *L'Albania nella cartografia italiana dei secoli XVI e XVII* (Florence, Istituto Geografico Militare, 1940).

261 Bogumilism was a Christian neo-Gnostic or dualist sect founded in Bulgaria by the priest Bogomil in the tenth century. It most probably arose in what is today the region of Macedonia. The Bogomils called for a return to early spiritual teaching, rejecting the ecclesiastical hierarchy, and their primary political tendencies were resistance to the state and church authorities. This helped the movement spread quickly in the Balkans, gradually expanding throughout the Byzantine Empire and later reaching Ukraine and Bosnia, where itencountered a large diffusion and the creation of a Bogumil Church. Bogumilism found adepts also in Dalmatia, Italy and Serbia. In Bosnia, their condition as heretics favoured the passage of the Bogumil believers to Islam.

31. *Serhaddkulu* infantry, Bosnian foot soldier, 1715.

According to a coeval eyewitness, there were few differences between the dress of the Slavic population who sided with Venice and those under the Porte, except for the headdress, which for the latter was the classic turban. White cotton turban with black velvet *kavuk* cap; black *jacerma* doublet with white metal accessories; red *koret* short jacket with black piping; buttons, *kov* and *tucle* of pewter; dark orange sash, *benevreci* breeches of white linen, black *tozluci* gaiters with red embroidery and pieces of glass; *opanke* shoes in natural leather with grey stockings. (Author's reconstruction after Gravenboch, Tilke and contemporary prints; early eighteenth century, *tançitsa* musket, traditional Albanian–Bosnian pattern, Museo de Armas, Lima, Perù; seventeenth century Venetian *Schiavona* sword, Museo Correr, Venice)

in the Western sources as Arnauts. Montecuccoli encountered Albanians and Bosnians as enemies at the battle of Szentgotthárd, and quoted them among the 'chosen militias'.[262] In the War of the Holy League in 1682–99, the Ottoman commanders enlisted several thousand of these volunteers in an attempt to contain their enemies in Hungary, Greece and the Balkans. The most significant contribution came from 1689, during the years when the Imperialists were advancing in the Balkans, and occupied part of Bulgaria and northern Albania. The Arnauts answered enthusiastically the grand vizier's appeal. Their presence is mentioned at Nissa (1689) and in the reconquest of Belgrade (1690), then at Slankamen (1691). They distinguished themselves particularly in the disturbing actions against the Imperialists in Bosnia and in Serbia, where the Arnauts were even mounted on horseback to undertake the warfare of the Ottoman border irregulars.

In those years, while the regular army indulged in disorders and palace struggles, these mercenaries represented the only force on which to rely for every action. The Porte recruited additional troops in the course of the campaign starting from 1688. Their enlistmentment provided the payment of salary in advance and consequently it affected the financial policy of the Porte in this critical age. Years before, the Ottoman treasury paid a monthly allowance of 271,800 *akçe* for 906 foot soldiers summoned from the province of Rumelia.[263] The unit was divided into 18 companies, each commanded by a *bölükbaşı* (captain) and three subordinate officers: *bayrakdar* (standard bearer), *ser-oda* (lieutenant), *çavuş*, NCO.

Many Turks, Albanians, and especially Islamised Slavs who had settled in Hungary, emigrated to the northern regions of Bosnia following the loss of the province. After 1690, the Porte favoured the settlement of these populations to fill the void left by the over 200,000 Serbs fleeing the regions returned to Ottoman rule.[264] Thanks to this transfer of peoples, the Ottomans were able to recruit a first-rate light infantry, motivated and experienced in the frontier war. The new troops were used against Venice and the Habsburgs when the battlefield moved to the Sava and the Drina rivers in the conflict of 1714–1718. In the winter of 1715–1716, the Bosnian *paşa* gathered 4,000 infantrymen in Travnik, the same number in Livno, a further 2,000 in Lubno and 1,000 in Glamoc. In July, 7,000 foot soldiers took the camp near Banjaluka and another 3,000 in Zvomik.[265] Further north, the Serdar Demir Ali could oppose the Venetians with at least 12,000 Bosnian and Albanian infantry; as many forces guarded the border with Croatia and Dalmatia along the fortified

262 Montecuccoli, 'Della Guerra contro il Turco', in Luraghi, *Opere di Raimondo Montecuccoli*, vol. II, p.446.

263 Kolçak, *The Composition, Tactics and Strategy of the Ottoman Field Army*, p.80: 'The number of company officers suggests there was tight control of the soldiers; a company of approximately 50 warriors was commanded by at least two officers. Most probably, the mercenary cavalry was even smaller in numbers; again a corps of four officers commanded a division of nearly 37 mounted soldiers. It appears that the mercenary units and probably the units recruited for pasha households alike, were well-adjusted for positional warfare where the infantry units equipped with muskets played a key role.'

264 Matuz, *Das Osmanische Reich*, p.188.

265 K.u.K. Kriegsarchiv, *Feldzüge des Prinzen Eugen*, vol. XVII, p.253.

places in the region. The fortress of Novj, assaulted by Croatian *Grenzer* in August 1716, repulsed the enemy; less fortunate was the defence of Lesica, on the Drina, which was conquered and then destroyed by the Imperial frontiersmen. The local garrison comprised 'three banners of Bosnians and the same number of Albanians'.[266] The same destiny fell upon Derbent, in September 1716. Other encounters involved the frontiersmen of both sides at Brod, Gradiska, Mirolam and Dobor. Often, these kinds of actions were carried out by a few hundred soldiers, whose goal was some *palanka*,[267] old fortresses built on the top of a hill or by cattle in enemy territory,[268] but in July of 1718, while the conference of Passarowitz was already ending, the *serasker* Mustafa Paşa led 4,000 Albanian and Bosnian infantry against the Venetians who were leaving the siege of Ulcinj.[269] The Arnauts also fought at Belgrade. Despite the uncertainty over the figures dating back to the preliminary phases of the campaign, the Austro-Hungarian Kriegsarchiv estimated at least 5–6,000 Albanians and Bosnians would have arrived in Smedarevo on 27 July 1717, while a further 2,000 Bosnians had been in the city since the start of the summer.[270]

Halfway between the provincial force and the native troops, it is necessary to remember the *martolos* (from the Greek 'Αρματολός' or men-at-arms), employed alongside the units of *kapikulu* and *serhaddkulu* in the repression of brigandage or internal revolts.[271] Despite the rhetoric of both the Ottomans and their Western enemies portraying their conflict as a religious one, there were Christians willing to serve the Porte fighting against their co-religionists. Although the rank and file of the *martolos* units were Christian, the officers were Muslims. The leader of the *martolos* in a fort was called *martolos ağası* or *martolos başı*. In the early years of Ottoman rule in Hungary some of these officers were granted *timar* revenues. Like the other infantry specialities of the *serhaddkulu*, *martolos* units were called *cemaat* and were subdivided into *odas*, each comprising between five and 10 men and commanded by a *ser oda*. By the seventeenth century, *martolos* units are listed with a more elaborate officer corps. Payroll records for Hungarian fortresses list *cemaats* with an *ağa*, a *kethüda* and an *alemdar*. Contingents as small as 16 *martolos* are recorded with six officers.[272] All the senior officers were Muslims, but the *ser odas* could be Christians. These troops played an important part in the frontier defences of the Ottoman Empire, particularly in Hungary and Bosnia, and were engaged against bandits and other outlaws. However, their loyalty to the Ottoman lordship did not always remain constant. The most important event that involved *martolos* coming from Bosnia, was the expedition against the

---

266 *Ibidem*, p.256.
267 Wooden fortifications, usually of small dimensions, which are discussed later.
268 The cattle were the target of the encounter of Brod, fought on 8 August 1716. K.u.K. Kriegsarchiv, *Feldzüge des Prinzen Eugen*, vol. XVII, p.253.
269 *Ibidem*, p.260.
270 *Ibidem*, p.54.
271 Forms of the word are found in Bulgarian, Serbian, and Hungarian. Despite its Greek origin, it is interesting that the term itself is not securely documented in the Greek sources until the eighteenth or early nineteenth centuries.
272 Stein, *Guarding the Frontier*, p.90.

Montenegrins of the *vladika* Danilo I Petrovic, who in 1711 joined the Russian tsar and launched a series of attacks against the villages of Herzegovina and Albania. Although not registered in the *serhaddkulu* corps, the *martolos* are often confused with it.

Hisar-Erleri

As discussed in the section dedicated to the permanent army, the *kapikulu* artillerymen were joined on campaign by auxiliary personnel. These troops belonged to the *serhaddkulu* and were called *hisar-erleri* (or *hisar eri* or even *hisarli*). Originally, a certain number of men was mobilised as personnel of the artillery train or to serve as artillerymen in the fortresses for replacing the *topçu* when these latter joined the field army, no differently to what happened with *azabs* and janissaries. Though the *hisar-erleri*s were essentially garrison gunners, gradually they also took part in field operations. The Ottoman payroll refers to these troops as *müstahfız* when in garrison, and this term derives from Arabic and means one 'who appoints one to defend a place' or more simply 'defender'. Information from seventeenth-century sources helps to provide a fuller understanding of the role of the *müstahfız* corps in Ottoman garrisons. Each detachment of *hisar-erleri-müstahfız* served under the local *dizdar* appointed by the province governor. They served under a *topçu odabasi* artilleryman who was assisted by a variable number of non-commissioned officers, called *bolükbasi*, having the function of constables and adjutants. They acted also as specialised craftsman and made repairs to the walls and defensive works when necessary. Because of the importance of artillery in fortress defence, they worked closely with the *topçu* units, who also served under the supervision of the *dizdar* when in garrison.[273]

It is very hard, even approximately, to establish the strength of this speciality. Documents from Kanisza show that there were usually between 80 and 90 *müstahfız* artillerymen in the *cemaat* assigned to the garrison.[274] However, when the *hisar-erleri*s joined the army their number was confused with the one of the *kapikulu* artillerymen. According to the Ottoman list of the troops available on 7 September at Vienna, about 4,000 *serhaddkulu* artillerymen would have joined the Ottoman field army on campaign.[275]

Marsigli stated that in all the fortresses there were artillerymen of the *serhaddkulu*, and to establish the number to enlist, the commander or the *dizdar* took into account the calibre and the quantity of guns of the stronghold where they were required.[276] In relation to the number of artillery pieces at the fortresses and on the basis of the records of eyewitnesses, it is possible to reconstruct the number of *hisar-erleri*s mobilised on some fronts. The first defence of a city of considerable size was undoubtedly the one sustained in

---

273 *Ibidem*, p.87. The authors state that some Ottoman sources say the *müstahfız* did not have to leave the fort to join the army on campaign.
274 *Ibidem*, p.88.
275 *Kurtze Erzehlung*, pp.78–79.
276 Marsigli, vol. I, p.127.

Buda in 1684. On that occasion, Marsigli outlined how the artillery of the defenders outnumbered that of the besiegers, and this would have caused the Imperialists' failure.[277] Probably, there were also many *topçus* of the *kapikulu* within the city, since two years later, in the second Imperialist attempt, the *beglerbeg* of Buda was able to deploy only two batteries with just 200 men. In early July, Baron Michele D'Aste wrote that three weeks after the siege began, 'the enemy does not respond with his cannon, but [only] with 10 mortars.'[278] Evidence of the diminished effectiveness of the Ottoman artillery fire is confirmed by the low casualties suffered by the besiegers: in fact, 'many of the artillery shots had gone high.'[279] The explosion of the castle's ammunition depot, on 22 July, accelerated the surrender of the city.

The explosion of the artillery depot was one of the central episodes also in the siege of Athens in 1687. The Ottomans first demolished the Temple of Athena Nike to erect a cannon battery, and on 25 September, a Venetian cannonball exploded a powder magazine in the Propylaea. Even worst the damage suffered by the Parthenon. The Ottoman used the temple for ammunition storage, and when, on the evening of 26 September 1687, a mortar shell hit the building, the resulting explosion killed 300 people and led to the complete destruction of the temple's roof and most of the walls.

On other occasions, the performance provided by the *serhaddkulu* artillerymen was more satisfactory. During the siege of Belgrade, in 1693, and Bihac, in 1697, a few hundred well-directed artillerymen fought bravely and, particularly in Bihac, guaranteed the success of the defence.[280] In the autumn of 1710, about 7,000 artillerymen destined for the field army in Moldavia, including those of the *kapikulu*, were mobilised for war against Russia.[281]

As usual, war remained endemic on the borders, and even after the Truce of Carlowitz several encounters engaged the two sides, forcing the Porte to maintain the presence of these reservists.[282] The sieges of the two last major strongholds of the Hungarian–Balkan theatre, namely Temeşvár and Belgrade, once again saw the *hisar-erleri*s engaged in the defence of the places. In 1716, at Temeşvár, the fire of the Ottoman mortars and cannons was particularly accurate in the opening phase of the siege, then the Imperial artillery deployed its power and forced the defenders to withdraw their guns.[283] However, even after the loss of the external *palanka*, on the night between 1 and 2 October, the mortars continued to fire without rest against

277 Marsigli, vol. II p.152.
278 D'Aste, 'Diario dell'assedio di Buda', in Piacentini *Diario dell'assedio e liberazione di Buda*, p.134.
279 *Ibidem*, p.137.
280 K.u.K. Kriegsarchiv, *Feldzüge des Prinzen Eugen*, vol. II, p.108.
281 Chandler, *The Art of Warfare*, p.74.
282 Many examples of such behaviour exist with reference to the Balkan borders. For instance, the Habsburgs behaved in this way after the Treaty of Carlowitz, during the talks for the new Venetian–Ottoman–Imperial border. On 10 June 1699, about 1,000 horse and 500 Imperial foot marched against the fortress of Zuonigrad and asked it to surrender. After a refusal, they attacked it, whereas only three artillery shots could be made from the walls; 100 Imperial soldiers got into the fortress through a breach and took possession of the building, which they would possess even after the border agreement. See M.P. Pedani, 'The Ottoman-Venetian Border, 15th–18th Centuries', in *Hilal – Studi Turchi e Ottomani* (Venice: Edizioni Ca' Foscari, 2017), p.60.
283 K.u.K. Kriegsarchiv, *Feldzüge des Prinzen Eugen*, vol. XVI, p.201.

the Imperial soldiers who had penetrated inside. After the surrender of the city, the Imperial commissars registered the capture of 48 guns, 10 mortars and 10 howitzers; a further 80 pieces were damaged. In overall, the number of *herar-erleri*s who fought at Temeşvár rose to 1,000 men. One year later, the artillery personnel inside Belgrade were less numerous and not as well trained: the Imperial artillery reduced the Ottoman batteries to silence in a few days, and the servants paid with their lives for the unbridgeable military gap. The belonging of the *hisar-erleri*s to the garrison of a fortress coincided with their residence in the city itself and this happened more often than in the other specialties of the *serhaddkulu*.

Compared to all the members of the corps, the *hisar-erleri* belonged to a more qualified group of personnel and among them served a significant percentage of non-Muslims, including many renegades of all nationalities. The Porte sought in various ways to removet specialised military personnel from their enemies, and effectively the desertions of Christian technicians constituted a fairly frequent phenomenon. Many renegades were Italian and southern French sailors, but there were also Dutch, Maltese and even Scandinavians.[284] Even a minimal professional experience could guarantee a better standard of living than the one left behind at home. If skill and shrewdness were combined with the spirit for the adventure, it was not uncommon to find dizzying ascents of these deserters into the highest offices of the Empire.

Lağımcı – Miners

The wars fought in Europe in the seventeenth and eighteenth centuries were marked by sieges much more than field battles. Even the conflicts between the Ottomans and Christians saw their respective armies engaging in a large number of siege operations, which almost always constituted the primary objective of a campaign. To this end, in the Ottoman army had been established corps of engineers and miners, usually recruited among the Christian populations of Asia and Balkan Europe, to be employed as skilled personnel for all the works required in a siege. This speciality was composed of a variable number of miners, called *lağımcı*s, recruited directly in the region close to the war theatre, or in the Empire's provinces from the governors. Each squad of miners obeyed a *lağımcısbasi*, who was also the technical director of his men. The activities were organised as in a normal construction site: team leaders were named, turns were organised and compensation was paid for particular jobs. In 1645, the year of the Ottoman invasion of Crete, the *lağımcı*s were used in large numbers for the sieges of the island fortresses. At the beginning of the campaign there were 30,000 Armenian auxiliary workers with the army that besieged Chaniá, and at least half were miners.[285] The number increased with further miners and diggers

284 In 1709, when the army of Charles XII of Sweden took refuge in Moldavia after the defeat suffered at Poltava, some Swedish privates and NCOs agreed to enter Ottoman service. See also Seaton-Watson, *Histoire des Roumains*, p.106.
285 P. Morachiello, *Candia: i baluardi del Regno*, in 'Venezia e la Difesa del Levante, p.139.

recruited among the islands' population. They experienced the war of mines in Kandije through a spectacular offensive effort between 1648–1649 and 1667–1669. The Armenians were considered the most skilled miners in the Empire, and for this reason they were much sought after, but together with them also Serbs and Bulgarians occasionally provided personnel for this task, as well as miners from central Anatolia.

The salaries received were high, but the life in the mine was very hard. In the years of the siege of Kandije, the Venetians sought by all means to face the enemy's underground activity, not least by the use of poison. The *lağımcı* were the most exposed and less-surveyed personnel, and soon became the target for the strangest and most nauseating devices spread in water and food destined for them.[286] Along the poison there were the countermeasures thought up by the defenders. In the defence of Kandije, the Venetians demonstrated a great ability to intercept the enemy works, causing the collapse of numerous mines. Kandije represented for many years the greatest siege carried out by the Ottoman *lağımcıs* and contributed to the development of a working method adopted also in subsequent years. Marsigli succeeded in questioning some 'Armenian masons' who had taken part in the siege of 1667–69. From them he obtained much information about the techniques employed and about other aspects of the life in the mine; this is their testimony:

> … to measure the distance to the curtain, which they (the miners) wanted to ruin, they entrusted a capable and daring miner, who had a stone attached to a cord, and in the night, where they had decided to open the tunnel, he threw the stone to the wall and then cut the superfluous cord … then he measured the distance, calculating the remaining feet.[287]

The extreme simplicity of the technique was functional to the speed of execution requested in this kind of action. Usually the galleries were very narrow, no more than 'half-man', but the dimensions facilitated the construction of the explosion chamber. To maintain the right direction they used goals made with wooden poles, whose direction was indicated by a candle placed at the beginning of the tunnel. For air, they provided themselves with augers to make holes. The Armenian interlocutors of the Count admitted the great dangers of

286 On 22 March 1645, even before the war began, a Venetian merchant suggested an expedient to 'destroy and annihilate the enemies' with poison. Periodically the Venetian officials sent letters requesting poisons to be used against the Ottomans. In June 1646 Dalmatia's provveditor, Lunardo Foscolo, urgently asked for 'poison at time' to be thrown into the wells near the besieged Novigrad. In the meantime he tried himself to prepare some poison, which did not cause serious damage. At the end of the month, he used 1,000 pounds of arsenic 'to harm the enemy in the use of water'. Then, in July, a box containing poisons finally arrived from Venice, but in the meantime Novigrad had surrenderd. Seven years later, Foscolo again left an extensive report on the stratagem devised to pollute the wells of the Ottomans in Crete. Implacable, Foscolo proposed the use of the poisons prepared by the physician Michiel Angelo Salomone, to dip 'Albanian caps' and other clothing to be issued in the enemy camp. By way of curiosity, the substance had been obtained with 'a liqueur made from bile, bubos and sick coals combined with other ingredients'. *Ibidem*, note at page 94.
287 Marsigli, vol. II, p.37.

this work, but the wages they received were high and the miners received extra prizes for every mine successfully carried out.

The same technique used in Kandije was revived in Vienna. During the two months of siege, the effort sustained by the miners was considerable, and in comparison with Kandije, the success was even greater, because the countermeasures put in place by the defenders were much less effective than those devised by the Venetians. In the opening phase of the siege, the Imperialists intercepted and destroyed just two mines. The ravelins of the Burg and Löbel bastions, with the counterscarps between them, were the targets against which eight mines were exploded in just 13 days. Rain delayed the Ottoman miners' progress, but the advance continued and culminated in mid August, when the external defence of the Burg bastion collapsed after three well-placed mines exploded simultaneously. From there the Ottomans penetrated into the chambers under the *Hofburg*, which became a battlefield of terrifying fights in the darkness. At the end of the siege, more than 40 mines had exploded in both sectors, and 11 were failed attempts.[288]

After Vienna, the *lağımcıs* had no other opportunity to take advantage of their art, as the Ottoman army did not undertake sieges of considerable proportions for over 30 years. The last operation of any importance was the siege of Corfu, in July–August 1716. The assault, conducted with great deployment of forces, concentrated against the external defence of the *Fortezza Nuova* and continued up to the curtain, which became the main target of the Ottoman mines.[289] The Venetians lost an advanced defence and an entrenchment, but their sorties destroyed the works of the enemies and on more than one occasion: 'the Turks, so superior in strength, did not know how to take advantage of the success obtained. They lacked neither the value nor the number, they lacked art.'[290] Too much time had elapsed since, under the light of a candle and under metres of terrain, the veterans of Crete and Vienna had aroused the admiration of the world for the speed and audacity of their enterprises.

Musellim – Engineers and Pioneers

In the same way as the miners, personnel were also recruited for the excavation of the trenches and other necessary carpentry and building works. These workers belonged to the *musellim* of the *serhaddkulu*, and mainly came from the Christian populations of the Empire. In the *beglerbeglik* of Anatolia, 17 *sancakbegs* were called *musellimleri* and, together with two others in Rumelia, they had the task of recruiting these specialised personnel. The workers obeyed a chief designated by the governors of the districts where they enlisted, ranked with title of *musellimbasi*. In every campaign, the *musellims* contributed not a little to increase the number of the army. Whenever the main army assembled, the vanguard travelled the planned

---

288 Hammer-Purgstall, *Geschichte des Osmanischen Reiches*, vol. XII, p.103.
289 Prelli, Mugnai, *L'Ultima Vittoria della Serenissima*, p.117.
290 K.u.K. Kriegsarchiv, *Feldzüge des Prinzen Eugen*, vol. XVII, p.267.

route in advance and provided an escort to the *musellims* who had to restore the roads, to reinforce bridges or even build new ones when the situation demanded. However, sieges were the operations that required the highest number of *musellims*. Though the infantry was engaged in the excavation of the approach trenches, and sometimes even the cavalry, in every siege thousands of auxiliary engineers made the soldiers' work less hard.

As an eyewitness in the campaign of Vienna, Marsigli related on the arrival of *musellims* and soldiers into the trenches. He stated that the janissaries did not show great commitment to the excavation tools, while the *musellim* progressed rapidly. Marsigli claimed that the Christians wanted to humiliate the proud soldiers of the sultan and for this reason, a sort of rivalry had been triggered among them.[291] To instil courage in the workers and keep up the morale of the infantry, the commanders offered prizes for the achievement of a goal. A typical oriental atmosphere reigned in the trenches: tobacco sellers, servants and coffee makers offered their wares to the soldiers, 'since it would have been impossible to make him accept the job without these comforts.'[292] Marsigli again explains how the Ottoman trenches were less deep than those usually made by the Christian armies, not due to negligence or laziness, but due to the habit of the Turks to work seated with crossed legs. Even the repairs were much lower compared to the Western ones, and judging by the name, these should not have been acceptable even to the Ottomans, who in fact called them *domuz dami* (pigsty). The schematic pattern of the approaches was composed of a main trench, called *meteris*, which constitutes the parallel, from which started the winding approaches perpendicular to the walls, called in an equally picturesque way, *sicari yolu*, translatable as 'mouse path'. At the end of the parallels it was customary to dig a semicircle to build a firing place for the muskets. As excavations progressed from the lower part, other trenches were used for communication between the approaches. According to Marsigli, the Ottoman trenches did not conveniently protect soldiers and workers from enemy fire, and this occurred because of the poor direction of the works.[293] Whether it was the merit of the officers or not, the allied officers who inspected the Ottoman trenches at Vienna, after the decisive battle of 12 September, extensively praised the work of the besiegers. Despite the apparent complexity, the system of approaches and parallels fit perfectly on the terrain. The defenders' sorties were hindered not only by the soft soil due to the excavations, but above all by the network of trenches, as successfully exploited at Kandije.[294]

Usually the command of the *musellim* corps was entrusted to the janissary officers, but they were not always sufficiently trained on the recent techniques developed in Western countries. However, despite the many critics, the

---

291 Marsigli, vol. I,. p.97.
292 *Ibidem*, vol. II, p.133
293 *Ibidem*, p.140: 'There is nothing more disproportionate to see than these approaches, so tortuous and unequally deep … as effects of the lack of skilled commanders for these works, and because the janissaries work without guidance of a line of faggots or other item, and therefore they proceed tortuously.'
294 J. Stoye, *The Siege of Vienna*, p.214.

32. Armenian *lağimçi* miner, early eighteenth century. The fur-trimmed cap is a typical Anatolian headdress and essentially this Armenian 'architect' wears a dress no different to that worn by Ottoman civilians.

Ottoman trenches turned out to be as effective in countering the opposing sorties. Marsigli mentions the inextricable labyrinth of parallels and approaches in Kandije that had trapped the French soldiers when they attempted the great sortie of June 1669. Similar difficulties met the Imperials in Belgrade, on the morning of 16 August 1717, during the assault on the encampment of the Ottoman relief army.

During the sieges, the *musellims* worked also under the direction of the artillery officers, digging and building the cannon batteries. To carry out these works, a high point was preferably chosen behind the first line of the parallels, because once the guns were positioned, the Ottoman artillerymen did not try to advance towards the enemy walls.[295] The large calibres allowed only a modest mobility and even the smallest pieces could not be moved quickly due to the intricacy of the trenches. For this reason, the preparation of the battery required a considerable initial effort to ensure the best possible position for cannons and mortars. The huge battery built for the siege of Érsekújvár in 1663 occupied an area of 2,000 square metres and almost 10,000 Serbian and Hungarian *musellims* were used to build it. Equally impressive was the battery built under the *serasker* Kara Mustafa before Chirigin in 1678, during the campaign against the Ukrainian Cossacks. Both episodes were remembered as the most significant even by Count Marsigli.[296] These great works suffered a certain decline due to the progress achieved by mining techniques; however the *musellims* continued to support the troops when the conditions of the ground did not allow the use of the *lağımcıs*, just as happened at Érsekújvár, which was surrounded by an extensive swamp.

The Ottomans generally used thousands of gabions filled with earth, stones, or other material during their sieges, and they were able to protect their advancing sapper parties with elaborate tactics, alternating gabions and trenches. By stacking a couple of layers of gabions, Ottoman besiegers obtained an effective system to provide elevation, often matching the height of the opposing walls. In the last phase of the siege of Kandije, the Ottoman *musellims* built a cavalier before the bastion that protected the haven's access, in order to target the supply ships. From the top of these artificial hills, the Ottoman artillery could comfortably shoot at point-blank ranges. Casualties

295 This tactic was not the same as in the last phase of the siege of Kandije, when the Ottoman artillery supported the advance of the approaches with the close fire of the cannons. Evidently this tactic caused high losses and was therefore no longer employed.
296 Marsigli, vol. II, p.132.

were high, but the Ottomans managed after weeks of 'tremendously tiresome work', to build up a platform of 'astonishing height'.[297]

The Ottoman commanders continued to employ the *musellims* not only to restore roads and bridges, but also to build temporary defensive works or to destroy those of their enemies. In almost all the clashes that took place after 1686, in Hungary and the Balkans, the Turkish commanders directed their engineers' work in the construction of shelters for the troops on foot. At Eszék (today Osijek in Croatia), Harsány, Nissa, Slankamen, Ollaschin and Zenta, the Ottoman infantry fought behind the entrenchments dug with the work of the *musellims*.[298] Also in 1716 and in 1717 the Ottoman commanders protected their encampments with powerful ramparts, both at Peterwardein and Belgrade. The gathering of the armies required months of preparation and, once the assembled contingents started up, their marches proceeded with great slowness.

The crossing of a river and the need of bridges to cross it caused many delays. The practice of equipping convoys with pontoons and mobile bridges was in fact unknown to the Ottomans, who adopted it only in the late seventeenth century. According to the Austro-Hungarian War Archive, the first Ottoman pontoons appeared in 1696, when they mounted French-style pontoons for crossing the Temes River.[299] One year later, under the direction of a 'Genoese renegade' pontoons on boats were used to cross the Theiss River before the battle of Zenta. In the 1683 campaign, 10 wooden bridges were built on the Raba river, and an equal number on the Rabnitz river, to allow the large army of Kara Mustafa to reach Vienna. The Ottoman commanders made up for their technological handicap with the ease of mobilising a labour force. Nevertheless, stable bridges required the presence of soldiers, as happened on the same campaign, when Kara Mustafa was forced to leave the *beglerbeg* of Hungary with a strong corps of infantry and artillery to guard the bridges at Eszék, and later the ones on the Raba River. Even when the *beglerbeg* marched to join the besieging army before Vienna, the bridges passed into the control of the Grand Prince of Transylvania's troops. Obviously, the loss of bridges constituted a source of danger for every army, and certainly, Kara Mustafa knew the problems caused in 1664 by the Imperialist *Grenzer* under Miklós Zrínyi, who destroyed the poorly surveyed Ottoman wooden bridges near Eszék with sudden cavalry assaults.

Though the building of new bridges was preferred, the Ottomans resorted to local resources for crossing the rivers with improvised pontoons when their work force was unavailable. This occurred during the siege of Vienna, on 3 August 1683, when all the boats found in Klosterneuburg and Nussdorf were moved along the *Donaukanal* in order to arrange a passage to replace the bridge burned by the defenders days before.[300] The Ottomans built another improvised bridge on boats at Párkány across the Danube, which on

---

297 G. Brusoni, *Historia dell'Ultima Guerra tra Veneziani e Turchi* (Venice, 1673), Libro IX, p.208.

298 Marsigli, vol. II, p. 132.

299 K.u.K. Kriegsarchiv, *Feldzüge des Prinzen Eugen*, vol. II, p.87. According to Marsigli, the Ottomans would have employed the first pontoon on boats in the campaign of 1697.

300 Hammer-Purgstall, *Geschichte des Osmanisches Reiches*, vol. XII, p 101.

9 October 1683 proved to be of very bad quality, because it ruined the critical phase of the retreat and sealed the Imperial–Polish victory.[301]

Perhaps also for this, the practice of built bridges *ex-novo* was not completely interrupted, however, in the eighteenth century, pontoons became a stable military device also in the Ottoman army, which was finally able to master this technology. In 1710, about 1,500 *musellims* were enlisted for the campaign in Moldavia, expressly entrusted with the service of pontoons on boats.[302] Six years later Grand Vizier Damad Ali Paşa ordered the building of two stable bridges on the Danube near Visnika, downstream of Belgrade, and another at Semlin on the Sava river, to allow the passage of the army that would fight against the Imperialists at Peterwardein. On that occasion, about 3,000 workers were employed in this task. However, although the pontoons came together with the field army train they were not used.[303] During the campaign of 1717, about 2,000 *musellims* transported pontoons on boats from Viddin to Belgrade following the relief army, and were sighted by Imperial reconnaissance in mid July.[304]

Other characteristic achievements of the *musellims* were the wooden fortresses, known as *palanka* and *kale*, placed to control the vast European frontier of the Ottoman Empire. In its essential lines, the *palanka* was an elevated fort, enclosed within a ditch and preferably built on the top of a hill, or protected by a stream or a swamp. The same defences were built in the opposite field, especially in Hungary and Croatia. The Porte used these simplified field-engineering techniques to improve the stone wall forts or to provide a defence for the border intruder parties of the *serhaddkulu*. Count Marsigli depicted these fortifications in his work and the illustrations show the Ottoman *palanka* was a much more specific type of military construction than has previously been recognised.[305] Since the use of stacked gabions to build elevated artillery firing platforms had been a significant part of Ottoman military techniques, it is likely the case that the basic military engineering structural elements used in Ottoman *palanka* were designed to serve the exact same function. This allowed the Ottomans to practice firing overhead using elevated platforms, over another line of artillery or infantry, while these fired as well.[306] Sometimes the *palanka* constituted the external defence of a fortress, such as in Szeged and Kanisza, before their destruction in 1687, at Nissa in 1688 and again in Novy and Temeşvár in 1716. The palisade was

---

301 *Ibidem*, p.127; the defeat suffered at Párkány cost 7,000 dead and 200 prisoners.
302 Chandler, *The Art of Warfare*, p.74.
303 K.u.K. Kriegsarchiv, *Feldzüge des Prinzen Eugen*, vol. XVI, p.131.
304 *Ibidem*, vol. XVII, p.91.
305 C. Flaherty, 'Classical Ottoman Field Engineering: a Revaluation', in *History and Uniforms* n. 4–2016, p.28.
306 *Ibidem*. Two illustrations of Marsigli were published as a set of architectural depictions of a typical Ottoman *palanka* made with an enclosure of wattle fencing. It is suggested that these fence-like barriers were approximately the height of a man. Likewise, these wattle fencing enclosures followed the same design convention as the larger frontier *palanka*, and usually had simple rectangular or regular plans. The wattle fencing enclosures were also like the larger *palanka* surrounded by a ditch. Other features seen in the Marsigli illustrations show the wattle fencing enclosing the *palanka* had an entrance guarded by a watch tower, which was covered by a roof; and this sat over an entrance connected with a small bridge over the ditch.

usually strengthened with earth, while shooting pitches could also be created for small-calibre cannons, and then the Ottoman distinguished the *palanka* from the *kale*, which has no artillery.

The Ottoman frontier defence system was the result of the expansion of the Empire. The conquered territories did not increase the resources of the state treasury; on the contrary, the new frontiers required subsidies from the centre. Everywhere the border zones were loss-making.[307] In Asia, a large part of income from the provinces of Aleppo, Diyarbakir and Erzurum was spent in neighbouring former Iranian territories, which had been conquered by the Porte.[308] Here the defences required less fortification, given the often inaccessible terrain. Thus, the largest expenses were incurred on the Hungarian frontier, where the Habsburgs strengthened and modernised their frontier fortresses according to the most updated techniques. This action effectively prevented any further Ottoman expansion. Consequently, the Hungarian frontier became rigid, and the Ottomans were required to station a disproportionately large number of soldiers in Hungary to defend their positions. Since paying garrisons and constructing and maintaining fortresses represented a massive expense, where possible the Porte attempted to encourage local leaders to take responsibility for the construction and maintenance of frontier fortifications, and naturally to bear the costs. It is not surprising, therefore, that although the Ottomans were well aware of the latest technology in fortress-building, such as the bastioned fort that

33. The external citadel of Negroponte (Chalkis) on the island of Euboea, known as *karabba*, is one of the best-preserved Ottoman fortresses in Greece. The citadel was the theatre of the bitter siege of 1688, which marked the end of the Venetian offensive in Greece. The final appearace is the result of the works provided by the Ottoman *musellim*s, who upgraded the defences shortly before the siege.

---

307 Ágoston, *Ottoman Warfare in Europe*, p.133.
308 *Ibidem.*

34. Illustrations concerning the border *palanka* forts in Marsigli's **Stato Militare dell'Imperio Ottomanno**. It is interesting to note, these defences were likely transportable once constructed, and like modern prefabricated components could be dismantled and transported to a new location to be reassembled.

Above: A *Palanka* using timber and wattle fencing. Marsigli relates that these fence-like barriers were 'approximately the height of a man'. Likewise, the wattle fencing enclosures followed the same design convention as the larger frontier forts, and: 'usually had simple rectangular or regular plans'. The wattle fencing enclosures were also, like the larger frontier *palanka*, 'surrounded by a ditch'.

Below: A more elaborate type of *palanka* was also made with timber and wattle fencing. The illustration shows three musket slits in the timber front side of the tower's platform parapet wall. The bridge is also shown with cross-bracing visible, and this may indicate that it could have been hauled up like a small drawbridge.

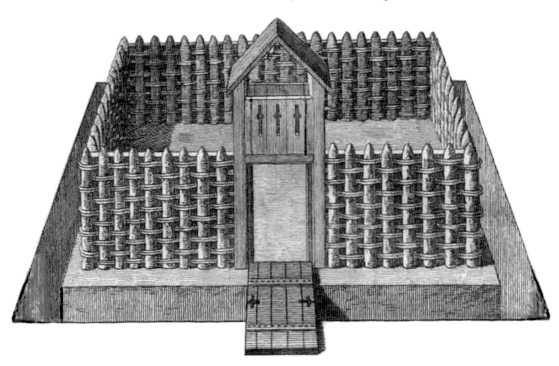

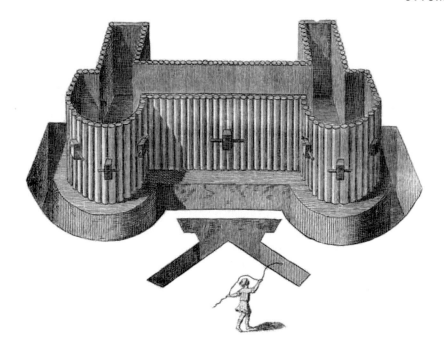

Above: The figure shown iis throwing a line across an additional trap ditch, or firing trench, and gives an indication of scale, illustrating that the log fence was more than twice a man's height. Both versions, unfilled and filled, give no indication of any parapet wall being included, suggesting that the log fence version was intended only to provide an elevated platform for musketeers and artillery.

Below: The Marsigli illustrations show the heads of the securing traverse/cross beams held by pins. For this structural system to have worked effectively to stabilise the wall sections, clearly there was required an additional set of horizontal beams, which the outer logs were spiked onto. This would allow a large number of prefabricated sections to be made, including the semi-circular end sections (thanks to Chris Flaherty for this information).

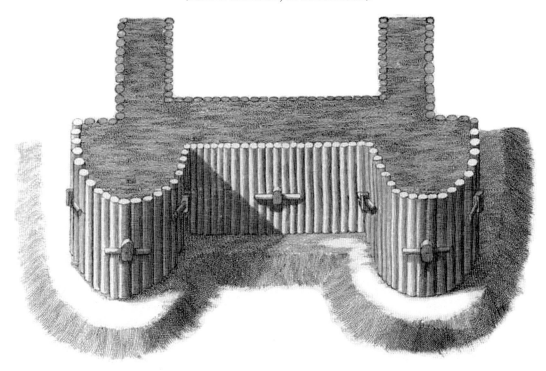

was introduced from the sixteenth century onwards, such forts were only built sporadically, in key locations, mainly on the border with the Habsburg domains, or against the Venetian fleet in the Dardanelles. Though less modern compared to the Western forts, in the seventeenth century the number of Ottoman strongholds reached the number of Habsburg fortresses and thus it remained almost until the end of the century. Such a strongly militarised area obviously had great geo-political importance for the Porte; in comparison, the Ottoman–Safavid border, which was almost twice as long, was much less defended and more vulnerable.[309]

The Ottoman siege technique for the defence of the fortresses was less advanced than that developed in the West. Therefore their defences often became obsolete and incapable of lastingly resisting to modern siege techniques. Many commenters attributed this delay to the Ottoman confidence in offensive means, which convinced the Ottoman commanders that they would never faced a prolonged defensive strategy.[310] Instead, after the disastrous outcome of the Vienna campaign, the technological gap came to light in all its gravity. In the 1690s, only a few fortresses were reinforced with some upgrades of European imitation. The Ottoman bastions, with their characteristic circular shapes, or the ones equally typical with five sides, were endowed with some little lunettes or small ravelins. In Belgrade, the restoration was directed by an Italian engineer, Sebastiano Corner, captured after the surrender of the city in 1690, who then passed into the service of the Porte.[311] The improvements turned out to be effective for rejecting the Imperial attempt in 1693. The most significant traces of the Ottoman domination in Europe are characterised by the defensive works of the *musellims* that, although obsolete compared to Western European works, represented valuable fortifications. Even today is possible to admire the monumental *barbakan* of the royal castle of Budapest, or the one of Pecs, in Hungary. Fortified complexes of great importance are preserved in Bulgaria, such as in Viddin and Belogradtschik. The citadel of the *Kalemegdan* in Belgrade still preserves the signs of the many sieges sustained. Less known by mass tourism, but equally important, are the walls of Kamieniec, restored after 1676, another testimony of the fine work of the Ottoman *musellims*.

Cavalry: *Gönüllü, Beslü* and *Dely*

According to Marsigli, the mounted units of the *serhaddkulu* constituted a border military force immediately available for every war operation, 'ready-to-use' troops, and for this reason they were maintained in high efficiency.[312] The customary stereotypes of a society of the frontier draws

---

309 Pedani, *The Ottoman–Venetian Border*, p.24.
310 In this regard, Montecuccoli remarked: 'the Turk does not seem to fortify many squares, because no one would dare to risk an assault to any of his fortresses without a powerful army which could well withdraw him. In addition, when the Turk doubts whether someone wants to attack, he throws in eight or ten thousand soldiers, and so does not care about other fortification'; 'Trattato della Guerra', in Luraghi, *Opere di Raimondo Montecuccoli*, vol. I, p.231.
311 Marsigli, vol. II, p.151.
312 *Ibidem.*

usually a male environment, where women are few and children do not exist; the living conditions are violent; killings and heinous crimes are committed in the name of religion (or profit, or the necessity to appropriate someone else's space). In addition, heroic and savagely romantic characters, however, belong to this category of men: spurred by an ideal drive, they fight against the enemy, hostile nature or a people different in religion, culture and origin. Similar ideas may be found not only in historiography, but also in the chronicles or contemporary literature. An illuminating example of this frontier society may be the so-called 'blood brotherhood', which was created with a formal rite and was present in the Balkan area and in Hungary since the sixteenth century at least. Similar customs strengthen the idea of a society where the ideal of the *ǧihād* (Holy War) made room for different lifestyles. Also the great traveller Evliya Çelebi, who was witness to a similar episode in 1660, gapingly talked about it. He told the story of a *gazi* who took part in a border skirmish with the Venetian troops and was discovered while hiding a Christian soldier.[313] As surprising as it may be, this and other episodes show how the frontier society was very liquid and that the communities, although enemies, followed a code of mutual respect. It was not uncommon for business relations with Ottoman counterparts to exist between the Venetian as well as the Hungarian or Croatian border leaderships. Military rivalry focused more on robberies than on destruction and extermination, therefore, this kind of warfare relied upon mounted troops.[314]

The Ottomans distinguished three types of soldiers on horseback: the main component was represented by the *gönüllü*, gathered in units of large size and under the direct authority of the commanders settled in the border

35. Ottoman *dely*, sixteenth or seventeenth century (copy after Jacopo Ligozzi, 1547–1627). In 1682, the attachè to the Venetian ambassador in Constantinople, Antonio Benetti, described the Ottoman dely riders wearing a similar dress, including lynx's fur and plumed headgear.

313 'When it was time to kill the prisoners who had been captured, the Ottoman warrior prostrated himself before the *paşa* asking to have mercy on his enemy: Mercy, Grand Vizier! I have sworn brotherhood with this captive on the battlefield; we have pledged each other our faiths. If you kill him, he will go to paradise with my faith and that will be an injury to me, wretch that I am; and if I die, the faith of this captive, with whom I have sworn brotherhood, will stay with me and we will both go to hell, so that again I am the loser.'; in Pedani, *The Ottoman–Venetian Border*, p.34.
314 This kind of mutual respect disappeared after 1683. Reciprocal distrust and atrocities removed any mercy and the war became a total conflict aiming at the destruction of the enemy. Often the actions were taken as reprisals for Ottoman atrocities, though it is pointless to speculate who began this vicious spiral of violence.

provinces, the *alaybeg*. These officers were usually chosen among the natives of the border regions and they had to be acquainted with more languages in addition to Turkish, mainly Hungarian, Croatian and also Italian.[315] Directly under their orders, some *cehays* were chosen as lieutenants. The *gönüllü* were recruited from the Muslim population settled in the same district where they served. *Gönüllü* troops served in both the field army and in fortresses. When serving in garrisons they came under the command of the local *dizdar*. These soldiers could serve as both cavalry and infantry and were organised in *cemaats* and *bölüks* like the *kapikulu* units.

In a similar way, every township and village near the border recruited one or more 'flying corps' destined for the garrisons of the small fortified places and trained in tasks such as exploration and intruding: they were the *beslü*. Marsigli does provide information concerning the strength of both corps, however it can be assumed that the *gönüllü* formed corps of 2–300 of horsemen, while the latter raised squadrons of 50–100 men. However, there is some indirect information that suggests the actual size of this cavalry. Records from the seventeenth century show that *gönüllüs* were usually one of, if not the largest element in the garrison, comprising 20–25 percent of the garrison's strength.[316] In 1663, when the garrison at Érsekúivár was established, 153 *gönüllüs* were assigned to the fortress. After the Ottoman defeat at Szentgotthárd in August 1664, the garrison was strengthened. Perhaps in an effort to keep regular troops with the field army, a majority of the troops sent to the fort were *gönüllü*. A corps of 248 *gönüllü* soldiers is finally recorded at Érsekúivár in the autumn of 1664.[317]

Both corps were organised in tactical troops, called *faris*, ranging between 20 and 50 men divided in *odas*. The total number of *faris* assembled in each district took the name *cerna'at*. Within the corps operated the officials in charge of administrative services, such as the *kàtib* with one or more *çavuş* as adjutants. Each detachment included in its ranks also a standard bearer, the *bayrakdar*, plus a certain number of *odabasis* according to the number of *odas* forming the *faris*. In 1701, the Bosnian village of Gradale housed a *faris* under the command of a *cehay*, which included one scribe, one standard bearer, one adjutant, four *odabasis* and 40 horsemen.[318]

The structure of this mounted border corps was functional for the organisation of the service. The Ottomans did not set up a continuous defensive line of fortified places, but left the main garrisons rather isolated from each other. The task of maintaining the connections was entrusted to the *gönüllü* and the *beslü*, who were able to intervene in the threatened sector in a short time thanks to their mobility. Furthermore, since the Ottomans conceived the war only as an offensive action, the defence of the borders was guaranteed more by the rapid breaks into enemy territory than by a line of fortresses.

---

315 *Ibidem*, vol. I, p.96.
316 Stein, *Guarding the Frontier*, p.97.
317 *Ibidem*.
318 Z. Grbasic and V. Vuksic, *Cavalry, the History of a Fighting Elite* (London: Cassell, 1993), p.140.

The establishment of a broad border strip and the maintenance of this structure with relatively minor changes created a special situation for soldiers serving in the border fortresses, Imperial–Hungarian and Ottoman alike. Namely, it offered opportunities to the soldiers of both sides to launch raids into the border that were protected by the forts of the enemy and therefore more wealthy, even into the regions beyond, primarily in order to collect tributes and taxes. Owing to the taxing of the two sides by one another in the Ottoman–Hungarian territories and in Transylvania – the so-called 'dual sovereignty' region – tending to either side of the border zone there were a large number of subjects liable to double taxation. However, at least in theory, each were only obliged to pay half the amount of tax officially prescribed.[319]

Along with the mobilisation of the *cemaat*, small corps of chosen horsemen were also created. They were responsible for the most dangerous tasks, and usually opened the actions in enemy territory. They were the *delys*, which in Turkish means 'crazy' but also 'bold' or 'reckless'. The *dely* usually belonged to the circle of clients close to the governors of the provinces or their relatives. These horsemen are the most famous members of the *serhaddkulu* cavalry, and often they are considered as the only mounted units of the border cavalry.

Belonging to the border cavalry granted special privileges, and compared to the infantry, the duration of the service had a different regulation. Ultimately, a *faris*'s horseman remained a soldier for life, alternating service in the army with trade, or to the usual economic activities managed by the Ottoman classes. The rank of *alaybeg* often coincided with the chief of the community. He was directly responsible for his unit and often acted as an independent commander, leading raids or reprisals against the enemy target even in period of truce. As a senior officer, each *alaybeg* chose his men and appointed the adjutants.[320]

Generally, the *serhaddkulu* cavalry acted autonomously from the main army once the offensive campaign started. The border cavalry certainly represented one of the most feared components of the *serhaddkulu*, and

---

319 According to some scholars, the taxing of enemy territory was much more important and necessary for the soldiers of the Habsburg royal fortresses equipped for defence than it was for the continually advancing Ottomans. See G. Pálffy, 'Scorched-Earth Tactics in Ottoman Hungary: A Controversy in Military Theory and Practice on the Habsburg–Ottoman Frontier', in *Acta Orientalia Academiae Scientiarum Hungaricae*, vol. 61, No. 1/2 (Budapest: Akadémiai Kiadó, March 2008), pp.181–200.

320 The Muslim Slavic communities of Bosnia and Macedonia had the identical social structure of their Christian Serbian neighbours. The chief of the village assumed the role of political and legal leader, as well as being responsible for the military education of adults. However, all decisions stemmed from a collegial discussion. This led to a strong spirit of cohesion and the formation of a leading class credited with considerable political abilities. Even in the smallest villages, this pattern was reflected in the *zadruga*: the great patriarchal family. In this context the authority of the 'chief of the family' guaranteed to all the members the use of the goods belonging to the community and his action could be discussed in the assemblies. From this social scenario, the mobilisation of the warriors took place very quickly and this constituted a characteristic trait of the whole Slavic world from the dawn of their history. Moreover, even in the Second World War, both the southern Slavs and the Russians were able to organise in a short time efficient partisan formations. See F. Conte, *Gli Slavi, le civiltà dell'Europa centrale e orientale* (Turin: Einaudi. 2006), pp.248–249.

until the Porte was able to take advantage of its military power, they constituted a considerable threat for the neighbouring states. In 1658 the rapid mobilisation of these troops was experimented with by the Grand Prince of Transylvania György II Rákóczy, when the *beglerbeg* of Buda, Seidi Ahmed, led a punitive incursion into the princedom as a response to the invasion of Poland. The *beglerbeg* gathered a force of 6,000 horsemen of local troops, including the *serhaddkulu* cavalry, forcing Rákóczy to hastily return to Transylvania.[321] Some authors state that in the 1670s, the Porte could still gather 8,000 horsemen on the Hungarian border, ready to be employed against the Habsburgs.[322] The action carried out by them involved the enemy regions close to the border as a mere threat or to support rebellions in enemy territory. In August 1681, the *paşa* of Várad led one of the largest raids ever carried out against Habsburg Hungary in peacetime. The action had been planned to support the rebellion of the Hungarian 'malcontents' and involved a force of nearly 6,000 horsemen, who plundered and collected contributions in enemy territory for almost two months.[323]

After the loss of the Hungarian domain, these troops also suffered the same fate as the *azab* corps. The disappearance of the border cavalry deprived the Ottoman army of a valid instrument of war, skilled in the reconnaissance service and usually well informed about the ground. During the War of the Holy League, the Ottomans turned more often to the Tatars, and only partially with the Muslim refugees who had immigrated to Bosnia. With these latter, it was possible to reorganise an efficient border cavalry, even if deprived of its most talented ranks and files. Therefore, it took a lot of time to train a cavalry capable of performing the tasks entrusted to the border riders in the task required by the 'small war', as classified in the West. Information on the *serhaddkulu* cavalry became confused starting from the 1680s. The strength of the corps considerably diminished and its men merged with the rest of the Ottoman cavalry. The turning point of numerical superiority no longer allowed the deployment of the mounted forces in autonomous isolated operations.

The conflict against the Habsburgs and Venice of 1714–18 reopened border warfare on the secondary fronts of Dalmatia, Croatia and Transylvania. Several bloody episodes occurred near the Croatian–Bosnian border along the Sava and Drava rivers. In the spring of 1716 the Ottoman commander of Banyaluka gathered a mobile force of 5,000 horsemen, a part of which, together with reinforcements from the field army, carried out raids against Eszék and Sombor.[324] The reaction of the Imperial *Grenzers* forced them to cross back over the Sava; then the news of the Peterwardein defeat interrupted further planned actions. On the Croatian border, near Carlstadt, the Ottoman border cavalry was particularly daring and achieved some significant goals between July and August 1716. The *alaybeg* of the *serhaddkulu* of Bihac, the Bosnian Bessirevic *Beg*, led small cavalry corps and

---

321 Payer, *Armati Hungarorum*, p.106.
322 Marsigli, vol. I, p.65.
323 Payer, *Armati Hungarorum*, p.107.
324 K.u.K. Kriegsarchiv, *Feldzüge des Prinzen Eugen*, vol. XVII, p.254.

infantry in enemy territory with the aim of making cattle raids. In Brujavac, the Ottomans attacked and destroyed the Imperial *palankas* and finally clashed with the Croatian *Grenzer* near Carlstadt.[325] The reprisal ordered by the Imperial command materialised in an expedition against Bihac. Here, the Croats burned some wooden forts on the Unna river, then sustained numerous cavalry assaults for over a week, before being forced to retreat, not being able to move their artillery in time to target Bihac. As reinforcement for the stronghold, 'feudal troops' came from Macedonia under a *paşa*.[326] Mutual retaliatory actions continued throughout the summer. In response to the attempted Imperial siege of Novj, the Ottomans carried out an assault on Zrin, where they destroyed the enemy *palanka* and plundered some villages. The cold season did not stop the actions of the Imperial *Serasseners*, led by the *Grenz-Hauptmann* Petrasch, who caused much damage on the Lower Sava. However, on 10 October, the Bosnian *serhaddkulu* soldiers managed to intercept a column of enemies directed against a *palanka* near Sabek. The battle resulted in a victory for the Ottoman horsemen, who pursued the fleeing enemies for a long time. The *Serasseners* also lost their artillery.[327]

In January 1717, in response to the new Imperial incursions against Doboj, Dobor and Mirolam-Cocak, about 2,000 Bosnian horsemen stormed into the district of Vukovar, destroyed the border posts, dispersed all the *Grenzers* and finally headed for Peterwardein, after setting fire to the fortress of Mitrovitz which had been abandoned by the enemy. The episode caused great alarm on the Imperial side and induced the commanders to send part of their troops that had already taken to winter quarters. New incursions from both factions occurred in February and in the following months, but no action reached the violence of the previous ones.

Before the battle of Belgrade, groups of *serhaddkulu* horsemen appeared behind the Imperial rear in April 1717. A month later the Ottoman border horsemen reappeared before Belgrade and destroyed the Imperial wooden forts at Kruçedol and Carlowitz, where they set fire to the chapel erected for commemorating the truce of 1699.[328]

The study of the frontier society of the Ottoman Empire and its defence has produced much research, which however has obscured the military organisation of the eastern border. After the treaty signed in 1639, a new border between Iran and the Ottoman Empire was established. The Ottomans and the Safavids did not engage in any large-scale conflict during the remaining part of the seventeenth century, which enabled the Ottoman Empire to focus on integrating its territories into the Ottoman political and administrative system. The inhabitants of this region were mainly Kurds. As a frontier region, Kurdistan demanded close attention from the Ottoman Empire. Realising the strategic importance of the region, the Ottomans aimed at integrating Kurdish tribes fully into the Ottoman system. This was not an easy task, since the Kurdish political units demonstrated complicated structures, unfavourable to

---

325 *Ibidem*, p.255.
326 *Ibidem*.
327 *Ibidem*, p.262.
328 *Ibidem*, p.263.

any single administrative policy. There were powerful confederacies as well as highly fragmented and diffuse Kurdish tribes.

The Porte was extremely careful to ensure that power remained in the hands of the same ruling families.[329] The Ottoman administration in Kurdistan was initially flexible, with the Kurdish emirates enjoying the privileges granted to them. However, historian and traveller Evliya Çelebi affirms that by the mid seventeenth century the degree of autonomy in the Kurdish emirates had greatly diminished.[330] Because of this policy, however, most Kurdish leaders became heavily dependent upon Ottoman assistance to maintain their position of power, and the Porte found a favourable environment in which to interfere with Kurdish tribal structures.

Evliya Çelebi specifies two different types of administration besides the Ottoman *paşalik* of Diyarbakir. The first was similar to the ordinary Ottoman province. Therefore, the Kurdish *sancaks*, like ordinary *sancaks*, contained the *timar* and *zeamet*, whose holders, mostly Kurdish tribesmen, were subject to the same military obligations as those in the rest of the Empire. The second kind of administrative variation in Kurdistan, the *hükümet*, enjoyed the highest degree of autonomy. They were generally located in the most inaccessible territories. The *hükümets* did not have the *timar* and *zeamet*. They neither paid taxes to the Porte nor provided regular military forces, except to secure the border. It is difficult to form a picture concerning the strength deployed on the eastern frontier, but here existed a similar corps of borders men, which operated under the command of the local leaders. This frontier was almost deprived of large fortresses and it is reasonable to guess that the border troops were essentially horsemen.

Marine and River Infantry

The Ottoman fleet had a stable guard corps called *azab* based at Galata, rising to 1,364 men in 1670, divided into 650 *odas* (chambers).[331] Each of two or four men were in charge of presiding over the arsenal, escorting wagons or convoys that transported the materials for the dockyards; the oldest among the *azabs* also provided surveillance in the harbour area, others controlled the prison of the convicted oarsmen, while about half of their force could be used for carpentry work under the masters. The command of the whole corps was entrusted to one *reis*, with one *odabaşi* as lieutenant and one *ascybaşi*, the cook, as second junior officer. The various positions taken by the *azabs* included gendarmerie, craftsmanship and naval duties, considering that

---

329 This policy was apparently aimed at creating strong leadership. In no case was the leadership allowed to go to anyone outside of the ruling dynasty. If the *sancakbeg* had no son to succeed him, then the other *sancakbegs* of Kurdistan would nominate the successor, probably a person from a different branch of the same family. It is noteworthy that the sultan did not favour non-Kurdish rulers. See H. Özoglu, *Kurdish Notables and the Ottoman State. Evolving Identities, Competing Loyalties, and Shifting Boundaries* (New York: State University of New York Press, 2004), pp.34–35.

330 *Ibidem.*

331 Marsigli, vol. II, p.139.

they also knew the use of a compass, nautical cartography and explosives.[332]

Alongside the permanent *azab* corps, the infantry embarked on warships were represented also by the *levend* and *mensugat*. While the first corps was recruited by *paşas* and governors of the major provinces, the second was formed with non-professional naval soldiers in the minor departments, namely *beg* and *zeamet*, and mainly used as reserve troops. Both these categories of soldiers also provided personnel for naval artillery, as well as for landing troops, garrisons in the ports and coastal fortifications. These footmen were involved in the amphibious actions during the Cretan War of 1645–71, and in the War of the Holy League of 1684–99, again on the Aegean front, facing the feared Venetian fleet. They performed alternately and often with modest successes, entrusted in the difficult task of defending the Peloponnese's ports, faced with the overwhelming Venetian offensive under Francesco Morosini in 1684–1687.

Organised like the navy, the Ottomans also possessed a considerable fleet operating on the Danube and on the major tributaries. This force comprised the river boats and crews, under the command of the *kapudan paşa* of the Danube, who usually resided in Ruse, in Bulgaria. In the mid seventeenth century, the town was the main operational base of the river fleet. In Ruse there was also an arsenal and a yard.[333] Through its port and another in Orsova,[334] Belgrade, Semlin and, before their loss, Titel, Peterwardein and Eszék, the Porte controlled a large network of navigable waterways. Along the course of the rivers sailed supplies for the field army, while the units of the fleet provided the escort. The Turkish river ships were larger than the corresponding Imperial ones and were reputed as better in terms of manoeuvrability. The Ottoman sailors came from the regions crossed by the Danube, especially from Bulgaria, but not even Hungarians and the Serbs were rare. They were crews skilled in fluvial navigation, with whom light troops were also set up, aboard *chaikas* and on other small, oared ships capable of operating in shallow waters.

36. Ottoman *levend*, 1680–1700. *Levend* soldiers were the Ottoman marine infantry and were usually equipped with a short *tüfek*, one or two *kandjar* knives and a *pala* sabre. They dressed like the southern Mediterranean sailors, and as members of the navy, they wore a shirt with the sleeves held above the elbow. (Author's illustration)

---

332 For further details concerning the Ottoman navy, see B. Mugnai, *The Cretan War, 1645–1671* (Warwick: Helion & Company, 2018), pp.33–38.

333 Marsigli, vol. II, p.172.

334 Orsova was also known as 'the Iron Gate'.

37. Navy *azab*, mid seventeenth century. (*Icones Habitus Monumenta Turcarum*, between 1586 and 1650, Biblioteka Jagiellońska, Krakow)

On many occasions, the Danube fleet supported the field army on campaign. At Viddin, in 1689, a squadron of three 'half-galleys', six brigantines and other minor units intervened against the Imperialists who were besieging the fortress.[335] In 1691, a raid conducted by the crews of the *chaikas* set fire to the Imperial supply boats north of Slankamen, in the days before the bloody battle. In 1694, during the long siege on the Imperial fortified camp at Peterwardein, the Ottoman river fleet continually supported the efforts of the field troops.[336] In the 1690s, the Danube's *kapudan paşa* Ali introduced some changes in order to rationalise the fleet, maintaining only three types of ships. The larger ship was the *ciktere*, corresponding to the Mediterranean 'half galley', with 18 or 20 banks of rowers. The *birgende*, similar to the brigantine, was smaller with 16 banks of rowers. A ship with only 10 benches closed the series. All had six- or eight-pound artillery pieces on board and a variable number of smaller calibre pieces. The *ciktere* boarded two larger pieces and an indeterminate number of smaller guns; the *birgende* and the smaller model had various combinations of light pieces. The new ships received their baptism of fire in August 1693, when they opposed the Imperial attempt to reconquer Belgrade. To improve the quality of the fleet the *kapudan paşa* introduced in the river fleet the most experienced crews from the sea units, but this expedient did not bring significant benefits.[337] Ali Paşa also planned the construction of floating

335 Marsigli, vol. II, p.171.
336 *Ibidem.*
337 *Ibidem*, p.172.

pontoons to transport wagons, horses and troops on the Danube, but there is no information on their actual use.

The Danube fleet continued to support the field army until the end of the War of the Holy League. In 1696 a squadron of 106 ships blocked the fortress of Titel and targeted the city with artillery. The following year, large sums were invested to arm 22 new ships with low draught; another 39 *chaikas* were built at the state treasury's expense, which sent them to the Danube ports along with 10 galleons, 13 frigates and 100 rafts.[338]

Also against Russia, the Ottoman commanders used the fleet to support infantry often embarked on small ships based in the ports of the Kuban River and the Sea of Azov. Before the fall of Azov, 20 among *cikteres* and *galiottes*, alongside 25 *chaikas* crossed the Black Sea to face the piracy of the Cossacks.[339] In 1711, the river fleet was mobilised for the campaign in Moldova and in 1716–18 for that in the Banat against the Imperialists. Already in 1715, the Ottoman river ships sailed up the Sava bringing supplies to the troops deployed on the Venetian border in Dalmatia. Other preparations were undertaken in the spring of 1716. Many of the largest ships were gathered in Belgrade, where, under the command of the *kapudan paşa* Ibrahim, 1,500 men with 70 *chaikas* served between Belgrade, Rama, Smedarevo and Orsova, as well as at Sabac on the Sava River.[340] In 1717, during the siege of Belgrade, the Ottoman *chaikas* alongside the larger units of the fleet threatened on several occasions the besiegers' supply lines.

Together with their naval soldiers, the sultans could often count on the non-negligible naval power of Barbary pirates. Although the most important military activity of the Northern African *re'is* was the war on the sea as privateers or corsairs, in 1646 and 1667, from Tunis, Algiers and Tripoli, several ships arrived in Crete and their crews took part in the fighting for the possession of the island.[341] The North Africans provided the escorts for the convoys that transported the troops destined for the siege of Kandije, and during the years of the blockade of the Dardanelles they escorted the merchantmen that from Smyrna or Egypt supplied the garrisons that remained isolated in the Mediterranean.

During the War of the Holy League, the Ottomans occasionally used African crews to reinforce their garrisons in the Peloponnese and Ionian. After the surrender of Prevesa, which took place in July 1684, the Venetians discovered among the defenders many 'privateers'. While the garrison was granted evacuation from the city, the pirates ended up slaves to the oars of Christian ships.[342] In the eighteenth century, the political events of North Africa caused a relaxation of Ottoman authority on the region, which except for Tripoli, Algiers and Tunis less and less willingly provided men for the sultan.

---

338 K.u.K. Kriegsarchiv, *Feldzüge des Prinzen Eugen*, vol. II, p.98.
339 *Ibidem*.
340 *Ibidem*, vol. XVII, p.55.
341 R. Mantran, *L'Evolution des relations entre la Tunisie et L'Empire Ottoman du XVI au XVII siècle*, p.325, and 'Le Statut d'Algerie, de la Tunisie et de la Tripolitaine dans l'Empire Ottoman', p.6 in *L'Empire Ottoman du XVI au XVII siécle*.
342 ASFi, 'Relazione del gran Priore Vandomi', *Mediceo del Principato*, in 'Carteggi e Miscellanea'.

4

Allies and Tributaries

In all the wars fought by the Ottomans since the late sixteenth century, their armies were joined by numerous auxiliary contingents sent by their allied and tributaries of Eastern Europe. The cavalry represented the largest part of these forces, usually employed to provide reconnaissance and a screen for the field army on campaign. The commanders were awarded the symbols of the Ottoman hierarchy and the number of men was established on the basis of agreements signed with the Porte.

Tatars

Through the treaty signed in 1629 between the Ottoman sultan and the *han* of the Crimean Tatars, it was established that 12,000 soldiers on horseback would form the contingent to be sent on campaign in case of war. The Porte paid a sum of money equivalent to the men requested, assuming also their maintenance. The contingent included horsemen recruited among the Bucak Tatars and sometimes the Noghay. The single unit composing the corps took the name *kazan* (cauldron) under the command of a *mirza*; the high command of the Tatar contingent was entrusted to a member of the *han*'s family or to his lieutenant. Usually the *han* personally led their men on campaign. In 1676, during the campaign against the Poles in Podolia, the command was held by the *han* Murad Giray, while in 1683, the *han* led his horseman to Hungary, but eventually they acted under the command of *han*'s nephew, Mehmet Ali Giray, who assumed the title of *kalgay*. The rank of *kalgay* meant that the officer held the office of first vice-*han*, followed hierarchically by the *nureddin*, the second lieutenant of the souvereign.[1] A third and final grade, corresponding to the post of governor of the Crimean peninsula, was the *olu bas*. The commander of the Bucak Tatars had the rank of *beg*, while the leader of the Noghay assumed the title of *sultan*.

---

1   Marsigli, vol. I, p. 66.

Each Tatar went to war leading with him up to four horses, so as to always have a fresh animal.[2] Tatar warfare required constant mobility and therefore they were used to feeding themselves in the saddle, and their encampment consisted of tents made with skins and improvised pickets. Even the baggage travelled quickly, loaded on camels or on small two-wheeled carts. The Tatars anticipated the field army entering early on campaign, dispersing the border outposts and facing the enemy vanguards, to cover the direction and the strength of the army. Usually the Tatars avoided encounters against large regular forces, but constantly maintained pressure on the enemy with raids and skirmishes. The Polish king Jan Sobieski described very well this tactic, claiming that, '[the Ottomans] employ them [the Tatars] as we use the hunting dogs.'[3]

Regarding the actual strength of the Tatar contingents, information is once again uncertain. Due to their ability to move quickly, to appear in very distant places in a short time, the Tatars were a very elusive force. Some sources estimate their strength at 40,000 men; however the large number of horses could confuse the reports.[4] In any case, their presence alongside the Ottomans was constant and significant for a large part of the seventeenth century.

The Tatars were involved in the expeditions against Transylvania in 1657–59. The *han* sent their men to relieve the Poles in the war against Sweden and Transylvania; then the Tatars repressed the anti-Ottoman uprisings in Moldavia and Walachia in 1660, and finally fought in Hungary against the Imperialists in the war of 1663–64. An Imperial report of late 1662 gave the number of Tatars in Hungary as 8,000 horse.[5] The traces of their passage were observed by the soldiers of General Montecuccoli and described as 'stripes of lightning'.[6] One year later, the number of Tatars had increased considerably. On 2 September 1663, a force of 'over 20,000 Horse' crossed the Vah river under the protection of the field army and advanced into northern Hungary, where it threatened the Hungarian Diet at Bratislava. In mid September, the incursion reached the inland regions of Moravia and Silesia, from which the Tatars enslaved several thousand civilians. The German historian Joseph von Hammer-Purgstall left an impressive narration on the Tatar incursion:

> Tatars travelled to Nikolsburg to Rabensbourg and Brno, burning everything they found and then arrived within three miles of Olmütz. The domains of the princes Dietrichstein and Liechtenstein were looted and [they] burned thirty-two villages belonging to the second. Then they moved to Pressburg (Bratislava), reduced the suburbs to ashes, and Geyersdorf St. George, crossed by swimming the river Waag, and came to Rosincko, in the county of Hradisch. Meanwhile fourteen thousand Tatars ravaged around Brunau and Klobach, killed, burned, plundered

---

2   Montecuccoli, 'Della Guerra contro il Turco', in Luraghi, *Opere di Raimondo Montecuccoli*, vol. II, p.322.

3   J. Sobieski, *Listy do Marisyenka*, edited by J. Zeller (Berlin: Buchverlag der Morgen, 1974), p.33.

4   Montecuccoli, 'Della Guerra contro il Turco', in Luraghi, *Opere di Raimondo Montecuccoli*, vol. II, p.323.

5   *Ibidem*, p.396.

6   *Ibidem*, p.397.

and hunted before them like breed all the prisoners they brought back to Hungary with four carriages trailed by sixteen horses transporting many unfortunate girls … The number of Christians taken into slavery by the incendiary hordes which traversed Moravia, Silesia and Hungary, amounted to eighty thousand.'[7]

The Imperialists tried to intercept them by sending General Sporck with 2,000 cuirassiers, but the Tatars: 'like a flashing light and from a tired horse to a fresh one … from now on throwing, and causing the slightest clash, they plundered, burned, destroyed and finally returned to their bases, where the retreat was supported by the Turks'.[8] Before the end of the month, the Croatian *banus* Miklós Zrínyi intercepted with his hussars a large column of Tatars which was fording the Raba river, he routed them and freed over 20,000 captives.[9]

If the Tatars were feared for their fierce action and the cruelty they practised for the trade of slaves, nevertheless against regular troops they never offered good proofs, suffering defeats in almost all encounters, even against numerically inferior forces. It also happened that their raids ended as soon as they collected a satisfying loot, and then they disappeared to return to their home. This behaviour made them even disliked by the Ottoman commanders, increasing their contempt for the *han*.

In 1672, a contingent of 10,000 Tatars horsemen joined the Ottoman field army in Podolia for the opening campaign against the Poles. Similar contingents fought alongside the Ottomans in Ukraine against the Cossacks and their Russian allies from 1678 to 1681, distinguishing themselves for the violence committed against the civilian population. It is remarkable that Tatars were strongly involved in both the conflicts, providing on several occasions more soldiers than those gathered by the Porte.

During the War of the Holy League, the Tatars were present with 20,000 horsemen at the siege of Vienna.[10] According to Marsigli, after this episode their participation in the campaigns on the Danube and in the Balkans diminished, due to the entry into the conflict of Poland, and in 1686 also Russia joining the alliance. The new scenario forced the *han* to face the enemy attacks almost alone. The presence of Tatar contingents in the Hungarian war theatre is mentioned in 1684, when in February they invaded Upper Hungary, and then the following year, during the struggle for the defence of Érsekúivár. In 1686, they came to Hungary with 4,000 horsemen, employed by Grand Vizier Süleyman in the inconclusive actions against the enemy cavalry. After the fall of Buda, in October the Tatars were surprised in Szeged by the Imperial cavalry which at night attacked the camp, dispersing the whole contingent. One year later, a Tatar cavalry corps

---

7   Hammer-Purgstall, *Geschichte des Osmanischen Reiches*, vol. XI, p.153.

8   Montecuccoli, 'Della Guerra contro il Turco', in Luraghi, *Opere di Raimondo Montecuccoli*, vol. II, p.418.

9   Payer, *Armati Hungarorum*, p.107 and *Geschichte des Osmanischen Reiches*, vol. XI, p.153: 'He [Zrínyi] was assaulted in his turn by the pasha of Aleppo, who obliged the Banus to retire under the fortress of Komarom.'

10   Podhorecki, *Weiden 1683*, pp.42–44, states 15–20,000, while most other sources relate 20,000 or more.

38. Tatar Horseman, late seventeenth century. Each mounted Tatar conducted on campaign one or more horses in order to always have a fresh one. Usually the Tatars' war equipment consisted of a light spear, most with a bamboo pole, pre-contracted bow, sabre and sometimes two or three javelins. Firearms such as short rifles and pistols become quite frequent from the late seventeenth century. As defence weapons, the Tatars wore thick coats quilted of wool of horse or sheepskin with fur inside; armour plates of metal, imitating the Ottoman–Persian models, and iron mail shirts were worn by officers and commanders. The fur-lined leather cap constituted the most widespread protection for the head, but the Tatars used also turbans wrapped around black cloth caps or, less common, on metal helms. (Author's illustration, after Jean Struys, *Les Voyages de Jean Struys en Moscovie et Tartarie*, Amsterdam, 1681. This work is a very interesting and detailed source relating the Tatars of the late seventeenth century, which includes accurate descriptions of their dress and weapons)

of 5–6,000 men formed the vanguard of the Ottoman army at Eszék and then at Harsány, where it was almost completely destroyed. The last major action carried out by the Tatars in Hungary took place in September 1693, when they became the protagonists of a series of well-planned raids which ended a month and a half later with the deportation of 6,000 civilians.[11] Against the Poles and the Russians, the *han* of Crimea with his Bucak allies gathered a force of over 30,000 men until the Peace of Carlowitz.[12] Infantry garrisons were also organised to guard the fortresses, such as Azow, besieged by the enemy, while an average of 7–8,000 horsemen fought in Transylvania and then in the Balkans until 1698.

The Tatars returned to fight outside their home in 1711 against Tsar Peter I and in 1715 even further, in Greece. In the spring about 5,000 cavalry arrived at the field of Thebes under the orders of an *aǧa*.[13] Later they were sent to Bosnia to reinforce the Ottoman cavalry on the Dalmatian border.

The last significant operations carried out by the Tatars took place in the Banat and Transylvania during the war of 1716–17. The episodes that occurred in these campaigns showed not only the decline of Ottoman offensive power, but also the poor fighting spirit of the Tatar cavalry and its cruel greed.

For the campaign of 1716, the *han* assured the Porte he would raise 40,000 men, but by midsummer only a fifth had arrived on the Danube, and hurriedly fled at the sight of the Ottoman rout at Peterwardein. In the spring of 1717 the new *han*, Seadet Giray, promised to arm 70,000 men, and to send them to the Balkans under the orders of his lieutenant the *nureddin* Sultan.[14] The Tatars arrived in small groups, gathering in Belgrade, but altogether they numbered only a few thousand: many of them had lost their horses and their equipment was inadequate, and so at the end of May almost all of them joined the garrison of the city.[15]

The protests of the Ottoman officials in Bakcisaray forced the *han* to recruit further cavalry, and in this way a new contingent of 10,000 horsemen moved from Crimea and Dobruja in the early summer, initially directed to Wallachia and then to Moldavia. After various setbacks and a considerable loss of time for planning the campaign, the grand vizier decided to invade Eastern Transylvania. For this goal, the Ottoman commander appointed the *serasker* Regeb Paschià, with a force of 20,000 men among Ottomans and Tatars, including Moldavian auxiliaries on foot and on horse.[16] As reinforcement, 100 Hungarian exiles belonging to Prince Rákóczy's party were added before the start of the offensive. On 22 August the Tatars formed the vanguard that marched to Bistritz, where they prevailed over a small corps of dragoons and frontiersmen, and then headed towards the interior of the region, devastating and burning the countryside. While the Tatars continued with their raids, the rest of the forces remained at Bistritz for a few

---

11   Payer, *Armati Hungarorum*, p.115.
12   Marsigli, vol. II, p.101.
13   Brue, *Journal*, p.8.
14   K.u.K. Kriegsarchiv, *Feldzüge des Prinzen Eugen*, vol. XVII, p.54.
15   *Ibidem*, p.55.
16   *Ibidem*, p.187.

days, plundering the suburbs and finally, having tried unsuccessfully to enter the city, they separated into small groups to escape the Imperialists that were coming to relieve Bistritz.

The Tatars penetrated as far as Upper Hungary, riding for three days without stopping. On 28 August, the incursions spread along the Szamos River. Here the Tatars plundered many small villages and captured numerous civilians. Until the end of the month the Tatars did not meet resistance, but soon the Hungarian and Transylvanian *Grenzer*, who had chased them, began to block the roads. Even the civilian population began to react by attacking and fleeing the isolated Tatars and forcing them to flee. Pressed from all directions, the Tatars divided into two groups. A thousand sought refuge in Transylvania but found the local militia waiting for their arrival, who repulsed them, took away their loot and freed the prisoners. The surviving Tatars fled to the mountains, but the armed peasants pursued them and killed all at the end of a ruthless hunt.[17]

In early September the bulk of the Tatars headed towards the Polish border, but they found all the roads blocked by the Hungarian militiamen and were forced to withdrew, trying to force the pass of the Maramureş to get safely into Transylvania and from there into Moldavia. After being repeatedly assaulted by the Transylvanian *Grenzer*, the Tatars headed to Barczànfalva and eventually exited into the opposite valley, a few miles from the border with Moldavia. In three days they had travelled 120 km, a considerable march taking into account the inaccessible paths crossed, and the large number of prisoners: 'who marched before as a herd of cattle.'[18]

On the evening of 3 September, the Tatars crossed the narrow road before the pass of Szrimtura, but they found it blocked by boulders and timbers; therefore they had to stop and spend the night in the place. At dawn they were attacked by frontiersmen and peasants: 'the Tatars fled in a confused crowd, desperately trying to save their lives ... but they lost 5 to 6,000 men in the valley; the rest routed.'[19] A few hundred Tatars were saved by escaping on foot and eventually reached Moldavia, still chased by the *Grenzer* hussars. The Tatars lost all their baggage, even the loot was returned to the Hungarians. About 3,000 civilians had survived the terrible march but more than 1,000 had died along the way.[20]

Transylvanians

In the mid seventeenth century, the *kiral* ('king' in Hungarian, but actually grand-prince) of Transylvania had his own national army which, together with the militias gathered with the general call to arms, rose to almost

---

17 *Ibidem*, p.188.
18 *Ibidem*.
19 *Ibidem*, relation of the *Grenz Obrist* Andras Dettina von Pivoda.
20 *Ibidem*, p.189.

39. Hungarian *kuruc* officer, portrayed in the 1670s in the book of costumes *The True and Exact Fashion of all Nations in Transylvania*. The Hungarian rebellion against the Habsburgs found in Transylvania an asylum from where the exiles continued their struggle, joining the Ottoman army in 1683. The officer wears a red fur-trimmed headdress, a long crimson *attila* lined with yellow, azure trousers, and a pair of high yellow leather boots.

90,000 men on paper, of which 40 percent was formed by cavalry.[21] The composition of the army had maintained several characteristic of the original Royal Hungarian army, however in the organisation of the troops, the Transylvanians had adopted some Western features. As occurred in Habsburg Hungary, in Transylvania the establishment of the army depended on the Estates voting in the Diet, where the three nations were represented. The troops were grouped together in regiments and in companies of 1,000 and 100 men respectively, and joined by artillery, maintained by the state treasury and directed by professional officers. All the officer class belonged to the nobility: the captains of the companies received the title of *vajda*, while the senior commander held the rank of *elsò vajda*.

The cavalry was divided according to the princedom's nationality into Hungarian and Székely (the Sequi or Siculi and also Szekler in German) regiments. The main *speciality* was the light cavalry equipped as the Hungarian hussars, but there were also companies of heavy cavalry, trained to fight in close order, armed like the Polish winged hussars and protected by armour, who usually formed the lifeguard for the *kiral* and other magnates. The common infantry soldiers was the *hajduk*, similarly equipped as the janissaries, but trained to fight in small, very mobile groups, and always in close contact with the cavalry. In the field, they also used a defensive deployment with wagons mixed with the artillery. The Transylvanian army enjoyed a considerable reputation and, in an emergency, could be joined by an indeterminate number of militia, on foot and on horseback, recruited by the cities and by the nobles at the head of the committees into which the state was divided.

The Transylvanian army originally consisted of three corps: the noble troops, the *Militia Portalis*, and the general levies (called the 'insurrectionis'). Every aristocrat was liable for military service, the so-called *Primipilus*, and further he had to recruit a representative number of soldiers that depended on the value of his property. If the prince announced the general call to arms or 'insurrection', the *masserias* would add one additional horseman, and one foot soldier to join the army on campaign. Without the general 'insurrection', the numerical size of the troops assembled by the counties would have been a very meagre force. Moreover, the battle quality of these inexperienced and often poorly armed soldiers was low, and in the mid seventeenth century their presence as fighting force had declined drastically.

---

21 *Ibidem*, vol. I, p.160. In 1648 the Transylvanian army, which joined the Swedish under Torstensonns in Moravia, had 22,000 soldiers of which half were cavalry.

Alongside the Hungarians, also the Székely followed this pattern. These Hungarian-speaking folk of Turkish origin settled along the eastern borders and formed a political majority with the status of autonomy and self-government. They were also the leading political group in seven provinces or *sedes*: Udvarhely, Maros, Aranyos, Csík, Sepsi, Kézi and Orbai. In return for their privileges, each Székely male was nominally a soldier as well. In the mid seventeenth century, the Szekély organised an effective militia of some 20,000 men. The Saxen, a German-speaking people settled in Hungary and Transylvania from the twelfth century, constituted the third 'nation' of Transylvania. Protestant immigrants also arrived in the sixteenth century from the Rhine, Mosel and Saxony. They settled in the central south, around the Saxon cities of Hermannstadt, Kronstadt and Bistritz (today respectively Sibiu, Brașov and Bistrița in Romania), and these were the three main trade centres of the Princedom. Saxen communities had the same status of self-government and autonomy as the Székely. Each Saxen town and village organised a militia for garrison duty and employed it on campaign with the main army. Saxens traditionally comprisedd the personnel for the artillery also. Other militia units were formed in the principal towns, which had been granted fiscal autonomy. The major ones were Koloszvár, Várad and Marosvásárely (today respectively known as Clui-Napoca, Oradea Mare and Tirgu Mures in Romania), each with a permanent garrison of 5–600 men. Some of the small towns and villages had a company of barely 50 men or less. Another kind of semi-permanent military unit of Transylvania was the *praesidiarius* or frontiersmen, who formed in 1550 the force in charge of guarding the southern and western borders and providing a first line of defence before the mobilisation of the army. In the 1650s the prince ordered a new organisation for these troops, exchanging their border service for fiscal benefits. Approximately 4–5,000 horses and foot were deployed along the border. On the south-west border, the major fortresses were Lippa and Boros-Jenő, guarding the passing point across the Maros and Fekete-Kőrös rivers. Other strong fortresses on the southern border were Tokay, Huszt, Kővar, Szamosúivár, Várad and Szatmár. The latter two were the most important and well protected, with modern walls and bastions.

Since the beginning of the seventeenth century the princedom's military had become standing mercenary units enlisted in the *comitates* and over the border, especially in Poland, Hungary, Germany and the Balkans. Prince Rákóczy György I enlisted his private guard and some foreign infantry 'regiments' who were trained in Western tactics, and equipped them to be the most modern infantry army in Eastern Europe. These permanent and disciplined modern troops came under the direct control of the ruling prince, removing the aristocracy from influencing the formation of the army. During the reign of György II, the *kiral*'s omnipotent supremacy turned to move the balance more in favour of the Prince, in the absolutist spirit of that age. In 1650 Rákóczy recruited a whole German infantry regiment, known as the *Vörös Németek*, Red Germans, by the colour of the uniforms. In the campaign against Poland of 1657, György II led an army of 21,000 men, almost completely formed by mercenary soldiers. In January, Rákóczy reviewed 10,000 horsemen, 5,000 Transylvania foot and 6,000 from

Wallachia and Moldavia.[22] Since 1650, the Prince had already reformed the army's administrative corps, with the commissars and officers posted to the general command of infantry, cavalry and artillery.

The Transylvanian princedom had an efficient arsenal and foundry in Gyulafehérvár, where several calibres of cannon were produced using modern methods and technology. Another foundry was activated at the beginning of the seventeenth century, at Fogaras (today Făgăras in Romania). Powder storage and mills were to be found in the Saxen cities and other major towns. Contemporary writers recorded that the Transylvanian artillery was a significant and efficient force, and they estimated 300 pieces, both siege and field guns.

The presence of foreign professional soldiers did not change the traditional composition of the Transylvanian army, which maintained a large percentage of cavalry. When in July 1658 Rákóczi György II returned to Transylvania, having lost his army in Poland, he turned to the towns' militiamen to reconstitute his military force, while other soldiers were recruited in Hungary, Wallachia, Moldavia and Germany.[23] In 1662 the pro-Habsburg faction led by Kemény János assembled a 4–5,000-strong army, which included Croatian light cavalry and German mercenary infantry.

The great magnates usually recruited mercenary contingents too as private corps. However, the limiting factor on the military effectiveness of the Transylvanian army was the paucity of great landowners capable of raising military contingents. Only the great and rich families, such as the Bocskay, Bethlen and Rákóczy organised permanent troops, recruiting their subjects and joining them in companies known as *bandeira*. Theoretically, there were no limits to forming private contingents, but in the second half of the seventeenth century, there were very few standing units larger than 500 men. These troops, quartered in their castles or villages, were exempted from military service outside their residence. The function of the *Bandeiras* was mainly for the defence of towns and villages, so they posted only temporary small units in the field.

Once the Ottomans had regained control of the princedom, at the end of the bloody wars of 1657–62, and that against the Habsburgs which ended in 1664, they prevented the reconstitution of the Transylvanian army, keeping it slightly above the strength that, in case of war, the *kiral* was obliged to send to the sultan. In 1670 the contingent was established at 8,000 cavalry, while further infantry units had to be available to replace the Ottoman garrisons in the fortresses close to the Hungarian border.[24] The Porte strictly controlled the princedom's military affairs. In 1677 a spy reported that the prince could field only 1,500 soldiers as household troops, and the overall size of the Transylvanian army was estimated at 13,900 men in all.[25]

---

22   Payer, *Armati Hungarorum*, p.105. The Transylvanians was later joined by 20,000 Cossack horse and foot.

23   *Ibidem.*

24   Marsigli, vol. I, p.95.

25   S. Papp, 'Splendid Isolation? The Military Cooperation of the Principality of Transylvania with the Ottoman Empire (1571–1688) in the Mirror of the Hungarian Historiography's Dilemmas', in G. Kármán and L. Kunčević', *The European Tributary States of the Ottoman Empire in Sixteenth and Seventeenth Centuries* (Leiden, Boston: Brill, 2013), p.311.

In August 1681 the grand vizier ordered the raising of 8,000 infantry and cavalry, to be joined by another 19,000 Ottomans under the *paşa* of Várad Saidi Ahmed, for the planned offensive in Upper Hungary to support the Hungarian Protestant rebels against the Habsburg Emperor.[26]

The Hungarian refugee army under Count Imre Thököly had to join this force in the action that one year before could have opened the war with the Habsburgs. However, the struggle between Thököly and the Emperor would later have a significant weight in the dispute between Constantinople and Vienna as well as in the Transylvanian events. In 1677, the Hungarian rebels organised an armed force of almost 15,000 men in Transylvania, with which they intensified the attacks against the Imperial garrisons in Royal Hungary. The Porte supported these actions with foodstuff and ammunitions, while the *kiral* Apafy Miklós allowed Thököly to use the border fortresses in Transylvania as operational bases. However, decisive support came from Louis XIV, who sent officers to train the recruits, as well as an annual financing of 100,000 *thaler* signed in 1677.[27] The war against the Emperor led to the fall of numerous Hungarian fortresses in the hands of the *Kuruc* ('crusades') party. At the end of 1679 almost all Upper Hungary was under the control of the rebels, who intensified their attacks up to Moravia.[28]

A truce interrupted the hostilities in 1680, but two years later, when the Porte declared war on the Emperor, about 9,000 horse and 6,000 foot *kuruc* soldiers joined the Ottoman field army for the campaign against Vienna. Thököly achieved the greatest personal success when the city of Bratislava (Pressburg-Poszony), home of the Hungarian Diet, opened its doors to him. Disagreements and poor collaboration between Thököly and the Ottoman *serasker* Abaza Kör Hüseyn contributed to the failure. On 11 July, Thököly joined the Ottomans' 7,000- strong corps at Győr and marched to Esztergom where both forces crossed the Danube. Here initial disagreements among the commanders delayed the march to Bratislava, which was finally resumed on 24 July. The *kuruc* leader was obviously focused on conquering the capital of Habsburg Royal Hungary, while the Ottoman commander had as his task controlling the moves of the enemy relief army, regarding which there was little information. On 25 July, the Ottoman–Hungarian vanguard sighted a small detachment of Imperial infantry marching to reinforce the garrison of Bratislava. They forced the Imperialists to retreat, but the news of encounter alarmed the Duke of Lorraine, who was camped 15 km from the Hungarian capital. The next day, the Imperial commander moved the army in the direction of Marchsegg, on the Morava River, where he learned that Bratislava had opened its gates to Thököly's men. The plan to establish an autonomous Hungarian state, allied to the Porte, seemed to have come to pass. Considering the terrible consequences that the rebels' success could have on the current campaign, the Duke waded the Morava on 28 July with all the cavalry available. Marching in the night along the narrow road leading to Bratislava, he arrived in front of the city the following day. Lorraine did

---

26 József Bánlaky, *A magyar nemzet hadtörténelme*, vol. XVII (Budapest, 1928–1942), p.429.
27 Payer, 'Armati Hungarorum' p.233.
28 See volume II of this series: 'The Imperial Army, 1657–87', pp.161–170.

not know the size of the opposing force, and ordered a reconnaissance. The Hungarian sentinels spotted the enemy and gave the alarm. Thököly overestimated the enemy strength, and realising he would receive no support from Abaza Kür Hüseyn, who obstinately performed his own personal campaign, he ordered the retreat.[29] Some infantry companies joined the 12,000 Imperial and Polish cavalry and dragoons, who advanced in the early morning of 30 July, allowing Ludwig of Baden to re-take Bratislava with little effort, while the cavalry approached the retreating enemies south of the city. Probably Charles of Lorraine doubted that he had enough forces to attack the bulk of the enemy army, but the war council expressed a wish for a general assault, and therefore the Imperialists came to battle.[30] The reports of the encounter are somewhat confusing, and the battle appears to have been just a skirmish. Even Lorraine had lost control of his men; however, the battle was celebrated with great resonance by the Imperialists, because it was their first victory in a war against a such numerous enemy.[31]

Much less dramatic was the Transylvanian participation on the campaign. In August 1682, the Grand Prince of Transylvania was compelled to gather a contingent of 6,000 horse, 2,000 foot and 500 diggers to join the Ottoman army at Fülek.[32] Under his command, Visegrad, Győrszentmárton (today Pannohalma in Hungary) and some minor forts were occupied in early 1683. In mid August *kiral* Apafy Miklós moved his force to guard the bridges on the Raba River, 90 km south of Vienna, in order to replace the Ottoman corps recalled to replace the casualties suffered in the siege. When the defeated Ottoman army withdrew from Austria, the Transylvanians provided an escort to Grand Vizier Kara Mustafa, forming a large square of cavalry around his person, and in this way they headed to Belgrade.[33]

In February 1684 Apafy returned with his troops into Transylvania, concluding his participation in the war against the Holy League. In 1686 the Imperial troops completed the occupation of the princedom, obtaining the submission of the new *kiral*, Apafy Miklós II.

The outcome of the Vienna campaign also had a negative impact on the Hungarian rebel forces; however the *Kuruc* army continued to fight against the Imperialists until 1699. With their rapid cavalry actions, the rebels caused considerable damage to the enemy along the routes of communication with Austria, providing a significant contribution to exploration and the gathering of information. In 1684, the *Kuruc* army controlled the Upper Hungary towns of Károly, Késmárk (today Kežmarok in Slovakia) Ungvár (Užhorod in Ukraine) and Munkács (Mukachevo in Ukraine), while besieging the fortress of Besztercebánya (Banská Bystrica in Slovacchia), but in November the rebels were defeated at Eperjes and forced to leave the country. All the

---

29   J. Bánlaky, *A magyar nemzet hadtörténelme*, p.122.
30   Stoye, *The Siege of Vienna*, p.163.
31   *Ibidem*.
32   S. Papp, 'Splendid Isolation? The Military Cooperation of the Principality of Transylvania with the Ottoman Empire', p.328.
33   Marsigli, vol. II, p.38.

fortresses were lost, except Munkács, which resisted until January 1688 under Imre Thököly's wife Ilona Zrínyi.

The desperate strategic situation prompted the Porte to sacrifice its ally, in the hope of arresting the Imperial advance in Hungary. Thököly thus became an exchange pawn, offered by the Porte to the Emperor, in the negotiations for opening talks for an armistice. On 15 October 1685 the Count was arrested by the *paşa* of Várad and transferred to Belgrade, but the negotiations failed, and the Ottoman treason caused the passage of thousands of rebels to the Imperial side. Thököly was finally released on 2 January 1686, and sent to Transylvania to organise the struggle against the plenipotentiary of Prince Apafy, Tekeli Mihaly, who agreed with the Emperor about the passage of the princedom into the control of Vienna. On 21 August 1690 the Count defeated his rival at Zernest, and a Diet was called in Kereszténysziget, to elect Thököly as new grand prince of Transylvania with Ottoman support; nevertheless, he could only maintain his position against the Habsburg armies with the utmost difficulty. His desperate struggle could not slow down the course of events, and in October 1690 the rebels suffered a decisive defeat at Hatség opposed to the Imperialists under Margrave Ludwig of Baden. Thököly and the remains of the *Kuruc* army finally left Transylvania in early 1691 and joined the Ottomans, continuing to fight alongside them until the Peace of Carlowitz. Hundreds of rebels participated in the campaigns on the Danube and in the Balkans; their presence was signalled at Slankamen (1691), Peterwardein (1694), Lugos (1695), Ollaschin (1696) and Zenta (1697), where the residual hopes of the *kuruc* cause were laid down once and for all in bitter defeat. Thököly spent the rest of his life in exile in Anatolia, and there he died, now alone and forgotten, in 1705.[34]

Wallachians and Moldavians

In the mid seventeenth century, the army of the Wallachia *hospodar* maintained the original structure received at the beginning of the century. Together with a nucleus of regular troops on foot and on horseback, directly under the command of the prince or his lieutenant, the *hataman*, each boyar had to recruit a variable number of between 100 and 200 horsemen, known as *cálárasi*. The city and the countryside contributed to increase the strength of the army, organising infantry and engineer units.[35] In Moldavia, the military structure imitated that of the neighbouring state. To ensure border security, armed and trained infantry formations similar to the Hungarian *hayduk* were created; the name of these frontiersmen was *dorubanti*. Mercenary units, mostly Serbians, called *seimeni*, supported the other infantry units, composed mostly of feudal levies. Small artillery units were located in the fortresses, equipped with poor quality guns.

---

34 The French traveller La Mottraye met Thököly in 1698, leaving a moving account in his first book *Voyages en Europe, Asie et Afrique*, pp.218–220.

35 N. Stoicescu, 'The Greater Army of Wallachia and Moldavia', in *Pages from the History of the Romanian Army* (Bucarest: Editura Academiei Republicii Socialiste, 1975), pp.56–57.

40. Transylvanian *hayduk* infantry, dating to 1670. (After *The True and Exact Fashions of all Nations in Transylvania*).

Altogether about 25,000 fighters could be gathered in Wallachia and 20,000 in Moldova in a reasonably short time. The restless political situation of both states did not contribute to improving the quality of the troops. In Wallachia in February 1655, *seimeni* and *dorubanti* provoked a violent uprising that soon spread to Moldavia. They were joined by the peasants, and for four months rebel bands crossed the two states, attacking the boyars' residences and the nobles' cavalry. The revolt was finally defeated thanks to the intervention of the Transylvanian prince and Tatars sent by the Ottomans. The repression caused the dissolution of almost all the *seimeni* units and most of the *dorubanti*, reserving to the boyars the task of raising the infantry in case of need, and recruiting soldiers from the peasants. Consequently, the cavalry units were strengthened, becoming the only regular force in the two princedoms.

Armament and equipment reflected the classic Ottoman-pattern cavalry, but usually both Wallachian and Moldavian troops were armed even worse with old and poor firearms, and favouring the use of bows and arrows. Ther fighting technique was similar to the Tatars, with whom the Ottomans often merged them. Also, in Wallachia as well as Moldavia the Ottomans required contingents of horsemen in time of war, with a force of 4,000 men each.[36]

---

36 Marsigli, vol. I, p.134.

Normally it was the ruler princes who conducted their contingents; to them the Ottomans assigned a *tugh* ensign and a *mehter* like the *paşas*.

The actual number of soldiers provided by Wallachia and Moldavia to the Ottoman armies is a vexing question.[37] Certainly, the Ottoman commanders seem to have doubted the loyalty of the two Romanian princes. This distrust was not unfounded. In the seventeenth century, Wallachian and Moldavian sources often record the two princes' desire to join the Porte's enemies. In 1663, at the eve of the campaign against the Imperialists, the Italian traveller Antonio Zani relates that messengers from both princes informed Montecuccoli that they were forced to fight against him and that their troops were poorly armed and ill-disciplined.[38] Concerning the combat effectiveness of this cavalry there are further unflattering testimonies: 'the Turks treated them [the Wallachians and Moldavians] with great contempt … they were considered cowards, and also cruel and thieving against enemies and friends, and even treacherous, because they often left the battlefield without understandable reason and disappeared from the army.'[39] The most sensational case in which was demonstrated the unreliability of Wallachians and Moldavians, occurred during the battle of Chocim (1673), when the whole contingent escaped into the Polish camp.

About 3,000 Wallachians and Moldavians participated in the war in Hungary of 1663–64. In the autumn of 1661 before the war against the Emperor, they were joined with the Ottoman cavalry and formed the rearguard of Koprülü Ahmed's army.[40] One year later, the Wallachians participated with the Tatars and the Ottoman border cavalry to the raids in Upper Hungary; then, towards the end of the campaign, they attempted an assault on the fortress of Fágaras, but were repulsed by a sortie of the Imperial garrison, and left eight ensigns to the enemy. After this defeat, they left the army and quickly crossed back over the border. In September 1663, Wallachians and Moldavians formed the vanguard that opened the way to the Tatars in the great incursion into Styria and Moravia. One year later, under the *hospodar* Gheorges Ghica, the Wallachians participated in the campaigns in Upper Hungary.[41] Together with the Ottoman cavalry their

---

37 'The first difficulty for establishing the field forces of the princedoms is the unreliability of the original sources. According to authoritative authors, there are still disagreements about when and how a Wallachian or Moldavian prince first joined a military expedition of the Porte. Sometimes a Romanian presence on campaign can be deduced from Ottoman sources, while Christian accounts often ignore their number, or identify them as 'Auxiliaries'. Sometimes, however, the situation is reversed: Christian sources mention Wallachian or Moldavian involvement in a battle, while the Ottoman ones are silent.' O. Cristea, 'The Friend of my Friend and the Enemy of my Enemy: Romanian Participation in Ottoman Campaigns', in G. Kármán and L. Kunčević, *The European Tributary States of the Ottoman Empire in Sixteenth and Seventeenth Centuries* (Leiden-Boston: Brill, 2013), p.252.
38 *Ibidem*, p.268.
39 K.u.K. Kriegsarchiv, *Feldzüge des Prinzen Eugen*, vol. I, p.528.
40 Montecuccoli, 'Della Guerra contro il Turco', in Luraghi, *Opere di Raimondo Montecuccoli*, vol. II, p.402.
41 *Ibidem*, p.403.

presence is recorded at Leva, on 9 July 1664, where they were again defeated by the Imperialists.[42]

Approximately, 4,000 horsemen from Wallachia and 2,000 from Moldavia took part in the Vienna campaign of 1683, under the orders of their respective sovereigns, Serban Cantacuzeno and Georghes Duca.[43] The Grand Vizier employed them in rearguard tasks, avoiding contact with the defenders.[44] Indeed the true feelings of the Wallachian hospodar and his soldiers were revealed at the end of the siege, when, before fleeing, Serban Cantacuzenus erected a cross as a sign of gratitude for the salvation of Vienna. Wallachians and Moldavians appeared again with the Ottoman army in 1684, then in the fighting before the siege of Érsekúivár in 1685, in Bia in 1686, and finally in Esseg and Mòhacs, in 1687, deployed with the cavalry vanguard.[45]

The allied offensive also extended to the two Romanian states; Wallachia was run from 1686 by the Polish army, which occupied the fortresses of Suceava, Neamṭ and the northwestern border. Operations continued until 1691 and, still together with the Ottomans and their Tatar allies, engaged the Moldavian army in a gruelling war of raids and plunders. In an attempt to delay the Polish advance, the Ottomans resorted to the destruction of the countryside in the theatre of war, employing the same Moldavian cavalry in the destruction. Wallachia was threatened by the Habsburg army that, once it occupied Transylvania, penetrated the northern region of the country in 1690. Aliquots of Wallachian cavalry fought under Imre Thököly at Zernest and Hatség (1690), and finally at Lugos (1695).

After the Peace of Carlowitz, and following the political events of the two states, the Ottomans obtained from the local rulers a reduction of the armed force, gaining the direct control of the princedoms and increasing the Ottoman and Tatar military presence in both countries.

The experience of the War of the Holy League persuaded the Porte to rely less and less on the Wallachian and Moldavian forces. The Ottoman commanders, rather than assigning them an active role, preferred to employ the princedoms' troops in defensive roles.

The disarmament policy imposed by the Porte on the Romanian princes was secretly evaded by the Moldovan *voyevoda* Demeter Cantemir, in anticipation of the war between Russia and the Ottoman Empire in 1711. At the eve of the campaign on the Pruth, Cantemir had gathered four infantry 'German' regiments of 1,000 men each (possibly Transylvanians and Ruthenians), and four 'regiments' of Ukrainian Cossacks, with the

---

42 Gheorges Ghica kept up a secret correspondence with the Imperial command, informing Montecuccoli about the Ottoman plans and avoiding full commitment in the fighting. Montecuccoli refers several times to these agreements: 'Ghica never fought in favour of the Turks … and besides this he offered himself with more than a message to lend any good service to the Christian arms.' *Ibidem*, pp.420–421.

43 Seaton-Watson, *Histoire des Roumains*, p.96.

44 Hammer-Purgstall, *Geschichte des Osmanischen Reiches*, vol. XII, p.103. The lack of confidence of the Ottoman commander against them is confirmed by the orders issued on 4 August 1683, when Kara Mustafa assigned the troops of two *paşas* to better control the Wallachian–Moldavian contingent.

45 Marsigli, vol. II, p.90.

same strength. This professional mercenary force joined the local troops consisting of the Cantemir's lifeguards with 60 horsemen, a palace corps with 10 companies of 100 men, 20 Moldavian mounted companies, four 'banners' of Lithuanian Tatars, two 'banners' of Muslim *beslü* as mounted police, a levy of 1,000 horsemen from each of the 19 Moldavian provinces, 8,000 *dorobant* infantry, and one private company of boyar *hinsary* (hussars) cavalry.[46] This 'secret army' had to join the Russians on the Pruth, but the plan failed and the units immediately disbanded.

At the beginning of hostilities against the Habsburgs in 1716, the two states had almost no more than an army that could be defined as such. The tragic end of Prince Costantin Brâncoveanu and the harshness of the government of the new *hospodar*, Nicolaos Mavrocordatos, led the majority of the Wallachian boyars to take refuge in Transylvania, followed by numerous volunteers of the dissolved cavalry corps. After the fall of Temeşvár, an Imperial expeditionary corps occupied the north of Wallachia and under the protection of *Feldmarschall Lieutenant* Steinville a Diet was convened in Tirgovist, charged to form a new government. The *hospodar* sent letters to Vienna to protest against the occupation of the country, then turned to the Bucak Tatars. In November 1716, taking advantage of the weakness of the princedom and the internal disorder, the Imperial *Grenzer* of Transylvania scored a bold achievement against Prince Mavrocordatos himself. After sustaining an encounter with a corps of Tatars north of Bucharest, the Transylvanians entered the city on 25 November and headed for the Prince's residence. Altogether the Imperials raised 500 horsemen, but they easily prevailed against the guards of the palace, then they also dispersed a corps of Ottoman and Tatar cavalry encamped outside the city, and finally captured the *hospodar*. During the return to Transylvania, hundreds of peasants and a good number of horsemen who had been sent against the *Grenzer* joined them: 'the ferocious hatred against Mavrocordatos put his life in great danger. In vain he offered a ransom of 100 bags of gold, but the Transylvanians took him along with a great booty and also the Harem.'[47] The prisoner was interned in Cronstadt, where the Imperialists arrived carrying the ensigns in triumph, all the instruments of the *Mehter* and the personal flag of the *hospodar*.[48]

The Ottomans placed on the throne Mavrocordatos' brother, Joannis, appointing him as new *hospodar*: 'without much ceremony, throwing on his shoulders a caftan'.[49] The outcome of the successful action of the Transylvanian *Grenzer* encouraged the Imperial command to attempt a similar action in Moldavia against the *voievoda*. At the end of January 1717, a small corps of dragoons and mounted militiamen crossed the border and arrived at Jassy without encountering resistance. However, as they prepared to enter the city by storming a *palanka*, hundreds of Tatar and Moldavian horsemen came out of the surrounding woods and threw themselves at them.

---

46 *Oderint dum Prebunt*: <http://rusmilhist.blogspot.com/2010/10/moldavian-army-in-prut-campaign-1711.html>
47 K.u.K. Kriegsarchiv, *Feldzüge des Prinzen Eugen*, vol. XVI, p.241.
48 *Ibidem.*
49 *Ibidem*, p.245.

Surrounded, and targeted by arrows and fire, almost all the Imperialists fell in combat or were taken prisoners. The few survivors were chased across the border by the *voievoda*'s horsemen and the Tatars, who then attacked some fortified villages on the Transylvanian border. In February, 1,000 horsemen from Moldavia fired and destroyed the Imperial fort of Niamt, abandoned by the *Grenzer*.[50] At the end of August 1,000 Moldavian knights, alongside the Ottoman and Tatar cavalry under Regeb Paşa, participated in the raids into Transylvania with the *voievoda* Mihaly Rakovita.

Moldavians and Wallachians also supplied a work force to the Ottoman field army, and the horsemen usually supported the *musellims* in their duties.[51]

---

50 *Ibidem*, p.249.
51 Hammer-Purgstall, *Geschichte des Osmanischen Reiches*, vol. XII, p.102.

1. Grand Vizier, 1658–1691; 2. *Beglerbeg* of Rumelia, 1650–1660

(Illustration by Bruno Mugnai, © Helion & Company 2020)

See Colour Plate Commentaries for further information.

Plate B

1. Janissary *çorbaci*, mid 17th century;
2. Janissary in parade dress, 1680–1690; 3. Janissary in quarters dress, 1650–1700
(Illustration by Bruno Mugnai, © Helion & Company 2020)
See Colour Plate Commentaries for further information.

ii

Plate C

1. *Topçu*, artilleryman, 1650–60;
2. *Cebeci*, armourer, mid 17th century; 3. *Solak*, 1658
(Illustration by Bruno Mugnai, © Helion & Company 2020)
See Colour Plate Commentaries for further information.

1. Horseman of the grand vizier's household cavalry, 1658;
2. *Kapikulu* cavalry, *sipahi ulùfely*, mid 17th century
(Illustration by Bruno Mugnai, © Helion & Company 2020)
See Colour Plate Commentaries for further information.

Plate E

1. Janissary in campaign dress, 1660–1670;
2. *Serdengeçdi*, mid 17th century; 3. *Topçu*, campaign dress, 1660–80
(Illustration by Bruno Mugnai, © Helion & Company 2020)
See Colour Plate Commentaries for further information.

1. European *azab* infantryman, mid 17th century;
2. Anatolian *azab* infantryman, 1650; 3. European *azab* infantryman, 1686
(Illustration by Bruno Mugnai, © Helion & Company 2020)
See Colour Plate Commentaries for further information.

1. Egyptian *çavuş*, 1658; 2. Egyptian *sipahi*, mid 17th century;
3. Kurdish standard bearer (*tugh*), 1640–50
(Illustration by Bruno Mugnai, © Helion & Company 2020)
See Colour Plate Commentaries for further information.

Plate H

1. Ottoman *sancakbeg*, Syria or Egypt, 1650–1700;
2. Eastern Anatolian horseman, mid 17th century; 3. *Matbah*, driver, 1650–1700

(Illustration by Bruno Mugnai, © Helion & Company 2020)

See Colour Plate Commentaries for further information.

Plate I

1. Arnaut, Albanian Infantryman, 1700–1718;
2. Mounted Arnaut, 1690–99; 3. Bosnian Frontiersman, early 18th century
(Illustration by Bruno Mugnai, © Helion & Company 2020)
See Colour Plate Commentaries for further information.

Plate J

1. Crimean Tatar *kalgay*, late 17th century; 2. Tatar foot soldier, 1670–90;
3. Moldavian *călăraşi* horseman, late 17th century
(Illustration by Bruno Mugnai, © Helion & Company 2020)
See Colour Plate Commentaries for further information.

Kapikulu cavalry, *sipahi*, 1690–1718
(Illustration by Bruno Mugnai, © Helion & Company 2020)
See Colour Plate Commentaries for further information.

Plate L

Serhaddkulu cavalry, *dely*, mid 17th century
(Illustration by Bruno Mugnai, © Helion & Company 2020)
See Colour Plate Commentaries for further information.

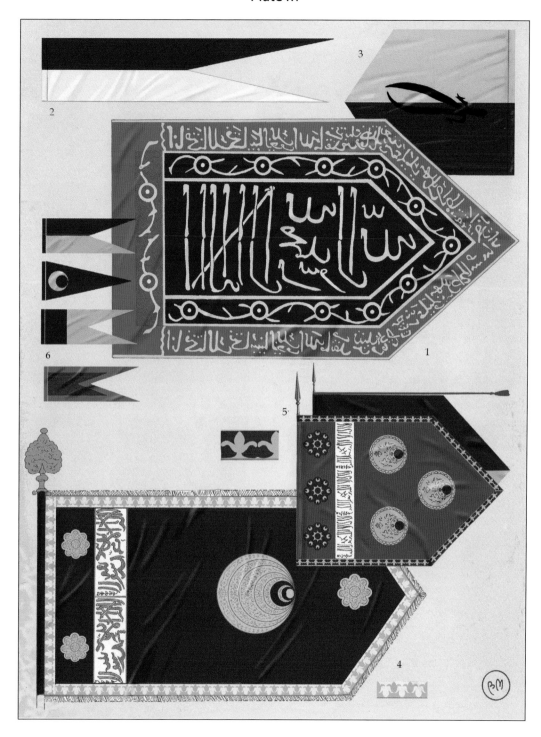

Ensigns

(Illustration by Bruno Mugnai, © Helion & Company 2020)

See Colour Plate Commentaries for further information.

Plate N

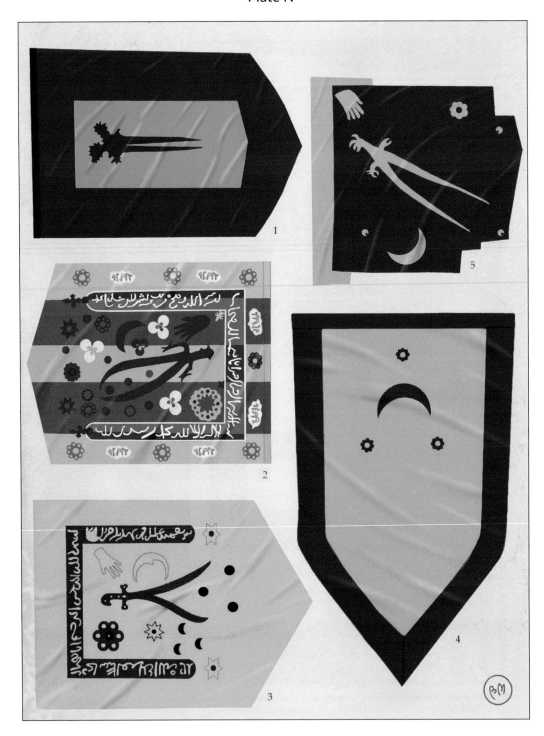

Ensigns
(Illustration by Bruno Mugnai, © Helion & Company 2020)
See Colour Plate Commentaries for further information.

1

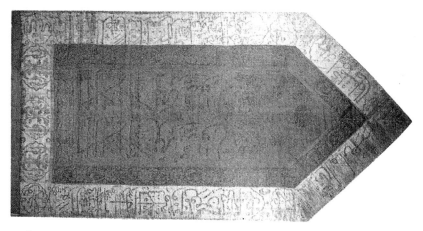

2

Ensigns captured at Vienna, 1683
(Wavel Museum, Krakow)
See Colour Plate Commentaries for further information.

Plate P

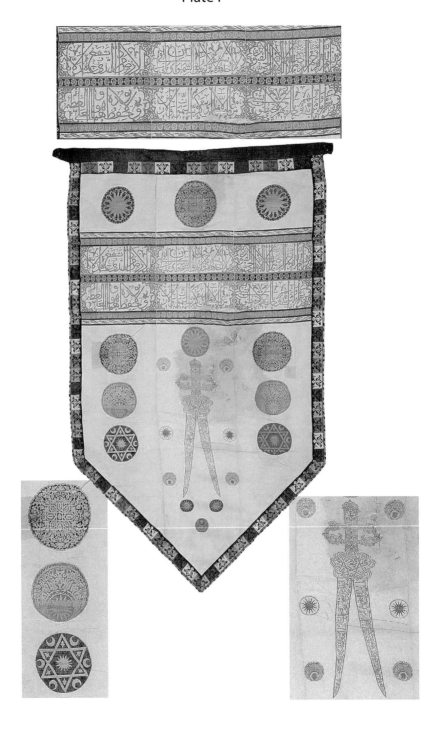

Large *sancack* captured in 1686
(Museum of Fine Arts, Budapest)
See Colour Plate Commentaries for further information.

5

The Ottoman Art of War

'The Turks did short but great war.'

(Montecuccoli, *Aforismi applicati alla guerra possibile col Turco in Ungheria*,
chapter III, aphorism XIII.)

The Ottoman Empire was a determining world power of the seventeenth century; in modern terms, the Empire was a superpower. The Porte held this rank by virtue of the geopolitical scenario, its enormous territory and population, its wealth of economic resources, as well as a central and provincial administration capable of mobilising these resources to support the policy of the state. Before the balance of forces in favour of the Porte turned to the Christian side in the war of the Holy League (1682–99), the Ottomans had always adopted a unique strategy of war, developed since their arrival in Europe and perfectly integrated with the political structure of the Empire.[1] The Koran, alluding to the division of the world into two parts: the *dhar ul Islam* (the land of the faithful) and the *dhar ul arb* (the land of conquest), had provided the mystic-ideological basis to Ottoman warfare. Consequently, since territorial conquests were one of the main affairs of the state, the military campaigns had a distinctly offensive character. Thanks to this, the Ottoman commanders could anticipate the moves of their enemies and almost always hold the strategic initiative.

Offensive campaigns consumed huge resources, but also in this regard, the Porte could access considerable reserves. The Christian enemies knew as the efficient use of resources constituted the base of the Ottoman army, which continued to be one of the most fearsome armies in Europe at the time. Though Ottoman trade remained excluded from the routes of the Atlantic Ocean, the Empire constituted an alternative 'world economy' and, unlike many of its rivals, was self-sufficient in the production of weaponry and ammunition.[2] With the exception of tin, the Porte possessed all the necessary

---

1   Montecuccoli, *Aforismi applicati alla guerra possibile col Turco in Ungheria*, chapter III, aphorism XIV. 'The coherence of his states and the permanent troops make it easier for the Turk to maintain large armies.'
2   G. Ágoston, *Ottoman Warfare in Europe*, p.130.

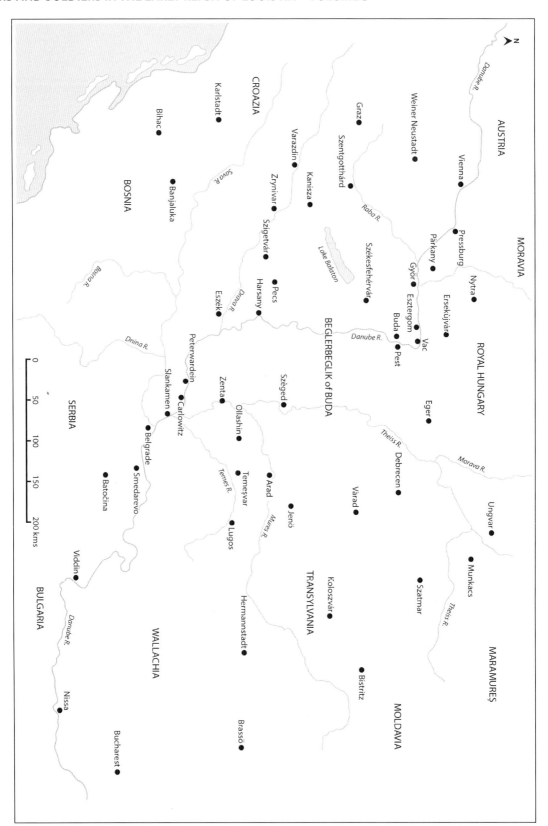

Map 5. War Theatre in Hungary and the Balkans.

raw materials to cast ordnance and to supply the artillery with cannonballs and gunpowder. Iron was excavated in large quantities in Anatolia at Bilecik, Kigi near Erzurum and Keban. In the European part of the Empire, there were iron mines in Bulgaria, Bosnia and Serbia, and in Greece. There were important copper mines in Anatolia and further in Bosnia. Next to the mines, furnaces produced hundreds of thousands of cannonballs. Wood and charcoal needed to operate the war industry plants and used in the construction of ships and fortresses could easily be obtained from the wooded areas of the Empire. Most of the wood came from the forests along the Black Sea coast. Wood for the workshops in Constantinople came from a section of the European coast that extended from Constantinople to Varna and from a section of the Asian coast from Constantinople to Samsun.

The Porte also had plentiful supplies of the raw materials needed for the manufacture of gunpowder. Large quantities of saltpetre were to be found in Egypt (especially in Old Cairo), in Syria, in Lebanon, in Palestine and in Iraq (especially in the Basra area). Saltpetre could was also to be extracted in Asia Minor, especially at Karaman, Malatya, Içe1 and Van, and in the European part of the Empire in Greece, Bulgaria, Hungary and Crimea. The main sources of sulphur, which was the other main constituent of gunpowder, were located in the vicinity of the Dead Sea, in the region of Van, in Moldavia and on the island of Melos. There were gunpowder factories in Constantinople, Gelibolu, Thessalonica, Smyrna, Belgrade, Buda, Temeşvár, Karaman, Van, Erciş, Cairo, Baghdad, Aleppo, and several other localities. These powder mills were capable of manufacturing the required quantity of gunpowder for the army and the navy. In short, the Empire did not have any difficulty in mass-producing, and was not dependent on the import of European weaponry and ammunition, as has been suggested by many historians.[3]

Supply and Logistics

The key to Ottoman superiority was also the result of the work managed by an impressive corps of officials in charge of organising the supply system for the field army, directed by operational bases that were the same capitals and administrative centres of the Empire. While in the rest of the seventeenth-century Europe, supplies constituted a significant problem for the conducting of military campaigns, the Porte succeeded with relative ease in assuring its troops of all necessary items. This achievement appears even more significant, considering that in the seventeenth century, the campaigns were launched with three times as many soldiers and five to six times as many firearms and cannons than in the previous century.[4]

The ability to quickly prepare for conflicts was an advantage particularly feared by the sultan's enemies. In his 'aphorisms' Montecuccoli affirmed that

3   Ágoston, 'Firearms and Military Adaptation: The Ottomans and the European Military Revolution, 1450–1800', in *Journal of Military History*, vol. 25/1, March 2014, pp. 107–108.
4   Uyar-Erickson, *A Military History of the Ottomans*, p.86.

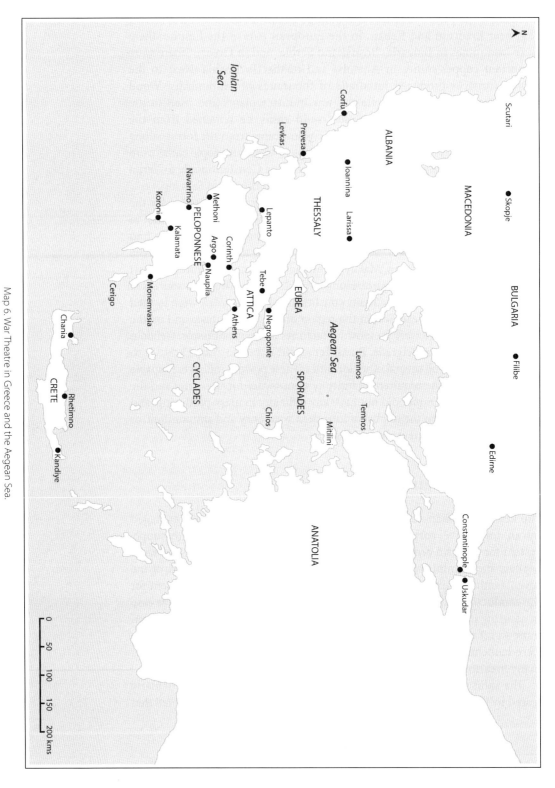

Map 6. War Theatre in Greece and the Aegean Sea.

'the Turk does not wait for war, but he takes it into the enemy country.'[5] The constant threat on the borders aimed to maintain exposed the peripheries of the Christian states, a condition that the Ottoman plenipotentiaries tried to maintain in every truce negotiation. It is worth remembering that one of the clauses of the armistice between the Porte and the Habsburg emperor at Vasvár in 1664, declared that incursions with fewer than 5,000 men without artillery did not mean a breaking of the truce.[6]

Research has clarified the dimensions of the Ottoman logistics system and its efficiency. As in the West, the regular distribution of provisions was the best way to preserve the armies from disintegration, even if the cost could be exorbitant. In this regard, in the last siege campaign in Crete, the Porte prepared a budget of 47,700,000 *akçes* just for military provisions, including foodstuffs.[7]

The coordination of supplies and the preparation of ammunition and food for the troops fell within the sphere of activity of the supreme financial authority of the Empire, the *defterdar paşa*, which made use of a corps of commissioner-employers, the simple *defterdar*, in turn assisted by the administrative officials of the provinces, the *defter kàtibi*.

The army *defterdars* were the administrators responsible for the field army, and occupied an important place in the army. They were entrusted with the war cash, with which they faced the costs of maintaining the troops mobilised for a campaign, namely the provincial cavalry and the *serhaddkulu*; since the *kapikulu* had its own autonomous administration with the budget established for the whole year. Before each war campaign, in anticipation of the number of men mobilised, a network of magazines was set up, around which operated the personnel in charge of preparing the necessaries for the army, joined in the *matbah*. This term identified the personnel in charge of the provisioning, along with the drivers and other service personnel, usually recruited for a single campaign in the provinces close to the war theatre.

In addition to supplies of ammunition and weapons, every soldier of the permanent corps enjoyed food provision established by the *kapikulu* regulations. Marsigli devotes several lines about the janissaries' feed, which included wheat, biscuit, meat and of course rice and butter for the preparation of the traditional dish: the *pilav* rice. He also recalled the Greek, Armenian and Jewish butchers, accredited directly by the *yeniceri agasi* and subjected to the control of the *meydanbasi*.[8] In the matter of foodstuffs, the Ottoman army had other crucial advantages as well. In the seventeenth century, the average Ottoman soldier was sturdier, consumed fewer luxury goods, and contended more easily with the difficult conditions of being on campaign than his European counterparts. Even the turbulent janissaries demonstrated on more than one occasion that they were more accustomed

---

5   Ágoston, 'Firearms and Military Adaptation', p.108
6   K.u.K. Kriegsarchiv, *Feldzüge des Prinzen Eugen*, vol. I, p.148.
7   Murphey, *Ottoman Warfare*, pp.94–95.
8   Marsigli, vol. I p.82 and vol. II p.67. Each janissary received every day 420 grammes of bread, 210 grammes of biscuit, 240 grammes of beef or mutton, 210 grammes of rice or legumes, and 100 grammes of butter only on Friday. The rations were divided into two meals: the first at 11:00 and the second at 7:00 in the evening, prepared by the cook of the *orta*. Meat and rice were boiled with the addition of spices. According to Marsigli, the janissaries' cuisine was of very high level.

than the Christian soldiery to the hard conditions of campaign, and even more so when spurred on by the promise of prizes and awards.

The daily supply of the marching army and its billeting was the duty of the districts along the routes crossed by the marching army. The local officials were tasked to coordinate and make available prearranged amounts of provisions at the billets, the *menzil*, which were positioned at intervals from four to eight hours of marching distance from each other. Like the European soldiers, every Ottoman soldier bought his food and fodder for his animal at his own personal expense. To accommodate this, the government was under obligation to provide enough supplies at a reasonable price to standing army units. For this task, the Porte turned to authorised dealers who dealt with supply for the army. They were qualified as *orducu*, who consisted of artisans, contractors, and various types of tradesmen authorised by the *defterdar* to supply foodstuffs or perform services for the army in peacetime as well as on campaign. Most of these civilians were tasked by their respective guilds, and on several occasions they successfully provided for the army during the military campaign in Europe and in Asia.[9] The Porte only provided security and sometimes transportation. Every individual soldier, and units as well, had to buy logistical support for themselves from the *orducus*, which had a monopoly for specific items. Additionally, villagers were encouraged to sell their products at reasonable profit to the *orducu* and other military contractors. Authorised *orducus* and peasants were subject to the control of the army *defterdars* and senior commanders. Thanks to these meticulous preparations, the movement of the army most often worked quite well, especially in the European theatre of operations.[10] There, the Ottoman government was able to solve the logistics of campaigning relatively easily, thanks to the agricultural capacity of its vassal states. The Porte tried to protect border regions from pillaging and foraging, but not always successfully. The Crimean Tatars especially created problems, and Ottoman control measures rarely worked on them. During the campaigns, carrying enough necessary provisions with the army itself was the least desirable logistical choice, but Ottoman soldiers generally received qualitatively and quantitatively superior treatment compared to their contemporaries, because of better rations, more reliable supply systems, and better sanitation and health services. Even though the personnel strength and the baggage train of the armies increased, the Porte still managed to maintain a high standard of logistics, and in some respects exceeded it.

---

9   Uyar-Erickson, *A Military History of the Ottomans*, pp.83–84.
10 *Ibidem*, p.84: 'However, several factors were critical for the efficient functioning of this system. These were regular payment of the soldiers, good harvests, law and order and, most importantly, terminating campaigns quickly and prior to the end of the season. In this respect, the Iranian campaigns were always difficult due to the lack of productive villages and farmlands along the corridors, greater marching distances, hostile nomads, and the scorched-earth tactics of the Iranians. For these campaigns, the government continuously tasked adjacent provinces to supply provisions and arranged additional sea or land transportation. Despite these arrangements, the Ottoman army continued to suffer privations during nearly all of the Iranian campaigns (which certainly was an important part of its poor performance there).'

In February 1682, the Imperial diplomat Alberto Caprara noticed the intense work of preparation of food and other supplies for the Ottoman army, while he was on his way to Constantinople. He could observe the continue logistical activity for the incoming war against the Habsburgs: 'Everywhere there is the presence of new armed bands and the setting up of huge stocks of ammunition in arsenals and storages close to the border … flocks of animals for slaughter and road maintenance …'[11] These activities were coordinated by the assistants of the *defterdar* and by the *çavuş* of the army. The transport of ammunition and foodstuffs, as well as all the troops and officers' baggage, required a large number of vehicles and often forced the *defterdars* to engage peasants with carts and draft animals from the province close to the theatre of war. Marsigli criticised the Ottoman train, stating that wagons and carts had four wheels of equal size and deprived of iron circles 'and these [the wagons] always very bad'.[12] The draft was formed by pairs of oxen, to which were added numerous mules, camels and dromedaries. For the campaigns in Hungary, many supplies were also loaded on ships, which sailed on the major waterways. To move along the rivers Danube, Sava and Drava more quickly, boats and drafts were trained by the shore using oxen, mules and even donkeys.

The Porte was able to set up an enviable network to supply its armies when engaged on different fronts, but the most strategically relevant, and the most extended, was the Hungarian supply network. It becomes clear that the importance of transport in terms of logistics and strategy brought fundamentally different situations for opposing forces, depending on which part of the Danube they were fighting at. During the siege of Vienna, the two supply apparatuses undoubtedly had completely different tasks to solve the problem. It also becomes clear that as the war shifted south, the problems of the Imperial supply apparatus worsened, while that of the Ottomans diminished. Consequently, the strategic situation of the opposing armies was either less favourable, or cheaper. Although historians do not know exactly how the Ottomans resolved food supply during the siege of Vienna, some scholars conclude that the flour deliveries were essentially secured if the Christians captured 24,000 quintals of flour after the battle on Kahlenberg. It is reasonable to think that this amount would have covered the needs of 60,000 soldiers for 40 days. However, historians also know that Kara Mustafa had called on the Hungarian population of the surrounding areas in a manifesto to visit the Ottoman camp and sell superfluous food at a good price. Of course, the farmers followed this call.[13]

The scenario was different with the fodder for the horses. In each army, one of the biggest problems was finding food for the riding and draft horses. If, in addition, it were possible to have relatively large cavalry troops, and the army was in one place for a long time, the food stocks of that area were exhausted quite quickly. Such was the case with the siege of Vienna

---

11 Eickoff, *Venedig, Wien und die Osmanen*, p.384.
12 Marsigli, vol. II, p.63.
13 G. Periés, 'Verproviantierung und Strategie im Befreiungskrieg', in *Acta Historica Academiae Scientiarum Hungaricae* n. 33–1 (2–4), (Budapest, 1987), p.273.

in 1683. Chroniclers relate that the horses needed dry fodder in the sixth week of the siege, but it was lacking in the first days. Since dry fodder was generally not delivered on site, but was transported from the magazines, it is probable that there were difficulties in transport. The transport capacity was probably fully consumed by the need for foodstuffs and artillery materials in particular, so that it was no longer sufficient for oat or barley deliveries. In fact, it can be proven that the Ottomans brought along a tremendous amount of artillery equipment for the siege of Vienna, included gunpowder for the mines. Although minor disturbances and delays occurred, they resulted not so much from inadequate organisation of the supply apparatus, but from financial difficulties and from the misunderstanding of the military leaders. It must be remembered that this was a siege campaign, and that the Ottoman commanders did not have to coordinate the movement of troops and transport, which was otherwise the most difficult logistical task.

There are many accounts relating the large quantities of foodstuffs following the Ottoman armies on campaign. The loot of Vienna is considered one of the largest and richest in the whole century, but even more striking was the amount of resources lost after the battle of Harsány, in 1687. It comprised 6,000 cattle, 5,000 draft horses, 1,000 donkeys, 300 camels and dromedaries, 400 buffalos, and also sheep and lambs in large numbers, then coffee, rice, sugar, lemons, chocolate and honey capable of sustaining an army for weeks.[14]

In the years in which the Ottoman Empire was at the height of its power, it was common to see the procession of wagons and animals with an immense amount of baggage. Marsigli cites as an example the drawing made by the Venetian provveditor Giovanni Morosini, in which the train gathered for the campaign of 1672 against the Poles, which included 'all the Arts necessary for food and luxury.'[15]

During the marches, the train occupied the central part of the column and was divided into two parts: the one managed by the *defterdars* and the one belonging to the *kapikulu*. In the first section was included the war cash, the baggage of the commander-in-chief and the major officers, the tents of the soldiers, the foodstuffs, the tent of the tribunal of war and even a carriage containing some *kaftans* destined as prizes for the more deserving soldiers; then the *kapikulu*'s baggage followed.

Each *kapikulu*'s *sipahi* owned along with six or seven other comrades a pack animal for transporting personal effects, and also the janissaries and all the *kapikulu* infantry used one horse for every nine or 10 soldiers; moreover the Egyptian janissaries proceeded on horseback in all the marches. Cairo and Damascus janissaries used horses also in their engagements. There are several accounts concerning the Ottoman mounted infantry on battlefield. Ottoman narrative and archival sources firmly confirm that Kıbleli Mustafa

---

14   *Theatrum Europaeum*,vol. XIII, p.29. The text describes in detail the campaign of 1687 and lists the rich *Türkenbeute*, which naturally included war equipment and siege tools, more than 50 flags, ammunition and tons of gunpowder.

15   Marsigli, vol II, p. 66, Marsigli insinuates that 'giganticmania' and taste for pomp were the actual reason for these apparatuses, which ultimately served to impress the enemy.

Paşa, as the governor-general of Damascus, had among his troops 500 *sam kulu*,[16] who were famous for their use of firearms on horseback.[17]

Camels, dromedaries, mules, oxen, buffalo and even donkeys were typical pack animals of the Ottoman armies. Camels and dromedaries, in comparison to the buffalo, were the favourite pack animals, because of their freight capacity.[18] Both were even faster and better suitable for the climate and had a load capacity of approximately 250kg.

Combat Tactics

According to Marsigli, in the open field the Ottoman commanders continued to deploy the troops, following a form that essentially remained unchanged throughout the seventeenth century.[19] The order of battle was large and deep, composed of several ranks, with the cavalry and infantry separated from each other. Generally, the troops on foot occupied the centre, called *dibolai*; while one the wings, the *sagacol* (right wing) and the *solcol* (left wing), the cavalry occupied the space. The *kapikulu* cavalry usually occupied the position behind the centre as tactical reserve. The first rows of the *dibolai* were occupied by groups of 100 men formed by volunteers from the janissaries, the *serdengeçdi*, in charge of leading the assaults. The deployment assumed the characteristic form of a semicircle, with the cavalry wings stretched for enveloping the enemy flanks. The need to deploy and exploit their own mobility favoured the Ottoman cavalry to take advantage of open spaces. Gathered in wide columns, the *sipahis* tried to disunite the enemy with a continuous movement made of assaults and rapid retreats. With this tactic, they tried to attract the enemy towards unfavourable terrain, or to isolate the troops imprudently launched to pursuit them. The continuous alternation of assaults and fake retreats were substantially the evolution of the ancient tactic of the Central Asian riders, already known by Roman times as 'Parthian war'. The agility of their cavalry allowed the Ottomans to easily overcome obstacles in the terrain and this made them insidious even on rough terrain. Competing with the Ottoman cavalry in terms of sudden mobility and sudden attacks was a matter in which Poles, Cossacks or Hungarian and Croatian hussars could engage themselves, while the Imperial armoured cavalry was forced to adopt a particular formation, arranging itself in actual squares of squadrons to resist the unbridled assaults of the *sipahis*.[20]

Effectively, the Ottoman cavalry never performed well against well-trained formatios. Similarly, a square of infantry could easily repel the *sipahi*'s charges. In this regard, Montecuccoli rightly stated that facing the

16 The *sam kulu* were cavalrymen from the garrison of Damascus, or 'Damascene janissary' in Ottoman terminology, who held the same privileges as the Egyptian janissaries.
17 Kolçak, 'The Composition, Tactics and Strategy of the Ottoman Field Army', in *A szentgotthárdi csata és a vasvári béke*, p.83.
18 F.Ardalı, *Food for the Army in the Ottoman Empire* (Istanbul Bilgi Üniveristesi, Ottoman Material Culture, Fall-Semester 2011–12), p.11.
19 Marsigli, vol. II, pp.119–20.
20 K.u.K. Kriegsarchiv, *Feldzüge des Prinzen Eugen*, vol. I, p.456.

41. 1) The figure is a reconstruction after Jean Guer's *Mœurs et usages des Turcs*. The author relates that at the end of the seventeenth century, in order to provide recruits for the janissary corps, the *kapikulu* enlisted soldiers from the *azab* infantry. Before they became true janissaries, the recruits received a 'Thessaloniki green' (turquoise) *kaftan*, faced and lined in different colours. Their headgear was the typical red felt *tekke*. 2) Egyptian janissaries held the privilege of marching on horseback. In some encounters, they fought like the Western dragoons (Reconstruction after Marsigli and van Moor). 3) The *serdengeçdi* 'head riskers' were the volunteers opening the infantry assaults. When in quarters they wore special dress, a fur-trimmed cap with plumes and embroidered *kaftan* with tassels and piping. Further distinctive marks were metallic or cloth stripes around the legs, carried by the veterans. Special distinctions issued to the bravest soldiers were great belts with metallic or enamelled accessories. In service, the leaders carried a long-bladed *tirpan* axe, similar to the Russian *bardiche*. (Author's illustration. After Van Moor, *Recueil de cent estampes représentant les diverses nations du Levant.*)

Ottoman cavalry should be the infantry, while cuirassiers and dragoons could fine work against the janissaries.[21] Before 1687, the limits of Ottoman combat tactics consisted in the lack of compactness of the battle order, which, once the attempts to disrupt the enemy failed, easily entered into crisis. If the adversary was able to launch a counter-attack, restricting the space for manoeuvring, the cavalry became dangerously exposed, being less trained to fight in close formation. Even disciplined and well-conducted armies, such as the one under Köprülü Ahmed in 1664, routed after they faced critical events. In the last phase of the battle of Szentgotthárd, which he witnessed, Evliya Çelebi describes the Ottoman soldiers overwhelmed by the allied assault 'like a mere drop in the ocean of the enemy forces.'[22] Köprülü Ahmed ordered the infantry to move back to the entrenchments guarding the bridgehead; but when the other troops saw this relocation, they assumed the infantry were fleeing the battlefield. The Ottoman army was in total panic. Only a few succeeded in getting back across the river to their camp. In Evliya's words: 'it was like the Day of Judgement'. Similar events occurred during the wars in Hungary, Greece, Podolia and Banat until 1717.

Apart from the *kapikulu sipahis*, the rest of the Ottoman cavalry consisted of irregular soldiers, who knew of no other warfare than that learned by their ancestors. Certainly, there were commanders who tried to adapt tradition to the new challenges posed by the most updated tactics of their Western enemies. Nevertheless, traditional tactics allowed the Ottomans to achieve considerable successes when they could outnumber the enemy, or fought against less disciplined adversaries, as occurred at Szentgotthárd. In the opening phase of the battle, the sequence of assaults and retreats induced the inexperienced German troops to pursue their enemy, and they were then overwhelmed by the sudden counter-attack. More than half a century later, at Carlowitz, the *sipahis*' charges succeeded in breaking the iron wall of the Imperial cavalry vanguard, causing the enemy to retreat in disorder; numerous prisoners were captured.

Speed and agility remained the only qualities of the Ottoman cavalry, which continued to perform the same tactics until the eighteenth century. A bizarre but eloquent narrative on the Ottoman incursions against the Imperial siege camp at Belgrade is reported in the 1717 campaign volume of the *Feldzüge des Prinzen Eugen* of the Austro-Hungarian war archive:

> For a couple of days about 3–4,000 horsemen continually appear in front of our trenches and ride up and down. Many volunteers went out of the trenches to try their luck, and they succeeded in throwing down several Turks … undressing them and also taking several horses with red tails. These skirmishes continue between our soldiers with Tatars and spahys, and on both sides, some come back without the head, because the Turks do not leave one, and for this they receive

---

21 Montecuccoli, in Luraghi, *Opere di Raimondo Montecuccoli*, vol. II, p. 440.
22 Cited in M.F. Çalişir, 'The Grand Vizier Köprülüzâde Fazil Ahmed Pasha and the Battle of Mogfersdorf-Saint Gotthard (1664)', in *Die Schlacht von Mogersdorf-St. Gotthard und die Friede von Eisenburg-Vasvár 1664*, edited by K. Sperl, M. Scheutz, A. Strohmeyer (Eisenstadt: Burgenlandische Forsungen, 2014), Band 108, p.209.

a ducat for each. This craze has also been introduced among us, but we do not receive money.[23]

Regarding the same events, a Bavarian officer added:

> The next day (the Ottoman cavalry) occupied the hills outside our encampment. Soon many horsemen gathered before our entrenchment, as they should make a reconnaissance, and with growing boldness, they risked running around here and there without stopping. They left the reins on the horses' necks and advance to the edge of our ditches, and then they stopped the horses and in a twinkling of an eye turned their backs. But first, they discharged the weapons shouting loudly: Allah! Allah! This challenge caused a lot of low-ranking soldiers, but also officers and cadets, to find something to do, to leave the entrenchments for shooting the enemies. And so we spent time, like a game, without much hurting each other.[24]

The awareness of the low effectiveness of the Ottoman cavalry in the open field now appeared obvious to all. On the eve of the battle of Belgrade, Prince Eugene of Savoy dictated to his officers the prescriptions to be observed for the incoming encounter, and when he introduce the Ottoman cavalry he recommended as follows:

> Our soldier must understand that we are dealing with Turks, Tartars and similar light enemies, from whom nothing is to be feared if the soldier remains in good order and does the right thing, while if he runs into danger he does badly. And the soldier must understand that these light horsemen always try to outflank us from behind, and then, if something similar happens, no one turns around for this, but has trust in the officers, who will be able to face the threat.[25]

Once the cavalry threat became inoffensive, the rest of the army was destined to defeat, exposing its weak points to the enemies: the artillery, due to the poor mobility, was always lost without the support of the cavalry, and infantry, not trained to defend themselves in squares, were overwhelmed by the charges of the enemy cavalry.

With the decline of the Ottoman cavalry, its presence in the battle diminished in percentage. At the siege of Vienna the troops on horseback still represented 40 percent of the army; at Zenta, 14 years later, the horsemen had fallen to less than 25 percent, and finally, in the following century, the highest percentage rarely exceeded 20 percent.[26]

The change in battle tactics therefore transferred the main role on the battlefield to the infantry. The favourite tactic of the janissaries consisted of mass assaults, which, after a general volley, were performed witho cold steel with a deafening background of shouts of incitement. The assaults, sudden

---

23 K.u.K. Kriegsarchiv, *Feldzüge des Prinzen Eugen*, vol. XVII, p.94.

24 M. de La Colonie, *Memoires de Monsieur De La Colonie*, Livre III, pp. 240–241.

25 K.u.K. Kriegsarchiv, 'Feldzüge des Prinzen Eugen', vol. XVII, p.119

26 Ágoston, 'The Ottoman Wars and the Changing Balance of Power along the Danube in the Early Eighteenth Century', in C.W. Ingrao, N. Samardžić, J. Pesalj (eds), *The Peace of Passarowitz, 1718*, p.95.

and violent, were launched several times and in these actions the Ottoman infantry showed great skill, especially in taking advantage of the advantages offered by terrain or by buildings present on the battlefield. The military laws of the janissaries prescribed a maximum of three assaults, after which it was necessary to suspend combat, but this rule was not always respected, and in many encounters the infantry carried out a greater number of assaults.

Several accounts report that the elite infantry faced the enemy in a state of spiritual exaltation, brimming with confidence, courage and daring. The English ambassador Sir Robert Sutton wrote about the battle on the River Pruth in 1711. He reports that a janissary coming before the grand vizier's tent, cried out: 'Shall we lie here to die of sickness and misery? Let all true Muslims follow me to attack the infidels'. Then he snatched up one of the ensigns that stood before the tents and went forwards. Sutton continues: 'He was immediately followed by other janissaries, the hand-picked assault troops (*serdengeçdi*) and the desperados (*deli*) gathered together and with their usual cries moved towards the enemy.'[27]

The same tactic was also adopted in the defence of fortified places, not only by the better-trained *kapikulu* infantrymen but also by local *azabs*. The coeval western European commenters outlined the effectiveness of the Ottoman sorties:

> This morning [9 July 1686], with the dawn of day, the enemy made a sortie that, if it is not stronger than 200 men, nothing less seemed to be very numerous; those who left did not have anything but a sabre in their hands and invested the posts held by the Brandenburg soldiers … and the enemy, not forgetting to pursue the fugitives, cut off about 100 among the Imperial and Brandenburg footmen.[28]

Savage hand-to-hand fighting ws a characteristic feature of the Ottoman infantry. The Roman Baron Michele D'Aste, author of the following lines, complained during the siege of Buda that the Allies had never been able to effectively repulse the Ottoman sorties:

> According to the usual, after the sunrise, the enemy has come out and already has succeeded not only to cut in pieces many people of Saxony, but also to nail three cannons and a mortar. This sortie is the most beautiful that they have ever done throughout the course of this siege, and on the other hand we can with shame observe that it has never been possible for us to reject one.[29]

Before D'Aste, Montecuccoli recommended constantly maintaining musket fire per platoon, because the over-long pauses between one volley and the

---

27 *A Letter from an eminent Merchant in Constantinople to a Friend in London*, cited by A. Wheatcroft, *The Enemy at the Gate: Habsburgs, Ottomans and the Battle for Europe* (New York: Basic Books, 2008), p.164. The assault turned in a failure: the Ottoman soldiers were repulsed three times with about 8,000 casualties.

28 D'Aste, 'Diario dell'Assedio di Buda del 1686, in Diarii degl'Assedii di Vienna del 1683, e di Buda del 1686, distesi e scritti dal Baron Michele D'Aste che vi si trovò presente in tutte le sue Azzioni', in E. Piacentini, *Diari del barone Michele D'Aste* (Rome, Budapest: Bulzoni-Corvina, 1991), p.139.

29 *Ibidem*.

42. A Janissary assault. The favourite combat tactic of the janissaries was massive assaults with swords and knives, repeated mostly after a general volley. If the action was performed with energy, the janissaries easily prevailed against poorly disciplined enemies. Montecuccoli warned his readers concerning this tactic, and suggested that the janissaries were prepared with a special drink. This drink – to which Montecuccoli devoted a concise description – revealed a great competence in botany: it was the 'Turkish *maslach*', namely 'a honey juice obtained from a umbellifer, which, dissolved in hydromel and immediately drunk, excites a wonderful animosity in the soldiers, and sometimes makes them similar to furies, and therefore, particularly in war, they do not fear any danger however great it may be.' (Author's illustration)

next favoured the Ottoman assault.[30] Thirty years later, the Margrave of Baden returned to this topic: 'experience having taught that the Turks respect the enemy more with continuity of the volleys than with the violent fire'.[31]

Although the tactics typical of the Ottoman armies were above all offensive, on many occasions, especially during sieges, the infantry engaged the enemy with protracted duels of musketry. During the siege of Kandije, starting from the middle of 1668, Grand Vizier Köprülü Ahmed reduced assaults and employed small corps of marksmen for neutralising the key positions of the enemy defence with musketry fire. A similar tactic had been developed years before. In his chronicle dating back to 1664, the Ottoman historian Evliya Çelebi, as an eyewitness, reports the conquest of Zrínyivár occurred on 7 July. He writes that the Imperial soldiers fleeing from the fortress were decimated by Ottoman fire while they tried to escape crossing the river. In his dramatic account of the event, he says: 'However, our soldiers fired several thousand shots and so many bullets at the enemy fleeing in the water that the Mura River was boiling as if it were boiling water in a cauldron.

---

30 Montecuccoli, 'Della Guerra contro il Turco in Ungheria' (1668), in R. Luraghi (ed.) *Le Opere di Raimondo Montecuccoli*, voll I–II (Rome: USSME, 1988), p.342.

31 K.u.K. Kriegsarchiv, *Feldzüge des Prinzen Eugen; Puncta des General-Lieutenant Ludwig von Baden*, vol. I, p.704.

Recent studies have introduced aninteresting theory concerning the effectiveness of Ottoman infantry fire. Since the Ottomans had already in the sixteenth century introduced infantry units equipped exclusively with firearms, they would have experimented with firing 'en masse' before this occurred in Western Europe. Ottoman sources prove that the janissaries were already using volley fire by 1605, and possibly before. This evidence remained unnoticed, but clearly describes the janissaries practising volley fire during the campaign of 1606.[32] According to this study, the janissaries deployed in two ranks and fired alternately, preferably behind shelters and wagons, in order to maintain a regular fire rate.

Another source confirms that Ottoman marksmen performed very well inside the besieged Buda in 1686. Baron Michele D'Aste remarks that the Christian stormings in late July collapsed because the officers leading the columns were all shot.[33] Another eyewitness described the effectiveness of the Ottoman fire during the early phase of the siege:

> While the Hungarians descended from the ravelin without artillery preparation, the Turks occupying the advanced enemy posts took advantage of the ditches for firing on them. When our soldiers approached the ditches, the officers were all killed by well-aimed Turkish bullets, and the troops looked hesitantly to climb the high walls without a leader.[34]

Although the attack was repeated several times, the result did not change.

The Ottoman infantry was particularly feared in night fighting also. In June 1686, a corps of 3,000 janissaries penetrated at night into besieged Buda; on that occasion, a part of the infantry used horses to take full advantage of speed and surprise. With equal ability, infantrymen and river units eluded the surveillance of the enemy to set fire to the Imperial supply ships at Slankamen, on the night between 17 and 18 August 1691. During the campaigns in Hungary, when the battle gap between the Ottomans and their enemies had become increasingly unsustainable, a dramatic change occurred in combat tactics. Mobility and unrestrained offensive switched to a tactic based on entrenchments and the choice of an easily defensible position.

This was a well-established tactic of the Ottoman infantry. Already at the battle of Szentgotthárd, once the Ottoman infantry crossed the Raba River, Köprülü Ahmed had cleverly exploited a loop of the river to protect

---

32 For Further reading on this topic, see G. Böreckçi, 'A Contribution to the Military Revolution Debate: The Janissary use of Volley Fire during the Long Ottoman–Habsburg War of 1593–1606 and the Problem of the Origins', in *Acta Orientalia Academiae Scientiarum Hungaricae*, vol. 59 (4), 407–438 (2006).

33 D'Aste, 'Diario dell'Assedio di Buda del 1686', in E. Piacentini, *Diari del barone Michele D'Aste*, p.141.

34 Archivio di Stato di Venezia, *Dispacci degli Ambasciatori e Residenti*, 'Germania' f.224, *Lettere*. Francesco Grimani's letter, which can be considered an objective source for evaluating the effect of the Ottoman musketry fire on the besiegers' morale: 'The failure of these actions changes the expected state of things and produces a result that contradicts rationality, desires and expectations. In the wake of the failure, people here are not sure that this city will be overthrown … and they are even afraid, and they see that the Emperors will be defeated.'

his flanks from an enemy counter-attack. In this phase, the infantry took possession of the terrain, awaiting the arrival of further troops from the other banks, engaging in a musketry duel by improvised defences. On 29 July 1687, the soldiers of Charles V of Lorraine sighted the Ottoman field army at Eszék, on the right bank of the Drava River, deployed behind a large defensive embankment. Some cavalry was outside the embankment, and before it, further horsemen followed the approach of the Imperials advancing to Eszék. All day long, the two armies remained facing each other without making any move. The Imperialists preferred to avoid an assault against such a strong position, protected even from behind by an extensive swamp, while the Ottomans, because they were satisfied at having arrested the enemy, maintained the defensive. The Ottoman commander, Grand Vizier Süleyman Paşa, engaged the Imperialists with his cavalry vanguard, which with the customary tactic, tried to attract the enemy to pursue them. Behind the embankment, the Ottoman artillery targeted the Imperialists until late evening, but from such a distance most of the shots failed. In Constantinople, the news of Eszék was celebrated as a great victory and great importance was given to the deployment adopted by the Grand Vizier.[35]

With this arrangement, the Ottoman commanders could only slow down the inevitable course of the conflict. Apart from some modest success, as achieved at Ollashin in 1696, this tactic failed to avoid disastrous defeats, such as the one suffered at Harsány in 1687, and especially at Zenta in 1697. In this last episode, the excess of trust in the static defence was one of the causes of the disastrous outcome of the battle. However, the Ottoman commanders continued to protect the armies behind defensive embankments and trenches for the rest of the war, avoiding any manoeuvres to engage with the Imperialists in the open field. This tactic did not change even when the enemy was forced on the defensive, as happened at Peterwardein in the summer of 1695. In front of the enemy trenches, Grand Vizier Sürmeli Ali laid the encampment and began to entrench himself, starting a confrontation destined to last 20 days. Marsigli judged the episode 'a senseless war of sap and cannon'.[36] The same happened at Belgrade in 1717, when the Ottoman relief army opened the trenches around the encampment and began to dig approaches against the besieger's circumvallation.

The Ottoman field defences generally consisted of a linear embankment reinforced with timbers and sandbags, and interrupted more or less regularly by a semicircle ledge in which a shooting pitch for the artillery was built. The infantry deployed in two rows and, when it fired, the first row occupied the outer edge of the embankment, allowing the soldiers behind to unload their weapons at the same time and therefore they could maintain an effective volume of fire. Throughout the defensive system large passages were left to allow the cavalry to retreat into the entrenched camp. In some actions, as happened at Ollashin and at Zenta, carts and wagons were also used to carry

35 Marsigli, vol. II, p.87: 'Great praises were made of this entrenchment, saying finally that they [the Ottomans] has found a way to face effectively the Imperialists in the open field.'
36 *Ibidem*, p.154.

out a temporary defence: practically an updated version of the ancient *Tabur Cengi* formation.

Parallel to the decline of the strategy, in the last decades of the seventeenth century, the Ottoman army suffered a severe reduction in combat efficiency. In the 1660s, Montecuccoli still declared that: 'The Turk is brave in combat',[37] emphasising the resistance qualities of the soldiers to fatigue and the blind fanaticism with which they obeyed their commanders:

> I have seen many Turks, broken by Christians on the field, or forced to stay in the stormed *palankas* to perish, instead surrendering and obstinately resisting to the last. I saw them before Zrínyivár deploy in full sun meridian, protected only by light shelters, neither to stop the advance, neither to slow down the approaches for the mortality of the soldiers fallen by our fire, and one above the other dead fell. I saw them throwing with the sabre into his mouth twice inside the walls … and so swimming [the Raba River] at Szentgotthárd.[38]

Equally positive is the comment of the Baron D'Aste at the siege of Buda in 1686, notwithstanding the Imperial soldiers mainly faced irregular infantrymen: '… comparing the one [the Ottomans] with the other [the Imperialists], there is none of them who, in close combat, did not prevail over almost two of ours.'[39]

Western commenters outlined the obstinacy of the Ottoman soldiers in defending the forts:

> It is beyond the human powers of comprehension to grasp … just how obstinately the Turks defend themselves. As soon as one fortification is demolished, they simply dig themselves another one. It is easier to deal with any conventional fortress and with any other army than with the Turks when they are defending a stronghold.[40]

There are many other testimonies to the individual value of the Ottoman soldiers in the seventeenth century, and apart from some significant exceptions, before the 1680s, the discipline in the Ottoman army was also better than at any other period. According to several authors, unrest occurred

---

37 Montecuccoli, in Luraghi, *Opere di Raimondo Montecuccoli*, vol. II, p.209.
38 *Ibidem*, pp.485–496. According to Montecuccoli, another strong point of the Ottoman army was 'executive virtue', namely the ability to translate plans into operations and, more generally, to manage war effectively. This virtue quality came 'from the authority, which is despotic and undivided' because it reflected: 'the fundamental laws of the Ottoman kingdom', where there is 'only one Prince and all subjects are slaves', and that consequently guaranteed to the army commander 'free commissions, absolute and with full and undivided authority', since 'he does not have another senior officer neither in the task, nor auxiliary, nor connected to consult them on campaigns and in the dissensions to reconcile them; but to him all blindly obey.' See also Del Negro, 'Raimondo Montecuccoli e la guerra contro i turchi', in *American Legacy, La SISM ricorda Raimondo Luraghi*, p.273.
39 D'Aste, 'Diario dell'Assedio di Buda del 1686', in E. Piacentini, *Diari del barone Michele D'Aste*, p.139.
40 V. von Renner, *Wien in Jahre 1683, Geschichte der zweiten Belagerung der Stadt durch die Türken* (Vienna, 1883), p.361.

WARS AND SOLDIERS IN THE EARLY REIGN OF LOUIS XIV - VOLUME 3

mainly due to the delay of salary than for other matters. However, desertions occurred frequently, also among the allegedly well-disciplined janissaries. According to some Hungarian relations, after the battle of Szentgotthárd the Ottoman troops lost numerous soldiers due to desertion, which according to some testimonies of the Hungarian frontiersmen were constant.[41] However, when Count Marsigli began to form his own experience to write it in the *Stato Militare*, the Ottoman valour no longer aroused much admiration. In the same period, further reports relate cases in which the determination to fight only took place behind the promise of money, or threats and even swindles. Between the age of Montecuccoli and that of Marsigli, there is the crucial moment in which Ottoman military power suffered the most humiliating defeats, beginning with the disaster of Kahlenberg in 1683.

Among all the factors that contributed to the decay of the combat efficiency, was the modest quality of the officers, both of the senior commanders and the subordinate ones. Although the Porte was able to gather numerous contingents, the difficulty of finding commanders with leadership and knowledge became ever greater. Many of the *beglerbegs* and *paşas* had been soldiers before becoming governors, but – in addition to gaining office due to the aberrant dynamics of nepotism and corruption – they were almost more like leaders capable of leading a raid, than modern officers able to lead composite corps, coordinate the activities of subordinates, take care of logistics and oversee the many tasks required by a campaign of war. In vain, the government tried to remedy this by offering rewards to the veterans who had left the army and promulgating amnesties for disgraced officers. In 1686, Grand Vizier Süleyman went so far as to extend the amnesty even to the leaders of the outlaws in Anatolia; among them a former raider named Jegen was even appointed with the title of *paşa*, and obtained the command of the rearguard at Harsány. The rapidity with which certain military careers evolved was the macroscopic symptom of the declining quality of the Ottoman officers.

Moreover, the command structure of the tactical units had a vertical rather than pyramidal pattern and this made it difficult to carry out complex operations. The number of officers and non-commissioned officers was also inadequate compared to the troops. At the highest levels, the hierarchy reflected all the negativities that afflicted the Ottoman state, with the result that the key posts were occupied by officers in close relation to some protector or the commander-in-chief. Moreover, the commander's authority was always absolute, while the subordinate officers had limited decision-making autonomy. Despite the choice of simple and easy-to-implement strategies and tactics, each time the action took on a more complex aspect, offensive power faded and the whole army entered crisis. Any coordination became therefore precarious and in the crucial moments the soldiers often remained without orders.

---

41 During reconnaissance, some Hungarian *Grenzer* met a great number of 'fugitive Turks' coming from the Ottoman camp a few miles away: 'The deserters said they were all janissaries, and three of them were immediately baptized to testify their intention to change sides. Later, a Hungarian captain learned of many former Ottoman soldiers who had joined the army of the grand-prince of Transylvania.' See F. Végh, 'A török haderö visszavonulása a Balaton-felvidéken a Szentgotthárdi csata után, 1664 augusztus' (2003), in *Hadtörténelmi Közlemények*, 116 (2003), p.597.

There were innumerable cases in which the transmission of orders, or their execution on the battlefield, were badly applied or remained unaddressed, granting the enemy decisive advantages. These errors constituted a problem of all armies during the period, and they were not only a prerogative of the Ottoman army, but misunderstandings and negligence seems to have considerably increased in the last phase of the War of the Holy League. In the weeks preceding the siege of Buda in 1686, Michele D'Aste noted the disorder with which the Ottomans conducted operations. Their cavalry seemed unable to coordinate the moves to prevent the approach of the Imperial reconnaissance.[42] When the Imperialists came in sight of the city they witnessed, between incredulous and amused, how the Ottomans had not even thought of placing an outpost to guard the access to Szent Gellert hill, a position from which they could dominate the city, and notwithstanding two years earlier it had been one of the main objectives of the besiegers.

Probably the most sensational case in which misunderstanding and negligence combined with a clumsy application of orders and caused disastrous consequences, occurred at Zenta on 11 September 1697. Protected behind the usual embankments and wagons and leaning against the Tisza River, the Turks were crossing the river and had transferred most of the cavalry to the other bank. On the right side of the deployment, an extensive area abutting the back of the Ottoman defence remained unguarded. Prince Eugene of Savoy ordered his dragoons and infantry to occupy the terrain, while all the Imperial troops moved to the assault supported by the artillery fire.

An Ottoman cavalry corps moved to the first line, feinting an assault, but was repulsed by the Imperial artillery. At the same time, perhaps worried by the resolute decision of the enemy to attack, Grand Vizier Elmas Mohammed summoned the *sipahis* who had already crossed the Tisza. On foot, hampered by the troops that continued to cross the river, the Ottoman horsemen reached the embankment causing great confusion and turmoil throughout the other troops. Meanwhile, the Imperialists were advancing through the open space behind the Ottoman right wing and quickly reached the first bridges. Panic spread among the defenders, and:

> …what followed cannot be described. Many [of the Ottomans] threw themselves into the river, trying to save themselves with desperate efforts, or they were pushed by the throng crowded on the bridges, but here the Imperialists followed them furiously and made a horrible massacre.[43]

From the other bank, Sultan Mustafa II observed, horrified, the epilogue of that tragic day. Desperately, Elmas Mohammed rushed into the field, but was killed while trying to rally the troops. The survivors fled in disorder; near the bridges the corpses piled up to hinder the current and above them the enemies passed the river, seizing all the baggage and heavy artillery.

---

42 D'Aste, 'Diario dell'Assedio di Buda del 1686', in E. Piacentini *Diari del barone Michele D'Aste*, p.65.
43 K.u.K. Kriegsarchiv, *Feldzüge des Prinzen Eugen*, vol. II, p.141.

The limitations of their officers and the disadvantage in terms of coordination of the troops on the battlefield against a modern disciplined army was well known to the Ottoman commanders. This handicap therefore favoured siege warfare, especially in Hungary, the Balkans and Greece. The Ottomans developed highly successful siege methods through their experiences in the late sixteenth and seventeenth centuries, and enjoyed a great reputation for conquering modern fortresses. The Long War with the Habsburgs, the sieges of Baghdad in the 1620s and 1630s, and especially the campaigns in Crete with the long siege of Kandije gave the Ottomans ample opportunity to test and refine their technique. Officers who fought at Kandije in the early years of the siege later used their knowledge at Kamieniec and Vienna. Contemporary Habsburg and Ottoman writers alike refer to Kandije as a training-ground for future sieges. Some of the skills the Ottomans acquired there were learned from foreign experts. Assistance from the Dutch, English, and French was important in the final resolution of that siege. This help was particularly useful in the effective use of bombs and mortars.

The Ottomans were seen as relentless in pursuing their military goals. In this regard, with his unmistakable style, Raimondo Montecuccoli wrote:

> They [the Ottomans] break the walls and ramparts with continuous batteries, using a large number of artillery of large calibre, dig ditches to the water, fill them with sacks of sand and wool, fascines, and other materials. They make galleries, push up mountains of dirt able to withstand many projectiles, which are the height of the walls and earthworks of the besieged fort. They make mines, plain, double, and triple the size of ours, set deep and which can use 120, 150, or more barrels of powder, undermining, as the Romans did, the walls and wood supports, making them susceptible to fire in such a way to bring down a long face of the walls. They worry constantly, and are stubborn in attack and defence.[44]

Montecuccoli also praised their organisation in the siege, writing that the Ottomans did not waste time and money in 'expeditions of small moment,' and that they worked methodically, reducing forts along the way to their goal, rather than bypassing one fort to attack another.[45]

When the Ottoman engineers arrived in front of a fortress, they were careful to choose where they would focus their attack and begin their trenches. They would reconnoitre the fortress and find its weak points. Ottoman sources record how the Ottoman commander at the siege of Novigrad in Dalmatia, Kaplan Mustafa Paşa, fully scouted the fortress, town, suburbs, and surroundings before beginning the siege. The Ottomans usually attacked on a wider front than their European enemies did. Also, unlike their opponents, the Ottoman commanders established their camp without a fortified line of circumvallation protecting the rear. This is not to say that the Ottomans were unconcerned about attacks from armies sent to relieve the siege. Instead of fortifying their camp against such onslaughts, they relied on

---

44 Montecuccoli, in Testa, *Le Opere di Raimondo Montecuccoli*, vol. III, p.525.
45 *Ibidem*, p.524.

the Crimean Tatars and their superiority in cavalry to cover their sieges: a certainty destined to cause bitter consequences in 1683.

Still, large cannon were necessary for siege duty, and the Ottomans had a variety of battering guns at their disposal. One difficulty in developing a typology of Ottoman artillery is that the same names were used for guns of a variety of different sizes. Thus, cannon called *balyemez*, usually considered the largest of Ottoman guns, were recorded firing a variety of shot.[46] However, as mining techniques progressed, siege artillery lost its importance. The large gun called a *şayka* was another type associated with sieges, but usually on the defensive side.[47] In the sieges, it was the field artillery that played a relevant and unprecedented offensive role, because the Ottoman artillerymen used to place the cannons to support the approaches, in order to target the external defensive works such as palisades and embankments.[48]

Field Operations

Although the high level of logistical organisation was a major pride of the Ottoman army, the complexity and length of the preparations considerably delayed the start of operations. Once again, Montecuccoli effectively synthesised this characteristic by writing: 'The Turk comes on campaign late in the year and soon he retires.'[49] This normally stretched over a four and a half month period beginning with the *ruz-i kasim* 'day of division' on 6 November, marking the end of summer and ending with the *nevruz*, equinox, on 21 March, which marked the end of winter, leading to the army mobilisation in springtime.

---

46 Claims for the origin of the name *balyemez* are equally varied. Evliya Çelebi gave a fanciful etymology for this term, writing that it was named for a gun-founder who ate no honey (Turkish *bal yemez*, literally 'one who does not eat honey'). More convincing sources trace it to a famous German gun called *Faule Metze*, or to a gun large enough to fire two balls connected by a metal bar, a device called in Italian *palla ramata*. See Stein, *Guarding the Frontier*, p.41.

47 Again, there is some confusing nomenclature, as there was also an Ottoman boat called a *şayka*.

48 Concerning the raising of the Ottoman siege technique, see also Veysel Göger, 'Taş Yasdanup Toprak Döşenenler: Kandiye Kuşatması Örneğinde Osmanlı Askerlerinin Metristeki Mücadele ve Yaşamı (1667–1669)', in *Osmanlı Araştırmaları Dergisi*, 52 (2018): pp. 41–78.

49 Montecuccoli, *Aforismi*, chapter II, aphorism XLVI. In another place Montecuccoli admirably synthesised the Ottoman strategy of war in seven points: I – to give battle; II – to deploy high number of cavalry; III – to consume food and to destroy the countryside; IV – to surround the enemy; V – to use large contingents in the conquest of fortresses; VI – to launch great raids; VII – to exit the campaign late. To this strategy, the Imperial army had to oppose: I – to have a great advantage from nature and from the Armies; II – to occupy the terrain and strategic places, to seize fortresses; III – to never move too much from the magazines, and from the advantages, and when it is possible from a great river; IV – to prevent the enemy from going out on campaign, and to conquer some places before the Turk goes out; V – to continually march the infantry and horses, 'because they constantly diminish'. Once again the result of this analysis was very comforting: 'one can even go to engage the Turk because, notwithstanding that he is able to do battle, he can never conquer the terrain, not being able to fortify his army because it is too large, and for not having enough infantry in proportion to the cavalry to hold the lines, and to defend them.' Vol. III, pp.138–136 and 142–144.

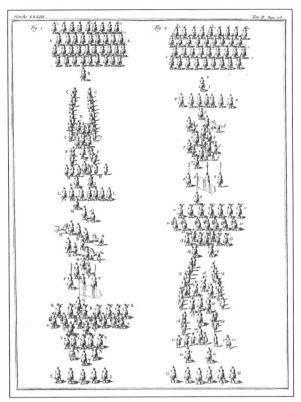

43. Ottoman field army marching, after Marsigli's *Stato Militare dell'Imperio Ottomanno*. The Porte usually formed a single field army. This force, with all its units gathered and ready to march, was called the *sefer*. It left the barracks after the *nevruz*, equinox, on 21 March, and closed the campaign with the *ruz-i kasim* 'day of division' on 6 November, which marked the end of summer. The objective was usually only known by the sultan with his close entourage and by the grand vizier. Never in its history did the *sefer* perform against two different targets, but after 1684, when the Porte was engaged against the Holy League, the Ottoman commanders were forced to face a new strategic scenario.

Alongside a curious series of causes, among which the poor resistance of soldiers to the rigours of winter, due to their diet free of alcoholic beverages,[50] the Italian general underlined the coincidence between the beginning of operations and the full ripening of fodder and fruit, to allow feeding of the horses and the other draft animals. Observing the beginning of operations in the war against the Habsburgs in 1663–64, the Ottomans reached full offensive capacity only at the end of May and began to retreat in the last days of October or at the latest in early November.

The need to accommodate troops coming from the most remote provinces of the Empire, forced the Ottoman commanders to concentrate operations over short periods. Considerable organisational effort was therefore aimed at a lightning-fast and as devastating as possible action of war. The short operative period of the Ottoman armies represented a remarkable disadvantage when enemies were able to prolong their permanence on campaign. In November 1672, the Polish commander Jan Sobieski successfully led an assault against the troops under Genç Hüseyin, *paşa* of Silistra, while they were encamped at Chocim, after the bulk of the army had already moved into winter quarters. However, Chocim represented an isolated case in the context of the wars between the Ottomans and Christians; normally, in the seventeenth century, not even the enemies of the sultan were able to gather their troops more

---

50   *Ibidem*, 'Discorso della guerra contro il Turco', in Luraghi, *Opere di Raimondo Montecuccoli*, vol. II, p.227. In this work, dated 1 March 1664, the previous topic was taken up and developed in an organic way. Montecuccoli identified 16 'principles' relating to the Ottoman warfare, to which he opposed 20 'maximum', namely as many proposals to allow the Imperial army to advantageously stand against the Ottomans in sieges and on the battlefields: 'The scheme of the *Discorso* identified the Turks and the Christians as protagonists, but Montecuccoli effectively reversed the usual pattern of the religious war, subordinating, to some extent, religion to war or, better, using military efficiency as a key of reading for evaluate the validity of the 'civilization' choices, including those dictated by religion'; in P. Del Negro, 'Raimondo Montecuccoli e la guerra contro i turchi: riflessioni su strategia e arte militare', in *American Legacy, La SISM ricorda Raimondo Luraghi*, (Roma: Società Italiana di Storia Militare, 2016).

quickly, and moreover the operations ended with the arrival of the cold season almost simultaneously for both sides.[51]

Since the conquest of Constantinople, the Ottoman army had established an assembling area and routes to reach the European fronts. The principal route was the so-called 'Royal Road', which joined Constantinople to Belgrade and Buda, and passed through the main centres of the Balkans and the Danube basin.[52] In the seventeenth century, the Danube plain was very different from the one we know today. The countryside was subject to frequent flooding and large areas crossed by the Danube and major tributaries were reduced to swamps, making it difficult to move troops and wagons with supplies. The descriptions of the landscape of those years paints a nightmare scenario for parties coming from Royal Hungary: villages and cities stood isolated several miles from each other and in the deserted countryside the grass grew so high that it exceeded height of a man, so much so that it was necessary to trace paths so as not to get lost in the tangle of the marshes.[53] Moving troops across the vast expanses of this region was a constant preoccupation, where disease-inducing marshes and floods decimated troops and animals alike. The unhealthy air favoured the spread of diseases, to which was added the pitfalls represented by stray dogs and wolves that attacked men and cattle. Large watercourses that were difficult to cross limited the theatre of war. The cities that were at the confluence of the emissaries and straddling the major rivers were of considerable strategic value and were the main objective of the campaigns. The north–west–south-east route followed the natural course of the Danube and intersected close to Belgrade with the southern base of the theatre of war, represented by the semicircle between the rivers Drava to the north and Sava to the south. The arrangement of the rivers made the march more difficult for those coming from the north than those coming from the opposite direction, yet those coming down from the north could exploit the current to transport troops and supplies by ship, which current instead slowed down adversaries, who were forced to go up the course of the rivers using a tow from the shore. The main direction of the Imperial advance was, however, exposed to the east to the outbreaks of rebellion in Upper Hungary, fed by the Ottomans through the principality of Transylvania, whose control allowed the sultan the rapid transit of the Tatar contingents. Another non-secondary front extended south-west along the Croatian–Bosnian border, where the Ottomans were masters of the most important fortified sites, from which disturbing actions could be launched on the opposing sides.

---

51 Montecuccoli, in Luraghi, *Opere di Raimondo Montecuccoli*, vol. II, p.512. In this regard, in the 1670s, conceiving a plan of war against the Porte, Montecuccoli suggested concentrating offensive actions in the winter season: 'Great advantage would be for us to make war in winter, since the Turk does not know how to do it, having never fought with the cold, and before he gets used to it, he will have suffered irreparable losses'.

52 Marsigli, vol. II, p.120.

53 P. Wilson, *German Armies. War and German Politics, 1648–1806* (London: UCL Press, 1998), p.39. A surgeon in the Brandenburg corps in 1686 described the Hungarian war theatre as 'a wilderness … for 30 miles and more there would be neither town nor village, and the grass was as tall as a man, so that we often had to clear a path for ourselves. As for the countryside it was full of wild dogs, which attacked men and cattle just as wolves do.'

To the south, Edirne was the first gathering point, followed by Filibe (today Plovdiv, in Bulgaria) and Sofia. The route turned westward towards Viddin, on the Danube, and from there it continued north. Before arriving in Europe, the troops coming from Anatolia arrested their march at Usküdar, on the southern shores of the Black Sea, and after crossing the Dardanelles, made camp east of Constantinople. The infantry coming from the more eastern provinces of Anatolia embarked in Trabzon and sailed to Gelibolu. Once reunited with the other Asian troops, they marched to Edirne. The Asian cavalry reached the Dardanelles by land and crossed the sea on large rafts. All the troops on foot from southern Anatolia, Syria, Palestine, Arabian Peninsula and Egypt landed in Thessalonica and from there moved in the direction of Edirne, while the cavalry proceeded by road to Constantinople and crossed the Dardanelles in the aforementioned ports. From Edirne, Sofia and Filibe all the contingents made camp at Belgrade and once there they waited for the troops coming from Bosnia, Albania, Macedonia and the auxiliaries from Transylvania, Wallachia and Moldavia. The Tatars followed a path that from their base brought them to central Bulgaria, passing through Izmail, Silistra, Ruçuk and Tarnova; normally they made their camps in the middle of the woods along the route.[54]

The *kapikulu* was the last to march, from its quarters in Constantinople, Bursa and Edirne, and as the other troops headed in the direction of Belgrade along the Royal Road, allowing supplies and troops to exploit the great river route. Belgrade was considered 'the gate of Hungary' and under its walls, for centuries, the Ottoman troops made their camp before heading to the Habsburg borders. However, further strategically important centres in the Danube and Balkan area were Bihac, Banjaluka and, until their loss, Nitra, Esztergom, Eszék, Buda and Temeşvár. For the operations in Ukraine and Podolia, the field army gathered at Sofia and then marched to Craiova, Bucharest, Jassi and finally Kamieniec, the main base for actions against the Poles. The same route continued to Azov, another important logistic centre for the operations against Russians and Cossacks.

The main route for the gathering of troops destined for the Peloponnese joined Kavala, Thessalonica, Larissa and, through the pass of the Thermopylae, stopped at Thebes, where usually the troops made their main camp. In 1685, Thebes became the main base for the operations against the Venetian offensive in the Peloponnese, and its importance increased in the last decade of the seventeenth century, when the Porte built magazines and facilities to supply the troops. From here, in 1692 and 1694 started the great incursions into the Peloponnese and Attica. In 1715, the camp at Thebes returned to being the base of the troops gathered for the new war against Venice. To better accommodate the soldiers, it was necessary to expand the magazines and the area destined for the encampment.[55]

The march of the troops took place at more or less regular intervals of one or two days, but once the last camp in friendly territory had been raised,

54 Marsigli, vol. II, p.120.
55 G. Silvini, *La Fine del Dominio Veneto nel Levante* (Udine: Editrice Grillo, 1979), pp. 38–39.

all the forces prepared to cross the border, keeping in close contact. The advance in enemy territory involved the army into three sections: the çarhaci (vanguard), the main corps, and the *dundar* (rearguard).

The vanguard was entrusted to an officer chosen by the commander-in-chief, called çarhacibasi, and preceded the rest of the army by five or six hours. Generally, it was formed by selected troops of the provincial cavalry, to which could be added infantry to occupy the strategic places in the war theatre. The çarhaci marched, preceded by a screen formed by Tatar cavalry. Behind the vanguard followed the janissaries with the *cebeci*, the artillerymen together with their train and then the commander with his own *mütefferika* (the mounted lifeguards), the officers and the adjutants, the administrative staff and the *ulùfely sipahis*. The army's baggage and all the other troops on foot and on horseback closed the column. Another corps of cavalry proceeded about six hours behind, to form the extreme rearguard. While the army was proceeding in the marches, the rearguard was responsible for providing the escort to that part of the train and baggage inevitably in delay, as well as to the wagons used to collect the wounded and the sick.

The contemporary commenters agree in affirming that the Ottomans entered the campaign with all their forces and very rarely divided it into two or more corps, not even when the nature of the terrain or the strategic scenario would reasonably have required it. The advance into enemy territory proceeded in close order, covered by as strong a vanguard as possible. Objectives were usually assaulted by Tatar horsemen and mounted raiders of the *serhaddkulu*. Montecuccoli cited an episode occurred in 1661, in the phase preceding the war between the Habsburgs and the Porte, when the Serasker Ali Paşa of Temesvar moved from the Tisza River keeping his army compact, confining himself to launching only some Tatar raids against the Imperial corps advancing on Koloszvár.[56]

Whenever the Ottoman commanders could count on the numerical superiority of the cavalry, they often resorted to incursions, sometimes directed very deep into enemy territory, while avoiding advancing more than two days away from the field army. However, the great Tatar raid of 1663 penetrated into Moravia, and 20 years later the Tatars alongside the Hungarian *kuruc* rebels travelled to Austria, travelling over 300 kilometres from the main army.

Incursions served to achieve strategic results, and forced the enemy to scatter its force for protecting key places. Usually, the Ottomans opened every war with this kind of action. After the Tartar raids in Summer 1657, Grand Vizier Köprülü Mehmed ordered the invasion of Transylvania and in May 1658 he mobilised the *kapikulu* corps, but not to its full strength. The bulk of the Ottoman army was almost completely composed of contingents from Buda, Temeşvár and Bosnia, supported by the Tartar auxiliary cavalry. Overall strength rose to 45–50,000 soldiers, who could stay on campaign for

---

56 Montecuccoli, *Della Guerra col Turco in Ungheria*, in Luraghi, *Opere di Raimondo Montecuccoli*, vol. II, pp. 398–399.

a limited period only.[57] At the end of the campaign season, the Ottoman army was accustomed to returning to their home provinces or peacetime barracks. This was very important for the provincial *sipahis* as well as the irregular units, as they had to deal with their estates, collect taxes, and protect their own personal interests. Once the campaign ended, the *zeamets* and *timars* eagerly returned to their peacetime occupations or bases, especially when a military operation had ended unfavourably. Increasingly, however, the Porte had to maintain part of its army in winter quarters near the frontiers to maintain reserve forces against possible out-of-season enemy attacks or to start the next year's campaign early. This strategy always created serious tensions within the retained provincial units, causing numerous disciplinary problems and occasional disorders. In addition to these problems, winter quartering required strict order and discipline as well as detailed planning beforehand so as to arrange provisions, and numerous other logistical needs.[58]

During the war against the Habsburgs of 1663–64, the Porte employed three times more soldiers and five to six times more firearms and cannons than in the sixteenth century. The Ottoman logistical transformation becomes more impressive when compared to the experiences of the Thirty Years' War, during which the concentration of more than 20,000 soldiers in a given area became the exception rather than the norm. By contrast, the Ottoman government was able to move and concentrate up to 50,000 soldiers with few problems, thereby securing decisive numerical superiority on campaign. Moreover, the government demonstrated an understanding of the importance of balancing local and military needs and managing to preserve regional economies, whilst milking their capacity, so as to keep the military corridors intact but never turning them into economic wastelands. However, the frontier regions did not profit from this policy, due to constant siege and counter-siege operations as well as a never-ending stream of raids and counter-raids. Moreover, the two sides considered the destruction of the border districts under respective rule to be necessary and advantageous for the disruption of the enemy's advance and provisioning.[59] Therefore, the Ottoman–Hungarian, Bosnian and Greek domains slowly managed to fully recover completely from the damage of the war campaigns, and only partly managed to support the needs of the Ottoman permanent garrisons, whereas they had managed to supply all their needs during the previous century.[60] Surprisingly, even during the campaigns of 1658–62 in Transylvania, and later in 1663 in Hungary, Ottoman commanders tried to limit forced

---

57 *Ibidem*, p.98, and Payer, *Armati Hungarorum*, p.106. In the campaign of 1658, *kapikulu* corps numbers could reach 25–30,000 men.

58 Ágoston, 'Habsburg and Ottomans. Defence, Military Change and Shifts in Power', in *Turkish Studies Association Bulletin*, vol. 22 (1998), p.36.

59 On this topic, see in Pálffy, 'Scorched-Earth Tactics in Ottoman Hungary', in *Acta Orientalia Academiae Scientiarum Hungaricae*, vol. 61, No. 1/2, pp.181–200.

60 *Ibidem*, p.187: 'The Hungarian military leadership, too, employed scorched-earth tactics on a number of occasions in certain parts of Hungary. Evidently, the economic and political disadvantages that accompanied these actions were more than outweighed by the strategic advantages that accrued from them.'

requisitions, managing to pay for the provisions provided by the peasants.[61] Similar cases occurred on the Venetian–Ottoman border in 1645–1671, in 1684–1699 and 1714–1718.

As occurred in Dalmatia and Bosnia against the Venetians between 1645 and 1648, and in the war against Transylvania and the Habsburgs, the Ottomans commanders displayed a general lack of battlefield competence, with poor communications and a lack of coordination of their troops. In the campaigns before 1663, these failings proved only minor and the resulting losses had no long-lasting consequences, as the Ottomans had seemingly unlimited numbers of troops and war materials, but now the effects were to prove more significant. Confidence in their own ability and the knowledge that even a defeat could not ever be disastrous had convinced the Ottoman commanders not to change their military model. Luck remained an indispensable ingredient of their strategic warfare, whilst contemporary Ottoman leaders failed to realise that warfare was changing: an excessive belief in ancient strategies and tactics proved to be catastrophic 20 years later. Before the war against the Emperor, the Porte had mobilised its permanent forces of the *kapikulu* as recently as 1658, when Grand Vizier Köprülü Mehmed led the Ottoman army on its devastating summer campaign in Transylvania. The offensive action had been energetic but short, largely due to the fact that the Venetians were still maintaining their blockade of the Dardanelles. The Venetian danger was still alive, considering that the year before, the enemy fleet threatened to penetrate the Marmara Sea and assault the Ottoman capital. The campaigns against György II Rákóczy were conducted employing the provincial corps from Bosnian and Hungarian *beglerbeglik*. The contingent, under Seidi Ahmed *serdar* of Transylvania, and Ali Paşa of Silistra, included the *kapikulu* infantry from Buda and Sarajevo. The first campaigns were erratic and lacked coordination between the forces involved. Both the Ottoman commanders conducted indecisive offensives against the Transylvanians under Rákóczy, also because the presence of the Imperial corps, under *Feldmarschall* Louis de Souches in Western Transylvania, were certainly forced to act with caution, but this threat was not as concrete as the obstacles presented by a well-garrisoned enemy fortress.[62] However, in 1661 the strategic situation turned in favour of the Porte. On 22 January 1662, the fate of the unfortunate Kemény Janos, the Transylvanian pro-Habsburg pretender, was sealed at Nagyszöllös. Over 2,000 heads were sent as trophies to Constantinople, among them the prince's. The weakness of the Imperialists convinced the Porte to assume a more aggressive stance in relation to Hungary.[63]

---

61 Stein, *Guarding the Frontiers*, p.154.
62 In 1660, the Transylvanian fortress of Várad, defended by the town militia and just 850 mercenaries, held out for 45 days against Ali Paşa's army of 50,000 men. The Ottoman siege took place in relative safety, however, as the Imperialists camped a few miles away made no attempt to relieve the besieged garrison.
63 The Porte asked for the evacuation of the Imperial forces from all the Transylvanian fortresses, because the princedom was a vassal of the sultan and the Imperial army had violated the peace treaty by invading and occupying its western fortress. The Emperor wanted to keep at least the

Facing page: 44. Wallachian boyar and *cǎlǎraşi* cavalrymen, late seventeenth century. The Romanian nobility employed the same Ottoman fashions, such as a *kaftans* with long false sleeves and silver or gilded metal war maces. Defensive weapons of local production are exemplified in the helm worn by this boyar, which was a typical head protection of Romanian officers in the late seventeenth century. Helm in black polished metal with gilded accessories; azure brocade *kaftan* with crimson linings and false sleeve cuffs; silver buttons; turquoise waistcoat with yellow cuffs; white silk sash; yellow leather boots. (Author's illustration. Reconstruction after *A Mintjan of the Prince ov Wallachia*, in 'The True and Exact Fashion and Dress of all Nations in Transylvania' 1670; seventeenth-century eastern Europe helm, Oriental collection of the Musée de l'Armée, Paris).

Negotiations were opened to find an agreement. Ottoman demands were not limited to the evacuation of the Transylvanian fortresses and the demilitarisation of the Croatian border, but also included the handing over of Szatmár (today Satu Mare in Romania) and Tokay as well as the re-establishment of an annual tribute of 30,000 gold ducats to the Sultan. The Emperor was slow to react, the decision making process faltered and, as a result, full war broke out on 12 April 1663.[64] Possibly for the last time in the seventeenth century, in 1663 and 1664 the Porte faced the Imperialists with a powerful military force, mostly composed of well-disciplined troops, supported by adequate resources, and backed up by a formidable cavalry strength reinforced by the feared Tatar contingents. The Porte was also able to introduce improvements in its siege warfare using other methods, such as mining, complex trench systems, field constructions. The Ottoman advance caused great alarm since by August 1663 the Habsburg forces had almost completely been eradicated from Royal Hungary.

However, the traditional perception that depicts Ottoman warfare as a devastating series of campaigns seems not to be respected in the war of 1663–64. Even in the context of Christian–Muslim enmity, it should not be supposed that seventeenth-century warfare was always characterised by episodes of brutal, unyielding, bitter fights to the death. Alternating cruelty with non-violent tactics was typical of Köprülü Ahmed's command. Probably, he entered the war aiming to avoid an open encounter with the Imperialists in order to agree a profitable truce. In this regard, in several cases the Grand Vizier considered an easy surrender as the best way to avoid Ottoman casualties. From an account of Ottoman army movements in 1663 and 1664, it can readily be seen that the conclusion of a confrontation between seriously mismatched, or sometimes disproportionate, opponents by non-violent means, involving a conditional but otherwise voluntary surrender, was by no means unusual. In the seventeenth-century Ottoman–Habsburg context, it seems clear that the conclusion of an encounter by the voluntary

---

fortresses of Tokay and Szatmár. The Ottomans replied that the border fortress of Zrínyivár, recently built, had to be dismantled in exchange.

64 It is interesting to note that negotiations between Emperor Leopold and the Porte continued even after the start of hostilities. The Imperial delegates, Reininger and Goes, met Köprülü Ahmed in Belgrade and later in Eszék, following the march of the approaching Ottoman army. The last negotiations took place in Buda in July of 1663, but this time the Imperial delegates held discussions with the governor of Silistra, Ali Paşa, while the Grand Vizier secretly listened to the talks, hidden behind a curtain. See Hammer-Purgstall, *Geschichte des Osmanischen Reiches*, vol. XI, p.137.

surrender of the obviously weaker side bore no stigma or implication of treachery. Instead, it was regarded, on both sides, as a natural and everyday fact of military life. The practical advantages which such conclusions for military confrontations offered, especially when the outcome was a foregone conclusion, were obvious enough. Typically, in addition to the avoidance of unnecessary bloodshed, conditional surrender often included transport and the accompaniment of a military escort, for the safe evacuation of the defeated side and their personal belongings to a nearby friendly fortress.

The Ottoman army's initial opening gambit in the war was the siege of Érsekúivár, in August 1663, directed by Köprülü Mehmed with the main army, whilst 6,000 horse executed a raid in Croatia against Zrínyivár. The Porte mobilised a large contingent, which also included the whole *kapikulu* from Constantinople and Edirne. Thousands of Tatars, and even Cossacks, joined the army that laid siege to Érsekúivár in the summer of 1663.

In late July, Köprülü Mehmed ordered Küçük Mehmed, *serdar* of Transylvania, to join the main army in the siege of Érsekúivár. The 8,000-strong vanguard corps, under Ali Paşa and Küçük Mehmed, advanced to Esztergom, where they crossed the Danube over a single bridge, confident enough not to form screens or outposts as defence.[65] The Imperial attempts to intercept the Ottomans by joining their forces failed at Párkány on 7 August 1663 with heavy casualties. The siege of Érsekúivár proceeded slowly but every phase was planned to perfection. Ottoman miners diverted channels that filled the moats of the fortress, while approach trenches were dug by soldiers and manpower recruited among the local peasants. For this task, the Grand Vizier divided the detachments into four corps, which were employed to raise an elevated platform. According to the Ottoman chronicles, Köprülü Ahmed himself placed him at the head of the first corps composed by *muteferrikas* and *çavuş*, The vizier Hüseyn Paşa of Buda, was charged with inspecting these troops.[66] Köprülü Ahmed deployed his siege battery, 21 great cannon with calibres between 22 and 64 pounds, which created hugely destructive volleys. This battery comprised weapons of disparate provenance, such as a sixteenth-century heavy cannon cast in Brunswick, nicknamed 'the wallbreaker'. Each night the Grand Vizier ran through the trenches, and encouraged miners and labourers to push their work to the base of the bastions. The siege of Érsekúivár was, with the exception of Várad in 1660, the first large-scale siege since the Ottoman capture of Chania and Réthimno in Crete in 1645–46. Fighting was fierce, with the Ottoman artillery firing an estimated 18,000 projectiles. Although the Ottoman exploits, achieved years later in Kandije, are incomparable in relation to the siege of Érsekúivár, their skill in siege warfare at this time was already extensive. The Ottomans stormed the breached bastion three times, but each time they were repulsed. In early September, Köprülü Ahmed offered surrender terms to the Imperial garrison.[67] Realising that the

---

65 Hammer-Purgstall, *Geschichte des Osmanischen Reiches*, vol. XI, pp.139–140.

66 *Ibidem*, p.157.

67 An honourable surrender was proposed. The Grand Vizier agreed to write a declaration commending the valiant resistance put up by the besieged Imperial forces. This example of the surrender of Érsekúivár is an interesting precedent of the Ottomans offering face-saving

Imperial field army would not bring relief to the city, and aware of the low morale of the inhabitants, the Imperial commander Forgách accepted the Ottoman proposal.[68]

In the short period between the events of Érsekúivár and the final clash at Szentgotthárd, military activity followed a common pattern of strike and counterstrike operations, with the difference that in this instance reaction times were reduced to a fraction. Instead of returning to Constantinople – the regular practice in the absence of any significant threat of off-season counter-attacks – a significant part of the Ottoman army, including a part of the Tatar cavalry, remained in the field and made their winter quarters at Szeged, Szombor and Pécs, allowing a much faster response time. The Grand Vizier transferred to Buda and later to Belgrade.

The last phase of the war lasted for a 10-month period from autumn 1663 to the early summer of 1664. The period between the Ottoman conquest of Érsekúivár in late September 1663 and the battle of Szentgotthárd saw most of the full variety of military activity that typifies eastern warfare.

The Tatars launched their devastating raids into Styria and Moravia, while the Imperialists, under Miklós Zrínyi, performed an aggressive winter campaign against the Ottoman outposts in Slavonia from his fortified base of Zrínyivár. However, during this period, the Ottoman commanders turned to a strategy of low-intensity warfare, characteristic across Europe, but unusual for the Ottomans. Moreover, Köprülü Ahmed underestimated the threat coming from Zrínyi and when he tried to face the enemy action, he realised he had insufficient manpower. Gürcü Mehmed, the Ottoman *serdar* in command of the winter quarters at Eszék, was ordered to organise a force to oppose Zrínyi, drawing on local *serhaddkulu*, but most of the army's main units had been assigned to winter quarters five to 10 days' march away. Although the Grand Vizier moved quickly from Belgrade to set up field headquarters at Zemun, across the Sava River, his whole force amounted to little more than an escort troop of 4,000 men. Infantry immediately available to Gürcü Mehmed's command were, when the alarm was first raised, no more than half that number.

---

concessions to encourage local military figures to lay down their arms. See Murphey, *Ottoman Warfare*, pp.127–128.

68 Officers and soldiers left Érsekúivár not just with their personal belongings intact, but also allowed to leave the fortress bearing arms. This concession, a point of honour not commonly agreed to, was granted by the Ottoman commander despite the fact that the garrison had, at least for an initial period, offered determined resistance. Mühürdar's account, cited by Murphey in *Ottoman Warfare*, p.127: 'He (the grand vizier) agreed to draft a letter to the defenders' sovereign Leopold confirming the bravery and determination of the garrison's resistance to the Ottoman attack (Condition no. 4) and to provide adequate supplies of grain to cover them during their retreat (Condition no. 6). Although Köprülü Ahmed reduced the provision of wagons from the 1,000 requested in Condition no. 3 of the surrender agreement to 400, still by general standards even this level of transport assistance was quite generous. From the Érsekúivár example and a comparison with similar terms of surrender offered to lesser forts it is readily apparent that humane, even face-saving alternatives were routinely sought by the Ottomans as an alternative to the senseless continuation of the blood-letting on both sides that resulted from the needless prolonging of a siege. *Aman* [voluntary surrender] was used not only as a means for terminating conflicts, but was also commonly offered to adversaries to avoid the inception of violence.'

On 2 February 1664, Köprülü Ahmed learned the bad news concerning the destruction of the bridges at Eszék performed by Zrínyi. These facilities permitted supply and communication between the Hungarian front and vital Ottoman resources and reinforcement links along the Danube. A few weeks after, the Ottomans could do little more than helplessly watch while the enemy systematically destroyed the outer defences of Pécs. The destruction was so complete that Ottoman sources acknowledge the devastation resulting from the enemy bombardment as wide enough to allow grazing animals to pass in and out of the city walls without obstruction.[69] Although Zrínyi raised the siege of Pécs on 6 February, without having captured the inner citadel, the whole of the operation carried out between the last week of January and the first week of February cost the Ottomans dearly. The effect of the enemy's winter offensive in the early months of 1664 had been to eliminate a vitally important period of winter rest and recuperation. Losses were great both in terms of the financial cost for repairs and the inevitable delays that would result in their spring campaign.

Surprisingly, the Imperialists under Zrínyi had prevailed in a matter in which the Ottomans were normally masters, and this was certainly a serious mistake. Furthermore, a lightly armed force composed mostly of irregulars, who advanced unopposed into Ottoman territory, had inflicted these damages, taking advantage of the Ottoman army that had taken to winter quarters. After a season of engagements in Habsburg Hungary, the Ottoman troops were not very favourably disposed to listen to the Grand Vizier's urgent orders to reopen the campaign. This pattern of uncontested or only minimally-contested offensives was not confined to the relatively unusual occurrence of winter actions. It was, as the Ottoman counter-offensive of spring 1664 would show, a common feature of many military encounters even in the principal campaigning season. In the spring of 1664, the full Ottoman army was redeployed to the sectors where immediate repairs were required, and to make good the damage inflicted in the winter raids carried out by the Croatian and Hungarian *Grenzers*. However, Köprülü Ahmed had barely advanced beyond Mitrovica, the second stage for the Ottoman army after Belgrade. At the time of his return to Belgrade on 11 February, the Grand Vizier had already set in motion plans for organising work crews to carry out the extensive repairs that would be required, before the critical bridges at Eszék could be restored.

Because of Zrínyi's offensive, Ottoman engineers and pioneers were kept busy throughout the winter and beyond just restoring bridges, forts and paths, let alone attending to preparations for the Ottoman counter-offensive. Seventy-five days later, the *musellims* were dispatched to Eszék. Even then, the arrival of the Grand Vizier, with his assembled troops, at the river crossing on 15 May 1664, still managed to coincide with a last-minute flurry of activity to complete the final phase of reconstruction of the bridge.

In addition, some border fortresses needed restoration. The 36-day Imperial siege of Kanizsa ended in failure. Nevertheless, before Zrínyi was

---

69 Murphey, *Ottoman Warfare*, p.124.

able to move ahead with his own offensive plans, the Ottomans were once again burdened with the task of repairing the damage done to this fortress, which formed a key element of their border defences along that sector of the frontier. The scale of these repairs was such that, according to an Ottoman account, even with input from peasant work crews mobilised from seven outlying districts – in open contradiction to normal Ottoman military practice – the work was not completed until 13 July, long after the normal start of seasonal operations.

The immediate challenge facing Grand Vizier Köprülü Ahmed in the spring of 1664 was the mobilisation of the field army in areas scattered throughout the Danube. Even after the bridges at Eszék had been finally restored, and regular army units attached to the Grand Vizier had crossed the river on the 20 May, Köprülü Ahmed advanced slowly to allow time for his army's strength to increase. He had only reached Szigetvár by 29 May, where he was joined by irregulars from Bosnia and Albania enlisted in place of regular units still lingering in their winter quarters. It should be noted that swifter mobilisation was difficult due to the need for cavalry mounts – on whom the army would depend in the later phases of the campaign – to complete their spring pasturing before proceeding to the front. News from Upper Hungary informed Köprülü Ahmed about the loss of Nitra on 7 May, and the defeat suffered by Küçük Mehmed Paşa at Szent-Benedek nine days after.

A strategic decision had already been taken to leave behind most of the heavy siege guns and other cumbersome equipment to allow the army to advance as quickly as possible. In fact, only seven out of the 27 heavy guns stored in Eszék accompanied the army during its onward march.[70] This decision was based on a calculated risk, but given that the four-week-old Imperial investment of Kanizsa was then entering its most critical phase, there was no real alternative. The decision was, moreover, based on a clear-headed assessment of the enemy's offensive capabilities, and the design and actual state of repair of local fortress defences gained from scouting intelligence. The decision was, of course, reversible should military developments take an unexpected turn, but for the army's immediate purposes the logic that suggested the shedding of unnecessary weight was irrefutable. The wisdom of this decision was clearly demonstrated only a few days later when the Ottoman army was delayed for two days covering the 20 km separating the army's base of departure at Szigetvár and its camp at Darány. In order to complete the march, it had to raise bridges in four places to pass over marshy terrain. Once the Ottoman army was up to full strength and had brought the Kanizsa relief operation to a successful conclusion, it was able to proceed with its real purpose, which was to launch an offensive of its own. The fortress of Zrínyivár, situated only two hours' march to the west of Kanizsa, was the first objective. Zrínyivár's relatively sophisticated defences occupied Ottoman siege engineers for 21 days, before it finally yielded to an Ottoman frontal assault on 30 June. The conquest of this outpost gave Köprülü Ahmed relatively free hand in deciding where to turn next. After some further delays in overseeing the demolition of

---

70 Hammer-Purgstall, *Geschichte des Osmanischen Reiches*, vol. XI, p.455.

45. Battle scene between Imperial cavalry and *kuruc* rebels, in a late seventeenth-century print. After the definitive loss of their bases in Upper Hungary, the rebels joined the Ottoman army and continued to fight against the Imperialists until 1699. After the Truce of Carlowitz, hundreds of Hungarians followed their leader Imre Thököly into exile. (Author's archive).

Zrínyivár, on the one hand, and the rebuilding of Kanizsa on the other, the Ottomans decided to move against a new, previously untested region along the Hungarian frontier to the north of Kanizsa towards the natural boundary formed by the Zala and Rába rivers.

The Ottoman army set out on 14 July with its sights set on the lightly fortified, central frontier zone that stretched for some 80 km between Kanizsa, in the south, to Körmend, in the north. There were numerous diversions during late July; the Ottoman offensive had to be launched on both primary and secondary fronts in Croatia and in Upper Hungary from Transylvania. One after the other, seven Imperial forts in the area between Kanizsa and Körmend fell into Ottoman hands in just two weeks. The sieges were extremely brief and opened the way for the Ottoman advance on the Rába River.[71] Only a couple of forts offered an initial determination to defend, but the methodical tactics and the large amount of resources and facilities of the Ottoman army always prevailed over enemy resistance. Fortuitously, in all sieges mounted during this phase of the campaign, the Ottomans were able to achieve their military objectives with the application of a minimum of force, whilst committing only small numbers of their available troops. Ottoman siege preparations for Pölöske, one of the forts that offered resistance, had included siege technicians and miners standing by, equipped with a quantity of five kantars (620 pounds) of gunpowder,

71　For more details regarding the campaign of 1664 and the battle of Szentgotthárd, see Mugnai, *Wars and Soldiers in the Early Reign of Louis XIV; vol. II, The Imperial Army, 1657–1687* (Warwick: Helion & Company, 2019), pp.155–161.

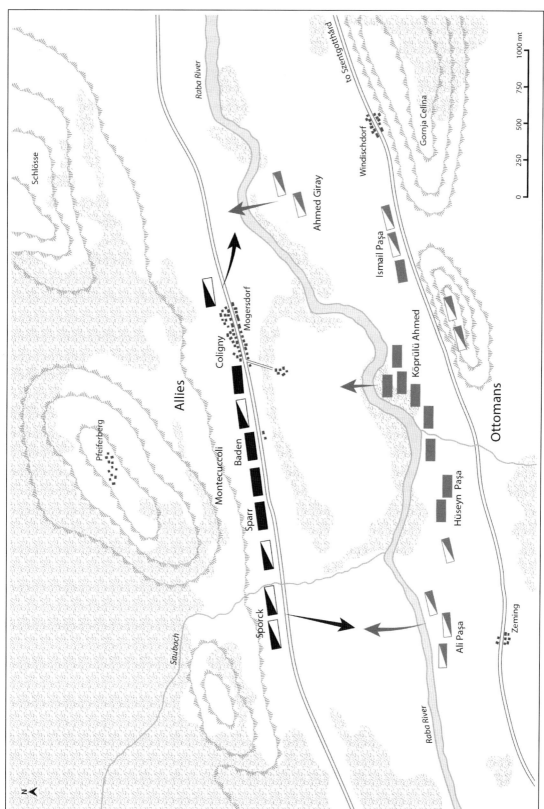

Schlösse

Raba River

to Szentgotthárd

Windischdorf

Gornja Celina

Ahmed Giray

İsmail Paşa

Mogersdorf

Köprülü Ahmed

Coligny

Allies

Pfeiferberg

Montecuccoli

Baden

Ottomans

Sparr

Hüseyn Paşa

Spořck

Ali Paşa

Saubach

Zeming

Raba River

1000 mt

750

500

250

0

Map 7. Battle of Szentgotthárd, 1 August, 1664. Opening phase.

N

whose use in the event proved unnecessary.[72] The main purpose of this phase of the campaign was not to extend the Ottoman frontier or conquer new territories, but to neutralise their potential as a base for counter-attacks aimed against nearby Ottoman settlements. To secure his plan, the Grand Vizier also planned an offensive campaign to threaten Upper Hungary with an assault from Transylvania. To this end, he had directed Ali Paşa with a force of 20,000 provincial and auxiliary Tatar and Wallachian–Moldavian troops to advance from the east. The Imperial commander, Louis Radouit de Souches, anticipated his opponent's moves and after besieging Léva (today Levice in Slovakia), defeated the Ottoman relief corps on 19 July. The failure of this action had little effect on the outcome of the battle of Szentgotthárd, which was a decisive battle, but more for the Imperialists than for the Porte.[73]

Though the Hungarian campaigns of 1663 and 1664 had been characterised by the exensive use of infantry, against enemies such as the Poles and the Russians, the Ottoman commanders directed operations by entrusting the main offensive role to the cavalry. The boundless plains of Podolia and Ukraine favoured rapid offensives and constant displacements. The infantry served only to occupy fortified sites or to conquer them with a siege. The fortresses of those regions, almost always in woodland, were not able to withstand assaults for long, and forced the defenders to intervene at the threatened points, resorting in turn to the mobility of the cavalry. This was a kind of warfare in which the Ottomans usually showed remarkable skill. Led by daring commanders such as *saitan* Ibrahim Paşa, even modest contingents achieved excellent results during the campaigns against the Poles from 1672 to 1676. In the spring of 1675, Ibrahim launched an offensive into Volhynia. Making an effective use of the Tatars and Cossacks, the diabolical *serasker* held the Poles in check with the unpredictable moves of his horsemen. In August 1675, the raids performed by the Tatars of the *nureddin* Selim Safa Giray arrived before the walls of Lvov, where the Polish royal family was. A disastrous rainstorm disrupted the main corps and slowed the Ottoman progress, allowing Sobieski to repel the enemy at the end of a spectacular two-hour cavalry battle.[74] A similar scheme was also employed in operations against the Russians in the war of 1678–81, but the campaigns were also limited by physical constraints. Operations in the open field were of course constrained by the climate, and by natural barriers, such as mountains, marshes, deserts. These could be surmounted, but only at great effort and expense, therefore the moves of the Ottomans were hindered by the poor conditions of the terrain, and the remoteness of the theatre of war also influenced the provision of supplys, slowed down by lack of roadways. Inevitably, Ottoman campaigns against Russia concentrated on

---

72 Murphey, *Ottoman Warfare*, p.129.
73 An Ottoman victory would have had incalculable consequences for the Habsburgs, while the Ottoman army, although defeated, was still a considerable force. The armistice of Vasvár, which would have so irritated the Hungarians against the Emperor, was in fact a continuation of that of Zsitvatörök in 1606. The strategic scenario effectively put back the one before 1663, with the Ottoman advantage deriving from the control of Transylvania and from the conquest of Ersekuivar, while the emperor had been forced to return the fortresses conquered in 1664 with a few exception. See also in 'Wars and Soldiers in the Early reign of Louis XIV, vol. II' pp.160–161.
74 Eickoff, *Wien, Venedig und die Osmanen*, p.311.

more accessible areas, which explains the Ottoman conduct of the operations. Unlike in Podolia, in this conflict the unpredictable *saitan* Ibrahim performed very poorly, and his obstinate attempts to seize the fortress of Chirigin resulted in heavy casualties.[75]

The Gamble of Vienna

Before the war against the Holy League, the Porte had always managed to disengage rather quickly from conflicts. Apart from the long siege of Kandije, which undoubtedly constituted an anomalous case,[76] all the wars fought by the Ottomans had been resolved within three or at most five years, and above all, they always avoided facing more than one enemy at a time. In 1682, the decision to go to war to support Hungarian Protestants against the Emperor also brought this risk.

Much has been written on this subject, but there are still several details to clear regarding the actual Ottoman strategy of this campaign. Although the authority of the Grand Vizier was extensive, it has never been clarified whether the conquest of Vienna was the main goal of the war, and whether this had been more or less agreed with the sultan.[77] Unfortunately, the primary Ottoman sources contribute to make this issue uncertain. One of the greatest difficulties encountered in defining the actual design of the Porte derives from the scarcity of reliable sources from Ottoman officials. Nevertheless, even when these sources are accessed, the military tradition of the Ottoman Empire made dignitaries and military leaders little inclined to draw up state documents and instructions for the army on the Western model, or write memoirs to explain or justify the actions taken. In this way, certain episodes and decisions remain in a mysterious and ambiguous context. Even men of culture who accompanied the armies on campaigns left only succinct reports about the events to which they assisted. Yet, there was no one better than them in the best position to observe and judge certain episodes.[78]

---

75 This time, the *serasker* paid his failure with arrest and prison in Constantinople. Hammer-Purgstall, vol. XI, p.355.

76 Montecuccoli, 'Aforismi', in Luraghi, *Opere di Raimondo Montecuccoli*, vol. II, p.507. 'Usually the Turk does not engage in two wars simultaneously, And if the Turk moved war against Caesar but had not yet concluded the one against Venice, it was because he conducted this latter only passively.'

77 F. Cardini, *Il Turco a Vienna Storia del Grande Assedio del 1683* (Bari: Laterza, 2011), p.260: 'Doubt remains as to when Kara Mustafa actually matured his plan to besiege Vienna. Is it possible that he had kept the idea hidden since the first meeting in Constantinople in August 1682? Other doubts persist as to whether he really dared to hide his design to the sultan. It was objectively unthinkable, however, that the Grand Vizier was transgressing a formal prohibition. Kara Mustafa knew well that his head was at stake, but he thought that if the siege were successful he would bring an invaluable gift to the sultan. However, reports dating back to days after the siege began, say that Mehmd IV learned of his grand vizier's decision and expressed disappointment.' According to Cardini, possibly the actual inspiration for the conquest of Vienna was the Grand Vizier's spiritual advisor, Mehmed Vani *efendi*, who was constantly with him.

78 There are essentially two major Ottoman sources regarding the Vienna campaign. The *Vekayi'-i Beç* exists in two manuscript copies, one in London, the other in Constantinople. The parts of the work concerning the siege and its aftermath has been translated into German and annotated by R.F. Kreutel in *Kara Mustafa vor Wien: das Türkishe Tagebuch der Belagerung Wiens verfasst vom*

It is certain, however, that from the early stages of the campaign, there was a strong divergence within the Ottoman command regarding the plan to follow. At Székesfehérvár, on 27 June 1683, Kara Mustafa presided over a war council. At that meeting was discussed which route to follow for the invasion of Austria, and on that occasion Kara Mustafa expressed his intentions to besiege Vienna. Now, it became clear to everyone that it was not an expedition in force, but limited, only to support of the Hungarian rebels, a ruse initially attempted to deceive the spies and Imperial diplomats who were guest-hostages in the Ottoman camp. The actual goal was the 'Golden Apple'.[79] There were doubts and protests at that news. Buda's *beglerbeg*, Ibrahim Paşa and the *han* of the Crimean Tatars, Mehmed Ali Giray, expressed their opposition. Both claimed that such an objective should have been discussed the previous year in Constantinople, and added that the risk was too high, because to besiege Vienna would have attracted the whole of Christian Europe against the sultan. Instead of marching to Vienna and threatening a siege with an uncertain outcome, the army could easily have conquered Komárom and Győr and forced the Emperor to accept an unfavourable armistice.

In various moments of the crucial campaign of Vienna misunderstandings and disagreements occurred, as well as real quarrels between the Ottoman commanders and their Tatar and Hungarian allies. Nevertheless, despite the poor convergence of intent, the campaign proceeded well. On 7 July the Tatars, supported by the Ottoman border riders, defeated at Petronell the Imperialist rearguard while it marched to north after being forced to leave the siege at Érsekújvár. The news of the unfavourable encounter caused the flight of the Emperor Leopold I with the court from Vienna. The Imperial convoy, heading for Linz, risked being intercepted by the Tatars, who appeared before Krems and occupied the northern bank of the Danube. It was by a matter of minutes that they missed an unrepeatable opportunity.

On 10 July the Ottoman army halted at Ungarisch-Altenburg, 86 km from Vienna. Kara Mustafa had under his command a very large army, further increased after the arrival of Tatars, tributary contingents and Hungarian *Kuruc* allies.[80] The actual strength of the Ottoman army for the campaign of 1683 is one of the most debated topics in seventeenth-century military

---

Zeremonienmeister der Hohen Pforte (Graz: Styria Verlag, 1960). This chronicle is supposed to be an official diary written by the anonymous Master of Ceremonies of the Ottoman court. Its eyewitness description reflects first-hand knowledge about the abortive Ottoman siege of Vienna. The second major source is the aforementioned *Silihtar Tarihi*, written by *silihtar* Findiklili Mehmed ağa. The chronicle contains interesting political details on the campaigns. According to Findiklili Mehmed, the *ulemas* would not permit the war, and in this regard they issued a *fatwa*. However, Grand Vizier Kara Mustafa ignored it and persuaded the sultan to proceed with a military campaign against Austria.

79   The golden apple is an element that appears in various national and ethnic folk legends or fairy tales. For the Ottomans, the golden apple indicated the city to be conquered and therefore the object of the sultan's wishes. At first, the name referred to the city of Constantinople, which thanks to its mighty city walls had repeatedly managed to escape conquest. Once the expansion route on the Balkan Peninsula was completely cleared, the main target of the Ottomans first became Buda; after the conquest of the latter, the turn of Vienna came, which for the Ottomans thus became the new golden apple.

80   Cardini, *Il Turco a Vienna*, p.290.

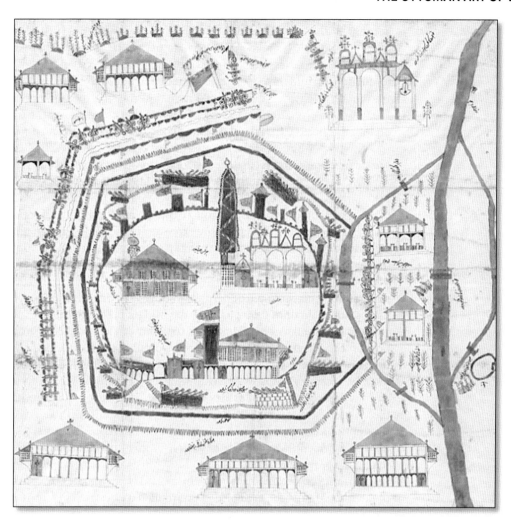

46. Ottoman map of Vienna, illustrating the siege camp around the city, mid July 1683.
(Museum of Vienna)

history. Unfortunately, as discussed in another chapter, the reliability of coeval documents is somewhat questionable. Apart from the exaggerated reconstructions circulating in those years, and those proposed until the 1930s,[81] there is an anonymous French document that reconstructs in detail the transit through Győr of the Ottoman troops and personnel following the army heading to Vienna.[82] The document, dated early July, registered 302,000 men in all. An even bigger figure, 400,000 men, is reported by a neutral eyewitness, the Venetian provveditor Lunardo Donado, who each week transmitted a detailed

---

81 Among these exaggerated estimates, the most durable is the one relating 300,000 soldiers stated by Jan III Sobieski, repeated by L. von Pastor in *Storia dei Papi dalla fine del Medioevo* (Roma, 1932), p.124. Hammer-Purgstall, in his *Geschichte des osmanishen Reiches* vol. XII, p.95, states the strength of the Ottoman army at Vienna at 200,000 men, but without specifying whether the figure included auxiliary personnel. Even a classic on the subject, such as Stoye's *The Siege of Vienna* is ambiguous on this matter. However, some recent reconstructions also relate unreliable and inaccurate information. In this regard see S. Millar, *Vienna 1683, Christian Europe repels the Ottomans*, Campaign 191 (Osprey Publishing, 2008), p.22.

82 Bibliothèque Nationale de France, Ms. fr, 24482, ff. 40–45, cited by Ph. Roy, in *Louis XIV et le second siege de Vienne* (1683) (Paris: Honoré Champion, 2000), pp.87–88.

account of the campaign to the *Serenissima*.[83] Considering that about two fifths of the total was made up of civilian personnel and servants, estimates suggest that a little less than 200,000 Ottoman and allied soldiers had arrived to Vienna in mid July. This total would include *musellims* and *lağımcıs*, who totalled together about 30,000 men,[84] decreasing the fighting force to 170,000 men. This strength is close enough to that estimated by the Imperial diplomat Alberto Caprara, who refers about 160,000 men in late June.[85]

Among the most accurate sources published after the siege, the Viennese *Kurtze Erzehlung* reports a detailed list of the troops that arrived before Vienna, which the anonymous author would have found amongst the documents belonging to Kara Mustafa, relating the figure of 168,000 men, including *lağımcıs* and *musellims*, mustered on 7 September.[86] Regarding this document, several doubts persist. The figures are expressed in thousands: a strange enough detail for a muster. However, this strength is far from the initial number stated in the aforementioned French document. Furthermore, some estimates produced during the siege by the defenders propose 80,000 or 120,000 men maximum.[87] This gap could be partially filled considering the 6–8,000 Ottoman troops under Ibrahim Paşa guarding the bridges on the Raba River, and the 6,000 Transylvanians who did not join the army at Vienna. Further troops did not come to Vienna because they were involved in the blockade of Győr and Komárom, as well as the contingents in charge of guarding the Danube Island. Moreover, cavalry corps were plentiful in the environs of Vienna to plunder and fire the countryside. Possibly the 20,000 Tatars also are not included in these latter estimates, as well as the 15,000 *Kuruc*s under Thököly. Another assumption can be considered to explain this difference: desertions. There is no direct evidence concerning desertion in great numbers, but it is certain that many protests were addressed to Kara Mustafa when the actual objective of the campaign became known. In this regard, some sources report that half of the troops under the *paşa* of Aleppo would have deserted before arriving at

---

83 A. Prelli, 'L'Assedio di Vienna nei Dispacci del Provveditore Lunardo Donado (1682–1684)', in *Quaderni del Civico Museo Storico della Città di Palmanova* (Palmanova, 2006), p.12. Probably, this figure was deduced from the first Imperial estimates produced in 1682. In another letter, received by Donado from a correspondent in Vienna after the battle of 12 September, the Ottoman strength is now different. From these notes, he learned that the Ottoman army numbered in early July 168,000 'fighters', including 40,000 Tatars, 26,000 'miners, diggers and artillerymen' and a further 30,000 'servants, Jews and similar people'. It was therefore credible, the letter pointed out, that the enemy had moved away from Vienna with at least '120,000 soldiers'.

84 *Ibidem.*

85 L. Anguissola, *Assedio di Vienna d'Austria, intrapreso li 14 luglio 1683 dagli Ottomani sotto il comando generale di Mustafà Carrà Primo Visire* (Modena, 1684), pp.17–18; I. Reiffenstuel, 'Tagebuch der Belagerung. Die Eiregnisse in und um Wien vom 7 july bis 12 september 1683', in G. Düriegl (ed.) *Die Türken vor Wien* (Vienna: Wien Kultur, 1983), p.57, and *Hollandse Mercurius verhalende de voornaemste saken van staet, en andere... in het Jaer 1683* (Haerlem, 1684), pp. 127–128. The latter source proposes the lower estimate: 83,000 soldiers in all. Further details in the appendix.

86 *Kurtze doch warhaffte und mit denkwürdigen Umständen verfasste Erzehlung, Der im Julio 1683. Zeit Jahre von dem Erb-Feinde vorgenommenen Welt-erschollenen Belagerung, Wie auch hernach klüglichst angeſtellten und mit Aufschlagung dess ganzen Ottomanniſchen Heers am 12. September desselben Jahre* (Vienna, 1684), pp.78–79. Further details in the appendix.

87 Cardini, *Il Turco a Vienna*, p.292.

Vienna.[88] Uncertainty about the actual strength of the Ottoman army remains a question that increases as the siege progressed.

However, the overall strength of the army appeared impressive. An eyewitness wrote that the dust raised by the marching army was so thick that a soldier could not see his comrades close to him.[89] Three days later, the Grand Vizier arrived before Vienna and immediately led a reconnaissance between Schwechat and the Austrian capital. Kara Mustafa established his residence at Neugebäude, a palace built by the Habsburg emperors in the same place where Süleyman the Magnificent had camped in 1529. The palace imitated the Ottoman architectural style, was surrounded by magnificent gardens, and travellers from Constantinople had admired and praised its construction. For this and other reasons, the Grand Vizier had taken possession of the building, in the hope of surpassing his illustrious predecessor.

According to reports in the coeval sources, the approach of the army to the city continued chaotically, causing some drawbacks.[90] On 14 July, a large quantity of timber was lost during an encounter with the enemy at Fischamend, while the columns of the army waited for a long time before they could set up camp. Finally, the Grand Vizier and his commanders rode up to the slopes from which it is possible to see the city from the south. Vienna lies at the centre of the valley, and around it they could see the other most important points: the Donaukanal, the Danube River, the Wienerwald hills to the north and the suburb of Leopoldstadt.

In that same place, Kara Mustafa convened the war council. The commanders discussed the siege plan, also with the support of the *lağımcıbasi* and other officers. Vienna posed considerable difficulties for even the most inspired engineer. Rivers ran past two sides of the city. To the east, one of the many branches of the Danube had been turned into a sluggish channel, the Donaukanal, which followed the line of the city walls on the northern and eastern sides, before bending back to join the main line of the river. This was Vienna's port and at one time it also provided the water for the ill-starred ditch that ran around the curtain. Nevertheless, water remained the most effective barrier against mining, but by 1683 the ditch no longer served its original purpose. On the channel side, to the east of the city, a century of erosion and the constant dumping of rubbish had made the channel shallower. Where it had dried out in summer, holes and cracks appeared in the banks through which the water would drain away. On the southwestern side of the city, a narrow river called the Wien ran down from the high ground of the Vienna Woods to join the Danube. However, it too was often dry during the summer, but after only a few days' heavy summer rain it could turn into a torrent, overflowing its banks almost up to the city walls close to where it joined the Donaukanal. Unfortunately for the defenders, the two rivers – the Danube canal and the Wien stream – made it impossible to build a strong, modern defence in depth. The weakest point in the city's perimeter was undoubtedly the eastern flank facing Leopoldstadt Island, which was surrounded by the

---

88   Roy, *Louis XIV et le second siège de Vienne*, p.95.
89   *Vekayi'-i Beç*, in Kreutel, *Kara Mustafa vor Wien*, p.14.
90   *Ibidem*, p.29.

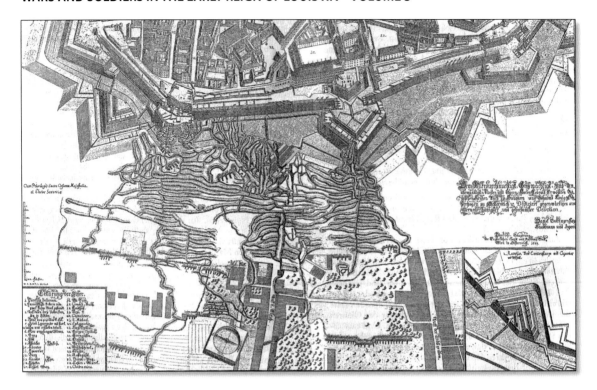

47. The west side of Vienna with the bastions of Lobel and Burg, with the adjacent ravelin, in the drawing of Daniel Suttinger, one of Georg Rimpler's assistants in restoring the defences of the Austrian capital. The drawing shows the Ottoman progress as it appeared at the end of August 1683. The besiegers had consolidated their positions in the counterscarp of the Löbel and Burg bastions and in the adjacent ravelin, and they were very close to penetrating beyond the curtain.

Danube on all sides, both by the canal and by the main stream of the river. Kara Mustafa and his officers examined the maps and discussed the different options. Excluding the sides encircled by the channel and the Wien, the decision turned to the west side.

The plan was based on the belief that it was possible to open a breach between the Hofburg and Löbel bastions. In that sector, the Wien stream curved away from the walls and there it was possible to take advantage of the elevated terrain to advance with the approaches to the counterscarp of the bastions. The stream was often dry during the summer, but the heavy summer rain of July, it could turn into a narrow river, overflowing its banks almost up to the city walls close to where it joined the Donaukanal. In favour of an assault from the south, there was also the fact that the gradient of the terrain facilitated the drainage of the water, and therefore would have favoured the digging of the trenches more than in other sectors.

Examining the progress of the siege operation, the mines were the principal instrument for supporting the approaches against the city's defence. The artillery, although numerous, was represented by field guns and mortars, while the calibres suitable for a siege were scarce. This has fuelled a debate among modern historians about the responsibilities of Kara Mustafa, who would not have taken into account the insufficient number of siege guns.[91] Instead, the heavy artillery, especially mortars, was used to hit the city, while the field guns supported the advancement of the approaches targeting the

---

91   Cardini, *Il Turco a Vienna*, p.293.

palisade, ravelins and the other external defences, according to a scheme tested in Crete 14 years before, which had produced good results.

Meanwhile, Ottoman riders and Tatars overran the surrounding area in every direction. Hundreds of villages were ravaged and fired; only Bruck, Sopron and Eisenstadt, whose inhabitants had implored the protection of Thököly, no less powerful than one of the grand viziers, were spared.[92] Also the troops of the main army, widespread across the surroundings, were engaged in looting and burning. On 14 July, Ottoman soldiers arrived under the walls of Perchtoldsdorf and the next day, bombs having set fire to the city, the inhabitants took refuge in the church and the fortified tower. On the third day, they negotiated with a *paşa* sent expressly from Vienna to Perchtoldsdorf, and obtained free withdrawal by paying a sum of 4,000 guilders.[93] Despite some adjustments, Kara Mustafa's orders concerning the civilian population had been clear: hit hard and wreak havoc.[94]

On 15 July in the morning the Ottomans troops made their encampments, while Kara Mustafa sent an officer to Vienna to submit the traditional formal request to surrender, which Ernst Rüdiger von Starhemberg, the Imperial commander in the city, indignantly refused. The Grand Vizier disposed his troops to close the city in a large circle, to lay out an encampment that extended for 24km. Part of the infantry made camp on the opposite bank of the Wien stream, between the villages of Gumpendorf and Hernals. Other detachments were deployed from west to north to occupy the terrain up to the village of Döbling. Other troops encamped around the suburb of Rossau, near the Donaukanal, while the tents of the Grand Vizier and his staff were prepared between Gumpendorf and Saint Ulrich. A corps of European and Anatolian infantry made camp to the north-east with part of the janissaries, while behind them was placed a composite cavalry contingent from Anatolia. A smaller camp was made in the south-east, close the village of Saint Marx.

On the opposite bank opposite to Leopoldstadt, as a reserve, was disposed the Wallachian and Moldavian cavalry. Transylvanians were involved in the

---

92 Hammer-Purgstall, *Geschichte des Osmanischen Reiches*, vol. XII, p.92

93 *Ibidem*, p.95.

94 A miraculously surviving eyewitness describes the events that occurred: 'Just as the day broke on the 15th July, with us still fast asleep, the enemy arrived at our market square. On the cry and report from the lookout, we quickly gathered in and around the church, where the walls protected us. The enemy completely occupied the market, and it was therefore impossible for anyone to ward them off. Thus, we left ourselves to God's mercy. The enemy had assured us of our personal safety, even in writing, so that should any other groups [of them] appear, we were to present the document and nothing evil would befall us. Thus, in the name of God, we opened up [the church].We mingled with them, and they with us, without the slightest fear … We brought them food … Once they ate their fill, leaving very little for us, they called out, bring the arms! … Two Turkish pashas sat at the cemetery gate, listed all of the males among us, then ordered us at the church to raise our right hands. We bade one another farewell. The enemy, in the meantime, each with a saber on his side [and] another weapon in his hand, stood ready to our left. We never imagined that they would slaughter us on the spot, but thought that they were going to take us to Vienna, to use us as storm troops and to dig trenches. Once they saw that all of [our] men were out of the church, their commander gave a hand sign … after which they fell upon and hacked away at us hideously, an act of cruelty that left us all falling atop one another, screaming for mercy the whole time.' In P. Sutter Fichtner, *Terror and Toleration. The Habsburg Empire Confronts Islam, 1526–1850* (London: Reaktion Book, 2008), p.9.

seizing of the Imperial places in Upper Hungary, while the Tatars moved north to survey access to Vienna and the Imperial army under Lorraine, which was reorganising somewhere north of the Wienerwald. The Viennese witnessed with dismay the deployment of the troops, and at dawn the following day, the encampments offered a spectacle of a boundless tent city that far exceeded Vienna itself.[95]

July 15 was also the first day of siege. With classical oriental indolence, approaches were started towards the Burg and Löbel bastions, while the mortars opened the fire against the western side of the city.[96] Three large corps of troops, supported by *musellim* diggers, each received a sector towards which to advance. This area had its centre of gravity on the road leading to the Burg, which gently descended to the advanced defences of Vienna. At this point, about 400 metres from the walls of Vienna, Kara Mustafa had his personal advanced position placed, from which he could control the development of the siege. This post became the command centre of operations, in which a small number of collaborators and commanders participated in the war councils, such as the *yeniceri agasi*, the *yeniceri efendi* and the *beglerbeg* of Rumelia, who held the command of the central corps. The troops to the right operated under the *beglerbeg* of Anatolia, Ahmed Paşa, with the trustworthy governor of Diyarbakir, Kara Mehmed as vice-commander, while on the left the approaches were directed by the vizier Ahmed, with the *paşa* of Jenö and Sivas as deputies. The approaches of the right advanced against the Burg bastions; the left proceeded against the Löbel; while the centre directed its approaches against the counterscarp before the ravelin of the Burg. The Ottomans completed the encirclement of Vienna on 16 July. Kara Mustafa himself reconnoitred the terrain between the Donaukanal and the suburb of Leopoldstadt. Then he ordered the *paşa* of Damascus, Genç Hüseyin, to wade the shallow waters of the canal, and supported by the Wallachian and Moldavian cavalry, Hüseyin assaulted a small detachment of Imperialists, which retreated in the direction of the last bridge over the Danube north of the city. Leopoldstadt was set on fire and some wooden bridges were built to maintain communications with the other troops. Even this sector was manned by a strong corps, supported by artillery batteries to face the city also from that side. The Ottomans did nothing to disguise the objectives towards which they directed their efforts, amassing the largest number of troops and artillery before the western walls of Vienna, allowing defenders to concentrate their reserve in the most threatened sectors.

Historians point out the error made by the Grand Vizier in the failure to build a complete circumvallation trench to protect the troops against an assault from the north-west. Although the Tartars moved across an extended area westward from Vienna, Kara Mustafa seems to have done nothing to gain information from them about the enemy's movements, as he had on the march northwards through Hungary. Kara Mustafa was commanding the largest army ever seen in Europe, but the number of trained musketeers and disciplined assault troops, of artillerymen and engineers, was limited.

---

95   Reiffenstuel, *Tagebuch der Belagerung*, p.69.
96   This first bombardment lightly injured the Imperial commander Ernst Rüdiger Starhemberg.

Despite these concerns, the work of the miners proceeded and achieved their first successes in a relatively short time. Kara Mustafa was sure that his miners would demolish the walls before the arrival of the enemy relief army, and the prize would be his.

The huge encampments, extending around the city, were for the most part filled with men doing nothing much, apart from occasionally patrolling the space before the approaches and palisade. Otherwise, they were half-hearted, like the horsemen from Moldavia and Wallachia, who had reluctantly joined the campaign under threat. The provincial *sipahis* had little enthusiasm to dig trenches, and their firearms were insufficient to perform a regular battle siege, although they later proved as zealous serving on foot as they did on horseback. Contemporary accounts describe the life in the trenches and in the encampments, and in both there was a typical oriental atmosphere. Tea and other beverages were issued to soldiers, and even the work in the trenches respected the pauses for drinking. Strange as it may seem, besiegers and defenders found ways to trade.[97] The relative initial quiet was interrupted in the second week from the beginning of the siege, in conjunction with the sorties of the defenders and the first assaults of the besiegers.

Apart from the failure to guard his sprawling camp, the Ottoman plan of attack made sense, concentrating the best troops where they would do most good. Historians have discussed the actual possibility of an Ottoman victory, and most lean to a negative outcome, but on several occasions the Ottoman were close to prevailing. The first danger occurred on 25 July, when a mine exploded under the ravelin of the Burg. The explosion destroyed the palisade and killed 100 Imperial musketeers.[98] Two days after, a well-coordinated assault left the Ottoman soldiers master of the covered road in the Burg bastion. The defenders reacted immediately and repulsed the enemy, throwing them in the ditch.[99] Moreover, an epidemic of dysentery caused great concerns inside Vienna, almost causing the collapse of the defence.

Some testimonies describe the savagery of these attacks. They describe how the defenders fixed long hooks on poles to drag the besiegers to their deaths on *Schweinsfeder* and swords,[100] and how the flayed skins of Ottoman soldiers would be nailed to the palisade in view of their comrades.[101]

Kara Mustafa realised that the city was well defended. The enemy commander stripped the garrison inside the city to man the outer defence line and the ditch behind. Moreover, there was a sudden steep incline up to the palisades, and then the strength of the palisades itself to hinder the besiegers. The Imperial commander provided new timbers hammered deep into the earth and strongly buttressed by cross-beams. Ottoman artillery might blow away a section, but it could be quickly repaired and replaced.

---

97 Stoye, *The Siege of Vienna*, p.147: 'On 23 July, Starhemberg informed the municipal authorities that Viennese women used to leave the city to exchange bread for vegetables and other food with the Ottomans.' This fact alarmed the Imperial command, which forbade any type of contact, but it seems that the exchange of products never stopped.

98 Reiffenstuel, *Tagebuch der Belagerung*, p.73.

99 Stoye, *The Siege of Vienna*, p.152.

100 Hammer-Purgstall, *Geschichte des Osmanischen Reiches*, vol. XII, p.107.

101 *Vekayi'-i Beç*, in Kreutel, *Kara Mustafa vor Wien*, p.62.

By the time the charging Ottoman infantry reached the palisades, their impetus was slowing in the last few yards. There was no flat ground where they could place scaling ladders, no space for their men to mass before the bastion. Reports of those first assaults and the evidence of his own eyes made the Grand Vizier realise that this bank of earth and line of stakes was as formidable an obstacle as the great walls of the main defences of the city, almost 12 metres in height. The palisades were too strongly defended to be rushed; it would have to be besieged and undermined section by section, like the city behind it. All this would take time.

The Ottoman lines reached the palisade on 20 July; 10 days later it had still not been overwhelmed. After the first assaults were driven back with heavy casualties, the Ottoman *lağımcıs* began the slower task of digging under the palisade and exploding powerful mines below them in an attempt to break through. But still the assaults failed. The mines exploded, creating a huge mound of soft earth and a great pit, but the Ottoman infantry were driven off yet again.

In the first week of August, the besiegers were still desperately seeking to break through the external defences. By 5 August, they had built earth mounds on either side of their assault saps so that they were higher than the palisade. From these elevated positions they could now shoot down on to the enemy musketeers defending it. Then the Ottomans moved their artillery forward in a concentrated bombardment of the palisade, and for the first time waves of infantrymen also armed with grenades managed to push across through the open space to the edge of the ditch. On 7 August, the 25th day of the siege, Kara Mustafa's soldiers had finally achieved the conquest of the ravelin before the Burg and Löbel bastions. As the first Ottomans entrenched themselves in the conquered positions, they stared up at the main defences of the city that now towered above them. To each side as far as they could see there were massive brick walls; in the ditch before them there were trenches filled with musketeers.

On 9 August, at eight in the morning, a huge roar shook the city. The Ottoman miners had set off a gigantic mine under the Burg bastion, opening access to the dungeons of the building. The fighting raged for hours above and below the bastion. The Ottoman losses were very high and the assault was eventually suspended. The infantrymen of each side engaged in a duel of musketry, and the irregular crackle of gunfire lasted until sunset. Alongside the musketry, the Ottoman artillery continued to fire, causing serious damage to the defenders. Soon they learned which were the most deadly weapons. At various points the city walls were edged with dressed stone, and when hit by a cannonball these copings would shatter into sharp fragments, which caused terrible wounds.[102]

The Ottomans maintained the pressure on both the bastions, but the counter-attacks from the city erased the progresses achieved after costly and fierce fighting. On 10 August, after the explosion of a mine under the Burg and another at Löbel, the Ottomans launched an assault against both

---

102 Stoye, *The Siege of Vienna*, p.215.

bastions, but were repulsed by a well-coordinated sortie. Now, one of the most violent battles of the whole siege began, which cost heavy losses for both sides. For two days the Ottomans conquered, lost, reconquered and finally lost again the trenches from the ravelin to the Burg's counterscarp. The fighting extended to the approaches of the Löbel's external defences, where the defenders destroyed all the besiegers' works. On 13 August a strong rainstorm interrupted the assaults, but a day later a mine exploded under the gate of the Burg bastion, while new approaches advanced against the curtain. On 16 August, a successful Imperial sortie killed all the Ottoman diggers pressing hard on the Löbel bastions, setting fires that spread rapidly. The defenders succeeded in destroying the depots of the gabions and the timbers used for galleries and approaches, but the human cost was very heavy. One hundred Imperialists had died in the sortie, and these offensives called for the best and most spirited members of garrison.[103] Even the Ottoman casualties were considerable. Prisoner interrogations reported that in August the besiegers had lost 11,000 soldiers. Two *paşas* died along with a large number of officers and a further 10,000 men lay injured.[104] As the siege was prolonged, the discipline which normally prevailed gradually broke down. Ottoman commanders met constantly with their soldiers, offered them rewards for their courage, spoke to them of the great prospects that victory offered them, of the richness of the prize that lay into Vienna.

There is a vacuum of information from both sides between 14 and 17 August, however indirectly is possible to guess that Kara Mustafa was running out of soldiers, because, as reported by an Ottoman chronicle, the Grand Vizier called the troops from Győr, the Danube islands and the bridges on the Raba River, to reinforce the infantry fighting in front of the bastions of Burg and Löbel.[105] According to the Ottoman sources, Kara Mustafa would not listen to those more experienced commanders who suggested that he should not underestimate the enemy.[106] It was less that the Ottomans had no intelligence from the Tatars and the Hungarian rebels sweeping far to the west, than that their leader was not interested in hearing it. It seemed that only the city interested him and the actions of the hatred infidels were of no importance.[107] Nor was he concerned that the overextended Ottoman encampment was losing all the order and discipline that westerners had so long admired. Dead animals were swelling and rotting under the heat of the sun, and even human corpses, buried in shallow graves, distended with the gases of corruption and began to

---

103 Reiffenstuel, *Tagebuch der Belagerung*, p.77.
104 *Ibidem*. Regarding the Ottoman manpower in August see also Stoye, *The Siege of Vienna*, p.165: 'Even Charles V of Lorraine tried to have a picture of the situation and to obtain information about the numerical strength of the besiegers. In August, two Austrian peasants who had worked for the Ottomans, and a captive *ağa*, were interrogated. The Duke received further information from the inhabitants of Bruck an der Leitha, then from a 'Catholic Cossack' and from a man who declared himself as a German deserter of the Ottoman army, but who was later revealed to be an Italian Jew.' Their information was screened and compared, but casualties and the actual size of the enemy army remained uncertain.
105 *Vekayi'-i Beç*, in Kreutel, *Kara Mustafa vor Wien*, p.78.
106 *Silihtar Tarihi*, in Kreutel, *Kara Mustafa vor Wien*, pp.153–154.
107 *Ibidem*.

push up through the loose soil above them. Mutinies also began in late August. The first was the Egyptian janissaries, who abandoned the trenches, followed by the rest of the Egyptian contingent, under the orders of the *paşa* of Aleppo.[108]

Despite these difficulties, the siege continued uninterrupted. On 23 August, after a series of furious assaults, supported by the field guns placed at short range from the enemy positions, the Ottomans finally seized the counterscarp between the Burg and Löbel bastions. The success, achieved at a very heavy cost, slowed the fighting, which turned in a war of mines. However, in early September the city defence entered its most critical phase.[109] On one side the Ottomans dominated the huge mound of earth that had once been the outer bastion, and every night hundreds of infantrymen and engineers shovelled soft earth into the ditch below. Underground, hundreds of diggers worked in gallery shored up with wooden staves and props as they moved forward, laying thick timbers on the top, under a layer of soil, while the artillery targeted the city with mortars. Projectiles and gunpowder were diminishing, but despite this, the Ottoman pressure continued for further 12 days.[110]

On 3 September, the assaults resumed with violence. After the explosion of a mine under the Löbel bastion, the besiegers occupied the counterscarp and immediately entrenched there. Taking advantage of the night, they introduced two field guns and two mortars, in order to target the nearby bastion of the Burg.[111] The next day a vast mine burst at this bastion, where 3–4,000 men assaulted the covered way for an hour and a half, and they succeeded in planting their ensigns there. The intense fire of the Imperialist musketry and artillery from the flank caused heavy casualties and soon the Ottoman infantrymen could not stand the position. The breach opened by the mine explosion was immediately filled with timbers and sandbags by the defenders.

The last Ottoman attempt to seize the city occurred on 6 and 7 September. Kara Mustafa gathered 6,000 soldiers and as many diggers and miners for a new powerful assault. On 6 September, at one in the afternoon, a mine exploded under the Löbel bastion. A portion of the curtain crumbled and the infantry began the assault. At the same time, the artillery opened fire against the Burg bastion, and a series of furious assaults were launched to seize the counterscarp. The struggle continued into the night and through the following day. In the pauses between one assault and the next one, the artillery targeted the city with mortars, while flares were launched from the tower of Saint Stephen's cathedral to warn the relief army to hurry in succour

108 Hammer-Purgstall, *Geschichte des Osmanischen Reiches*, vol. XII, p.109.
109 According to Starhemberg the situation into the city had become desperate. In letters sent to Lorraine by the defenders, and delivered by messengers disguised as Ottoman soldiers, great concern was expressed about the state of the defences. The valiant Imperial commander declared that the garrison would fight to the last man, but the city could collapse and surrender within a few days. See Cardini, *Il Turco a Vienna*, p.313, and Stoye *The Siege of Vienna*, p.171. In particular, Cardini cites the letter of the Imperial general Enea Silvio Caprara, who dramatically described the situation inside Vienna, adding that succour was indispensable: 'otherwise, we will go under the tyranny of barbarians who invade the country like Attila'.
110 To remedy the shortage of projectiles the Ottoman artillerymen loaded the cannons with metal scraps, stones and even sword pommels. See Hammer-Purgstall, *Geschichte des Osmanischen Reiches*, vol. XII, p.107.
111 *Ibidem*, p.110.

of the city. On 8 September there was another assault against the bastion of the Burg, but it lasted only a couple of hours.[112] The day after, a night assault interrupted the quiet, and the day after a mine exploded under the Burg bastion. These were the last episodes of the celebrated siege of Vienna. The defences of the city had resisted once again; the Ottomans had failed to penetrate the bastions, which were now reduced to a pile of rubble.

On 8 and 9 September, during two dramatic war councils, Kara Mustafa received from his commanders the request to deploy the army to the north-west, to face an enemy assault from that direction.[113] The first serious consideration of the Grand Vizier concerning the dangers that could have come from the Wienerwald dates back to 4 September. The interrogation of a prisoner revealed that a large relief army was about to arrive in Vienna. Four days later, another prisoner said that the Imperial and Polish armies had crossed the Danube at Tulln and were marching through the hills north-west of Vienna. Reconnaissance confirmed the presence of a strong corps of troops marching to Klosterneuburg, while other officers and cavalry coming from Krems confirmed the arrival of a large army. The Grand Vizier complained to the Tatar *han* and *kalgay* for having paid little attention to the progress of the approaching enemies.[114] Nevertheless, he wanted to maintain the siege ring around Vienna, because news concerning conditions within the city encouraged him to continue the siege.[115] Further considerations maintained the Grand Vizier in his obstinacy. In fact, the distance from Tulln to Vienna was little more than 32km, but there was only a single high road winding up through the Wienerwald.

However, both Ottoman chronicles report that between 8 and 12 September the Grand Vizier deployed the army to receive as assault from the allies. Initially, on 7 September, he placed a corps of 2,000 horse on the hills north-west of the city to guard the routes to the city, but there is still much uncertainty about the actual position of the troops deployed for the

---

112 Reiffenstuel, *Tagebuch der Belagerung*, p.79.
113 *Silihtar Tarihi*, in Kreutel, *Kara Mustafa vor Wien*, pp.161–162.
114 *Ibidem*, p.163. According to the Ottoman chronicler, Kara Mustafa had a bitter argument with the Tatar *han*, Murad Giray, accused of not having sufficiently surveyed the bridges on the Danube. This episode served in the Ottoman historians of the following centuries to explain the defeat of Vienna. The story maintained that the *han* had previously been warned by the Grand Vizier about the future, hoped-for, division of the Vienna booty; the *han*, offended by the demeanour of the Ottoman commander, allegedly refused to guard 'a stone bridge north of Vienna.' All this, simply as a revenge on the Grand Vizier. This unreliable tale is still repeated today as popular belief and even some recent articles in the press and on websites repeat that Murad Giray refused to prevent the passage of the enemy army from the stone bridge over the Danube, six hours from Vienna. Recently, this tale has been exposed by an eminent member of an historical association in Turkey. The author of this book has also tried to explain the inconsistency of such a legend in the chat of a well-known social network. Although the Tatars provided a poor service at Vienna it is unthinkable that, without artillery, and with only mounted troops, they could have prevented the enemy relief army from crossing the Danube. Furthermore, the Imperialists and Poles could have crossed the river in at least five other places between Krems and Tulln.
115 A letter delivered by the servant of an Armenian doctor in Vienna stated that the city did not contain more than 5,000 soldiers, who were in disagreement with the citizenship, and the commander was in a perilous position. See Hammer-Purgstall, *Geschichte des Osmanischen Reiches*, vol. XII, p.111.

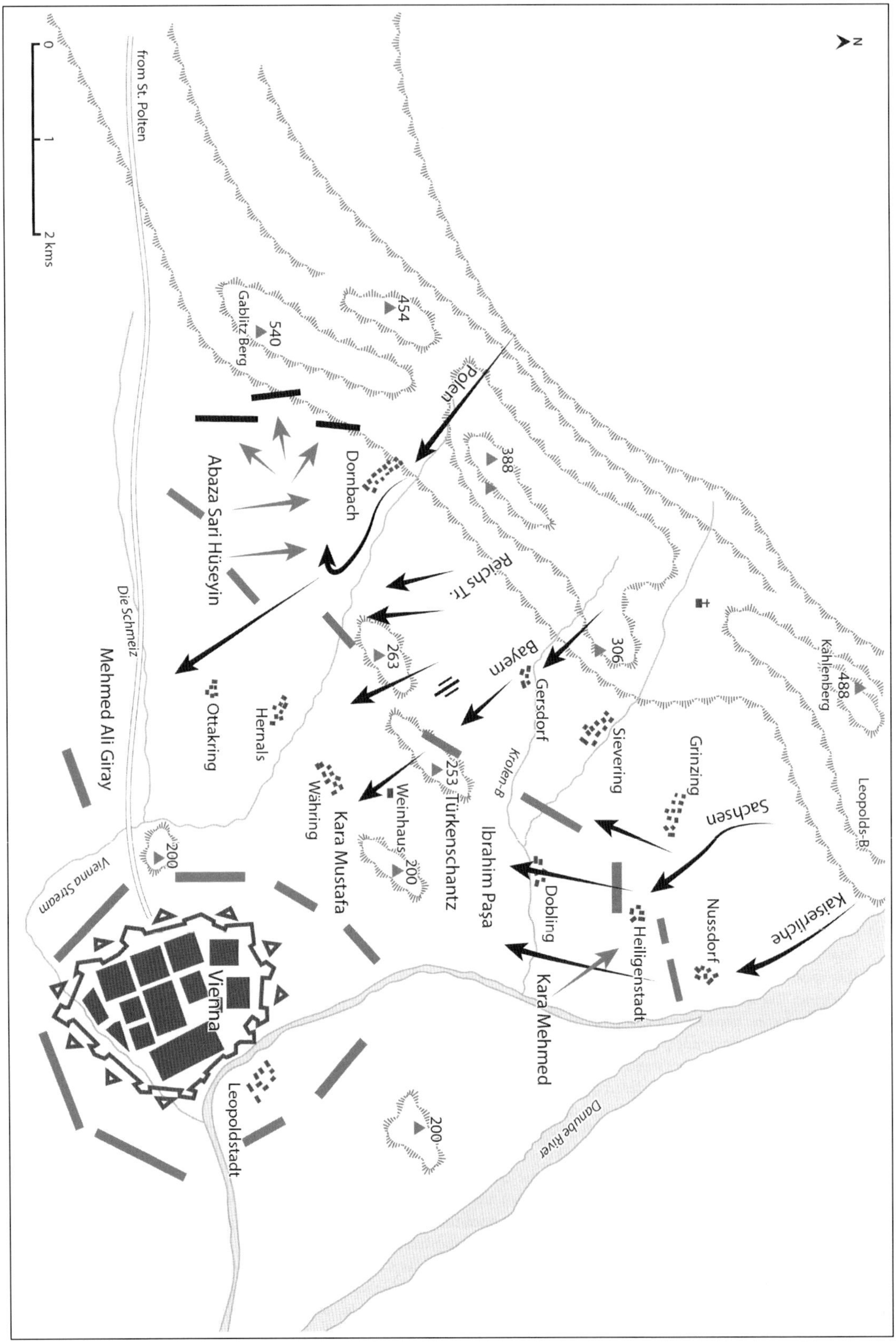

Map 8. The Battle of Kahlenberg, 12 September 1683.

oncoming battle. Significantly, information about the positions occupied by the troops, and the earthworks prepared to better resist the enemy's assault, is also uncertain. Despite the absence of a regular circumvallation, fallen trees and embankments were prepared to protect the village of Nussdorf, on the right bank of the Danube. Other testimonies report improvised *palankas* and a large redoubt built at Währing, a village about three kilometres south-east, indicated in the western sources as *Türkenschanz*, of which some traces still remain today. On the opposite side of the terrain, above the hills on the left bank of the Wien stream, the Ottomans reinforced some posts with trenches, embankments and artillery. Between Währing and the Wien stream, Kara Mustafa thought of taking advantage of the buildings and low walls among the lower vineyards. Behind these posts remained a large area of free terrain, probably to facilitate the manoeuvre of the cavalry deployed as a tactical reserve. On 8 September 6,000 infantry and 60 field guns were withdrawn from the siege, and alongside 22,000 cavalry, they manned the outer defences, for about 28,400 men in all.[116] This force had to face about 74,000 infantry and cavalry of the enemy relief army. News coming from sentinels and reconnaissance persuaded Kara Mustafa to modify the deployment, realising the urgency of preparing new countermeasures. On 9 September he deployed a cavalry screen with 5,400 men under the new *kaimakan* Kara Mehmed, *paşa* of Diyarbakir, between Heiligenstadt and Neustift. The cavalry reserve, with 16,000 horsemen under the *beglerbeg* of Buda, Koca Ibrahim, divided into corps of 2,000 troopers, occupied the terrain behind the vanguard. Their task would have been to hinder the advance of the enemy with a series of assaults and retreats, in order to disrupt them. The infantry, about 6,000 men, held the fortified positions from north to south. The Grand Vizier would have directed the battle from his quarter at Saint Ulrich, while two further corps of cavalry under Abaza Sari Hüseyin were deployed for defending both the banks of the Wien stream. The Tatars covered the space between the Ottoman battlefront and the Wienerwald. The idea, quite reckless, was to focus the defence on a centre of gravity represented by the Grand Vizier's camp, in order to employ all the troops available in case of need. Preparations were intensified the next day, but news indicated that the assault would come further north, from the area between and hills of the Kahlenberg and Leopoldsberg. On 10 September, the Imperial–Polish forces were advancing into the hills of Sauberg, next to Kahlenberg. Lorraine and Sobieski discovered that a few Ottomans had occupied the two high points at the end of the ridge, but only as observation posts. They had recently dug some ditches and might have been about to strengthen the position further. It was fortunate that the Ottomans had not occupied the ridge and built field fortifications: even a few musketeers well entrenched there would have caused problems to approaching enemies. By dusk the infantry and German cavalry had encamped by the village of St Andra on the western edge of the Wienerwald, while the Polish force, arriving late in the day, bivouacked a few miles to the west. It was well after nightfall before the advance guard arrived

---

116 *Vekayi'-i Beç*, in Kreutel, *Kara Mustafa vor Wien*, p.131.

at the agreed mustering point, with an additional demanding climb the following day. As the whole army gathered beyond the first line of foothills in the deep valley cut by the Weidling River, a small group of volunteers (including the 20-year-old Eugene of Savoy), and some musketeers were sent ahead in the evening. Their task, guided by local hunters, was to find their way up the maze of forest pathways to the summit of the Kahlenberg ridge. Once it was dark, they were to capture the Ottoman outposts with a sudden assault. By dawn on Saturday 11 September they had surprised the small Ottoman outpost on the Kahlenberg and slaughtered all the enemy men they could find. But some of the soldiers slipped away in the dark, returning to the main camp on the plain below, bearing news of the impending attack. To respond to the new threat, the entire Ottoman deployment turned to the right, leaving the southern sector uncovered. The front was so extended that Kara Mustafa could not defend in equal strength all along the line, and he relied on Tartars encamped on the far left of his positions to provide emergency cover.

Again, calculating the forces on the field poses a challenge for many historians. Coeval sources give some detail, suggesting that between 50,000 and 60,000 horse and foot with 60 field guns were deployed from Dornbach to Währing along a five kilometre-wide front.[117] A further 48,000 soldiers, diggers and miners still besieged Vienna, while the Tatars could add 18–20,000 horse. These figures would permit the possibility that at least 40,000 soldiers and auxiliaries had died, were wounded or had deserted in the 60 days of siege. The number of troops still available was considerable, but the janissaries and other elite infantry had lost half of their original strength; the most part of this force comprised provincial troops and, except for the *azabs*, were poorly trained to fight behind embankments or in the trenches.

By 11:00 a.m. on the morning of 11 September, the Austrian and German troops had arrived along the ridge. They made camp on the slopes of the three peaks – the Kahlenberg, the Vogelsangberg, and the Hermannskogel – company by company, in accordance with the allied battle orders. Closest to the Danube on the Kahlenberg were the Imperial troops of Charles of Lorraine; next to them below the summit of the Vogelsangberg were the contingents from the Holy Roman Germanic Empire under Count Georg Friedrich of Waldeck, with the Saxons under the direct command of Julius Franz, Duke of Lauenberg, covering the lower slopes of the Hermannskogel. When the Poles arrived on the ridge, they took up position on the slopes below the last three hilltops, farthest from the river: the Dreimarkstein, the Gränberg and the Rosskopf.

The terrain along the ridge was laid out in lines, corresponding to the plan of attack. Nevertheless, when Charles V of Lorraine and Jan III Sobieski rode up to the vantage point on the Kahlenberg in reconnaissance, it became clear that the maps they had and the reality they faced were different. The maps had presented a set of flat, open, rectangular fields below the hills, even showing the neat lines of the plough. There was not a slope running smoothly

---

117 *Kurtze Erzehlung*, pp.70–71.

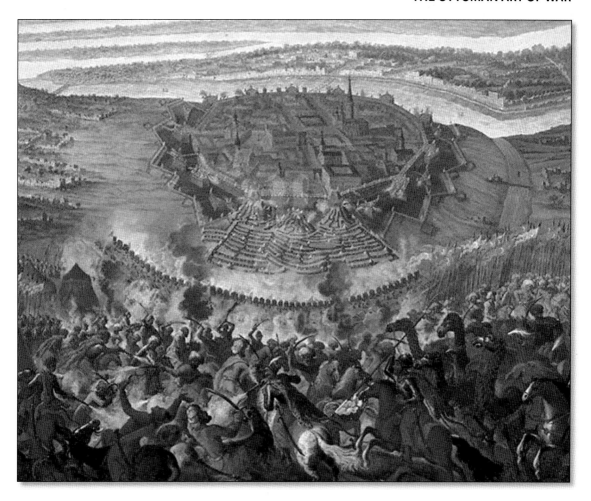

48. The battle of Kahlenberg engaged in succession the whole Ottoman line of defence from Nussdorf to Dornbach. The arrival of the enemy was announced by the scream 'Gavur yakindir!' (The Infidels are coming!). The Ottoman troops fought strenuously, but the Imperial–German–Polish troops took advantage of the terrain, and advanced supported by the field artillery, overwhelming the static Ottoman line. Kara Mustafa's attempt to re-establish the situation with a cavalry charge failed, and the retreating Ottoman *sipahis* routed the troops and caused complete defeat. Despite the multinational composition of the confederate army, an effective leadership structure was established, centred on the Polish King Jan III Sobieski. The Ottoman commander, was less effective at ensuring the coordination of his forces, and in preparing the commanders to better collaborate with him.

down towards the city, but a pockmarked, rocky landscape enfolded into a succession of clefts and ridges. There were little villages clustered amid the fields. The fields were not flat, but steeply sloping, and often bounded by stone walls, thick hedgerows or dense scrub. Worst of all the descent was precipitous. It was difficult ground for infantry, but for cavalry it might be murderous. The only hope was strong support from musketeers who could exchange fire with the Ottomans, and Sobieski had few of these. Lorraine agreed to change the order of battle and transferred some of his infantry to the Polish wing. This event forced the allies to postpone the assault to the day after.

The Ottoman advance guard commanded by Kara Mehmed had taken possession of Nussdorf, and the *paşa* had sent small groups of dismounted cavalry with muskets further up the hill, in plain sight of those on the

Kahlenberg. Reconnaissance confirmed Kara Mustafa on his superiority in cavalry. However, there was no sign of activity in the hills to the west of the city. There was, indeed, nothing to see, because the Poles did not arrive on the crest, after a terrible struggle uphill, until after nightfall on 11 September. As Kara Mustafa watched the activity of the enemy army on the Kahlenberg, the emplacement of gun batteries and signs of movement, he was certain that this was where the attack would come. He pushed more and more men into positions facing the expected assault. He sent some of his personal troops to take up position above the village of Währing, in the *Türkenschanz*.

In the early morning of 12 September, Lorraine told the gunners to target Nussdorf, but the Ottoman skirmishers who had crept very close in the night opened fire sporadically from behind a small rise of ground, and with more success from behind a sturdy fence further down the slope. The Ottoman muskets outranged the lighter Imperial weapons, and it was easier to shoot accurately uphill than down. Lorraine order the infantry to displace the enemy from their posts, and two infantry battalions overwhelmed the skirmishers and carried on moving slowly forward. The Saxon troops, closer to the Imperialists, formed up and began to descend the slope. In the space of an hour, the left flank of the relief army had begun to move downhill. Far above them on the high point of the Kahlenberg, according to the allied reports after the battle, the engagement began before the planned moment. At 8:00 a.m. Lorraine ordered his dragoons to move quickly down to block any Ottoman attack up from Nussdorf along the Danube side of the battle, with the aim of outflanking the Imperial troops. Two hours after, the advance paused on the lower slopes of the Nussberg hill, and began to take heavy enemy fire. The two sides exchanged volleys. The Ottoman Master of Ceremonies later wrote in his diary for the early morning of 12 September that a huge army of the *gavur* (Christians) was advancing upon the Ottoman line: 'it looked as if a flood of black pitch was pouring downhill, crushing and burning everything that opposed it.' Thus the Imperialists attacked 'in the vain hope of encircling the soldiers of Islam from both sides.'[118]

The impetuous advance followed the course that Kara Mustafa's commanders had anticipated. The Ottomans were outnumbered by the army moving steadily down the hill, and they had cannon and well-chosen positions. Still, the battle did not go as the Ottomans anticipated. After a hard fight and taking casualties, the Christian forces stormed the crown of the Nussberg, and directed their artillery fire down into the village. Observing the fight from a distance, and certain that this was the decisive moment, Kara Mustafa ordered his strategic reserve forward, and he himself moved with all his remaining bodyguard and household troops to the prepared positions on the *Türkenschanz*. No general had given the order to start the battle, but it had begun nonetheless. If it was to be won, then all the commanders needed to keep control of the action on the ground. Once Lorraine had set the army in motion, he rode off at speed to meet Sobieski. The Poles had arrived under cover of darkness, and had assembled in battle order covering

---

118 *Vekayi'-i Beç*, in Kreutel, 'Kara Mustafa vor Wien', p.107.

the ground below the Dreimarkstein and the Rosskopf peaks. Both parts of the relief army were in position. They had, as far as was possible under the conditions, decided on a common plan, which reflected the reality on the ground. Sobieski would command the attack of the right wing, while Lorraine would push his men forward to a decisive encounter against the Ottoman position near Währing and the *Türkenschanz*. In contrast, Kara Mustafa had abandoned any attempt to coordinate his troops in front of the Ottoman camp or the Tartars in their camp to the south-west.

In the early afternoon, the Habsburg advance steadily converged on the newly fortified village of Nussdorf, while the Saxons pushed down the little Muckenthal valley towards the village of Heiligenstadt. The Ottomans immediately counterattacked, with the *kapikulu* elite cavalry engaging in savage close-range fighting all along the line, with the more numerous Ottoman cavalry pressing hard into any gap. However, Imperial and Saxon cuirassiers held back behind the line of infantry then surged forward to join the fight, striking the *sipahis* at a fast trot. Nussberg finally fell to the Imperialists after a house-to-house battle. With both Nussdorf and Heiligenstadt securely in his hands, and the Ottomans concentrated in their posts above the two villages near Döbling, Lorraine called for a halt. The battle cries of both sides had ceased; there was considerable movement atop the Ottoman strongpoint but no cannon fire. The relief army had taken all the villages: Neustift, Sievering, Grinzing and nearly down to the *Türkenschanz*, where the Grand Vizier had his headquarters. But the Ottoman defence line still blocked any closer advance on the city, which might fall at any moment. As the two front lines grew silent, the soldiers of both sides were watching movements on the hills above them to the south-west. A cloud of dust from horses' hooves appeared above the ridge. The Polish host was drawn up in three columns: on the far right was Stanislaw Jablonowski, one of the most renowned soldiers in the host; next came the King himself, with his troops grouped on the slopes of the Gränberg; to Sobieski's left, with his men lined up on the Rosskopf, Nicolas Hieronymus Sieniawski. Behind the horse were lines of Polish infantry, stiffened by the German musketeers and pikemen sent by Lorraine. Sobieski led the army slowly downhill over the rough ground, to be followed by Jablonowski and Sieniawski with their columns, each taking a different route through the ravines and rough ground. The three columns moved slowly downhill, until the whole Polish army was lined up on flat and easy ground for cavalry. The Polish cavalry turned from a dust cloud into lines of horsemen, visible to the Ottomans and Imperial–Saxon–Bavarian forces alike. Ottoman *sipahis* and some infantry made vain attempts to impede their advance, and eventually, by about 4:00 p.m., Sobieski and Sieniawski's columns were drawn up in a long line stretching westwards from the village of Gersthof, past all the hills and foothills that led up to the Wienerwald, in order to secure a solid position from which to launch the charge.

The Ottoman static defence was turning into a serious crisis. The Döbling villages had fallen and Lorraine ordered his army to concentrate on the Türkenschanz from the northern side. At 5:00 p.m. the Poles began to launch a series of cavalry charges into the heart of the vast Ottoman encampment. Here the defenders had concentrated their field guns and the cavalry reserve. They trotted off in the direction of the enemy, their black and gold pennant visible above the dust kicked up by the Ottoman gunfire and the horses' hooves.[119] The Poles prepared to launch their final attack just before 6:00 p.m. Sobieski had at his disposal almost 3,000 hussars, and probably double that number of other horsemen. Before them was a confused mass of Ottoman cavalry and some infantry, demoralised and with no space left in which to manoeuvre. Kara Mustafa had seen and heard the first assaults by the Poles, and he watched as their squadrons in three great columns stopped, and then moved laterally, slowly spreading across the flat ground. The Poles' power and weight were devastating against Ottoman troops in the open field, either cavalry or infantry. They were much less effective against an enemy entrenched behind field fortifications, with field guns in support. The Ottomans' best hope was to tempt the Poles to attack a well-defended position, but despite the camp before Vienna being full of beams, gabions, wooden stakes and the like, none were put to use. This oversight, indolence or mere carelessness, cost the Ottomans dearly. They faced the Polish charges out in the open, lined up before their tents. The final resistance of the Ottoman soldiers lasted less than an hour before they broke out, abandoned the camp, and fled. Some *sipahis* blundered into the flank of Jablonowski's hussars, and attacked them fiercely; but soon they broke off the engagement to resume their flight. Also Kara Mustafa had left his headquarters to join the fight, charging into the flank of Jablonowski, but was finally forced to leave the battlefield escorted by his lifeguard. The campaign of Vienna was turning in the heaviest defeat in the history of the Ottoman Empire. To worsen the already dramatic situation, a sortie from the besieged city also intervened. During the battle, the Ottomans suffered about 9,000 casualties and further 5,000 men were taken prisoner. The *Silithar* Findiklili Mehmed wrote: 'Everything is lost, the catastrophe: irreparable.'[120]

The Long Road to Carlowitz

The traditional strategy to engage only one enemy at once had permitted the Porte to concentrate all their forces on a single war front. Nevertheless, after the disastrous defeat of Vienna, the always-feared threat became concrete, namely the coalition of its enemies.[121] The Holy League alliance, well determined to continue the struggle to drive out Islam from Europe, rejected all requests of the Porte to agree an armistice, forcing it to a long-lasting war fought on

---

119 The Polish historian Vespasian Kochowski was present at the battle for Vienna, and in 1684 published his commentary on the great victory. He described how: 'No sooner does the hussar lower his lance / Than a Turk is impaled upon its spike / Which not only disorders, but terrifies the foe / That blow that cannot be defended against or deflected … Oft transfixing two persons at a time, others flee in eager haste from such a sight / Like flies in a frenzy'. Cited in Wheatcroft, *The Enemy at the Gates*, p.183.

120 *Silihtar Tarihi*, in Kreutel, *Kara Mustafa vor Wien*, p 168.

121 The alliance of the sultan's Christian enemies made the prophecies about the end of the Ottoman monarchy more concrete. A few weeks after the defeat of Vienna, a cross with the letters A.E.I.O.U. was found in Germany, and thus soon interpreted 'Austrian Erunt Imperii Ottomani Victores'. This and other similar prophecies were spread in the Ottoman Empire by Christian propaganda to undermine the morale of the Ottoman soldiers. See also Preto, *Venezia e i Turchi*, pp.537–538.

multiple fronts, namely to a duel with incalculable consequences for the traditional Ottoman strategy. It immediately became clear that the aftermath of the conflict was linked to the confrontation with the Habsburgs on the crucial Hungarian front, and in fact, the Porte concentrated most of its forces on that front, engaging in the only actual field operations of the conflict.

The analysis of post-1683 war campaigns shows the effects caused by the new strategic scenario. The Ottoman war machine showed great difficulty in adapting to the changed situation, and also the complexity of the organisation contributed to amplify the difficulties. The command structure and military organisation grew outmoded, the 'Turkish crescent' battle formation reflecting the cultural and geographical divisions within the Ottoman Empire rather than modern military requirements. The heavy losses suffered at Vienna, the unpreparedness of the commanders and the demoralisation of the soldiers swept away any attempt at resistance, precipitating the army's total confusion. Except for the modest success achieved in the campaign of 1684, when the siege of Buda was thwarted, the field army under the orders of Grand Vizier Ibrahim was forced to concentrate its actions around the main Hungarian fortresses, but now, without the conditions necessary to launch an offensive, ended up in risky situations that were easily exploited by the enemy. The defeat suffered at Esztergom in August 1685, when the field army was even subjected to a surprise attack by the enemy under the city walls, is emblematic in this regard. The impoverishment of the economy, after the great expense sustained in 1682 and 1683, combined with the chaos caused by the climate of emergency, evolved in ever greater delays for gathering troops, making every war plan uncertain. In 1686, Grand Vizier Süleyman waited at Edirne for the arrival of the contingents for the entire month of May, but losing all possibility of avoiding the allied siege of Buda. When finally the Ottoman relief army left the camp in early June, the Imperialists had already begun the siege of the city. Süleyman resolved to attack only in mid August, having waited two more months for the arrival of further troops.[122] The besiegers were able to repulse the Ottoman attempts to relieve Buda, sealing the fate of the prestigious Hungarian stronghold. One year later, the defeat suffered at Harsány on 12 August marked the final collapse of the Ottoman defence in Hungary, involving the logistics structure, and opening the road into the heart of the Balkans to the Imperialists. The network of facilities that had allowed the Ottomans to maintain their threat to Central Europe for over a century ceased to exist. Moreover, in 1687 a disastrous and unpredictable drought reduced crops, which caused turmoil across the Empire. In this darkest scenario, the Ottoman soldiers themselves destroyed roads, magazines and other resources not only in a desperate attempt to hamper the enemy advance, but as a consequence of the army mutiny that occurred in early September.[123] The disappearance of this network would have had repercussions for many years, determining the profound change in Ottoman strategy, and tactics too underwent a drastic reform. The continuous defeats suffered induced the commanders to modify the disposition of the corps in

---

122 Hammer-Purgstall, *Geschichte des Osmanischen Reiches*, vol. XII, p.201.
123 *Ibidem*, p.223. The janissaries removed the Grand Vizier and marched to Constantinople, where they dethroned Sultan Mehmed IV.

49. The looting of Buda's castle occurred on 3 September 1686. The surrender of the capital of Ottoman Hungary was marked by atrocity and unheard of violence. The struggle between Christian and Muslim soldiers shows a reciprocal hate unknown in Western Europe. Imperial–German troops often went into battle fortified with drink, while their opponents used mild narcotics. Ottoman soldiers, as well as Imperial *Serassener* or Venetian Morlachs, were traditionally given a gold coin for each enemy head brought back from the field, encouraging them to mutilate corpses as well as decapitate prisoners, and these actions exasperated both sides. In this regard, it was said that a pair of Ottoman kettledrums, taken by Brunswick–Lüneburg troops after the battle of Szentgotthárd, were found to be covered with human skin. If anything, the level of inhumanity seems to have increased as the wars lengthened, suggesting that the participants experienced the same incremental brutalisation witnessed among soldiers on the Eastern Front in the Second World War. (Heeresgeschichtliches Museum, Vienna)

campaign. The field army marched with vanguard and rearguard no more than three hours away from the main corps. When the situation was favourable, a cavalry corps formed by Tatar and Wallachian and Moldavian cavalry preceded the vanguard remained at a greater distance, as had already occurred at Harsány. The new marching scheme was no longer abandoned, and in 1695 Sultan Mustafa II issued a special *firman* to emphasise its application.[124] If in this way the strength of the army was concentrated to the maximum, however, marches became even slower. The columns advanced slowly and prudently, protected by wagons and surrounded by cavalry, 'appearing to the eyes of the enemies as a mobile fortress.'[125]

The Ottoman commanders tried on two levels, in tactical and strategic conceptions, to balance the superiority of their western enemies. In tactics, they gave defence priority. This innovation was completely in contrast to the attacking traditions of the Ottoman armies and correspondingly aroused in the contemporaries great attention. The defence's inherent superiority was enhanced by technical work, by entrenchments and embankments. With mastery, the Ottomans developed massive defensive positions, so that the Western army commanders were either forced to give up their attacking intentions or were forced to modify their main tactics, based on compactness and discipline, and to outflank the Ottomans with wider-ranging and therefore more dangerous manoeuvres. When the enemy attacked such positions head-on, they always had high losses to complain about. Regarding strategy, the Ottoman commanders did not introduce a new method, but were intent on the conscious exploitation of flexibility and speed, and on the performance of the unexpected, and simultaneously tried to perform high accuracy manoeuvres.[126]

With such countermeasures they often drew enemy army leaders into difficult predicaments, hoping to compel the Christian commanders to commit some error. This aftermath was close to becoming reality in the Hungarian campaign of 1691. In April 1689, when the freshly appointed Grand Vizier Köprülü Mustafa took the command of the army against the Imperialists, the situation was so dramatic that many European courts believed the Porte was near to an unconditional surrender. For the oncoming campaign, command was held by the *serasker*s Ahmat and Rustam Paşa, because the dramatic political climate had forced Köprülü to stay in Constantinople. At the cost of bitter sacrifices, a network of supplies was organised to support the field army gathered in Sofia.[127] After the surrender of Belgrade in 1688, in 1689 the Porte suffered a further defeat at Batocina; in the summer, the important logistic centres of Nissa, Orsova and Viddin had fallen into the enemy hands. Despite these losses, the Porte provided renewed proof of its considerable reserves. Moreover, the war was about to change its course, and the events that occurred confirmed the foresight of the

---

124 K.u.K. Kriegsarchiv, *Feldzüge des Prinzen Eugen*, vol. I, p.534.

125 Marsigli, vol. II, p.88.

126 Periés, *Verproviantierung und Strategie im Befreiungskrieg*, p.279.

127 Funds for the army had been collected by turning to the sultan's treasure, because the government had exhausted any source of income. See Hammer-Purgstall, *Geschichte des Osmanischen Reiches*, vol. XII, p.259.

50. In the Hungarian campaign of 1687, Grand Vizier Sari Süleyman deployed his troops on the battlefield behind embankments and ditches, protected with poles and sacks of sand. At regular intervals, the Ottomans prepared artillery places, alternating them with open spaces to allow the manoeuvre of the cavalry. This deployment was experimented with at Eszék, and proved to be a very hard obstacle for the Imperial army, which avoided the encounter. (Author's illustration)

Ottoman commander. In the winter of 1689–90, the Imperial garrisons in Serbia surrendered and evacuated the fortresses one after the other.[128] From 1690, the year in which the operations were directed by Köprülü Mustafa, the Ottomans achieved important successes by taking advantage of enemy weaknesses. The increase in the distance between the lines of communication, with the consequent enlargement of the war front, combined with the vulnerability of the Imperialists to the guerrilla warfare performed by the Bosnian and Albanians bands, and, overall, the reopening of hostilities between France and the Empire, allowed the Porte to reopen the game. However, another significant source of support was the irreducible tenacity of the Hungarian rebels, especially in Transylvania, where the arrival of Count Imre Thököly could be exploited to reopen the war behind enemy lines.

These opportunities were the only ones that the Porte could avail itself of on strategic grounds against powerful enemies like the Habsburgs. The campaign of 1690 returned to the Ottomans the important strongholds of Nissa, Viddin and Belgrade. In these actions, French military advisers accompanied the Ottoman army on the field.[129] Meanwhile, in Transylvania, Thököly succeeded in isolating and defeating his adversaries, and forcing the Imperial commander, the Margrave Ludwig of Baden, to intervene with the bulk of his forces to restore control in the princedom. The Imperialists could not take the offensive because their strength had decreased after the

---

128 In February 1690, the Margrave of Baden suggested in Vienna that Serbia be abandoned altogether. In his opinion, the Ottomans in addition to their 50,000 men main army could easily set up a smaller army of 15,000 men, which would recapture Orsova together with the fleet on the Danube. Therefore, his suggestion was to move the line of defence back to the line of the Una–Sava–Orsova–Transylvanian Carpathians. See Periés, *Verproviantierung und Strategie im Befreiungskrieg*, p.278.

129 Hammer-Purgstall, *Geschichte des Osmanischen Reiches*. vol. XII, p. 320.

return of 12 infantry and 16 cavalry regiments to Austria, to face the French on the Rhine. Now the Margrave risked being isolated and deprived of supplies on such an overextended front. In July, after leaving some garrisons in Transylvania, Baden headed to Hungary. On 19 August 1691, the valour of the Imperial soldiers and the hasty decision of Köprülü in accepting battle at Slankamen, without waiting for the arrival of the forces returning from Transylvania, delivered to the Margrave of Baden a glorious victory and the nickname of 'Türkenlouis'. The Imperial triumph of Slankamen has obscured many aspects of the campaign and especially those concerning the Ottoman army. The battle has been synthetically described as a heroic proof of resilience of the Imperial army under the Margrave of Baden, and rarely mentions the strategic errors committed by the Ottomans, which undoubtedly favoured the outcome. In mid June 1691, the Ottoman field army had gathered between Sofia, Edirne and Constantinople, but the start of the campaign had to delayed because the enthronement of Sultan Süleyman III. In late July, the Ottomans

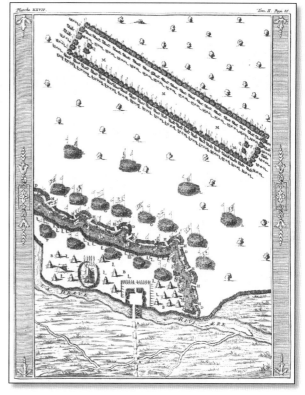

sighted the enemy marching along the Tisza River, when the first Ottoman columns arrived at Belgrade. The Grand Vizier set up camp around the village of Semlin, at the confluence with the Danube and the Sava rivers, and waited for reinforcements behind fortified trenches. Imperial reconnaissance reported that strong and well-constructed defences, with at least 200 cannons on the higher hills, protected the Ottoman encampment. Their right wing lay on the left bank of the Danube while the left one was deployed in the direction of the Sava River. The Imperialists estimated the Ottoman strength as 90–100,000 men, while they had 45,000 soldiers in all. Therefore, the Margrave decided not to launch an assault. On the other side, the Ottoman officers asked to Köprülü Mustafa to attack immediately but he dissuaded them, because he had not learned of the enemy position. The Grand Vizier lacked the vital Tatar cavalry, which was still travelling south to join the field army.

Both armies deployed in each other's view, but despite the numerical advantage, the Ottomans did not attack. By mid August the climate, disease and desertion had reduced both armies to 33,000 and 55,000 able men.[130] Bad news came to the Imperial command on 18 August, relating that the enemy had achieved the destruction of the river supplies in navigation on the Danube. The Margrave of Baden tried to provoke an attack, by withdrawing slowly to a fortified position near Slankamen. When the next day began, however, Ludwig of Baden and his soldiers were dismayed to find

51. The Ottoman army entrenched at Eszék, in July 1687, defending the bridge over the Drava River. Note the *palanka* protecting the bridge. Four Tatar cavalry corps follow the approaching Imperial army, while a further screen of horsemen is deployed behind them. (Marsigli, *Stato Militare dell'Imperio Ottomanno*)

---

130 Periés, *Verproviantierung und Strategie im Befreiungskrieg*, p.280.

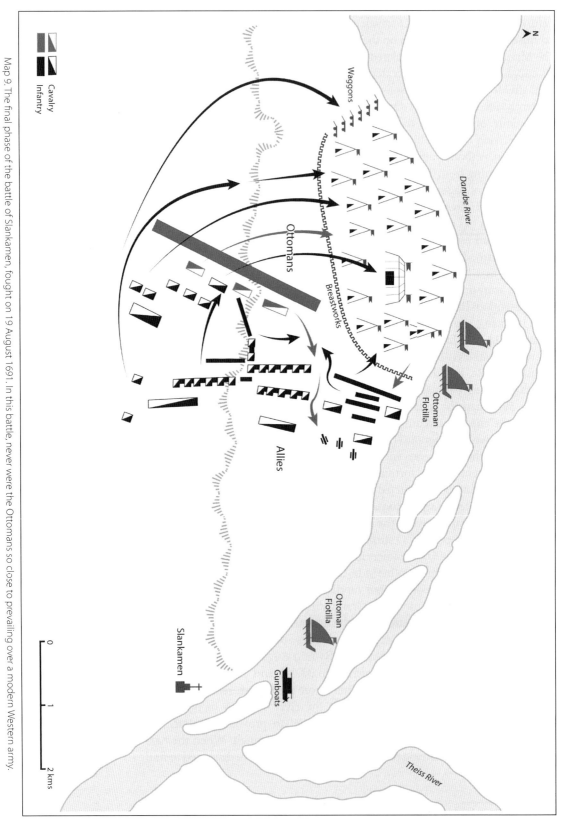

Cavalry

Infantry

Waggons

Danube River

Ottomans

Breastworks

Ottoman Flotilla

Allies

Ottoman Flotilla

Slankamen

Gunboats

Theiss River

0   1   2 kms

Map 9. The final phase of the battle of Slankamen, fought on 19 August 1691. In this battle, never were the Ottomans so close to prevailing over a modern Western army.

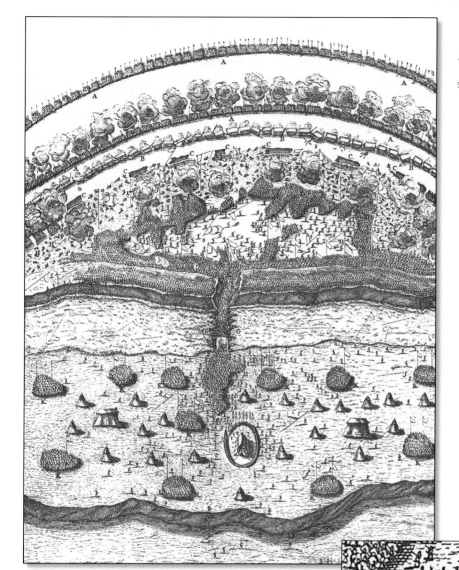

52. The Ottoman army at Zenta, 11 September 1697, after Marsigli. Note below the tent (see magnified section) seven *tugh* ensigns, signalling the presence of the sultan. (Zenta, Marsigli, 1697)

that the Ottomans, who had been standing before them the day before, were now behind them. Köprülü Mustafa had silently bypassed them in the dark, an action that testifies to unprecedented masterful leadership. On that day, the Grand Vizier ordered the cavalry to move against the enemy. Unfortunately, it is difficult to understand the decisions taken by Köprülü Musafa in the absence of primary information.[131] The position held by the Ottoman

---

131 Some historians suggest that lack of foodstuffs could have forced Köprülü Mustafa to decide for a general assault. See C. Greiner: 'Der 'Türkenlouis' – Markgraf Ludwig von Baden-Baden (1655–1707)', in *Militärgeschichtliche Beiträge*. Bd. 3, (1989), p.31.

troops seriously endangered the survival of the opposing army, now short of supplies and unable to receive others. It would have been sufficient to wait for the adversaries' exhaustion and force them to surrender.

The clash between the two forces took place on the west side of the Danube, opposite the outlet of the Tisza River. Initially, Köprülü Mustafa took advantage of his superiority in cavalry strength. The *sipahis* advanced and soon outflanked the Imperial army. During the action they isolated the enemy baggage and burned 800 Imperial supply wagons; a whole Imperial regiment of dragoons was almost destroyed.[132] The battle evolved into a series of disorganised charges; however, the Ottoman cavalry were poorly armed and no match for the infantry squares and field guns of the Imperialists. Louis of Baden, in a desperate situation, broke out of his position, and turned the Ottoman flanks with his heavy cavalry, inflicting fearful carnage. The Ottoman cavalry routed and overwhelmed its own infantry, which remained isolated under the fire of the approaching enemies. After a hard battle, the Imperial army was victorious over the larger Ottoman force. The Ottomans had been very close to victory, which would have changed the course of the war because the destruction of the army would have obligated the Habsburg emperor to call for a truce. Certainly, at Slankamen, the Ottomans lacked Tartar support, and the Imperialists could achieve a great victory because the small but battle-hardened Imperial regiments could respond precisely and effectively to the Margrave's command. But perhaps the most important factor of all was a lucky chance of war: a stray bullet killed Köprülü Mustafa and his troops immediately disintegrated. The death of the Grand Vizier caused such loss of morale that the army dispersed and retreated, abandoning the artillery and even the army war cash, and fleeing back towards the safety of Belgrade.

With the death of their commander in battle, the Ottoman counteroffensive on the Danube ended. Nevertheless, after 10 years of battles not even their enemies were able to gather enough forces for a new assault. When the Imperial attempt to recapture Belgrade failed, the conflict took on the character of a war of position, aggravated by epidemics of typhus and plague that decimated men and animals of both factions.[133]

However, the plan of Köprülü Mustafa, centred on the expansion of the war front and the never-appeased desire of the followers of Thököly, was again undertaken when Sultan Mustafa II assumed direct command of the army.[134] It was the first time in nearly a century that a sultan returned to command his soldiers on a war campaign. Assisted by his most trusted commanders, Mustafa II scored the last Ottoman victories on the Hungarian battlefields: at Lugos on 21 September 1695 and Ollashin on 26 August 1696.

---

132 *Dragoner Regiment Bucquoy*, see A. von Wrede, *Geschichte der K. u. K. Wehrmacht* (Vienna: 1901), vol. III, part two, pp.647–648.

133 In 1694, at Peterwardein, the epizooty left the Imperial cavalry almost completely without horses, and even the Ottoman cavalry began to decrease significantly a few days after the beginning of the campaign.

134 Also in the spring of 1697, a new anti-Habsburg rebellion broke out in Upper Hungary and threatened to spread into Transylvania, forcing the Imperial army to intervene to suppress the unrest, and delaying the start of the campaign. See K.u.K. Kriegsarchiv, *Feldzüge des Prinzen Eugen*, vol. II, p.116.

However, these successes were limited and inconclusive. In both campaigns, the Imperialists could not deploy a strong army, due to their involvement on the Rhine and in Piedmont in the West. Nevertheless, the Ottomans failed to take full advantage of the enemy weakness. As soon as the Habsburg Emperor could field an army of greater size, the modest advantage achieved by the Porte in the two previous campaigns vanished with the disastrous defeat suffered on 11 September 1697 at Zenta.

The loss of the Hungarian *beglerbeglik* together with the *paşalik* of Várad and the control of Transylvania represented the first major loss in the history of the Ottoman Empire. Demoralisation and resignation marked this age with a bitter aftermath for Imperial policy. The war in Hungary has always been regarded as the crucial duel between the Porte and the Holy League, as outlined for centuries by Western historians. As a result, the events that occurred in the Hungarian theatre have overshadowed thoses on the other fronts of the war. In this regard, the campaign against the Poles and Russians has been less investigated, especially on the Ottoman side. After their participation in the Hungarian campaigns of 1683 and 1684 alongside the Imperialists, the Poles turned their attention to the southern border of the *Rzeczpospolita*. The Polish war plans had been worked out in early December 1685 by King Jan III Sobieski. He devised a project of action by the Polish forces in summer 1686, in order to set up camp on the right bank of Dniester River and launch an offensive in the direction of the Danube. Having captured some enemy forts in the area, he would cut off the Ottomans from Kamieniec and Moldavia. The plan also aimed to subdue the princes of Moldavia and Wallachia and routing Tatar forces, but the first goal of Sobieski's army was to lay siege to and seize Kamieniec. Sobieski also expected the Moldavian and Wallachian troops to join his army. The parliament agreed to continue the war and decided to raise an army of about 45,000 soldiers. Polish–Russian negotiations were opened in Moscow with the aim of liquidating the political tension between the two states and reaching an agreement directed against the Porte, Poland not being able to face the Ottomans without her eastern borders properly protected. In spring 1686, Sobieski assembled his army in the south-eastern part of the country.

For the purpose of an operation in Moldavia he allotted about 36,000 men.[135] The army was well equipped and prepared for the incoming military campaign. The Porte could gather on this front just 20–22,000 troops in all, mostly irregulars and militiamen, able to perform only a static defence; while on the part of local tributary princes, not much was to be expected. The only prospects for military aid was that provided by the Crimean *han*, but only after a rich payment.

A further, modest, Ottoman advantage was knowledge of the terrain. In fact, the enemy lacked accurate maps because the territory of the Romanian principalities was almost unknown to European cartographers. On 21 July 1686, the Polish army left the camp and headed to Moldavia whose borders were reached four days later. Without encountering resistance, Sobieski's

---

135 M. Klimecki, 'A Polish Military Expedition to Moldavia in 1686', in *Acta Historica Academiae Scientiarum Hungaricae* 33 (2–4) (1987), pp.385.

troops crossed the Bukovina forests and advanced along the Pruth valley, leaving small garrisons. Some Wallachian boyars joined the Polish army with their own troops. On 14 August the Poles reached Cecora, where the King's great grandfather, *hetman* Stefan Zólkiewski, had died 66 years before. Two days later, Jan III entered the capital of Moldavia, Jassy. He was welcomed by, among others, the pro-Polish-orientated metropolitans, but the Moldavian Prince Constantin Cantemir had declined cooperation and left the town before the Poles arrived. In Jassy, Sobieski established a garrison in charge of restoring the fortifications and building food magazines. Jassy was to become a Polish military base for the wars against the Porte. The first serious encounters with the enemy took place in mid August. The enemy cavalry made forays difficult for the Polish army. They attacked with a stretched-out troop column, defeated isolated groups of soldiers, pressed hard on night encampments, and set the steppe on fire. At the same time, the Tartar and Ottoman horsemen always avoided a pitched battle, at which the Polish king was aiming. Broiling heat and droughts made the situation for the Polish army still worse. Having left Jassy, the Poles moved along the left bank of the Pruth and headed for the territory of the Bucak Tartars, between the Dniester and Danube estuaries. Because of difficult terrain and forage shortages, the Poles had to get to the left bank of the river, and in late August made their way towards Wallachia. Unfortunately, the Ottomans had destroyed all resources in the area, leaving the Poles with a serious shortage of foodstuffs and fodder. This resulted in human diseases and the death of horses. The King summoned the council of war on 2 September and most commanders advocated a return to Jassy. The officers who opposed the continuation of the march into enemy territory summarised his argument: the Ottoman strategy of war, the avoidance of a pitched battle; lack of support by Moldavian and Wallachian princes; insufficient food, water and forage supplies because it was destroyed by the enemy. These arguments forced Sobieski to give orders for retreat. After about two weeks marching and skirmishes with Tatars and Ottomans, the Poles arrived in the capital of Moldavia. The fire that broke out in Jassy on 15 September lasted until the next night and caused damage to a considerable part of the town and its fortifications. It also engendered anti-Polish public feeling. The King abandoned attempts to leave a strong garrison in Jassy, and on 17 September in the afternoon all Polish forces headed back to Poland.[136] Intensified attacks by Ottoman and Tatar cavalry on the withdrawing Polish army restored the King's hope that the enemy want to fight a pitched battle. Nevertheless, the only important fight took place on 2 October at Perehorce. A strong corps of Polish horse routed a 2,000-strong Ottoman–Tartar cavalry force under the *sancakbeg* of Neszty-Szobel (today Nestyuki in Ukraine). The Poles engaged in the last skirmish on 8 October. The Moldavian campaign resulted in a failure. The Polish army lost 20–30 percent of its strength.[137] The campaign appeared to have been a diversionary action to aid the Habsburg emperor's troops that were besieging Buda. Once again, in 1691, Sobieski attempted to capture Moldavia but failed then also. Poland

---

136 They were joined by about 40 boyars and their families, who feared repressive measures from the Ottomans as punishment for their support of Sobieski. *Ibidem*, p.386.
137 *Ibidem*, p.387.

regained Podolia with Kamieniec and the Ukrainian domains lost in 1672, only in 1699, with the truce of Carlowitz.

Passarowitz and Aftermath

The Ottoman ideology of a superior Islamic empire was evidently shattered as a result of 16 years of defeat at the hands of Christians. Unsurprisingly, this was not only a tremendous blow to the Ottoman Empire and its long and rightful claim of being a world empire, but also to the imperial ideology on its own. It was in fact the first occasion that the Porte not only officially accepted the mediation of neutral European states, but also admitted to the heavy defeat of its armies.

In the vast debate about the 'Military Revolution' several scholars have tried to explain in different ways the radical change both in tactics and technology that gradually gave significant advantage to the West over various non-Western powers, the Ottoman Empire included. Some authors appropriately noted that the definition of 'the nature and chronological location of Military Revolution' has become a scholarly obsession in recent years.[138] Other historians had previously tried to give technocentric explanation for the rise of European power, however recent works challenge these theories, focusing on the crucial importance of the economic and social-political factors in these changes.[139] The success of the West against the Ottoman Empire has usually been credited to various factors, such as new tactical discipline, effective military leadership, better-equipped and trained troops and a higher standard of artillery above all, while in recent studies some authors have underlined the significance of the economic domination of Europe in the creation of its political hegemony. It seems to be a consensus that military technological superiority alone cannot be accountable for the Ottoman military decline.[140] Amongst more recent studies there are numerous scholars who less propend to 'an inexorable stagnation and decline' of the Ottoman Empire.[141] In several respects, the term 'decline' itself reflects a judgement passed by Europeans convinced of their superiority than

---

138 See also J. Childs, *Warfare in the Seventeenth Century* (London: Harper Collins, 2006), p.16.

139 John A. Lynn, *Military Revolution Debate*, pp.185–6; C.J. Rogers (ed.), *The Military Revolution in History* (Boulder CO: Westview Press 1995); and J. Black, *A Military Revolution? Military Changes and European Society, 1550–1800* (London: Palgrave Macmillan 1991).

140 In the debate on the 'Military Revolution' it is possible to note that most of the authors failed to examine the Ottoman case. Jeremy Black, for instance, complained that Parker treats quite impressively even the non-European theatre and subsequently he neglects the Austro-Ottoman warfare. See *A Military Revolution?* p.99.

141 See J. Grant, 'Rethinking the Ottoman Decline: Military Technologies diffusion in the Ottoman Empire, 15th to 18th Centuries', in *Journal of World History*, 10 (1999), p.176. According to Grant, the word 'decline' always suggests a kind of comparison and in the case of the Ottomans, this comparison may be measured against either other states. On the following pages Grant makes a good point when he tells us that the comparison of the Ottoman Empire with England, France or the Dutch Republic, for instance, is a dubious proposition since the Ottoman armies operated mainly in Eastern Europe and Eastern Mediterranean and not in Western Europe.

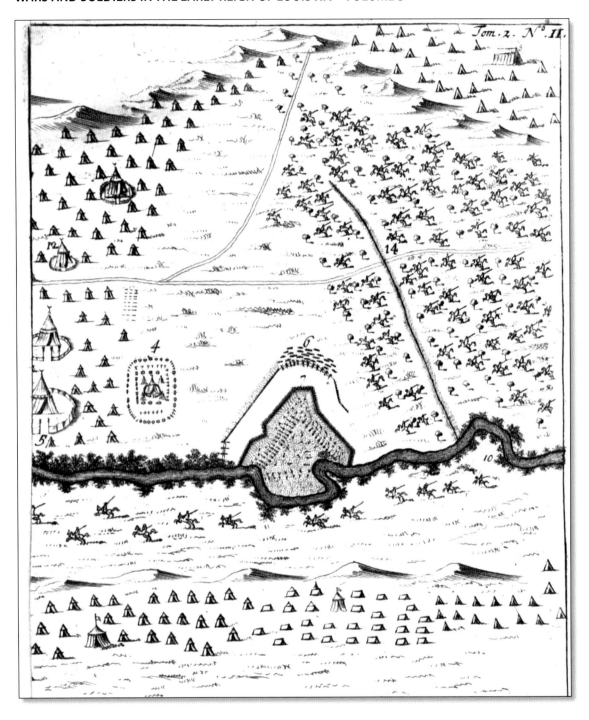

53. Map of the battle on the River Pruth, fought on 24 July 1711, by William Hogarth. The battle resulted in a great success for the Ottomans, who were able to encircle the enemy, taking advantage of their better knowledge of the terrain. Tsar Peter I Romanov was forced to sign a humiliating treaty, which returned Azov to the sultan.

an accurate assessment of Ottoman military capabilities in the seventeenth century.[142]

In the last two conflicts before 1718, the Ottoman conduct of war assumed the characteristics of a prudent strategy aimed at the conquest of limited goals. The field army carefully avoided entering too deep into enemy territory, continuing to maintain a strict contact between the corps. The raids, once so feared in the West, now occurred very rarely, or were conducted only by Tatars, Moldavians and Wallachians on secondary objectives. In these campaigns, the slowness of the marching columns worsened further and with this even the delay for the gathering of the troops. The marching qualities of the Turkish soldier, once considered good, did not hold up even with the speed of march performed in the last years of the War of the Holy League. Already in 1715, the preparations for the campaign in the Peloponnese had continued until late summer, and only because of the Venetian inaction was Grand Vizier Damad Ali able to continue war operations undisturbed.

Dwelling on some episodes that occurred in the last positively ended campaign for the Ottomans, namely that in the Peloponnese in 1715, it is clearly possible see how the overall level of the official corps continued to be inadequate. Certain details regarding the events would seem unlikely if they did not come from a neutral observer, such as the interpreter of the French ambassador, Benjamin Brue, who accurately described the dark climate reigning in the Ottoman camp.[143] Grand Vizier Damad Ali was at his first experience as commander, and in fact the campaign had been planned by the *kapudan paşa* Koca Jamun, while the direction of field operations was assumed by the *beglerbeg* of Rumelia Sari Ahmed, of whom the Grand Vizier had a deep distrust. The janissaries contributed to making the picture even more gloomy, because through their *ağa* they had informed the Grand Vizier that they were not satisfied with the rewards for completing the campaign. At the first major action, the siege of Corinth, Damad Ali did not take part, preferring to leave to Sari Ahmed the honour, and the risk, the direction of the action. During the five days of siege, the janissaries took advantage of every episode to extort money. The head of a Greek spy, beheaded by the Venetians and thrown out of the city, was found by the janissaries and exhibited to the leader as a trophy of their action against the enemy.[144] When the truth emerged, it was impossible to proceed against the culprits for fear of a mutiny. Meanwhile the siege progressed, and on 25 June the Ottomans crossed the Isthmus of Corinth and entered the Peloponnese. The fortress of Acrocorinth, which controlled the passage to the peninsula, finally surrendered alongside Corinth on 1 July. The Grand Vizier granted the Venetian garrison free evacuation, while the citizenry was assured of the safety and security of their property, but once again the janissaries protested

---

142 *Ibidem*, p.180. It is interesting to read that the authoritative Inalcik Halil, who always speaks about Ottoman decline in the late sixteenth century, is rather convinced that this issue cannot be narrowed down only to technological inferiority. See also *An Economic and Social History of the Ottoman Empire*, vol. I; 1300–1600 (Cambridge: Cambridge University Press, 2008), p.22.

143 Brue, *Journal*, pp.23–24.

144 *Ibidem*.

and demanded to loot the city. Taking advantage of the accidental explosion of a gunpowder depot, they attacked the inhabitants, despoiling each of the unfortunates that ended up in their hands. Many soldiers of the garrison were slaughtered and others enslaved.[145] The wrath of the Grand Vizier at the news concerning massacre and plunder was turned against a *paşa*, guilty of having arrived late for the gathering of the troops at Thebes.

Even in the following siege of Nauplia, from 11 to 19 July, the direction of operations took place in a rather chaotic manner and the favourable outcome of the action was due to the initiative of single units and to fate. The city had a good defensive curtain and housed a garrison of 3,000 men. To silence the criticisms circulating inside the janissary corps, the Grand Vizier personally assumed command, and not feeling sure about the force under his command, he sent a *çavuş* to Castel di Morea (today Rion in Greece) to order the return of the 15,000 men who were besieging the fortress. The key to the Venetian defensive system of Nauplia was the fort on Mount Palamida. This stronghold was protected by a large half-moon, from which the defenders dominated a large part of the coast and a considerable sector of the hinterland. The Ottoman approaches progressed quite quickly along the flat terrain in front of the city, but in the direction of the fort of Palamida it was not possible to dig any trench due to the rocky terrain. On this side, Damad Ali sent 8,000 janissaries and *sipahis* on foot, forced to position themselves behind the rocks of a cliff, but exposed to enemy muskets and mortar fire.

On the night between 13 and 14 July the Ottoman artillerymen, with great effort and numerous losses, placed five field guns on the slope in front of Mount Palamida, without however, succeeding in placing them in position due to the uneven ground, and the intense fire coming from the fort. Two days passed with the troops massed on the rocky slope being unable to move from their precarious position, and even unable to receive aid and food. Thirsty and exasperated by the sun of the Greek summer, the janissaries and *sipahis* suddenly jumped to the assault, although they had not received orders. The attackers advanced to the slope and even though they suffered terrible losses, they managed to penetrate into a small redoubt and occupy a part of the covered way. This action cost the Ottomans at least 2,000 dead and wounded, but the janissaries and *sipahis* did not leave the position, although the Venetian artillery continued to target them from the fort. Such a modest result, paid at such a high price, caused much nervousness in the Ottoman command, which was about to leave the siege. However, the events took a favourable course thanks to the arrival of the Ottoman fleet, which began to bomb the city from the sea. The turning point occurred on 19 June, when an inopportune order of the Venetian artillery commander precipitated events. By misinterpreting the order, the artillerymen nailed their cannons on Mount Palamida and the Belvedere redoubt, and finally retreated into the city. With the decrease in the fire of the Venetian batteries the Turks took courage and at the end of the same day penetrated into the bastions. 'Fortune helped the

---

145 Only 180 Venetian soldiers were saved and transported to Corfu; see G. Finlay, *The History of Greece under Ottoman and Venetian Domination* (London, 1856), p.268.

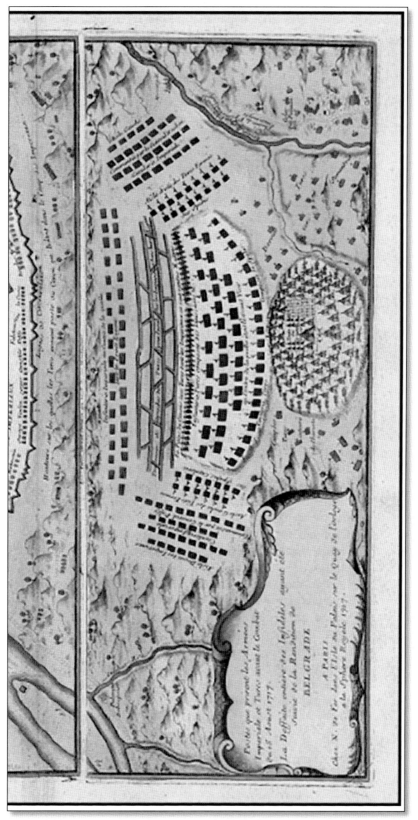

54. The initial deployments at the battle of Belgrade, 16 August 1717. The Imperialists, under the Porte's most feared enemy, Prince Eugene of Savoy, outmanoeuvred the Ottoman relief army after a fierce fight. The defeat led to the surrender of Belgrade the day after.

Ottomans, and since happiness was far exceeding expectations, they went saying that Allah had blinded the Venetians.'[146] The desperate courage of the janissaries and *sipahis* had undoubtedly contributed to saving the situation, but as far as the work of the Ottoman commanders was concerned, '[they] were too busy plotting intrigues against each other to be of any use.'[147]

Great concern accompanied the Ottoman army in the following campaigns. The commander's uncertainty and unresolved problems regarding his leadership seem to be reflected in the slow march towards the Danube. In 1716, Damad Ali left the capital with the *kapikulu* troops in mid April heading for the Hungarian border; after marching for nine days, the army arrived at Edirne and stayed there 12 days before resuming his journey to Belgrade. The Imperial spies transmitted to Prince Eugene of Savoy the phases of approach of the enemy columns: from Edirne to Plovdiv there were seven marches with a stop of 10 days; in Sofia the first unit arrived after six marches followed by another one-week stop. From Sofia to Nissa there were five marches and finally 10 marches before setting up the camp before Belgrade.[148] For completing the approximately 750 kilometres from Constantinople to Belgrade, it took over two months, an average of 11 km per day. The heavy defeat at Peterwardein, where the Grand Vizier was killed, reverberated in the loss of the strategic fortress of Temeşvár after 34 days of siege.

One year later, the march of the army led by the new commander, Grand Vizier Haci Bostançi Halil, remained slow, and came to the relief of Belgrade in early August, almost a month after the siege began. Trying to accelerate, he sent forward all the cavalry, and after three days' march it came in sight of Belgrade on 28 July 1717. The rest of the army camped at Smedarevo, a little less than 50 kilometres from Belgrade, where it waited a few days for the supply ships sailing from Orsova.[149] Once the camp was made in front of the enemy contravallation trenches, the artillery began to target the Imperial position. For more than two weeks, the Tatar and Ottoman cavalry engaged the enemy with continued skirmishing. No concrete attempt at assault was ever attempted. The plan of the Grand Vizier aimed to bleed the enemy between the city and their field, but in the end Prince Eugene of Savoy's decision to engage Damad Ali in battle completely reversed the situation, deciding the campaign, and the whole war.

At the beginning of the eighteenth century, the Ottoman Empire fell from being a great power into a condition of internal crisis and weakness. In the 1600s it was one of the most powerful in the world, surpassed perhaps only by China, but in the eighteenth century it was becoming the 'sick man' of Europe. This scenario was reflected in its population, which, during this period, slipped from being one sixth of that of western Europe to only one tenth, and from about one eighth that of China to one twelfth.

In Europe, the Empire suffered huge territorial losses, beginning with the treaty of Carlowitz on 26 January 1699 and continuing with the treaty of

---

146 Brue, *Journal*, p.32
147 *Ibidem.*
148 K.u.K. Kriegsarchiv, *Feldzüge des Prinzen Eugen*, vol. XVI, p.130.
149 *Ibidem*, vol. XVII, p.94.

Passarowitz on 21 July 1718.[150] At this stage, the Ottomans were confident that their past could provide them with a solution to their dilemma: namely, to strengthen their defences and to reform their army, whether by introducing new equipment or by education and training and replacing the less effective elements.

The best weaponry technology, organisation and training had been the principal reason for the Christian tactical victory. The influx of American silver and the associated price revolution, demographic pressures, rise of Western European military states, and economic hegemony were instrumental in the corruption of the classical Ottoman military system. The standing army, which consisted mainly of janissaries, helped to perpetuate this situation and to entrench the status quo, serving as a formidable obstacle to any change.

The campaigns of war had changed at a tactical as well strategical level, and this compelled the Ottoman commanders to modify their traditional warfare. After 1683, the Imperialists and their allies had successfully raised standing armies able to enter campaigns earlier than half a century before. Increasingly, the Ottoman commanders had to maintain part of the army in winter quarter barracks near the frontiers so as to have ready their forces and reserves against possible out-of-season enemy attacks, or to start the next campaign early; whereas, the Ottoman army was accustomed to return to their home provinces and quarters at the end of the campaign season. This was very important for the *toprakli sipahis* and other provincial units, especially since they had to deal with their estates, collect taxes, and protect their interests. The new strategic scenario created serious tensions within the retained provincial units and created numerous disciplinary problems and occasional disorders in the *kapikulu* troops also. In addition to these worries, winter quartering required strict order and discipline as well as detailed planning previously to arrange provisions and other logistical needs for a period longer than usually expected. Moreover, if the presence of gunpowder mills, cannon casting foundries and strong artisan guilds in main staging

---

150 The Treaty of Carlowitz established a borderline between the Porte and the House of Habsburg for the first time, and for this reason historians consider it as the moment when the Porte finally accepted the European legal principle of the state border. This historiographical idea has been challenged, but it is important to note that the event represents the actual turning point of Ottoman military history. Carlowitz and later Passarowitz represented a radical change in Ottoman diplomacy and consequently in geostrategy. Both treaties contained the promise that the deal would remain valid as long as the Ottoman ruler maintained his power. 'The same thirty-three chapters are found in the capitulations sworn by Mustafa II in 1701 and by Ahmed III in 1706. In 1718 with Passarowitz he returned instead to the plenipotentiary system. The document signed by them is called *temessükat* (receipt confirming an agreement) in a contemporary *name-i hümayun*, while the Venetian secretary Giovanni Francesco Businello calls it a peace treaty and *instrumentum pacis*. It consisted of twenty-six chapters and the sultan ratified it within thirty days. From the truce of arms and the safe conduct used in the Middle Ages as the only means to establish peaceful relations between Muslims and Christians, it was therefore by now the threshold of the treaty in the modern sense. In spite of western requests, which pressed to obtain perpetual peace from the sultan, in Passarowitz they regulated themselves according to the custom that had always been followed in this matter, for which a valid agreement was signed as long as the sultan remained on the throne. Only on 16 November 1720, at the time of renewing the agreements with the Russian Empire, the Ottomans for the first time agreed that there was talk of perpetual peace, that is, valid as long as the Ottoman Empire existed.' M.P. Pedani-Fabris, 'La Dimora della Pace. Considerazioni sulle capitolazioni tra i paesi islamici e l'Europa', in *Quaderni di Studi* n. 2 (Venice: Università Ca' Foscari, 1996), p.38.

55. *Gönüllü* horseman, late seventeenth century. White turban with green *kavuk* hat and black feathers; yellow ochre *hirka* short jacket over a long coat of mail with golden edge; black *kusak* sash; red breeches; natural leather foot dress and gaiters; dark brown cloak with black decorations; white lance with dark red tassels (Author's reconstruction after *Foggie diverse del vestire de' Turchi*, Venice, mid seventeenth century, and Marigli, *Stato Militare dell'Imperio Ottomanno*)

areas provided a large advantage to the Ottoman army, during their winter quartering these personnel increased the problems of supply. Economic shortage and the need to maintain a large army accelerated the crisis, and forced the Porte to a radical transformation of its strategy of war.

Alongside the changing warfare scenario, the Porte experienced further internal crisis and uprisings in the periphery. In this regard, the military history of Egypt under Ottoman rule is symptomatic of the difficulties encountered by the Porte in controlling its domains, and the increasing power achieved by local leadership. The acts of government reveal the principles of the Ottoman policy towards Egypt in general and the army in particular. After the Ottoman conquest, the army of Egypt was organised in seven *ocaks*, corps: two of infantry and five of cavalry. The infantry *ocaks* were the *mustahfizan-i qal'a-i misir* (guardians of the citadel), later known as Cairo's janissaries, and the *azabs*, organised like the European and Asian counterparts. The mounted corps were the *sipahis*, and included two elite units, the *müteferrika* and *çavuş* corps, who naturally were the best paid. The fifth corps was the *cherakise*, the Circassians; then the other two corps were the *gönüllü* and the *tüfenk*, horseman equipped with firearms. Initially, the main task of the *ocaks* was the control of the internal order of the newly acquired province and the securing of the countryside from the marauding Bedouins. The Porte constantly maintained any effort not to lose control of the army, understandably so, because of the local revolts and the general centralised nature of the Ottoman state. No appointments, even of the lowest ranking soldiers, were allowed without confirmation from Constantinople. Initially, discipline was extremely strict and insubordination was punishable by dismissal from service or death. The Porte's thriftiness is also evident when it specified the maximum number of soldier in each *ocak*, and a stern warning is given against enlisting men before a vacancy occurs. As in Constantinople, where a violent rivalry between janissaries and *sipahis* had arisen, also the military history of Egypt was marked by bitter factional struggles. The military class of Egypt was divided into two factions, the *faqariyya* and the *qasimiyya*, whose fierce and often bloody rivalries marked the political history of the seventeenth and early part of the eighteenth centuries.[151]

The Ottoman government attempted to control the two factions by dividing the rural governorships and key administrative positions evenly between them, maintaining in theory a *faqari* pilgrimage commander, and a *qasimi defterdar* as main administrator. In actual fact, particular grand viziers and *beglerbegs* favoured one faction or the other according to their own interests; meanwhile, each faction strove mightily to fill both positions.[152] In the late seventeenth century, the seven *ocaks* (primarily of the local janissaries), become even more demanding and conditioned the governor's action.[153] However, even a weak governor could make his will prevail if he acted with determination. In the recurrent crisis experienced during the military unrest, the governors flew an Imperial banner and ordered all the sultan's loyal servants to assemble under it; those failing to do so were threatened with expulsion from the army. This dramatic manner of addressing the loyalists and isolating the rebels was repeated several times by later governors. However, the reprisals returned peace for a short time. As happened in other parts of the Empire, stability led to economic and financial decline. Hurt by inflation, the soldiers tried to compensate themselves by forcing artisans and tradesmen into partnerships, extorting protection money in the cities and imposing an illegal tax, the *tulba*, on the peasants.[154]

The most important event in seventeenth century Egypt was the emergence of the *beylik* as a major political force. It signified not only an effort by the powerful military chiefs to establish their privileges against a weakened central government and its representative, the Ottoman governor, but also and more importantly, the reassertion of Mamluk traditions and ambitions. One expression of Mamluk political culture was the emergence of factionalism, namely, the continual feuds between the *faqariyya* and the *qasimiyya* factions. The most prominent representative of the beylicate in the seventeenth century was Ridwan Bey al-Faqari, who held the office of *amir al-hajj* for about a quarter of a century, until his death in 1656. Ridwan was a wealthy and powerful emir, who succeeded in thwarting the efforts of his *qasimi* rivals and several governors to remove him from his position as emir. They tried to have him appointed governor-general of the province of Habesh, a promotion that would have been akin to exile. His position was strengthened by his

---

151 'A myth mentioned in the introduction of 'Abd al-Rahman al-Jabarti's history of Ottoman Egypt, explains that the eponyms of these factions were two young Mamluks, whose competition as horsemen before Sultan Selim I developed into bitter strife. In fact, the Qasimiyya and the Faqariyya are not mentioned before the beginning of the seventeenth century, and the appearance of the two factions and their rivalry is related to the advent of the beylicate. Each faction had its bedouin allies: the Faqariyya, the Sa'd; the Qasimiyya, the Haram. Among the ocaks, the Azab were traditionally Qasimis, whereas the majority of the Janissaries were Faqaris.' See Winter, *Egyptian Society under Ottoman Rule*, p.39.
152 Hathaway, *The Politics of Households in Ottoman Egypt*, p.52.
153 Winter, *Egyptian Society under Ottoman Rule*, p.18.
154 J. Hathaway, *A Tale of Two Factions. Myth, Memory, and Identity in Ottoman Egypt and Yemen* (Albany NY: State University of New York Press, 2003), p.6.

alliance with other *beys*. He exercised ascendancy over the Mamluks thanks to his alleged origins.[155] Ridwan's experience shows that Mamluk political consciousness and memories were very much alive in the seventeenth century, more than 100 years after the Ottoman conquest of Egypt.

During the last quarter of the seventeenth and the first quarter of the eighteenth century, the centre of political gravity was held by the janissaries, the largest, richest, and most powerful of the seven *ocaks*. The quarrels between the janissaries and the *azab* corps, the second largest and strongest *ocak*, replaced the rivalries of the Mamluk houses in Egyptian annals. The office of the *bey* was no longer in demand; the governor could not exact as much money from candidates to the beylicate as before. Most significantly, it became accepted practice to promote an *ocak*'s officer to the now powerless *beylicate*. As had been the case among the *beys*, the struggles among and within the military corps had political and economic aspects, since the *ocaks* controlled numerous lucrative tax farms. As the career of Küçük Muhammad, an *odabaşı* of the janissaries shows, a junior officer could for a while become the most influential man in Cairo. He could use his power to force down the price of wheat against the interests of the grain speculators and to abolish the payment of the illegal protection levies, thereby assuming the role of a popular tribune. Muhammad's career from 1676 when he seized control of the Cairo janissaries until his assassination in 1694, reveals some of the complex political conditions in Egypt at the time. Muhammad's enemies attempted to oust him from his decisive position in the janissary headquarters by banishing him to Cyprus or transferring him to other garrisons, but he succeeded in establishing himself as the master of Cairo for two and a half years until his death.

The next crisis also revolved around the janissaries. The key figure was Ifranj Ahmad, another janissary *odabaşı*. A group of eight janissary officers, supported by the *azabs*, attempted to remove him. Initially they were successful, and Ifranj Ahmad was forced to accept the rank of *bey*, but eventually he was able to return to his original position in the *ocak*. The military forces in Egypt split into two hostile camps, but Ifranj Ahmad was just an excuse for the strife. The main reason was the resentment of the other corps, primarily the *azabs*, at the privileged position and the profits the janissaries were enjoying. From March to June 1711, hostilities between the two camps culminated in armed battles. The composition of the camps gives an idea of the political and military complexities. Siding with Ifranj Ahmad were the majority of the janissaries, the *paşa* Muhamad Bey, the *faqari* governor of Upper Egypt who brought with him reinforcements of the Hawwara bedouins, some elements of the other *ocaks*, and most of the Faqari *beys* and their Mamluk households. On the other side were almost all the *azabs* and the other regiments, 600 janissary defectors, the *qasimiyya beys*, and Qaytas Bey, a *faqari* grandee who had quarrelled with Ayyub Bey, the *faqari* leader, and had joined the *qasimiyya*. Fierce battles raged

---

155 A genealogy written for Ridwan Bey connected him with the Mamluk sultans and claimed that he was a descendant of Quraysh, the Prophet's tribe. The assertion of Ridwan Bey's noble descent was a challenge to Ottoman authority. To quote the words of Holt: 'The genealogy implies that Ridwan Bey exercised his functions (as amir al-hajj) not as a delegate of the remote Ottoman sultan, but by a species of hereditary right derived from Mamluk and Qurayshi ancestors'. *Ibidem*, p.21.

in and around Cairo during the fighting, in which the Citadel was bombarded. Iwaz Bey, an important Mamluk *qasimi* leader, was killed, but finally, the *faqaris* were defeated. Two of the *qasimi* leaders, Ayyub Bey and Muhammad Bey, the above-mentioned governor of Upper Egypt, left the country for Constantinople, and Ifranj Ahmad was captured and put to death on 22 June 1711.[156]

The Ottomans took appropriate lessons from their defeats at the hands of their great and respected adversary, Prince Eugene of Savoy. Though the very nature of the Porte did not allow the implementation of the regimental system into the Ottoman army, even the arch-pragmatist Ottoman commanders learned to play to their strong points to tip the scales against the enemy. Increased use was made of border light cavalry forces, to conduct relentless hit and run raids against the enemy supply lines. After all, supply was the Achilles' heel of all the armies. A reformist movement began as early as the mid seventeenth century and it matured into a significant force in Ottoman military affairs in the 1700s. Much of the discussions regarding the direction of reform pitted traditional Ottoman ideas from the classical period against the modern tactical innovations of contemporary Western Europe. Many of the reformers themselves were not exclusively men with military backgrounds, and the time and thrust of reform efforts varied through the years. Reversals of policy took place as well, which both accelerated and retarded overall progress.[157] However, the result was positive, at least in the short term. In the 1730s, personalities such as the Frenchman Claude Alexandre de Bonneval (later Humbaracht Ahmed Paşa)[158] brought significant progress in the artillery field. These advantages matured in the years following the Passarowitz treaty, but contributed significantly to the positive result in the war of 1736–1739 against Russia and the Habsburgs.

---

156 The civil war marked not only the defeat of the janissaries and the *faqariyya*, but more significantly, the eventual decline of the *ocaks* and the ascendancy of the beylicate, which lasted until the French occupation in 1798. After the armed conflict, the leadership of the victorious *qasimiyya* passed to Isma'il Bey, the 16-year-old son of Iwaz Bey, who had been killed. After murdering the emirs who competed with him for supremacy, Isma'il himself was assassinated in 1724. See Winter, *Egypt under Ottoman Rule*, pp.20–22.

157 Uyar-Erickson, *A Military History of the Ottomans*, pp.81–82.

158 Claude Alexandre, Comte de Bonneval (1675–1747), was a French-born military officer, later in the service of the Ottoman Empire, eventually converting to Islam. After escaping from France in 1704 and from Austria in 1725, Bonneval offered his services to the Porte. He was appointed to organise and command the Ottoman artillery, eventually contributing to the Austrian defeat at Nissa and the conquest of Belgrade. As a reward, he received the governorship of Chios, but he soon fell under the suspicion of the grand vizier, and was banished for a time to the shores of the Black Sea. Repairing to Venice, he tried to come back to Constantinople, where he died in March 1747.

6

Dress, Equipment and Designs

The 'Ottoman style' was the result of multiple contacts with other Asian cultures, such as the Chinese, the Mongolians, the Arabians and the Iranians. Other characteristic elements came from the encounter with the European world, which decisively is the influence of the Greek-Byzantines, or that of Hungarians and Italians too. Ultimately: 'at the sultan's court there was a melting pot of different influences and prescriptions which led to the formation of a new style of high quality.'[1] Generally the Ottoman style is divided into three periods, each with a relative style: the first is the original, coinciding with the arrival of the first descendants of Osman in Europe, and ended with the conquest of Constantinople. It is followed by an intermediate period, which lasted until the end of the seventeenth century, and finally one characterised by Western influences, in particular from France, destined to last until the end of the nineteenth century. The intermediate style is also called 'Imperial' or 'Classical' and may be divided into two phases: one of a more aulic character, formed during the reign of Sultan Süleyman the Magnificent (1520–1566), and established through the *kanun-i tesrifat*, a collection of laws intended for court ceremonial, and a second one, begun in the mid seventeenth century, where the first external influences can be identified, as well as the tendency towards extravagance typical of the years of the sultanate of Ahmed III (1703–30).[2]

The quality of Ottoman manufacture reached its peak in this period; the soundness of the fabrics, the softness of the silks imported from every corner of Asia,[3] the beauty of the equestrian weapons and equipment, reflected the love of the Ottomans for splendour and luxury, characterising in an unmistakable way the age of their maximum territorial expansion.

---

1   Z. Zigulski, *Ottoman Art in the Service of the Empire* (New York, London: New York University Press, 1992), p.105.

2   *Ibidem.*

3   The trade with China, India and other parts of Asia had considerably increased already in the early seventeenth century: 'The Ottoman ruling class began to surround itself with precious objects and fabrics, coming from every corner of Asia, to underline its aspiration to the Universal Monarchy', in Mantran, *L'Empire Ottoman*, pp.107–108.

Many descriptions and drawings depicting court life between the seventeenth and eighteenth centuries are preserved in the Topkapı library and in several European collections. Generally these sources deal with the dress of the court and the soldiers of the *kapikulu*, while those concerning the lower classes are not so numerous. The greatest iconographic document depicting Ottoman society as a whole is undoubtedly the *Codex Vindobonensis*, created as a gift for the Emperor Rudolph II of Habsburg at the end of the sixteenth century. The more than 170 colour plates of the work offer a very detailed view of the social life of the Ottomans, whose clothing would have remained almost unchanged throughout the seventeenth century. Copies and imitations of the *Codex Vindobonensis* were made somewhat throughout Europe, sometimes adding new elements and descriptions, and permitting investigations into changes and transformations. The mass of these sources is huge, and possibly the Ottoman army is the best-documented concerning dress and weaponry of this age.

'Ottoman Uniformology'

Every citizen of the Ottoman Empire occupied a place in the hierarchical scale of the state and his social ascent was marked by the clothing he could wear. Already in the last years of the sixteenth century, it was noted that the sultan's subjects respected a very severe *Lex Vestiaria*, and the punishments inflicted to people who did not respect this rule could be very hard.[4] Similar prescriptions were observed in the army, particularly among members of the *kapikulu*, so it was possible to identify the hierarchy of the body from

56. Battle scene with Christian and Ottoman horsemen, attributed to Jacques Courtois, known as 'il Borgognone'. The battles between Christians and Ottomans represented the ideal subject for exalting courage and religious zealotry. Often, the commissioners of the paintings were the same Christian aristocrats who had participated in a campaign in Crete, or in Dalmatia, or perhaps in Hungary. The *kaftan*, a short *hirka*, or just an iron mail coat, are frequently represented as the battle dress of the Ottoman horsemen; the most common colours are red, blue, yellow and the whole range of green. (Fondazione Federico Zeri, Bologna)

---

4   M. Ciccarini, *Il Richiamo Ambivalente*, p.125.

57. Turban with cotton spirals from the war spoils of Kahlenberg, 11 September 1683. Note the white metal *celeng* with a medallion as a sign of bravery (Heeresgeschichtliches Museum, Vienna).

the clothes worn by its members. Though it is not correct to speak of uniformology in the modern meaning, the dress of the *kapikulu* soldiers was subject to rules that prefigure one of the traditional requirements of permanent armies, namely the state's control on clothing and equipment. Therefore, the Ottoman army represents an absolutely original and stylistically characteristic model that could be treated as something very close to a uniformology matter.

There were two fundamental items in Ottoman dress: the turban, called *tülpend* and the *kaftan*, the long single-breasted coat. Both items belonged to the Eastern and Muslim world in general, however certain details allow the identification of the style typical of a region, or of a social class, based on the shapes, colours and accessories used. The turban had been adopted by the Turkic nomads of Central Asia in the ancient age. The turban contributed to the monumentalisation of the human figure.[5] The head, the most important part of the body, increased its volume and could be further adorned with feathers, jewels and other accessories, for which the turban was an excellent place for increasing the aesthetic of the people who wore it. It also represented the ideal item to protect the head from the rays of the sun and also guaranteed in battle a simple and cheap defence. In the Imperial age, three different types of turbans can be identified: a simple cloth drape around the head; a model wrapped around a hat, and finally one made from the overlapping of several layers of fabric. The Ottomans used all three types but the model consisting of the simple drape belonged to some minorities or to the poorer classes. The turbans of the third type were only created to respect court ceremonial. There were three models: the *seilimi*, the *kallavi* and the *mücevveze*. The *tulpend selimi*, so called because it was introduced by Sultan Selim I (1512–20), was cylindrical in shape and could measure up to 70cm in height. This turban was made with fine fabrics, usually with very fine white muslin, or entirely in silk in the most expansive models, and ended at the top with a characteristic convex shape. Usually the *selimi* was decorated with feathers. The *kallavi* turban, equally cylindrical in shape, but smaller than the previous one and slightly flared at the top, still existed for court ceremonial. The *kallavi* resembled a vase and such was the meaning of the Arabic word from which it came. Occasionally, *selimi* and *kallavi* both had a piping of silver fabric on the front. As an exclusive prerogative of the heads of the greatest dignitaries, the *mücevveze* was an actual sculpture of fabric. Shaped like a quadrangular sugar loaf, this turban was made with

---

5   Zigulski, *Ottoman Art*, p.106.

layers of white muslin and decorated with a band of golden silk. The *mücevveze* was the classic turban worn by the grand viziers.

The turbans belonging to the second group were the most widespread and can be considered the ordinary headgear of all the inhabitants of the Ottoman Empire. The hat around which the fabric was wrapped took the name *kavuk* and was almost always made of velvet; the drape could instead be cotton, wool, or muslin or silk. The *kavuk* usually had a cylindrical, crown-shaped or convex shape; the models pointed or truncated cones are less common; the most widespread colours were carmine red, scarlet, green and dark grey.

To make a turban, about 20 metres of fabric were used, wrapped around the *kavuk*, or applied in several layers and shaped as to give it the desired shape: cylindrical, globe-shaped or melon-like. The classical turban with the cloth twisted in more than one spiral, and with one end falling on the back, was common among the janissaries and in the rest of the

58. Turbans with *celeng*, dating 1683 (Heeresgeschichtliches Museum, Vienna)

kapikulu infantry, who normally wore them in active service on campaign. Substantially similar to the previous one, the turban was also worn by the *ulùfely sipahis* both in service and on campaign. A small turban made with spirals of white fabric also belonged to the sailors and to the *kapudan paşa*, the admiral of the Ottoman fleet, which thus underlined his belonging to the navy.

In action the turban was the most-used headgear. Marsigli recalled how on the morning of 12 September 1683, along the slopes of the Kahlenberg, he could see the turbans of the Ottoman soldiers waving: 'like a white tide'[6] under the assaults of the Allies. Thirty-four years later, at the battle of Belgrade, another eyewitness reported how all the cavalry that arrived with the relief army wore turbans, including officers.[7] In the infantry, in particular among the janissaries, it was usual to decorate the headgear with thin metallic strips fixed to a medallion, the *çeleng*, a special distinctive conferred on the soldiers as a sign of bravery. There are still at least three original turbans dating to the last quarter of the seventeenth century today preserved at Vienna in the Heeresgeschichtliches Museum, bearing the metal *çeleng*. They belonged to soldiers who participated at the siege of 1683. The *çeleng*s are in brass or tin with inserts of turquoise and coral, typical decorations of the Imperial style.

The turbans also served to identify officers from the the troops even in ordinary clothing. Normally the *çorbaci* of the janissaries and other officers of

---

6   Marsigli, vol. II, p.121.
7   La Colonie, *Memoirs* vol. III, p.180: 'many of them [the officers] had clothing and turbans cleaner than the ones worn by the soldiers.'

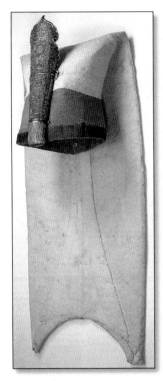

59. Janissary *ak börk*, preserved in the Badisches Landesmuseum of Karlsruhe, dating presumably to the 1680s, war spoil of the battle of Slankamen, 1691. The golden lanyard around the lower edge has been lost, but this is the only seventeenth-century *ak börk* still preserved. However, some scholars assume that this headgear belonged to Polish janissaries. (Badisches Landesmuseum)

the *kapikulu* infantry wore a large turban with the characteristic flared shape, which hid the *kavuk* around which it was wrapped. The turbans intended for high-ranking officers were subject to a series of rules to distinguish the rank of their owner. The classic *paşali kavuk* was the most common turban and made its appearance in the mid seventeenth century. This headgear spread rapidly across the Empire. Its dimensions ranged between 35 and 50cm in height. The *paşali kavuk* had a characteristic cylindrical shape and a slight flaring at the top; almost always the drape hung over the inner *kavuk*. On the top, the classic grey heron plumes were inserted, and their number established the rank of the officer. The plummet took the name *balikcil* and was fixed to the turban with a precious metal setting, *sorguç*, which gave its name to the whole plummet. The *sancakbegs* adorned their headdress with a single *sorguç*, while *paşas* and *beglerbegs* could have two, and the sultan up to three. A special distinction was granted to the first 12 Egyptian *sancakbegs*, privileged with the permission to carry two plummets; the same privilege belonged to the *yedekçi* corps of the *kapikulu* cavalry.[8]

The classic pumpkin-shaped turban was the *tulpend örf*, which compared to the other models was considered the most outdated, however it continued to be worn throughout the seventeenth century, particularly in religious circles. Imams and *Mullahs* had their turbans wrapped with dark green cloth, a prerogative reserved also to the caliphs descending from the Prophet Mohammed.

Brightly coloured turbans were worn by *mehter* members,[9] especially on solemn occasions. On campaign they followed the fashion adopted by the other corps of the Ottoman army. Even the Egyptian Mamluk favoured coloured turbans, almost always in red or black fabric. There were particularly complex local patterns, similar to those that can be seen in the paintings of exotic atmosphere by Charles Vernet, or those by Jean Luis David, depicting some episodes of the Napoleonic campaign in Egypt. We also find the taste for colourful turbans in the Kurdish tribes of eastern Anatolia and northern Iraq, where the influence of the peoples of the Caucasus and Iran was more marked.

The typical janissary headdress, 'the blessing sleeve of Allah', belonged to court ceremonial and was therefore used only on special occasions. The *ak börk*, such as its name, consisted of a cylinder-stitched fabric with a floating end. The part that slipped into the head was joined to a circular felt band and adorned by a golden cord with a wave pattern. On the front there was a cylindrical metal case decorated with corals, turquoises and other stones, inside which the *pilav* spoon was maintained. The original meaning of this tool came from the symbolism of the corps, and in fact the upper part of the case had the shape of a stylised spoon, useful only to show the skill of the craftsman who had made it. Judging by the iconography depicting the janissaries in parade, it would seem that each soldier competed in decorating his own *ak börk* with any sort of feather or artefact. The elaborate compositions of feathers exalted the sensuality and charm of whoever

---

8   Marsigli, vol. I, p.126.
9   Masala, *Il Mehter*, p.30.

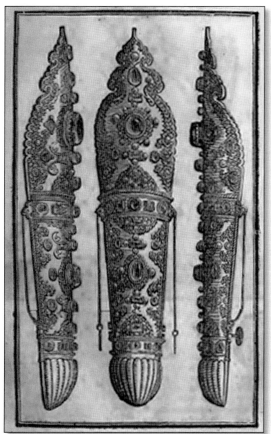

60. Janissary spoon cases, late seventeenth century. The original items, in gilded metal, are preserved in the City Museum of Vienna and date to 1683. The drawing with detail belongs to the *Thesaurus Exoticorum*, published in 1688 in Hamburg.

wore them,[10] even importing feathers from distant countries to satisfy the desire to show themselves in all possible splendour.[11] A beautiful description of the spectacle offered a procession of janissaries during a court ceremony, comparing the weaving of the feathers to a field of multicoloured tulips.[12]

The most elaborated headdress accessories imitated the plumage of peacocks, but apart from this symbolic context, the feather, with its swaying, was reminiscent of a banner in the wind and served to stimulate the erotic imagination.[13]

Even the janissary non-commissioned officers and junior officers wore headdress similar to those of the common soldiers; the greater or lesser richness and elaboration of the spoon case and other items marked rank and authority in the corps. In general the *odabasis* decorated their headgears with *çeleng* or with elaborated and large plumage; the *çorbaci*, on the other hand, wore on parade a white cloth cap, ending with a heron-shaped head-piece, adorned with a large white feather; around the base a circular band of

10 Zigulski, *Ottoman Art*, p.113.
11 *Ibidem.*
12 Lady Mary Montague, 'Turkish Letters, 1717–18', in *I Turchi*, edited by F. Unterkicher and A. Arbasino (Parma: Franco Maria Ricci, 1971), p.122.
13 Zigulski, *Ottoman Art*, p.113.

61. Janissary *çorbaci kalafat* headdress, with metal *celeng* imitating feathers, early eighteenth century. Note the unusual presence of the spoon case on the front (Hermitage Museum, Saint Petersburg).

felt was decorated with a golden cord like the one used for the janissary's ak börk. This headdress was known as *kalafat*. The headdress was the peculiar item of all the other members of the *kapikulu* infantry. The *acemi-oglanis* wore indifferently in parade or in active service the *külah*, a felt hat painted in white with a characteristic conical shape.

The *cebeci* are often depicted with metal helmets with the case for the spoon like the janissaries. The *topçus* wore instead a cloth cap, normally black or very dark green, and garnished with a golden or scarlet cord around the base; one or two rooster feathers fixed on the right side completed the headdress. This hat is indicated in several ways: a Bosnian hat or *bareta* representing one of the rare cases in which the forehead remained obscured by the brim. Both brims, front and rear, had a pointed pattern and fell limp; if viewed from above the hat had the shape of an 'X'. On campaign, the *topçus* replaced the *bareta*, and like the *cebecis*, wore the turban like the janissaries, or a simple cap of cloth, the *tekke*, practically a sort of fatigue cap. However, the *bareta* was very popular among the Balkan populations who wore it instead of the turban. Very often the *serhaddkulu* infantry and cavalry from Bosnia used *baretas* of various colours, with twisting brims.

A slouch hat with a flap at the base was typical of the Albanian soldiers. The most common colour was scarlet or carmine red; its shape resembled the Phrygian cap. In the *azab* infantry and in the *serhaddkulu* troops, as well as among the *toprakli*, the headgear typical of the regions of origin were worn as an alternative to the turban. Montecuccoli and Marsigli describe the border militia of the Hungarian war theatre who dressed in Hungarian style, with headdresses similar to those of the Imperial *hayduks*.[14]

Cylinder-shaped hats of velvet or felt were quite common throughout the Ottoman Empire. Dimensions and accessories varied, but the most frequent colour was carmine red or scarlet; sometimes a tassel on a black cord, fastened to the top, fell to the shoulders. These were the precursor caps of the *fez*, the typical headgear of the nineteenth-century Ottoman Empire. Some models were produced in North Africa and were already worn throughout the Maghreb at the beginning of the eighteenth century.[15] In the Asian regions of the Empire, local typical headgears represented an alternative to turbans, such as the cap with a felt or fur brim, typical of Eastern Anatolia, Armenia and Kurdistan, and very widespread throughout the Caucasus and Central Asia; the most expansive models were made with the precious *kedifé* velvet.

Adopted among the Turkish populations already at the end of the fourteenth century, the *zamt* continued to be popular among the lower classes. This headdress was a wool cap painted in red and combed in imitation of human hair. Among the Ottomans the *zamt* is almost always worn by valets, esquires and servants in general.

---

14 Montecuccoli, 'Aforismi', in Luraghi, *Opere di Raimondo Montecuccoli*, vol. II, p.478, and Marsigli, vol. I, p.84.

15 R. Mantran, 'Le Statut de l'Algerie, de la Tunisie et de la Tripolitaine dans l'Empire Ottoman', in *Atti del I Congresso Internazionale di Studi Nordafricani* (Cagliari,1965), p.212.

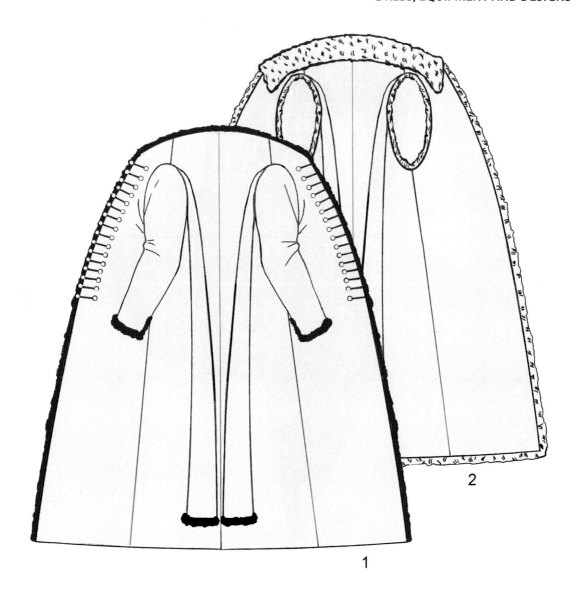

1

2

62. Court *kaftans*.

1: *erkan-i kürkü kaftan*;

2: *üst kürkü kaftan*. Alongside the *divoan-kurku kaftan*, represented on page 25, these were the classic clothing of the Ottoman dignitaries. (Author's illustration)

Finally, it must be remembered that, as an example of courage and contempt for pain, many soldiers went into combat with their heads uncovered, with feathers or arrowheads strung on the scalp. It was a widespread practice among the *serdengeçdi*, the volunteers for the most risky missions, or among the most fanatical dervishes, or even the *delys* of the border cavalry, who adopted the most impressive hairstyles to encourage and spread the spirit of emulation among the troops.

The ceremonial laws of court established by Süleyman the Magnificent prescribed precise regulations also on the fabrics, cut, shape, colours and ornaments of court dress. These codified rules also prescribed the dress of the princes and the highest officers, including all the *divoan*'s members with their subordinates. From the mid sixteenth century, in their essential lines, style and pattern of the court dress remained unchanged for almost two centuries.

63. *Kapikulu* infantry *dolama kaftan* for parade dress, late seventeenth century. (Author's illustration)

As a part of the sultan's apparatus, the regulations comprised the military dress. The typical symbol of the oriental world, the *kaftan*, was the ordinary coat of all the inhabitants of the Ottoman Empire. *Kaftans* manufactured for the upper classes were made with brocade, *kedifè*, or with fabrics mixed with silk, and in length almost reached the ankle. These large *kaftans* usually had only a single breast and no collar flap, and were usually lined with fur. For this purpose, sable skins were the most sought after due to their resistance, the amount of hair and range of colours, ranging from dark brown, almost black, to the white of albino specimens; alternatives to the sable were the fur of squirrel or fox. Fur was the distinctive mark of important personalities and was a welcome gift even for the sultans. In the seventeenth century it was customary to present a *kapaniça*, a large coat copiously lined with fur, to the grand viziers or to the princes of blood. Moreover, commanders about to leave for a war campaign received a special fur coat, called *veda-kürkü*, the cloak of the goodbye, as a symbol of good luck.[16]

The high-ranking *kaftan* was usually provided with false sleeves, almost as long as the *kaftan* itself, in imitation of the Byzantine *dalmatica*; sometimes the cuffs showed the inner lining. The shape of the sleeves could be more or less elaborate, in some cases the sleeves were double. The buttons were made of wood covered with silk or brocade, or directly with precious stones and even gold. Beside the *kapaniça*, there were three other *kaftan* specifically designated for higher officials: the *divoan kürkü*, lined with fur, made of wool and with double sleeves; the *ust kürkü*, made of brocade, with false sleeves and a wide collar, and finally the *erkan-i kürkü*, always made in brocade, but lined with white sable fur. The most common colours of the fabrics were carmine red, crimson, turquoise and gold brocade; embroidery and decorations of golden, silver, or combinations of both, were applied to attain the usual pomp.

The seventeenth-century sultans, as well as their major dignitaries, favoured sumptuous *kaftans* of red *kedifè* velvet, embroidered with elaborate floral compositions codified by the *saz* style, which remained dominant until the early eighteenth century. All sources confirm the tendency of the Ottoman upper classes to adopt the classic Imperial colours, red and golden yellow, inherited from the Byzantines after the conquest of Constantinople. The general rules on colours and fabrics could grant some licences to personal taste, to environmental factors or climatic ones. An Ottoman miniature from a collection of the second half of the seventeenth century and today preserved in the Correr Civic Museum in Venice, shows the participants in a *divoan* who probably met under Grand Vizier Köprülü Mehmed.[17] Similar images are very common and can be found in many libraries throughout the world, but this is particularly significant because it belongs to the period immediately before the religious prohibitions on figurative art, and the dress of the

64. The *yeniceri ağasi* is patrolling the street of Constantinople with an escort of *acemi oglanis* to arrest janissaries out of their barracks without permission. The *ağasi* carries a broom to touch the guilty soldiers, while his assistant carries the *kalka*, a two-pole weapon to bind the ankles and to beat the soles of the convicted janissary's feet.

Yeniceri ağasi: white *kallavi* turban; azure-turquoise *üst kürkü kaftan*, silver buttons and black buttonholes; pale blue *entari* waistcoat with white *kusak* sash; red *salvar* breeches; yellow leather *basmak* boots.

Acemi oglani: yellow ochre headgear; azure-turquoise *dolama kaftan*, natural wood buttons and black buttonholes; pale blue breeches and *kusak* sash; white grey stockings (or gaiters); black *mest* shoes. (Author's graphic after *Foggie diverse del vestire de' Turchi*, Marciana National Libray, Venice, mid seventeenth century)

---

16 Zigulski, *Ottoman Art*, p.125.
17 Correr Civic Museum, Venice, 'Memorie Turche', Inventory n. ms. Cicogna 1971.

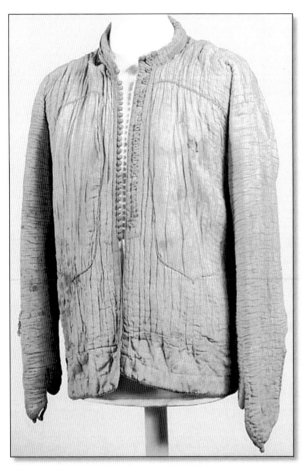

65. Marsigli and Montecuccoli related that Ottoman infantry went in battle with short coats or quilted jackets. Possibly these latter derived from the typical Ottoman *kazaghand*, a jacket with a cloth outer layer, a layer of padding, with mail shirt hidden inside. There are only two known examples, both manufactured in the 16th century. Note the end of the sleeves are peaked to cover the back of the hand. (Royal Armouries, London)

personages date back to the years here examined. In this scene, the Anatolian and Rumelian *beglerbeg* are represented wearing a turban of the *örf* model, and a large red *kaftan* with *saz*-style embroidery. The Grand Vizier, instead, wears a turban and a *kapaniça* of gold brocade, on a scarlet waistcoat with silver embroidery. The other dignitaries wear *kaftans* of scarlet, carmine, turquoise or golden brocade; those of the vizier, the *beglerbegs*, the treasurer and the master of ceremonies are lined with fur. All the *kaftans* have false sleeves that allow a glimpse of those of the waistcoat. The long one-breasted waistcoat, the *entari*, was worn under the *kaftan* and was of lighter fabric, variously decorated with embroidery, piping and trimmings. The waist was encircled by a sash, the *kusak*, of silk or other fabrics, usually very decorative. Sometimes the sash was replaced or accompanied by a metal belt, the *kemer*, invariably studded with turquoises. Under the *kaftan* and the *entari*, the shirt, *gömlek* and the breeches, *salvar*, were completely invisible. The shoes worn by the leading class were boots, *basmak*, shoes, *mest*, and also sandals, *cedik* or *cizme*, this latter usually worn also by the lower classes. The boots did not entirely cover the leg and reached at maximum the mid leg, then, towards the end of the seventeenth century, Hungarian-style boots became more common, especially in the cavalry. The sacredness of the *mehter* was reflected by their dress, which was strictly codified. All the musicians wore *kaftans* without double sleeves of green, turquoise or black cloth, with red leather shoes.[18] The officers were distinguished by certain more refined details, such as a brocade sash at the waist or a turban of fine white muslin.

Many descriptions of the Ottoman court ceremonial have come down to us thanks to the memories of travellers or Western residents in the Empire. The most interesting testimonies on the appearance of the *kapikulu* soldiers belong to the famous Italian travellers Pietro Della Valle and Giovanni Francesco Gemelli-Carreri, the Swedish diplomat Claes Rålamb, the French diplomat Jean Baptiste Tavenier, the geographer Aubry de la Mottraye and the aforementioned Imperial resident Count Fleischmann;[19] but once again one of the most accurate descriptions was recorded thanks to Count Luigi

---

18 Masala, *Il Mehter*, pp.30–31.
19 P. Della Valle, *Viaggio in Levante*, 1640–50; G. Francesco Gemelli-Careri, *Il giro del Mondo* (1703) ; Antonio Benetti, *Osservazioni fatte dal fu dottor A.B...* (1690); Jean Baptiste Tavernier, *Nouvelle relations du l'interieur du serrail du Grand Seigneur* (1675); Antoine La Mottraye, *Voyages en Europe, Asie et Afrique* (1726).

66. Late seventeenth century *mest* shoes in natural yellow leather, preserved in the Badisches Landesmuseum, Karlsruhe.

Ferdinando Marsigli.[20] In the years in which he was in Constantinople he took note of the costumes worn by the members of the janissaries' *divoan* in the parades held on the occasion of some festivities, such as the solstice of spring, the circumcision of a prince, or the departure of the sultan for the annual hunt.

Marsigli describes the procession of the permanent army's soldiers opened by the *yeniceri ağasi*. He wore a *kaftan* of red velvet embroidered in gold and lined with sable; on his head he wore a *Paşali kavuk* decorated with two *sorguçs*. The senior officer proceeded on horseback, while an esquire walked beside him ready to support his stirrup. The horse had a saddle cover in gold brocade; all the harnesses and the reins were covered in silver, stirrups and saddle included. Another assistant led four horses with the same equipment. Behind him came the *yenikgibasi*, the chief of the *ağasi's*

67. Late 17th century *basmak* boots in natural yellow leather, preserved in the Badisches Landesmuseum, Karlsruhe.

esquires, dressed entirely in red, with the janissary *ak-börk* headgear, and with the waist wrapped by a *kusak* of gold brocade. The *segmenbasi* wore turban and a velvet *kaftan* devoid of decoration. There was similar dress for the *Istanbul-agasy*, *kethüda beg*, *kethüda yeri*, and *muhzir ağa*, but all with the *çorbaci* headdress, adorned with a large *sorguç* with white feathers; all wore yellow leather boots and their *kaftans* were turquoise or red. The headdress of the *muhzir ağa* had a band of golden brocade. The *fodla kàtibi* dressed similarly but with the heron feather less showy than that of the previous officers. The *bas çavuş* proceeded wearing a *kaftan* of simple damask and his turban had only one *sorguç*; the other two *çavuş* wore red

---

20 Marsigli, vol. I, p.76.

kaftans, with a golden brocade sash; they also wore the *kalafat* caps. The Imam dressed like the Sunni religious clerics, namely in dark green *kaftan* and the *örf* turban; similar to him but with other colours followed the *yeniceri efendi*.

The other senior officers, the *çorbaci* and the commanders of the janissariey *ortas*, wore turquoise or red *kaftans*, with long false sleeves that left uncovered the waistcoat's sleeves, and were tied to the waist with colourful sashes. Marsigli specifies that the veteran *çorbaci* of the *hasseki*, *deveci* and *solak*, were dressed similar to the *kethüda beg*;[21] while the commander of *orta* 54, the *talimhaneciler*, always wore the turban with the insignia of *paşa* and on parade he carried a bow and quiver with arrows. A further accurate description is that provided by the Venetian *balivo* Antonio Benetti, who took notes about the parade that occurred in Constantinople on 6 October 1682, for the farewell to the army marching against the Habsburgs. He provides a very interesting picture, detailing the items in order to identify the different ranks of soldiers amd officers, such as weapons, headgear and shoes.[22]

The footwear was another sign of the distinction of the *çorbaci*. The *yayabeg* officers wore boots of yellow leather, because on parade and during active service they moved on horseback. The other commanders of the *segmen* and *bölukler* categories proceeded on foot, so their shoes were simple red leather shoes. This rule excluded the *muhzir ağa* and the *kethüda yeri*, who, despite being commanders of *segmen* and *bölukler*, held the privilege of being mounted on horseback. The janissary *odabasis* wore *kaftans* mostly turquoise or red, devoid of false sleeves, and with abundant layers that ended at the bottom with a characteristic pointed shape. This *kaftan* took the name *dolama* and was easily recognisable by the long front flaps and sometimes also by the back ones; to allow the soldier to walk, he fixed the flaps at waist height under the sash. The lining was almost always of the same colour as the outer fabric and in some cases a couple of Hungarian-style cuffs completed the *dolama kaftan*. The collar ended with a pointed flap, usually of different colour, but *dolama kaftans* were common also without the collar flap.

The differences between the *odabasi* and common janissaries were then very small. The most common colour of the *kaftans* were turquoise, but carmine red and green were also common. The sultan provided for the dressing of his soldiers, who received the cloth for manufacturing their dress every year and this could be the cause of the large variations, because there were no precise prescriptions regarding the colour of the fabrics to be used. According to Marsigli, the soldier himself could buy the fabric to make the kaftan, and then deliver it to the *terzilar* guild, the tailors, who manufactured the items following the rules codified by the original regulation.[23] Therefore, within each *orta* it was possible to see *dolama kaftans* of different colours, but the pattern and the accessories remained very similar to each other. The

---

21 *Ibidem.*

22 A.Benetti, *Osservazioni fatte dal fu A.B. nel viaggio a Costantinopoli dell'Illustrissimo et Eccellentissimo Signor Gio. Battista Donado, spedito Bailo alla Porta Ottomana, dall'anno 1680* (Venice, 1690), pp.21–25.

23 Marsigli, vol. II, p.4.

sash helped to establish the rank of the soldiers, generally a sash of a single colour was retained for the common soldiers; combinations of two or more colours, and more and more elaborate and rich fabrics appeared proceeding up the hierarchical scale.

Even *cebeci*, *acemi-oglani* and *topçu* soldiers, including their non-commissioned officers wore *dolama kaftans* similar to those issued to the janissaries. Among the *cebecis*, however, the most diffused colours were dark green, light green, red-scarlet and grey-blue. Their *kaftans* had also a different coloured lining, which shown the lining when the flaps were folded. Acemi-oglani wore *dolama kaftans* like the janissaries mostly of turquoise, as well as the *topçu*, who had it mostly of green. When the janissaries and the other *kapikulu* soldiers circulated in Constantinople, or in the cities where their garrison was located, permission being granted as long as they were not armed, they wore a large overcoat with lapels on the breast. The most popular colours were turquoise, red and green in various nuances, but also dark brown and butternut were common. It seems that the lapel served to highlight the elaborate decorative patterns of the inner linings. Under the overcoat, the soldier wore the *entari* waistcoat with or without a flap collar over a wide skirt; a leather belt or a sash completed the 'city dress'. This was certainly the winter version, and indeed other testimonies and images show the janissaries circulating in the city dressed with lighter items, consisting of a short jacket, breeches and turban.[24]

68. Janissary in field dress, early eighteenth century. (Illustration from the *Neu-eröffnete Welt-Galleria*, drawings by Caspar Luyken; engraved and published by Christoph Weigel, Nuremberg, 1703)

The janissaries who did not come from the *acemi-oglanis* also received a dress from the government. Jean Guer, a tireless compiler of books on the uses and customs of ancient and modern peoples, wrote that these recruits wore a brown *kaftan*, 'Thessalonica green' (turquoise), collar, trousers and other 'vestments' of various colours. As headgear they wore a simple red cap, the *tekke*.[25]

The breeches usually worn by all Ottoman soldiers had a wide shape on the legs, which narrowed downwards, where strings held them to the ankles. From the beginning of the seventeenth century, linen strips began to be used to wrap the leg up to the knee. The final appearance was similar to the gaiters of the First World War. These stripes were used above all on campaign, in order to preserve the breeches from mud and dust. The breeches varied

---

24 Towards the end of the seventeenth century, short padded fur jackets became fashionable. The French traveller La Mottraye noted the janissaries of Constantinople dressed in a very informal way, spending their time smoking large wooden pipes and serving the girls of popular neighbourhoods. See *Voyages*, vol. I, p.240.

25 Guer, *Moeurs et Usages*, vol. II, p.205.

69. Portrait of Jerzy Franciszek Kulczycki, the volunteer who crossed the Ottoman lines during the siege of Vienna to deliver a message from the besieged garrison to Duke Charles V of Lorraine. His disguise, in imitation of the Ottoman battle dress, proved effective and allowed him to repeat the mission by crossing the enemy lines to return into Vienna. (Author's archive)

much more in the range of colours compared to the *kaftan*, but usually they were of the same colour as the cuffs, collar, or waistcoat. The shoes were manufactured of leather or fabric with a reinforced sole. The colours were yellow, the prerogative of the *yayabeg* category, or red, reserved to *segmen* and *bölük*. *Cebeci* and *topçu* had yellow shoes.

Even the *ulùfely sipahis* were easily recognisable by their yellow leather shoes.On parade they wore a rich and elaborate dress, including armour and chainmail; their horses had saddle blankets and accessories always of exquisite workmanship. The most common colours of the cavalry *kaftans* were turquoise, red, azure and dark green; occasionally collar and cuffs showed the colour of the lining. Austere and marked by simplicity, the clothing of the *sakka* contrasted not a little in the midst of the lavish costumes of the *kapikulu* soldiers. They wore a simple turban of rough canvas, and the typical leather waterproof coat.[26] As members of the *kapikulu*, the older *sakkas* were allowed to let their beards grow.

The rules of Ottoman society prescribed rather precise norms also on hair, moustache and beard. Every *kapikulu* soldier had to shave his head and sometimes let a tuft of hair grow on the top of his skull. The moustache, of all shapes and sizes, was flaunted by every soldier as well as adult male; the beard was instead reserved for the ruling free classes, but exceptions were frequent. The officers of the janissaries, the *kapikulu* horsemen, as well as *timars*, *zeamets*, prince governors and naturally all the members of the court and government, wore a beard – the virile symbol par excellence – outlining the sign of their status.[27] Another symbol of high social status was the archer ring, the *zihgir*, worn on the thumb of the right hand and a traditional accessory of the warriors. It was made in horn, ivory, jade or gold, more or less embellished with jewels and other precious materials.

During military campaigns, the soldiers dressed freely and in a more practical way. Only the major officers wore *kaftans* related to their status, when they too did not opt for another dress. Soldiers and officers of the infantry and artillery wore a short single-breasted jacket, the *hirka*, or quilted short coats,[28] or just the shirt, worn under a sleeveless *yelek*: the Eastern forerunner of the vest. Undoubtedly, it must have been difficult to distinguish one unit from another in action and this may have been one of the reasons why the number of regular and irregular soldiers could be easily confused in

26 Marsigli, vol. II, p.30.
27 Guer, *Moeurs et Usages*, vol. II, p.195.
28 Montecuccoli, in Luraghi, *Opere di Raimondo Montecuccoli*, vol. II, p.475.

the Western sources. Even the cavalry eschewed its ceremonial clothing to wear more practical attire. The appearance of the Ottoman cavalry is largely illustrated in the numerous paintings belonging to the seventeenth and eighteenth century, currently known as *battaglismo* or *peinture de bataille*. While the coeval prints more willingly show the pomp and exoticism of the Ottoman world, in the paintings reproducing the cavalry encounters with the Christians, despite some conventional aspects, the vivid and fierce image of the protagonists of the struggle is more adherent to the reality of so many other iconographies. Among the famous painters who dedicated themselves to the genre of battle may be mentioned Salvator Rosa (1615–73) Jacques Courtois (known as *il Borgognone*, 1621–76), Pandolfo Reschi (1630?–96) and Francesco Simonini (1689–1753).[29]

Starting from the early years of the eighteenth century, Ottoman dress began to show eccentricity, willingly welcoming influences from the most disparate regions and often trespassing into true unruliness. The somewhat unkempt appearance of the Ottoman soldiers must have struck the Imperial ambassador Count Fleischmann, when, in the spring of 1715, he defined the *sipahis* escorting Sultan Ahmed III as *miserablen*.[30]

Over the years, this tendency became even more radical, to the point of provoking the reaction of the commanders. The Polish writer Ian Potocki, at the end of the seventeenth century, wrote about the decision to prohibit the janissaries in garrison on the Black Sea to wear Tatar bearskin.[31] To defend themselves from the cold, *kapikulu* cavalry and infantry were provided with woollen coats of various colours, almost always provided with pointed caps. The cloaks of the cavalry reached a considerable width, and usually also covered the horse; the cloaks of the foot troops reached below

70. In the Austrian *Codex Vindobonensis*, made in the late sixteenth century, are represented Ottoman soldiers and civilians with their dress, relating the Imperial style of clothing. Dress patterns and accessories remained unchanged for almost a century, and some particularities identify the main characteristics of some units. The figure is reconstructed after the plate illustrating some *Büchsenmeister* (senior artillerists, *kapikulu topçu*) dressed in parade dress and marching with *tüfek* muskets. This artilleryman wears a dark green *bareta* with red cords and black-white feathers, iron grey *dolama kaftan* lined of medium green; azure breeches; yellow leather shoes. Other figures are dressed in red. These are valuable exceptions for the *kapikulu topçus*, who are usually dressed in dark green.

29 The book edited by Patrizia Consiglio, *La Battaglia nella Pittura del XVII e XVIII secolo* (Parma: Editoriale Silva, 1983), represents the most important study on the subject.
30 K.u.K. Kriegsarchiv, *Feldzüge des Prinzen Eugen*, vol. XVI, p.14.
31 I. Potocki, *Viaggio in Turchia, in Egitto e in Marocco* (Rome: Edizioni E/O, 1980), p.9: 'because the Turks have great contempt for them [the Tatars]'.

71. *Kapikulu topçu* artilleryman in field dress, wearing dark green headdress and *kaftan* with black collar, red breeches and *kusak* sash; white gaiters and red leather shoes, after Rålamb's *Book of Costumes*, mid seventeenth century.

the knee; the soldiers also used them as blankets for the night.

A decisive influence in the evolution of Ottoman military clothing came from the Muslim populations of the Balkans, when their presence on the battlefields increased considerably between the seventeenth and eighteenth centuries. Following the Ottoman occupation, the clothing of the Bosnian and Albanian populations had adopted many elements of the new masters' dress, but certain peculiarities of the pastoral and mountain society remained intact for a long time. Among the characteristic elements of their clothing there were linen trousers, very broad for the soldiers coming from the plains, and of wool, close-fitting, and long to the ankle, those of soldiers living in the interior; in both cases the name was *benevreci*. Wool was the main material of the fabrics produced in the Dinaric-Balkan region; coats, jackets and cloaks were made with simple fabric, and wool was boiled to make heavier clothes like hats and gaiters. The colours most commonly used were red, dark green, or brown, black, grey or natural wool.

The area of origin of the Balkan warriors could easily be identified by their footwear. Normally the populations of the plains or the coast had *opanke* or *bivce*, consisting of a linen sock collected in a sole of bound skin with strings over the foot, and then passed around the ankle. Volunteers from the mountains also wore woollen gaiters, usually dark in colour (white was intended for women and children), high to mid calf, or below the knee. The gaiters were decorated with coloured cord, small pieces of glass or metal buckles; the season determined their thickness. The sole was attached to the foot as in the *opanke*, but the name of the footwear *tozluci* or *terluci*, reveals its Illyrian–Albanian origin.[32]

Alongside the *kaftan*, used also as overcoat, Bosnian soldiers wore the *koret*, the typical short Balkan jacket. It had a single breast and was closed by an 'olives' button inside a loop of cord; but the most important element of male dress was the *jacerma*, the richly decorated doublet, piped with silver cord, or with applications in metal, the so-called *kov* and *tucle*.

Since this 'important' dress coincided with what men were wearing on military duty, the striking Arnaut clothing frequently made use of elaborate and eye-catching accessories like these. They were worn by the chiefs of families, or in any case to the most important personalities, who on festive days matched them to showy sets of weapons. Their presence in the clothing

---

32 See in *Bull Collection*, Museo Stibbert, Florence, vol. II, pp.42–43.

of the Bosnian and Albanian populations has been documented since the first millennium of the ancient era.

The Albanians also used the skirt as traditional male clothing. It had an ancient apotropaic meaning, and consisted of a large rectangle of white linen or cotton, worn over the trousers, which encircled the hips and fell right under the knee. The skirt also belonged to the Ottoman and Mughal fashion of the seventeenth century, and in both cases it was often made of silk, like the one worn by the *solaks* of the *kapikulu*. The existence of a relationship between them is unlikely. The skirt was also common in Dalmatia, where it was common among the *oltramarini* soldiers of Venice. In this regard, an eyewitness of the late seventeenth century stated that there were very few differences between the dress of the soldiers, either Christians and Muslims, from those regions.[33]

Another rather common garment of the Balkan populations was the wool overcoat, long below the knees and tailored in several layers to make it waterproof. It was called in various ways: *kaban*, *kaput* or *kabanica*, but always provided with a hood and complete with long sleeves to protect the arms in the cold season. To allow greater freedom of movement, under the armpits were openings from which the arms came out, with an aesthetic result similar to the courtly Ottoman *kaftans*. At other times the soldier covered himself with a simple cloak, or with a fleece of mutton or lamb's wool.

As a distinctive symbol for authoritative personalities, fur found specific employment in the clothing of the border regions. Similar to the fashion of the Hungarian cavalry, extensive use was made of shoulder jackets or whole fur coats, especially by the commanders of the *serhaddkulu* cavalry. The most prominent leaders used skins of exotic animals, such as lion or leopard; the others resorted to those of the local fauna, namely wolves, bears and lynxes. The use of fur of wild animals was also a symbol linked to war dress among the populations of the Maghreb.[34] The fur was used to manufacture cloaks, caps and saddle blankets, all accessories generally reserved for members of the local ruling class. Typical of North African clothing were the loose trousers of light fabric, indispensable for facing the climate of the southern Mediterranean. It must be remembered that throughout the Maghreb the descendants of the Turkish conquerors, the *kuloglu*, tended to distinguish themselves from the Arab or Bedouin natives, by wearing typically Ottoman clothing, often in the aulic, if not obsolete, forms. Therefore it was easy to see members of the ruling class circulating in Algiers or Tunis with large turbans or *kaftans* fashioned as in the previous century.[35]

---

33 Letter of the French ambassador La Haye, in E. Concina, *Le Trionfanti Armate Venete* (Venice: Filippi, 1972), p.33.

34 The Tuscan doctor Giovanni Pagni, sent in April 1667 to the bey of Tunis, Mohammed El Hafsi, left an interesting relation of his journey in the letters to Francesco Redi. He described the trade in lion fur and the use made of it, including the making of amulets with the skin of its forehead. See in 'Lettere di Giovanni Pagni, medico ed archeologo pisano, a Francesco Redi, in ragguaglio di quanto egli vide e operò in Tunisi', in *Storie di Viaggiatori Italiani: l'Oriente* (Milan: Electa, 1985), p.102.

35 La Mottraye, *Voyages*, vol. I, p.110.

Infantry and Cavalry Weaponry and Equipment

The weapons of Asian peoples are one of the best keys to study their societies and their history. For the Ottoman Turks their weapons represented a cultural viaticum inherited from the nomad warriors of the Central Asia, as well as the awareness of belonging to the *sunna* of the believers, the defenders of the true faith. The high spiritual significance of the weapons was reflected in the great quantity of mottoes and proverbs in which sabres and daggers took on ethical and religious meanings; the same blades, or the plates of the armour and even the rings of the iron ribs, were engraved with words or lines from the Koran.

The weaponry and equipment of the Ottoman soldiers at the beginning of the seventeenth century had by now established stable characteristics and did not undergo significant changes until the mid eighteenth century. Some scholars outlined that one of the symptoms of the Ottoman Empire's military crisis can be seen precisely in the immobility of their technology. Nevertheless, the beauty and artistic value of the works dating back to those years reach their peak, up to becoming the actual symbol of the Ottoman military world.

The major European arms production centres were in Edirne and Constantinople, where the famous arsenal of St Irene was operating from the end of the fifteenth century. In Asia, there were important centres in Smime, Baghdad, Damascus and Yerevan. All these arsenals produced firearms, as well as armour and blades. The very symbol of the Ottoman world, the sabre, or more precisely the curved blade sword, was the noble weapon par excellence. In the Turkish language it is called *kiliç* and indicates not only the curved sabres, but all the weapons with the characteristic curvature because *kiliç* simply means 'sword'. With the exception of the *sakkas* and *acemi-oglanis*, sabres were part of the equipment of all *kapikulu* soldiers and Ottoman troops, both on foot and on horseback. The blades manufactured in the seventeenth century had assumed a rather pronounced curvature, destined to be further accentuated in the following century. After the mid seventeenth century, the Ottoman arsenals began to produce sabres with a sharp edge highlighted by an enlargement of the metal near the tip. The maximum size of the blades could reach up to a metre, but generally the smaller ones were preferred, lighter and more manageable. The superb blades of the most admirable Damascus steel or the one with showy decorations on precious metal were naturally the prerogative of the senior commanders, but also sabres of natural metal were conspicuously decorated with calligrams and ornamental figurations gathered in medallions, the *higab*, endowed with talismanic meanings. Among the recurring motifs, a prominent place belonged to the name of God, 'Allah', as well as the typical crescent, or the six-pointed star, the so-called *khateh Süleyman*, the seal of Solomon. The hilt was made of horn, wood, or bone; sometimes there were ivory or velvet-covered hilts with encrustations of turquoise and coral in the richer models.

The shape of the hilt establishes the age and place of production of the sabres. From the middle of the seventeenth century, the models with a curved profile prevailed, almost specular to the blade, and ending in an obtuse angle. The hilt had a cross shape with straight uprights and an oval or pointed end,

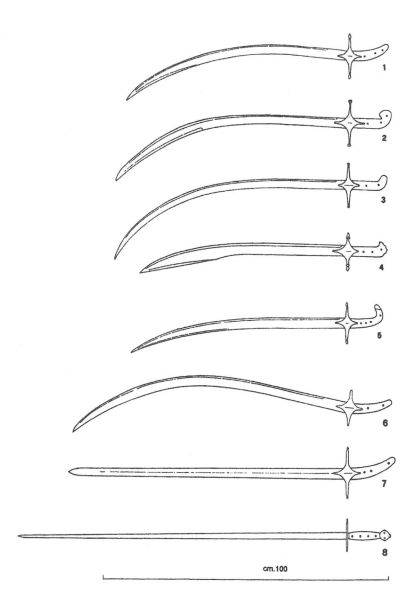

72. Ottoman Sabres
1 – Ottoman *qilij* with classical hilt (seventeenth century); 2 – Egyptian *pala* with pistol handle hilt (early eighteenth century); 3 – Iranian *samsir* or Ottoman *acemi-qilij* (early eighteenth century); 5 – Syrian-Arabian *qilij* (early eighteenth century); 6 – Saddle *qilij* (late seventeenth century); 7 – Saddle *palas* with Hungarian hilt (mid seventeenth century); 8 – Balkanian *meç* (late 17th century). (Author's illustration)

cm.100

and extended symmetrically along the direction of the blade and ended with a more or less pronounced rounding. At the end of the century, the *karabela* hilts became equally common. The terms derived from the town of Karabel, near Smyrna (for others from the city of Karbala, in Iraq), with the final part having the typical eagle head profile. Appearing as early as the late sixteenth century, the *karabela* hilt would have given its name to a new type of sabre with a less curved blade compared to the *kiliç*, and between the seventeenth and eighteenth century became the typical *kapikulu* infantry weapon. The *karabelas'* hilts were shorter and more massive, or they had the shape of an inverted 'U'; in the more elaborate models the final section was modelled in the shape of a dragon's head.

Another type of sabre, with a straighter and broader blade, made its appearance in Armenia in the mid seventeenth century, spreading throughout the Empire and becoming popular also in Poland and Russia alongside the *karabela*.[36] Its name was *pala*, recognisable for the very short blade and for the thickness of the counter-cutting edge. The section of the blade had the shape of a 'T' and in general the overall weight was higher than the other sabre. At the beginning of the eighteenth century, the *pala* was used especially by the cavalry, much appreciated for its power and manageability.

As already seen in the other sabres the blade also had different hilts and grips depending on the period. The most common hilt was the *karabela* type, but in the last years of the seventeenth century century, *palas* with hilts ending with a more rounded end made their appearance. These models were the first types of *pistol* grip, a pattern destined to last for over two centuries and typical of the classic Ottoman sabre.[37] These creations imitated the hilts of the Arab–Syrian sabre, particularly suitable for delivering the slash without running the risk of losing the weapon. In Egypt, sabres were produced with very curved blades already at the end of the seventeenth century,[38] while in Syria and Yemen the blades maintained a more upright shape.

In the Ottoman world, the mutual influences of the many cultures favoured the penetration of styles coming from across the border. In particular the Iranian style assumed connotations of elegance and refinement, and with it some parts of the armament were gladly adopted by the Ottoman ruling class. The Iranian sabre, the *samsir* (scimitar) was among the Ottoman weapons and, next to the imported ones, imitations were produced with the name *acem kılıç*, namely 'Iranian sword'. The *samsir* had a longer and thinner blade compared the Ottoman sabre (the Iranians said it was inspired by the lion's tail); the hilt was similar to the Arab– Syrian one, but with a rounded final that was almost bent at a right angle.

Not all Ottoman swords were curved: rarer, but still produced between the seventeenth and eighteenth centuries, there were the *qaddara* and the *palas*. The first was reserved to the court, whereas the *palas* consisted of a long pointed blade, double or single sided and used by the cavalry, who carried it hanging from the saddle. It was a weapon widespread throughout Eastern Europe and substantially similar to the *hegyesztòr* of the Hungarian hussars, from which the Ottoman models sometimes copied the hilt; its dimensions ranged between 110 and 120cm.

Always hanging from the saddle, there were also some 'proto-sabres', different from the *palas* due to the marked curvature of the blade and the hilt- like the *kılıç*. Smaller than the *palas*, these weapons were used by the senior officers. The hilts of the *palas* could be of various shapes, while the *qaddaras* had trilobate hilts, a variant of the *karabela* pattern. Other straight blades were part of the equipment of the Balkan soldiers, especially the Bosnian

---

36 Lebedinski, *Les Armes Orientales*, p.66.
37 See the *pala* preserved in the city museum of Vienna, dated 1683; inventory n. 126447.
38 See the Egyptian sabre dated about 1700 preserved in the Victoria and Albert Museum of London.

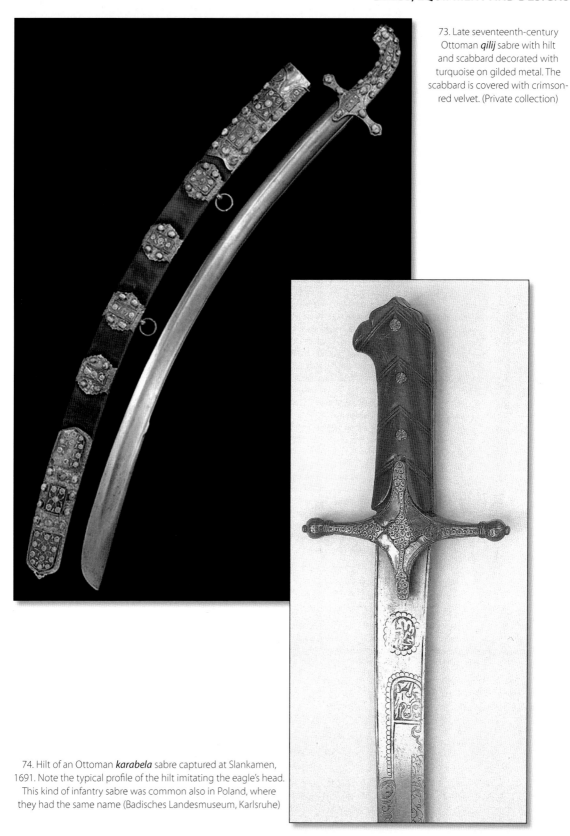

73. Late seventeenth-century Ottoman *qilij* sabre with hilt and scabbard decorated with turquoise on gilded metal. The scabbard is covered with crimson-red velvet. (Private collection)

74. Hilt of an Ottoman *karabela* sabre captured at Slankamen, 1691. Note the typical profile of the hilt imitating the eagle's head. This kind of infantry sabre was common also in Poland, where they had the same name (Badisches Landesmuseum, Karlsruhe)

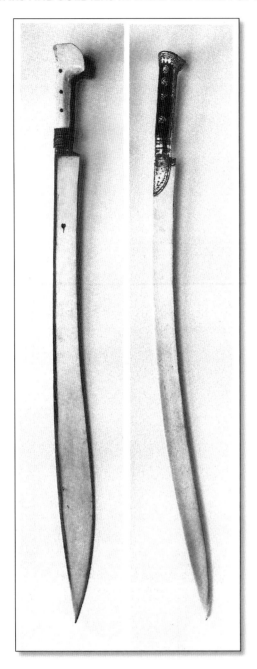

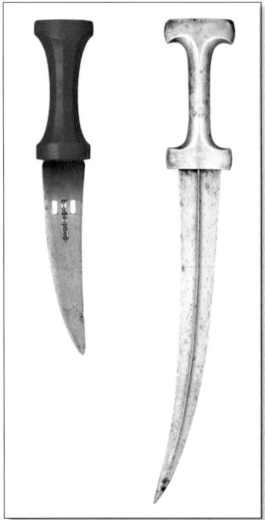

76. Ottoman knives, late seventeenth century. To the left, a curved double-edged blade, pierced with four rectangular and one circular apertures, the central three filled with nine coral beads (the others missing); a faceted hardwood grip of characteristic form, 15.5cm. To the right, a curved double-edged blade formed with a long raised central rib on each face, and well-formed hilt encased in sheet silver, 28cm.

75. Ottoman *yataghans*, war spoils from the battlefield of Slankamen, 1691. Note on left the hilt with the typical final in thighbone pattern. (Badisches Landesmueum, Karlsruhe)

Arnauts, armed also with swords *alla schiavona*, which imitated those of the contiguous Venetian *oltramarini* or were spoils of war.

The scabbards for all the sabres were made with two strips of wood covered with leather or velvet; metal reinforcements, and rings for the straps completed the whole. At other times, they made entirely metal sheaths with stones and other precious materials. Even on scabbards, the Ottoman artisans vented their passion for ornamentation. The most common motif was floral decorations, similar to the *Iznik* ceramics of the classical age.[39] Often, the upper end was flared outward to facilitate extraction of the weapon; another flare was used for housing the hilt.

Equally widespread as the sabre, daggers and knives mainly equipped the janissaries and other infantry soldiers, who carried them alone or in pairs under their sashes. From the middle of the seventeenth century the most widespread type was the *kandjar* (cangiarro), with a slightly curved cutting blade and a straight T-shaped hilt. Some models reached 60cm in length, but usually the *kandjar* ranged between 35 and 45cm, including the hilt.

This knife was the most widespread throughout Anatolia and Caucasus, where there was also another type of knife, with a straight and double-edged blade, called *kindjal*. It was not unusual to see both these weapons among the panoply of the Ottoman or Egyptian Mamluk soldiers. The fine workmanship and quality of Dagestan and Georgian knives frequently met with the approval of the Ottoman ruling class. At the end of the seventeenth century another knife, the *yataghan*, began to spread especially within the janissary corps: it was a large knife with a long, single-cutting S-shaped blade. The origin of the *yataghan* is probably to be found in the Balkans and more precisely in Albania, but in any case similar weapons existed throughout the Mediterranean already in ancient times, just think of the Greek–Macedonian *makhaira* or the Iberian *falcata*. The blades had always a decoration that thickened the edge at the base of the blade, in order to strengthen the insertion point into the hilt. This latter constituted the sign of recognition for the *yataghan* and was formed by a hilt without a guard terminating with two 'ears', or 'wings', with a typical rounded shape similar to a femoral head. The end of the scabbard carried a metal sphere or the stylised head of a monstrous animal. The diffusion of the *yataghan* intensified through the mid seventeenth century as a result of the increase in Albanian and Bosnian soldiers, and spread rapidly, reaching ever more elaborate forms and ornamentations. Numerous *yataghans* are preserved in the Austrian and German *Türkenbeuten* (Turkish booties), but the ones coming from the wars of the sixteenth and seventeenth centuries are less numerous compared the *kandjars*. The length of a *yataghan* exceeded 55cm, and some specimens even 70cm.[40] Several eyewitnesses recalled how the janissaries circulated with daggers on various occasions,[41] and according to Marsigli it was a sign of ostentation, but later he added that they also used it 'during the arguments

---

39 A. Jacob, *Les Armes Blanches du Monde Islamique* (Paris : Jacques Grancher, 1985), p.92.
40 See the *yataghan* dated 1715, Inventory n, 127.369, preserved in the civic Museum of Vienna, length 72.2cm.
41 Marsigli, vol. II, p.12, and La Mottraye, *Voyages*, vol. I, p.240.

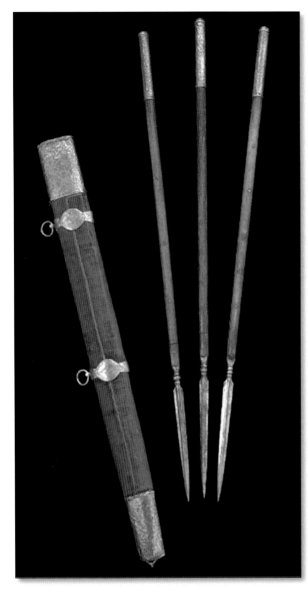

77. Javelins and quiver, Turkey, c. 1680. Black leather scabbard with brass accessories. (Private collection)

and the disputes, wounding more with the point than with the cut'. Other war knives came from Arabia and among the most common was the *djambiya*, easily recognisable by the curved blade and the 'J'-shaped metal scabbard.

The long lance was a part of the traditional equipment of the Ottoman cavalry, but according to finds dating back to the seventeenth century today preserved in museums and collections, they had lost their military purpose and were mainly used on parade, especially for hoisting banderols and other small ensigns. All lances can be divided into two categories: the long lance, properly in Turkish *mizrak* or *sünü*, and the numerous variants called *kostanica*. The former reached a considerable size, some weapons measuring up to 430cm in length, and belonged to the *kapikulu sipahis*. The *kostanica*, on the other hand, was smaller in size, at most 200/250cm, and was used mainly by the border cavalry. In the lower portion the spears often had a globe that served as a guard for the hand; some lances had a smaller globe also at the top of the pole. Both ends terminated with a metal tip: on one side of the actual spearhead, double-edged, cross-sectioned or even with three blades, and on the other side there was a little ferrule.

The dimensions of the *mizrak* and the striking colours of the poles betray the decorative use of these weapons. The surviving known examples are painted with red, green, or black with white spirals, and sometimes ornamental figures or motifs appear on the pole as tassels, circles or flames of various colours. Even the *kostanicas* were decorated, but compared to the others they were used more frequently in combat.

In the infantry, the use of pole weapons was confined to the *kapikulu* corps. The janissary *odabasis* were equipped with a partisan about two metres high with two iron beaks at the base of the blade, similar to the medieval Italian *corsesche*; they were used in the same way as the halberds of Western infantry, but more in ceremonies and parade than in battle.

Even in the early years of the eighteenth century, there was among the armaments of the *kapikulu* an infantry polearm 120/140cm long, provided with a large blade with a single cutting edge, used even in action. This weapon was substantially very similar to the *berdiche* of the Russian strelitzi and preferably equipped the storming parties formed by the *serdengeçdis*, the volunteers who led the assaults.

With a use similar to the long swords hanging on the saddle, there were metal poles with a square or triangular section, completed by a hilt, and ending with a very sharp point. It was the *meg* (estoc), up to 125cm long, with which the horsemen faced armoured enemies. It was a very common weapon in the border cavalry, but it was also used by the *kapikulu sipahis*. The hilts were the same of the Hungarian–Polish sabre, while other types were fitted with a characteristic discoid guard, with a large spherical knob at the end, suitable for carrying the blow as far forward as possible. Due to the fact that it was transported inside a scabbard similar to the *palas*, it is possible to fclassify the *meg* like the aforementioned long swords.

Finally, the javelin, *çerid* in Turkish, completed the cavalry weapons. It measured about 80/90cm and consisted of a thin wooden rod, with a tip and a metal hilt. Usually the javelins were carried in groups of three inside a scabbard hanging from the saddle. This weapon was a piece of horse furniture much appreciated by the officers of the *sipahi ulùfely*. The *çerids* were more often part of the war equipment of the Asian cavalry, but their use decreased considerably from the middle of the seventeenth century, finally being relegated to solely a decorative function.

Among the traditional weapons, a prominent place belongs to axes, maces and war hammers, all weapons that qualified the rank of the owner. The mace, called *gürç* and derived from the analogous Iranian *gourz*: a weapon intended for the most important officers and heroes; just think of the legendary bull head-shaped mace belonged to Rustam, the mythical hero of the *Shahname*.[42] The maces were often made of precious materials, silver, gold and even diamond,[43] or in Damascus steel. The pole, cylindrical or polygonal, reached 50/70 cm in length; the head had the shape of a globe, more or less elongated or flattened depending on the example; the winged edge also, inspired by Western models, was quite common. Even the axes were manufactured with precious materials and normally they reached dimensions identical to those of the maces; these followed in hierarchical order but, particularly in Asia, they were the preferred weapon of the senior officers, who imported rich examples from Iran and India.[44] On other occasions, the axes equipped the *kapikulu* cavalry and infantry officers. Small axes were part of the equipment of the janissaries and the infantry, used for preparing the bullets from the lead bars issued to each soldier. Occasionally, officers were armed with war hammers, above all in the *serhadkulu* cavalry, but while maces and axes were exclusively command symbols, war hammers were used also in action, especially by the *dely* raiders.

ancient origin. Sporting and hunting competitions, in which large groups of archers participated, were a widespread pastime throughout the Empire, both in Asia and in Europe. In the seventeenth century the bows were still produced following the ancient method of overlapping tendons and horn

---

42 V. Enderlein and W. Sundermann (eds), *Shāhnāme, das persische Königbuch, Miniaturen und Texte des Berliner Handschrift von 1605* (Leipzig-Weimar: Gustav Kiepenheuer, 1988).

43 Zigulski, *Ottoman Art*, p.136.

44 See the famous mace of jade and ruby preserved in the Topkapı museum, manufactured in Constantinople around 1650.

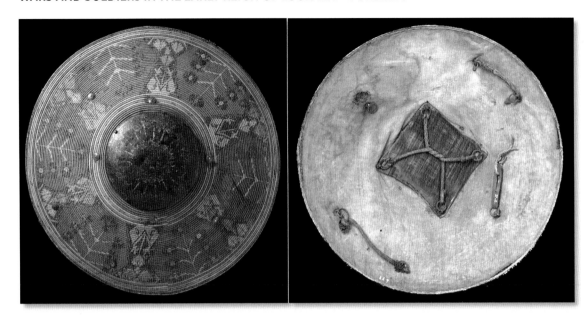

78. Front and back of an Ottoman late seventeenth century *kalkan* shield. Red fabric cover with yellow and black decorations. 59.5cm diameter. (Badisches Landesmueum, Karlsruhe)

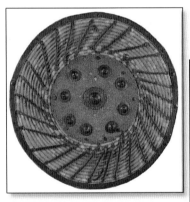

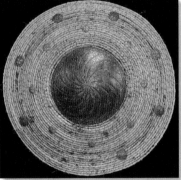

79. Round woven Ottoman *kalkan* shield, with ray skin and iron. seventeenth or eighteenth century; 38cm diameter. This rare shield displays a central, round decorative circle made from ray skin on top of which is an iron shield boss. It is surrounded by eight further, smaller decorative bosses. The shield is reinforced by a surrounding iron border and 28 diagonally placed iron struts. The reverse side is covered with an old, light brown fabric and has a plaited leather hilt on a leather cushion to support the hand. Historically this is an extremely interesting piece and is in very good condition. (Private collection)

80. Ottoman *kalkan* shield, late seventeenth century; 55.8cm. diameter. Plain covered Rattan palm, willow or dogwood, with brass studs of stylised floral form and mounted with a central gilt steel boss decorated in relief with a spiral, and embellished with cartouches of abstract floral motifs, the border with a band of cursive calligraphy, This form of shield widely used by the Ottoman light cavalry, which provided the defence for those wielding a sabre or bow and arrows. (Badisches Landesmueum, Karlsruhe)

81. Gilded metal shield, coming from the Kahlemberg battlefield, 1683; 56cm diameter. Circular form with a central boss encircled by 12 minor and major engraved palmette roundels, pierced by rivets with rosette-shaped heads retained on the inside by iron washers with attached loops, the outer edge with lining rivets, felt interior, the leather cover embossed with a radial design, the interior edge threaded with leather strap.

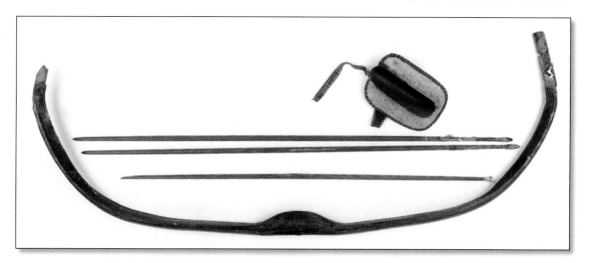

82. Complete set of bow, arrow and armlet, mid seventeenth century. (Topkapı Museum, Constantinople).

flakes on a wooden core, then they were covered in leather or fabric. The size never exceeded 90cm in length. All the bows were carried on the right side, inside a case hanging from a belt; in another case, hanging on the left side, arrows were held, 50 to 70cm long, stabilised with feathers or wooden fins. Both cases were called with the name *terkeç* (quiver) but more precisely this term would identify only the case for the arrows. In the mid seventeenth century, the bow still equipped the Ottoman cavalry, and in fact Montecuccoli confirms its use among the Ottoman cavalry weapons, but outlining its ineffectiveness against the armoured Horse.[45]

Marsigli described various types of arrows, including one with the point covered with incendiary material and another with a round tip, 'to be used for game'.[46] However, the use of bow in battle was diminishing quite rapidly towards the end of the seventeenth century. Baron Michele D'Aste, an officer in the Imperial army killed in 1686 at the siege of Buda, collected during the four campaigns fought against the Ottomans the unenviable record of seven different wounds, but only once was the arrow to injury him, and this happened at the siege of Ersekujvàr, where many Tatars were present. Numerous witnesses agree that at the end of the seventeenth century bows and arrows were used less in battle, and that only horsemen from Asia continued to use them. In the 1717 campaign, the Bavarian captain De La Colonie mentioned among the weapons of the *sipahi* sabres, lances, spears and muskets, while bows and arrows are never mentioned.[47]

Like all traditional weapons, the bow, and above all the quiver, became a symbol of rank and certain models made with fine fabrics, and decorated with inserts of gold, silver and jewels, were coveted gifts for dignitaries and officers, as well as for foreign ambassadors and princes. The bows preserved in the museums of Vienna, dating back to the siege of 1683, are all covered in velvet or silk, mostly carmine red, with gold and silver decorations. It seems

---

45 Montecuccoli, in Luraghi, *Opere di Raimondo Montecuccoli*, vol. II, p.477.
46 Marsigli, vol. II, p.9.
47 La Colonie, *Memoirs*, vol. III, pp.179–180. The French-Bavarian officer reports that the Ottoman also did not use pistols.

Left: 83. Ottoman *terkeç* quivers, 1690s. To the left in azure fabric with yellow-gold and red decorations; to the right in red velvet with silver embroidery. (Badisches Landesmuseum, Karlsruhe)

Right: 84. Detail of Ottoman *terkeç* quivers by Wenceslas Hollar, 1660–70. (Author's archive)

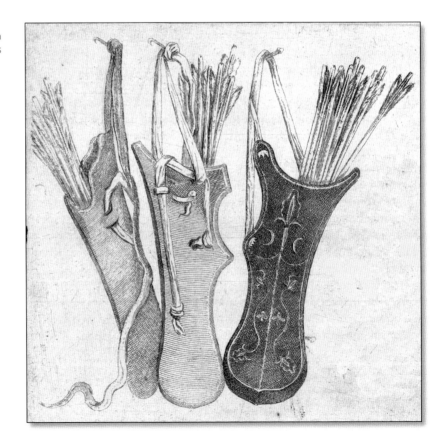

evident that even while these weapons would allow normal function, they accomplished only a decorative purpose. Some metal bows, manufactured exclusively for symbolic use, are preserved in several European collections.

Muskets and other Firearms

All military historians agree that the Ottoman sultans were among the first to equip their infantry with firearms long before the other princes. The Ottoman gunsmiths therefore boasted a consolidated tradition and a degree of technical skill able to stand comparison with the achievements of their adversaries, but progress stopped at the seventeenth century. The firing mechanisms, independently developed in the Ottoman arsenals, can be divided into two classes, matchlock and flintlock; regardless of the firing system, the name used was *tüfek* or *tüfenk*. The flintlock mechanism was introduced in the first half of the seventeenth century and was very similar to the Catalan system; in the Western world it was identified as the Spanish *patilla* system. The matchlock system, on the other hand, had a different mechanism compared to the Western European models, due to the inversion of the trigger transmission, with the result that in the Ottoman weapons the serpentine was placed behind the ignition stove. Several matchlock *tüfeks* became war trophies in the loot after the battle of Kahlenberg, but the flintlock ones are definitely greater in number. In 1683, when the Christian infantrymen were using matchlock or mixed mechanism muskets, at least 80 percent of the janissaries and possibly 60 percent of the other infantry had already received the flintlock *tüfek*. Certainly the quality muskets intended for elite troops were very different from those issued to the other infantry. In this regard, some commenters declare that the effectiveness of the latter did not go beyond the noise caused by the shot.[48]

Ottoman firearms were altogether shorter than the Western European manufactures, but not much heavier; on average a *tüfek* reached 120–140cm in length and weighed 4.5 to 6.5kg. The calibre was heavier than Western ones, between 12 to 16mm, and some weapons reached calibres of 18mm. Marsigli was impressed by the size of the muskets of the Egyptian janissaries, which forced them to adopt a particular position to resist the recoil.[49] The *kapikulu* infantry preferably used heavy trench muskets, known as *metris tüfenkçi*, sometimes with a support at the end of the barrel to facilitate aiming. In siege warfare or when defending fortresses the Ottomans employed this musket, provided with eight-sided or cylinder barrels, usually 130–160cm long and with bore diameters of 20–29mm. In addition, there were pieces with larger bore diameters (35 and 45mm) often used for firing grenades or other inflammable shells.[50] When European sources claimed that Ottoman handguns

---

48 Marsigli, vol. I, p.85.
49 *Ibidem*, vol. II, p.16.
50 G. Ágoston, *Guns for the Sultan. Military Power and the Weapons Industry in the Ottoman Empire* (Cambridge: Cambridge University Press, 2005), p.89.

were heavier than European ones, they probably referred to these trench guns, which they certainly could have seen in Crete, Kamieniec or Vienna.

In the late seventeenth century there were common in siege warfare long muskets, called *dahlian*. These were long-range barrelled rifles with calibres ranging from the usual 12–16mm to heavy 25 or 30mm heavy muskets, similar to the Western wall musket, which required two soldiers to operate.

Regarding the quality of Ottoman muskets, the sources are contradictory. A former janissary in the first half of the seventeenth century complained that the muskets manufactured in state-operated workshops in Constantinople were of inferior quality compared with the ones obtainable from private gun-makers.[51] Raimondo Montecuccoli, on the other hand, claimed that the metal of the Ottoman muskets was of good quality and that their range and force were greater than those of the Christian muskets.[52] The great Italian captain also describes the powder charge used by the Ottomans. The soldiers prepared the charge by introducing a quantity of powder equivalent to the weight of the projectile; this guaranteed a longer range compared to the Western muskets, but the loading operations were more complex, above all due to the lack of prepared cartridges.[53]

Several muskets dating back to the seventeenth and eighteenth centuries are preserved in the Askeri Museum in Constantinople and in the major collections of Ottoman trophies around the world, allowing us to admire the great variety of designs and decorative techniques. Most of the wood is painted in red or azure, but there are examples entirely covered with velvet or with tortoise shell tassels. Some muskets show all the wood painted in white or, more rarely, in black; while turquoise, coral and mother-of-pearl are mixed in refined ornamental combinations. Even the metal parts show elaborate decorations, sometimes the firing mechanism, and almost always the fixing bands of the barrel, are in brass. Some muskets have the barrel in Damascus steel, or in black polished metal and provided with decorations on gold or silver. Certainly, the muskets issued to the *kapikulu* infantry were the most lavish and most artistically ornamented, and once again the weapons of the Egyptian janissaries were to be noticed for their beauty.[54] In its general aspect the *tüfek* did not undergo significant changes, and with few differences the same type was widespread in the Caucasus, Ukraine and Iran, easily recognisable by the heavy wooden pentagonal section of the stock.

Towards the end of the seventeenth century, a new model of musket with a characteristic stock began to spread. It was the *tançitsa*, the typical firearm of the Albanian and Bosnian Arnauts, also mentioned by Marsigli with the name *schioppo lungo* (long musket).[55] These muskets were equipped with a mechanism identical to the Ottoman ones and were easily recognisable by the curved and very thin cross, ending in the shape of a fish tail. The wood was often covered with iron, stones or silver, and abundantly decorated in the same

---

51 *Ibidem*, p.90.
52 Montecuccoli, in Luraghi, *Opere di Raimondo Montecuccoli*, vol. II, p.210.
53 *Ibidem*.
54 Marsigli, vol. II, p.17.
55 *Ibidem*.

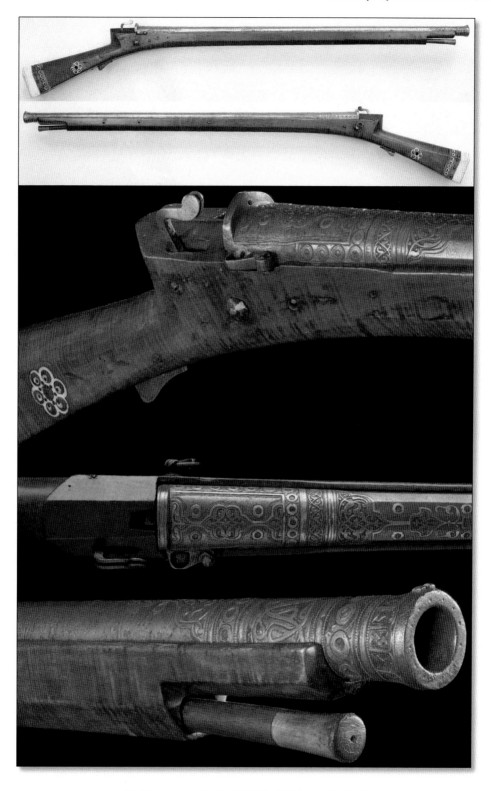

85. Ottoman matchlock *tüfek*, 1650–70 (Private collection)

86. Ottoman matchlock *tüfek*, 1660–70 (Private collection)

Left: 87. Ottoman janissary equipped with long *tüfek* musket, late seventeenth century. This kind of firearm was used by marksmen during the siege. (German print by anonymous artist, 1670-80, author's archive)

Below: 88. Ottoman flintlock, late seventeeth century. (Badisches Landesmuseum, Karlsruhe)

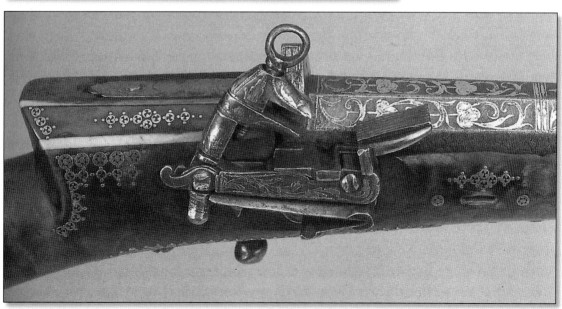

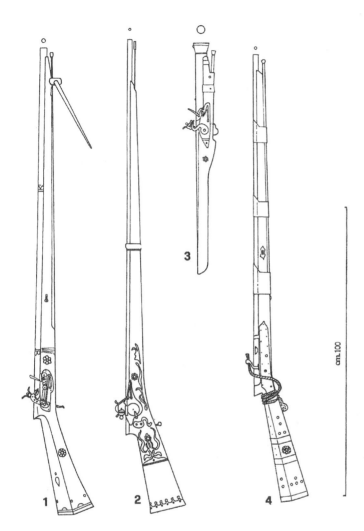

89. Ottoman and Tatar muskets. (Author's illustration)

1. Trench flintlock ***tüfek*** with aim staff (early eighteenth century)

2. Wheel-lock ***tüfek*** with imported mechanism (1660–70)

3. Siege handgun (early eighteenth century, Askeri Museum, Constantinople)

4. Iranian–Caucasian matchlock, carried by Tatar infantry (late seventeenth century, in Lebedinski, ***Les Armes Cosaques et Caucasiennesi***).

The Ottomans equipped their forces with muskets almost as soon as their European enemies did. However, concerned Ottomans watched with much apprehension the rapid advance of European technology already in the sixteenth century, as well as the growth of the European economy and military capability increased by the Industrial Revolution, which sparked changes at all levels, all of which contributed to Western Europe's power. Considering this scenario, and the maintenance of the original Ottoman military technological capabilities, the Ottoman military model acted until the early eighteenth century in an immutable context, where multiple factors determined choices, and mistakes also.

style as the *yataghan* daggers. A marked difference between the *tançitsa* and the *tüfek* lay in the length. In fact, the Balkan weapons could reach a total of 165cm, the calibre rarely exceeded 14mm and also the weight was much lower.

Among the Balkan warriors, particularly in the cavalry, blunderbuss *tüfeks* were diffused. This firearm was considered more effective than pistols, also because blunderbuss could shoot multiple projectiles, and the horseman loaded it more easily and, not least, the blunderbuss had a notable psychological effect on the enemies. Two basic blunderbuss models are known, both characterised by the shape of the barrel: one with a pentagonal section as for the *tüfek*, and another type with a stock similar to the Balkan model; in both cases it was common to weight the wood with the insertion of metal elements according to the decorative style characteristic of the place of production. Small blunderbusses were used both in Asia and in Europe with the name 'blunderbuss-pistol', and measured no more than 60/70cm; instead the classic Ottoman blunderbuss reached a metre in length and could be held up like a gun. The calibre was usually more than 15mm. The

90. Dagestan pistols, 1697. A pair of saddle pistols captured at Zenta, possibly belonging to Grand Vizier Elmas Mohammed. According to the museum's archive, Prince Eugene of Savoy presented these weapons to his cousin Vittorio Amedeo II in 1706. (Dagestan manufacture in silver, late seventeenth century; Armeria Reale, Turin)

blunderbuss was also a typical weapon of the Mamluk horsemen and other North African soldiers. The firing mechanisms mounted on these weapons were always of the Spanish *patilla* type, but starting from the eighteenth century flintlock systems of the French type were imported, especially in Egypt and the Maghreb. However, as early as the mid seventeenth century, several Wesern European firing mechanisms began to be imported for completing the production of muskets in the Constantinople arsenal. In some cases, imported mechanisms consisted of wheel systems produced in the Netherlands,[56] followed by more modern flintlock mechanisms imported from France. In this regard is famous the exchange of wheat and rifles which took place in 1709, between the king of France and the sultan.[57] The large variety of calibres made it difficult to produce balls fit for all the *tüfeks* issued to the *kapikulu* soldiers, therefore the *cebeci* distributed to the soldiers a barrel of lead, with which the men themselves prepared the ammunition balls, cutting the barrel with an axe or a knife.

Along with daggers, the *kapikulu* infantry and cavalry went into battle with one or two pistols under their waist sash. Sometimes the cavalry also carried one or two pairs of pistols in holsters. At the end of the seventeenth century the war equipment of the cavalry officers and *ulùfely sipahi*, as well as that of the senior commanders, often included a pair of pistols covered by Western imitation holsters. The Ottoman pistols, identifiable from the typical final pattern of the stock, the 'mouse's tail', underwent very few changes during the seventeenth century and proliferated until the nineteenth together with

56 Montecuccoli, in Luraghi, *Opere di Raimoindo Montecuccoli*, vol. II, p.210.
57 In the summer of 1709 Louis XIV offered to the Porte 10,000 flintlocks produced in France as payment for the Ottoman wheat. This episode has been discussed as a legend, but it is mentioned by Voltaire in *Le Siècle du Louis XIV* (Paris, 1735–39).

91. Early eighteenth-century pistol holsters, yellow fabric with floral decorations embroidered in green, red and white. Ottoman cavalry went in battle with firearms later than their Western enemies, and until the early eighteenth century, saddle pistols equipped almost officers and commanders. (Private collection)

another type, introduced at the beginning of the eighteenth century, characterised by a rounder end on the stock. The stock was almost always made of wood covered with metal plates, and thanks to its shape it was also an effective club. The calibres were normally between 10 and 14mm. In most cases the pistols had the classical Spanish *patilla* firing mechanisms but, especially in the Balkans, weapons were produced with Western flintlock systems, whether they were imported or captured in war. In tune with the taste for decoration, the pistols were decorated with inserts of corals, turquoises, mother-of-pearl and ivory.

According to the Ottoman passion for exotic weapons, a fair number of firearms produced in the Caucasus were also imported. The weapons from those regions were easily recognisable by the stock, ending with a fully decorated globe, marked by rich combinations of various precious materials. The name of this kind of pistol was *topança*, and it was used for gifts intended for important court personalities, such as the superb pair of Dagestan pistols that belonged to the Grand Vizier Elmas Mohammed, a war trophy of Prince Eugene of Savoy at Zenta in 1697.[58]

The Ottoman pistols lacked a ramrod, so independent metal rods, called *souma*, were used, suspended on the belt or powder flask. Sometimes, the *soumas* were combined with tools such as hammers, screwdrivers and brushes, and they constituted a pretext to stimulate the decorative imagination of the artisans.

Indispensable accessories for firearms, the Ottoman powder flasks were recognisable by their characteristic crescent shape and were mostly made of metal or wood, covered in leather, reinforced with brass accessories. *Kapikulu* infantry, especially the *cebecis*, were always equipped with two powder flasks, and also janissaries are represented often with a couple of powder flasks. While many metal powder flasks are today practically intact, there are very few pieces of equipment made with other materials that have followed the same destiny. For instance, belts and ammunition bags are today rather rare.[59] The iconographic sources depicting janissaries and other *kapikulu* infantry show that they were equipped with small leather bags variously decorated and painted, fixed to the belt or on a leather strap across the right shoulder. *Serhaddkulu* infantry, cavalry and artillery used different types and shapes, made of leather, canvas or natural leather, and inspired by the style of the region of origin. All the Ottoman infantry and cavalry military equipment

---

58 This pair of pistols is today preserved in the collection of the Armeria Reale of Turin.
59 The only seventeenth-century items are preserved in the Karlsruhe *Türkenbeute* and in the Vienna *Waffensammlung*.

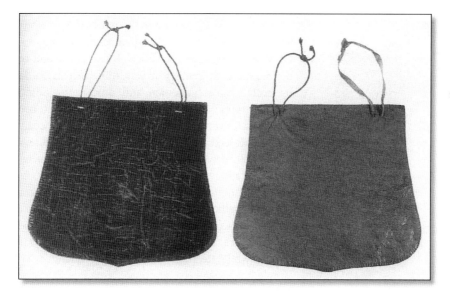

92. Front and back of a cover for ammunition bags or pistol holster(?) in natural red-brown leather, as part of the Slankamen war spoils, 1691; size 28.2cm high x 32cm wide. (Badishes Landesmuseum, Karlsruhe)

was marked by lightness and small dimensions, indispensable requisites for performing the most congenial tactics of warfare.

Armour and Horse Equipment

In the mid seventeenth century, the cavalry in particular still retained parts of their defensive armour such as metal plates, iron chainmail, quilted jackets, helms and shields. Later, the protective metal parts for the body and head in particular gave way to increasingly lighter versions and then disappeared altogether. This phenomenon, similar to what happened in the Western European armies, recorded a notable impulse starting from the penultimate decade of the seventeenth century, namely during the War of the Holy League. The helms continued to be used into the beginning of the eighteenth century, although to a much lesser extent than in the past, while the use of metal plates almost completely disappeared. Only the 'four mirror armour' of Iranian origin, the *çahar aìné*, was used for some time, but only for ceremonial purposes by the *kapikulu* cavalry or carried by senior commanders as distinctive of rank. Probably, some horsemen continued to wear armoured plates under the *kaftan*, re-using equipment belonging to a generation or two before, but the cavalry had long since renounced metal protection to achieve the greatest possible agility and speed. In the third book of *Della guerra contro il Turco in Ungheria* (The War against the Turk in Hungary, 1670), Montecuccoli remarks on this feature, writing that the Ottoman cavalry 'has no breastplates, armours, tassets and vambraces ... and then if the horseman does not have heavy protections, he becomes even more agile thanks to the speed of the horses, and lightness of the weapons.'[60]

---

60 Montecuccoli, 'Aforismi applicati alla guerra possibile col Turco in Ungheria', in Luraghi, *Opere di Raimondo Montecuccoli*, vol. II, p.475.

93. *Chahar aina*, or four mirrors armour, used by cavalry mainly in Asia, the Middle East and Eastern Europe, including India, Persia, Tibet, Russia and the Ottoman Empire. A distinctively Ottoman model consisting of large round steel plates in the front and back connected by mail.

The mail coat, or rather the shirt of iron rings, was the *zirh* and it enjoyed a great favour among the Ottoman cavalrymen, so much so that at the end of the seventeenth century it was still worn in battle by both simple horsemen and officers, including infantry ones.[61] There were simple shirts or those padded with canvas, rope or velvet; some mail coats were reinforced on the breast or around the kidneys with small metal plates, others coats had gilt metal ornamentations. In length, the Ottoman mail coats fell to the thighs and usually had sleeves. The forearm could be further protected by a vambrace, the *kulluk*, with its typical pointed shape near the elbow. The *kulluk*s were usually manufactured with precious details, while steel-only models were intended for simple horsemen. The vambrace remained in vogue until the eighteenth century, and as a decorative accessory it was used for a long time by the *ulùfely sipahis*, including officers. Usually the *kulluk* only protected the right arm, while the left one carried the round shield, known as *kalkan*. Because the Ottoman sabres, due to their curved shape, did not allow an effective defence against slashes, an additional protection was required. The originality of the Ottoman shields lay in their form, and in the manufacturing technique, which remained unchanged for centuries. The *kalkan* was composed of a central metal boss from which various circles of woven fabric or rope radiated, applied on a base of wood or light metal. There were also *kalkan*s manufactured entirely of metal or leather for ceremonial use. The average diameter of the shield was between 60 and 70cm. The surface offered itself to be decorated with inscriptions and images of various colours, while the boss and all the metal parts were occasionally worked with engravings. Along with the *kalkan*, long asymmetrical quadrangular left-pointed shields were also used. This was a widespread weapon among the Hungarian and Balkan border cavalry, whose origins date back to the fifteenth century; its use continued until the end of the seventeenth century. Like defensive armaments, the Ottoman helms also derived from ancient models. The two fundamental protections for the head still worn by the Ottoman cavalry were the *çiçak* and the *külah-kud*. The *çiçak* was very similar to the western lobster helm, which it had mutually influenced. The Ottoman helm was usually distinguished by the more pointed shape. Some models had reinforcing grooves to facilitate the deviation of blows from above. The *çiçak* weighed up to 2.5 kg, and usually included iron mail as additional protection. The *çiçak* was the most used helm by the *ulùfeli sipahis* and for them there were even types manufactured in gilded metal. Even more

---

61   The most prestigious example is the coat of mail belonging to the *yeniceri ağasi* Rodosti Mustafa, janissary commander in 1691, captured by the Margrave Ludwig of Baden at Slankamen, 1691. The coat is today preserved in the Landesmuseum of Karlsruhe.

Left, top and bottom: 94. Ottoman *çiçak* helm, sixteenth to seventeenth century, forged from watered steel and decorated in gold with arabesques and Koranic inscriptions. It is very similar to one now in the Kunsthistorisches Museum, Vienna, manufactured about 1560 for a grand vizier of Sultan Süleyman the Magnificent (reigned 1520–66). Both helms presumably were made in one of the Imperial workshops, possibly in the Constantinople arsenal of Saint Irene. Although this helm is a practical military object, judging from its fine materials and ornamentation it must have been created primarily as part of parade armour and as a symbol of rank. (Metropolitan Museum of Art)

Below: 95. Ottoman *çiçak*, dating to the 1620s, in gilded copper. Note the feather holder as a symbol of the *kapikulu sipahi* cavalry. (The Art Institute of Chicago)

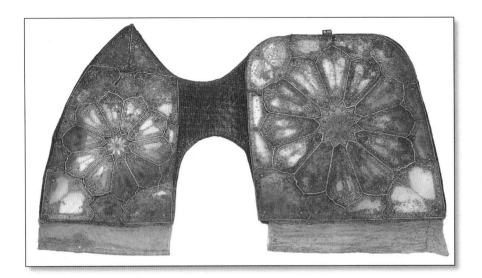

96. Horse furniture in white metal and red fabric, and its frontal section. (Badisches Landesmuseum, Karlsruhe)

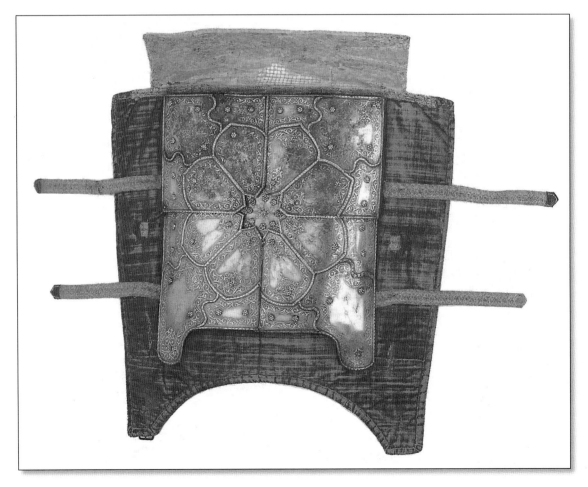

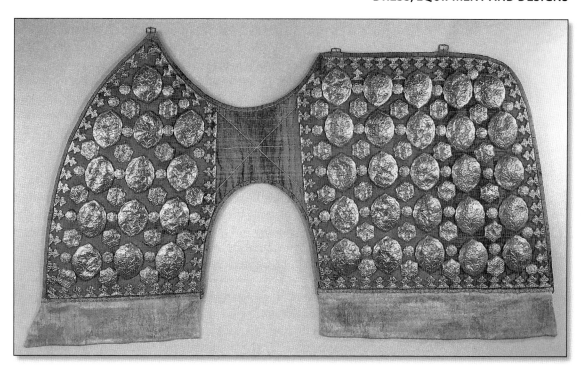

Above: 97. Horse furniture in gilded metal and azure fabric. (Badisches Landesmuseum, Karlsruhe)

Below: 98. Horse furniture in white metal with floral saz-style decoration and azure fabric. (Badisches Landesmuseum, Karlsruhe)

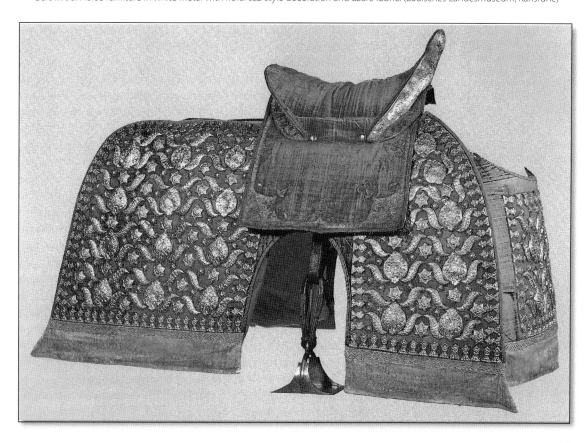

widespread than the *çiçak*, the *külah-kud* was widespread in Egypt, Iran and the rest of Asia, and through the Ottomans it was also adopted by the Polish and Russian cavalry. It was a very simple helm and therefore of very low cost – it could be used as a headdress under the turban, thus remaining invisible, but there were some items with very fine decorations in gilded or silver. Furthermore, inspired by the Iranian fashion, the Ottoman artisans decorated the *külah-kud* with the insertion of two peacock feathers. Iron mail was applied along the edge and fell back down to the shoulders, in some cases even protecting the neck.

With the reduction of the defensive armament of the cavalryman, the protections for the horse also considerably diminished. Except for the metallic protections for the head, the *tombak*, destined for the richest horse equipment of the officers, the only defence still widely used was the *bojunduruk*, formed by a strap of fabric or leather placed behind the ears of the horse, on which metal scales or simple iron mail were fixed. The strap gathered under the horse's head, then it was garnished with a metallic globe from which long tails of horsehair started. Along with the hair, strips of coloured silk or wool were inserted. Originally, the *bojunduruk* served to protect the neck of the horse from enemy blows, over time it became a typical ornament of the Ottoman cavalry. *Bojunduruk* with gold or silver decoration were reserved for the high dignitaries' horse equipment; other items, of very simple construction, belonged to the common horsemen. In the Balkans there was a variant with formed only by a leather protections ending with a metal crescent. Also parts of the bridle, especially those above the mouth, occasionally carried protective reinforcements, consisting of metal plates or pendants, which on the horses of the highest officers took the form of medallions; on the forehead, feathers were usually inserted.

The magnificence of the dress worn by commanders and high dignitaries was matched by the pomp of their horses. Heavy brocade saddle covers, studded with traditional accessories of the Imperial style, appeared alongside other creations in silk or *kedifè*. Sometimes, the Ottoman saddle covers were made in several pieces which also covered the horse's chest, very similar to the harnesses used in the European Middle Ages. This kind of apparatus was intended for ceremonial purposes, but it was employed also on campaigns, as testified by the items captured at Vienna and Slankamen, today preserved in Vienna, Krakow and Karlsruhe. The most common colour employed was red, in all its shades, combined with gold or silver brocade; blue and turquoise harnesses are frequent also. To enhance further the decorative splendour, sometimes grey horses had their tails and lower bodies painted with red henna. Although much simpler, even the saddle covers of the cavalry were usually of fine manufacture, evidence of the high artistic level achieved by Ottoman textiles. Saddle covers from Anatolia have kept unchanged the patterns and designs of the main decorative motifs, the same ones that can still be seen today on Usak and Sivas-style carpets. Regarding size and shape, there were no established rules and only the *kapikulu* cavalry showed greater homogeneity in their saddle blankets, while with regards the colours and the decorative motifs there was no limitation other than that imposed by personal taste.

According to the saddle covers, the Ottoman saddles reproduced unchanged the same design, characterised by the rather high seat and the lightness of the

materials used, and substantially similar to the Hungarian model. The saddles, *eger* in Turkish, were made in wood, occasionally covered with leather. The horsemen used the cloak or other patches 'of bad blankets' for preparing a more comfortable seat.[62] The saddle, symbol of the cavalry, was a welcome gift among the Ottomans and to this end were manufactured types covered with metal and precious stones, quilted with *kedifè* velvet. Today, the donor and the beneficiary of some saddles are well known, such as the harness that belonged to Grand Vizier Köprülü Mustafa, a gift from Sultan Süleyman II, or the superb saddle offered to the Polish ambassador Malachowski during the Carlowitz conference.[63]

99. Mid seventeenth century saddle cover and saddle in red fabric and silver embroidery, complete with a *meç* (estoc) in gilded copper scabbard and hilt with turquoise and mother of pearl accessories. (Museum of Applied Art, Budapest)

62 Marsigli, vol. II, p.47.
63 This horse equipment became a war trophy of the Margrave Ludwig of Baden after the battle of Slankamen (1691) and today is preserved in Karlsruhe, while the second saddle is in the Wavel

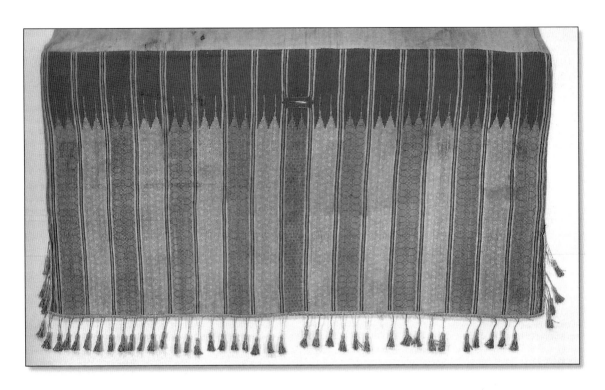

100. Saddle covers from the battlefield of Slankamen, 1691, in red fabric with yellow embroidery. (Badisches Landesmuseum, Karlsruhe)

101. A set of saddle covers in a horse-market scene, mid seventeenth century Ottoman miniature. (Private collection)

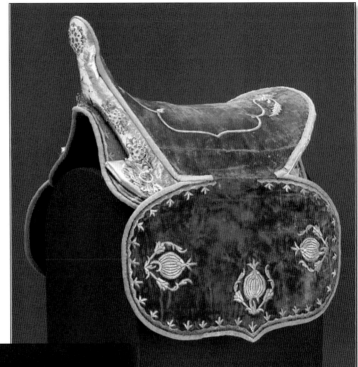

Right: 102. A very well preserved saddle in gilded copper and red fabric, with yellow gold embroidery, mid seventeenth century. (Museum of Applied Art, Budapest)

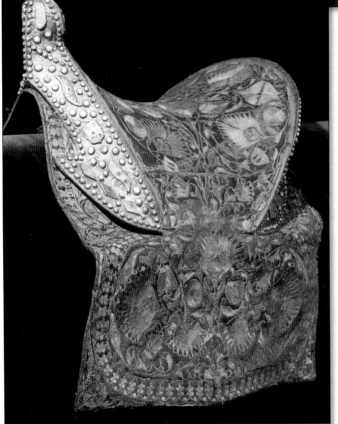

Left: 103. Ottoman saddle with gilded surface and carmine red velvet with golden decorations. (Wavel Museum, Krakow)

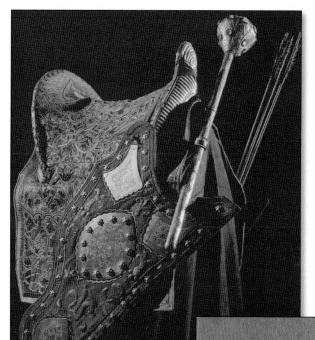

Left: 105. Allegedly the saddle of Kara Mustafa, with his war mace. (Museum of Vienna)

Right: 104. Complete Ottoman saddle and saddle cover from the Kahlenberg war spoils. (Wawel Museum, Krakow)

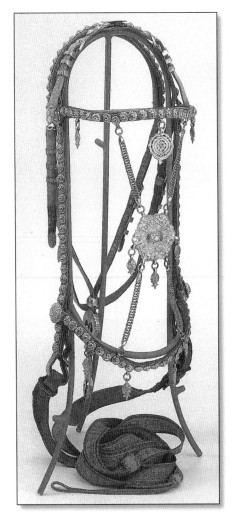

Above: 106. Bridle and reins in red leather and gilded accessories, late seventeenth century. (Badisches Landesmuseum, Karlsruhe)

Above, right: 107. Horse bridle in red leather covered with gilded metal and turquoise, captured at Vienna, 1683 and belonging to a senior Ottoman officer. (Wawel Museum, Krakow)

Cannons, Mortars and Artificial Fires

Classic works on the Ottoman army focusd on the great variety of guns employed, outlining the technological gap and the disorder caused by the attempts with which it tried to remedy them. Towards the middle of the seventeenth century cannons of calibres between 1 and 48 pounds were used, and mortars up to 100 pounds. Some gigantic stone mortars reached 400 pounds;[64] the intermediate measures were innumerable.

Recent research has contributed to provide more light on this matter.[65] The data support the notion that contrary to the general view suggested in

---

Museum of Cracow.

64 K.u.K. Kriegsarchiv, *Feldzüge des Prinzen Eugen*, vol. I, p.529.

65 Ágoston, *Guns for the Sultan*, pp.186–187. According to this authoritative work, also the research on the supposed 'metallurgical inferiority' of Ottoman cannon, which is based on the superficial assessment of random evidence, begs for re-evaluation. The author adds: 'In addition to the general problems of Orientalist and Eurocentric approaches, the literature regarding

earlier studies, the majority of guns cast in the seventeenth century in the Ottoman foundries were small and medium-calibre field guns. On the late seventeenth century, information is fairly consistent. In 1685–86 and 1693–96 are especially valuable, for they reflect the largest inventory and output figures of the foundries short before 1700. In the 1680s and 1690s, the great majority – 62–90 percent – of newly cast guns consisted of very small calibre pieces, except for 1695–96 when their proportion was only 44 percent. Medium-calibre guns were the second largest group, except again for 1695–96 when they comprised the majority with 55 percent. The proportion of large siege guns of the cannon class is surprisingly small, except for the years 1691–92. This fluctuation might partly be explained by the Ottoman practice by which large fortress guns, suitable for sieges, were mobilised during campaigns. Since most of these guns were deployed in border garrisons close to enemy territory, the difficulties of transporting large siege guns and the associated

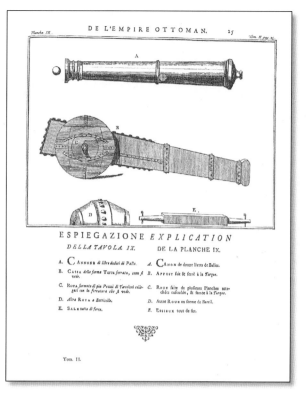

costs could somewhat be reduced by mobilising such fortress pieces.[66] While large guns remained the minority in the early eighteenth century, there is a change between the proportions of the smallest and medium-calibre pieces. The latter category had become the dominant one, medium-calibre guns comprising the majority of newly cast cannons in 1704–06, and 1712–13.

Following the experience gained in the war of 1663–64 against the Imperialists, colubrines of eight and 12 pounds were produced largely in Constantinople by the Italian founder Pietro Sardi, who set up a Western-style field artillery, but Ottoman achievements never reached the technological level of the enemy's.[67] Alongside the Italian gun caster, the Porte enlisted several 'renegades' coming from the United Provinces of the Netherlands and Germany, as well as English and French professional artillery technicians.[68]

In the mid seventeenth century, Ottoman field guns employed on the battlefield were generally single-piece cast bronze, firing stone or cast iron projectiles, and it is known that the artillery units accompanying

108. Heavy gun carriage and barrels, late seventeenth century. Note the wheel below with metal accessories to improve movement on muddy ground. After Marsigli, *Stato Militare dell'Imperio Ottomanno*. Although Ottoman sources state that the *topçu* were masters of their profession, it is rather questionable as to what kind of training they had received, especially in geometry and ballistics.

Ottoman weapons technology suffers from serious methodological deficiencies. Of these the most important are: 1 – lack of understanding of the bewildering terminology of Ottoman guns and thus of the various types of Ottoman artillery pieces; 2 – lack of any attempt to compare Ottoman and European pieces and thus failure to understand the similarities and differences between guns employed by the Ottomans and by their European adversaries; and 3 – ignorance of the rich archival material preserved in the Ottoman archives with regard to the technical characteristics of individual guns upon which more solid conclusions can be drawn.' p.62.

66 *Ibidem*, p.185.
67 K.u.K. Kriegsarchiv, *Feldzüge des Prinzen Eugen*, vol. I, p.529.
68 Ágoston, *Guns for the Sultan*, p.193.

DE L'EMPIRE OTTOMAN.   27

Planche X.

ESPIEGAZIONE *E X P L I C A T I O N*

DELLA TAVOLA X.   DE LA PLANCHE X.

A.   Cassa.   A.   Affut.

B.B.   *Forchette di ferro su cui posavano gli Ori-*   B.B.   Fourchettes de fer sur lesquelles les O-
glioni del Cannone.   rillons du Canon s'appuyoient.

109. Ottoman gun carriage, after Marsigli, *Stato Militare dell'Imperio Ottomanno*. This carriage was captured by the Imperialists during the campaign of 1686. It was one of the many failed attempts to improve the mobility of the field artillery.

expeditions carried an ammunition load of 100 balls and gunpowder for each cannon. In general, the Ottomans from the early seventeenth century tended to use guns that ranged, according the Ottoman measurement of mass-weight in *okka* (an *okka* approximately 1.29kg), from eight to 22 *okka* calibre, firing 10–27kg balls. The mobile field *kolunburna* (very similar to the classical European colubrines), was the most diffused of the Ottomans' light field guns. This kind of gun ranged between 1.5 to 7 *okka* calibre guns, which fired a 1–9kg ball.[69]

Although bronze guns were much more expensive than cast-iron pieces of the same calibre, they were considered much safer and of better quality. Since the Empire had abundant quantities of copper, the most important constituent of bronze, the Ottomans cast their large and medium-sized pieces of bronze, unlike their European opponents who used cheaper iron guns. The Ottomans used iron to cast hundreds of small pieces that weighed only 25–100 pounds and fired projectiles of about five to 16 ounces in weight, and usually issued these weapons to their river flotillas. Archival records show that the proportions of copper and tin used in the composition of Ottoman bronze cannons was similar to those cast in Europe, suggesting that the weapons themselves were of good quality.[70] On the other hand, some European contemporaries, especially the Venetians, expressed a less favourable opinion of Ottoman guns. While chemical analyses have eventually provided more precise figures, the very modest technical advances in weapon design and effectiveness before the industrial age meant that guns in 1700 were very similar to those made two centuries before.[71]

Large siege guns are referred in the Ottoman sources as *kale-kob* (from the Persian *qal'eh-kub*), however the sources also use the word *şahi* to designate the larger version of a gun. The same terms identifies also very light and small guns. Modern Turkish–Ottoman dictionaries state briefly that the *şâhî* is 'an ancient form of brass muzzle-loading cannon or an old, long field gun'.[72] They were indeed relatively long pieces, especially considering their very small calibres. Weapons inventories from the latter part of the seventeenth century list 242 and 330cm long field guns. The great majority of them were very light pieces firing shots ranging from 150 grams to 1.8kg in weight. The

---

69   *Ibidem*, p.78.
70   Ágoston, 'Firearms and Military Adaptation:The Ottomans and the European Military Revolution, 1450–1800', in *Journal of Military History*, vol. 25/1, March 2014, p.102.
71   *Ibidem*, p.104.
72   Ismail Hakkt Uzunfarjili, *Osmanl Devletinin Merkezve Bahriye Teşkilan* (Ankara, 1984), New Redhouse Turkish–English Dictionary (Istanbul, 1988), p.1045.

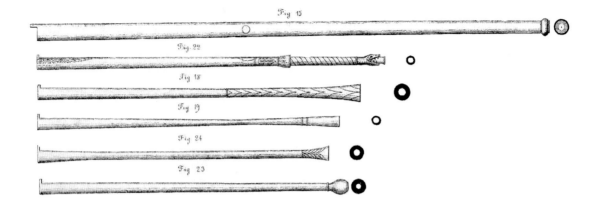

110. Seventeenth-century gun barrels of small calibres, used in the *palanka* and by the river fleet, from Ahmed Cevad's *Etat Militaire Ottoman*, 1882.

weight of these guns could have varied according to the length of the barrel. The minimum and maximum weight of the 0.5 *okka* calibre and 110cm-long *şaykas* cast in Constantinople in the early eighteenth century varied from 159 to 182kg, the average being 169kg. Several of the single *okka* calibre *şayka* guns weighed around 325–395kg, though the ones cast in 1704–05 and 1712–14 weighed considerably more, around 510 and 620kg, respectively. While the above data represent the majority of *şâhî* guns, occasionally there are larger pieces firing three and five *okka* projectiles.[73]

Saçma guns were among the smallest Ottoman field guns and often fired grapeshot. They were such small pieces that inventories usually treated them separately from other cannons. The average weight of the *saçma* guns cast in 1687–88 and in 1695–96 was around 35.6kg. The pieces cast in 1704–05 weighed around 42kg, while the pieces cast in 1697–98 were much heavier, almost 190kg each.[74] *Saçmas* were among the favourite naval guns, widely issued to the fleet of the Danube and Black Sea. Even smaller were the guns called *eynek*. Sixty-two *eynek* guns cast in 1695–96 weighed only 22.7kg on average, while those cast in 1697–98 weighed just 11.5kg. Eleven medium-sized *eynek* guns, issued to the fort of Selanik in 1659–60, fired projectiles of 150 *dirhems* (461g) in weight.[75] They were used mainly aboard ships operating on major rivers of the Empire.

The Ottomans distinguished their artillery not only in terms of tactical employment, but also regarding the projectiles. Cannon firing stone balls were common in the mid seventeenth century. According to Evliya Çelebi, 'Guns throwing stone balls that are too large to be carried by humans are called *şaykas*.' He also noted that 'such guns cannot be put on carriages and transported to campaigns but only slid on sleighs and installed at castles. No one in the world, but the Ottomans have cannon of this kind.'[76] The

73   Ágoston, *Guns for the Sultan*, pp.85–86.
74   *Ibidem*, pp.86–87.
75   *Ibidem*.
76   *Ibidem*, pp.75–76: 'These cannons were named after the şayka (Slavic *cliaika* or 'seagull') boats that were usually equipped with three guns. This seems to contradict Evliya Celebi's description of these guns as so enormous. The contradiction, however, is easily resolvable: initially şayka

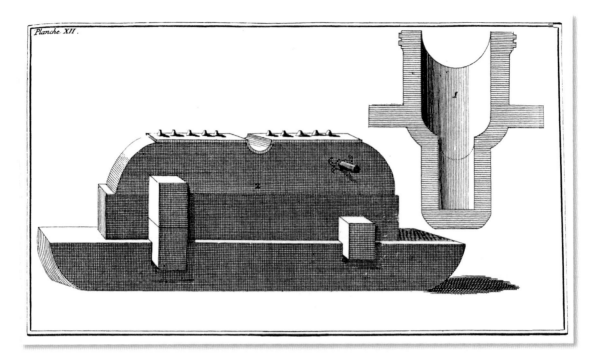

111. Ottoman gun carriage for mortar, and mortar section, after Marsigli, *Stato Militare dell'Imperio Ottomanno*.

Ottomans differentiated between large, medium-sized and small *şayka* guns, often without specifying their calibres. While in certain cases the above distinction was made according to the calibre of the piece, in other cases it was the length of the barrel that determined whether a particular piece was designated as large, medium or small. The length of the Ottoman *şaykas* also shows a great variety. The shortest pieces were 176, 198 and 264cm long, while the longest ones to be found in inventories were 396, 418, 440 and 462cm in length. In addition to these small and long pieces, the Ottoman sources also list 308, 330 and 352cm long *şaykas*. In the early eighteenth century 44 *okka* calibre *şaykas* weighed around 4,060kg, while the smaller 36 and 22 *okka* pieces weighed 3,666 and 2,707kg respectively.[77] In addition to *şaykas* deployed as siege and fortress cannons, large *şayka* guns were also used aboard Ottoman ships.

Cannons called *balyemez*, a name of uncertain origin, were another type of large siege guns, similar to the *şaykas* with which they are occasionally listed. It appears, however, that most *balyemez* guns were closer to the medium and small calibre *şaykas*. Evliya Çelebi, whose interest in curious objects and events is well known, mentioned *balyemeze*s firing shots of 25, 30, 40, 50 and 60 *okka* in weight. He also noted that there existed only four examples of the largest 60 *okka* calibre gun in the whole Empire.[78]

guns may have been used on boats sent to defend river mouths. Later they were carried from these boats into riverside forts, which enabled the Ottomans to install şayka guns of ever larger bore sizes. Archival sources also reveal that şayka guns were made with various bore sizes. Evliya Celebi, obsessed with size and numbers, mentioned only the largest pieces.'

77 *Ibidem*.
78 *Ibidem*, p.77.

Externally, there were few differences between one kind of cannon and another. The typical Ottoman cannons were free of dolphins and had a typical cylindrical shape that made aiming easier, but it greatly reduced their manageability; moreover, the metal of the barrel was of much lower quality than the one used in Western Europe.

By the mid sixteenth century, mortars were present in several major Ottoman arsenals. This indicates that by that time mortars firing bombshells had become regular weapons in siege warfare. Mortars firing explosive shells were produced in various calibres. In the 1690s the most popular ones fired explosive projectiles of 30, 43, 44 and 98kg in weight and are designated in the sources as 24-, 35-, 36-*okka* mortars. Due to their shorter barrel and thinner tube, mortars were lighter than cannons of the same calibre. The average weight of a 35 *okka* calibre mortar was 636kg in 1693–94.[79] The mortars had a shorter burst chamber than normal, and this was the cause of frequent burns and accidents among the servants. Furthermore, they were less precise due to the rudimentary systems of aiming employed. At the end of the seventeenth century, iron cannons and howitzers were also produced, but the Ottomans always tried to recycle Western material obtained by conquest or by purchase. Cannons and howitzers fired iron bullets, grapeshot and more rarely stone balls; no chained balls were used, but double balls linked by metal bars were common until the end of the seventeenth century. According to coeval testimonies, the howitzers' grenades were often defective, so much so that the same projectiles as the cannons were preferred instead; the large mortars fired stone ammunition instead. Several Ottoman large stone balls are today preserved in the courtyard of the Museum of Military History in Budapest, or a well-recommended visit would be that to the Neustädterhof palace in Vienna, at number 3 Stemgasse, where in the frontage is still incorporated a stone ball of 79 pounds, fired during the siege of 1683.

The cannons produced in the Ottoman arsenals carried decorations as *mirhab*, Koran's verses and other talismanic inscriptions on the barrel and the muzzle; sometimes a *tughra* was reproduced with the name of the sultan. Except for the mortars, positioned on carriages without wheels, the other artillery pieces were placed on wooden carriages larger than the ones normally used in the Western armies, and characterised by solid wooden wheels mounted on particularly low axles. It allowed the artillerymen to carry out in a short time an embankment for protecting the cannon and men. In this regard, Count Marsigli declared himself enthusiastic, and proposed the adoption of analogous carriages for the Imperial artillery.[80] Other cannons were fitted with barrel-shaped wheels, with metal heads nailed on the external side to facilitate grip on the ground. In the 1686 campaign in Hungary, some eight-pound pieces mounted on four-wheeled carriages appeared. They were one of the many attempts made to increase the mobility of the field artillery and to make towing operations faster. The Imperialists

---

79 *Ibidem*, pp.69–70. According to the author, the Ottoman 35 *okke* mortars were lighter than the 30-pounder European mortars that weighed 680 kg (1,500lb).
80 Marsigli, vol. II, p.23.

112. Before the battle of Batocina (1689), the Ottomans arranged some artillery pieces like the one here illustrated: 'and considering the vain attempt, the Turks retired immediately their artillery. It was an entertainment for our Imperial side to see the foolish idea and all we smiled about this stratagem.' (Marsigli, *Stato Militare dell'Imperio Ottomanno*)

captured some of these cannons, and Marsigli reproduced them in his work.[81]

However, the most singular attempt to improve the mobility of the artillery was undoubtedly the one experienced at Batocina in 1689. At the end of the battle, the Imperialists captured a dromedary with two three-pound guns placed on either side of the hump. The poor animal carried all the equipment to load the weapons, including a servant who manoeuvred the cannons by means of ropes. The brief summary released by the eyewitnesses does not include other comments.[82]

Despite the attempt to conform as much as possible to Western models, chaos continued to reign in the Ottoman artillery. The presence of the wide variation of calibres remained a constant in the sultan's armies until the second decade of the eighteenth century.

Examination of the Imperial inventories of captured guns offers idea of how the Ottomans set up their field artillery. After the battle of Zenta, 80 bronze cannons were counted, 69 of which had a three-pound calibre, two a one-pound calibre, two a four-pound calibre and three an eight-pound calibre. Four more cannons were entirely in iron and had calibres between half a pound and three pound; three of them were five-barrel organs. The list included 58 *spingarde*; among the three-pound bronze cannons, four were of Austrian origin. The use of foreign artillery material was widespread even among Christians, but the Ottomans even reused cannons cast in the sixteenth century. In 1716, after the battle of Peterwardein, among the cannons captured by the Imperialists there was a Hungarian two-pound colubrine cast in 1541, while two other cannons were dated 1565 and 1583; a three-pound cannon had been cast at Košice in 1655, while three other two- and three-pound pieces came from Austrian foundries, cast between 1681 and 1683. Finally, two cannons turned into howitzers had been produced in Austria in 1529.[83] Three months later, on the surrender of Temeşvár, out of 156 captured artillery pieces, as many as 40 were Hungarian or Austrian pieces dating back to the sixteenth and seventeenth centuries.[84]

The projectiles required by the many calibres generated a considerable confusion in the preparation of the artillery train. At the end of some

---

81 *Ibidem*, p.26.
82 K.u.K. Kriegsarchiv, *Feldzüge des Prinzen Eugen*, vol. II, p.345.
83 *Ibidem*, vol. XVI, pp.285–287. See details in the appendix.
84 *Ibidem*, p.207

encounters, carts of ammunition loaded with balls from all calibres remained in the hands of the enemy, without taking into account the actual presence of the relative guns.[85]

Horses were rarely used for the train; in most cases oxen were exploited for this task for both cannons and ammunition wagons, with consequent negative consequences on the speed of march. In 1715, on the narrow streets of the Peloponnese, it was necessary to employ up to 18 pairs of oxen for the siege artillery park, but despite this, 'it was only possible to proceed slowly and with fatigue.'[86] The Ottoman infantry used different types of hand grenade. Montecuccoli reported the use of 'fireballs' in the war of 1661–64.[87] These consisted of a mixture of pitch and straw. Later, versions were produced in Western imitation, in metal, in glass and in clay, all provided with a trigger for the fuse, but whose effectiveness left much to be desired. On the other hand, the more artisanal leather bags, filled with gunpowder and pieces of metal, proved to be particularly fearful. The Ottoman infantrymen would have used them for the first time during the siege of Buda in 1686, demonstrating considerable skill when they threw it from the ramparts.[88]

Further flammable devices were formed by a metal case filled with bitumen, sulphur and other flammable substances. These weapons were usually attached to poles and were used to set fire to the wooden fortifications and the palisades. Iron pots filled with bitumen and hung on the walls, were also used to light the terrain in case of attacks. Among the fireworks devised to shed light there were also simple mixture balls, grates with straw and bitumen and canvas lanterns supported by poles. All these variations were successfully used in 1693, to repulse the Imperialists' night assault at the covered way of the fortress of Belgrade.[89] A canvas lantern attached to a pole was used to illuminate the night marches.

During the siege of Érsekúivár in 1663, Montecuccoli recalled the use of 'noisome fumes' by the Ottoman artillery.[90] This device would constitute a unique case, and probably it was an experiment abandoned in subsequent years. However, in 1711, some records refer again to the use of this kind of expedient during the Pruth campaign.[91]

Ensigns

The variety of Ottoman ensigns is very large in terms of shapes, sizes and colours. There are in fact banners of rectangular shape, as well as rectangular pointed, triangular, double-pointed and trapezoidal-cut banners; the most used colours were carmine, scarlet, purple, green, yellow and white, alone

85 *Ibidem*, vol. I, p.530.
86 Brue, *Journal*, p.42.
87 Montecuccoli, 'Discorso della guerra contro il Turco in Ungheria', in Luraghi, *Opere di Raimondo Montecuccoli*, vol. II, p.210.
88 D'Aste, 'Diario dell'Assedio di Buda', in Piacentini, *Diario*, p.158, and Marsigli, vol. II, p.34.
89 Montecuccoli, in Luraghi, vol. II, p.210.
90 *Ibidem*, p.475.
91 M. Cazacu, 'I Veleni degli Zar', in *Storia & Dossier*, IV-35, 1989, pp. 43–49.

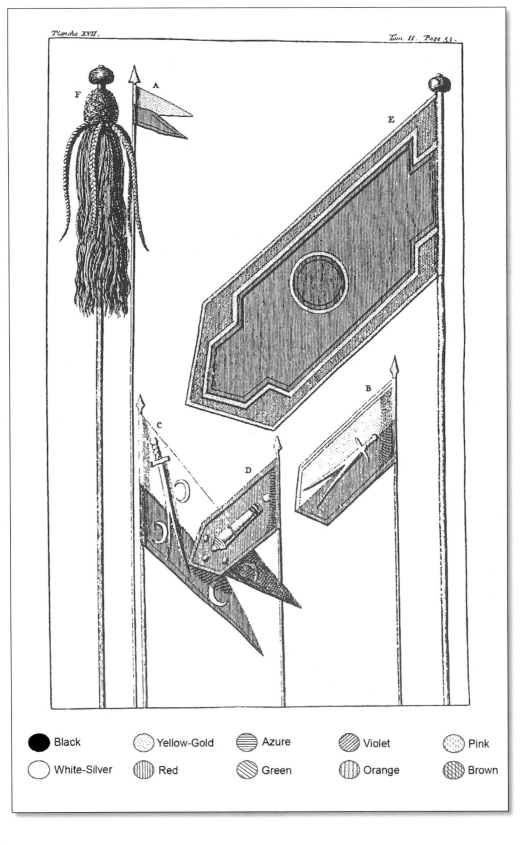

Planche XVII.

Tom. II. Page 53.

Black

White-Silver

Yellow-Gold

Red

Azure

Green

Violet

Orange

Pink

Brown

Facing page: 113. Illustration from the second volume of Marsigli's *Stato Militare dell'Imperio Ottomanno*, depicting some Ottoman *sancak* ensigns, *bayrak* pennants and a *tugh* horsetail. The simplification of the decorative motives compromise accuracy, but well represent the essential appearance of the Ottoman field ensigns. A) Little pennant fastened to the *kapikulu* cavalry lances. B) Janissary flag. C) Provincial cavalry standards. D) *Topçu* artillery standard. E) Flag for *paşas* and viziers. F) *Tughs* or horsetails.

or in multiple combinations. Equally important are the symbols depicted, the inscriptions, the disposition and the richness of the decorative elements, which contribute to qualifying the importance of the ensign.[92] In fact, the right to display a flag was closely linked to the hierarchy and the actual name of the flag, *sancak*, was an explicit allusion. Each army detachment and each unit received its own *sancak*, while the smaller units received small-sized banners, the *bayrak*, closely related to the tactical division of the military corps. *Beglerbeg*, *paşa* and *sancakbeg* each had their own banners, with which they led their contingents; other flags belonged to the janissaries' *orta*, the artillerymen and the *sipahis* of the *kapikulu*.

During marches or in action, the banners of every order and rank occupied the first line of the deployment. In the encampments, the ensigns were hoisted to a pole into the ground or fixed to the tents. The impression aroused by the spectacular mass of colours of a marching Ottoman army, shines through the words of the Count of Coligny, commander of the French expeditionary corps at the battle of Szentgotthárd: 'Now we saw masses of people walking, a moment later a multitude of horsemen and then always new units, each with innumerable and different flags, banners and small ensigns with all the colours imaginable. And even if those masses advanced without order and rule, we saw in that disorder a charm that enchanted us.'[93]

Very often, the lances of the cavalry had small ensigns or long coloured flames, which would seem to have an identifying function. For some commenters, this peculiarity constituted instead a trick to make the adversaries believe that they had a force superior to reality. During the siege of Vienna, to cite the most emblematic events, small ensigns were attached to cannons, wagons and even to the horns of draught animals: in war there were no limits to the stratagem.[94]

Following the hierarchical order of the banners used in battle by the Ottoman armies, in first place is undoubtedly the sacred flag of the Prophet, the *sancak-i serifi* or the *al-rāyat al-'uqāb*, 'the banner of the eagle'. Around this flag circulated numerous tales, including the one concerning its capture, which took place in Vienna on 12 September 1683. The Polish soldiers of Jan Sobieski sent it to Rome, to exhibit the trophy in St Peter's, but instead the alleged *'uqāb* was hung from a nave of the church of S. Giovanni in Laterano. The flag remained in the church until the early eighteenth century, and then lost. In reality, the true banner of the Prophet had been saved and even after other defeats, although in a daring manner, the Ottomans always succeeded

---

92 Zigulsky, *Ottoman Art*, p.25.
93 'Relation of Count Couligny-Sovigny to the King of France, 1664', in Eickoff, *Venedig. Wien und die Osmanen*', p.228.
94 Marsigli, vol. II, p.51.

114. Large *sancak* with zulfiqar sword, inscriptions and crescents, captured at Vienna, 1683. This is one of the larger Ottoman seventeenth century ensigns (460x240 cm) in excellent condition and still preserved. It was manufactured in Constantinople, or perhaps in Baghdad. Wawel Museum, Krakow. See the following illustration for a more detailed analysis.

in bringing it to safety. It cannot be established with certainty whether the ancient religious relics belonged to the sultans were actually the flag of Muhammad; in any case, the longevity of certain oriental artefacts is surprising and no concrete proof has ever been exhibited to refute this statement.[95] When Western sources (and even Turkish ones) describe the *'uqāb* they mention a 'green flag', without describing size, shape or other elements and representations of the field; the same Marsigli, while quoting it many times, declared that he had never seen it. The reference to the green colour was due to the linen case in which the flag was enclosed, or rather a part of it, since, as the chronicles relate, when the fabric began to deteriorate, the *uqab* was cut into three pieces, resulting into three new *sancaks*.[96] One flag remained along with the other relics of the Prophet in the Topkapı palace, another accompanied the sovereign in all his travels, and finally the third one was destined for the army. It can therefore be said that the *'uqāb* looked more like a small cylinder than a real flag, and this certainly served to save it from capture.[97] The sacred *sancak* was intrusted to the grand viziers upon the assumption of the command of an army, through a ceremonial complex in which the grand mufti and the sultan participated.

The ordinary ensigns of the Ottoman army can be divided into three categories based on the elements depicted on the field. The subdivision allows us to establish some rules to identify the hierarchy and the usage. The first category includes the *sancaks* bearing only inscriptions, usually of a religious nature and in Arabic. Text and words came mostly from the Koran; otherwise the artisans used the traditional *hadiths*, the mottoes of the Prophet,

---

95 Zigulski, *Ottoman Art*, p.18.
96 *Ibidem, Silhitar tarihi*, p.20.
97 *Ibidem*, p.24. In 1938, the Turkish art historian Kurtoglu Fevzi examined the treasures contained in the Topkapı palace, including the sacred flag. Inside a huge cage of silver bars, Kurtoglu found a basket covered with velvet. Inside it, under many layers of fabric, there was a small flag of green silk with a crimson satin stripe and a Koranic inscription with calligrams dating back to the seventeenth century. Linked to this flag, there was a green taffeta bag containing fragments of black wool. Very probably, it was the remains of the famous *'uqab*, transferred from Syria or Egypt, to Constantinople during the reign of Süleyman the Magnificent.

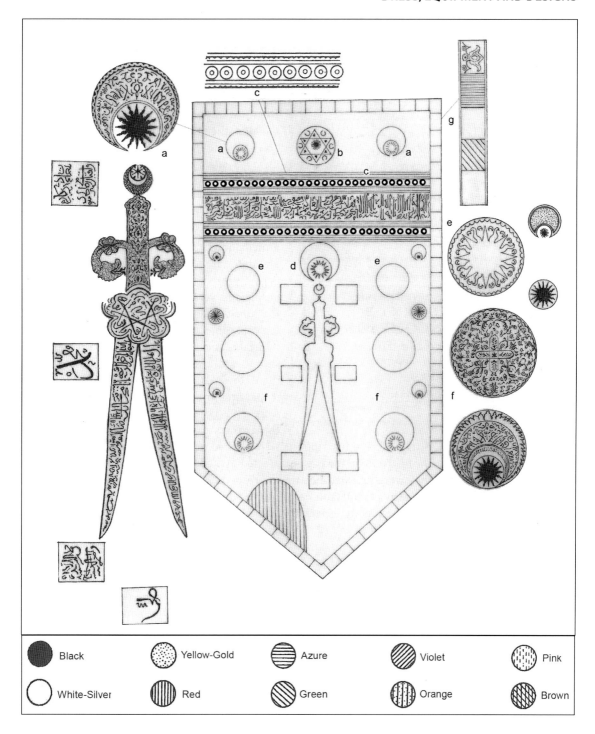

	Black		Yellow-Gold		Azure		Violet		Pink
	White-Silver		Red		Green		Orange		Brown

115. Large *sancak* (see previous illustration). Background in carmine-red silk; the two crescents above (a) are embroidered in dark red silk on silver brocade; Solomon's seal (b) is embroidered in dark red on carmine red; the edges of the inscription (c) are in azure with little red spheres and white stripes separated by a black weave motive on carmine red. The inscription, the *zulfiqar* sword, the medaillons, and the crescent (d) are in dark red. The great stars above (e) are in azure on carmine red; the globes and the crescents framed below (f) are both in red on silver. The border floral motive (g) is carmine red on white. (Author's illustration)

Difegno dello STENDARDO del Primo Vifire
Leuato fotto VIENNA dal Sereniſsimo, & Inuittiſsimo

GIOVANNI TERZO RE' DI POLONIA,
E DA SVA MAESTA' MANDATO ALLA SANTITA' DI NOSTRO SIGNORE

PAPA INNOCENZO VNDECIMO,

Aggiuntaui la vera interpretatione delle parole Arabiche, che in detto Stendardo
fono artificiofamente inteffute.

Del Reuerendiſs. Padre Lodouico Maracci della Congregatione della Madre di Dio,
Confeſſore di Noſtro Signore.

ALL' EMINENTISSIMO, E REVERENDISSIMO
SIG. CARDINALE
GIROLAMO BONCOMPAGNO
Arciuefcouo di Bologna, e Principe
del Sacro Romano Imperio.

IN ROMA, ET IN BOLOGNA,

Per Giacomo Monti, MDCLXXXIII. Con licenza de' Superiori.

116. Print depicting the alleged 'Sacrd Standard' captured at Vienna and presented to pope Innocent XI by Jan Sobieski in 1683.

to formulate short slogans. The words evoked the true essence of faith and recalled the prohibition against all forms of idolatry, a fixed point of the Sunni doctrine, and with their elegant and monumental form they enchanted the faithful.[98] The most important of the inscriptions was the *shahàda*, the profession of faith of the Muslims: أشهد أن لا إله إلا الله أشهدأو الله الإ اله ال نأ رسول الله (*la ilàha illa Alláh, Muhammadun rásul Alláh*: there is no other god than Allah and Muhammad is the Prophet). The inscriptional ensign could also carry short invocations or only the name of Allah, composed in elegant calligrams forming a medallion.[99] Texts of non-Koranic derivation are quite rare, but on one of the most beautiful flags captured in Vienna in 1683, appear some auspicious verses addressed to the owner of the *sancak*.[100] The inscriptional style, clear and logical, came from the ancient insignia used by Islam, and for a certain period it remained simple and austere even in the Ottoman area; then, towards the early seventeenth century, it became more sophisticated. The writings were ever larger and more elaborate, forcing the artisans to set up a special compositional discipline. The inscriptions were applied on the *sancak* in different ways on the field and on the edges, collected in medallions or cartridges; on the verso they were repeated inverted to respect the symmetry of the decoration. In the early seventeenth century it tended to elaborate the writings more and more frequently, especially the *tughra*, the monograms with the name of the sultan. Still in the same years, it was the calligraphic style *sulu*, originated from the Iranian *naskhi* style, characterised by wide rounded signs. In general, the *sancak* of the inscriptional type belonged to the major officials of the Empire and to the sultan himself. The *sancaks* of the monarch were normally of enormous size; the Ottomans called these flags *alem-i padisàhi* (standard of the sultan), or *alem-i osmani* (Ottoman standard), which accompanied the sultan on the war campaign. The Ottoman chronicles report that when occurred the enthronement of a new sultan, seven flags were made with the embroidered monogram on the field.[101] However, based on the examples today preserved, there is not always evidence in this regard;

---

98 *Ibidem*, p.33.

99 Among the favourite verses, those of sura 48 of the Koran, *surat al-fatah* (the Victory), are found quite often. Equally appreciated are the verses of sura 61, *surat as-saff* (the Battle), in particular verse 13: *nasrun min Allahi wa-fathun qarihun wabashshiri lmu'minì* (the help of God and a easy victory proclaims glad news for the faith).

100 See the flag preserved in the Wavel Museum of Cracow, inventory n. 3981.

101 *Silihtar tarihi*, in Zigulski, *Ottoman Art*, p.20.

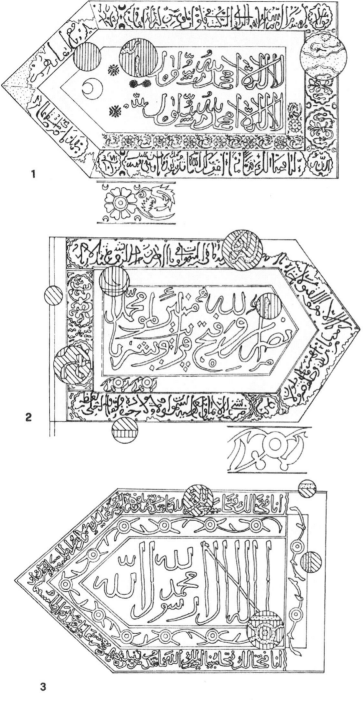

1

2

3

117. Three large inscriptional *sancaks*.

1) Ensign captured at Vienna by the Poles in 1683. The *shahad* text appears twice in the main camp, while on the edge is reproduced a fragment of *sura* 48, 'the Victory'. The floral decorations are in dark red brocade silk with gilded filaments (the particular is magnified to the left); size 374x178cm (Wawel Museum, Krakow).

2) Ensign captured at the battle of Slankamen in 1691, by the Imperial general Federigo Veterani, who sent it to his native town of Urbino. The particular of the decorative design is reproduced to the right; size 395x186cm (Urbino Cathedral Museum).

3) Ensign captured at Parkany, 1683; size 325x167cm (Heeresgeschichtliches Museum, Vienna)

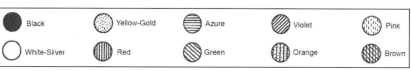

● Black	⦿ Yellow-Gold	⊖ Azure	◍ Violet	◉ Pink
○ White-Silver	▥ Red	◈ Green	▨ Orange	◍ Brown

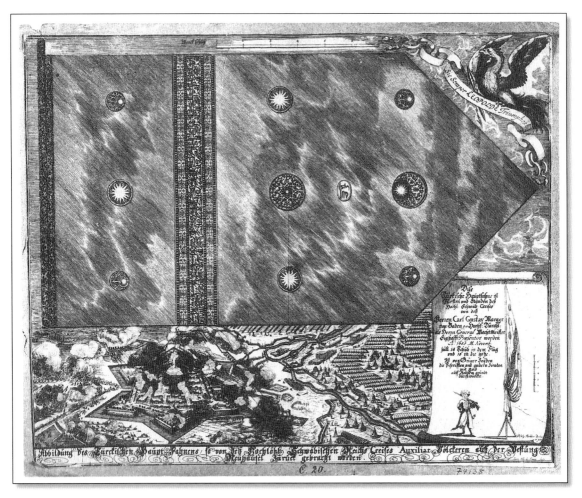

118. The large *sancak* captured at Vienna by the Swabian troops. The image suggests a green background with silver or golden symbols. Note at bottom right, the size comparison with the human figure.

in some cases, the attribution of a flag to the sultan is identifiable by the inscription engraved on the top of the pole, or more often by its enormous dimensions. Even with regard to the colours, information does not coincide at all. For some scholars the colour of the sultan would have been white, while on the other hand red, yellow and green *sancaks* are frequent. Some miniatures, albeit in a conventional way, show the sultans accompanied by seven flags of red, green, white, and red combined with yellow and green.[102]

When the army marched on campaign, the seven *sancaks* of the sultan preceded in the hierarchy the ensigns of viziers, *beglerbegs*, *paşas*, and *sancakbegs*. However, these were the flags carried in battle and which today are preserved in numerous collections outside Turkey, as they constituted most of the trophies lost on the battlefield. Based on their colours and the testimonies of eyewitnesses, it is possible to assume that the grand vizier used green ensigns, *beglerbegs* and *paşas* had crimson, and the *sancakbegs* scarlet. Frequently, it

---

102 *Ibidem*, p.25. The Turkish art historian Nur Ruza attempted a systematic investigation of the 158 Ottoman flags and standards preserved in different collections. Although he has not defined the symbolism and hierarchy of the ensigns, Nur lists the following colours in order of frequency: green, red, yellow, white, blue and purple.

happened that edges and decorative elements of different colours were added to the ensign, resulting in a particularly wide variety of combinations.

Regarding their size, the variety is even bigger. There are generally flags of considerable size, such as *sancaks* of 470cm in length and 270 in height; in most cases their shape is trapezoidal. Because of their large size, they were hoisted to a pole planted in the ground in the centre of the encampment, or on the tower of a fortress.

Along with the inscriptional type, a series of symbols representing the sky and the other astral elements also developed. The ensigns depicting figurative elements constitute the second category of *sancak*; those formed simultaneously by inscriptions and symbols belong to the third and last category.

The most famous of the astral symbols, destined to become the Ottoman heraldic symbol par excellence in the nineteenth century, was undoubtedly the crescent, or half-moon. The crescent had ancient origins and probably derived from the symbol of the horns, known by the peoples of Central Asia already 1,000 years before our era. Another explanation about its adoption by the Ottomans can be found in the crescent engraved on Byzantine coins starting from the fourth century AD.[103] Originally, the crescent symbolised the moon deity and later assumed the meaning of royalty; in the Islamic world it was enriched with other meanings, such as the imprint of the Prophet's horse.

Apart from all these explanations, the crescents depicted on the Ottoman flags are of two types. The first is very similar to a new moon in the first quarter, and is then called 'open crescent'; the other appears as the eccentric conjunction of two circles, in which the smaller one touches the circumference of the larger, and in this case it takes the denomination 'closed crescent'. The latter type is the most common, in the form associated with one or more stars, and abounds on the Ottoman flags until the twentieth century. Even the star, together with the crescent or alone, appears in a great variety of forms. The astral symbol par excellence, in the Islamic world the star represented the eye of God, in particular when it was formed by the crossing of two equilateral triangles. In that form it was also known as the seal of Solomon and identified the concept of royalty. In other case, the star presented eight tips, the result of the conjunction of two squares, but these were rarer. The last astral symbol used on the Ottoman *sancaks* was the *czintamani*, consisting of three diskettes similar to three closed crescents, arranged in a triangle with the tip pointing upwards. No explanation of its meaning has yet been identified; according to some theories, it would imitate the leopard's fur, while other scholars identify the Central Asian shamanic signs symbolising the domination on the three elements of the world: earth, air and water.[104] The Ottomans introduced the *czintamani* on their *sancaks* starting from the second half of the seventeenth century.

The use of astral symbols on flags would seem to follow hierarchical rules. In general these images appear on the *sancak* issued to the single units, such as the janissary *ortas*, but in some cases, above all the crescent, they are

---

103 The sultans considered themselves the heirs of the Eastern Roman Empire and therefore adopted the symbols and colours of their predecessors.
104 Zigulski, *Ottoman Art*, p.41.

formed by inscriptions, or enclose the calligrams on the large banners of the *paşas*. From a territorial point of view, the astral symbols are usual on the ensigns coming from every province of the Empire, among these the crescent was common on the *sancaks* of the navy and of the Northern African states. A figurative symbol often adopted in the army's flag was the double-bladed sword, the *dhu al-fiqàr* (Zulfikar), commonly known as 'the sword of the Prophet' or also 'the sword of the janissaries'. In the sixteenth century the first depictions of Zulfikar began to appear on the army's ensigns and from the following century the favour of the Ottomans towards this image increased considerably. The representative style followed two main trends: a traditional one, with a straight bifid blade; the other depicted the Zulfikar with curved blades like a sabre. Often the final knob had the appearance of a dragon's head or the shape of a crescent; at other times the hilt ended in a snake" head. Zulfikar was widely represented on the *kapikulu*'s flags, especially the infantry; the most used colours were red on yellow and vice versa; on some fine *sancaks*, the sword appears entirely formed by inscriptions.[105]

Each janissary *orta* carried its *sancak* in battle, while the tents were decorated with different symbols and colours to identify the unit. Some drawings are extremely realistic and natural, contravening the strict rules on Islamic figurative art, and allow the easy recognition of the *orta* to which they belong. Some symbols allude explicitly to the unit when it represent the original task or qualification assumed. Therefore, the dog is the symbol of *orta* 71, *samsoncu*, and the dromedary identifies *orta* 1, the *deveci*, originally tasked with escorting the army baggage. The same symbols were tattooed on the hand or on the forearm of the soldiers; instead, on the flags, appeared more easily the crescent, the Zulfikar, or combinations of two or three colours arranged in various patterns. The janissary corps had a further and singular symbol that distinguished them, the *kazan*, the cauldron that was carried in parade in all ceremonies and preceded by the *asci* of the *orta*.

Other *kapikulu*'s *sancaks* are described by Marsigli and La Mottraye. The latter witnessed a parade of the *ulùfely sipahis* with yellow, red, white and green standards.[106] The first two ensigns belonged to the two wings into which the corps was subdivided, while the others identified the two subdivisions of the left wing; but unfortunately the authors give us no description concerning the symbols depicted. All the lances carried flames with the same colours previously mentioned or combinations of the same. Other authors report different information about the *sancaks* carried by the *sipahis*. They describe six 'banners', of which the first four were identical to the ones mentioned by La Mottraye, plus one with white and green bands and another in white and red. Their belonging to the various units of the *kapikulu* cavalry corresponds only in part to the other direct sources.[107]

---

105 See the two *sancaks* captured at Vienna, with inscriptional Zulfiqars preserved in the Museum of the Royal Castle of Wavel, Inventory n. 859 and 3981.

106 La Mottraye, *Voyages*, vol. I, p.243.

107 H.D. Oldhafer. 'Die Osmanischen Sipahis', in *1683, die neue Mölkerbastei*, 4/82, pp.9–10. A similar article by the same author appears in *Gorget and Sash* vol. II, n. 22. Oldhafer attributes the yellow banner to the *silihtar* squadron, the green and white-green ones to the right and left

119. Three plates of Marsigli's *Stato Militare dell'Imperio Ottomanno* portray 162 ensigns and symbols of the janissary *ortas*. Despite the conventional style of the illustrations, the plates show the principal details and the colour of the flags, notwithstanding the absence of decorations and symbols.

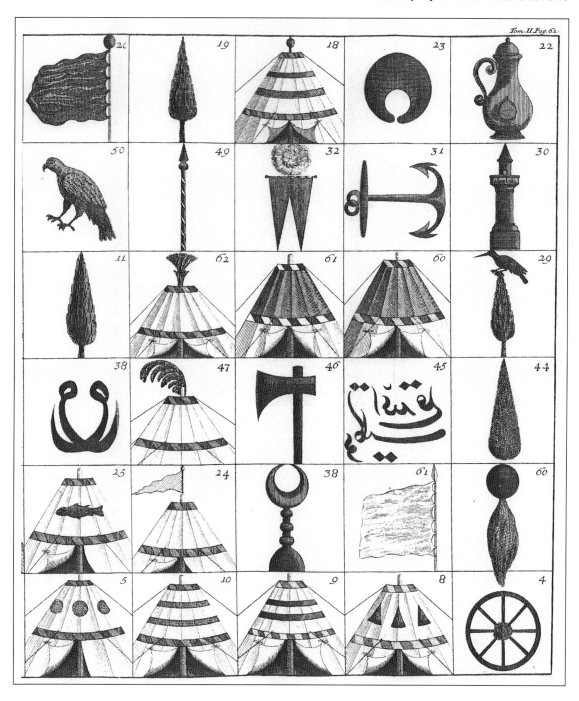

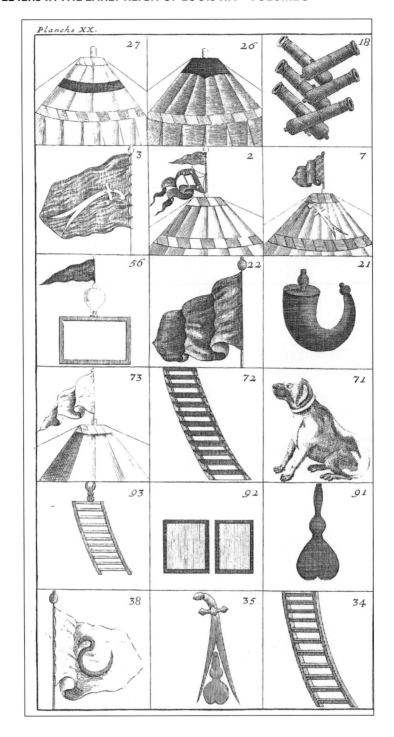

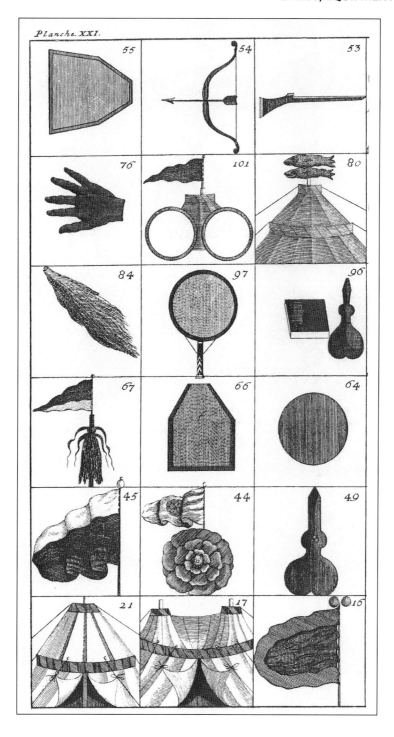

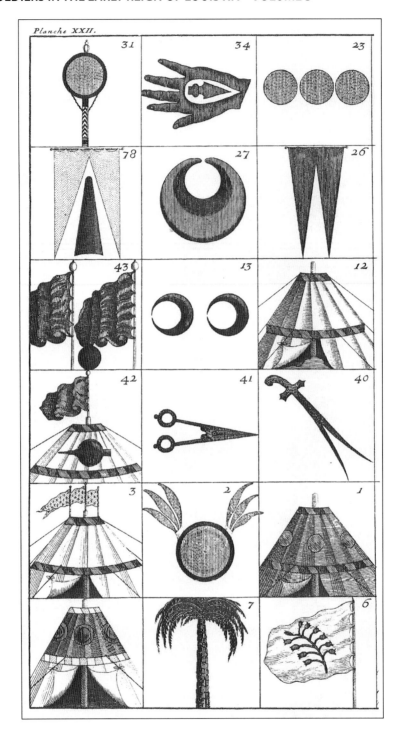

120. Late seventeenth century *tugh* horsetails coming from the battlefield of Vienna. (Wawel Museum, Krakow)

In the second volume of Marsigli's work, some ensigns are represented, including the flag of the *topçu*, and others belonging to the provincial cavalry, as well as to the *paşa* and *beglerbeg*. Although the design denotes a conventional style, the artillery *sancak* and the one of the janissaries show some details of the field, such as a cannon and the Zulfiqar sword, including colours and the shape of the pole with the accessories. Until the end of the seventeenth century the pole ended with a golden metal tip in the shape of an inverted heart, on which were inscribed texts in Arabic. Equally widespread, another pole had a metal globe at the top. As the years progressed, the latter completely replaced the pole in the shape of a heart. Some testimonies affirmed that a copy of the Koran was kept inside the globe, and for this purpose small copies of the Holy Book were produced, called *sancak mushafa*.[108] All the *sancaks* were rolled up on their poles, protected by a green canvas, and unfolded only in parade or before the battle.

The variety of colours and shape of the Ottoman flags had as a counterpoint the substantial uniformity of the most typical ensign, the *tugh*, also known in the West as a 'horsetail'. The kinship of the Ottoman *tugh* with the similar Mongolian and Chinese ensigns is evident and a suggestive interpretation of their meaning, the image of a spirit with a face reflecting the sun's rays and framed by a long beard,[109] evokes religious symbols of the shamanic world of Central Asia. A large number of Ottoman *tughs* dating back to the seventeenth and eighteenth centuries are preserved in Turkish museums and in those of the countries that were enemies of the Porte.[110] The classic *tugh* consists of two parts. The larger upper part is a long wooden pole with a gilded metal ball on the top, three or four circular brush-

wings, the white *sancak* to the *gureba* of the right wing, and the white-red to the *gureba* of the left wing. The red banner is generally assigned to the *sipahi* corps. Unfortunately, the author does not mention the sources from which his information comes. However, this could be a misinterpretation of Ottoman texts, translated into German in the nineteenth century.

108 Zygulski, *Ottoman Art*, p.32.

109 *Ibidem*, p.83.

110 *Ibidem*, pp.84 and 89. There are 67 *tughs* still existing dating back to the seventeenth and eighteenth centuries.A further 25 *tughs* are preserved in the Topkapı museum and another 10 in the Askeri museum. Six *tughs* are in the Magyar Nemzeti Muzeum (Hungarian National Museum) and in the Honved Tòrteneti Muzeum (Military History Museum of Budapest). Single *tughs* are preserved in Dresden, Karlsruhe and Ingolstadt; a further eight are in the Viennese collections and the same number are preserved in Venice. Six *tughs* belong to the Polish museums of Cracow, Czestochowa and Poznan. A fine *tugh*, perhaps belonging to the *levend* of the Ottoman navy, is preserved in the Danish National Museum of Copenhagen, donated to

121. This pavilion belonged to the Ottoman *serasker* Caffer Ismail, captured by the Venetians in 1686, depicted in a coeval Tuscan chronicle,. The tents in the centre are in medium green and the curtain are in pink. (After Cassigoli Collection; Florence, Biblioteca Nazionale Centrale)

like layers of horsetail beneath, and four or six falling braids; the baluster-shaped stem is covered with intricate and colourful horsehair plaitwork, while in the middle there is a loosely falling black, white, red or green horsetail. The stem is in the lower part. It is covered with the same plaitwork, is hollow and reinforced at the bottom with a metal band. Altogether the tugh could measure between 200 and 350cm. In the *tughs* still existing, the metallic globe is never perfectly spherical, its shape being oval, slightly flattened at the top, or onion-like.[111]

Like flags and standards, the *tughs* were also assigned to the various military units. Each janissary *orta*, as well as *cebeci* and the two divisions of the *ulùfely sipahis* received one *tugh* and during the march they carried it at the head of the column. More than the *sancak*, the *tugh* served to establish

the king by Admiral Cort Adler, who participated in the Cretan War in 1667 as commander of a naval squadron.

111 The Vienna *Waffensammlung* has a splendid example of a pendulous *tugh* that is often wrongly described as being Ottoman. This *tugh* is crested with boars' teeth in crescent-like form but the decoration of the metal mounting, with small human figures, is surely the work of European hands. This imitation was commissioned by Archduke Ferdinand of the Tirol, in the late sixteenth century. It is well known that the Ottoman symbols have sometimes been misinterpreted, and in fact this *tugh* had been wrongly represented as Ottoman in Osprey Man-At-Arms Series n. 140, *Armies of the Ottoman Turks, 1300–1774.*

the rank of the owner. As discussed in another chapter, the *ulùfely sipahis* marched with seven *tughs* when the sultan was present and with five if the command of the army belonged to the grand vizier. Their *tughs* were the highest and in the encampment they were planted in the ground in front of the commander's tent. Four *tughs* signalled the presence of a vizier, three for a *beglerbeg* or *paşa* and only one for the *sancakbeg*. When the call to arms were announced, the *tughs* fluttered on the towers of the governors' palaces. A single *tugh* was also assigned to the *yeniceri ağasi*, but in war marched preceded by the *çavuş basi* who carried the *melala*, a torch of resinous wood, symbolising its function as head of the messengers.

The *tugh* was the actual war ensign of the Ottoman army and therefore used across the Empire. The Egyptian Mamluk *begs* carried *tughs* like the Ottoman ones, as did the Tatar *han*. Also the princes of the vassal states, such as Transylvania, Wallachia and Moldavia, had their own *tughs* when they joined the Ottoman army on campaign.

Appendix

Tabular Data and Orders of Battle

Succession of the Grand Viziers, 1645–1718

Semin Mehmed Paşa	1644–1645
Defterdar Salih Paşa	1645–1647
Kapdan Musa Paşa	1647
Hezarpâre Ahmed Paşa	1647–1648
Sofu Mehmed Paşa	1648–1649
Kara Murad Paşa	1649–1650
Melek Ahmed Paşa	1650–1651
Siyavuş Paşa	1651
Gürcü Mehmed Paşa	1651–1652
Tarhoncu Ahmed Paşa	1652–1653
Kapdan Derviş Ahmed Paşa	1653–1654
Ibşir Mustafa Paşa	1654–1655
Kara Murad Paşa (2nd term)	1655
Ermeni Süleyman Paşa	1655–1656
Gazi Deli Hüseyin Paşa	1656
Zurnazen Mustafa Paşa	1656
Siyavuş Paşa (2nd term)	1656
Boynueğri Mehmed Paşa	1656
Köprülü Mehmed Paşa	1656–1661
Köprülü Ahmed Paşa	1661–1676
Merzifonlu Kara Mustafa Paşa	1676–1683
Kara Ibrahim Paşa	1683–1685
Sari Süleyman Paşa	1685–1687
Siyavuş Paşa (3rd term)	1687–1688
Nisançi Ismail Paşa	1688
Tekfurdağli Bekri Mustafa Paşa	1688–1689
Köprülü Mustafa Paşa	1689–1691
Arabaci Ali Paşa	1691–1692
Çalik Ali Paşa	1692–1693
Biyikli Mustafa Paşa	1693–1694
Sürmeli Ali Paşa	1694–1695
Elmas Mohammed Paşa	1695–1697
Amucazâde Hüseyin Paşa	1697–1702
Daltaban Mustafa Paşa	1702–1703

Rami Mehmed Paşa	1703
Kavanos Ahmed Paşa	1703
Morali Enişte Hassan Paşa	1703–1704
Kalaylokoz Ahmed Paşa	1704
Baltaci Mehmed Paşa	1704–1706
Çorlulu Ali Paşa	1706–1710
Köprülü Numan Paşa	1710
Baltaci Mehmed Paşa (2nd term)	1710–1711
Ağa Yusuf Paşa	1711–1712
Silihtar Abaza Süleyman Paşa	1712–1713
Hoca Ibrahim Paşa	1713
Damad Ali Paşa	1713–1716
Haci Bostançi Halil Paşa	1716–1717
Kayserily Nişanci Mehmd Paşa	1717–1718

Army Expenditure, 1687–1701

Source: G. Ágoston, *Ottoman Warfare in Europe, 1453–1826*, p.138.

Fiscal year	Salaried Troops (*kapikulu*)	Garrisons (*serhaddkulu*)	Total	Salary (*akçe*)	% total exp.
1687–1688	58,974	?	?	440,431,988	48.88
1690–1691	69,247	?	?	458,474,172	56.40
1691–1692	59,956	74,280	134,236	495,379,604	52.13
1692–1693	62,593	70,351	132,944	503,172,351	54.75
1693–1694	79,786	?	?	527,255,974	57.17
1695–1695	114,012	75,971	189,983	640,013,576	58.15
1696–1697	107,403	77,168	184,571	603,990,096	55.09
1698–1699	103,913	86,395	190,308	668,041,167	55.14
1700–1701	81,853	87,310	169,163	636,569,460	57.35

Kapikulu – Permanent Troops (1652–1712)

Source: G. Ágoston, 'Ottoman military organization (up to 1800)', p.4.

Date	Janissary (and *cebeci*)	Artillery	Cavalry	TOTAL
1652	55,151	7,246	20,479	82,876
1654	51,047	6,905	19,844	77,796
1660–1661	55,150	7,246	?	?
1661–1662	54,222	6,498	15,248	75,697
1665–1666	20,467	?	?	?
1666–1667	47,233	?	?	?
1669–1670	39,470	8,014	14,070	61,544

Date	Janissary (and *cebeci*)	Artillery	Cavalry	TOTAL
1694–1695	78,798	21,824	13,395	114,017
1696–1697	69,260	14,726	15,217	99,563
1698–1699	67,729	15,470	13,447	96,646
1700–1701	42,119	11,485	13,043	66,647
1701–1702	39,925	10,893	12,999	63,817
1702–1703	40,139	10,010	12,976	63,125
1704–1705	52,642	11,851	17,133	81,626
1710–1711	43,562	5,510	15,625	64,687
1712	36,383	?	?	?

Janissary Strength
Source: G. Ágoston, *Ottoman Warfare in Europe, 1453–1826*, p.135.

1660–61	1665	1669	1670	1680
54,222	49,566	51,437	49,868	54,222

Garrisons in Kanisza and Érsekúivár (1652–1665)
Source: Mark L. Stein, *Guarding the Frontier. Ottoman Border Forts and Garrisons in Europe* (London, New York NY: Tauris Academic Studies, 2007), pp.109 and 112–113.

Kanisza	1652	1653	1655	1657–58
çavuş	3	3	3	3
mehter	6	6	6	6
top arabaci	7	7	7	7
cebeci	25	25	25	25
janissaries	64	74	83	147
hisar erler	87	87	87	87
topçu	89	89	89	89
azab	826	829	849	692
cavalry	625	624	624	625
religious officials	17	17	17	-

Érsekúivár	1664	1665
çavuş	4	16
kátib	4	5
cebeci	14	13
martolos	22	21

Érsekúivár	1664	1665
janissaries	80	165
cavalry	81	100
topçu	6	13
hisar erler	108	96
azab	120	123
gönüllü	154	248
religious officials	6	14
river fleet sailors	30	24

Toprakli – Provincial Cavalry Strength

Sources: L.F. Marsigli, *Stato Militare dell'Imperio Ottomanno*, vol. I, pp.104–132.

The data refer to the contingents recruited by the provinces and come from the work of Count Luigi Ferdinando Marsigli. The count transcribed these figures from the *kanun-name* (the general register) which he consulted during his time in Constantinople as an official of the Venetian *bailo* (ambassador) at the Porte. The situation would be that dating back to the 1670s. In the transcription, the calculation errors committed by Marsigli have been taken into account and, where possible, figures have been integrated with others coming from different sources.

Beglerbeglik of Anatolia:	Troops under *beglerbeg* and *sancakbegs*:	*Zeamets* with their troops:	*Timars* with their troops:
beglerbeg (residence in Kütahya)	240	39–52	949–949
other *sancakbegs*: 15	423	269–395	6,253–6,253
16	663	308–447	7,184–7,184
Total: 15,802			

Paşalik of Karaman:	Troops under *paşa* and *sancakbegs*:	*Zeamets* with their troops:	*Timars* with their troops:
paşa (residence in Kroira)	158	18–27	512–512
other *sancakbegs*: 6	514	49–72	1,515–1,515
7	672	67–99	2,027–2,027
Total: 4,794			

Paşalik of Sivas:	Troops under *paşa* and *sancakbegs*:	*Zeamets* with their troops:	*Timars* with their troops:
paşa (residence in Sivas)	216	494–738	953–953
sancakbeg of Turhal	96	16–24	310–310
sancakbeg of Divricy	60	1–1	310–310
sancakbeg of Zile	84	7–7	344–344
sancakbeg of Elazig	50	2–3	144–144
other *sancakbegs*: 5	177	34–48	1,159–1,159
10	683	553–823	3,229–3,229
Total: 8,626			

Paşalik of Maras:	Troops under *paşa* and *sancakbegs*:	*Zeamets* with their troops:	*Timars* with their troops:
paşa (residence in Maras)	148	10–15	1,018–1,018
sancakbeg of Gazanteb	58	9–12	119–119
sancakbeg of Malatya	120	8–12	27–27
other *sancakbegs*: 4	160	2–3	656–656
7	486	29–42	1,820–1,820
Total: 4,204			

Paşalik of Cildir:	Troops under *paşa* and *sancakbegs*:	*Zeamets* with their troops:	*Timars* with their troops:
paşa (residence in Cildir)	222		
sancakbeg of Ardahan	110	9–12	186–186
sancakbeg of Ardanuk	67	4–6	49–49
sancakbeg of Adigeny	87	2–3	127–127
sancakbeg of Ispir		4–6	14–14
other *sancakbegs*: 11	249	74–106	401–401
16	735	49–133	777–777
Total: 2,531			

Paşalik of Djarbakir:	Troops under paşa and sancakbegs:	Zeamets with their troops:	Timars with their troops:
paşa (residence in Djarbakir)	288		
sancakbeg of Siverek	55	4–6	163–163
sancakbeg of Nussaibin	48	1–1	5–5
sancakbeg of Derik	71	1–1	
sancakbeg of Kulp	38	3–3	24–24
sancakbeg of Sirt	53		
sancakbeg of Genc	66		
other sancakbegs: 26	823	56–81	290–290
33	1,442	67–92	482–482
Total: 2,597			

Paşalik of Mosul:	Troops under paşa and sancakbegs:
paşa (residence in Mosul)	192
sancakbegs: 3	206
4	398
Total: 402	

Paşalik of Aleppo:	Troops under paşa and sancakbegs:	Zeamets with their troops:	Timars with their troops:
paşa (residence in Aleppo)	192	98–147	295–295
sancakbeg of Kilis	125	2–3	19–19
sancakbeg of Ma'arat			
other sancakbegs: 6	196	4–6	371–371
9	513	104–104	685–685
Total: 4,204			

Paşalik of Syria:	Troops under paşa and sancakbegs:	Zeamets with their troops:	Timars with their troops:
paşa (residence in Damascus)	240	87–129	772–772
sancakbeg of Zefaat	89	5–6	123–123
sancakbeg of Gaza	121	6–9	108–108
sancakbeg of Nabulus	71		–
other sancakbegs: 11	249	22–30	261–261
15	770	120–174	1,264–1,264
Total: 3,606			

Paşalik of Tripoli in the Lebanon:	Troops under paşa and sancakbegs:	Zeamets with their troops:	Timars with their troops:
paşa (residence in Tripoli)	168	12–18	82–82
sancakbeg of Hamah	94	35–51	161–161
other sancakbegs: 6	154	28–39	312–312
8	466	75–108	555–555
Total: 1,767			

Paşalik of: Kars	Troops under paşa and sancakbegs:
paşa (residence in Kars)	52
other sancakbegs: 5	309
3	651
Total: 367	

Paşalik of Erzurum:	Troops under paşa and sancakbegs:	Zeamets with their troops:	Timars with their troops:
paşa (residence in Erzurum)	291	56–84	2,219–2,219
sancakbeg of Passin	64	9–12	654–654
sancakbeg of Jueman	39	1–1	253–253
other sancakbegs: 10	528	66–99	2,031–2,031
13	922	132–196	5,517–5,517
Total: 11,577			

Paşalik of Van:	Troops under paşa and sancakbegs:	Zeamets with their troops:	Timars with their troops:
paşa (residence in Van)	271	48–72	147–147
sancakbeg of Kacizman	108	72–39	101–101
sancakbeg of Erçis	72	14–21	104–104
sancakbeg of Pervary	48		
other sancakbegs: 18	634	75–108	564–564
22	1,133	163–240	916–916
Total: 3,390			

Paşalik of Al Raqqah:	Troops under paşa and sancakbegs:	Zeamets with their troops:	Timars with their troops:
paşa (residence in Al Raqqah)	148	3–3	149–149
sancakbeg of Al Bab		3–12	291–291
sancakbeg of Medinat	60		
sancakbeg of Busayrah	67		
sancakbeg of Tail Al Ahmar	24		
other sancakbegs: 3	144	16–20	376–376
8	443	28–39	672–672
Total: 1,862			

Paşalik of Kirkuk:	Troops under paşa and sancakbegs:
paşa (residence in Kirkuk)	264
other sancakbegs: 23	
24	
Total: 288	264

Paşalik of Baghdad:	Troops under paşa and sancakbegs:
paşa (residence in Baghdad)	288
other sancakbegs: 20	1,482
21	1,770
Total: 1,791	

Beglerbeglik of Rumelia:	Troops under beglerbeg, paşa and sancakbegs:	Zeamets with their troops:	Timars with their troops:
beglerbeg (residence in Sofia)	264	48–72	1,107–1,107
paşa of Morea	121	100–150	343–343
paşa of Viddin	79	12–18	195–195
paşa of Silistra	108	75–111	4,022–4,022
paşa of Tirana	108	36–54	529–529
other sancakbegs: 19	1,135	685–1,012	4,736–4,736
3	1,815	950–1,417	10,842–10,842
Total: 25,890			

Beglerbeglik of Buda:	Troops under beglerbeg, paşa and sancakbegs:
beglerbeg (residence in Buda)	280
paşa of Kanisza	
paşa of Eger	
paşa of Belgrade	92
sancakbeg of Smedarevo	109
sancakbeg of Esztergom	57
sancakbeg of Szeged	108
sancakbeg of Szymontornia	48
sancakbeg of Mohács	58
other sancakbegs: 12	777
20	1,249
Total: 1,269	

Paşalik of Crete:	Troops under paşa and sancakbegs:	Zeamets with their troops:	Timars with their troops:
paşa (residence in Kandije)	480	8–12	14,000–14,000
sancakbeg of Chania	192	5–6	800–800
sancakbeg of Réthimno	49	4–6	350–350
3	720	17–24	15,150–15,150
Total: 31,067			

Paşalik of Bosnia:	Troops under paşa and sancakbegs:
paşa (residence in Sarajevo)	160
sancakbeg of Eszék	49
sancakbeg of Knin	128
other sancakbegs: 6	426
9	763
Total: 772	

Paşalik of Temeşvar:	Troops under paşa and sancakbegs:
paşa (residence in Temeşvar)	161
sancakbeg of Lippa	40
sancakbeg of Gyula	58
sancakbeg of Jenö	38
other sancakbegs: 4	262
8	559
Total: 567	

Paşalik of: Várad	Troops under paşa and sancakbegs:
paşa (residence in Várad)	
Total: unknown	

Beglerbeglik of Egypt:*	Troops under beglerbeg, and sancakbegs:
sancakbegs: 15	20,000
Total: 20,000	

*According to a coeval account, at the beginning of the eighteenth century the Egyptian province could assemble a force of 20,000 horsemen under the first 12 *sancakbegs* while a further 18,000 men could be gathered as second-line troops. Guer, *Mœurs et Usages des Turcs*, vol. II, pp. 223–224.

Paşalik of Bassora:	Troops under paşa and sancakbegs:
paşa (residence in **Bassora**)	
Total: unknown	

Paşalik of Yemen:	Troops under paşa and sancakbegs:
paşa (residence in **Saana**)	500
sancakbegs: 21	
Total: 21	

Provincial Cavalry Strength: *Zeamets* and *Timars*, 1709

	zeamets	timars
Anatolia	629	8,570
Rumelia	75	8,194
Bosnia	63	1,621
Caraman	73	2,165
Diyarbakir	118	873
Sivas	108	3,029
Erzurum	22	5,548
Maras	27	512
Tripoli	63	570
Rika (Al Raqqah)	60	666
Aleppo	117	1,044
Cildir	106	959
Kars	78	2,111
Mosul	58	1,340
Babylon (Baghdad)	180	7,924
Trabzon (?)	56	398
Cyprus (?)	40	1,067
Unidentified	185	826
	94	2,450
	124	1,152
	128	560
TOTAL	2,504	51,579

Source: A. Hill, *A Full and Just Account of the Present State of the Ottoman Empire* (London, 1709), p.25.

Hungarian Campaign, Buda, April 1663

Commander-in-Chief: Köprülüzade Fazil Ahmed, grand vizier

With Ismail Paşa, *beglerbeg* of Rumelia
      Infantry: 10,000 janissaries and cebecis
      Cavalry: 14,000 *ulùfely sipahis* and *çavuş*
      Artillery: 300 field and siege guns

With Ali Paşa of Temeşvar
      Infantry: 8,000 *azabs*
      Cavalry: 3,000 provincial *sipahis*, 2,500 *beslü*, 10,000 Tatars, 8,000
      Wallachians and Moldavians

With Küçük Ahmed, *sancakbeg* of Jenö
      Infantry: 7,000 *azabs* and *segmens*
      Cavalry: 5,000 Transylvanians, 6,000 Tatars

With Hüseyin Paşa, *beglerbeg* of Buda
      Infantry: 6,000 *azabs*, 8,000 Arnauts
      Cavalry: 12,000 provincial cavalry and *serhaddkulu*

18,000 *musellims* and *lagimçis*

Sources: Reconstruction after Luraghi, *Opere di Raimondo Montecuccoli*, vol. II, pp.205–220; Hammer-Purgstall, *Geschichte des osmanischen Reiches*, vol. XI, pp.144–146; Kolçak: *The Composition, Tactics and Strategy of the Ottoman Field Army*, pp.73–92.

Troops Before Vienna, 15–16 July 1683

Bekri Mustafa Paşa, janissary Aga:	20–30,000
Sipahis and Silihtar:	10–15,000
Topçu, *Top arabaci*, Cebeci:	7–9,000
Ibrahim, *beylerbeg* of Egypt:	3,000
Kiiczick Hassan Paşa, *beglerbeg* of Rumelia:	33,000
Mehmed Paşa, *kaimakan*, from Diyarbakir:	1,500
Kurd Bekir Paşa of Aleppo:	2,550
Ahmed Paşa, *beglerbeg* of Anatolia:	16,000
Ahmed Paşa, governor of Temesvar:	2–3,000
Binamaz Chechil Paşa of Sivas:	6,500
Sziszman Mehmed Paşa of Karaman:	4,900
Sary Husein Paşa of Damascus:	2,250
Sarchos Ahmed Paşa of Marasu:	1,130
Chyzyr Paşa of Bosnia:	4–5,000
Ibrahim Paşa of Erzerum:	11,580
Husein Paşa of Eger:	2–3,000

Sejdioglu Mehmed Paşa of Kanisza:	1,000
Mustafa Paşa of Ochakow from Mitelen:	3,000
Celebi Husein Paşa of Janowan:	2–3,000
From Belgrade:	3–4,000
From Cyprus:	1,000
Koca Arnavut Ibrahim Paşa, *beglerbeg* of Buda (on the Raba River):	8,000

TOTAL:	**111–116,000**

Murad Gyrey, han of Crimea:	15–20,000
Imre Thököly, Hungarians:	15–20,000
Jerzy Duca, *voievoda* of Moldavia:	5–6,000
Serban Kantakuzin, *hospodar* of Wallachia:	5–6,000

TOTAL:	**40–52,000**

Source: Podhorecki, *Weiden 1683*, pp. 42–44.

Troops Before Vienna (August 1683)

Kara Mustafa, grand vizier:	6,000
Kara Mehmed Paşa, *kaimakan*:	5,000
Hüseyin Paşa of Bosnia: 6,000	
Ibrahim Paşa of Buda (*beglerbeg*):	5,000
Huseyn Paşa of Damascus:	3,000
Hassan Paşa of Temeşvar:	1,000
Mustafa Paşa of Silistra:	500
Sei Ahmed Paşa of Armilia:	1,000
Cori Agi *beglerbeg* of Rumelia:	6,000
Bekier Paşa of Aleppo:	1,000
Ahmed Paşa of Manisa:	800
Ahmed Paşa of Zygra:	600
Hassan Paşa of Hamina:	500
Halil Paşa:	500
Ali Paşa of Sebasta:	1,000
Ali Paşa of Anzira:	500
Ahmed Paşa of Aferos:	,000
Ali Paşa of Canamina:	1,000
Mustafa Paşa of Eufek:	500
Husami Paşa of Dolin:	600
Emir Paşa of Adera:	500
Hassan Paşa of Nicopol:	1,000

Hosani Paşa of Nitra:	500
Ali Paşa of Benis:	300
Hasa Paşa of Sermin:	300
Jarigi Paşa of Eger:	600
Ahmed Paşa of Quarissat:	1,000
Osman Paşa of Kutalia:	1,000
Ibraim Paşa of Wardein:	600
Mustafa Paşa, janissary *ağasi*	16,000
Osman Ağa, *kapikulu sipahis*:	12,000
The *ağa* of provincial *sipahis*:	5,000

TOTAL: **83,000**

Source: *Hollandse Mercurius*, 1683 (1684), pp.127–128.

Troops Deployed Between Nussdorf and Währing, 6–7 September 1683

Under Kara Mehmed Paşa of Diyarbakir, with	2,000 men
Paşa of Sivas:	1,500 men
Paşa of Aleppo:	1,000 men
Paşa of Adana:	900 men
Paşa of Maraş:	1,200 men
Paşa of Karaman:	1,000 men
Troops from Damascus:	600 men
Paşa of Bosnia:	2,000 men
Hüseyin Paşa of Bolu:	300 men
Ali Paşa of Teke:	200 men
Paşa of Saruhan:	300 men
Hüseyin Paşa, quartermaster:	150 men
Troops from Egypt:	1,000 men
Hasan Paşa of Hamid:	400 men
Ahmed Paşa of Aydin:	500 men
Harmuş Paşa of Menteşe:	200 men
Yusuf Paşa of Érsekúivár:	500 men
Dilâver Paşa of Kaysariye:	150 men
Abdülmümin Paşa von Içil	200 men
Omer *sancakbeg* of Karahisár:	200 men
Hüseyn *sancakbeg* of Kanğiri:	150 men
Ibrahim *beglerbeg* of Buda:	4,000 men
Mehmed *beg, sancakbeg* of Beyşehir:	150 men
Mustafa Paşa of Herzegovina:	300 men

Janissaries:	5,000 men
Cebecis:	1,500 men
Kapikulu Sipahis (4 squadrons)	3,000 men

TOTAL: **28,400 men**

Source: 'Vekayi'-i Beç', in R. Kreutel, *Kara Mustafa vor Wien*, p.131.

List of Turkish Troops available for the siege, from the Muster Roll found in the tent of the grand vizier at Vienna... (dated 7 September 1683)

Mustafa Kara, grand vizier, Commander-in-Chief:	6,000
Kara Mehmed, Paşa of Diyarbakir:	5,000
Hayra Paşa of Bosnia:	6,000
Ibrahin Paşa of Buda:	5,000
Hussein Paşa of Damascus:	3,000
Hassan Paşa of Temeşvar:	1,000
Mustafa Paşa of Silistra:	1,500
Sei Covi Ahmed, Paşa of Manisa	1,000
Covi Ogli, beglerbeg of Rumelia	6,000
Bekier Paşa of Aleppo:	1,000
Ahmed Paşa, beglerbeg of Anatolia:	2,000
Harmos Paşa of Meneschem:	500
Ahmed Paşa of Tyra:	600
Hassan Paşa of Honima:	500
Ali Paşa of Teke:	500
Ali Paşa of Sebasta:	1,000
Ali Paşa of Ancira	500
Ahmed Paşa of Meros	1,000
Ali Paşa of Karaman:	1,000
Mustafa Paşa of Ersek:	500
Hussain Paşa of Bolin:	600
Emir Paşa of Adana:	500
Aslan Paşa of Nikopol:	1,000
Hassan Paşa of Nitra:	500
Ali Paşa of Bursa:	300
Hassa Paşa of Sermen:	300
Jurigi Paşa of Erla:	600
Ahmed Paşa of Karahisar:	1,000
Osman Oglu Paşa of Kuthaya:	1,000
Ibrahim Paşa of Waradein:	600
Mustafa Paşa, *yeniceri ağasi*:	16,000
Osman, *sipahylar ağasi*:	12,000
Dilly, *ağa* of the *timars*:	5,000
The *ağa* of the assault troops	5,000

The *topçu basi*:	1,500
Other servants under the *topçu basi*:	4,000
Egyptians from Cairo:	3,500
Miners:	5,000
Volunteers:	20,000
Tatars:	20,000
Thököly with his Hungarians:	18,000
Transylvanians:	6,000
Wallachians:	4,000
Moldavians:	2,000
TOTAL:	**168,000**

Troops Before Vienna, 7 September 1683

Paşas:	3
Çorbaci:	16
Officers of the assault troops:	25
Volunteer Officers:	500
Janissaries:	10,000
Volunteers (*serdengeçdi* or *azabs*?):	16,000
Provincial Cavalry:	12,000
Miners and artillerymen:	6,000
Tatars on foot:	2,000
Officers:	2,000
TOTAL:	**48,544**

Source: *Kurtze doch warhaffte und mit denkwürdigen Umständen verfasste Erzehlung, Der im Julio 1683. Zeit Jahre von dem Erb-Feinde vorgenommenen Welt-erschollenen Belagerung, Wie auch hernach klüglichst angeftellten und mit Aufschlagung dess ganzen Ottomannifchen Heers am 12. September desselben Jahre* (Vienna, 1684), pp.78–79.

Campaign in Hungary, Field Army Marching From Eszék to Mohács, Early August 1687

Commander-in-Chief: Süleyman Paşa, grand vizier

Vanguard: Selim Paşa, *çarkacibasi*
Troops under Osman Paşa of Sofia: 1,000 provincial *sipahis*; 5,000 Tatars; 4,000 Wallachians and Moldavians

5,000 janissaries
5,000 *musellims*

Main Army:
8,000 janissaries under Ali *çavuş*, *serasker*; 500 *cebecis* under Süleyman *cebecibasi*; 5,000 *ulùfely sipahis*. Troops under Omer Paşa of Erzurum: 1,000 provincial *sipahis*

Troops under Süleyman Paşa of Bosnia: 9,000 *azabs*, 6,000 Arnauts
Troops under Mehmet Paşa, *zagarcibasi*: 5,000 janissaries; 800 provincial *sipahis*

Artillery, under Hassan *topçubasi*: 70 field guns, 10 mortars.
Rearguard; Jegen Paşa, *dumdarbasi*
500 provincial *sipahis*

Source: Marsigli, *Stato Militare dell'Imperio Ottomanno*' vol. II, pp.116–117.

Campaign on the Pruth River, 2 April 1711

Janissaries:	20,000
Cebeci:	10,000
Topçu:	7,000
Top arabaci:	1,500
Janissaries from Egypt:	3,000
Rumelian infantry (incl. Albanians and Bosnians):	20,000
TOTAL INFANTRY:	61,500
Kapikulu *sipahis*:	20,000
Gedikly *sipahis*:	400
Provincial cavalry (*zeamet* and *timar*):	36,500
TOTAL CAVALRY:	56,900
TOTAL:	**118,400**[1]

Source: Военно-походный журнал фельдмаршала графа Б.П. Шереметева 1711, и 1712 (Military Journal of Field Marshal Count B.P. Sheremetev, 1711–1712), 1898/9.

Campaign in the Peloponnese, Camp at Thebes, 9 June 1715

Commander-in-Chief: Damad Ali Kumurci, grand vizier

Corps of Ahmed Paşa, *serasker*: 10,500 janissaries; 24,360 *azabs*; 2,000 *segmens*; 500 *ulùfely sipahis*; 194 *mutefferika* and *çavuş*; 3,000 artillerymen

---

1   British ambassador Satton confirmed this amount at the end of 1710, but related that actual strength could be about 80,000 combatants. Later he reported that the Albanian and Bosnian infantry numbered about 8,000, instead of the planned 20,000.

Corps of Kior Ali, Paşa of Sivas (arrived in late-June): 2,000 Egyptian janissaries; 1,000 provincial *sipahis*; 1,000 Egyptian *sipahis*

Corps of Mustafa Paşa (destined for the siege of Castel di Morea): 5,000 janissaries, 1,000 *cebecis*, 9,000 *azabs*

1,200 provincial *sipahis* under Sesuvar Oglu Mehmed, *beglerbeg* of Anatolia. 15 siege guns and 5 mortars; 5,000 *musellims* and *lagimçi*

Troops under Topal Osman *ağa*: 5,000 Arnauts; 100 *azabs*; 7,000 *musellims* and *lagimçis*

Troops under Sari Ahmed, *beglerbeg* of Rumelia: 7,000 *kapikulu sipahis*; 2,300 provincial *sipahis*; 2,000 *beslü*

Troops under Türk Ahmed, Paşa of Aydin: 240 *azabs*; 300 provincial *sipahis*

Troops under Yusseuf Paşa of Karaman: 240 *azabs*; 300 provincial *sipahis*

Troops under Maktuloglu Ali, Paşa of Aleppo: 200 *azabs*; 500 provincial *sipahis*

Troops under Cürd Paşa of Akseray: 100 provincial *sipahis*

Troops under Daud Paşa: 100 provincial *sipahis*

Troops under Umer Paşa of Vize: 30 *azabs*; 20 provincial *sipahis*

Mustafa *ağa* with 5,000 Tatars

Source: Brue, *Journal de la Campagne que le Grand Vesir Ali Pacha a faite en 1715 pour la conquête de la Morée* (Paris, 1879), pp.65–68.

Campaign in the Banat, Camp Between Vezirac and Peterwardein, 4 August 1716

Commander-in-Chief: Damad Ali Kumurci, grand vizier
Mehmet Ali *defterdar*

Right Wing: Cürd Paşa of Akseray, *çarkacibasi*
10,000 *azabs* and *segmens*; 7,000 provincial *sipahis* under Osman Paşa of Erzurum; 2,000 Egyptian *sipahis*

Centre: Türk Ahmed, *beglerbeg* of Anatolia
18,000 janissaries under Husseyn yeniceri agasi; 2,000 cebecis, 2,000 topçus; 11,000 *kapikulu sipahis*; 5,000 *musellims*

Left Wing: Sari Ahmed, *beglerbeg* of Rumelia
8,000 Arnauts; 4,000 *azabs* and *segmens*; 4,000 provincial *sipahis*, 3,000 *serhaddkulu* cavalrymen

Reserve: Ali Giray, *nureddin*: 8,000 Tatars

Source: K.u.K. Kriegsarchiv, *Feldzüge des Prinzen Eugen*, vol. XVI.

Spezification of Cannons, Howitzers and Mortars Captured on 5 August 1716 (after the battle of Peterwardein)

Cannons:
1 colubrine of 30 pound, 29 calibres long, with Turkish inscription on the breech and the muzzle.
2 'large half-cannons', 27 calibres long, one with two Turkish inscriptions, the other with eight Turkish inscriptions on breech and muzzle.
4 colubrines of 20 pound, 26 calibres long, with Turkish inscriptions on the breech and the muzzle.
4 colubrines of 20 pound, 27 calibres long, with Turkish inscriptions on the breech and the muzzle.
4 colubrines of 20 pound, 28 calibres long, with Turkish inscriptions on the breech and the muzzle.
4 colubrines of 20 pound, 30 calibres long, with Turkish inscriptions on the breech and the muzzle. 8 colubrines of 16 pound, 29 calibres long, with Turkish inscriptions on the breech and the muzzle.
5 colubrines of 12 pound, 32 calibres long, with Turkish inscriptions on the breech, one of which unserviceable.
1 colubrine of 8 pound, 30 calibre long, with dolphins without signs, unserviceable.
1 colubrine of 6 pound, 34 calibres long, with flowers and dolphins.
2 colubrines of 5 pound, 31 calibres long, without signs.
2 colubrines of 5 pound, 34 calibres long, with dolphins and Turkish inscriptions on the breech and the muzzle.
7 Colubrines of 5 pound, 32 calibres long, without signs.
4 Colubrine of 5 pound, 26, 27, 28 and 29 calibres long, with Turkish inscriptions on the breech and the muzzle.
24 Colubrines of 4 pounds, 31, 32, and 33 calibres, some with Turkish inscriptions, some without, two of them are Imperial with inscription: *Psal.58, Vl Exurgat Deus et confundantur inimici nostri.*
1 Colubrine of 3 pound, 27 calibres long, with double-headed eagle on the breech and Hofkirch's coat of arms at the muzzle.
3 Colubrines of 3 pound, 35 calibres long, with Turkish inscriptions, all nailed and 1 useless.
1 Colubrine of 3 pound, 28 calibres long, with Hofkirch's coat of arms over it, one eye in the clouds, two hands, in one the sword in the other the sceptre and below the earth globe with a crown, the breech with a double-headed eagle and the inscription: *LR.J.S. AA0 1683.*

1 Colubrine of 3 pound, 27 calibres long, with this emblem (Hofkirch) and the inscription: *Ernst Graf von Abensperg und Traun, General-Land und Haus Zeugmeister*; below: *Ferdinandus 2dus D.G.R.J.S.A.G.B.R. Axchidux Austriae 1655, goss mich Hermann Littich in Kaschau 1655* (casted by H. L. in Kaschau).

1 three-pound Colubrine, 30 calibers long, with the Hofkirch coat of arms and the inscription: *E.L. Graf von Hochkirch röm. Kais.Maj.Hofkriegsrath General Oberst Land und Feld Haus Zeugmeister, BJE.OJB General Oberster der Grafschaft Gross Komorni*, and below a double-headed eagle with the inscription: *L.R.J.SAA0 1681, goss mich Baldasar Herold in Wien*.

10 colubrines of 3 pound, 32, 33 and 34 calibres long, part with Turkish inscriptions and part without.

1 Colubrine of 2 pound, 36 calibres long, with dolphins and with this inscription: *Durch das Feuer bin ich geflossen* (the fire has liquefied me), *Martinus Blasi Rupensis hat mich gegossen* (M.B.R. casted me) and with a nightingale, under which it is written: *Assidue et cause* (?) and then *will niemand singen; sing aber ich über Berg und Thal, und hört man mich!* (nobody wants to sing with me; but I sing over hills and valleys, and you may hear me!), and under the dolphins *Martinus Emmerich Richter 1681*.

1 two-pound colubrine, 41 calibres long, with a double-headed eagle and the inscription *Rudolphus 2dus R.J.H.BJR*, with dolphins.

1 two-pound colubrine, 42 calibres long, with the inscription above the muzzle: *wer will den wider, so Gott ist mit uns?* (who against us, if God is with us?); below *Zur Zeit Lukas Hirscher 1583, gegossen durch Paul Neydel* (at the time of L.H, casted by P.N.), with dolphins.

1 two pound colubrine, 40 calibres long, with a coat of arms, within which an eagle holding the cross in its beak, to the right the sun, to the left the moon and on both sides a lion with a dagger.

1 two-pound colubrine, 38 calibres long, with this inscription *Haec machina fusa est judice domino Joanne Fux AD 1541*.

1 two-pound colubrine, 41 calibres long, with two crossed swords, and *1567*.

58 colubrine of 11.5 pounds, 34, 35 and 36 calibres long, some of which with Turkish inscriptions, the others without, 1 useless and 1 nailed.

6 one-pound colubrines, 34, 36 and 38 calibres long, without inscriptions.

Total: 160 cannons.

Howitzers:

1 piece of 60 pounds with 2 images of the crucifix on the left and right, with this inscription *Fernandus rex Z.C. me fecit 1529*, with Imperial coat of arms;

1 piece of 24 pounds with Turkish inscription.

1 piece of 13 pounds, with inscription *Rudolf Binger goss mich, 1529*, with Imperial coat of arms

Total: 3 howitzers.

Mortars:

4 mortars with Turkish signs;

5 mortars of 60 pound, 2 of which without signs.

1 mortar of 40 pound without signs

2 mortars of 30 pound with Turkish signs.

1 mortar of 24 pound without signs.
7 mortars of 16 pound with Turkish inscriptions

Items on 11 August were delivered in the castle of Peterwardein:
1 mortar of 100 pound with Turkish inscription.
1 mortar of 80 pound without signs.
1 mortar of 15 pound without signs.
Total: 23 mortars.

[Signed] *L.S. Johann Karl Strassberg,* captain of the Imperial artillery.

Source: K.u.K. Kriegsarchiv, *Feldzüge des Prinzen Eugen,* vol. XVI, pp.285–287.

Procession of the Ottoman Army in Constantinople, 6 October 1682

'The *zagarci* janissary officers opened the procession on horseback, and behind each company, came the cook (*asci*) whose approach was announced by a clicking of chains and silver spoons. The captain on horseback, covered in bright armour, wore a plume of crescent-shaped heron feathers on the turban. He was armed with a bow and a quiver each of them had behind him his servant and his gun holder … Then came the janissary *ağasi* with two horsetails [*tughs*] and three flags of silk. He was followed by fifty volunteers [*serdengeçdi*], on whose shoulders were rejected leopard skins. They preceded twenty pages, aged twenty to twenty four years, armed with chainmail, sparkling helms and dressed in red silk cloths, carrying on their shoulders quiver decorated with rich embroidery. In their hands, they carried bamboo spears, while fifty others janissaries were armed with muskets, and four standard bearers held white, green, red and yellow flags. The musicians, among whom we noticed six flute players, six drums, four cymbalists. They were followed by the *topcu-basi* [commander of the *kapikulu* artillery], surrounded by fifty adjutants with three flags, two red and one green. Then came the *ağas* with the pages of the *kaimakan* Ibrahim Paşa, armed with spears, arrows, quivers and helms. Forty *muteferrikas* with rich weapons, proceeded on their horses. accompanied by twenty lancers on foot, and eight horsemen. Forty chamberlains (*çavuş*) in ceremonial turban, dressed in white kaftans, followed each by forty pages with shields, arrows and bows, marched mounted on horses whose sides disappeared under the richest armour. We then saw appearing the court of the favourite vizier, followed by forty *ağas*, wearing sable fur and mounted on horses covered with sumptuous saddle cloths, with their feet rested on silver stirrups. They were followed by hand horses with thirty pages richly equipped; the favourite's *kiaya* was advancing with two horsemen bearing horsetails carried at the end of blue and red sticks; the shield fixed on the saddle, the war mace and the sabre hanging on each side, all more richly harnessed each other and led by servants. Then passed the members of the State Chancellery, the two Masters of Requests, the Chancellor of State, the Secretary of the Treasury with a band of twenty-seven musicians. Fifty *delis*, wearing red caps which were surmounted by the wings of different birds, and their appearance was very strange, wore sable furs and spears to which were hung tassels of green, yellow and English silk. Others designated by the name of *gonüllü*, namely 'brave', were dressed in carmine red and leopard skins; moreover, similar to the previous ones, except for their caps there were *gonüllü* in green. After them another fifty *deli*s came with headresses similar to the one worn by the Hungarians; they were covered with larger lynx furs. Next came the grand-vizier's household, the brightest and most numerous that had been seen to date. We could see a hundred and seventy *segmen*s on horseback (mounted musketeers) armed with rifles, shields and sabre. Then followed twenty-four pages, two hundred *cavus*, two hundred valiant *ağa*s … Further forty *ağa*s of the grand vizier marched, each accompanied by thirty pages who carried bamboo spears, and forty pages in lemon-coloured dress, quivers gold embroidered, reins and stirrups of silver. Two hundred other pages advanced, divided between two corps, each of which distinguished by a particular colour and followed by one hundred and twenty-five servants of the grand-vizier, and the governor of Mosul with his men armed with muskets. The first followed by one hundred and fifty pages and fifty *ağa*s of Kara Mustafa, carrying quivers embroidered with gold and three standards. Then followed the *kiaya* [Minister of the Interior], surrounded by six armed adjutants and finally twelve *çavuş* with the musicians of the grand vizier. The latter succeeded the captain of the life guard and the provost, opening the way for the Sultan. Seventy horsemen and seventy *çavuş*, with their large turbans and their silver sticks and twenty-two fouriers preceded the judges, the counsellors, the *mullah*s and other court's officials. These latter were followed by the four masters of hunting, the grand huntsman for the falcon, vulture, hawk and kite hunting. The standard bearer carried the flag, the great green standard of the Prophet; in the midst the dervishes of all the orders filled the air with their cheers. After them advanced a hundred and fifty emirs, descendants of the Prophet, green turbans, proceeded by their chief, and twelve sheiks elected from the nobility. Preachers, whose clothes were woven in camel hair, proceeded one hundred and fifty *çavuş*, and before them, they creased the air of their cheers. The *çavuş* advanced in front of four flags, which preceded the two highest magistrates: the judge of Constantinople and the grand judge of Europe and Asia, distinguished by their enormous turbans rolled up in the form of bulges. Then came to the right and to the left the highest ministers and the *kaimakan*s, escorted by forty soldiers on foot, covered with leopard skins and armed with sword sticks … two viziers wearing ceremonial turbans [*kallavis*] around which a large gold braid snaked like a golden river in a silver sea. They were escorted by servants who carried their arms. The grand-vizier, dressed in scarlet fur lined with sable, advanced on a horse richly harnessed and covered with a rich armour. His reins and spurs were of gilded silver. Twenty-four servants followed him on foot, dressed in red velvet kaftan, and wearing belts with gold scales. At short distance behind the grand vizier walked his *odabasi*, the *muhzir ağa*, and the captain of the grand vizier's life guard. To the left of the latter, we saw the *mufti*, dressed in white furs and wearing a huge turban. Behind him, came the lieutenant-general of the janissaries [*kethüda yeri*], who was in the same commander of the guardians of sultan's mastiffs. The dogs had cover of damask embroidered with gold. Four horsemen had the same number of leopard cats trained for hunting on the rump. Sixty-four *sipahy*s armed with lance followed, wearing golden and silver feather caps, their waist girded with precious scarves [*kusak*], whose stockings barely reached the knees. Then came four hundred archers [*solaks*], whose headdress was surmounted by a tuft of crescent-shaped feathers, like the ones of the janissary *çorbagi*, dressed in golden doublets. Then passed the *silihtar*s of the *serai* in ceremonial turbans, leading twenty-four horses with golden saddle covers, shields and weapons also gilded, and more adorned with emeralds, rubies, turquoise and pearls; the stirrups and the reins were also gilded.'

Source: A. Benetti, *Osservazioni fatte dal fu A.B. nel viaggio a Costantinopoli dell'Illustrissimo et Eccellentissimo Signor Gio. Battista Donado, spedito Bailo alla Porta Ottomana, dall'anno 1680* (Venice, 1690), pp.21–25.

Major Field Operations, 1645–1717

Key to siege tables (see following tables):

All.	Allies
Cos.	Cossacks
Cro.	Croatians
Imp.	Imperialists
Hun.	Hungarians
kpk.	*kapikulu*
Krc.	*Kuruc*
Mil.	Militiamen
m/l	*musellim* and *lagimçi*
Ott.	Ottomans
Pol.	Poles
Rus.	Russians
srk.	*serhaddkulu*
Tat.	Tatars
tpk.	Ottoman provincial troops
Trn.	Transylvanians
Ven.	Venetians
d.	dead
w.	wounded
pr.	prisoners

Conflicts:
1. Cretan War (1645–1671)
2. Expeditions against Transylvania (1657–1662)
3. Habsburg–Ottoman War (1663–1664)
4. Second Polish–Ottoman War (1672)
5. Third Polish–Ottoman War (1673–1676)
6. First Russian–Ottoman War (1678–1681)
7. Holy League War (1682–1699)
8. Second Russian–Ottoman War (1711)
9. Austria–Venetian–Ottoman War (1714–1718)

Major Sieges

Place	Date	Conflict	Besiegers (A)	Besieged (B)	Casualties (a)	Casualties (b)	Outcome
Chaniá	1645, 24 June–7 August	1	Salih Yussuf, 50,000 kpk. and srk., 30,000 m/l, 80 cannons	Navagero, 800 Ven., 500 Mil.	8,000	unknown	garrison surrender
Réthimno	1646, 2 June–20 October	1	Baltaoğlu Hüseyin, 20,000 kpk. and srk.	Corner, 300 Ven., 400 Mil.	2,000	unknown	garrison surrender
Novigrad	1646, 2 June–20 October	1	Ibrahim Paşa, 18,000 tpk. and srk.	Loredan, 700 Ven., 400 Mil.	unknown	unknown	garrison surrender
Zemunik Donji	1647, 14–19 March	1	Pisani, 1,200 Ven.	800 Ott.	100	600 d.	Venetians storm the fortress
Novigrad	1647, 30 January–2 February	1	Foscolo, 5,000 Ven.	Ahmed Beg, 1,000 srk.	unknown	unknown	garrison surrender
Klis	1648, 10–18 March	1	Foscolo, 6,000 Ven.	Tekely Ali, 2,200 srk.	unknown	unknown	garrison surrender
Šibenik	1648, 21 August–10 September	1	Tekely Mustafa, 30,000 tpk. and srk.	Degenfeld, 2,000 Ven. and Mil.	6,000	350	besiegers leave siege
Kandije	1648, 1 May–10 November	1	Baltaoğlu Hüseyin, 50,000 Ott., 90 cannons	Gonzaga, then De Haes, 4,500 Ven.	15,000	650	besiegers leave siege
Kandije	1649, 21 August–2 October	1	60,000 Ott., 120 cannons	De Haes, 6,000 Ven.	9,000	800	besiegers leave siege
Várad	1660, 14 July–27 August	2	Ali Paşa, 12,000 kpk., 15,000 tpk., 18,000 srk. and Tat.	Rákóczy, 850 Trn., 1,000 Mil.	2–3,000	800 d.	Ottomans storm the fortress
Érsekújvár	1663, 16 August–23 September	3	Köprülü Ahmed, 28,000 kpk. and tpk., 22,000 srk. and All., 10,000 m/l	Forgách, 3,500 Imp. and Hun.	1,800 d	450 d.	garrison evacuates the fortress
Zrínyivár	1664, 5 June–7 July	3	Ismail Paşa, 45,000 Ott. and Tat.	Strozzi, 3,000 Imp. and Cro.	1–2,000	1,000 d. and pr.	Ottomans storm the fortress
Kamieniec	1672, 25 July–27 August	4	Köprülü Ahmed, 50,000 Ott. and Tat., 90 cannons	Sieniavski, 2,000 Pol.	6,000 d	2,000 d.	Ottomans storm the fortress

Place	Date	Conflict	Besiegers (A)	Besieged (B)	Casualties (a)	Casualties (b)	Outcome
Ladyżyn	1674, 17–18 August	5	Silisade Mehmed, 11,000 Ott. and Tat.	unknown, 1,000 Pol.	unknown	800 pr.	garrison surrender
Uman	1674, 1–4 September	5	Mustafa Kara, 12,000 kpk. and tpk., 32 cannons	Kaczorwski, 900 Pol.	unknown	900	Ottomans storm the fortress
Çigirin	1678, 13 June–3 August	6	Kara Mustafa, 40,000 Ott. and All.	Rodomovoski, 4,000 Rus. and Cos.	8–9,000	1,500	garrison leaves the fortress
Esztergom	1683, 20–27 October	7	Lorraine, 32,000 Imp.	Ibrahim Paşa, 1,200 kpk. and srk.	unknown	500 d.	garrison evacuates the fortress
Ercsi	1684, 13–22 July	7	Leslie, 8,000 Imp.	Hamza Beg, 1,000 srk.	unknown	unknown	garrison surrender
Lefkas	1684, 21–26 July	7	Morosini, 12,000 Ven.	Ibrahim Beg, 900 srk.	unknown	unknown	garrison evacuates the fortress
Érsekújvár	1685, 8 July–16 August	7	Caprara, 55,000 Imp and All.	Ali Paşa, 4,000 kpk. and srk., 1,000 Tat.	4,000	3,000 d., 1,000 pr.	Imperialists storm the fortress
Buda	1686, 18 June–2 September	7	Lorraine, 60,000 Imp and All.	Abdi Abdurrhaman, 6,000 srk, 3,000 tpk.	6,000	3,600	Imperialists storm the fortress
Navarino	1686, 8–2 June	7	Königsmark, 10,000 Ven.	Hüseyn Paşa, 2,300 srk.	800	1,500	garrison surrender
Methoni	1686, 22 June–27 July	7	Königsmark, 11,000 Ven.	Ahmed Ağa, 1,500 srk.	300	unknown	garrison evacuates the fortress
Nauplia	1686, 7–30 August	7	Königsmark, 10,000 Ven.	Mustafa Paşa, 2,000 srk.	500	unknown	garrison surrender
Corinth	1687, 6–7 August	7	Morosini, 14,000 Ven.	Mehmet Paşa, 1,000 srk.	unknown	unknown	garrison evacuates the fortress
Athens	1687, 23–29 September	7	Königsmark, 10,750 Ven.	Murat Beg, 1,500 srk.	unknown	300	garrison surrender

Place	Date	Conflict	Besiegers (A)	Besieged (B)	Casualties (a)	Casualties (b)	Outcome
Belgrade	1688, 11 August–6 September	7	Bayern, 53,000 Imp. and All., 65 cannons	Ibrahim Paşa, 8,300 kpk. and srk.	1,300	5,300 d., 3,000 pr.	Imperialists storm the fortress
Monemvasia	19 June 1688–12 August 1690	7	Morosini, then Corner, 8,500 Ven.	Hassan Paşa, 3,000 srk.	2,500	unknown	garrison surrender
Negroponte	1688, 14 July–24 September	7	Königsmark, later Morosini, 25,000 Ven.	Mustafa Paşa 5/6,000 srk.	12,000	unknown	besiegers leave siege
Nis	1690, 16 August–8 September	7	Köprülü Mustafa, 65,000 Ott., 90 cannons	Starhemberg, 4,000 Imp.	unknown	unknown	garrison evacuates the fortress
Belgrade	1690, 19 September–8 October	7	Köprülü Mustafa, 60,000 Ott., 100 cannons	Aspremont, 2,400 Imp.	7,000	1,400 d., 1,000 pr.	Ottomans storm the fortress
Chaniá	1692, 12 July–29 August	7	Trauttmansdorf, 12,000 Ven., 18 cannons	Hassan Paşa, 800 kpk., 2,200 srk.	unknown	unknown	besiegers leave siege
Belgrade	1693, 12 August–10 September	7	Croy, 35,000 Imp., 25 cannons	Bocoglu Mustafa, 6,000 srk. later reinforced by 5,000 kpk. and tpk.	unknown	unknown	besiegers leave siege
Chios	1694, 16–24 October	7	Zeno, 15,000 Ven.	Davud Paşa, 2,500 srk.	unknown	unknown	besiegers leave siege
Temeşvar	1696, 18 July–18 August	7	August II of Saxony, 38,000 Imp. and All.	Ahmed Paşa, 6,000 kpk. and srk.	unknown	unknown	besiegers leave siege
Bihac	1697, 21–23 June	7	Auersperg, 13,000 Imp. and Hun.	Mehmet Beg, 2,200 srk.	1,200	unknown	besiegers leave siege
Corinth	1715, 28 June–2 July	9	Sari Ahmed, 40,000 Ott.	Minetto, 400 Ven., 500 Mil.	unknown	unknown	garrison surrender
Nauplia	1715, 11–19 July	9	Damad Ali, 25,000 kpk., 35,000 tpk. and srk.	Bon, 1,700 Ven., 1,100 Mil.	8,000	800 d.	garrison surrender
Methoni	1715, 12–16 August	9	Sari Ahmed, 15,000 kpk., 20,000 tpk. and srk.	Pasta, 700 Ven.	unknown	unknown	garrison surrender
Corfu	1716, 25 July–20 August	9	Mustafa Paşa, 55,000 Ott., 110 cannons	Schulenburg, 6,000 Ven.	10,000	900 d.	besiegers leave siege

Place	Date	Conflict	Besiegers (A)	Besieged (B)	Casualties (a)	Casualties (b)	Outcome
Temeşvar	1716, 1 September–14 October	9	Eugene of Savoy, 45,000 Imp.	Mustafa Paşa, 18,000 Ott. And Tat.	4,500	3,000	Imperialists storm the fortress
Belgrade	1717, 20 July–18 August	9	Eugene of Savoy, 95,000	Mustafa Ali, 25,000	20,000	4,500	garrison surrender

Major Field Engagements

Place	Date	Conflict	Ottomans (A)	Opponents (B)	Casualties (a)	Casualties (b)	Outcome
Messara	1647, 28 June	1	Baltaoğlu Hüseyn, 6,000 Ott.	Della Marra, 2,500 Ven. and Mil.	400	1,000 d. and pr.	Ottoman success
Lippa	1658, 26 June	2	Seidi Ahmed, 18,000 Ott. and Tat.	Rákóczy, 11,000 Trn.	3,000 d., 1,200 pr.	1,800	Transylvanian victory
Szászfenes	1660, 22 May	2	Seidi Ahmed, 6,000 kpk., 12,000 srk., 7,000 Tat.	Rákóczy, 6,500 Trn.	5,000	3,800	Ottoman victory
Léva	1664, 19 July	3	Ali Paşa, 22,000 Ott. and All	Souches, 12,600 Imp. and Hun.	2,000	200	Imperial victory
Szentgotthárd	1664, 1 August	3	Köprülü Ahmed, 20,000 kpk., 22,000 tpk., 18,000 srk. and Tat.	Montecuccoli, 25,000 Imp. and All.	8,000 d.	4,000	Allied victory
Komarnem	1672, 9 October	5	Sultan Giray, 10,000 Tat., 400 Cos.	Sobieski, 3,000 Pol.	1,500	250	Polish success
Chocim	1673, 11 Nov	5	Ibrahim Paşa, 32,000 Ott. and All.	Sobieski, 30,000 Pol, 65 field guns	7,500 d. and pr.	2,000	Polish victory
Lvov	1675, 24 August	5	Ibrahim Paşa, 20,000 Ott. and All.	Sobieski, 6,000 Pol.	unknown	unknown	Polish success
Żurawno	1676, 25 September–14 October	5	Ibrahim Paşa, 36,000 Ott. and All.	Sobieski, 16,000 Pol.	7,000	5,000	Armistice

Place	Date	Conflict	Ottomans (A)	Opponents (B)	Casualties (a)	Casualties (b)	Outcome
Sula River	1677, 28 August	6	Ibrahim Paşa, 30,000 Ott. and Tat.	Shepelev, 25,000 Russians	5,000	unknown	Russian victory
Petronell	1683, 8 July	7	Kara Mehmed, 18,000 Ott. and Tat.	Baden, 3,500 Imp.	unknown	800 m.	Ottoman success
Párkány	1683, 12 October	7	Kara Mehmed, 18,000 Ott.	Lorraine and Sobieski, 27,000 Imp. and Pol.	9,000 d., 3,000 pr.	1,200	Allied victory
Vác	1684, 27 June	7	Ibrahim Paşa, 18,000 Ott.	Lorraine, 32,000 Imp.	100	3,000	Imperial victory
Ercsi	1684, 22 July	7	Süleyman Paşa, 20,000 Ott.	Lorraine, 30,000 Imp.	2,500	unknown	Imperial success
Esztergom	1685, 16 August	7	Ibrahim Paşa, 32,000 Ott. and Tat.	Lorraine, 20,000 Imp.	unknown	unknown	Imperial victory
Bia	1686, 14 August	7	Süleyman Paşa, 24,000 Ott. and Tat.	Lorraine, 32,000 Imp. and All.	3,000 d.	600	Allied success
Harsány	1687, 12 August	7	Süleyman Paşa, 55,000 Ott.	Lorraine, 50,000 Imp. and All.	7,000 d., 3,200 pr., 66 field guns	568 d.	Major Imperial victory
Batocina	1689, 30 August	7	Ahmat Paşa, 33,000 Ott.	Baden, 20,000 Imp.	4,000	1,500	Imperial victory
Nis	1689, 23 September	7	Ahmat Paşa, 25,000 Ott.	Baden, 17,000 Imp.	7,500	400	Imperial victory
Zernyest	1690, 21 August	7	Thököly 12,000 Hun. Ott. and Tat.	Heissler, 7,500 Imp.	unknown	1,000 pr.	Rebel victory
Hátseg	1690, 3 October	7	Thököly, 10,000 Hun. and All.	Baden, 32,000 Imp.	4,000	unknown	Imperial victory
Slankamen	1691, 19 August	7	Köprülü Mustafa, 55,000 Ott., 158 field guns	Baden, 33,000 Imp., 90 field guns	20,000 d. and pr.	7,900	Decisive Imperial victory
Peterwardein	1694, 14 September–3 October	7	Sürmeli Ali, 25,000 Ott.	Caprara, 18,000 Imp.	unknown	unknown	Imperial success

Place	Date	Conflict	Ottomans (A)	Opponents (B)	Casualties (a)	Casualties (b)	Outcome
Lugos	1695, 21 September	7	Mustafa II, 70,000 Ott. and All.	Veterani, 8,000 Imp.	4,000	6,000 d. and pr.	Ottoman victory
Ollashin	1696, 26 August	7	Mustafa II, 65,000 Ott. and All.	Sachsen, 45,000 Imp. and All.	2,500	1,000	Ottoman success
Zenta	1697, 11 September	7	Elams Mohammad, 62,000 Ott.	Eugene of Savoy, 40,000 Imp.	30,000 d., 5,000 pr.	2,100	Imperial triumph
Falltschi	1711, 24 July	8	Baltaci Mehmed, 75,000 Imp. and All.	Peter I Romanov, 40,000 Rus.	5,000	3,000 d., 900 pr.	Ottoman victory
Carlowitz	1716, 2 August	9	Cürd Paşa, 12,000 tpk. and srk.	Pálffy, 3,000 Imp.	1,000	700	Ottoman success
Peterwardein	1716, 5 August	9	Damad Ali, 68,000 Ott.	Eugene of Savoy, 59,000 Imp.	8,000 d., 2,000 pr.	4,400	Imperial victory
Belgrade	1717, 16 August	9	Bostançi Halil, 80,000 Ott.	Eugene of Savoy, 50,000 Imp.	20,000 d., 5,000 pr.	5,500 d. and w.	Imperial victory

Colour Plate Commentaries

Plate A

1. Grand Vizier, 1658–1691

The colorful *kapaniça* embroidered in 'saz' style, and the high *mücevveze* turban mark the high rank of this personality. The horse furniture is completed by a precious saddle cover with gilded decoration and bridle with metal and turquoise accessories. Source: Rålamb's *Book of Costumes* (1658); horse furniture: Smyrna manufacture, 1680–90, preserved in the Badisches Landesmuseun, Karlsruhe.

2. *Beglerbeg* of Rumelia, 1650–1660

The *beglerbeg*, lord of lords, was the governors of the major provinces. As the other high officials, he held the rank of military commander in his own province. Rumelia, corresponding to modern-day Greece, Albania and Bulgaria, was the first Ottoman *beglerbeglik* established in Europe, followed by Buda, in Hungary, in 1552. The *beglerbeg* wears an *erkan-i* kürkü silk *kaftan* lined with fur. Some seventeenth-century sources represent the *beglerbeg* of Rumelia with the typical *bareta* headdress. Source: Rålamb's *Book of Costumes* (1658), late seventeenth century war mace and sabre, Wavel Museum, Krakow.

Plate B

1. Janissary *çorbaci*, mid seventeenth century

The commanders of the janissary *orta*s wore in parade special clothing, such as the *kalafat* headdress and *dolama kaftan* with false sleeves. The commanders of the *yayabeg* category, mounted on horseback during parades and ceremonies and they were marked by yellow leather footwear. Sources: Ottoman miniatures from the Zamoysky Album, representing a parade procession of the sultan Ibrahim I (1640–48), National Library, Warsaw.

2. Janissary in parade dress, 1680–1690

The dress of the janissaries changed very little in the seventeenth century, but their elaborate 'uniforms' were actually worn only in the most important ceremonies. On this occasion, the janissary carried the finest weapons and special accessories, such as headgear with multi-coloured feathers or artefacts. This janissary is one of the 100 bravest soldiers chosen to form the escort of the *yeniceri ağasi*, the senior field commander of the corps. For this task, they received a distinctive lynx fur. On parade, the janissaries wore *dolama kaftan*s, usually in turquoise-azure, but also red and green were common. Sources; Antonio Benetti, *Osservazioni fatte dal fu A.B. nel viaggio a Costantinopoli; tüfek* flintlock, 1683; Waffensammlung, Vienna.

3. Janissary in quarters dress, 1650–1700

According to coeval descriptions, this was the ordinary clothing of the janissaries within the garrison when they were not engaged in active service. The great coat, worn in winter, was often dark grey, dark green or dark brown rough wool lined with linen, and decorated with elaborate embroideries or floral patterns. Source: *Foggie diverse del vestire de' Turchi*, mid seventeenth century, Marciana Library, Venice.

Plate C

1. *Topçu*, artilleryman, 1650–60

The European iconography compensates for scarcity of Ottoman illustrated sources of the late seventeenth century, when the prohibition to represent human beings was introduced and lasted until 1721. The artilleryman illustrated comes from one of the many works celebrating the enterprises of Christian commanders. This *topçu* wears a *dolama kaftan* similar to the one issued to the *kapikulu* infantry and a fine manufactured *Paşali* turban. Sources: Monument to Lazzaro Mocenigo, San Lazzaro de' Mendicanti Church, Venice.

2. *Cebeci*, armourer, mid seventeenth century

Like the janissaries, also the *cebecis* wore elaborate parade dress. The existing iconographic sources relating to the *cebecis* seems to refer to NCOs. Note the helm with the spoon plume holder, as with the janissaries. During peacetime, the *cebecis* kept the weaponry in the Constantinople arsenals, named *cefane*, and in the other arsenals where the janissaries formd the *ocak*-garrison. Usually, only a part of the corps marched on campaign. The *cebeci* corps were also in charge of patrolling the area around the Hagia Sophia mosque in Constantinople. Sources: Rålamb's *Book of Costumes* (1658); *tüfek* matchlock, Topkapı Museum Collection, 1660–1670.

3. *Solak*, 1658

The solak was the term for identifying *ortas* 60, 61, 62 and 63, which formed the foot escort of the sultan. They joined the field army only when the sultan marched with his troops, and on parade continued to carry bow and arrows as primary weapons and to wear a particular and colourful dress very different to that of the ordinary janissaries. Their headgear was the *kalafat*, the headdress with the heron's head form, like that worn by the *çorbaci* officers. Sources: Rålamb's *Book of Costumes* (1658).

Plate D

1. Horseman of the grand vizier's household cavalry, 1658

The Swedish diplomat Claes Rålamb commissioned a wonderful series of 20 large paintings, illustrating the *kapikulu* soldiers in full colour. In one of this painting are portrayed the officers of the grand vizier's mounted lifeguard.

Some horsemen are dressed as the *kapikulu sipahis*, while others wear *kaftans* and cloaks in red with a large *zulfiqar* sword in gold and *bareta* headdress. All the lifeguards carry long lances with red or white-red pennants. Sources: Sultan's procession, Rålamb's Album, Stockholm, *Tabula M*.

2. *Kapikulu* cavalry, *sipahi ulùfely*, mid seventeenth century

The *ulùfely* squadrons were equipped with the best and most highly decorated weapons produced in the Imperial arsenals, as well as weapons imported from Iran, or war trophies. Usually, the *kapikulu* cavalry wore armour and various other body and arm protections. This *sipahi* wears the complete Ottoman armour panoply with typical *chahar-aine* steel body plates for protecting the chest. This equipment marks the Imperial age, which lasted until the early eighteenth century. However, starting in the 1690s, later iconography represents the *kapikulu* cavalry wearing less metal protection. Sources: Zamoysky Album, c. 1645; National Library, Warsaw; mid seventeenth century *çiçak* helm, Furusiyya Art Foundation, Constantinople; late seventeenth century *kalkan* shield, *Karlsruher Türkenbeute*, Badisches Landesmuseum, Karlsruhe.

Plate E

1. Janissary in campaign dress, 1660–1670

This figure is reconstructed after a different description relating the true appearance of the *kapikulu* infantry on campaign. According to Marsigli and other eyewitnesses, the janissaries did not wear their elaborate clothing in battle, but wore more comfortable short jackets or quilted *jupons*. Even the *ak-börk* headgear was usually replaced with turbans or *tekke* caps. Sources: L.F. Marsigli, *Stato Militare dell'Imperio Ottomanno*; La Hay-van Moor, *Recueil de Cent estampes représentant differentes Nations du Levant* (1707–08); mid seventeenth century matchlock *tüfek*, Topkapı Museum, Constantinople; ammunition bag, 1683; Waffensammlung, Vienna.

2. *Serdengeçdi*, mid seventeenth century

The Imperial general Raimondo Montecuccoli wrote a concise account concerning the psychological expedients employed in the Ottoman army to encourage the troops. He gave some information about an 'opium potion' called *maslach*, issued to the volunteers of the storming parties, who drunk it before the assaults. Furthermore, as a sign of bravery, the *serdengeçdis* submitted their body to trial pain resistance, hurting themselves with arrows or cattle hooks under the skin. Some Western iconographies show these 'head riskers' with spears and even knives threaded into their flesh. Sources: seventeenth-century Hungarian print by an anonymous artist, Library of the Hungarian National Museum of Budapest; 1690s *karabela* sabre, Croatian National Museum, Zagreb.

3. *Topçu*, campaign dress, 1660–80

The Ottoman artillery played an important role in the army. On campaign, only a part of the corps joined the field army. They provided the professional personnel in charge of the direction of the artillery and the *hisar erleri* militiamen. This figure is based on the classical *kapikulu* dress for the artillerymen. Medium green *dolama kaftans* are generally associated with the household artillery corps. Sources: *Foggie diverse del vestire de' Turchi*, seventeenth century, Marciana Library, Venice.

Plate F

1. European *azab* infantryman, mid seventeenth century

This figure comes from a miniature of Kenan Paşa's campaign against the Albanian rebels in 1630. The infantry troops depicted in the miniature are *serhaddkulu* infantry from Rumelia. This miniature is commonly described as the main source for Ottoman *azab* infantrymen in the mid 1600s, and usually they are represented wearing a red coat *kaftan*. However, the miniature also includes soldiers in dark blue, brown and medium grey, and only the headdress, with two or more black feathers, is red for all. Sources: Paşaname, 1640–45, in Hans Sloan's Album: *The Habit of the Grand Signor's Court*; British Museum Library, London; seventeenth-century matchlock *tüfek*, Topkapı Museum Collection, Constantinople.

2. Anatolian *azab* infantryman, 1650

Azab infantrymen formed the bulk of the Ottoman foot troops and they were usually well-equipped with a short-barrelled *tüfek* musket and *pala* sabre. This infantry wore the clothing of the recruiting province, but some contemporary evidence shows that the units were uniformly dressed. This Anatolian *azab* wears an elaborate turban which strongly contrasts with a *kaftan* of dark grey cloth. The linen gaiters around the legs preserved the breeches during marches through muddy ground, a measure usually adopted by the Ottoman infantry of all the classes. Sources: Paşaname, 1640–45, in Hans Sloan's Album: *The Habit of the Grand Signor's Court*; British Museum Library, London.

3. European *azab* infantryman, 1686

Another typical *azab*, reconstructed after a description in a coeval source, referring to the garrison of Methoni, Greece. The author, the Tuscan Giovanni Fabroni, who participated in the campaign against the Ottomans in the Peloponnese as a knight of the Order of Saint Stephen, remarked that the Ottoman infantry was better armed than the Christian soldiers. Source: Cassigoli Collection (Manuscript), Biblioteca Nazionale Centrale, Florence; flintlock *tüfek*, 1680–90, Correr Museum, Venice.

Plate G

1. Egyptian *çavuş*, 1658

The word *çavuş* means 'messenger' but this term was used for different types of officer in the Ottoman army. These men acted as messengers, but the *çavuş* could be a category of the *kapikulu* cavalry, adjutant of the senior commanders or a junior officer. This Egyptian *çavuş* wore a high feathered *zamt* headdress, and a laced cloak, in typically Mamluk style. Sources: Ottoman miniature, mid seventeenth century, *Recueil de Costumes Turcs*, Bibliothèque National de France, inv. 10598 2.

2. Egyptian *sipahi*, mid seventeenth century

After the conquest of Egypt, the Ottoman governor forbade the local Mamluks to wear Ottoman dress, and ordered them to wear red *zamt* headdress and *maluta*, the traditional Mamluk greatcoat. Eventually, a further important distinction between the two groups was the *kaftan*, with tight sleeves for the Ottomans, and broad sleeves for the Egyptians. This feature remained typical through the seventeenth and eighteenth centuries, facilitated also by the climate. The Mamluks suffered discrimination under Ottoman rule; their social decline was evident and their salaries were paid several months in arrears. Source: Rålamb's *Book of Costumes* (1658).

3. Kurdish standard bearer (*tugh*), 1640–50

In the Iranian miniatures of the Firdousi's Shāhnāma, the Ottomans are identified with the archetypal enemy mentioned in the poem. In the copy preserved in the Berlin Library, produced in the golden age of the Safavid Empire, several enemy horsemen are depicted with typical Ottoman clothing and headdress. The figures show the typical dress of the Asian subjects, whose appearance is little different to the coeval Iranian cavalrymen, except for the headdress. This *tugh* bearer wears a mix of typical Ottoman clothing, like the *kaftan* with a folded tail, and Iranian clothing, like the large turban typical of Kurdish dress. Kurds contributed to the army with border troops along the frontier with Safavid Iran, and with provincial cavalry from the provinces of Diyarbakir and Mosul. Several Kurdish officers held command roles in the Ottoman armies, such as Behir Paşa in 1683 during the siege of Vienna, and the *serasker* Cürd Paşa in the campaigns of 1715 and 1716. Source: Shāhnāma of Firdousi, early seventeenth century, Deutsche Staatliches Bibliothek, Berlin.

Plate H

1. Ottoman *sancakbeg*, Syria or Egypt, 1650–1700

The *sancak* was an administrative and military subdivision of the Ottoman Empire. This term also carried the meaning of 'district', 'banner', or 'flag' as well, reflecting the Arabic word for standard, namely *sancaq*. Ottoman provinces (*vilayet*s) were divided into *sancak*s, and governed by the *sancakbeg* or, more simply, *beg*, who usually dealt with military matters leading the provincial troops. As a distinctive sign, the *beg* carried a single *sorguç*, a horsehair plume on the turban. In Egypt, the first 12 *begs* carried two *sorguç*s, which was the usual distinctive for *paşa*s and *beglerbeg*s. Broad sleeves were typical of Egyptian and Syrian dress. Source: Rålamb's *Book of Costumes* (1658).

2. Eastern Anatolian horseman, mid seventeenth century

In the miniature depicting the battle episodes of the *shānāma*, the Iranian book of kings, appear several eastern Anatolian horsemen. They balance the Turkish and Iranian influences in weaponry and dress, such as the fur-lined headdress here represented. This horseman, probably coming from Diyarbakir, or Van, carries a lance, a pre-contracted bow and a *samsir* sabre, a panoply widespread in the cavalry from Anatolia to India. Note the bow quiver in natural leather with brass accessories, decorated with *czintamani* in seashell, alternated with painted wave symbols. Sources: Shāhnāma of Firdousi, Deutsche Staatliches Bibliothek, Berlin; early seventeenth century bow case, Anatolian manufacture, armoury of the castle of Churburg, Austria.

3. *Matbah*, driver, 1650–1700

Auxiliary personnel normally constituted two fifths of an Ottoman field army. A large proportion of these personnel were drivers enlisted for a single campaign. The transport of ammunition and foodstuffs, as well as all the troops' and officers' baggage, required a large number of vehicles and often forced the Porte to engage peasants with carts and draught animals from the province close to the theatre of war. Camels, dromedaries, mules, oxen, buffalo and even donkeys were typical pack animals of the Ottoman armies. Camels and dromedaries, rather than the buffalo, were the favourite pack animals, because of their freight capacity. Both were even faster and better suited for the climate and had a load capacity of approximately 250kg. Sources: reconstructions after Marsigli, *Stato Militare dell'Imperio Ottomanno*.

Plate I

1. Arnaut, Albanian Infantryman, 1700–1718

Arnauts were irregular light infantrymen recruited in Albania. In the mid seventeenth century this term identified not only the Albanians, but Bosnian mercenaries as well. This Arnaut warrior wears the traditional Albanian dress, with influences from the Greek Adriatic regions. The firearm is an early *tançitsa* flintlock musket. Usually, the Albanian foot soldiers carried only knives, like the *yataghan* carried under the waist sash, and they did not carry sabres. Sources: La Hay-van Moor, *Recueil de cent estampes représentant les diverses nations du Levant, tirées d'après nature…* (Paris, 1714–15); early eighteenth century *tançitsa* musket, private collection.

2. Mounted Arnaut, 1690–99

The figure has been reconstructed from the description of the French traveller Aubry De La Mottraye, who was present at the arrival of the Ottoman delegation for the Truce of Carlowitz. The column was preceded by 500 mounted Arnauts armed with 'long muskets' and wearing red or black caps. Sources: Aubry De La Mottraye, *Voyages en L'Europe, l'Asie et l'Afrique* (The Hague, 1727), vol. II, p. 244; saddle cover, Albanian traditional design, in August Racinet, *L'Ornement polychrome: 100 planches en couleurs or et argent contenant environ 2000 motifs de tous les styles art ancien at asiatiaque, moyen age, renaissance, XVIIe et XVIIIe siècle* (Paris, 1873); early eighteenth century *tançitsa* musket, private collection.

3. Bosnian frontiersman, early eighteenth century

During the war against the Western European powers, the Porte enlisted many irregular troops among the Muslim population of Bosnia. The volunteers served in the irregular formations and received equipment and rifles from their local magnate, the *ayan*, who enlisted them on behalf of the provincial governors. There were no specific requirements regarding dress or even personal armament, which consisted usually of a knife-like *yataghan* and other cutting weapons, which reflected the province of origin. The long fulled wool coat with open sleeves, the *dalmatica*, was typical clothing worn by Bosnian males, although similar patterns were also common in southern Dalmatia. Source: reconstruction after Giovanni Ferrario, *Il Costume Antico e Moderno*, Venice, 1813; early eighteenth century flintlock *tüfek*, Stibbert Museum, Florence.

Plate J

1. Crimean Tatar *kalgay*, late seventeenth century
Much of our information on the Crimean Tatars comes from accounts written by travellers from Christian Europe. This figure is a reconstruction after an eighteenth-century Russian painting, depicting a North Caucasian or Tatar chief with very good details concerning dress and equipment. Iranian influences are evident, but some particulars are typically Tatar, like the *qilic* sabre with 'Circassian style' hilt, while other weapons are common among the Ottomans, such as the bow case and the gilded war mace as a distinction of rank. According to other sources, the Tatar commanders dressed also in Ottoman style, as related in the authoritative work of Johann Hammer-Purgstall, *Geschichte des Osmanischen Reiches*. The author relates that on 27 August 1663 the *han*'s son Ahmed Giray, who commanded the Tatar contingent, wore an Ottoman-style *kaftan* with fur lining, while his brother Mehmed had a *kaftan* in golden brocade, a red *kusak* sash and a sable fur cap. Source: oil painting of Vladimir Orlowski, in J. Lebedinski, *Les Armes Cosaques et Caucasiennes*; Anatolian bow case, second half of the seventeenth century, collection of the Museo del Bargello, Florence; saddle cover on traditional seventeenth-century Ottoman design, Museo Civico, Turin.

2. Tatar foot soldier, 1670–90
Little is known about the Tatar infantry, however weapons and equipment may be similar to that issued to the Ottoman *azab*s. This Tatar foot soldier carries an Iranian–Caucasian musket and an Ottoman *qilic* sabre. Source: Jean Struys, *Les Voyages de Jean Struys en Moscovie et Tartarie* (Amsterdam, 1681); late seventeenth century Caucasian flintock, in J. Lebedinski, *Les Armes Cosaques et Caucasiennes*.

3. Moldavian *călăraşi* horseman, late seventeenth century
Moldavian and Wallachian vassal principalities were obliged to supply mounted troops – called *călăraşi* – to the Ottoman field army on campaign. The quality of this cavalry were generally poor and the Ottomans employed them as scouts, joining them with the Tatars. Source: Corina Nicolescu, *Istoria costumului de curte in tarile romane*, Bucharest, 1980.

Plate K

Kapikulu cavalry, *sipahi*, 1690–1718
Çiçak helms and other defensive weapons did not completely disappear in the Ottoman cavalry, remaining in use particularly for parade or court ceremonies and processions when the *sipahis* escorted the sultan. The weaponry included a *mizrák* lance, long-bladed *palas* sword, and since the closing years of the seventeenth century, also a pair of saddle pistols. Further defensive items were

a mail coat and shield, both typical of the Ottoman cavalry of all classes. Source: Marsigli, *Stato Militare dell'Imperio Ottomanno*, vol. II, ill. V and XXXIII; late seventeenth-century *çiçak* helm, Askeri Museum, Constantinople; saddle cover, Anatolian manufacture, 1680–90, Fine Art Museum, Budapest.

Plate L
Serhaddkulu cavalry, *dely*, mid seventeenth century
The appearance of the *dely* invaders was often significant, in order to frighten civilians as well as enemies. Western iconography usually shows these riders mounted on a horse with a fur saddle cover, especially those of fierce animals, comprising legs and head. Similar dress was common also in their Hungarian counterparts, but the Ottomans preserved these features longer than their enemies. The use of furs, as well as feathers and even wings in the Ottoman *dely* cavalry is widely documented in iconographic sources since the sixteenth century however, similar dress for *delys* is also described by the Italian *balivo* Antonio Benetti in 1682. Source: *Codex Vindobonensis*; mid seventeenth century *meç*-stoc, Askeri Museum, Constantinople.

Plate M – Ensigns
Several Ottoman flags and standards of the mid seventeenth and early eighteenth centuries have survived intact, especially because they represented the most important military trophies. Regardless of the shape or size, all Ottoman ensigns were called *sancaks*.

1. Large flags with Koran inscriptions were usually carried by the senior commanders' corps. In the Ottoman world the symbolism of the colours had not the same Western heraldic meaning, however red and yellow-gold were considered the Imperial colours par excellence, adopted by the sultans from their Byzantine–Roman predecessors after the conquest of Constantinople. (Ottoman *sancak* captured at Parkány in 1683; Heeresgeschichtliches Museum, Vienna; size 325x167cm)

2. A white-red pennant is represented in the Rålamb paintings, carried by the grand vizier's escort in 1657–58. Further pennants are in red, and this one is carried by the aforementioned figure D1.

3. A late seventeenth century infantry ensign that probably belonged to a janissary *orta*. (Heeresgeschichtliches Museum, Vienna; approximate size 100x140cm)

4. Large *sancak* captured by the Venetians at Coron in 1685. The original has been lost, but the illustration shows a flag whose owner is known, namely the local *beg*. The illustration represents also the pole's final. (*Teatro della Guerra contro il Turco*, Venice 1687; approximate size 360x120cm)

5. Green, the traditional Sunni colour, symbolised the faith and often appears associated with red and yellow, especially on cavalry standards such as the

example here depicted. Until the early eighteenth century, the standards of Ottoman mounted units usually bore a single flame. (After the print preserved in the Museo di Roma, copy of the standard captured at Peterwardein and presented to Pope Clement XI; approximate size 90x160cm)

6. Cavalry pennants, after Rålamb and Marsigli. Size and pattern varied considerably and usually ensigns with the same colours were also carried by the artillery and baggage train. Im this regard, Marsigli states that during the march to Vienna, pennants were also tied to the horns of the oxen.

Plate N – Ensigns

1. *Sancak* with *zulfiqar* sword, captured at Slankamen, 1691. Size 188x 129cm; Badisches Landesmuseum, Karlsruhe.

2. Janissary *sancak* captured in 1683 at Vienna. In addition to the official insignia and symbol, each janissary *orta* used combat ensigns, most often of two colours, but also with bands or a full coloured background, with traditional symbols such as the *zulfiqar* sword, Koranic inscription, a closed or open crescent, a hand and *czintamani* (three crescents arranged in a circle). Even the size of the ensigns was variable, but generally did not exceed 180cm high or 260cm in length. (Museum of Vienna, 256x173 cm)

3. Another *sancak* captured in 1683, which probably belonged to a janissary *orta*. Alongside the *zulfiqar* sword are depicted the most important Ottoman symbols, such as the hand, star, crescent, and *czintamani*. (Infantry *sancak* captured at Vienna; Heeresgeschichtliches Museum; size 231x173cm)

4. Large *sancak*, with crescent and floral symbols, captured at Slankamen, 1691. (Badisches Landesmuseum, Karlsruhe, size 190x120cm)

5. Infantry *sancak* possibly captured at Harsány, 1687. The yellow edge was probably completed with a fringe now lost. (Badisches Landesmuseum, Karlsruhe, size 155x137cm).

Plate O – Ensigns

Ensigns captured at Vienna, 1683, and preserved in the Wavel Museum, Krakow.

1. Single-pointed inscriptional *sancak* (size 347x178cm)
2. Double-pointed inscriptional *sancak.* (size 330x230cm)

Plate P

Large *sancak* captured in 1686, preserved in the Fine Art Museum of Budapest. There are similar ensigns with *zulfiqar* sword, inscription and crescent, but usually on a red background, while white *sancaks* are relatively rare (size 430x210cm).

Glossary

acemi oglan: boy recruits for the *kapikulu* infantry
ağa: 'master', officer, senior field commander (especially janissary's *ağa*)
ağalan: junior officer of *paşa* and *beglerbeg*
alaybeg: border commander
akçe: silver currency
arnavut: Arnaut, Albanian; Balkan mercenary soldier
aşçi: 'cook'; non-commissioned officer of the janissaries
ayan: term used in the Ottoman Empire to refer to social elites, particularly landed notables or magnates in either cities or the countryside
beg or *sancakbeg*: governor of a district, roughly translated as 'Lord'
beglik: small district governed by a *beg*
çavuş: 'herald'; senior adjutant, junior officer
çavuşbasi: 'chief herald', senior officer, commander of a unit of the *kapikulu* household cavalry
cehay: lieutenant of the *gönüllü serhaddkulu* cavalry
çorbaci: 'the one who give the soup'; captain, commander of a janissary *orta*
davul: drum; musician of the military band or *mehter*
defterdar: commissar, administrator
defterdar paşa: minister of finance
dely: 'crazy' or 'bold', specialties of the *serhaddkulu* cavalry
derviş: dervish
dizdar: warden, responsible for a fortress
divoan: council of government, major staff
dökükübasi: administrator of the provincial revenues
dündarbasi: commander of the reaguard
duaci: master ceremony
fodla kàtibi: 'bread keeper', fourier of the janissary corps
fodla horan: pensionary or honorary member of the janissary corps
gàvur: infidel
gönüllü: horseman of the *serhaddkulu* cavalry
gureba: 'foreigner', unit of the *kapikulu* household cavalry
han: kahn, 'chief'; sovereign of the Crimean Tatars
hazinedar: treasurer; responsible for the keys of the war chest
hasseki: lifeguard
hetman: field commander of Wallachian, Moldavian and Cossack auxiliary cavalry
hisar erleri: auxiliary artillerymen, garrison gunner

hospodar: prince in Wallachia

ic oglan: sultan's page

kadilasken: military court judge

kaimakan: commander's lieutenant

kalgay: lieutenant of the Crimean Tatar *han*

katib: clerk

kethüda: junior officer, adjutant

kethüda beg: general adjutant if the janissary corps

kethüda yeri: prevost of the janissaries

kiral: (Hungarian) 'king', grand-prince of Transylvania

korucu: janissary veteran

humbaraci: 'bombardier', soldier of the *kapikulu* household artillery in charge of the mortars

lagimci: miner

lagimcibasi: mining commander

levend: marine; naval infantry

matbah: personnel in charge of the army baggage train

meydanbasi: provost of the *acemi oglans*

mehter: military band, instrumental ensamble

millet: an Ottoman Turkish term for a confessional community in the Ottoman Empire

mimar: engineer, craftsman of the *kapikulu* household artillery

mirza: Tatar clan leader

mullah: religious judge

mücevveze: headgear, court turban of the grand vizier

muhzir aga: 'butter manager', janissary senior officer

müteferrika: lifeguard cavalry, escort for sultans and grand viziers

müteferrika agasy: commander of the escort cavalry squadron

name: book, register

nureddin: Crimean Tatar third in command

ocak: garrison or corps

ocak yazidsi: administrative officer of the *ocak*

oda: 'kitchen', company, administrative sub-unit of a janissary *orta*

odabasi: 'chief of the room' non-commissioned officer

ösür: quota of provincial cavalry recruitment

otturak: category of honorary janissaries

orducu: authorised foodstuff dealer for the army

orta: 'battalion'; administrative unit of the janissary corps

padisah: 'emperor', synonym of sultan

paşa: pasha

Paşalik: province under the *paşa*

reis effendi: state chancellor

saray: 'serail', sultan's court, palace

segmen: i) levy en masse, militia, irregular soldier; ii) denomination of 34 janissary *ortas*

segmenbasi: janissary senior officer in charge of the command of the *segmens*

segmenbolükbasi: commander of irregular troops and militia

salàm agasy: chief master of ceremonies of the sultan's court *serasker*: general; commander of an independent corps

sercesme: officer of irregular troops

serdar: general in charge of regional command

silihtar: 'esquire', life guard, adjutant of the sultan, grand vizier and court dignitaries

sipahi: horseman

solak: janissary *ortas* in charge to escort the sultan

Stanbul ağasi: commander of the *acemi oglanlar*

timar: land holder with an income until 20.000 *akçe*. The revenues produced on this land acted as compensation for military service

tìmarli: provincial cavalry formed by *timars*

timar defterdari: commissar, administrator of the *timarli* troops

top arabaci: driver, personnel of the artillery train

top arabacibasi: commander of the artillery train

topçu: gunner, *kapikulu* artileryman

topçubasi: *kapikulu* household artillery commander

toprakli: provincial cavalry recruited by *beglerbegs, paşas, sançakbegs, zeamets* and *timars*

tüfekçi: musketeer

ulùfely: *kapikulu* household unit

vilàyet: province, major district

voinak: artillery train

vekilharc: fourier commissar of the janissary *orta*

yaya: footman, irregular infantry

yayabeg: i) senior commander of the foot militia; ii) denomination of 101 janissary *ortas* destined for the most important places

yedekci: 'stableman'; unit of the *kapikulu sipahis*

yoldas: 'fellow', comrade of arms in the janissary corps

yüruk: nomad

zeamet: land holder with an income until 70.000 *akçe*

Bibliography

Contemporary Sources and Memoirs

Anonymous, *Kurtze doch warhaffte und mit denkwürdigen Umständen verfasste Erzehlung Der im Julio 1683. Zeit Jahre von dem Erb-Feinde vorgenommenen Welt-erschollenen Belagerung, Wie auch hernach klüglichst angeftellte und mit Aufschlagung dess ganzen Ottomannifchen Heers am 12. September desselben Jahre* (Vienna, 1684)

Anonymous, *Nuova e Vera Relatione del sanguinoso Combattimento seguito tra gli Esserciti Imperiale e Ottomano al fiume Raab* (Bologna, 1664)

Anonymous, *Diario dell'Assedio di Negroponte, assieme a un Giornale delle Campagne in Dalmazia, 1687–1688* (Venice, without date)

Anonymous, *Diario di tutto il progresso fatto dall'Esercito Cesareo in Ungheria dal 1716 al 1717* (without place and date)

Anguissola, Leandro, *Assedio di Vienna d'Austria, intrapreso li 14 luglio 1683 dagli Ottomani sotto il comando generale di Mustafà Carrà Primo Visire* (Modena, 1684)

Benetti, Antonio, *Osservazioni fatte dal fu A.B. nel viaggio a Costantinopoli dell'Illustrissimo et Eccellentissimo Signor Gio. Battista Donado, spedito Bailo alla Porta Ottomana, dall'anno 1680* (Venice, 1690)

Brue, Benjamin, *Journal de la Campagne que le Grand Vesir Ali Pacha a faite en 1715 pour la conquête de la Morée* (Paris, 1879)

Chéron, Élisabeth-Sophie (author): *Recueil de cent estampes représentant les diverses nations du Levant, tirées d'après nature en 1707 et 1708 par les ordres de M. de Ferriol, ambassadeur du Roy à la Porte, et gravées en 1712 et 1713 par les soins de Le Hay* (Paris: 1714–1715)

D'Aste, Michele, 'Diario dell'Assedio di Buda del 1686, in Diarii degl'Assedii di Vienna del 1683, e di Buda del 1686, distesi e scritti dal Baron Michele D'Aste che vi si trovò presente in tutte le sue Azzioni', in E. Piacentini, *Diari del barone Michele D'Aste*'(Rome, Budapest: Bulzoni-Corvina, 1991)

De la Colonie, *Memoires de Monsieur de la Colonie, Maréchal de Camp de l'Armée de l' Électeur de Baviere, contenant les événemens de la Guerre depuis le siège de Namur en 1692 jusqu'à la bataille de Belgrade en 1717.*

De La Mottraye, Aubry, *Voyages en L'Europe, l'Asie et l'Afrique* (The Hague, 1727)

Demiryürek, Mehmet, and Dogan, Güner: *Boundary Letters. Ottoman Officials to Luigi Ferdinando Marsigli (1699–1701)* (Ankara: Tarcan Maatbacilik, 2015)

Frangipane, Odorico, 'Libro Primo di memorie estere, abozate da O.F.', in D. Frangipane, A. Vigevani, P. Zanetta, *L'Ultimo Crociato* (Udine: Centro Iniziative per l'Arte e la Cultura, 1983)

Marsigli, Luigi Ferdinando, *Stato Militare dell'Imperio Ottomanno* (The Hague, Amsterdam, 1727; Graz: Akademische Druck und Verlaganstalt, 1972)

Montecuccoli, Raimondo, 'Discorso della Guerra contro il Turco' (1661–1664), and 'Della Guerra contro il Turco in Ungheria' (1668), in R. Luraghi (ed.), *Le Opere di Raimondo Montecuccoli*, vol. I–II (Rome: USSME, 1988)

Nitri, Mauritio, *Ragguaglio dell'ultime guerre di Transilvania et Ungaria* (Venice, 1666)

Prelli, Alberto, 'L'Assedio di Vienna nei Dispacci del Provveditore Lunardo Donado (1682–1684)', in *Quaderni del Civico Museo Storico della Città di Palmanova* (Palmanova, 2006)

Adhal, Karin (ed.), *The Sultan's Procession. The Swedish Embassy to Sultan Mehmed IV in 1657–1658 and the Rålamb Paintings* (Stockholm: Swedish Research Institute in Istanbul, 2006)

Struys, Jean (Johan), *Les Voyages de Jean Struys en Moscovie et Tartarie* (Amsterdam, 1681)

Özcan, Abdülkadir (ed.), *Anonim Osmanlı Tarihi (1099–1116/1688–1704)* (Ankara: Türk Tarih Kumuru, 2000)

Reiffenstuel, Ignaz, 'Tagebuch der Belagerung. Die Eiregnisse in und um Wien vom 7 july bis 12 september 1683', in G. Düriegl (ed.), *Die Türken vor Wien* (Vienna: Wien Kultur, 1983) pp.73–87

Wagner, Johann Christoph, *Delineatio provinciarum Pannoniae et Imperii Turcici in Oriente oder Grundrichtige Beschreibung dess ganzen Aufgangs, sonderlich aber dess hochlöblichen Königreichs Ungarn, und der ganzen Türckey* (Augsburg, 1685)

General Documentary Sources (Ottoman Empire, Balkans and North Africa)

The Cambridge History of Turkey (ed. S. Faroqhii), vol III, *The Later Ottoman Empire, 1603–1839* (Cambridge: Cambridge University Press, 2006)

Asztalos, Miklos, and Petho, Sandor, *Storia dell'Ungheria* (Milan, 1930)

Bombaci, Alessio and Shaw, and Standord J., *L'Impero Ottomano* (2nd Edition, Turin: UTET, 1981)

Chéron, Élisabeth-Sophie (author): *Recueil de cent estampes représentant les diverses nations du Levant, tirées d'après nature en 1707 et 1708 par les ordres de M. de Ferriol, ambassadeur du Roy à la Porte, et gravées en 1712 et 1713 par les soins de Le Hay et van Moor* (Paris: 1714–1715)

Adhal, Karin (ed.), *The Sultan's Procession – The Swedish Embassy to Sultan Mehmed IV in 1657–1658 and the Rålamb paintings* (Stockholm: Swedish Research Institute in Istanbul, 2006)

Ciccarini, Marina: *Il Richiamo Ambivalente. Immagini del Turco nella memorialistica polacca* (Bergamo:Jus Juvenilia, 1991).

Conte, Francis, *Gli Slavi* (Turin, Einaudi, 1991)

Canale Cama, Francesca; Casanova, Daniele; Delli Quadri, Rosa Maria, *Storia del Mediterraneo moderno e contemporaneo* (Naples: Guida Editori, 2017)

Genoviè, Lina, *L'Albania nella Cartografia Italiana dei secoli XVI e XVII* (Florence: Istituto Geografico Militare, 1940)

Hathaway, Jane, *A Tale of Two Factions. Myth, Memory, and Identity in Ottoman Egypt and Yemen* (Albany, NY: State University of New York Press, 2003)

Inalcik, Halil (ed.), *An Economic and SocialHistory of the Ottoman Empire*, vol. II (Cambridge: Cambridge University Press, 1997)

Kaleshi, Hasan, 'La Toponymie ottomane dan les pays yougoslave actuels', in *Studi Pre-ottomani e Ottomani' Conference Acts* (Naples: Istituto Universitario Orientale, 1976)

Kreiser, Klaus, 'Osmanischen Grenzbeschreibungen', in *Studi Pre-Ottomani e Ottomani' Conference Acts* (Naples: Istituto Universitario Orientale, 1976)

Mantran, Robert, 'L'evolution des relations entre la Tunisie et l'Empire Ottoman du XVI au XIX siècle', in *L'Empire Ottoman du XVI au XVII siècle* (London: Variorum Reprints, 1984)

Mantran, Robert, *L'Empire Ottoman du XVI au XVIII siècle* (London: Variorum Reprint, 1984)

Mantran, Robert, 'Le Statut de l'Algerie, de la Tunisie et de la Tripolitaine dans l'Empire Ottoman', in *Atti del I Congresso Internazionale di Studi Nordafricani* (Cagliari, 1965), pp.205–216

Matuz, Josef, *Das Osmanische Reich* (Darmstadt: Wissenschaftliches Buchgesellschaft, 1985)

Roux, Jean Paul, *Storia die Turchi* (Milan: Garzanti, 1988)

Özoglu, Hakan, *Kurdish Notables and the Ottoman State. Evolving Identities, Competing Loyalties, and Shifting Boundaries* (New York: State University of New York Press, 2004)

Pedani-Fabris, Maria Pia, 'La Dimora della Pace. Considerazioni sulle capitolazioni tra i paesi islamici e l'Europa', in *Quaderni di Studi* n. 2 (Venice: Università Ca' Foscari, 1996)

Preto, Paolo, *Venezia e Turchi* (Florence: Sansoni, 1975)

Seton-Watson, Robert W., *Histoire des Roumains* (Paris, 1937)

Valensi, Lucette, *Venezia e la Sublime Porta* (Bologna: Il Mulino, 1991)

Vaughn-Findley, Carter, *Ottoman Civil Officialdom. A Social History* (Princeton, NJ: Princeton University Press, 1989)

Winter, Michael, *Egyptian Society under Ottoman Rule 1517–1798* (New York, London: Routledge, 1992)

Winter, Stefan, *The Shiites of Lebanon under Ottoman Rule, 1516–1788* (Cambridge: Cambridge University Press, 2010)

Żygulski, Zdzisław, *Ottoman Art in the Service of the Empire* (New York: New York University Press, 1992)

Żygulski, Zdzisław, *Chorągwie Tureckie w Polsce. Na the ogólnej problematyki przedmiotu* (Krakow: Państwowe Zbiory Sztuki na Wawelu, 1968)

Military History

Adhal, Karin (ed.), *The Sultan's Procession – The Swedish Embassy to Sultan Mehmed IV in 1657–1658 and the Rålamb paintings* (Stockholm: Swedish Research Institute in Istanbul, 2006)

Ágoston, Gábor, *Guns for the Sultan. Military Power and the Weapons Industry in the Ottoman Empire* (Cambridge: Cambridge University Press, 2005)

Aksan, Virginia H., *Ottoman Warfare, 1700–1800. An Empire Besieged* (London, New York: Routledge, 2013)

Cardini, Franco, *Il Turco a Vienna. Storia del Grande Assedio del 1683* (Bari: Laterza, 2011)

Cevad (Kabaağaçlızade), Ahmed, *Etat Militaire Ottoman depuis la Fondation de l'Empire jusqu'à nos jours* (Constantinople, Paris: 1882), vol. I–XX

Chandler, David, *The Art of Warfare in the Age of Marlborough* (London: Batsford, 1976)

Hegyi, Klára, 'Ottoman Military Organization in Hungary', in *Studien zur Sprache, Geschichte und Kultur der Turkvölker* Nr. 25 (Berlin: Klaus Schwarz Verlag, 2018)

Heywood, Colin, *Writing Ottoman History: Documents and Interpretations* (Aldershot: Ashgate, 2002)

Imber, Colin, *The Ottoman Empire, 1300–1650. The Structure of Power* (New York: Palgrave Macmillan, 2002)

İnalcık, Halil, *The Ottoman Empire: The Classical Age, 1300–1600* (London: Phoenix, 1997)

Jacob, Alain, *Les Armes Blanches du Monde Islamique* (Paris: Jacques Grancher, 1985)

K.u.K. Kriegsarchiv, *Feldzüge des Prinzen Eugen von Savoyen. Nach den Feldacten und anderen authentischen Quellen hrsg. von der Abtheilung für Kriegsgeschichte des K.K. Kriegs-Archives*: vols I, II, XVI and XVII (Vienna, 1876–1892; Italian Edition, Turin, 1895–98)

Klein, Denise (ed.), *The Crimean Khanate between East and West (15th–18th Century)* (Wiesbaden: Harrassowitz Verlag, 2012)

Kreutel, Richard F., *Kara Mustafa vor Wien: das Türkishe Tagebuch der Belagerung Wiens verfasst vom Zeremonienmeister der Hohen Pforte* (Graz: Styria Verlag, 1960)

Masal, Anna, *Il Mehter: la Banda Militare Ottomana* (Rome: Università degli Studi di Roma, without date)

Murphey, Rhoads, *Ottoman Warfare, 1500–1700* (New Brunswick: Rutgers University Press, 1999)

Setton, Kenneth M., *Venice, Austria, and the Turks in the Seventeenth Century* (Philadelphia: The American Philosophical Society, 1991)

Silvini, Giorgio, *La Fine del Dominio Veneto nel Levante* (Udine: Editrice Grillo, 1979)

Stein, Mark L., *Guarding the Frontier. Ottoman Border Forts and Garrisons in Europe* (London, New York NY: Tauris Academic Studies, 2007)

Stoye, John, *The Siege of Vienna* (Edinburgh: Birlinn, 2006)

Sutter Fichtner, Paula, *Terror and Toleration. The Habsburg Empire Confronts Islam, 1526–1850* (London: Reaktion Book, 2008)

Uyar, Mesut, and Erickson, Edward J., *A Military History of the Ottomans. From Osman I to Atatürk* (Santa Barbara CO: ABC Clio, 2009)

Articles and Essays

Ágoston, Gábor, 'Habsburg and Ottomans. Defence, Military Change and Shifts in Power', in *Turkish Studies Association Bulletin*, vol. 22 (1998), pp.22–43

Ágoston, Gábor, 'The Cost of the Ottoman Fortress-System in Hungary in the Sixteenth and Seventeenth Centuries', in G. David and P. Fodor (eds), 'Ottomans, Hungarians, and Habsburgs in Central Europe: The Military Confines in the Era of Ottoman Conquest', in *The Ottoman Empire and its Héritage. Politics, Society and Economy*, vol. 20 (Leiden, Boston, Köln, 2000), pp.195–228

Ágoston, Gábor, 'Disjointed Historiography and Islamic Military Technology. The European Military Revolution Debate and the Ottomans', in M. Kaçar and Z. Durukal (eds), *Essays Honour of Ekmeleddin Ihsanoglu. Societies, Cultures, Sciences: a Collection of Articles* (Istanbul, 2006), vol. I, pp.567–582

Ágoston, Gábor: 'Empires and Warfare in East-Central Europe, 1550–1750: the Ottoman–Habsburg rivalry and military transformation', in *European Warfare, 1350–1750* (Cambridge: Cambridge University Press, 2010), pp.110–134

Ágoston, Gábor, 'Ottoman military organization (up to 1800)', in *The Encyclopedia of War* (Hoboken NJ: Wiley-Blackwell, 2012), pp.1–9

Ágoston, G., 'Ottoman Warfare in Europe, 1453–1826', in J. Black (ed.) *European Warfare, 1453–1815* (London: Palgrave Macmillan, 1999), p.137

Ágoston, Gabor, 'The Ottoman Wars and the Changing Balance of Power along the Danube in the Early Eighteenth Century', in C.W. Ingrao, N. Samardžić, J. Pesalj, (eds), *The Peace of Passarowitz, 1718* (West Lafayette, IN: Purdue University Press, 2011), pp.93–108

Ágoston, Gabor, 'Firearms and Military Adaptation:The Ottomans and the European Military Revolution, 1450–1800', in *Journal of Military History*, vol. 25/1, March 2014, pp.85–124

Ardali, Fehmi, *Food for the Army in the Ottoman Empire* (Istanbul Bilgi Üniveristesi – Ottoman Material Culture, Instructor, Prof. Dr. Suraiya Faroqhi) Fall Semester 2011–12

Calişir, Mohammed Fatih, 'The Grand Vizier Köprülüzade Fazil Ahmed Pasha (1635–1676) and the Battle of Mogersdorf/Saint Gotthard (1664)', in K. Sperl, M. Scheutz, A. Strohmeyer (eds), *Die Schlacht von Mogersdorf/St Gotthard und der Friede von Eisenburg-Vasvár*, Burgenländische Forschungen Band 108 (Eisenstadt, 2006), pp.207–214

Cristea, Ovidiu, 'The Friend of my Friend and the Enemy of my Enemy: Romanian Participation in Ottoman Campaigns', in G. Kármán and L. Kunčević, *The European Tributary States of the Ottoman Empire in Sixteenth and Seventeenth Centuries* (Leiden, Boston: Brill, 2013), pp.251–273

Ceylan, Ebubekir, 'The 'Millet' System in the Ottoman Empire', in J. Upton-Ward (ed.), *New Millennium Perspectives in the Humanity* (Constantinople, New York, NY: Fatih University, Brigham Young University, 2002), pp.245–266

Del Negro, Piero, 'Raimondo Montecuccoli e la guerra contro i turchi: riflessioni su strategia e arte militare', in *American Legacy, La SISM ricorda Raimondo Luraghi* (Rome: Società Italiana di Storia Militare, 2016)

Fehér, Géza, 'Magyar Gyűtemény Hódoltság Végeről Származó Török Vezéri Zászlaja', in *Művészet* n. 8, vol. IX; Budapest, 1968), pp.10–11

Flaherty, Chris, 'Classical Ottoman Field Engineering: a Revaluation', in *History and Uniforms* n. 4-2016, pp.28–36

Gârdonyi, Albert, 'Buda és Pest keresztény lakossâga a török hodoltsâg alatt. Tanulmânyok', in *Budapest Mùltjâbôl* vol. 5 (1936), pp.13–33

Greiner, Christian, 'Der 'Türkenlouis' – Markgraf Ludwig von Baden-Baden (1655–1707)', in *Militärgeschichtliche Beiträge*, Bd. 3, (1989), pp.27–41

Göger, Veysel, 'Taş Yasdanup Toprak Döşenenler: Kandiye Kuşatması Örneğinde Osmanlı Askerlerinin Metristeki Mücadele ve Yaşamı (1667–1669)', in *Osmanlı Araştırmaları Dergisi*, 52 (2018): pp. 41–78

Hegyi, Klára, 'Ottoman Military Force in Hungary', in Dâvid, G., Fodor, P. (eds), *Ottomans, Hungarians, and Habsburgs in Central Europe: The Military Confines in the Era of Ottoman Conquest. The Ottoman Empire and its Heritage. Politics, Society and Economy*, (Leiden, Boston, Köln: Brill, 2000), pp.131–148

Inalcık, Halil, 'Military and Fiscal Transformation in the Ottoman Empire', in *Archivum Ottomanicum*, n. 6 (1980), pp.283–337

Kizilov, Mikhail, Administrative Structure of the Crimea before and after the Russian Annexation of 1783, in *Oriens*, n. 5, 2016, pp.53–63

Klimecki, Mihal, 'A Polish Military Expedition to Moldavia in 1686', in *Acta Historica Academiae Scientiarum Hungaricae* 33 (2-4) (1987), pp.385–387

Kolçak, Özgür, 'The Composition, Tactics and Strategy of the Ottoman Field Army at Zrín-Újivár and St. Gotthard (1663–1664)', in *A szentgotthárdi csata és a vasvári béke: Oszmán Terjeszkedés-Európai Összefogás – La bataille de Saint Gotthard et la paix de Vasvár: Expansion Ottomane-Coopération Européenne* (eds F. Tóth Ferenc and B. Zágorhidi Czigány), Budapest: MTA Történettudományi Intézet, 2017, pp.73–92

Królikowska, Natalia, Sovereignity and Subordination in Crimean–Ottoman Relations (16th–18th Centuries), in G. Kármán and L. Kunčević (eds), *The European Tributary States of the Ottoman Empire in the 16th and 17th Centuries* (Leiden, Boston: Brill, 2013), pp.43–66

Langer, Herbert, and Dudás, János, 'Die Kämpfe in Ungarn 1684 bis 1686 und die Rückeroberung Budas im Spiegel des 'Theatrum Europaeum'', in *Acta Historica Academiae Scientiarum Hungaricae*, vol. 34, No. 1 (Institute of History, Research Centre for the Humanities, Hungarian Academy of Sciences, 1988), pp.17–25

Öztürk, Temel, 'Egyptian Soldiers in Ottoman Campaigns from the Sixteenth to the Eighteenth Centuries', in *War in History*, 2016, vol. 23 (1), pp.4–19

Pálffy, Géza, 'The Origins and Development of the Border Defense System Against the Ottoman Empire in Hungary (Up to the Early Eighteenth Century)', in G. Dávid and P. Fodor, *Ottomans, Hungarians, and Habsburgs in Central Europe* (Leiden: Brill, 2000), pp.3–70

Papp, Sándor, 'Splendid Isolation? The Military Cooperation of the Principality of Transylvania with the Ottoman Empire (1571–1688) in the Mirror of the Hungarian Historiography's Dilemmas', in G. Kármán and L. Kunčević, *The European Tributary States of the Ottoman Empire in Sixteenth and Seventeenth Centuries* (Leiden, Boston: Brill, 2013), pp.301–340

Periés, Géza, 'Verproviantierung und Strategie im Befreiungskrieg', in *Acta Historica Academiae Scientiarum Hungaricae* (Budapest, 1987), n. 33 (2-4), pp.271–250

Tóth, Ferenc, 'Le Journal de Charles V de Lorraine comme source pour l'histoire de la reconquête de la Hongrie sur les Turcs', in A. Colin (ed.), *Histoire, Économie et Société*, vol. 34, No. 3, *La Hongrie Ottomane, XVIe–XVIIe Siècles* (September 2015), pp.90–103

Yılmaz, Gülay, 'Becoming a Devshirme: The Training of Conscripted Children in the Ottoman Empire', in G. Campbell, S. Miers, J.C. Miller (eds), *Children in Slavery Through the Ages* (Cincinnati, OH: Ohio University Press, 2009), pp.119–134

Conferences

Atti del Convegno Sobieskiano (Udine: Università degli Studi di Udine, Istituto di Lingue e Letteratura dell'Europa Orientale Jan I.N. Baudouin de Courtenay, 1986)

Exhibitions and Collections

Borroni Salvadori, Fabia (ed.), *I Turchi da Lepanto a Vienna e oltre* (Florence: Biblioteca Nazionale Centrale, 1984)

Curatola, Giovanni, 'Il periodo ottomano in Turchia dal 680 al 1924', in *Eredità dell'Islam. Arte Islamica in Italia* (Milan: Silvana Editoriale, 1993)

Egyek, Edit, 'Az Iparművéseti Múzeum török zászlói', in *Az Iparművéseti Múzeum Évkönyvei* (Budapest: Képzőművéseti Alap Kiadóvállalata, 1960)

Jacobs, Alain, *Les armes blanches du monde islamique* (Paris: Phoenix, 1984)

Lebedinski, Iaroslav, *Les armes orientales* (La Tour du Pin: Editions du Portail, 1993)

Askeri Müze (Constantinople: Y&Y, 2010)

Bull Collection (Florence: Museo Stibbert, without date)

Collection oft he Royal Castle of Wavel (Krakow: Studów do dziezóv Wavelu, 1988)

Die Karlsruher Türkenbeute – Badisches Landesmuseum (Munich: Hirmer, 1991)

Führer durch die Wiener Waffen-Sammlung (Vienna, 1889)

Die Türken vor Wien. Europa und die Entscheidung an der Donau, 1683 (Vienna: Wien Kultur, 1983)

The Topkapi Museum and Collection (Constantinople: ETC, 1990)

The True and Exact Dress and Fashion of all Nations in Transylvania (ed. A. Várkony, Budapest: Corvina, 1990)

Venezia e la Difesa del Levante (1570–1670) (Venice: L'Arsenale Editrice, 1986)